Israel Smith Clare

The World's History Illuminated - Vol. 03

Israel Smith Clare

The World's History Illuminated - Vol. 03

ISBN/EAN: 9783744651523

Printed in Europe, USA, Canada, Australia, Japan

Cover: Foto ©Thomas Meinert / pixelio.de

More available books at **www.hansebooks.com**

MT. BLANC.

THE WORLD'S HISTORY
ILLUMINATED

CONTAINING A RECORD OF THE HUMAN RACE FROM THE EARLIEST HISTORICAL PERIOD TO THE PRESENT TIME. EMBRACING A GENERAL SURVEY OF THE PROGRESS OF MANKIND IN NATIONAL AND SOCIAL LIFE, CIVIL GOVERNMENT, RELIGION, LITERATURE, SCIENCE AND ART

COMPLETE IN EIGHT VOLUMES

Compiled, Arranged and Written by....... ISRAEL SMITH CLARE Author of "THE WORLD'S HISTORY ILLUMINATED," and "COMPLETE HISTORICAL COMPENDIUM."

REVIEWED, VERIFIED AND ENDORSED BY THE PROFESSORS OF HISTORY IN FIVE AMERICAN UNIVERSITIES, WITH AN INTRODUCTION ON THE EDUCATIONAL VALUE OF HISTORICAL STUDY

By MOSES COIT TYLER, A.M., L.H.D.

PROFESSOR OF AMERICAN HISTORY IN CORNELL UNIVERSITY.

"NOT TO KNOW WHAT HAPPENED BEFORE WE WERE BORN IS TO REMAIN ALWAYS A CHILD; FOR WHAT WERE THE LIFE OF MAN DID WE NOT COMBINE PRESENT EVENTS WITH THE RECOLLECTIONS OF PAST AGES?"—*CICERO.*

Volume III.—Alexander's Empire and Roman Empire

ILLUMINATED WITH MAPS, PORTRAITS AND VIEWS.

ST. LOUIS
WESTERN NEWSPAPER SYNDICATE

COPYRIGHT, 1897,

BY

R. S. PEALE AND J. A. HILL.

TABLE OF CONTENTS.

PART II.—ANCIENT HISTORY.—VOL. III.

SECTION XVIII.

DISSOLUTION OF ALEXANDER'S EMPIRE, 770-779
Consequences of Alexander's Death.—Arrangements of His Generals.—Philip Arrhidæus and Alexander IV.—The Lamian War.—Suicide of Demosthenes.—Quarrels of Alexander's Generals.—Regency and Death of Perdiccas.—Regency of Antipater.—Polysperchon and Cassánder.—Antigonus and Demetrius Phalereus.—Coalition against Antigonus.—Demétrius Poliorcétes.—Battle of Salamis in Cyprus. — Siege of Rhodes. — Battle of Ipsus and Death of Antígonus.—Dismemberment of Alexander's Empire.—Hellenization of Western Asia.

SECTION XIX.

MACEDON AND GREECE, ... 779-782
Demétrius Poliorcétes.—Pyrrhus,—Lysímachus.—Seleucus. — Ptolemy Ceraunus. — Invasion of Macedon and Greece by the Gauls.—Antigonus Gonatus and Pyrrhus.—Rise of the Achæan League under Aratus of Sicyon.—The Ætolian League and the Spartans.—Agis III. and Cleómenes.—Archæan and Macedonian Alliance.—Capture of Sparta.—Death of Aratus.—Sparta Subdued by Philopœmen, the Successor of Aratus.—Philip V. of Macedon at War with Rome.—Battle of Cynoscephalæ.—The Ætolians Subdued by the Romans.—Messenian Revolt and Death of Philopœmen.—Perseus, King of Macedon, at War with Rome.—Battle of Pydna.—Roman Conquest of Greece and Destruction of Corinth.—Table of Kings.

SECTION XX.

SYRIAN EMPIRE OF THE SELEUCIDÆ, . 782-789
Founding of the Syrian Empire by Seleucus.—Its Early Prosperity.—Founding of New Cities.—Antioch and Seleucia.—Baälbec or Heliopolis.—Reign of Antíochus Soter.—His Wars.—Antíochus II.—His Successors.—Antíochus the Great.—War with Egypt.—Reverses of Antíochus.—His Invasion of Parthia.—His Wars with Rome.—His Defeat.—Antíochus Ephíphanes.—He Drives the Jews into Rebellion.—Weak Reign of Antíochus Eúpator.—Demetrius I.—His Conflict with Rome.—Alexander Balas.—Demetrius Nicátor.—Made Prisoner by the Parthians.—His Captivity.—Antíochus Sidétes.—Decline of the Syrian Empire.—Civil Wars.—Syria Becomes Subject to Armenia.—Conquered by Pompey and Made a Roman Province.—Table of Kings.

SECTION XXI.

EGYPT UNDER THE PTOLEMIES, ... 790-799
Conquest of Egypt by Alexander the Great.—Alexandria Founded and Made the Capital.—Greek Civilization in Egypt.—Alexander's Death.—Ptolemy Soter Takes Possession of Egypt.—His Reign.—Character of His Kingdom. — Ptolemy Philadelphus.—Intellectual Greatness of Egypt.—Libraries of Alexandria.—The Septuagint,—Events of this Reign.—Commercial Prosperity of Egypt.—The King's Vices. — Ptolemy Euérgetes. — His Conquests.—His Relations with Rome.—Cruelties of Ptolemy Philópater.—Decline of the Kingdom under Ptolemy Epíphanes.—The Romans in Egypt.—Continued Decline of the Kingdom.—The Romans the Real Arbiters of the Destiny of Egypt.—Reigns of the Other Ptolemies.—Rapid Decline of Egypt.—Queen Cleopatra.—Julius Cæsar in Egypt.—Mark Antony.—Roman Conquest of Egypt.—Egypt a Province of the Roman Empire.—Table of Kings.

SECTION XXII.

THE SMALLER GREEK KINGDOMS, . . . 800-810
Rise of the Kingdom of Pergamus.—Eúmenes I.—Attalus I.—He Takes the Royal Title.—His Alliance with Rome.—Eúmenes II.—He is Rewarded by the Romans.—Intellectual Splendor of Pergamus.—Attalus Philadelphus.—Attalus Philométer.—He Bequeaths His Kingdom to the Romans.—Pergamus a Roman Province.—Growth of the Kingdom of Bithynia.—Prusías I.—His Wars.—Death of Hannibal.—Nicomédes Epíphanes.—Nicomédes III.—He Bequeaths His Kingdom to Rome.—Kingdom of Paphlagonia.—Growth of the Kingdom of Pontus.—Mithridates III.—His Conquests.—His Capture of Sinópé.—Mithridates IV.—He Aids Rome in Her Wars.—Mithridates the Great.—His Conquests.—His Wars with Rome.—His Defeat and Death.—Pontus Becomes a Roman Province.—Kingdom of Cappadocia.—Kingdom of Greater Armenia.—Tigránes.—Kingdom of Lesser Armenia.—The Greek Kingdom of Bactria.—Its Absorption by Parthia.

SECTION XXIII.

PARTHIAN EMPIRE OF THE ARSACIDÆ, . 810-818
Geographical Description of Parthia.—Characteristics of the Parthians.—The Parthian Kingdom Founded by Arsáces.—Its Growth.—Early Parthian Kings.—Wars with Syria.—Parthia Invaded by Antíochus the Great.—Alliance of Parthia and Rome.—Rome Makes War on Parthia.—Defeat and Death of Crassus.—Rome Undertakes to Conquer Parthia.—Wars between Parthia and the Roman Republic.—Reign of Arsáces XXV.—His Defeat by the Roman Emperor Trajan.—War between Vológeses III. and the Roman Emperor Marcus Aurelius. — Other Wars with Rome. — Arsáces XXX., the Last King of Parthia.—Rebellion of the Persians.—Sudden Overthrow of the Parthian Empire.—Table of Kings.

SECTION XXIV.

THE KINGDOM OF JUDÆA, ... 818-831
Conquest of Judæa by Alexander the Great.—Judæa under the Ptolemies of Egypt.—The Septu-

(iii)

iv   TABLE OF CONTENTS.

agint.—Judæa under the Seleucidæ of Syria.—Revolt of the Maccabees.—Exploits of Judas Maccabæus.—The War with Syria.—The Asmonæan Kingdom.—The Romans in the East.—Their Intervention in Judæa.—The Temple Plundered by Crassus.—End of the Maccabæan Dynasty.—Herod the Great.—Jesus Christ.—Judæa a Roman Province.—The Jewish War for Independence.—Siege, Capture and Destruction of Jerusalem by Titus.—Dispersion of the Jewish Nation.—Table of Kings.

SECTION XXV.

EDOM, OR IDUMÆA, ... 831–836

Geographical Description.—Early History.—Kings of Edom.—Extension of the Edomite Territory.—David's Conquest of Edom.—Edom Becomes Independent.—Edom Subject to Babylon.—Edomite Conquest of Southern Judæa.—Divisions.—The Nabathæans.—Their Wars.—The City of Petra.—Antiquities of Idumæa.—Description of Petra.

SECTION XXVI.

LATER GREEK SCIENCE AND LITERATURE, 836–842

Alexandria the Seat of Greek Science and Literature.—Aristóphanes and Aristárchus.—Euclid—Archimédes.—Eratósthenes.—Hipparchus.—Ptolemy.—Hippócrates.—Galen.—Meuander the Last Great Athenian Comic Poet.—The Pastoral Poets of Syracuse, Theócritus, Bion and Moschus.—The Four Great Alexandrian Poets, Lycóphron, Callímachus, Apollonius and Arátus.—Historians.—Manetho.—Berosus.—Apollodórus and Polyhistor.—Polybius.—Diodórus Siculus.—Dionysius Halicarnasséus.—Strabo.—Josephus.—Plutarch.—Arrian.—Appian.—Diogenes Laertius.—Herodian.—Lucian the Satirist.—Longínus the Critic.—The Greek Versions of the Old and New Testaments.—The Greek Christian Fathers.—St. Paul's Preaching in Greece.—Conversion of the Greeks to Christianity.—The Mausoléum at Halicarnassus.—The Colossus of Rhodes.

CHAPTER XIV.—ANCIENT ROME.

SECTION I.

GEOGRAPHY OF ANCIENT ITALY, ... 847–855

Position and Area of Ancient Italy.—Physical Features.—Gulfs and Bays.—Mountains.—Plains.—Rivers.—Lakes.—Islands.—Divisions.—Northern Italy.—Liguria.—Venetia.—Cisalpine Gaul.—Central Italy.—Etruria.—Latium.—Campania.—Umbria.—Picenum.—Sabine Territory.—Southern Italy.—Lucania.—Bruttium.—Apulia.—Calabria.—Islands.—Sicily.—Sardinia.—Corsica.—The Smaller Italian Islands.

SECTION II.

ANCIENT RACES OF ITALY, ... 855–856

Italian Races.—Iapygians.—Italians Proper.—Etruscans.—All the Italians Aryans, except the Etruscans.

SECTION III.

EARLY LEGENDS AND TRADITIONS, . . . 856–860

Character and Sources of Early Roman History.—The Romans a Latin Race.—Legend of Æneas.—Legend of Romulus and Remus.—Founding of Rome by Romulus.—Romulus First King of Rome.—Seizure of the Sabine Women.—War with the Sabines.—Treachery and Death of Tarpeia.—The Temple of Janus.—Peace between the Romans and the Sabines.—Union of the Two Nations.—Translation of Romulus.—Numa Pompilius.—Tullus Hostilius.—Combat Between the Horatii and the Curiatii.—Mettius Fuffetius.

SECTION IV.

ROME UNDER THE KINGS, ... 861–866

Modern Views Concerning the Founding of Rome.—King Tullus Hostilius.—His Constitution.—His Conquest of Alba Longa.—Ancus Martius.—Wars with the Latins.—Origin of the Plebeians.—Rapid Growth of Rome.—Tarquin the Elder.—He Increases the Roman Territory and Improves the City.—His Changes in the Roman Constitution.—Servius Tullius.—His Laws.—The Military Organization.—New Tribes Instituted.—Walls of Rome.—Tarquin the Proud.—He Sets Aside the Constitution of Servius Tullius.—His Tyranny.—Lucretia Outraged by Sextus.—Revolt of the Romans and Expulsion of Tarquin the Proud.—Abolition of Monarchy and Establishment of the Roman Republic.—Table of Kings.

SECTION V.

ROMAN RELIGION, ... 866–871

The Roman Religion a Polytheism.—Jupiter and Mars.—Religious Festivals.—Janus.—Vulcan.—Vesta.—The Vestal Virgins.—The Lares.—Other Divinities.—Oracles.—The Sibylline Books.—The Four Sacred Colleges.—Augurs.—Pontiffs.—Heralds.—Flamens.—Priests.—Purifications and Lustrations.

SECTION VI.

THE REPUBLIC'S EARLY STRUGGLES, . . 871–893

Founding of the Roman Republic.—The First Two Consuls.—The Lictors.—Republican Institutions.—Legends of Lucius Junius Brutus.—Wars with the Etruscans and the Latins.—Legends of Horatius Cocles and Mutius Scævola.—Legend of the Battle of Lake Regillus.—The First Dictator.—Tyranny of the Patricians.—Imprisonment and Enslavement for Debt.—Secession of the Plebeians and their Occupation of the Sacred Mount.—Menenius Agrippa.—Tribunes of the Plebs.—Return of the Plebeians to Rome.—Spurius Cassius and the First Agrarian Law.—The Law Nullified by the Patricians.—Exclusion of the Plebeians from the Consulate.—Plebeian Revenge.—The Fabii.—Murder of Genucius.—The Tribune Volero Publilius.—Publilian Law.—Wars with the Oscans and the Etruscans.—Struggle of the Plebeians for their Rights.—Dictatorship of Cincinnatus.—His Victory over the Æqui.—The First Decemvirs.—Laws of the Twelve Tables.—Appius Claudius Seizes Virginia, who is Slain by her Father.—Plebeian Revolt and Overthrow of Appius Claudius.—Second Secession of the Plebeians—Abolition of the Decemvirate.—Return of the Plebeians to Rome.—Reforms.—Roman Victory over the Sabines.—The Consuls Accorded a Triumph by the Plebeians in Spite of the Opposition of the Senate.—Impolicy of the Patricians.—Third Secession of the Plebeians.—Concessions to them.—Their Return to Rome.—Censors and Military Tribunes.—The Census.—War with Veii.—Siege and Capture of Veii by Camillus.—Discontents of the Roman People.—Invasion of Italy by the Gauls.—Their March to Rome.—Battle on the Allia.—Rome Taken and Burned by the Gauls.—Defense of the Capitol.—The City Ransomed.—Retreat of the Gauls.—Successes of Camillus.—Rome Rebuilt.—

TABLE OF CONTENTS.

Errors of the Romans.—Hard Terms of the Government.—Sufferings of the People.—Condemnation and Death of Marcus Manlius.—Lucius Sextius Lateranus and Caius Licinius Stolo.—The Three Licinian Laws.—Opposition of the Patricians.—Adoption of the Licinian Laws.—Second Invasion of Italy by the Gauls.—They are Defeated by Camillus.

SECTION VII.

SAMNITE WARS AND CONQUEST OF ITALY, 893-907

First Samnite War.—Mutiny of the Roman Army.—It Marches to Rome and Demands Redress for the Plebeians.—Concessions by the Government.—War with the Latins.—Titus Manlius.—Patriotic Devotion of Decius in the Battle of Vesuvius.—Roman Conquest of the Latins.—Second Samnite War.—Roman Defeat at the Caudine Forks.—Roman Reverses.—Rome Recovers her Supremacy.—The Samnites Subdued.—Rome's Supremacy in Italy.—The Latins Conciliated.—Roman Conquest of the Æqui.—Third Samnite War.—Patriotic Devotion of the Younger Decius in the Battle of Sentinum.—Final Conquest of the Samnites and the Sabines.—Distress of the Plebeians.—Curius Dentatus Proposes the Second Agrarian Law.—Fourth Secession of the Plebeians.—The Patricians Yield.—Hortensian Laws.—War with Tarentum.—Coalition against Rome.—The Allies Defeated.—Pyrrhus Called to Italy by the Tarentines.—The Tarentines Find Pyrrhus a Master.—Victories of Pyrrhus.—Noble Conduct of Fabricius.—Pyrrhus Fails to Induce the Latins and the Romans to Join him.—Cineas the Orator.—Rome Refuses to Treat with Pyrrhus.—Progress of the War.—Pyrrhus Disheartened.—He Aids the Syracusans against the Carthaginians in Sicily.—His Successes in Sicily.—His Return to Italy.—His Disasters.—He Retires from Italy and Returns to Greece.—Roman Conquest of Central and Southern Italy.—Roman Colonies in Southern Italy.—Roman Roads.—The Appian Way.—Roman Colonial System.—Admission of the Plebeians to Political Equality.

SECTION VIII.

PUNIC WARS AND FOREIGN CONQUESTS, 908-940

Wealth of the Romans Increased by their Wars.—The Republic Adopts War as a Means of Acquiring Riches and Territory.—The Romans Resolve upon the Conquest of Carthage.—A Pretext for War Found.—Origin of the First Punic War.—Roman Successes in Sicily.—Carthaginian Fleet on the Italian Coast.—Creation of the Roman Navy.— Roman Naval Victories.— Roman Conquests in Africa.—The Home Territory of Carthage Ravaged.—Defeat of the Romans.—Regulus a Prisoner.—Roman Fleets Destroyed by Storms.—Battle of Panormus.—Embassy of Regulus to Rome.—Story of his Death.—Roman Reverses in Sicily.—The Italian Coast Harassed by the Carthaginian Fleet.—The Wealthy Romans Build a Fleet.—Battle of Ægusa.—Roman Conquest of Sicily and the Neighboring Islands.—Humiliation of Carthage.—End of the First Punic War.—Rome a Great Naval Power.—Sicily, Sardinia and Corsica Become Roman Provinces.—The Romans Exterminate the Illyrian Pirates.—Roman Conquest and Annexation of Cisalpine Gaul.—All Italy under the Roman Dominion.—Conquests of the Carthaginians in Spain.—Their Wise Policy.—Hannibal.—He Succeeds to the Carthaginian Command in Spain.—Siege and Capture of Saguntum by Hannibal.—Roman Demands Rejected by Carthage.—Beginning of the Second Punic War.—Hannibal's March from Spain to the Alps.—His Passage of the Alps and Invasion of Italy.—His Great Victories at the Ticinus, the Trebia and Lake Trasiménus.—Cautious Policy of Fabius Maximus the Delayer.—Hannibal's Stratagem.—Battle of Cannæ.—Hannibal Master of Southern Italy.—Firmness of the Roman Senate.—Hannibal Winters at Capua.—Hannibal's Defeats at Nola and Capua.—Capture of Syracuse, Capua and Tarentum by the Romans.—Successful Campaigns of the Scipios in Spain.—Their Defeat and Death.—They are Succeeded in the Roman Command in Spain by the Younger Scipio.—He Defeats Hasdrubal, Hannibal's Brother.—Hasdrubal's March to Italy.—His Error.—Hannibal's March to Meet his Brother.—Hasdrubal Defeated and Slain in the Battle of the Metaurus.—His Bloody Head Thrown into Hannibal's Camp.— Hannibal's Retreat.—Scipio's Conquest of Spain.—His Invasion of Africa.—Hannibal's Return to Africa.— Battle of Zama.—End of the Second Punic War.—Carthage Made Tributary to Rome.—Splendid Triumph of Scipio Africanus.—Results of the Second Punic War.—War with Philip V. of Macedon.—Battle of Cynoscephalæ.—Philip V. Humiliated.—War with Antiochus the Great of Syria.—Battle of Magnesia.—Antiochus Forced to Cede a Large Part of Asia Minor to Rome.—Sad Fate of Hannibal and Scipio Africanus.—War with Perseus, King of Macedon.—Battle of Pydna.—Macedonia Made a Roman Province.— Roman Conquest of Greece.—Destruction of Corinth.—Origin of the Third Punic War.—Capture and Destruction of Carthage by Scipio Æmilianus.—Roman Wars in Spain.—Viriathus the Lusitanian Chieftain.—Siege and Fall of Numantia.—Heroism of the Numantians.—Spain a Roman Province.—Roman Acquisition of Pergamus.

SECTION IX.

RISE OF LATIN LITERATURE, ... 941-943

Origin of Latin Literature.—Results of Roman Intercourse with the Greeks.—Livius Andronicus.— Nævius.— Ennius.— Plautus.— Terence.— Cato the Elder.—Influence of Conquered Greece on Roman Civilization.—Degeneracy of the Roman People.—Corruption of Roman Manners.—Futile Efforts of the Elder Cato.

SECTION X.

CIVIL WARS—FALL OF THE REPUBLIC, 944-1004

Rome Mistress of the Civilized World.—Luxury and Corruption.—Loss of Patriotism and Civic Virtue.—Political and Social Condition of the Roman People.—Rapid Increase of the Population of the City of Rome.—Proportionate Growth of Pauperism.—Rome "a Commonwealth of Millionaires and Beggars."—Reasons Therefor.—Political Corruption.—First Servile War in Sicily.—Tiberius Sempronius Gracchus.—His Remedy for the Political and Social Troubles.—He Proposes an Agrarian Law and Procures its Passage.—Aristocratic Opposition to the Law.—Murder of Tiberius Gracchus.—Murder of Scipio Æmilianus.—Discontents of the Latins and the Italians.—Caius Sempronius Gracchus.—He is Elected Tribune.—His Measure for the Improvement of the Condition of the People.—The "Sempronian Granaries."—Increase of the Pauper Population of Rome.—Unpopularity of the Proposal to Extend the Roman Franchise to all the Italians.—Overthrow and Murder of Caius Gracchus.—The Lower Classes Take a Lesson in Violence from the Aristocracy.—The Jugurthine War.—Rise of Caius Marius.—He Brings the Jugurthine War to a Close.—Capture and Death of Jugurtha.—Marius Reëlected Consul.—Invasion of Gaul by the Cimbri and the Teutones.—Their Repeated Victories over the Roman Armies.—Marius Sent against them.—He Defeats the Teutones at Aquæ Sextiæ.—The Crimbri Invade Italy.—They are exterminated by Marius at Vercellæ.—Ambition of Marius.—Second Servile War in Sicily.—Drusus Proposes the Enfranchisement of the Italians.—Is Murdered.—Social War.—Rome Forced to Enfranchise the Italians.—First Mithridatic War. —Rivalry of Marius and Sulla.—Civil War.—Capture of Rome by Sulla.—Flight and Exile of Marius.—Cinna Driven from Rome.—Return of Marius.—He takes Rome and Massacres his Enemies. —His Seventh Consulship and Death.—Sertorius Slaughters the Marian Assassins.—Cinna in Power at Rome.—Sulla's Threats.—His Victories over King Mithridates the Great of Pontus.—His Return.—Civil War Renewed.—Sulla Takes Rome and Massacres his Enemies.—His Dictatorship.—His Resignation and Death.—Rebellion of Sertorius in Spain.—He is Murdered.—The Revolt Suppressed by Pompey.—Rebellion of the Slaves and Gladiators under Spartacus.—Their Victories over the Roman Armies.—They are Finally Subdued by Crassus.—Crassus and Pompey Elected Consuls.— Their Reform Measures.— Cicero.— Cilician Pirates Subdued by Pompey.—Pompey Sent to Command in Asia.—He Conquers Mithridates the Great of Pontus and Tigranes of Armenia and Annexes Syria and Pontus to the Roman Dominions.—His Return to Rome.—Catiline's Conspiracy.—Pompey Distrusted by the Senate.—Julius Cæsar.—The First Triumvirate.—Banishment of Cicero.—Cato the Younger Sent to Cyprus. —Cæsar's Conquest of Gaul and Invasions of Germany and Britain. Expedition of Crassus into Parthia.—His Disasters and Death.—Rivalry of Pompey and Cæsar.—Pompey Supported by the Senate.—Cæsar Driven into Hostile Measures by the Senate.—Civil War.—Cæsar Crosses the Rubicon and Marches to Rome.—Pompey's Flight to Greece.—Cæsar Master of Italy.—He Subdues Pompey's Adherents in Spain and Takes Massilia in Gaul.—He Pursues Pompey to Greece.—Battle of Pharsalia.—Pompey's Flight to Egypt.—Murder of Pompey.—Cæsar in Egypt.—He Sustains Cleopatra.—His Narrow Escape.—His Victory over Ptolemy.—Over Pharnaceles of Pontus.—Over the Pompeians in Africa at Thapsus.—Suicide of Cato the Younger.—Cæsar's Return to Rome.—His Triumphs.—His Victory in Spain over the Pompeians at Munda.—His Return to Rome.—His Dictatorship.—His Great Projects.—Assassination of Cæsar.—Mark Antony.—Octavius Cæsar.—Second Triumvirate.—Brutus and Cassius in Greece. —Antony and Octavius Take the Field against Them.—Battles of Philippi.—Suicide of Brutus and Cassius.—Division of the Roman World among the Triumvirs.—Octavius Triumphs over Lepidus and Sextus Pompey.—Antony's Foolish Conduct in the East.—He Becomes a Slave to Cleopatra's Charms.—His Debauchery.—Quarrel of Octavius and Antony.—Civil War.—Naval Battle of Actium. —Flight of Antony and Cleopatra to Egypt.—Conquest of Egypt by Octavius.—Suicide of Antony and Cleopatra.—Egypt a Roman Province.—Octavius Returns to Rome.—Octavius Sole Master of the Roman World.—End of the Roman Republic and Beginning of the Empire.

SECTION XI.

PROVINCES OF THE ROMAN EMPIRE, 1005–1021

Vast Extent and Greatness of the Roman Empire.— Boundaries.— Provinces.— Spain.— Gaul.— Britain.—Roman Germany.—Vindelicia.—Rhætia. — Noricum. — Pannonia. — Mœsia. — Illyricum. — Macedonia.—Thrace.—Achæa.—Asia Proper.—Bithynia.—Galatia.—Pamphylia.—Cappadocia.—Cilicia.—Syria.—Palestine.— Egypt.— Cyrenaica.—Africa Proper.— Numidia.— Mauritania.—Temporary Provinces of Dacia, Armenia, Mesopotamia and Assyria.—Inhabitants of the Empire.—Latin, Greek and Oriental Civilizations and Languages.—Native Languages.—Six Classes of People.—Peasantry.—Slaves.—Roman Citizens.

SECTION XII.

NEIGHBORS OF THE ROMANS, ... 1022–1026

The Germans.—Numerous Tribes.—Their Condition. — Institutions. — Assemblies. — Religion.— The Iberians and Albanians.—Gætuli of Africa.—India.

SECTION XIII.

THE CITY OF ROME, ... 1027–1032

Its Origin.—Pomœrium.—Comitium.—First Fortifications and Edifices.—Rome as Rebuilt after its Destruction by the Gauls.—Circus Maximus.—Capitol.—Temple of Jupiter Capitolinus.—Other Temples.—Forum.—Senate-House.—Campus Martius.—The Pantheon.—Flavian Amphitheater, or Colosseum.—Aqueducts.—Rome Under Augustus.—Walls.—Wealth, Luxury and Magnificence during the Empire.—Porticos and Colonnades.—Roads.—Works of Utility.—Ruins of Ancient Rome.

SECTION XIV.

AUGUSTAN AGE OF LATIN LITERATURE, 1032–1037

The poets Lucretius and Catullus.—The Historian Sallust.—Cicero.—Julius Cæsar.—Varro.—Augustan Age.—The Poets Virgil, Horace, Ovid, Tibullus and Propertius.—The Historian Livy.—Cornelius Nepos.—Character of the Augustan Age.

SECTION XV.

VIEW OF ROMAN CIVILIZATION, . . . 1037–1049

Architecture.—Sculpture.—Painting.—Dwellings. — Villas.— Food.— Meals. — Banquets.— Early Simplicity.— Later Luxury.— Dress. — Baths.— Circus, Theater and Amphitheater.—Other Amusements. — Gladiatorial Combats. — Private Amusements.—Early Characteristics.—Books and Writing.—Education. — Slaves.— Marriages.— Funerals.— Roman Army.—Legions.—Arms and Armor.—Military Rewards.—Order of March.— Encampment.— Exercises. — Catapults, Balista and Battering-Rams. — Besieging Towers.—Roman Ships.—The Triumph.

SECTION XVI.

FLOURISHING PERIOD OF THE EMPIRE, 1050–1087

The Emperor Augustus.—Glories of his Reign.— Wars with the Germans.—Defeat of Varus.—Birth of Christ.—Domestic Unhappiness of Augustus. —His Death.—The Emperor Tiberius.—His Cruelties.—Crimes and Fall of Sejanus.—Tyranny of Tiberius.—Crucifixion of Christ.—Missionary Travels of St. Paul.—Caligula's Cruel and Shameful Reign.—The Emperor Claudius.—Roman Conquest of Britain.—The Emperor Nero.—His Profligacy and Cruelty.—Burning of Rome.—First Persecution of the Christians.—Rome Rebuilt.—Revolt of the Provinces.—Overthrow and Suicide of Nero.—Short Reigns of Galba, Otho and Vitellius.—Follies and Crimes of Vitellius.—His Overthrow and Death.—Good Reign of Vespasian.—Jewish War for Independence.—Siege, Capture and Destruction of Jerusalem, and Dispersion of the Jewish Nation.—Good Reign of Titus.—Destruction of Herculaneum and Pompeii.—Cruel Reign of Domitian.—Nerva's Good Reign.—Trajan's Vigorous Reign.—Conquest of Dacia.—Cam-

TABLE OF CONTENTS.   vii

paigns against the Parthians.—Peaceful Reign of
Adrian.— His Travels.— Peaceful Reign of Antoninus Pius.—Marcus Aurelius.—Wars with the Germans and the Parthians.—Disgraceful Reign of Cómmodus.—Decline of the Empire.

SECTION XVII.

LATER LATIN LITERATURE, ... 1087-1089
Decline of Latin Literature.—The Poets Phædrus, Lucan, Perseus, Juvenal and Martial.—Claudian, the Last Ancient Roman Poet.—Seneca, the Philosopher.— Pliny the Elder.— Pliny the Younger.— Quintilian, the Rhetorician.— The Historians, Tacitus, Quintus Curtius and Suetonius.

SECTION XVIII.

COMMERCE UNDER THE ANTONINES, . 1089-1091
Roman Commerce with the East.—With Central Asia.—With the North.

SECTION XIX.

PERIOD OF MILITARY DESPOTISM, . . . 1091-1110
Good Reign of Pertinax.—The Prætorian Guards Sell the Imperial Dignity to Didius Julianus.—His Overthrow and Death.— The Emperor Septimius Sevérus.—He Breaks the Power of the Prætorian Guards.— Wars in Parthia and Britain.— Cruel Reign of Caracalla.—Macrínus.— His Defeat by the Parthians.—Shameful and Dissolute Reign of Heliogábalus.— The Good Emperor Alexander Sevérus.— War with the New Persians.— Cruel Reign of Maximin.— The Gordians.— Pupienus and Balbínus.— The Third Gordian.— Philip the Arabian.— Decius.— Great Persecution of the Christians.— Gallus.— Æmilianus.— Valerian.— Ravages of the Northern Barbarians.— War with the New Persians.—Valerian's Defeat and Captivity.—Gallienus and the Thirty Tyrants.—Odenatus of Palmyra.—His Widow, Zenobia, the "Queen of the East."— Flavius Claudius.— Aurelian's Vigorous Reign.—Overthrow of Palmyra and Capture of Zenobia.—Tacitus.—Probus.—Carus.— Great Reign of Diocletian.—He Destroys the Power of the Legions.— His Colleague, Maximian.— The Cæsars, Galerius and Constantius Chlorus.— Great Change.—Revolts Subdued in Britain, Africa and Egypt.— Galerius Defeats the New Persians.—Diocletian's Great Persecution of the Christians.— Abdication of Diocletian and Maximian.—Galerius and Constantius Chlorus.—Constantine the Great.—His Triumph over his Rivals.

SECTION XX.

TRIUMPH OF CHRISTIANITY, ... 1110-1139
Rise and Progress of Christianity.—Ten Great Persecutions.—Christian Martyrs.—Edict of Milan.— Constantine's Conversion.— The Labarum.—Triumph of Christianity.—Council of Nice and its Decisions.—Christianity the State Religion.—Constantine Founds Constantinople and Makes it the Imperial Capital.—Reorganization of the Empire.—His Wars with the Goths and the Sarmatians.—His Character.—His Death.—Constans, Constantine II., and Constantius II.—Their Rivals.—Final Triumph of Constantius II.—His Reign as Sole Emperor.—His War with the New Persians.—Julian's Victories over the Germans in Gaul.—Reign of Julian the Apostate.—His Futile Efforts to Overthrow Christianity.—His Expedition against the New Persians.—His Defeat and Death.—The Emperor Jovian.—Humiliating Peace with Persia.—Restoration of Christianity.—Valentinian I. and Valens.— Barbarian Inroads.—Revolt in Africa.—Invasion of Europe by the Huns.—The Goths in Thrace.— Defeat and Death of Valens at Adrianople.—Gratian and Valentinian II.— The Emperor Theodosius the Great.—His Suppression of Paganism.— His Massacre of the Thessalonians.— His Chastisement by St. Ambrose.—Arcadius Emperor of the East, and Honorius Emperor of the West.—The Christian Fathers.

SECTION XXI.

FALL OF THE WESTERN EMPIRE, . . . 1139-1152
The Emperor Honorius.— Invasion of Italy by the Goths under Alaric.—Their Defeat by Stilicho.—Invasion of Italy by the Vandals.—Their Migration to Spain.— Another Gothic Invasion of Italy.— Alaric's Plunder of Rome.— Death and Burial of Alaric the Goth.— The Visigoths settle in Spain, and the Vandals in Africa.— Reign of Valentinian III.— Invasion of Gaul by the Huns under Attila.—Battle of Chalôns and Defeat of the Huns.—Their Invasion of Italy.— Founding of the City and Republic of Venice.— Death of Attila.—The Emperor Petronius Maximus.—Rome Pillaged by the Vandals.—Count Ricimer.—Puppet Emperors.—Rapid Decline of the Western Roman Empire.— Dethronement of Romulus Augustulus by Odoacer, and End of the Western Roman Empire.— Founding of the Kingdom of Italy by Odoacer, Chief of the Heruli.—Cause of Rome's Fall.—Table of Emperors.

MAPS IN VOLUME III.

Empire of Alexander the Great.................774,775
Kingdoms of the Successors of Alexander...........776
Parthian Empire...................................819
Palestine in the Time of Christ...................820
Ancient Jerusalem.................................820
Ancient Italy.................................845,846
Ancient Italy Proper..............................847
Mediterranean Lands, Second Punic War............1007
Roman Dominions, Mithridatic War.................1007
Roman Empire, 2d and 3d Centuries A. D.....1008,1009
City of Ancient Rome.............................1010

Plan of Rome, Time of Augustus...................1031
Roman Empire at the Death of Augustus............1111
Roman Empire in Its Greatest Extent.........1112,1113
Roman Empire Extending East and West.............1112
Roman Empire, Greatest Extent Westward...........1113
Roman Empire under Trajan........................1114
Roman Empire Divided into Prefectures............1114
Britain under the Romans.........................1141
Europe during the Barbarian Inroads.........1142,1143
Scotland during the Roman Period.................1144

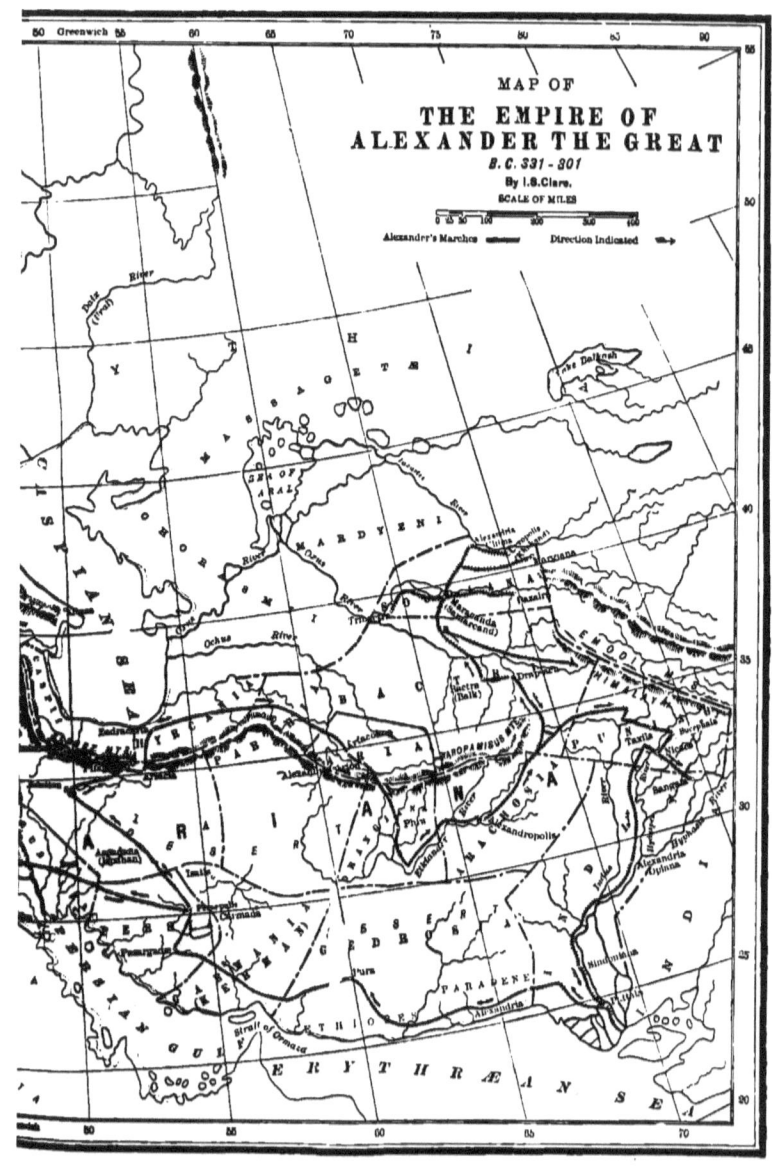

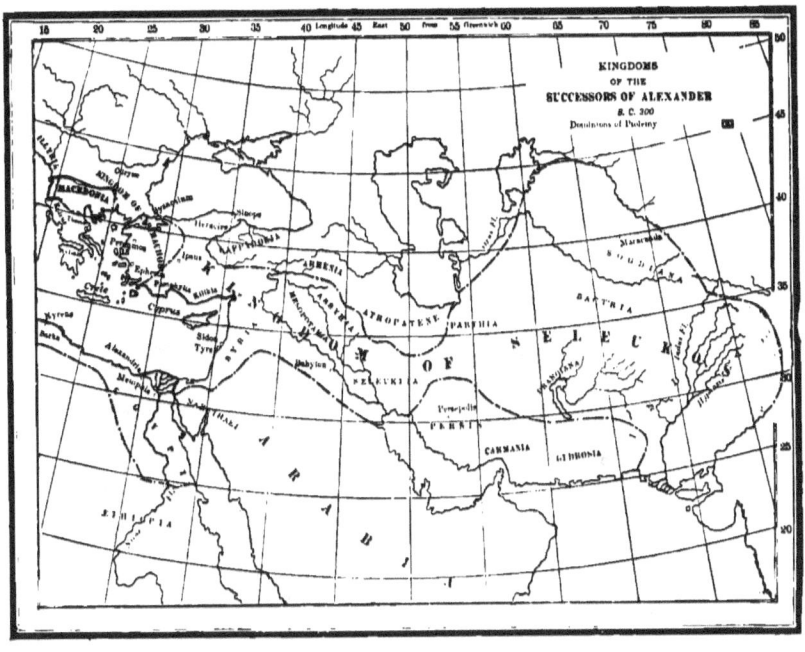

CHAPTER XIII.

ANCIENT GREECE.

SECTION XVIII.—DISSOLUTION OF ALEXANDER'S EMPIRE.

ALEXANDER the Great appointed no successor; he left no heir of his body, though both his widows, Statira and Roxana, were expecting to become mothers; his half-brother, Philip Arrhidæus, was weak-minded, and none of his other relatives was capable of holding the Empire together. To prevent its falling in pieces, a council of his leading officers, in the great palace at Babylon, agreed to support Philip Arrhidæus as nominal sovereign, with Perdíccas (to whom Alexander just before dying had left his signet-ring) as regent for themselves. If Roxana's child should be a son, he and Philip were to be joint sovereigns. But all the real power was to be in their own hands as viceroys—nearly forty of them, the most important being Antípater and Cráterus in Macedon and Greece; Ptólemy in Egypt; Antígonus in Phrygia, Lycia and Pamphylia; Leonnátus in Hellespontine Phrygia; Eúmenes in Paphlagonia and Cappadocia; and Lysímachus in Thrace.

Roxana did give birth to a son, and at once put Statira to death to prevent her doing likewise. This son was called Alexander IV., and proclaimed joint ruler according to agreement; but the real ruler was Perdíccas, who for two years held the Macedonian Empire together and loyal to the family of its illustrious founder. Four regents were appointed; two in Asia and two in Europe; but Perdíccas murdered his co-regent, thus becoming the sole ruler of Asia, while Antípater and Cráterus governed Macedon and Greece.

When intelligence of the death of Alexander the Great reached Greece, the Athenians, the Ætolians, and other Grecian allies decided upon rising in revolt against Antípater for the purpose of throwing off the hated yoke of Macedonian supremacy. The revolted allies assembled a considerable army and placed it under the command of the able Athenian general Leósthenes; while the Athenian people sent a galley to the island of Ægina and brought back Demosthenes, with enthusiastic demonstrations of respect. At the beginning of the struggle there seemed fair hope of permanent success. Leósthenes led the Grecian army into Thessaly, where he defeated Antípater in a spirited engagement. But Antípater sustained his military reputation by the excellent order of his retreat, and was enabled to throw his forces into Lamia, where he was besieged by the victorious army under Leósthenes. After an obstinate defense, Antípater finally made a successful sally, escaping with his troops through the lines of the besiegers. This enabled him to join the reinforcements which he had sent for from Asia, and soon afterward he encountered and defeated the allies at Cranon. The vanquished allies were obliged to sue for peace, which Antípater only granted on the most humiliating terms to the Athenians. Athens was required to abolish her democratic form of government; a Macedonian garrison was to be placed in the city, and Demosthenes and other orators were to be delivered to the Macedonians. Demosthenes fled, and on one of Antípater's tools attempting to decoy him from sanctuary, swallowed poison.

776 DISSOLUTION OF ALEXANDER'S EMPIRE.

COURT FESTIVAL AT SUSA AFTER THE DEATH OF ALEXANDER THE GREAT.

This struggle was called the *Lamian War*, because its seat was the Thessalian town of Lamia.

When Antípater was called to Asia soon afterward to quiet the dissensions prevalent there, the Ætolians embraced the opportunity to again attack the Macedonian territories, but failed as signally as in the previous enterprise. Peace was restored before Antípater's return.

The various viceroys, of course, considered their provinces as independent kingdoms, and refused to be governed by the regency. When Perdíccas saw that it was impossible to preserve the crown for the infant Alexander IV., he tried to gain the supreme power himself; but encountered opposition from Antígonus, one of the viceroys of Asia Minor, and Ptólemy, the viceroy of Egypt. Eúmenes, another viceroy of Asia Minor, supported him. Antígonus aimed at the sovereignty himself, while Ptólemy designed erecting his province in the Nile valley into an independent kingdom. Perdíccas was slain by his mutinous troops in a campaign against Ptólemy, and Cráterus perished in a battle with Eúmenes in Cappadocia, thus leaving Antípater sole regent of the entire Macedonian Empire. Antípater silenced Euridicé, the young wife of the puppet king, Philip Arrhidæus, who demanded to be allowed a share in the government, and caused the empire to be newly divided (B. C. 320). Antígonus, being assigned to the conduct of the war against Eúmenes, seized the larger portion of Asia Minor, under the pretext of upholding the royal authority.

Antípater died in Macedon in B. C. 319; and on his death-bed gave a striking proof of his disinterested regard for the interests of the Macedonian power, by appointing Polysperchon, the oldest of Alexander's generals then in Europe, as his successor to the viceroyalty of Macedon and Greece and to the regency of the entire Alexandrine dominions, thus disregarding the claims of relationship. When some one had once asked Alexander the Great whether Antípater ought not to have a crown, the conqueror replied: "Antípater is royal within."

One of Polysperchon's first acts caused the death of Phocion, the last of the Athenians worthy of being ranked with the great men of former times. Desiring to remove the governors appointed by Antípater, to concentrate the power of the empire in himself, Polysperchon ordered the Macedonian garrisons to be dismissed from Athens and other cities. The Athenians rejoiced at this decree; but Nicánor, the governor of the Macedonian garrison in Athens, declined to obey the viceroy's orders, and Phocion was charged with abetting his contumacy, and compelled to drink poison. Later, the Athenians remembered his virtues and the benefits they owed him, and erected a statue to him and paid other honors to his memory.

The appointment of Polysperchon as Antípater's successor disgusted Cassánder, Antípater's son, and Cassánder accordingly joined Antígonus, who was prosecuting the war against Eúmenes. Polysperchon and Eúmenes were endeavoring to uphold the unity of Alexander's great empire, while Cassánder, Antígonus and Ptólemy were seeking to dismember it for their own aggrandizement. Antígonus defeated a royal fleet near Byzantium, after which he drove Eúmenes beyond the Tigris, where the latter was joined by many of the Eastern satraps; but in spite of this reinforcement, Eúmenes was defeated after two indecisive battles, and was seized by his own troops and delivered up to Antígonus, who put him to death (B. C. 316).

In Macedon during the same year the puppet king, Philip Arrhidæus and his wife were put to death by order of Olympias, the mother of Alexander the Great. But Olympias herself fell into Cassánder's power at Pydna; and, in utter violation of the conditions of her surrender, was murdered by her enemies. Cassánder became master of Macedon and Greece. He secured his power by marrying Thessalonica, the half-sister of Alexander the Great, and founded in her honor the city bearing her name (B. C. 316).

The ambition of Antígonus now began

to alarm the other Macedonian generals and viceroys, as it was very evident that he was aiming at the undivided sovereignty of the whole of Alexander's dominions. He disposed of the Eastern satrapies at his pleasure, and drove Seleucus from Babylonia. Seleucus thereupon sought refuge in Egypt, and united with Ptólemy, viceroy of Egypt, Cassánder, viceroy of Macedon and Greece, Lysímachus, viceroy of Thrace and Bithynia, in a league against Antígonus. Thereupon a four years' war followed (B. C. 315-311), resulting in the recovery of Babylon and the East by Seleucus, while Antígonus gained power in Syria, Asia Minor and Greece. The peace of B. C. 311 provided for the independence of the Greek cities of Asia Minor, but permitted Ptólemy to hold Egypt and Lysímachus to retain Thrace; and left Cassánder as regent of Macedon and Greece until Alexander IV. should attain his majority, that prince being now sixteen years of age. But both Alexander IV., and his mother Roxana were murdered by order of Cassánder.

Cassánder entrusted the government of Athens to Demétrius Phaléreus, whose administration of ten years was so popular that the Athenians raised three hundred and sixty brazen statues to his honor; but at length, having lost all his popularity at his dissipated habits, Demétrius was compelled to retire into Egypt, all his statues but one being thrown down.

Seleucus, having recovered Babylon, also made himself master of Susiana, Media and Persia, and was not a party to the peace. All the allies probably considered him fully able to hold all his conquests. The peace of B. C. 311 lasted but one year, and was broken by Ptólemy, on the pretext that Antígonus had not liberated the Greek cities of Asia Minor, as provided for by the treaty, and that Cassánder still maintained his garrisons in the cities of European Greece. The war was thereupon renewed. Ptólemy gained an important success at first in Cilicia, but was finally checked by Demétrius, son of Antígonus, known as Demétrius Poliorcétes (the *town-taker*). Ptólemy then invaded Greece and occupied Sicyon and Corinth. He sought to marry Cleopatra, the sister of Alexander the Great, and the last survivor of the royal family of Macedon, but the princess was assassinated by order of Cassánder (B. C. 308). Demétrius Poliorcétes now arrived with a large fleet for the relief of Athens, whereupon Ptólemy retired to Cyprus and seized the island, but was followed by Demétrius Poliorcétes in B. C. 306. A great naval battle occurred off Salamis, in Cyprus—one of the most severe sea-fights in the world's history—in which Ptólemy was thoroughly defeated, with the loss of all but eight of his ships, while seventeen thousand of his soldiers and sailors were made prisoners by the victorious fleet under Demétrius Poliorcétes.

The five leading generals now assumed the royal title. Demétrius Poliorcétes vainly besieged Rhodes for an entire year; and that town, by its heroic defense, secured the privileges of neutrality during the remaining years of the war. During this year (B. C. 305) Cassánder made progress in his efforts to bring Greece under his authority. He had captured Corinth and was besieging Athens when Demétrius Poliorcétes arrived in the Euripus for the relief of the beleaguered city. Thereupon Cassánder relinquished the siege and marched against Demétrius, but was defeated by him in a battle near Thermopylæ, after which the victorious Demétrius entered Athens, where he was joyfully welcomed by the inhabitants. Demétrius assembled a congress at Corinth, which conferred upon him the title of generalissimo.

Cassánder, in great alarm, stirred up his allies to invade Asia Minor; and in the spring of B. C. 301, Demétrius was recalled to the aid of his father, who was menaced by the united forces of Lysímachus and Seleucus, the latter of whom had come from the East with a large army, including four hundred and eighty elephants. A great and decisive battle was fought at Ipsus, in Phrygia, B. C. 301. Antígonus and Demétrius being utterly defeated, and Antígonus slain in the eighty-first year of his age.

The battle of Ipsus resulted in a permanent division of the vast empire founded by Alexander the Great, after twenty-two years of sanguinary wars among his generals, during which the whole of Alexander's family and all his relatives perished. The triumphant Seleucus and Lysímachus divided the dominion of Asia between them; Seleucus receiving the Euphrates valley, Northern Syria, Cappadocia and part of Phrygia; while Lysímachus obtained the remainder of Asia Minor in addition to Thrace, which extended along the western shores of the Euxine as far north as the mouths of the Danube. Ptólemy was allowed to hold Egypt, along with Palestine, Phœnicia and Cœle Syria; while Cassánder was allowed to reign in Macedon and Greece until his death.

These twenty-two years of war among Alexander's generals had disastrous consequences for Macedon, by the exhausting expenditure of blood and treasure, and likewise by the introduction of Oriental habits of luxury and unmanly servility, in the place of the free and simple manners of previous ages. The minds of the Greeks were enlarged by a knowledge of the history and philosophy of the Asiatic nations, and by the observation of the physical world with its products in new climates and circumstances, but most of the influences which had kept the free spirit of the Grecian race alive no longer operated. Grecian patriotism was a thing of the past. Genius gave way to learning, and art to imitation.

The gains to Asia were many splendid cities and a vastly-increased commerce, along with the Greek military discipline and forms of civil government, which added new strength to her armies and states. The Greek language prevailed among the educated and ruling classes from the Adriatic on the west to the Indus on the east, and from the northern shores of the Euxine, or Black Sea, to the southern frontier of Egypt. The influence of Hellenic thought prevailed during a thousand years in Asia Minor, Syria, Palestine and Egypt, until the hosts of Mohammed changed the face of this quarter of the world anew by the establishment of a new Semitic dominion. The wide diffusion of the Greek language throughout the whole West of Asia was one of the most important preparations for the spread of the Christian religion. Had Alexander lived to complete his great project of amalgamating the Greek and Oriental nations, Asia would have been still more the gainer, and Europe more the loser, in consequence.

SECTION XIX.—MACEDON AND GREECE.

EMÉTRIUS Poliorcétes, son of Antígonus, proceeded to Greece, after the battle of Ipsus, but the Athenians refused to receive him. After entering into an alliance with Seleucus, King of Syria, Demétrius appeared before Athens, which, after a long siege, he captured; but instead of punishing the Athenians for their obstinate resistance, he treated them with unexpected magnanimity, supplied their wants, and did all in his power to relieve them from the miseries which the long siege had occasioned. After the death of Cassánder, Demétrius seized the throne of Macedon and Greece; but seven years afterward, Pyrrhus, King of Epirus, and Lysímachus, King of Thrace, successively possessed themselves of the kingdom of Macedon, and Demétrius died in captivity (B. C. 283). After Lysímachus had reigned over Macedon six years, a war broke out between him and Seleucus, King of Syria; and Lysímachus was defeated and slain iu battle near Sardis. Soon afterward, Seleucus was assassinated in Thrace by Ptólemy

Ceraunus, son of Ptólemy, King of Egypt, who then became King of Macedon and Greece (B. C. 280).

In the year 280 B. C., Macedonia was invaded by an immense horde of barbarians, called Gauls, under their chief, Brennus; and Ptólemy Ceraunus, who had usurped the throne of Macedon, was defeated and slain in battle against them. After frightfully ravaging Macedonia, the Gauls, under the leadership of Brennus, invaded Greece the next year (B. C. 279), and marched into Phocis for the purpose of plundering the temple to Apollo at Delphi. The Grecians met and defeated the barbarians at the pass of Thermopylæ, where their ancestors under the brave Leonidas two centuries before had made so heroic a defense against the immense Persian hosts of Xerxes; but the Gauls, like the Persians, marched by a secret path over the mountains, revealed to them by a traitor from the Grecian army; and the Greeks were finally obliged to retreat. Finding their way unobstructed, the barbarians then pushed forward to Delphi; but the Phocians soon arose against them and harassed their flank and rear, and at Delphi a very violent storm and earthquake so terrified the superstitious Gauls, and caused such a panic in their ranks, that they fought against each other, and were at last so weakened by mutual slaughter that they retired from Greece, many being slaughtered by the exasperated Greeks without mercy. The Gallic leader, Brennus, who had been severely wounded before Delphi, killed himself in despair. The shattered remnants of the Gauls then passed over into Asia Minor, and settled in the country named after them, Galatia.

After the death of Ptólemy Ceraunus, ANTIGONUS GONÁTUS, son of Demétrius Poliorcétes, seized the throne of Macedon and Greece; but he found a powerful rival competitor in the ambitious Pyrrhus, King of Epirus. After having failed in an expedition into Italy against the Romans, Pyrrhus aimed at reducing the whole of Greece and Macedonia under his own dominion, and with this end in view he invaded Macedonia; but he was soon obliged to retire into the Peloponnesus, and after being repulsed in an attack on Lacedæmon, he entered Argos, where a terrible conflict ensued, in which Pyrrhus was killed by a huge tile hurled upon him from a house top by an Argive woman, who was enraged at seeing that he was about to slay her son (B. C. 272). The death of Pyrrhus put an end to the long struggle for power among Alexander's successors in the West.

A new power now arose in Greece which soon became a formidable adversary to Macedonian supremacy in Greece, and which at one time promised fair to revive the former glory and influence of the Hellenic race. This power was the celebrated *Achæan League*, which at first consisted only of twelve towns of Achæa associated together for common defense and forming a little confederated republic, all the towns being equally represented in the federal government, which was entrusted with all matters concerning the general welfare, while each town retained the right of managing its own domestic affairs. The Achæan League did not possess much political influence until about the middle of the third century before Christ, when Arátus, an exile from Sicyon, with a few followers, took the city by surprise in the night, and, without the cost of a single life, liberated it from the sway of the tyrants who had long oppressed it with their despotic rule (B. C. 251). Dreading the hostility of the King of Macedon, Arátus induced Sicyon to join the Achæan League. Arátus soon became the idol of the Achæans, and soon after the accession of Sicyon to the League he was placed at the head of the Achæan armies. Corinth, which had been seized by a stratagem of Antígonus Gonátus of Macedon, and whose citadel was occupied by a Macedonian garrison, was delivered by a gallant enterprise of Arátus of Sicyon, and was also induced to join the Achæan League. Other cities joined the confederacy; but Argos and Corinth, influenced by the Spartans, at length seceded from the League. In wars with the Macedonians, the Achæans triumphed.

FLAMINIUS IN GREECE.

MACEDON AND GREECE.

Besides the King of Macedon, the enemies of the Achæan League were the Ætolian League and the Spartans. The Ætolian League, which was a confederation of the rudest of the Grecian tribes, had by degrees extended its supremacy over Locris, Phocis, Bœotia and other Grecian states. The valiant Spartan kings, Agis III. and Cleómenes, endeavored to restore the ancient glory and greatness of Lacedæmon by reviving the long-neglected laws of Lycurgus, the foundation of Sparta's former glory. They met with considerable opposition from the wealthy and aristocratic citizens of Lacedæmon, and Agis III. was cruelly murdered in prison; but Cleómenes succeeded in his endeavors by causing the opponents to his schemes to be removed by assassination. The ambitious Cleómenes aimed at the elevation of Sparta to the rank of the first power in Greece; and as the Achæan League was the chief obstacle in the way of his cherished designs, all his energies were directed to efforts for the dissolution of that formidable confederacy.

Seeing that the liberties of Greece were in greater danger from Spartan than from Macedonian ambition, Arátus of Sicyon, the Achæan chieftain, entered into an alliance with King ANTIGONUS DOSON of Macedon, the old enemy of the Achæan League. Cleómenes was defeated and Lacedæmon captured by the King of Macedon (B. C. 221). Afterwards, in a war against the Ætolian League, Arátus formed an alliance with PHILIP V., the successor of Antígonus Doson on the throne of Macedon; but when Arátus displeased Philip by advising him not to enter into an alliance with the Carthaginians in their war against the Romans, the Macedonian king caused the valiant leader of the Achæan League to be poisoned (B. C. 213).

The successor of Arátus of Sicyon in the administration of the affairs of the Achæan League was the talented and virtuous Philopœmen, who subdued the Spartans, and compelled them to abolish the laws of Lycurgus and to join the Achæan League. In a general assembly of the Greeks, Philopœmen was hailed as the restorer of Grecian liberty.

During the second war between Rome and Carthage, King Philip V. of Macedon entered into an alliance with the Carthaginians against the Romans. To give Philip sufficient employment in Greece, the Romans induced the Ætolians and the Spartans to wage war against the King of Macedon. After the conclusion of peace between Rome and Carthage, the Roman general Flaminius, who had been sent into Greece with a large army, defeated King Philip V. in a decisive battle fought in Thessaly, near a range of low hills, called from their peculiar shape, Cynoscéphalæ, or dogs' heads (B. C. 197). Philip V. was obliged to accept peace and to acknowledge the independence of Greece. At the Isthmian Games, the Roman general, to gratify the vanity of the Greeks, proclaimed the liberation of Greece from Macedonian oppression; but the Romans were now as intent on extending their supremacy over Greece as the King of Macedon had been in maintaining his sway there.

Several years after the defeat of Philip V., of Macedon, the Ætolians took up arms against the Romans, and formed an alliance with Antíochus the Great, King of Syria, the enemy of Rome. The Ætolians were completely defeated and deprived of their independence by the Romans; and their ally, the Syrian king, having suffered disastrous defeats by the Romans at Thermopylæ and in the great battle of Magnesia, in Asia Minor, was compelled to accept a disadvantageous peace (B. C. 190).

The Messenians attempting to secede from the Achæan League, Philopœmen was sent to reduce them to submission; but being taken prisoner, the valiant Achæan leader was compelled to drink the cup of poison (B. C. 183). The Achæans, however, conquered Messené the following year, and put the murderers of Philopœmen to death.

The wicked PÉRSEUS, who, on the death of his father, Philip V., had made his way to the throne of Macedon by the bloodiest crimes, was driven by the ambition of the

Romans into a war against that people; but he suffered a crushing defeat in the great battle of Pydna by the Roman army under the command of Paulus Æmilius (B. C. 168), and being soon afterward taken prisoner, the unfortunate king was carried to Rome, to grace the triumph of his conqueror; and Macedonia became a Roman province. One thousand Achæan chiefs, who were accused of having a secret understanding with Pérseus, were seized and carried to Rome as hostages. After many of these chiefs had died at Rome, the rest returned to Greece, burning with vengeance against the Romans.

Twenty years after the overthrow of the Macedonian monarchy, the arrogance of the Romans, who assisted the Spartans in a war against the Achæans, and who demanded that the Achæan League should be reduced to its original limits, induced the Achæans to take up arms in defense of the independence of Greece against Roman encroachments (B. C. 148). The Achæans were defeated in several bloody battles, and finally the Roman army, commanded by Consul Mummius, took Corinth by storm and reduced it to ashes. Greece then became a Roman province under the name of Achæa (B. C. 146). Thus ends the history of the celebrated and once-flourishing republics of Ancient Greece. We shall next proceed to a brief notice of the two most powerful and extensive kingdoms that arose from the dismemberment of the vast empire of Alexander the Great.

KINGS OF MACEDON.

B. C.	KINGS.	B. C.	KINGS.
795	CARANUS.	360	PHILIP THE GREAT.
	CŒNUS. } Dates uncertain.	336	ALEXANDER THE GREAT.
	THURYMAS.	324	PHILIP ARRHIDÆUS.
729	PERDICCAS I.	317	CASSANDER.
684	ARGÆUS.	298	PHILIP IV.
640	PHILIP I.	297	ALEXANDER IV. and ANTIPATER.
	ÆROPUS. } Dates uncertain.	294	DEMETRIUS I.
	ALECTAS.	287	PYRRHUS.
540	AMYNTAS I.	286	LYSIMACHUS OF THRACE.
500	ALEXANDER I.	281	PTOLEMY CERAUNUS.
454	PERDICCAS II.	280	MELEAGER.
433	ARCHELAUS.	278	SOSTHENES.
399	ORESTES.	277	ANTIGONUS GONATUS.
394	PAUSANIAS.	239	DEMETRIUS II.
393	AMYNTAS II.	229	ANTIGONUS DOSON.
369	ALEXANDER II.	220	PHILIP V.
366	PTOLEMY.	178	PERSEUS (to 168 B. C.)
364	PERDICCAS III.		

SECTION XX.—SYRIAN EMPIRE OF THE SELEUCIDÆ.

HE Syrian Empire of the Seleúcidæ dates from the year B. C. 312. After SELEUCUS had been restored to the government of Babylonia, in that year, he extended his dominion over all the provinces of Alexander's empire between the Euphrates on the west and the Indus on the east, and between the Jaxartes on the north and the Erythræan (now Arabian) Sea on the south. He also waged war against an Indian kingdom upon the western head-waters of the Ganges, thereby acquiring a vast extension of commerce, and the addition of five hundred elephants to his army. After the victory of Antígonus off the Cyprian Salamis, Seleucus assumed the royal title. The battle of Ipsus (B. C. 301) gave Seleucus the dominion of the country as far west as the Mediterranean, and gave him possession of Cappadocia, part of Phrygia, Northern Syria, and the right bank of the middle Euphrates, as his share of the territory which the conquerors divided between them; thus making his kingdom by far the most extensive that had been formed from the fragments of Alexander's vast empire.

Seleucus skillfully and thoroughly organized his extensive dominion, which was the most important of all the monarchies which sprang from the fragments of Alexander's empire. He divided his dominions into seventy-two provinces, all of which were placed under the rule of Greek or Macedonian governors. A standing army of native troops was organized and officered by Greeks or Macedonians. New cities sprang up in each of the seventy-two provinces, as monuments of the power of Seleucus, and as centers of Greek civilization. Sixteen of these cities were named Antioch, in honor of the father of Seleucus; five Laodicéa, in honor of his mother, Laódicé; seven Seleucia, in honor of himself; and several in honor of his two wives, Apaméa and Stratonicé. For the purpose of watching the movements of his rivals, Ptólemy and Lysímachus, more effectually, Seleucus removed his capital from Babylon to the new city of Antioch, on the Orontes, which for almost a thousand years remained one of the largest and most celebrated cities of the East. The new cities of Seleucia and Antioch in Syria became the centers of Grecian culture and refinement in Asia. The ancient Baälbec—the Greek Heliopolis—was a splendid city, as attested by its ruins.

In B. C. 293, Seleucus divided his empire with his son Antíochus, giving him all the provinces east of the Euphrates. Demétrius Poliorcétes, who had won and lost Macedonia, invaded the dominions of Lysímachus in Asia Minor in B. C. 287, for the purpose of acquiring for himself a new kingdom with his sword. Failing in this quarter, he invaded Cilicia and attacked the dominions of Seleucus, by whom he was defeated and held a prisoner the remainder of his life.

In B. C. 281 Lysímachus, King of Thrace, murdered his son, at the instigation of his Egyptian wife, Arsinoë, and her brother, Ptólemy Ceraunus; thus alienating the affections of his subjects. The widow of the murdered prince fled to the court of Seleucus, who espoused her cause and invaded the dominions of Lysímachus in Asia Minor. Seleucus and Lysímachus, now both aged, were the only survivors of Alexander's companions and generals. Lysímachus was defeated and slain in the battle of Corupédion (B. C. 281), and all his possessions in Asia Minor fell into the hands of the victorious Seleucus, who thus became master of the greater part of the empire of Alexander the Great. After committing the government of his present dominion to his son, Antíochus, the triumphant Seleucus crossed the Hellespont into Thrace and advanced to Lysimachía, the capital of his late rival, but was there assassinated by Ptólemy Ceraunus, who thereby became King of Thrace and Macedonia (B. C. 280).

ANTÍOCHUS I., Soter, the son of Seleucus, inherited his father's Asiatic dominions, and soon after his accession he waged war against the native kings of Bithynia, one of whom, Nicomédes, called to his aid the Gauls, who were then ravaging Thrace, Macedonia and Greece, and rewarded them for their assistance by assigning them a large territory in Northern Phrygia, which had formed part of the dominions of Antíochus, and which was thereafter called *Galátia.* North-western Lydia was likewise wrested from Antíochus and erected into the *Kingdom of Pérgamus.* Antíochus acquired the title of *Soter* (the Deliverer), from his only important victory over the Gauls (B. C. 275); but his operations were generally unsuccessful, and his kingdom was very much diminished in wealth and power during his reign. Antíochus Soter was defeated and killed in battle with the Gauls, near Ephesus, in B. C. 261.

ANTÍOCHUS II., Theos, (the God), who bore such a blasphemous title, succeeded his father Antíochus Soter. He was a weak and licentious monarch, and abandoned his government to his wives and dissolute favorites, who were neither feared nor respected in the remote provinces, and the empire rapidly declined. In the East, Bactria and Parthia revolted and formed themselves into independent kingdoms. These new monarchies greatly reduced the dominions of the Seleucidæ in the East. Through the influence of his wife, Laódicé, Antíochus Theos became involved in a war with Egypt, which he ended by divorcing his wife and marrying Berenicé, the daughter of Ptólemy Philadelphus, King of Egypt.

On the death of Ptólemy Philadelphus, Antíochus sent away Berenicé and took back his former wife, Laódicé, who, doubting his constancy, murdered him, along with Berenicé and her infant son, to secure the kingdom for her son, Seleucus (B. C. 246).

SELEUCUS II., Callinícus, the son of Antíochus Theos and Laódicé, succeeded his father, and was at once involved in a war with Ptólemy Euérgetes, King of Egypt, who invaded the dominions of the Seleúcidæ to avenge the murder of his sister and nephew, and who the next year conquered almost the whole Syrian Empire, becoming master of all Asia west of the Tigris, excepting part of Lydia and Phrygia; even Susiana, Media and Persia submitting to the invader, who carried his victorious arms as far east as the Indus. But his severe exactions aroused discontent, and a revolt in Egypt called him home, whereupon he lost all his conquests, Seleucus reëstablishing his authority from the Indus on the east to the Ægean on the west. Soon afterward Antíochus Híerax (the Hawk), younger brother of the king, only fourteen years old, revolted and was aided by his uncle and a troop of Gauls; while, at the same time, the Parthian king, Arsáces II., gained some important advantages in the East, and signally defeated Seleucus Callinícus in a great battle (B. C. 237). The civil war between Seleucus and his youthful brother continued until B. C. 229, when the rebellious prince was defeated and obliged to flee for his life. Seleucus Callinícus was killed by a fall from his horse (B. C. 226).

SELEUCUS III., Ceraunus, the son and successor of Seleucus Callinícus, reigned only three years; and in an expedition against Attalus, King of Pérgamus, he was killed by some of his mutinous officers (B. C. 223).

ANTIOCHUS III., the Great, the great-grandson of Seleucus, the founder of the dynasty of the Seleúcidæ, had an eventful reign of thirty-six years (B. C. 223–187). He began his reign by crushing the revolt of Molo, the ablest of his generals, who had made himself master of the provinces east of the Euphrates, and had annihilated every army sent against him. Antíochus finally defeated Molo in B. C. 220, after which he waged war with Ptólemy Philópator, King of Egypt, for the recovery of Phœnicia and Palestine, which had hitherto been held by Ptólemy. He first conquered those provinces; Palestine having become alienated from Egypt by Ptólemy Philópator's profanation of the Temple of Jerusalem, and willingly submitting to Antíochus the Great, who advanced southwards and encountered the Egyptian army at Raphia, where he suffered a great defeat, which deprived him of all his conquests except Seleucia in Syria, the port of Antioch (B. C. 217).

Archæus, the cousin of Antíochus the Great, and hitherto the loyal servant of Antíochus and his father, had revolted in consequence of the false accusations of Hermías, the king's prime minister. Archæus made himself master of all the provinces west of the Taurus mountain-range. After making peace with the King of Egypt, Antíochus the Great marched against the rebel chieftain, wrested all his possessions from him in one campaign, besieged him in Sardis two years, and finally captured him by treachery and caused him to be put to death (B. C. 214).

Antíochus then led an army to the eastern portion of his empire to meet the Parthian king Arsáces III., who was advancing toward Media. By a rapid march across the desert to Hecatómpylos, the Parthian capital, Antíochus took that city (B. C. 213), after which

SYRIAN EMPIRE OF THE SELEUCIDÆ.

he passed the mountains and entered Hyrcania, where he fought an indecisive battle with the Parthians, in consequence of which he agreed to a treaty of peace, by which he acknowledged the independence of Parthia and Hyrcania as one kingdom under Arsá- Euthydémus, and Demétrius, the son of Antíochus. Antíochus then crossed the Hindoo Koosh mountain-range and penetrated into India, where he renewed the old alliance of Seleucus Nicátor with the Indian kingdom of that region, after which he re-

SCENE IN THE REGION OF DECAPOLIS.

ces. Antíochus then made war on Bactria, but after he had won some successes he made peace with the Bactrian king, Euthydémus, leaving him in possession of Bactria and Sogdiana. A marriage was arranged between the daughter of the Bactrian king, turned home through Arachosia, Drangiana and Carmania, wintering in the last-named province. The next year Antíochus undertook a naval expedition in the Persian Gulf against the Arabs on the western shore of that body of water, to punish them for their piracies, after which he returned home (B. C. 205), after an absence of seven years, whereupon he received the title of *the Great*, by which name he is generally known in history.

Antíochus now renewed his designs against Egypt, in which country Ptólemy Epíphanes, a child of only five years, succeeded his father, Ptólemy Philópator, the government being conducted by a regent. Antíochus, considering the opportunity favorable for aggrandizing himself at the expense of the Egyptian monarchy, made a treaty with Philip V. of Macedon to divide the kingdom of the Ptólemies between them. Philip's designs were interrupted by his unfortunate war with Rome; but Antíochus prosecuted hostilities with great activity in Cœle-Syria, Phœnicia and Palestine, and recovered those provinces by the decisive battle of Páneas. B. C. 198. Antíochus gave his daughter Cleopatra, in marriage to Ptólemy Epíphanes, the young King of Egypt, and promised Cœle-Syria and Palestine as her dower, but neither Antíochus nor his successors fulfilled this promise. Antíochus then overran Asia Minor, crossed the Hellespont, and seized the Thracian Chersonésus.

In B. C. 196, the Romans, after having defeated Philip V. of Macedon and assumed the protectorate of Egypt, sent an embassy to Antíochus the Great, requiring him to surrender all the conquests of territory which he had made from Egypt and from Macedon. Antíochus rejected this intervention of the great republic of the West with intense indignation, and prepared for war, with the assistance of Hannibal, the great Carthaginian leader, who had found refuge at his court. In B. C. 192 Antíochus invaded Greece and took Chalcis, but he was decisively defeated by the Romans at Thermopylæ and forced to retire into Asia Minor. The Romans followed up their success, and by two naval victories wrested from Antíochus the whole western coast of Asia Minor. The Roman army under the two Scipios crossed the Hellespont into Asia Minor, and in the great battle of Magnesia, in Lydia, B. C. 190, reduced Antíochus to such straits that he was obliged to sue for peace, which he only obtained by ceding all Asia Minor except Cilicia to the Romans, and by agreeing to pay a war-indemnity of fifteen thousand talents, equal to about fifteen million dollars, and giving twenty hostages, among whom was his son, Antíochus Epíphanes, for the payment. The territory which Antíochus surrendered to the Romans was given to the Kingdom of Pérgamus, which was thus sufficiently powerful to serve as a check upon the Syrian Empire of the Seleúcidæ. These losses were followed by the revolt of Armenia, which succeeded in establishing its independence of the Seleúcidæ, (B. C. 190). While endeavoring to suppress the Armenian revolt, Antíochus, in order to obtain the money to pay the indemnity imposed upon him by the Romans, plundered the temples of Asia of their treasures, thus exciting a tumult in Elymaïs, in which he lost his life (B. C. 187).

SELEUCUS IV., Philópator, succeeded his father, Antíochus the Great, and had an uneventful reign of eleven years. His kingdom was exhausted, and the Romans were ready to seize any of its exposed provinces if he made the least hostile movement. Seleúcus Philópator was finally assassinated by his treasurer, HELIODORUS, who then usurped the Syrian crown (B. C. 176), but the usurper was soon overthrown by ANTIOCHUS IV., Epíphanes, the brother of Seleucus Philópator, who, aided by Eúmenes, King of Pérgamus, established himself upon the throne.

Antíochus Epíphanes had been a hostage at Rome thirteen years, and after his accession he introduced many Roman customs into his kingdom, to the utter surprise of his subjects. He waged war with Armenia, and, irritated at the demand of Ptólemy Philométor, King of Egypt, for the surrender of Syria and Palestine, which his father had promised as a dowry to the wife of Ptólemy Epíphanes, he invaded Egypt, and had almost conquered the country when the Romans interfered and compelled him to relinquish all his conquests. Being thus obliged to obey the Romans, Antíochus Epíphanes vented his rage upon the Jews by capturing Jerusalem by assault, and plundering and desecrating the Temple. His attempt to suppress the worship of Jehovah, and to introduce the Grecian polytheism into Judæa, aroused the Jews to revolt, and that people flew to arms under the leadership of the High Priest, Mattathías, and his heroic son, Judas Maccabæus, and several times defeated the army sent by Antíochus Epíphanes to subdue them. Antíochus, who was then in the East, set out in person to punish the Jews for this insult to his authority. On the way he stopped to plunder the temple at Elymais, but was seized with a superstitious insanity which caused his death (B. C. 164). Both the Jews and the Greeks believed that his madness was inflicted upon him as a punishment for his sacrilege.

ANTIOCHUS V., Eúpator, the son of Antíochus Epíphanes, succeeded his father. As he was only twelve years old, the government was conducted by Lysias as regent. Lysias and the youthful king proceeded to Judæa to prosecute the war against the rebellious Jews, and forced Judas Maccabæus to shut himself up in Jerusalem and besieged the city. Philip, whom Antíochus Epíphanes had appointed guardian of his son, now appeared at Antioch with the royal signet and seized the government. When Lysias heard of this, he immediately caused the young king to make peace with Judas Maccabæus, and at once returned to Antioch, defeated Philip, captured him, and put him to death. Lysias appears to have cared nothing for the interests of the kingdom, as he made no effort to check the Parthians, who were overrunning the eastern provinces of the kingdom, and as he did not resist the Romans, who were ravaging the kingdom on the west and harshly enforcing the terms of the treaty made with Antíochus the Great. In the midst of the serious danger thus threatening the kingdom of the Seleúcidæ, Demétrius, the son of Seleucus Philópator, escaped from Rome, where he had been kept for many years as a hostage, and seized the throne, after causing both Antíochus Eúpator and Lysias to be put to death (B. C. 162).

DEMÉTRIUS I. spent some years in unsuccessful efforts to crush the Jewish rebellion. He was at first successfully resisted by Judas Maccabæus; but when that valiant chieftain perished in battle, the Romans entered into an alliance with the Jews and forbade Demétrius to conquer the revolted province of Judæa, which they recognized as an independent kingdom under the Maccabees. Demétrius then endeavored to dethrone Ariaráthes, King of Cappadocia, and bestowed the Cappadocian crown upon Orophérnes, his illegitimate brother. The deposed satrap of Babylon instigated the impostor, Alexander Balas, an illegitimate son of Antíochus Epíphanes, to claim the Syrian crown. The pretender was aided by the forces of Rome, Cappadocia, Pérgamus, Egypt and Judæa, which had entered into an alliance in his interest; and when Demétrius was slain in battle, B. C. 151, his rival acquired the crown.

ALEXANDER BALAS reigned five years. His success was chiefly owing to Egypt, and he had married Cleopatra, the daughter of the Egyptian king, Ptólemy Philométor; but he proved himself wholly unfit for his royal station, as he relinquished the government to a worthless favorite named Ammónius, and abandoned himself to licentiousness and self-indulgence. His ingratitude to his father-in-law, Ptólemy Philométor, caused that monarch to withdraw his support, and to take his daughter Cleopatra from him and give her in marriage to Demétrius Nicátor, the son of Demétrius I., who had been encouraged to make pretensions to the crown in consequence of the hatred of the Syrians towards Alexander Balas. Demétrius Nicátor landed in Cilicia, and, aided by the Egyptian army under King Ptólemy Philométor, defeated Alexander Balas in a battle near Antioch, whereupon Alexander fled into Arabia, where he was assassinated by his own officers (B. C. 146).

DEMÉTRIUS II., Nicátor, soon alienated

the favor of his subjects by his tyranny and cruelty. The people of Antioch having rebelled against him, he permitted his bodyguard, composed of Jewish mercenaries, to plunder the city. Diódotus Tryphon, of Apaméa, now set up ANTIOCHUS VI., the two-year-old son of Alexander Balas, as a claimant for the crown. Three years later Diódotus removed this infant pretender, and, with the aid of Judas Maccabæus, declared himself king, assuming the name of TRYPHON (B. C. 143). After fighting ineffectually for seven years against his rivals, Demétrius left the government in Syria to his wife, Cleopatra, as regent, and took the field against the Parthians, who had almost conquered the eastern province of the Seleúcidæ; but Demétrius, after some successes, was defeated and made prisoner by the Parthian king, Arsáces VI., who kept him in captivity ten years, but treated him with all the honors of royalty, and gave him a Parthian princess for his second wife.

Unable to maintain her position without assistance, Cleopatra called to her aid her husband's brother, Antíochus Sidétes, who defeated and killed the usurper, Diódotus Tryphon, after a war of two years, and seated himself upon the vacant throne as ANTIOCHUS VII., Sidétes (B. C. 137). He married Cleopatra, his brother's wife, who considered herself free on account of her husband's captivity in Parthia and his marriage with a Parthian princess. Antíochus Sidétes made war on the Jews, captured Jerusalem, after a siege of almost a year, and again reduced Judæa under the dominion of the Seleúcidæ, in which condition that country remained two years (B. C. 135-133).

Antíochus Sidétes then led an expedition against the Parthians for the purpose of releasing his brother from captivity. He gained some success at first, but was finally defeated, with the loss of his army, and slain, after a reign of nine years (B. C. 128). Just before the death of Antíochus Sidétes, the Parthian king had liberated Demétrius Nicátor and sent him to Antioch to claim his crown, for the purpose of forcing Antíochus to retire from Parthia to preserve his kingdom. Demétrius Nicátor resumed his authority, and the death of his brother soon afterward left him without a rival for a short time. Ptólemy Physcon, King of Egypt, soon raised up a pretender named Zabínas, for the purpose of revenging himself upon Demétrius for the support which he had given the Egyptian queen Cleopatra. Zabínas, who claimed to be a son of Alexander Balas, defeated Demétrius near Damascus. Thereupon Demétrius fled to his former wife, Cleopatra, at Ptólemaïs (now Acre), but she refused to receive him. He then attempted to enter Tyre, but was captured and put to death (B. C. 126).

SELEUCUS V., the eldest son of Demétrius Nicátor, assumed the crown without the permission of his mother, Cleopatra, who then caused him to be put to death, and placed herself and her second son, ANTIOCHUS VIII., Grypus, on the throne as joint sovereigns. Zabínas, the pretender, at the same time reigned in part of Syria for seven years, during which he quarreled with his patron, Ptólemy Physcon, King of Egypt, who abandoned him (B. C. 124); and finally Zabínas was defeated and captured by Antíochus Grypus, who compelled him to take poison (B. C. 122). The next year Antíochus Grypus found his mother conspiring against his life, whereupon he caused her to be executed.

The Syrian Empire of the Seleúcidæ now enjoyed eight years of peace, and well did this kingdom need rest, as it was exhausted by the long foreign wars and the domestic commotions which distracted it, and had lost Parthia, Bactria, and all the other provinces east of the Euphrates, along with Judæa, thus becoming a mere petty state, without energy and thoroughly corrupt. The wealth of the country was in the possession of weak nobles enfeebled by luxury, the masses of the people being in a condition of abject poverty.

In B. C. 114 the king's half-brother, ANTIOCHUS X., Cyzicénus, the son of Cleopatra by her third husband, Antíochus Sidétes, headed a rebellion against the king, thus involving the kingdom in a bloody war of

SYRIAN EMPIRE OF THE SELEUCIDÆ.

three years, and finally compelling Antíochus Grypus to divide the kingdom with him. But the war was renewed in B. C. 105 and continued until B. C. 96, bringing dreadful loss and misery upon the kingdom, without any decisive gain to either party. During this period Syria was terribly ravaged by the Arabs on the east and by the Egyptians on the south. The province of Cilicia and the cities of Tyre, Sidon and Seleucia revolted and achieved their independence. Finally, in B. C. 96, Antíochus Grypus was assassinated by Herácleon, an officer of the court, who made an unsuccessful effort to seize the crown.

SELEUCUS V., the son of Antíochus Grypus, succeeded his father on the Syrian throne, and continued the war against Antíochus Cyzicénus, defeating him in a great battle. The vanquished pretender committed suicide to avoid capture, but his eldest son, ANTIOCHUS X., Eúsebes, maintained the pretensions of the rival house, assumed the royal title, and drove Seleucus V. into Cilicia. Seleucus endeavored to raise money by a forced contribution from the people of the Cilician town of Mopsuestia, but they seized him and burned him alive.

PHILIP, the brother of Seleucus V., and the second son of Antíochus Grypus, succeeded to the Syrian throne, and with the assistance of his younger brothers, Demétrius and Antíochus Dionysus, continued the war against Eúsebes for some years; and Eúsebes was finally defeated and obliged to seek refuge in Parthia. But peace was still not restored to the country, as Philip and his brothers could not agree upon a satisfactory division of power between them, and made war upon each other; and the unhappy kingdom only obtained rest when the Syrians, tired of these dynastic quarrels, invited Tigránes, King of Armenia, to become their sovereign.

TIGRÁNES readily accepted the invitation and governed Syria wisely and well for fourteen years (B. C. 83–69), and the country enjoyed tranquillity. Finally Tigránes incurred the vengeance of the Romans by assisting his father-in-law, Mithridátes the Great, King of Pontus, and was forced to relinquish Syria, whose crown was then conferred upon ANTIOCHUS XIII., Asiáticus, who reigned four years (B. C. 69–65), and was the last of the Seleúcidæ. In B. C. 65 the Roman general, Pompey the Great, defeated Antíochus Asiáticus and converted Syria into a Roman province.

THE SELEUCIDÆ OF SYRIA.

B. C.	KINGS.	B. C.	KINGS.
312	SELEUCUS NICATOR.	146	DEMETRIUS NICATOR (deposed).
280	ANTIOCHUS SOTER.	137	ANTIOCHUS SIDETES.
261	ANTIOCHUS THEOS.	128	DEMETRIUS NICATOR (restored).
246	SELEUCUS CALLINICUS.	125	ANTIOCHUS GRYPUS.
226	SELEUCUS CERAUNUS.	111	ANTIOCHUS CYZICENUS.
223	ANTIOCHUS THE GREAT.	95	SELEUCUS IV.
187	SELEUCUS PHILOPATOR.	94	ANTIOCHUS EUSEBES.
175	ANTIOCHUS EPIPHANES.	85	PHILIP.
164	ANTIOCHUS EUPATER.	83	TIGRANES OF ARMENIA.
162	DEMETRIUS SOTER.	69	ANTIOCHUS ASIATICUS (to B. C. 65).
150	ALEXANDER BALAS.		

SECTION XXI.—EGYPT UNDER THE PTOLEMIES.

THE conquest of Egypt by Alexander the Great in B. C. 332 entirely changed the character of Egyptian history and of the Egyptian people, and laid the foundation of their future greatness and glory. He made Alexandria the capital of Egypt, and conferred upon it the advantages of Greek civilization, which rapidly spread among the native population. This change brought Egypt into constant and familiar intercourse with the rest of the world, and the old exclusiveness of the ancient Egyptians was forever broken down. Thus the Macedonian kingdom in Egypt presented a remarkable and striking contrast to the native kingdoms and the Persian satrapy. When Palestine was annexed to the Macedonian-Egyptian kingdom, the Jews were specially favored; and the Græco-Macedonian conquerors, the native Egyptians, and the Jewish merchants—representatives of the Aryan, Hamitic and Semitic branches of the Caucasian race—were united as they had never been before. The native Egyptians, who had never been reconciled to the Medo-Persian dominion, hailed the Græco-Macedonians as deliverers. Commercial pursuits were adopted by the larger portion of the nation. The masses of the people zealously engaged in the new industries that promised wealth as the reward of enterprise. The learned class found delight in the intellectual society and in the rare treasures of literature and art for which the court of the Ptolemies was distinguished.

The Greek, Macedonian and Jewish elements were principally found in and about Alexandria. The native Egyptians in the interior of the country retained the language and religion which they had inherited from their ancestors; but they were also powerfully affected in manners and thought, and were brought more into intercourse and sympathy with the rest of mankind, by their commingling with the Greeks. They became the willing subjects of Alexander the Great and his successors, the Ptolemies, and under that dynasty they engaged actively in commerce and commenced the cultivation of a literature which soon made Alexandria the chief seat of Grecian learning and civilization, and one of the most renowned cities of the ancient world.

Upon the death of Alexander the Great, in B. C. 324, Egypt was conferred on PTOLEMY I., Soter, or Lagi, one of his most distinguished generals. Ptolemy immediately took possession of his share of the great conqueror's vast empire, and from the very beginning he intended to retain this renowned country for his own personal benefit, and proceeded, with great wisdom and energy, to its organization into an independent kingdom for himself and his posterity. He abandoned all other ambitious designs for the purpose of confining himself to the strengthening of this country and the development of its internal resources, restricting his conquests to those regions which could be acquired without too much risk.

Ptolemy's chief effort was to make Egypt a great maritime power, and in this enterprise he eventually succeeded far beyond his expectations. To secure the success of this design, he sought to conquer Palestine, Phœnicia and Cyprus, whose forests he needed for ship-building, and whose hardy sailors he wanted to man his fleets. He occupied Palestine and Phœnicia in B. C. 320, and retained possession of them for six years, after which he lost them in a war with Antigonus, and only fully recovered them after the battle of Ipsus, in B. C. 301. Many conflicts occurred in and about Cyprus, the most severe and decisive of which was the great naval battle off Salamis in B. C. 306. Ptolemy then lost Cyprus, but recovered it in B. C. 294 or 293, and that island constituted the most important foreign possession of the Ptolemies as long as their kingdom remained in existence. The first

Ptolemy also annexed Cyrênê and all the Libyan territory between it and Egypt.

The kingdom founded by Ptolemy Soter was an absolute monarchy, in which the political power was vested entirely in the king, and was administered by Macedonian and Greek officials exclusively. The rank and file of the standing army was likewise composed almost wholly of Macedonians and Greeks, and was entirely officered by those people. The Greek inhabitants of the cities alone possessed full civil and political freedom. No important changes were, however, made in the political system or the ancient laws of the land, and Ptolemy reconciled the native Egyptians to his rule by respecting their laws, religion and usages. The kingdom remained divided into nomes, each having its own ruler, who was generally a native Egyptian. The Ptolemies rebuilt the temples, paid special honor to the bull-deity, Apis, and took full advantage of all points of resemblance between the Greek and Egyptian religions. Ptolemy erected a magnificent temple to Serápis at Alexandria. The priests remained in possession of their privileges and honors.

As Ptolemy was an author himself, he was a liberal patron of learning and literature, and pursued the most munificent policy toward men of genius and letters. He collected the celebrated library of Alexandria and placed it in a building connected with the palace.

He also founded the *Museum*, which attracted students and professors from every quarter of the globe. No place ever surpassed Alexandria in its intellectual and literary activity, and that city was preëminently "the University of the East." Ptolemy induced the most renowned scholars of the world to take up their residence at his court; and under his auspices Alexandria became what Athens had previously been—the great center of Greek civilization, learning, wealth and refinement, and the great emporium of the world's commerce; while a mingled civilization—Greek, Egyptian and Jewish—arose in this famous metropolis of the ancient kingdom of the Pharaohs.

In that city Euclid first unfolded the "*Elements of Geometry.*" There Eratósthenes discoursed of geography; Hippárchus of astronomy; Aristóphanes and Aristárchus of criticism; Manetho of history. There Apélles and Antíphilus added their paintings, and Philétas, Callímachus and Apollonius their poems for the delight of a court which has never had a parallel in its munificent patronage of men of talent and scholarship.

Ptolemy adorned Alexandria with numerous costly and magnificent edifices, such as the royal Palace; the Museum; the great light-house on the island of Pharos, built of white marble, four hundred feet high, the light at the top of which could be seen at a distance of forty miles, and which was one of the *Seven Wonders of the World;* the mole or causeway connecting this island with the mainland; the *Hippodrome;* the temple of Serápis; and the *Soma*, or *Mausoléum*, to contain the remains of Alexander the Great. Ptolemy likewise rebuilt the inner chamber of the great temple at Karnak.

Ptolemy Soter died after a brilliant reign of forty years (B. C. 323-283), and was succeeded on the throne of Egypt by his renowned son, PTOLEMY II., Philadelphus, who was then twenty-six years old, and who had been carefully educated by the learned men whom his father had gathered at the court of Alexandria. Ptolemy Philadelphus encouraged science and literature on a still more liberal scale than did his illustrious father, and Alexandria reached its zenith of greatness and glory as the intellectual metropolis of the world. He increased the Alexandrian Library to five hundred volumes, and is often spoken of as the founder of that famous repository of ancient learning. He appointed agents to search Europe and Asia for every valuable and meritorious literary work and to obtain it at any cost. He founded the minor library at Serapeium, and invited learned men from every portion of the world to his court; and under his patronage and auspices literary works of the greatest value were undertaken.

AN ALEXANDRIAN ASTRONOMER.

EGYPT UNDER THE PTOLEMIES.

The most important of these literary enterprises was the translation of the Hebrew Scriptures into the Greek language, by which these sacred writings have become the common property of the Jewish and Christian world. Ptolemy Philadelphus had sent an embassy to the High Priest at Jerusalem to bring a copy of the sublime works of the Hebrew bards and sages, along with a body of scholars who were able to translate them into Greek. The king entertained the translators with the greatest honor. The books of the Pentateuch were completed during the reign of Ptolemy Philadelphus, but the remaining books of the Old Testament were translated by order of the later Ptolemies. The entire translation is called the *Septuagint Version*, either because it was the work of seventy translators—Greek and Jewish doctors—or because it was au-

PTOLEMY SOTER ORDERING THE ERECTION OF THE ALEXANDRIAN MUSEUM.

ANCIENT HISTORY.—GREECE.

thorized by the *Sânhedrim* of Alexandria, which consisted of seventy members. The Septuagint translation was an important event in history; and, by spreading knowledge of the Hebrew sacred literature, prepared the way for Christianity.

It was also during the reign of Ptolemy Philadelphus that the Egyptian priest, Manetho, wrote in Greek his celebrated *History of Egypt*. Ptolemy Philadelphus liberally encouraged painting and sculpture and adorned Alexandria with numerous grand and noble edifices. He reopened the great canal built by Rameses the Great, connecting the Red Sea and the Nile, founded the port of Arsinoë (now Suez), and also Berenicé, on the Red Sea; and established a caravan route from it to Coptos, near Thebes. Ptolemais, on the Red Sea, became a flourishing emporium of the ivory trade; and various industries flourished, such as the weaving of linen, glass-blowing and paper-making. Ptolemy Philadelphus boasted that no citizen was idle in Alexandria. His revenue was immense, being equal to that which Darius Hystapes had derived from the vast Medo-Persian Empire, thus amounting to fourteen thousand eight hundred talents,

THE PHAROS AT ALEXANDRIA.

equal to about seventeen million seven hundred and sixty thousand dollars of our money, without counting the tribute in grain. His army numbered two hundred and fifty thousand men, and his fleet embraced fifteen hundred vessels.

Under Ptolemy Philadelphus, Egypt reached the culminating point of her commercial prosperity. The rich products of India, Arabia and Ethiopia crowded the marts of Alexandria; and for centuries this commerce followed the route established by this great and enterprising monarch, and having its center at Alexandria, which was the point of its distribution to the European nations. The Ethiopian trade was particularly important.

Ptolemy Philadelphus did not inherit his father's military genius, and his wars were therefore not as successful as those of his illustrious predecessor's reign. His first war was against Macedon for the protection of the Achæan League. The second was against his half-brother Magas, King of Cyrênê, who cast off his dependence upon the Egyptian king, and marched against Egypt, about B. C. 266. Thereupon Magas entered into an alliance with Antíochus Soter, King of Syria, and invaded Egypt a second time in B. C. 264. The Egyptians prevented Antíochus from coming to Africa to aid Magas by vigorous movements in Asia, and checked the advance of Magas. In B. C. 259 Magas was recognized as independent sovereign of the Cyrenaica, and his daughter Berenicê was betrothed to the eldest son of Ptolemy Philadelphus. Ptolemy made himself master of the coast of Asia Minor and many of the Cyclades, during his war with Antíochus Soter of Syria. Peace was made in B. C. 249, and Ptolemy Philadelphus gave his daughter in marriage to Antíochus Soter.

The personal character of Ptolemy Philadelphus was not so amiable as that of his father. He began his reign by banishing Demétrius Phaléreus, merely because he had advised Ptolemy Soter not to alter the succession. Soon afterward he caused two of his brothers to be put to death. He was

2—51.-U. H.

first married to Arsinoë, the daughter of Lysímachus, King of Thrace; but afterwards became enamored of his sister Arsinoë, who had already been married to his half-brother, Ptolemy Ceraunus, whereupon he divorced his first wife and banished her to Coptos, in Upper Egypt. He then married his sister, to whom he was thenceforth most affectionately attached, though no children resulted from the marriage. The custom thus introduced by Ptolemy Philadelphus was followed by all his successors, and was the cause of untold mischief and misery to the kingdom of the Ptolemies. Ptolemy Philadelphus died in B. C. 247, after a glorious reign of thirty-six years from the death of his father.

PTOLEMY III., Euérgetes, the son and successor of Ptolemy Philadelphus, was the most enterprising monarch of this celebrated dynasty, and was a great conqueror, as well as a liberal patron of literature and art. He was the son of the first wife of his father. He departed from the defensive policy of his father and grandfather, and began a series of conquests, thus reviving the glories of Egypt under the Pharaohs, and extended his dominions far beyond those of his predecessors or successors of the Ptolemaic dynasty. He acquired the Cyrenaica by his marriage with Berenicê, the daughter and heiress of Magas. In the second year of his reign he waged war with Antíochus Theos, King of Syria, to avenge the wrongs of his sister Berenicê, who had been divorced by Antíochus and murdered by Laódicé. In B. C. 245 Ptolemy Euérgetes led an army into Syria and took Antioch, after which he crossed the Euphrates and conquered Mesopotamia, Babylonia, Susiana, Media and Persia, and reduced all the eastern provinces of the Seleúcidæ as far as Bactria; while his fleet ravaged the coast of Asia Minor and Thrace. But when he was suddenly recalled to Egypt by coming troubles, all his Eastern conquests were at once lost, and those provinces were soon recovered by Antíochus Theos. The Egyptian king, however, retained his conquests on the sea-coast, because his command of the sea, by means of his powerful navy, enabled him to hold them. Thus the Egyptian empire of Ptolemy Euérgetes was one of immense extent, following the Mediterranean coast from Cyrênê to the Hellespont, and embracing a part of Thrace and many islands of the Mediterranean.

In the latter years of his reign, Ptolemy Euérgetes annexed a part of the western coast of Arabia and portions of Ethiopia. He participated in the wars in Greece, first assisting the Achæan League until it made peace with Antígonus Gonátus of Macedon, when he aided Cleómenes, King of Sparta, against the Achæan confederates. During this war the Egyptian fleet defeated the Macedonian fleet off the island of Andros. Ptolemy Euérgetes remained on amicable terms with Rome, but declined the aid offered him by that republic against the King of Syria. He seems to have been suspicious of Roman ambition.

Ptolemy Euérgetes was likewise a great patron of literature and art, and added many valuable manuscripts to the Alexandrian Library. The native Egyptians were still more gratified by the recovery of some of the oldest images of their gods, which had been taken to Assyria by Sargon and Esar-haddon, and were brought back to Egypt by Ptolemy Euérgetes from his Eastern campaign.

Ptolemy Euérgetes died in B. C. 222, after a prosperous reign of twenty-five years; and with his death ended the glory of the Ptolemaïc dynasty. Under him Hellenized Egypt had reached the zenith of her power and prosperity. Under the nine succeeding Ptolemies, who were weak and generally worthless, Egypt rapidly declined from the exalted position which it had held under the first three monarchs of this famous Macedonian dynasty.

PTOLEMY IV., Philópator, the son and successor of Ptolemy Euérgetes, was suspected of having murdered his father, and, to allay this suspicion, he assumed the title given him—Philópator meaning *lover of his father*. He, however, began his reign by murdering his mother, his brother and his uncle, and marrying his sister Arsinoë, whom he also put to death a few years later, after she had borne him an heir to the throne. This last crime was committed at the instigation of a worthless favorite of the king Ptolemy Philópator was a weak and shamefully-licentious sovereign, and left the government to Sosíbius, a minister who was as wicked and incompetent as his master. Through his negligence the Egyptian army became so weak, on account of lack of discipline, that Antíochus the Great, King of Syria, considered the opportunity favorable to recover the lost possessions of the Seleucidæ, and he accordingly endeavored to reconquer Palestine and Phœnicia from the Ptolemies. The Syrian king was, however, defeated by the Egyptians at Raphia, and recovered only Seleucia in Syria, the port of Antioch (B. C. 217). No sooner had this Syrian war closed than a general revolt of Ptolemy Philópator's Egyptian subjects broke out, and continued through many years of his reign, requiring a vast expenditure of blood and treasure for its suppression. Although of so infamous a character, Ptolemy Philópator was a liberal patron of learning and the arts, and dedicated a temple to Homer. His excesses shortened his life, and he died B. C. 205.

PTOLEMY V., Epíphanes, was only five years old when he succeeded his father, Ptolemy Philópator, and was the son of the murdered Arsinoë, the sister and wife of his father. He was readily acknowledged king, and Agáthocles, one of his father's worthless favorites, was made regent. He soon fell a victim to the people's wrath, along with all his relatives; whereupon the honest but incompetent Tlepólemus was invested with the regency. The Kings of Syria and Macedon plotted to divide the dominions of the Ptolemies between them, and the incompetent ministers of Egypt had recourse only to Roman assistance. A united attack by the allies deprived Egypt of all her foreign possessions except Cyprus and the Cyrenaïca. In response to the appeals of Tlepólemus for Roman aid, the Romans sent M. Lepidus, in B. C. 201, to undertake the management of Egyptian affairs. By his efforts Egypt was preserved to the young Ptolemy Epíphanes, but Lepidus was either unable or unwilling to recover for Egypt her lost foreign dependencies. Lepidus was succeeded as regent by Aristómenes, an Acarnanian, whose energy and justice restored the prosperity of the kingdom for a time. Ptolemy Epíphanes was declared of age at the age of fourteen, and thenceforth the government was conducted in his name. He married Cleopatra, the daughter of Antíochus the Great of Syria, and was assassinated B. C. 181.

PTOLEMY VI., Philométor, succeeded his father, Ptolemy Epíphanes, at the age of seven, under the regency of his mother, Cleopatra, who ruled vigorously and wisely for eight years. At her death, in B. C. 173, the government passed into the hands of two corrupt and incompetent ministers, who involved Egypt in a war with Antíochus Epíphanes, King of Syria, who invaded Egypt, defeated the Egyptians at Pelusium, and gained possession of Ptolemy Philométor, whom he used as a tool to effect the conquest of the whole kingdom. The Alexandrians crowned the king's younger brother, Ptolemy Physcon, and successfully withstood a siege by the army of Antíochus Epíphanes, who was finally forced to retire by the intervention of the Romans.

The two brothers agreed to reign jointly, and Ptolemy Philométor married his only sister, Cleopatra. The two Ptolemies then renewed the war with Antíochus Epíphanes of Syria. The Syrian king seized Cyprus and invaded Egypt a second time in B. C. 168. He would have taken Alexandria and conquered the whole of Egypt, had not the Romans again interfered in favor of Egypt and again forced him to withdraw from the country. After reigning four years in peace the two Ptolemies quarreled, and Ptolemy Philométor went to plead his cause before the Roman Senate, which sustained him and reinstated him in the possession of Egypt, assigning his younger brother, Ptolemy Physcon, the dominion of Libya and the Cyrenaïca. Ptolemy Physcon refused to accept the adjustment of the Roman Senate, and went to Rome and obtained t.ie grant of Cyprus also; but Ptolemy Philométor refused to relinquish that island, whereupon the two brothers prepared for civil war, when a revolt in Cyrênê occupied the attention of Ptolemy Physcon. Nine years later he renewed his claim, and obtained from Rome a small squadron to aid him in seizing Cyprus; but he was defeated and taken prisoner by his brother, in B. C. 155. His life was, however, spared, and Cyrênê was restored to him. Some years afterward Ptolemy Philométor encouraged the rebellion of Alexander Balas in Syria, for the purpose of revenging himself upon the Seleúcidæ, and to gain possession of the Syrian throne. Disgusted with the ingratitude of Alexander Balas, Ptolemy Philométor espoused the cause of his rival, Demétrius, and aided him in hurling Alexander from the Syrian throne. Ptolemy Philométor was killed by a fall from his horse, in his last battle with Alexander Balas, near Antioch, B. C. 146.

PTOLEMY VII., Eúpator, succeeded his father, Ptolemy Philométor, but was assassinated a few days later by his uncle, Ptolemy Physcon, who, aided by the Romans, became King of Egypt and Cyrênê with the title of PTOLEMY VIII. Ptolemy Physcon married his sister, Cleopatra, the widow of his brother Ptolemy Philométor, and became a cruel tyrant. He produced such terror by his inhuman cruelties, and such disgust by his licentiousness, that the Alexandrians fled in such numbers that his capital became half depopulated, and those who remained were almost constantly in rebellion. He was so bloated and corpulent that he could scarcely walk. He repudiated his wife Cleopatra, although she had borne him a son, and married her daughter Cleopatra, the child of his brother. To grieve his first wife more deeply, he assassinated her son, and sent her the head and hands of the victim. This atrocity aroused the Alexandrians to rebellion, and they fought bravely for the elder Cleopatra, whom they made queen, whereupon Ptolemy Physcon fled to Cyprus, B C. 130. A civil war of three years followed.

In B. C. 127 the reigning Cleopatra imprudently solicited the aid of Démétrius II., King of Syria, whereupon the Alexandrians became so alarmed that they recalled Ptolemy Physcon, who so profited by the experience of his exile that he desisted from his cruelties and devoted his attention to literature, gaining some reputation as an author. But he did not desist from war, and, to avenge himself on Demétrius II. of Syria for the support he had given to Cleopatra, induced Alexander Zabínas, the son of Alexander Balas, to revive his father's claims to the Syrian crown. Aided by Ptolemy Physcon, Alexander Zabínas became King of Syria, but, like his father, ungratefully turned against his patron, who consequently hurled him from the Syrian throne and put Antíochus Grypus in his place, giving the latter his daughter in marriage.

PTOLEMY IX., Láthyrus, succeeded his father, Ptolemy Physcon, on the latter's death in B. C. 117. Ptolemy Physcon had bequeathed the kingdom of Cyrênê to his natural son, Apion, who at his death left it to the Romans, thus severing it from Egypt. Cyprus almost became a separate kingdom, being first governed by Alexander, Ptolemy Láthyrus' brother, as king. Ptolemy began his reign as King of Egypt, but the real power was exercised by his mother, Cleopatra, who compelled her son to divorce his sister Cleopatra and marry his other sister Selênê, who was more easily controlled by their mother. In B. C. 107 Ptolemy Láthyrus began a policy of his own in Syria antagonistic to that of his mother, whereupon forced him to retire to Cyprus and placed his brother, Ptolemy Alexander, King of Cyprus, on the Egyptian throne. Soon afterward the queen-mother attempted to deprive Ptolemy Physcon of Cyprus also, but he successfully maintained himself there as king.

After Ptolemy Alexander and his mother had reigned jointly over Egypt for eighteen years, they quarreled, whereupon Ptolemy Alexander put his mother to death, and proclaimed himself sole King of Egypt with the title of PTOLEMY X.; but the Alexandrians thereupon rose against him, drove him from the capital, and recalled his brother, Ptolemy Láthyrus, from Cyprus to resume the sovereignty of Egypt. Ptolemy Alexander soon afterward made an effort to recover Cyprus, but was defeated, and died shortly afterwards. Soon afterward a revolt broke out in Thebes, but the royal troops took and destroyed the city after a siege of three years (B. C. 89–86). Ptolemy Láthyrus reigned eight years in peace and died in B. C. 81.

BERENICE, the only legitimate child of Ptolemy Láthyrus, and his daughter by Selênê, succeeded him on the Egyptian throne, and reigned six months alone, after which she married her cousin, PTOLEMY XI., also called Ptolemy Alexander II., the son of Ptolemy X., or Ptolemy Alexander I. The claims of Ptolemy XI. were sustained by the Romans, and his marriage with Berenicé was consummated for the purpose of preventing civil war, with the agreement that the king and the queen were to reign jointly, but Ptolemy XI. murdered his wife three weeks after their marriage. The Alexandrians were so enraged at this that they rose in revolt against Ptolemy XI. and killed him (B. C. 80). During the next fifteen years (B. C. 80–65) a number of pretenders claimed the crown, and great confusion prevailed, while Cyprus became an entirely independent kingdom.

PTOLEMY XII., Aulétes, or "the fluteplayer," an illegitimate son of Láthyrus, obtained undisputed possession of the Egyptian throne in B. C. 65, though he dated his reign from the death of his half-sister, Queen Berenicé, in B. C. 80. Ptolemy Aulétes did not succeed in obtaining recognition from the Romans until six years after he had secured his crown (B. C. 59), when he accomplished this purpose by bribery, after Julius Cæsar had just become one of the Consuls of the Roman Republic. Ptolemy Aulétes had been obliged to deplete his treasury in order to buy the acknowledgment of his title by the Roman Republic, and he sought to replenish it by increased taxation. His profligacy and oppression so disgusted his subjects that they rose in revolt and drove him from the kingdom, thus forcing him to seek refuge in Rome. The Alexandrians then placed his two daughters, TRYPHŒNA and BERENICÉ, upon the Egyptian throne. Typhœna died a year afterward, and Berenicé ruled until B. C. 55, when her father returned to Egypt under the protection of a powerful Roman army under Gabinius, sent by Pompey the Great to restore him to the throne. Berenicé resisted, for the purpose of retaining the crown, but was overpowered and put to death. Ptolemy Aulétes reigned under the protection of the Romans until his death four years later (B. C. 51), when he left the kingdom on the verge of ruin.

The celebrated CLEOPATRA, the eldest daughter of Ptolemy Aulétes, aged seventeen, and Ptolemy XIII., his eldest son, aged thirteen, then became joint sovereigns, in accordance with their father's directions, and under the patronage of the Romans. Their father had ordered that they should jointly reign, and marry each other when Ptolemy XIII. was of full age. Ptolemy Aulétes also left two younger children, a son named Ptolemy and a daughter named Arsinoë. The Romans approved his directions, but Cleopatra was unwilling to submit to any control and quarreled with her youthful brother and husband, Ptolemy XIII., and civil war ensued between them. Cleopatra sought refuge in Syria, where she met Julius Cæsar, who was so fascinated with her wonderful beauty that he became her protector. With Cæsar's aid, she conquered her brother-husband, who perished in the struggle. Cleopatra then became sole sovereign of Egypt, on condition of marrying her younger brother when he became of age (B. C. 47). Three years later (B. C. 44) she formally complied with her agreement, but released herself by causing her second brother-husband to be poisoned soon after their marriage. Thenceforth she reigned without a rival, and in great prosperity for seventeen years, displaying marked ability, along with the unscrupulous cruelty characteristic of her race. Julius Cæsar, whom she had captivated, protected her during the remainder of his life; and after his death Mark Antony allowed himself to be enslaved by her charms, and finally abandoned his second wife and sacrificed all his interests, honor, ambition and power, to her slightest caprices. For the sake of this beautiful but wicked queen, this great Roman general deserted his country, and ungratefully left his army to its fate, after it had faithfully stood by him through prosperity and adversity. When Mark Antony's fleet was defeated by the fleet of his rival, Octavius Cæsar, during the civil wars of the Roman Republic, and Mark Antony was pursued in his flight to Alexandria by his triumphant rival, Cleopatra showed herself willing to abandon her guilty lover to secure her own safety and to retain her kingdom. Upon the capture of Alexandria by the triumphant legions of Octavius Cæsar, in B. C. 30, Antony and Cleopatra both committed suicide, and Egypt became a Roman province. Thus ended the Egyptian kingdom of the Ptolemies, after an existence of almost three centuries (B. C. 323–B. C. 30).

THE PTOLEMIES OF EGYPT.

B. C.	KINGS.	B. C.	KINGS.
323	PTOLEMY LAGUS, or SOTER.	89	PTOLEMY LATHYRUS (restored).
283	PTOLEMY PHILADELPHUS.	81	PTOLEMY ALEXANDER II. and CLEOPATRA I.
247	PTOLEMY EUERGETES.		
222	PTOLEMY PHILOPATOR.	80	PTOLEMY AULETES.
205	PTOLEMY EPIPHANES.	58	BERENICE and TRYPHŒNA.
181	PTOLEMY PHILOMETOR.	55	PTOLEMY AULETES (restored).
146	PTOLEMY PHYSCON.	51	PTOLEMY and CLEOPATRA II.
117	PTOLEMY LATHYRUS.	46	CLEOPATRA II. and the younger PTOLEMY (to B. C. 30).
107	PTOLEMY ALEXANDER I. and CLEOPATRA I.		

SECTION XXII.—THE SMALLER GREEK KINGDOMS.

BESIDES the three great monarchies whose history we have just related — Macedon and Greece, the Syrian Empire of the Seleúcidæ, and Egypt under the Ptolemies—a number of smaller kingdoms were erected from the ruins of the vast empire of Alexander the Great. The most important of these will now be noticed. One of these minor kingdoms—Thrace—was in Europe. The others were all in Asia.

The Hellenic KINGDOM OF THRACE has no important history. It contributed nothing to art, science, literature or general civilization, as did the kingdom of the Ptolemies in Egypt and that of the Seleúcidæ in Syria. The several Thracian tribes were powerful on account of their numbers, their hardy contempt of danger and exposure, and their uncontrollable love of freedom. Their strength was, however, too frequently exhausted in fighting against each other; and thus they were reduced either to the condition of subjects, or that of humble allies, of the more civilized nations to the south of them. Their position on the Danube also rendered them the most exposed, of all the ancient kingdoms, to the inroads of the fierce barbarians from the North.

As we have already related, the Greek Kingdom of Thrace was founded by Lysímachus, one of the generals of Alexander the Great, who was confirmed in its possession by the battle of Ipsus in B. C. 301. The Kingdom of Thrace was of short duration, Lysímachus being its first and last sovereign. By his defeat and death in the battle of Corupédion, in B. C. 281, his kingdom was absorbed into the dominions of his conqueror, Seleucus I. of Syria.

THE KINGDOM OF PÉRGAMUS.

The city of Pérgamus, on the river Caicus, in Mysia, was considered one of the great strongholds of Asia Minor. Lysímachus, King of Thrace, made it the repository of the treasures of his kingdom, placing it in charge of his eunuch Philetærus. When Lysímachus was slain in the battle of Corupedion, Philetærus kept possession of his principality for himself, and, with the help of the treasures of Lysímachus, succeeded in establishing himself as an independent ruler. He ruled twenty years, from B. C. 283 to B. C. 263, but did not assume the royal title.

Eúmenes I., the nephew of Philetærus, became his successor. Soon after his accession, Eúmenes was attacked by Antíochus I., King of Syria, whom he defeated in a pitched battle near Sardis, thus vastly increasing his territory. He died in B. C. 241, from the effects of intemperance, after ruling twenty-two years.

ATTALUS I., the cousin of Eúmenes I., became his successor. The Gauls, who had been then settled in the North of Phrygia, afterwards called *Galátia*, for about thirty years, made frequent predatory incursions into the territories of their neighbors. They made a descent upon the territories of Pérgamus, about B. C. 239, and were terribly defeated by Attalus. In consequence of this victory, Attalus assumed the title of king, which none of his predecessors had taken. Ten years afterwards he was obliged to defend his kingdom against an invasion of the Syrians under Antíochus Híerax, the brother of Seleucus II. This ambitious prince was seeking to make himself King of Asia Minor, but was defeated by Attalus and driven away. Attalus likewise succeeded in extending his dominions, which, by the year B. C. 226, included almost all of Asia Minor west of the Halys and north of Mount Taurus, but was deprived of his conquests by Kings Seleucus Ceraunus and Antíochus the Great of Syria, so that by the year B. C. 221 he was merely sovereign of the territory of Pérgamus. He recovered Æolis in B. C. 218 by wise management and by a judicious employment of Gallic mercenaries. In B. C. 216 he entered into an alliance with Antíochus the Great, by which he recoverd most of the territory which the Syrian king had wrested from him.

In B. C. 211 Attalus formed an alliance with the Romans and the Ætolians in their war against King Philip V. of Macedon and rendered efficient service to his allies, thus gaining the powerful friendship and patronage of Rome. After the peace of B. C. 204 Philip attacked Attalus, ravaged his territories and sought to drive his fleet from the Ægean sea; but the King of Pérgamus entered into an alliance with Rhodes, and in B. C. 201 the allies terribly defeated the Macedonian fleet off Chios. In B. C. 199 the second war between Rome and Philip V. of Macedon commenced; and Attalus, then seventy years old, ardently espoused the cause of the Romans and afforded them important assistance with his fleet. His efforts in their behalf caused his death in B. C. 197.

EUMENES II., the eldest of the four sons of Attalus I., ascended the throne of Pérgamus upon his father's death, and inherited his talents and policy. In the wars which Rome waged against Philip V. of Macedon, Antíochus the Great of Syria, and Pérseus, Philip's successor on the Macedonian throne, Eúmenes rendered such important assistance to the Romans that, after the battle of Magnesia, in B. C. 190, he was rewarded with a large addition of territory on both sides of the Hellespont. By this territorial increase, the Kingdom of Pérgamus became one of the greatest monarchies of the East. This kingdom now embraced Mysia, Lydia, Phygria, Lycaonia, Pamphylia and parts of Caria and Lycia, in Asia Minor; while in Europe it included the Thracian Chersonésus, with its capital, Lysimachía, and the neighboring portions of Thrace. A war broke out between Pérgamus and Bithynia in B. C. 183, by which Pérgamus acquired Hellespontine Phrygia. Pérgamus also became involved in a war with Pontus in B. C. 183, which lasted six years. In B. C. 168 Pérgamus also engaged in a war with the Gauls. In these wars Eúmenes II. acted on the defensive, simply fighting to keep possession of the territories he had won, and not seeking to conquer others.

Under Eúmenes II., Pérgamus rapidly grew to be one of the most brilliant cities of antiquity. His father had liberally patronized literature, science and art; but Eúmenes far surpassed him in the aid which he rendered them. He adorned his capital with magnificent and stately edifices, whose splendor is still attested by their ruins. He afforded liberal encouragement to painting and sculpture. He founded the great library of Pérgamus, which was surpassed only by that of Alexandria, and which attracted many learned men to his court. The school of grammar and criticism which arose at Pérgamus was only excelled by that of Alexandria. In the reign of Eúmenes II., parchment, a material far superior to the Egyptian papyrus for writing purposes, was introduced.

Eúmenes II. died in B. C. 159, leaving a son named Attalus, who was a mere child, too young to rule; and the crown was assumed by ATTALUS II., the brother of Eúmenes II. Attalus II. took the surname of Philadelphus, and reigned twenty-one years, more than half of which he passed in the defense of his kingdom against Prúsias II., King of Bithynia. To relieve himself of so powerful an enemy, Attalus Philadelphus supported the revolt of Nicomédes, the son of Prúsias, against his father, and assisted in establishing him upon the Bithynian throne; whereupon peace followed between Pérgamus and Bythynia. Attalus Philadelphus was celebrated as a builder, and employed the peaceful years of his reign in erecting cities and increasing his library. Among the cities which he founded were Eumenía in Phrygia; Philadelphia, in Lydia; and Attalía, in Pamphylia.

Attalus Philadelphus died in B. C. 138, and was succeeded by his nephew, ATTALUS III., the son of Eúmenes II. Attalus III. assumed the surname of Philométor (lover of his mother). His reign of five years was a reign of terror. He caused all the trusted friends of his father and his uncle, and their families, and also every office-holder in the kingdom, to be put to death. He finally murdered his mother and many of her relatives. Remorse for his crimes then caused him to relinquish the government of his kingdom, and to devote himself to painting, sculpture and gardening. He died in B. C. 133 and bequeathed his kingdom to the Roman people.

The Roman Republic very readily accepted the bequest. Aristoníeus, an illegitimate son of Eúmenes II., claimed the kingdom as his natural inheritance, and at first gained some important successes over the Romans. In B. C. 131 he defeated and captured the Roman general, Licinius Crassus, who had been sent to forcibly take possession of the kingdom; but he was himself defeated and taken prisoner the following year by Perpena, another Roman general; whereupon the kingdom of Pérgamus became a Roman province, (B. C. 130).

THE KINGDOM OF BITHYNIA.

While the Medo-Persian Empire was in existence, Bithynia was one of its tributary kingdoms, and was governed by its own kings. It easily regained its independence after the battle of Arbéla, and successfully defended itself against all the attempts of Alexander's generals to reconquer it. BAS, the king who made this successful resistance, died in B. C. 326, leaving a flourishing independent kingdom to his son, ZIPŒTES.

Zipœtes reigned forty-eight years, from B. C 326 to B. C. 278, and successfully resisted the efforts of Lysímachus and Antíochus Soter to conquer his kingdom. When he died a civil war broke out between his sons, Nicomédes and Zipœtes. Aided by the Gauls, NICOMÉDES I. defeated his brother and thus secured the crown. He founded the city of Nicomedía, on the Gulf of Astacus. He had two wives, and by the first of these he had a son named Zeilas. By the second wife he had three children, to whom he desired to leave his dominions. Aided by the Gauls, ZEILAS defeated his half-brother, and obtained the throne. He died B. C. 228, after a reign of twenty years.

PRUSIAS I.—called "Prúsias the Lame" —succeeded his father Zeilas, and reigned until about B. C. 180, a period of about forty-eight years. The first eight years were not marked by any important events, but the remainder were passed in continual wars of importance. In B. C. 220 he aided Rhodes in her struggle with Byzantium, and in B. C. 216 he defeated the Gauls. He entered into an alliance with King Philip V. of Macedon, in his war with the Romans; and in B. C. 208 he attacked the dominions of Pérgamus, compelling Attalus I. to return home to defend his kingdom. By this action Prúsias made an enemy of Rome, whose indignation was aroused still more in B. C. 187, in consequence of the refuge which Prúsias gave to Hannibal, the vanquished Carthaginian general. Aided by Hannibal, Prúsias attacked Eúmenes II. of Pérgamus and defeated him, but gained nothing by his victory, as Rome now intervened, thus forcing him to indemnify Eúmenes for his losses by ceding to him the whole of Hellespontine Phrygia. The Romans likewise demanded that Prúsias should deliver Hannibal into their power, threatening him with war if he refused; and Prúsias was alarmed into ordering Hannibal's arrest, but Hannibal poisoned himself to escape falling into the hands of the Romans. With his dying breath, the great Carthaginian general expressed his animosity toward the Romans and his contempt for Prúsias. The King of Bithynia then made war on Heracléa Póntica, and gained some successes, but received a wound which gave him the surname of *the Lame*, soon after which he died, about B. C. 180.

PRUSIAS II. succeeded his father, Prúsias I., and reigned until B. C. 149. He was the most wicked and contemptible of all the Kings of Bithynia, and experienced great calamities. He married the sister of Pérseus, King of Macedon, but refused to give him active assistance in his final struggle with the Romans. After the overthrow of Pérseus, Prúsias made the most abject submission to the Romans, who permitted him to retain possession of his kingdom. In B. C.

156 he made war on Attalus Philadelphus, King of Pérgamus, whom he would have conquered if the Romans had not intervened and forced him to make peace, to restore his conquests, and to pay Attalus Philadelphus an indemnity of five hundred talents. Seeing that his son Nicomédes was more popular with the people than himself, Prúsias II. sent him to Rome, giving his attendants secret orders to assassinate the prince; but Nicomédes discovered the plot, and, with the consent of the Roman Senate, left Rome and returned to Bithynia, where he raised the standard of revolt against his father. With the assistance of Attalus Philadelphus, King of Pérgamus, Nicomédes defeated his father, whom he made prisoner and put to death (B. C. 149).

NICOMÉDES II., upon coming to the throne of Bithynia, in B. C. 149, assumed the surname of Epíphanes, or *Illustrious*. He sought to secure the friendship of the Romans, and rendered them efficient aid in their war against Aristonícus of Pérgamus. He did not, however, always act with good faith toward the Romans; and in B. C. 102, as an ally of Mithridátes the Great of Pontus, he subdued Paphlagonia and seized a part of it for himself. When the Romans ordered him to restore Paphlagonia to its legitimate heir, he made a pretense of obeying, but obtained it for one of his own sons by trickery. In B. C. 96 Mithridátes the Great sought to annex Cappadocia to the dominions of the Kingdom of Pontus. Laódicé, the widow of the late Cappadocian king, fled for refuge to the court of Nicomédes Epíphanes, who married her and made her Queen of Cappadocia. She was soon afterward driven from her kingdom by Mithridátes. Nicomédes Epíphanes afterwards attempted to recover Cappadocia by trickery, but was unable to deceive the Romans, who deprived him of both Cappadocia and Paphlagonia. Nicomédes Epíphanes died in B. C. 91, at the age of almost eighty years.

NICOMÉDES III. succeeded his father, Nicomédes Epíphanes, but was soon afterward driven from his dominions by a revolt headed by his brother Socrates, who was assisted by Mithridátes the Great of Pontus. In B. C. 90 the Romans forced Socrates to retire, whereupon Nicomédes III. recovered his throne. Nicomédes III. now attempted to chastise Mithridátes the Great by making inroads into the Kingdom of Pontus, whereupon Mithridátes marched against the Bithynian king with a large army and defeated him on the Amneius river, B. C. 88, expelling him and his Roman allies from Asia Minor. This caused the First Mithridátic War between Rome and Pontus, which ended in the defeat of Mithridátes and the restoration of Nicomédes III. to the throne of Bithynia, B. C. 84. Nicomédes III. then reigned in peace ten years. As he left no children when he died, in B. C. 74, he bequeathed his kingdom to the Romans. This bequest involved the Roman Republic in the Third Mithridátic War.

THE KINGDOM OF PAPHLAGONIA.

It is not known when the Kingdom of Paphlagonia was founded. After the Medo-Persian Empire had been established, Paphlagonia was nominally subject to that colossal power, but never wholly submitted to it. As early as B. C. 400 the Paphlagonian king CORYLAS permitted the Ten Thousand under Xenophon to pass through his kingdom on their famous retreat from Cunaxa, without attempting to check them. In B. C. 394 the next Paphlagonian monarch, COTYS, or OTYS, entered into an alliance with the Spartan king Agesilaüs against Persia. About B. C. 365 THYUS, or THYS, another Paphlagonian sovereign, who was celebrated for his magnificent entertainments, was defeated by the Persian satrap Datámes, who carried him a prisoner to the court of Artaxerxes Mnemon, where he continued to live in extraordinary splendor.

When Alexander the Great conquered the Medo-Persian Empire, Paphlagonia did not become a part of his vast dominion in anything more than in name. It is not known when, or under what circumstances, it regained its independence; but after B. C. 200 it again appears to have been governed by native monarchs, who were engaged in wars to defend their independence against the Kings of Pontus on the one hand and those of Bithynia on the other. In B. C. 189 the Paphlagonian king, MORZES, or MORZIAS, fought against the Romans in the war with the Greeks and the Gauls in Asia Minor; and in B. C. 181 the same King was attacked and subdued by Phárnaces, King of Pontus, but was restored to his dominions and compensated in B. C. 179. Another Paphlagonian king, Pylæmenes I., aided the Romans in their war against Aristonícus, King of Pérgamus, B. C. 131, and is said to have bequeathed his kingdom to Mithridátes the Great of Pontus at his death, in B. C. 102, as he left no children. Thereupon Mithridátes the Great, and Nicomédes Epíphanes, King of Bithynia, both seized upon Paphlagonia; and Nicomédes Epíphanes established his own son, Pylæmenes II., on the Paphlagonian throne; but after Pylæmenes had reigned eight years he was driven out by Mithridátes the Great, who then annexed Paphlagonia to the Kingdom of Pontus (about B. C. 94).

THE KINGDOM OF PONTUS.

The Kingdom of Pontus was formed out of the Persian satrapy of Cappadocia, which Darius Hystaspes conferred on Onátes, one of the commanders who had aided him to overthrow the impostor Smerdis. Onátes was descended from the ancient Arian Kings of Cappadocia, and Darius Hystaspes made the satrapy hereditary in his family. In B. C. 363 ARIOBARZÁNES, the son of Mithridátes, the satrap, headed a successful revolt against Persia and made himself master of that part of Cappadocia bordering on the coast of the Euxine. He erected his territory into a kingdom which the Greeks called *Pontus*, because it bordered on the Pontus Euxinus (now Black Sea). The inland portion of Cappadocia remained a province of the Medo-Persian Empire.

Ariobarzánes died in B. C. 337, and was succeeded as King of Pontus by his son, MITHRIDÁTES I. When Alexander the Great subverted the Medo-Persian Empire, Pontus became a province of his vast empire (B. C. 331). In B. C. 318 Mithridátes I. cast off the Macedonian yoke and reëstablished the independence of Pontus. He was assassinated in B. C. 302 by order of Antígonus, who, as we have seen, had acquired Phrygia, Lycia and Pamphylia as his share of Alexander's dominions.

MITHRIDÁTES II., who succeeded his father, Mithridátes I., reigned thirty-six years, and enlarged his kingdom at the expense of Cappadocia and Paphlagonia. His son, ARIOBARZÁNES II., succeeded him in B. C. 266, and had an uneventful reign of nineteen years. At his death, in B. C. 245, his son, MITHRIDÁTES III., beame his successor. This monarch was more enterprising than any of the other early Pontic kings. He was a minor when he became sovereign, and upon arriving at his majority he at once married a sister of Seleucus II. of Syria and obtained the province of Phrygia with her as a dowry. In B. C. 222 Mithridátes III. gave his daughter Laódicé in marriage to Antíochus the Great of Syria, and gave another daughter, also named Laódicé, in marriage to Achæus, a cousin of the King of Syria. He never allowed these marriages to influence his political course, and waged war against Syria just as if he had not contracted such ties. Mithridátes III. is supposed to have died about B. C. 190.

PHÁRNACES I. succeeded his father, Mithridátes III., on the Pontic throne. In B. C. 183 he conquered the Greek city of Sinopé, on the Euxine, and made it the capital of his kingdom. In B. C. 181 he made war on Eúmenes II., King of Pérgamus, notwithstanding all the exertions of the Romans to prevent the struggle. He achieved some successes at first, but was finally obliged to agree to a peace by which he relinquished all his conquests except Sinopé.

Phárnaces I. died about B. C. 160, whereupon his son, MITHRIDÁTES IV., Euérgetes, became his successor. Mithridátes Euérgetes reigned about forty years, from about B. C. 160 to B. C. 120. He was the ally of Attalus Philadelphus of Pérgamus against Prúsias II. of Bithynia, B. C. 154; and in the Third Punic War he fought in alliance with the Romans against Carthage. He likewise assisted the Romans in driving Aristonícus out of Pérgamus, and when the war ended the Romans bestowed on him the Greater Phrygia as a reward for his aid. He was assassinated in B. C. 120 by his disaffected courtiers.

Mithridátes Euérgetes was succeeded on the Pontic throne by his illustrious son, MITHRIDÁTES V., the Great, the most renowned of all the Kings of Pontus. Mithridátes the Great was the ablest of the Pontic sovereigns, and one of the greatest of Asiatic monarchs. He was a minor when he became king, and the affairs of the kingdom were directed by his guardian for eight years, during which he diligently applied himself to study, and is said to have acquired twenty-five different languages. He engaged in constant hunting expeditions in the wildest portions of his kingdom, for the purpose of hardening his constitution. He very early commenced to accustom himself to antidotes against poison, in order to thwart any attempt upon his life, as he perpetually distrusted his guardians. He assumed the government at the age of twenty. He was then blessed with a hardy and vigorous physical constitution, while his mind was filled with knowledge. His wonderful linguistic attainments enabled him to transact business with every portion of his dominions in its own peculiar dialect.

When Mithridátes the Great ascended the throne of Pontus, he clearly perceived that his kingdom, on account of its location, would be exposed to the attacks of the Romans, who now aimed at the dominion of the whole of Asia Minor. He also clearly saw that, in order to encounter them successfully, he must strengthen and enlarge his dominions. Accordingly in B. C. 112 he commenced a deliberate and systematic attempt at conquest in the East, the quarter in which he was secure from the intervention of Rome. During the next seven years he annexed to his kingdom the Lesser Armenia, Colchis, all of the eastern coast of the Euxine, the Cimmerian (now Crimean) peninsula, and the region extending westward from the Crimea to the Dniester. He also strengthened himself by alliances with the wild tribes of the region of the Danube, and with the Kings of Armenia, Cappadocia and Bithynia. He endeavored to p'ace his own son on the throne of Cappadocia, in B. C. 93, and to seat Socrates on that of Bithynia, in B. C. 90, but failed in both efforts. The Romans demanded that he undo these actions, and, as he was not yet prepared to confront the gigantic power of the great Roman Republic, he considered it prudent to comply with this demand.

In B. C. 89 Nicomédes III. of Bithynia invaded Pontus, at the instigation of the Romans. Mithridátes the Great instantly took the field at the head of a large army, and in the following year overran Cappadocia and annexed it to his dominions. He then marched into Bithynia, defeated Nicomédes III. on the Amneius, and drove him and his allies, the Romans, out of Bithynia. Mithridátes now quickly overran Galatia, Phrygia and the Roman province of Asia, and made himself master of the whole of Asia Minor, with the exceptions of a few towns in Lycia and Ionia. He wintered in Pérgamus, where he committed the great error of his life in ordering the massacre of all the Romans and Italians in Asia. From that moment the tide turned against Mithridátes the Great. The Roman general Sylla defeated two large armies which he sent into Greece, at Chæronéa, and his generals were defeated in a great battle in Bithynia, while Pontus itself was invaded and Mithridátes compelled to flee.

The Pontic king was forced to agree to a humiliating peace, by which he relinquished all his conquests and a fleet of seventy vessels, agreed to pay two thousand talents, and recognized the Kings of Cappadocia and Bithynia, whom he had formerly expelled. The misfortunes of Mithridátes encouraged the subject nations to cast off his yoke. He was getting ready to reduce them to submission when Murena, the Roman general in Asia Minor, committed an unprovoked attack which led to the second war with the Roman Republic, but after the Romans had been defeated on the Halys, peace was again made (B. C. 82.).

During the next seven years Mithridátes subdued all his revolted subjects and exhibited the most indomitable energy in recruiting his forces. His army, composed of barbarians from the nations on the Danube and the Euxine, were drilled and equipped according to the Roman system, and his navy was increased to four hundred vessels. The bequest of Bithynia to the Romans brought on the third war between Mithridátes and the Roman Republic (B. C. 74). After seizing the country and gaining a land and naval victory over Cotta, Mithridátes failed in the sieges of Chalcedon and Cyzicus, and in the second year he was beaten by Lucullus. His fleet was first defeated off Tenédos, and then wrecked by a storm. In the third year Mithridátes was driven from his dominions and those of his son-in-law Tigránes, King of Armenia. For three years the war was carried on in Armenia, where Mithridátes and Tigránes were both defeated by Lucullus.

In B. C. 68 Mithridátes returned to his kingdom and defeated the Romans twice within a few months; but in B. C. 66 Pompey assumed command of the Roman forces in Asia; and after Mithridátes had lost almost his entire army, he abandoned Pontus and retired into the barbarous regions north of the Euxine, where he plotted the bold scheme of marching upon Italy with an army drawn from the wild tribes north of the Danube, but his officers did not exhibit the same intrepid spirit or the same military ardor. His own son headed a conspiracy against him; and the old king, deserted by all his trusty followers, attempted to poison himself, but the drugs had no effect, because his constitution had been so guarded by antidotes, and he was finally slain by one of his Gallic soldiers (B. C. 63). Pontus then became a Roman province, only a small part remaining under princes of its old dynasty.

THE KINGDOM OF CAPPADOCIA.

We have seen that the northern portion of Cappadocia became the independent Kingdom of Pontus. The southern part continued loyal to Persia until the conquest of the Medo-Persian Empire by Alexander the Great. In B. C. 331, after the battle of Arbéla, ARIARÁTHES, the Persian satrap of the province, assumed the state of an independent sovereign; but was conquered by Perdíccas after the death of Alexander the Great, when he was taken prisoner and crucified. Perdíccas transferred the province to Eúmenes I. of Pérgamus; but after the death of that ruler, Cappadocia revolted, and regained its independence under ARIARÁTHES II., the nephew of Ariaráthes I. He died about B. C. 280, leaving his crown to his son ARIÁMNES, who was succeeded by his son, ARIARÁTHES III. The reigns of these monarchs are obscure. Ariaráthes III. died in B. C. 220, and was succeeded by his infant son, ARIARÁTHES IV., who, when he had reached manhood, married the daughter of his cousin, Antíochus the Great of Syria, B. C. 192. He aided Antíochus the Great in his war against Rome and fought as his ally in the great battle of Magnesia, which destroyed the power of the Syrian Empire of the Seleúcidæ (B. C. 190). This course of the Cappadocian king exposed him to the vengeance of the Romans, but he succeeded in appeasing the great republic, obtaining honorable conditions of peace, and lived on friendly terms with Rome during the remainder of his long reign, which ended with his death, in B. C. 162.

ARIARÁTHES V., the son and successor of Ariaráthes IV., reigned thirty-one years, and presents the only example of a "pure and blameless" ruler in the three centuries succeeding Alexander. No cruel or deceitful action stands on record against him. He sought and won the affections of his subjects and the respect of his neighbors. During his reign, and under his patronage and example, Cappadocia became a renowned seat of philosophy and the abode of learned men. He continued faithful to the Roman alliance, notwithstanding the efforts to induce him to abandon it; and when the Romans attempted to drive Aristonícus from Pérgamus, he took the field to assist them and lost his life in their service, B. C. 131.

ARIARÁTHES V. left six sons, all of whom were minors at the time of his death. His widow Laódicé became regent, and poisoned five of her sons before they became of age, for the purpose of retaining the power in her possession; but she ultimately fell a victim to the vengeance of the people, and her youngest son obtained the crown as ARIARÁTHES VI. His reign was unimportant. He married a sister of Mithridátes the Great of Pontus, and was assassinated by an emissary of that great monarch, B.C. 96. Mithridátes instantly seized Cappadocia, but Laódicé, the widow of Ariaráthes VI., found refuge with Nicomédes II. of Bithynia, who married her and established her as Queen of Cappadocia. Mithridátes the Great succeeded in driving her out of the kingdom, and a war of several years followed, during which the King of Pontus set up two sovereigns of Cappadocia, while the Cappadocians themselves set up one. The old Cappadocian dynasty became extinct during this struggle. Pontus and Bithynia both set up pretenders to the Cappadocian throne; but the Romans allowed the Cappadocians themselves to decide the matter by choosing their own king, whereupon they raised ARIOBARZÁNES I. to the throne in B. C. 93. He was soon driven from his kingdom by Tigránes of Armenia, but was restored by the Romans in B. C. 92, and reigned undisturbed until B. C. 88, when he was overthrown by Mithridátes the Great, who held Cappadocia during the whole of his first war with the Roman Republic. Ariobarzánes I. was reëstablished on the Cappadocian throne by the treaty between Rome and Pontus, but was again driven from his kingdom by Mithridátes the Great and Tigránes in B. C. 67, and was reinstated again by the Roman general, Pompey the Great, in B. C. 66. He abdicated about B. C. 64, in favor of his son, who became king with the title of ARIOBARZÁNES II. This monarch sided with Pompey against Cæsar during the civil war between those great Roman leaders, but was generously forgiven by the triumphant Cæsar after the battle of Pharsália, and was permitted to extend his dominions. In the next civil war of the Roman Republic he sided with Antony and Octavius against Brutus and Cassius, aud was put to death by Cassius in B. C. 42. When Brutus'and Cassius were overthrown by the battle of Philíppi, Antony bestowed the Cappadocian crown on ARIARÁTHES IX., believed to be a son of Ariobarzánes II.; but soon turned against him, caused him to be put to death, and conferred his crown on ARCHELAUS, a creature of his own, who governed Cappadocia until A. D. 15, when he was summoned to Rome by the Emperor Tiberius, whom he had offended. Archelaüs died in Rome A. D. 17, whereupon Cappadocia became a Roman province.

THE KINGDOM OF GREATER ARMENIA.

Armenia constituted a part of the Syrian Empire of the Seleúcidæ from the battle of Ipsus, in B. C. 301, to the battle of Magnesia, in B. C. 190. After the defeat of Antíochus the Great at Magnesia, Armenia revolted from Syria and was formed into two independent kingdoms of . *Armenia Major* and *Armenia Minor*, or Greater and Lesser Armenia, the former including all of Armenia east of the Euphrates, and the latter embracing the portion of the country west of that great river.

ARTÁXIAS I., who had been a general under Antíochus the Great, and had led the revolt against that monarch, was the first King of Greater Armenia. He founded the city of Artáxata, the capital of his kingdom; and reigned until B. C. 165, when he was defeated by Antíochus Epíphanes, who made Armenia again a province of the Syrian Empire of the Seleúcidæ. This subjection continued for an indefinite period, but about B. C. 100 Armenia again appeared as an independent kingdom under ORTOADISTES, who was succeeded in B. C. 96 by TIGRÁNES, the greatest of the Armenian kings.

Tigránes commenced his reign by ceding a portion of his kingdom to Parthia; but about

B. C. 90 or 87 he achieved great victories over the Parthians, regained his lost territory, and annexed Atropatênê (Northern Media) and Gordyênê (Upper Mesopotamia) to his kingdom; after which he overran and conquered the dominions of the Seleúcidæ. For the next fourteen years—from B. C. 83 to B. C. 69 —his kingdom extended from the frontiers of Pamphylia to the shores of the Caspian; and during this period he founded the city of Tigranocérta, which he made the capital of his kingdom. Tigránes ravaged Cappadocia and carried away more than three hundred thousand of its inhabitants in B. C. 75, thus making an enemy of the Roman Republic. He afterwards received his father-in-law, Mithridátes the Great of Pontus, who had been driven from his kingdom by the Romans, and gave him active support. The Romans thereupon demanded that Tigránes should deliver up Mithridátes to them; and when he refused, they invaded Armenia, defeated Tigránes, in B. C. 69, and took his capital, Tigranocérta. The next year, B. C. 68, Tigránes, accompanied by Mithridátes, retreated to the highlands of Armenia, whither he was pursued by the Romans, who terribly defeated him at Artáxata. The mutiny of the Roman troops against their general, Lucullus, checked their victories, and enabled Tigránes and Mithridátes to assume the offensive in B. C. 67. But when Pompey assumed command of the Roman army and induced the Parthians to invade Armenia, Tigránes was obliged to abandon his father-in-law to his fate in order to save his own kingdom. After conquering Pontus, Pompey invaded Armenia, and Tigránes submitted, as he was not able to withstand both the Romans and the Parthians. He thereupon relinquished all his conquests. He died in B. C. 55.

ARTAVÁSDES, the son and successor of Tigránes, aided the Roman general Crassus in his expedition against the Parthians, B. C. 54, and thus gained the friendship of the Roman Republic; but he afterwards offended Anthony, who took him prisoner in B. C. 34, and in B. C. 30 he was put to death by order of Cleopatra.

When Artavásdes had been taken prisoner by Antony, the Armenians raised his son, ARTÁXIAS II. to the throne. This was displeasing to the Romans, and a period of trouble followed, which continued more than a century, until the reign of the Roman Emperor Trajan, the Kings of Armenia being simply puppets of Rome. In A. D. 114 Trajan made Armenia a Roman province, but it was relinquished by the next Roman Emperor, Adrian.

THE KINGDOM OF LESSER ARMENIA.

Armenia Minor, or Lesser Armenia, as we have seen, revolted from Antíochus the Great of Syria in B. C. 190, along with Greater Armenia. ZARIADRAS, the leader of the successful revolt, made himself King of Lesser Armenia; and his descendants governed the kingdom until Mithridátes the Great of Pontus conquered Lesser Armenia and annexed it to his own kingdom. When Mithridátes was overthrown, Lesser Armenia followed the fortunes of Pontus and became a Roman province (B. C. 65). The history of Lesser Armenia is uneventful, and the names of the successors of Zariadras are scarcely known.

THE KINGDOM OF BACTRIA.

In the meantime, while the preceding kingdoms had arisen from the fragments of Alexander's empire in South-eastern Europe, Western Asia and Egypt, two kingdoms arose from the wrecks of the same empire in Central Asia—Bactria and Parthia. After the death of Alexander the Great, Bactria became a portion of the Syrian Empire of the Seleúcidæ. In B. C. 255 satrap Diódotus cast off the yoke of the Seleúcidæ and founded the independent Kingdom of Bactria, which was purely Greek in its origin, thus forming a striking contrast to the Kingdom of Parthia, which was founded about the same time, after casting off its allegiance to the Seleúcidæ. Very little is known of the reign of DIODOTUS I. It is believed that he aided Seleucus Callinícus in his first expedition against Parthia, and that he was rewarded for his

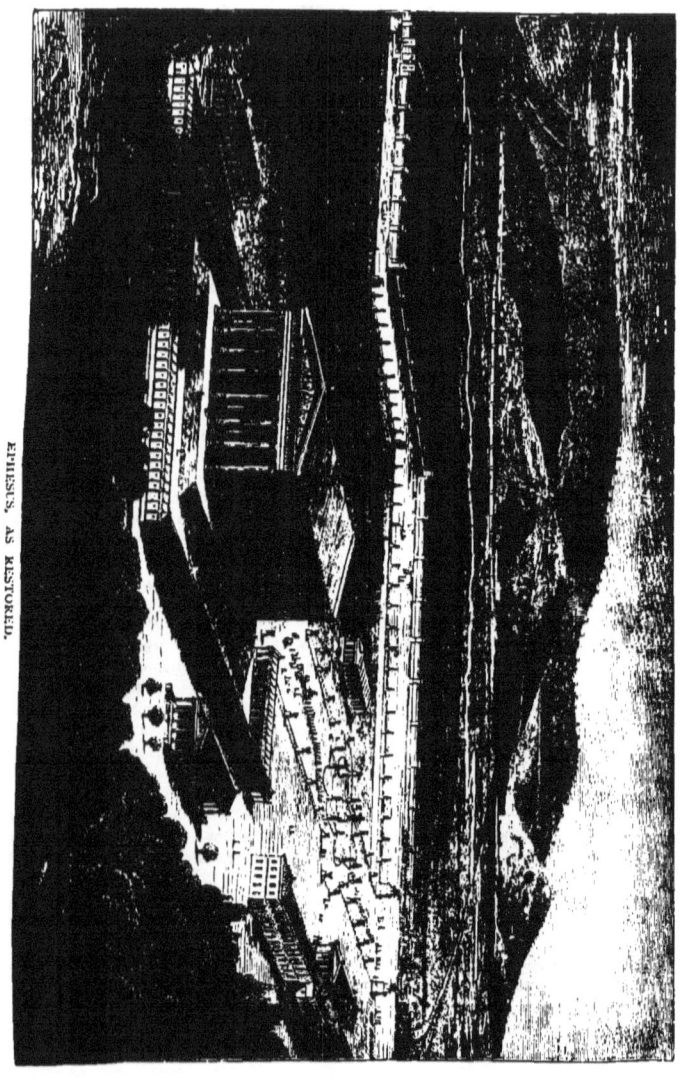

EPHESUS, AS RESTORED.

service by obtaining the recognition of Bactrian independence.

Diódotus I. died about B. C. 237, and was succeeded by his son DIODOTUS II., who reversed his father's policy by entering into an alliance with Parthia and aiding that country to achieve its independence. It seems that Diódotus II. was overthrown by a revolt headed by EUTHYDÉMUS, a native of Magnesia, who seized the Bactrian throne, becoming the third monarch of this remote Eastern Greek kingdom. Diódotus II. obliged to defend his kingdom against Antíochus the Great of Syria, and was defeated in a battle on the river Aríus, in which Antíochus was wounded. By the peace which followed, Euthydémus was left in possession of his kingdom (B. C. 206). His dominions were enlarged by the conquests made by his son, Demétrius, in the region of the modern Afghanistan and in India.

DEMÉTRIUS succeeded to the Bactrian throne upon his father's death, about B. C. 200, and continued his conquests in the East. While he was thus engaged, a leader named EUCRÁTIDES supplanted him at home, and made himself sovereign of Bactria proper, north of the Hindoo-Koosh mountains; while Demétrius continued to reign in the Bactrian dominions south of that mountain-range. The two monarchs thus divided the Bactrian kingdom between them until the death of Demétrius about B. C. 180, after which Eucrátides reigned over the entire kingdom as long as he lived. After he had become sole sovereign, Eucrátides carried his conquering arms far into the Punjab, but lost some of his western territories through the aggressions of the Parthians.

EUCRÁTIDES was assassinated about B. C. 160, while returning from a campaign in India, by his son HELIOCLES, who then ascended his father's throne. Very little is known concerning his reign, during which Bactria rapidly declined. The kingdom was sorely pressed on the north by the Scythian tribes, while the Parthians gradually wrested all its western provinces from its dominion. The Bactrian Greeks solicited aid from their kinsmen in Syria, and Demétrius Nicátor espoused their cause and led an army to their assistance, but was defeated and taken prisoner by the Parthians (B. C. 142). The reign of Heliocles had ended about B. C. 150, and no account of Bactrian history after his death has been transmitted to posterity. The Bactrian dominions were rapidly absorbed by the Parthians and the Scythians.

SECTION XXIII—PARTHIAN EMPIRE OF THE ARSACIDÆ.

PARTHIA and Bactria, besides being the most eastern of the monarchies which sprung from the wrecks of Alexander's vast empire, were also the only two of those monarchies not swallowed up in the overshadowing dominion of Rome; Bactria being absorbed by Parthia and the Scythic tribes, and Parthia existing side by side with Rome as a powerful rival empire for almost five centuries, when it was overthrown by a revolt of one of its subject nations, the Persians, who founded a new empire on its ruins.

Parthia proper occupied mainly the region of the modern Persian province of Khorassan, and was about three hundred miles long from east to west, and from one hundred to one hundred and twenty miles wide, thus embracing an area of about thirty-three thousand square miles, about equal to that of Ireland. It was bounded on the north by Chorasmia and Margiana, on the east by Ariana, on the south by Sarangia, and on the west by Sagartia and Hyrcania. This region included a mountainous tract in the North and a plain in the South. The elevation of the mountain-chains is not great, and the heights rarely exceed six thousand feet. The mountains are mainly barren and rugged, but the valleys are very rich and fertile, and some of them are very extensive. The plain lay at the base of the mountains, and was regarded as the true Parthia by the ancient writers. This plain is about three hundred miles long, and has always required irrigation for its fertility. In ancient times the fertile belt was much wider than at present, as irrigation was more extensively practiced then than now, but the plain could never have extended more than ten miles beyond the foot of the mountains, as the Great Salt Desert begins at that distance and renders cultivation impossible. In comparison with the countries around it, Parthia was a "garden spot," and the Persian monarchs regarded it as one of the most desirable portions of their dominions.

The Parthian Empire in its greatest extent embraced the countries between the Euphrates on the west and the Indus on the east, and from the Aráxes, the Caspian Sea, and the Lower Oxus on the north, to the Persian Gulf and the Erythræan (now Arabian) Sea on the south; thus comprising about the eastern half of the same domain occupied by the vast Medo-Persian Empire, and by the Syrian Empire of the Seleucidæ in its original extent. Its greatest length, from the Euphrates to the Indus, was almost two thousand miles, and its greatest width from the Lower Oxus to the Erythræan Sea was about one thousand miles; its area being almost one million square miles.

But a very large portion of this vast domain was scarcely inhabitable; as the Mesopotamian, Persian, Chorasmian, Carmanian and Gedrosian deserts occupied about one-half of the region between the Euphrates and the Indus, and were capable of sustaining but a scanty population. Thus the habitable portion of the empire comprised an area about one-third as large as that of the Roman Empire, but still larger than that of any modern European state except Russia.

The most important provinces of the Parthian Empire, or the countries under the suzerainty of the King of Parthia proper, or

2—52.-U. H.

Parthyênê, were Mesopotamia, Assyria, Babylonia, Susiana, Persia, Media, Atropatênê (or Northern Media, now Azerbijan), Hyrcania, Margiana, Ariana, Sarangia (Drangiana), Arachosia, Sacastané, Carmania (now Kerman), and Gedrosia (now Beloochistan). Excepting Sacastané, these have all been already described in our account of the geography of the Medo-Persian Empire, to which we refer the reader. Sacastané (the land of Sacæ) lay south of Sarangia, or Drangiana, and corresponded to the modern Seistan. Sacastané had probably been occupied by a Scythian colony during the interval between Alexander's conquests and the birth of the Parthian Empire. The minor provinces of this empire were Chalonítis, Cambadênê, Mesênê, Rhagiana, Choarênê, Comisênê, Artacênê, Apavarticênê, Arbelítis, Apolloníatis and others.

The capital of Parthyênê, or Parthia proper, and the early capital of the Parthian Empire, was Hecatómpylos. The later capital of the empire was Ctesiphon, in Assyria, on the east bank of the Tigris, in the vicinity of the modern Bagdad. Ctesiphon, as well as Seleucia, opposite, on the west bank of the Tigris, had been founded by the Seleúcidæ.

Besides Hecatómpylos, the important towns of Parthia proper were Apaméa, in Choarênê, near the Caspian Gates, and Parthaunísa, or Nisæa (Nishapur). The chief cities of the western provinces of the Parthian Empire besides Seleucia and Ctesiphon, were Arbéla and Apollonia, also in Assyria; Carrhæ, Európus and Nísibis, in Mesopotamia; Babylon, Borsippa, Vologesia, in Babylonia; Susa and Badaca, in Susiana; Gaza, or Gazaca, in Atropatênê; Ecbatana (now Hamadan), Bagistana (now Behistun), Concobar (now Kungawar), Aspadana (now Isfahan), Rhagas, or Európus, and Charax in Media; and Pasargadæ (now Murgab) in Persia, Persepolis having been destroyed by Alexander the Great. The most important cities in the eastern provinces were Carmania, in Carmania; Syrinx, Tapé, Talabrocé and Samariané, in Hyrcania; Antiochéa (now Merv), in Margiana; Artacoana (now Herat) in Ariana; Prophthasia in Sarangia; Sigal and Alexandropolis, in Sacastané; Alexandropolis, Demétrias, Pharsana and Parabesté, in Arachosia.

The Parthians were a Turanian race, like the modern Turks and Turkomans, and were closely related with the different Scythian tribes of Central Asia, whose descendants are the various Tartar or Turkish tribes forming a branch of the Mongolian race. Like their Turanian kinsmen, the modern Turks, the Parthians were treacherous in war, indolent and unrefined in peace, rude in arts, and barbarous in manners, even during the height of their empire; though they were brave and enterprising, and possessed a genius and love for war and a talent for government. Their appearance was repulsive. The Romans, after conquering the rest of the known world, were obliged to acknowledge their inability to subdue this fierce and warlike nation; so that the Parthian Empire remained independent under its own monarchs, while all the nations to the west of the Euphrates acknowledged the dominion of Rome, and that mighty river remained the boundary of the two great rival powers.

The ancestors of the Parthians are supposed to have been the tribe called Phetri or Pathri in the Hebrew Scriptures, but their early history, like that of other ancient nations, is very obscure. When the Parthians first became known to the rest of the world they were a hardy and warlike race, recognized as of Scythian origin. They were considered the most skillful horsemen and archers in the world. They fought on horseback, shooting their arrows with unerring aim, even at full gallop, and with equal effect, whether advancing or retreating; their flight being thus as dangerous to an enemy as their attack. This character they retained to the end of their history.

Parthia formed a part of the Medo-Persian Empire from the beginning to the end of that great power, having been conquered by Cyrus the Great, and being thus governed for two centuries by a Persian satrap. Upon the conquest of the Medo-Persian Empire by Alexander the Great, Parthia, with the rest of the Persian dominions, fell under the sway of that mighty conqueror. At Alexander's death Parthia became a part of the dominions of Seleucus Nicátor, who was confirmed in its possession by the battle of Ipsus. It remained under the dominion of the Seleúcidæ for a century and a half, until B. C. 255, during the reign of Antíochus Theos. In that year the independence of Parthia was asserted by Arsáces, the chief of a body of Scythian Dahæ, who led a revolt of the Parthian tribes and put to death the Syrian governor of the country. The chiefs of the various Parthian tribes supported Arsáces in this undertaking, and formed a government resembling the feudal aristocracy of Europe during the Middle Ages.

ARSACES I. was crowned King of Parthia B. C. 255, but he possessed only nominal authority. The Parthian crown was elective, with the restriction that the monarch should always be selected from the family of the Arsácidæ. The Parthian constitution was that of a kind of limited monarchy, the king being permanently advised by two councils, one comprising the members of his own royal house, the other the temporal and spiritual chiefs of the nation. When the *megistanes* had elected a monarch, the field-marshal, or *surena*, performed the ceremony of coronation. The megistanes claimed the right to dethrone a monarch who displeased them; but as any attempt to exercise this right would invariably lead to civil war, it was force, and not law, which determined whether the chosen monarch should retain or forfeit his crown. The anniversary of Parthian independence was annually celebrated by the Parthian people with extraordinary festivities. Arsáces I. spent the two years of his reign in consolidating his authority over the Parthian tribes, some of whom resisted him, and was finally slain in battle with the Cappadocians.

Arsáces I. was succeeded on the Parthian throne by his brother TIRIDATES I., who had aided him in his revolt against the Seleúcidæ, and who assumed the title of Arsaces II. The practice thus commenced passed into a custom, which lasted until the very end of the Parthian Empire. Arsáces II. reigned thirty-seven years (B. C. 253-216). He wrested Hyrcania from the Seleúcidæ, but when Seleucus Callinícus, King of Syria, led an expedition into Parthia, Arsáces II. fled into Scythia, but afterwards returned and defeated Seleúcus Callinícus, who was obliged to acknowledge the independence of Parthia.

Arsaces III., the son and successor of Arsáces II., is believed to have reigned twenty years (B. C. 216-196). He invaded Media, which he endeavored to wrest from the Seleúcidæ, about B. C. 214; whereupon Antíochus the Great marched against him (B. C. 213), drove him from Media, invaded Parthia and took its capital, Hecatómpylos, and pursued Arsáces III. into Hyrcania; but after an indecisive battle Antíochus the Great wisely made peace, confirming Arsáces III. in the possession of both Parthia and Hyrcania.

Arsaces IV., or Priapatius, the next Parthian king, had an uneventful reign of fifteen years (B. C. 196-181). His successor Arsaces V., or Phraates I., the son and successor of Arsáces V., reigned only seven years, but nothing is known of his reign except his attempted conquest of the Mardi, a powerful tribe of the Elburz mountain-region. He had many children, but left his crown to his brother Mithridátes I., also called Arsaces VI., who was regarded as the founder of the *Parthian Empire of the Arsácidæ*, because he extended the Parthian dominion over the neighboring countries and established the governmental system under which that empire was thenceforth ruled. Mithridátes I., or Arsáces VI., wrested several provinces from the neighboring Baćtrian kingdom on the east; after which he turned his conquering arms towards the west, and deprived the Seleúcidæ of many of their eastern territories, thus subduing Media, Persia, Susiana and Babylonia, and establishing the Euphrates as the western boundary of the Parthian dominions. He then renewed the war with the Baćtrian Greeks, and destroyed their kingdom, after a protraćted struggle of about twenty years (B. C. 160-140); while Demétrius Nicátor, who, in response to their appeals for aid, had marched to their relief, was defeated and taken prisoner by Mithridátes I., who held him in captivity until his own death, about B. C. 136.

Mithridátes I., or Arsáces VI., did not adopt the satrapial system introduced by the Medo-Persian kings and continued by Alexander the Great and his successors, but organized the Parthian Empire on the older and simpler plan which had prevailed in Western Asia under the empires of Assyria, Media and Babylonia, before the founding of the Medo-Persian Empire. This was the system of allowing the subjećt nations to retain their own native kings and their own laws and usages, and only requiring the subjećtion of all these kings to the monarch of the ruling nation as their feudal lord, or suzerain. Hence the title of *King of Kings* is often seen on the Parthian coins from the time of Mithridátes I. Each subjećt king was bound to furnish a contingent of troops when required, as well as an annual tribute; but in other respećts these subjećt monarchs were independent.

In the height of its prosperity, the Parthian Empire was one of the most powerful of all the Oriental monarchies. The Parthians were a nation of mounted warriors, sheathed in complete steel, and possessing a race of horses alike remarkable for speed and strength. They overran their Persian neighbors with scarcely any opposition, and converted themselves into a military aristocracy, the conquered Persians being degraded into a mere herd of slaves. The Parthian invaders thus became the feudal lords of the vanquished Persians, who remained attached to the soil in the condition of serfs. The Parthian cavaliers may thus be compared with the knights of mediæval Europe. These cavaliers constituted the strength of the Parthian army, and bore down everything in their way, while the infantry was comparatively disregarded.

The Parthians chiefly adopted Persian customs. The Arsácidæ maintained the same state as the Achæmenidæ. The Parthian court, like the Medo-Persian, migrated with the seasons, Ctesiphon becoming the winter capital of the Parthian Empire, and Ecbatana the summer capital. Hecatómpylos, so called from its hundred gates, the capital of Parthia proper, and the original capital of the Parthian Empire, was a splendid city. The Parthian monarchs, like other Oriental sovereigns, practiced polygamy on a large scale, as did also the Parthian nobles. The Parthians were not, however, enervated and corrupted by luxury, but remained to the end of their empire a rude, coarse and vigorous people. In a few respects they adopted Greek manners, as in the character of their coins and the legends upon them, which, being Greek from first to last, were probably copied from the coins of the Seleúcidæ. Grecian influences are also seen in the Parthian mimetic art, which, however, never reached a high degree of excellence.

Mithridátes I., or Arsáces VI., the founder of the Parthian Empire, was succeeded by his son, PHRAATES II., also called ARSACES VII., who reigned about nine or ten years (B. C. 136-127). About B. C. 129 Antíochus Sidétes, King of Syria, undertook an expedition against Phraates II., to release his brother Demétrius and humble the pride of the Parthians. He gained three victories and recovered Babylonia, and the insurrectionary spirit among the Parthian feudatories reduced Phraates II. to such extremities that he released Demétrius and sent him into Syria, but invoked the assistance of the Turanian tribes bordering his northern frontier, and before their arrival he attacked and overpowered the Syrian army in its winter-quarters, slaying Antíochus Sidétes himself in battle. The Parthian king was prevented from invading Syria by the conduct of the Turanians, whose aid he had invoked, and who, discontented with their treatment, attacked him and defeated him in the war which they waged against him. His army, consisting partly of captured Greeks, betrayed him, and Phraates himself was slain in the struggle, about B. C. 127. Phraates II., or Arsáces VII., was succeeded by his uncle, ARTABÁNUS I., or ARSACES VIII. The Seleúcidæ made no further attempt to recover their Eastern provinces, but the Turanian races north of the Oxus now began making constant raids into Hyrcania and Parthia proper, and Artabánus I. was fatally wounded in battle with a Turanian tribe called Tochari, about B. C. 124. He was succeeded by his son, MITHRIDÁTES II., also called ARSACES IX., who was a warlike and powerful monarch, and whose achievements won for him the title of *the Great*. He defeated the Turanian tribes in several engagements and broke their power, and extended the Parthian dominion in many directions in a long series of wars. He waged war against Ortoadistes, or Artavásdes, King of Armenia, whom he forced to accept a disadvantageous peace, and to give hostages for its fulfillment, among whom was Tigránes, a prince of the blood-royal of Armenia. Tigránes induced the Parthian monarch to assist him to gain the Armenian throne by ceding a part of Armenia to him about B. C. 96. But when Tigránes became King of Armenia, he declared war against Mithridátes II., recovered the ceded territory, invaded Parthia itself, conquered Adiabênê, and compelled the Kings of Atropatênê and Gordyênê to become his tributaries, about B. C. 90 or 87. Mithridátes II., or Arsáces IX., soon afterward died, after a reign of over thirty-five years (B. C. 124-89). Parthia now ranked next to Rome as the most powerful state of the ancient world at that time.

Thenceforth Parthian history is uncertain and uneventful for twenty years, during which ARSACES X. and ARSACES XI. are said to have reigned, the latter becoming king at the age of eighty and reigning seven years (B. C. 76-69), and being succeeded by his son, PHRAATES III., or ARSACES XII., who took the title of *Deos* or "God." He became king when the Romans compelled Mithridátes the Great of Pontus to seek refuge in Armenia; and in B. C. 66 he entered into an alliance with the Romans, and while Pompey the Great pressed Mithridátes of Pontus, Phraates III. attacked Tigránes of Armenia and thus enabled Rome to triumph. But the great republic ungratefully aided Tigránes against Phraates III. in B. C. 65, and took the province of Gordyênê from the Parthian king, who had in the meantime recovered it, and bestowed it on the Armenian monarch. Phraates III. vainly remonstrated, as Pompey was inexorable, and Phraates III. made peace with Tigránes about B. C. 63, ceding to him Armenia. Soon afterwards (B. C. 60) Phraates III. was poisoned by his two sons, Mithridátes and Orodes.

By the war with Mithridátes the Great of Pontus, the Roman and Parthian dominions became conterminous, as Syria, which now became a Roman province, was only separated from the Parthian province of Mesopotamia by the river Euphrates. A collision between the two great powers which now divided between them the dominion of the then-known world became imminent.

MITHRIDÁTES III., or ARSACES XIII., succeeded his father, Phraates III. He became involved in a war with Artavásdes, King of Armenia, the second son and the successor of Tigránes, in behalf of his brother-in-law Tigránes, the eldest son of the late king; but was unsuccessful in his efforts to place the rightful claimant upon the Armenian throne. After a reign of five years (B. C. 60-55), Mithridátes III. was deposed by the Parthian nobles, and, after a protracted resistance at Babylon, he was finally taken prisoner and put to death; while his brother, ORODES I., or ARSACES XIV., was elevated to the Parthian throne in his stead—about B.C. 55.

After its triumph over Mithridátes the Great of Pontus and Tigránes of Armenia, the Roman Republic cast longing eyes upon the greater and richer Parthian Empire; and without any pretext a Roman expedition under Crassus invaded the Parthian territories B. C. 54, but was entirely cut to pieces by the Parthians, Crassus himself being among the slain (B. C. 53). In B. C. 52 and 51 a Parthian army under Pacorus, the son of King Orodes I., crossed the Euphrates from Mesopotamia into Syria, thus invading the Roman territories and ravaging them far and wide, overrunning Northern Syria and Phœnicia, and defeating the Roman general Bibulus. But the Roman general Cassius gained some successes; and Orodes, suspecting the loyalty of Pacorus, recalled him and withdrew his army from the Roman territories. In B. C. 40 Pacorus, aided by the Roman refugee Labienus, again crossed the Euphrates and invaded Syria, destroyed a Roman army under Decidius Saxa, occupied Antioch, Apaméa, Sidon, and Ptolemaïs, plundered Jerusalem, and placed Antígonus on the Jewish throne as Parthian viceroy. The Parthians, being thus complete masters of Syria, Phœnicia and Palestine, invaded Asia Minor, which they plundered as far west as Caria, Ionia and the Roman province of Asia; but a Roman force under Ventidius defeated and killed Labienus in B. C. 39, and defeated Pacorus the following year (B. C. 38). The Parthians then retired from Syria, and thereafter only acted on the defensive against Roman aggressions.

On the death of Orodes I., in B. C. 37, his son PHRAATES IV. became his successor, and reigned under the title of ARSACES XV. Mark Antony led a great Roman expedition into the Parthian territories in B. C. 36, but was obliged to make a retreat almost as disastrous as that of Crassus.

For the next century and a half—from B. C. 37 to A. D. 107—Parthia was disturbed by internal troubles excited by the Romans. Phraates IV., or Arsáces XV., who reigned from B. C. 37 to A. D. 4, was annoyed by a pretender named Tiridátes, who was encouraged by the Roman Emperor Augustus, and was finally murdered by his female slave, Thermusa, whom he had married. His son and successor, PHRAATACES, or ARSACES XVI., the son of Thermusa, reigned only a few months, when he was put to death by the Parthians, who bestowed the crown on ORODES II., or ARSACES XVII., a member of the royal family, but he was soon put to death on account of his cruelty, (A. D. 5). The Parthians then sent to Rome for Vonónes, the eldest son of Phraates IV., who was sent to them by Augustus, and who reigned from about A. D. 6 to A. D. 14, as VONONES I., or ARSACES XVIII., when he was forced to yield his crown to ARTABÁNUS II., or ARSACES XIX., another member of the royal family, whose reign of thirty years (A. D. 14-44) was distracted by a revolt of the Babylonian Jews, by pretenders supported by Augustus, and by rebellions of the tributary kings. Upon his death two of his sons, Gotarzes and Vardánes, engaged in a civil war for the possession of the crown, which ended in the triumph of Vardánes, who reigned as ARSACES XX., for about four years (A. D. 44-48), when Gotarzes renewed the struggle, and the Parthians deserted and killed Vardánes and made Gotarzes king with the title of ARSACES XXI. Gotarzes reigned only two years (A. D. 48-50), and was disturbed by a war with Meherdátes, son of Vonónes I., who claimed the crown and was supported by the Romans, but was slain after a brief struggle. Upon the death of Gotarzes in A. D. 50, VONONES II., or ARSACES XXII., a member of the royal family, became king, but reigned only a few months. His son and successor, VOLOGESES I., or ARSACES XXIII., reigned forty years (A. D. 50-90). Vológeses I. had conferred the crown of Armenia on his brother Tiridátes, who was so harassed by the Romans that he renounced his allegiance to Parthia and consented to become a vassal of the Roman Emperor Nero (A. D. 65). After the death of Vológeses I., in A. D. 90, his son, Pacorus, succeeded him as ARSACES XXIV., and reigned seventeen years (A. D. 90-107), during which he beautified Ctesiphon.

At his death, in A. D. 107, Pacorus was succeeded by his brother, CHOSROES, or ARSACES XXV., who immediately asserted the Parthian supremacy over Armenia by dethroning its reigning king, Exedáres, and placing his nephew Parthamasiris, the son of Pacorus, upon the Armenian throne. This involved him in a war with the Roman Emperor Trajan, who thereupon invaded and conquered Armenia, driving out Parthamasiris, without a struggle; after which he quickly overran Mesopotamia and Assyria, capturing city after city, and annexing these Parthian provinces, along with Armenia, to the Roman Empire. Trajan then advanced southward, took Seleucia, Ctesiphon and Babylon, descended the Tigris to the Persian Gulf and conquered Mesêne, the Parthian province upon its northern shore, while his hosts advanced to Susa. But revolts broke out against the Romans at Seleucia, Edessa, Nísibis, Hatra and other cities, thus obliging Trajan to retire from the Parthian territories which he had conquered. To cover the humiliation of his retreat, Trajan held an assembly at Ctesiphon and placed his more southern conquests under the sovereignty of a puppet king, a native named Parthamaspates. Trajan strongly garrisoned his other conquests, Armenia, Mesopotamia and Assyria, and held them as Roman provinces during the remaining two years of his reign (A. D. 115-117), but they were relinquished by his successor, Adrian, who withdrew the Roman legions to the west of the Euphrates, which again became the boundary stream dividing the Roman and Parthian Empires. Chosroës returned to his capital, which was abandoned by Parthamaspates, who fell back on his Roman friends, who made him King of Armenia; and the Parthian Empire was restored to its former limits.

Chosroës died about A. D. 121, and was succeeded by his son, VOLOGESES II., or ARSACES XXVI., who reigned about twenty-eight years (A. D. 121-149). The Alani having invaded Media Atropatênê, Vológeses II. bribed them to retire. His successor, VOLOGESES III., or ARSACES XXVII., reigned about forty-three years (A. D. 149-192). He became involved in a war with the Roman Emperor Marcus Aurelius about A. D. 161, and invaded Armenia, which had become a Roman fief during the preceding reign. The Parthians defeated the Roman Prefect of Cappadocia and destroyed his army, the Prefect himself being slain. They then crossed the Euphrates and ravaged Syria, but were soon defeated and driven from Syria and Armenia, and the victorious Romans occupied Mesopotamia and took the cities of Seleucia, Ctesiphon and Babylon, burning the royal palace at Ctesiphon (A. D. 165). Thereupon Parthia sued for peace, which she only obtained by ceding Mesopotamia to the Romans and allowing Armenia to again become a Roman fief.

Vológeses III. was succeeded by his son, VOLOGESES IV., or ARSACES XXVIII., who reigned about twenty-one years (A. D. 192-213). Vológeses IV. became involved in a war with the Roman Emperor Septímius Sevérus, A. D. 193, in consequence of the aid which he had rendered Pescennius Niger, the rival claimant against Sevérus for the sovereignty of the Roman Empire. After the overthrow and death of Pescennius Niger, the Roman army marched across Mesopotamia into Assyria and occupied Adiabênê, descended the Tigris in ships to Ctesiphon, captured Ctesiphon, Seleucia and Babylon, and returned in safety after suffering a repulse at Hatra. Vológeses IV. purchased peace in A. D. 199 by ceding Adiabênê, or Northern Assyria, to the Roman Empire.

After the death of Vológeses IV. a civil war arose between his sons for the possession of the Parthian crown, which VOLOGESES V., or ARSACES XXIX., acquired after a short struggle. His successor, ARTABÁNUS III., or ARSACES XXX., was the last King of Parthia, and is supposed to have been a son of Vológeses IV. and a brother of Vológeses V. He reigned about ten years (A. D. 216-226). When he refused to give his daughter in marriage to the Roman Emperor Caracalla, at the demand of the latter, Caracalla instantly crossed the Euphrates, seized Osrhoënê, proceeded through Mesopotamia to the Tigris, invaded Adiabênê, took Arbéla, and drove the Parthians from the mountains (A. D. 216). Caracalla then returned to Edessa, in Osrhoënê, but was assassinated the next year by Macrínus, who renewed the war with the Parthian king, by whom he was twice defeated near Nísibis, in consequence of which Macrínus only obtained peace by the payment of a large amount of money and the cession of the Roman territory east of the Euphrates to the Parthian king.

The Parthian Empire thus recovered its old limits, and Artabánus III. exercised the old Parthian suzerainty over Armenia by supporting the claims of his own brother to the Armenian crown. But just at this moment, when the Parthian Empire appeared to have recovered its former strength and power, it suddenly received its death-blow. The Arsácidæ had never gained the affections of their Persian subjects in the southern part of their empire; and, after four centuries of Persian subjection to Parthian dominion, the conquering Parthians and the conquered Persians had not amalgamated or assimilated, but the Parthians continued to be an army of occupation, separated by habits, prejudices and feelings, from the mass of the Persian nation. In A. D. 226 the Persians under Ardeshír Bábegan, or Artaxerxes, the son of Sassan, who claimed descent from Cyrus, rose in rebellion and defeated the Parthian forces in three great battles, in the last of which Artabánus III. himself was slain. These victories suddenly put an end to the Parthian Empire by transferring the supremacy of the Parthian dominions from the vanquished Parthians to the triumphant Artaxerxes and the New Persians, who thus founded the *New Persian Empire of the Sassanidæ* (A. D. 226).

This important revolution put an end to the supremacy of the Turanian race in the East and restored the ascendency of the Aryans. The overthrow of the Parthian Empire in A. D. 226 holds the same place in Asiatic history that the subversion of the Western Roman Empire in A. D. 476 does in European annals—that of forming the connecting link between ancient times and the middle ages.

Scarcely anything is known of the domestic history of the Parthians, and in the Persian history the Parthian dominion is almost a blank, all that we know of Parthian political history being derived from Roman sources. Religion and literature were closely connected in Persian history, and under the sway of the Parthian kings the religious system of Zoroaster fell into utter neglect. After Christianity had begun to spread, the Parthian monarchs tolerated, if they did not directly encourage, this new religion, and liberally afforded a refuge to Christians fleeing from the persecutions of the pagans, and from such of their brethren as belonged to a different sect. But the expulsion of the Parthians from Persia was followed by the restoration of the religion of Zoroaster and the Zend-Avesta. The eastward advance of Christianity was checked, and it was thrown back upon the Roman world, leaving, unfortunately, too many marks of its close contact with Oriental mysticism and superstition. The foothold thus lost by Christianity in the East was never regained.

THE ARSACIDÆ OF PARTHIA.

B. C.	KINGS.	A. D.	KINGS.
255	Artaxerxes, or Arsaces I.	4	Phraataces, or Arsaces XVI.
253	Tiridates I., or Arsaces II.	5	Orodes II., or Arsaces XVII.
216	Arsaces III.	6	Vonones I., or Arsaces XVIII.
196	Priapatius, or Arsaces IV.	14	Artabanus II., or Arsaces XIX.
181	Phraates I., or Arsaces V.	44	Vardanes, or Arsaces XX.
174	Mithridates I., or Arsaces VI.	48	Gotarzes, or Arsaces XXI.
136	Phraates II., or Arsaces VII.	50	Vonones II., or Arsaces XXII.
127	Artabanus I., or Arsaces VIII.	50	Vologeses I., or Arsaces XXIII.
124	Mithridates II., or Arsaces IX.	90	Pacorus, or Arsaces XXIV.
89	Arsaces X.	107	Chosroes, or Arsaces XXV.
76	Arsaces XI.	121	Vologeses II., or Arsaces XXVI.
69	Phraates III., or Arsaces XII.	149	Vologeses III., or Arsaces XXVII.
60	Mithridates III., or Arsaces XIII.	192	Vologeses IV., or Arsaces XXVIII.
55	Orodes I., or Arsaces XIV.	213	Vologeses V., or Arsaces XXIX.
37	Phraates IV., or Arsaces XV.	216	Artabanus III., or Arsaces XXX, (to A. D. 226).

SECTION XXIV.—THE KINGDOM OF JUDÆA.

E HAVE seen that Palestine, or Judæa, as a part of the Persian satrapy of Syria, was conquered by Alexander the Great, along with the remainder of the Medo-Persian Empire (B. C. 332-331). After Alexander's death, in B. C. 324, Palestine was by turns the prize of the Seleucidæ of Syria and the Ptolemies of Egypt, and suffered severely from the invasions of both alternately. Ptolemy Soter besieged Jerusalem and stormed it on the sabbath-day. He carried one hundred thousand Jews captive to Egypt, Libya and Cyrenaïca, where their posterity continued to live as a distinct people for several centuries. During this period Simon the Just was High Priest. He was distinguished for his virtues as a ruler and also for his piety, and under his direction the canon of the Old Testament was completed (B. C. 292). At this time arose several Jewish sects. The *Sadducees*, who denied the doctrines of a resurrection and a future state, and who endeavored to modify the Mosaic laws in accordance with Greek doctrines, embraced mainly the rich and powerful. The *Pharisees*, who were noted for their strict adherence to the laws of Moses, and for their hypocrisy and their regard for outward ceremonies, comprised mostly the lower orders. The *Essenes*, a very small sect, held all their possessions in common, on the communistic principle, and served Jehovah by acts of penance and works of charity. Jesus Christ is believed to have belonged to this sect.

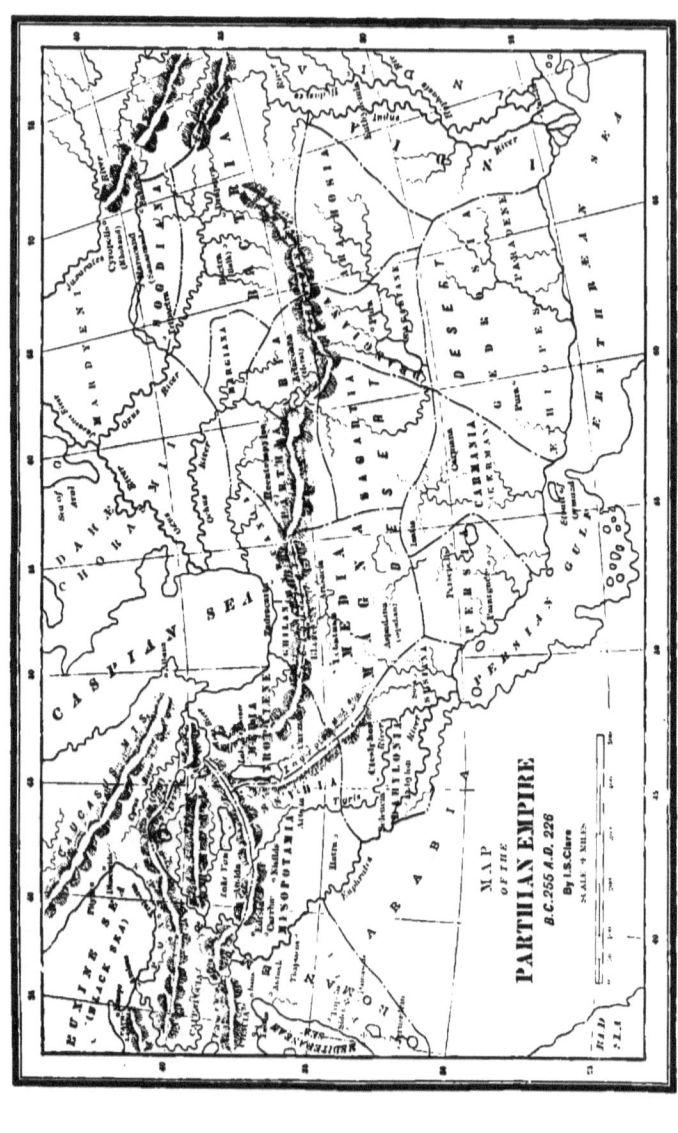

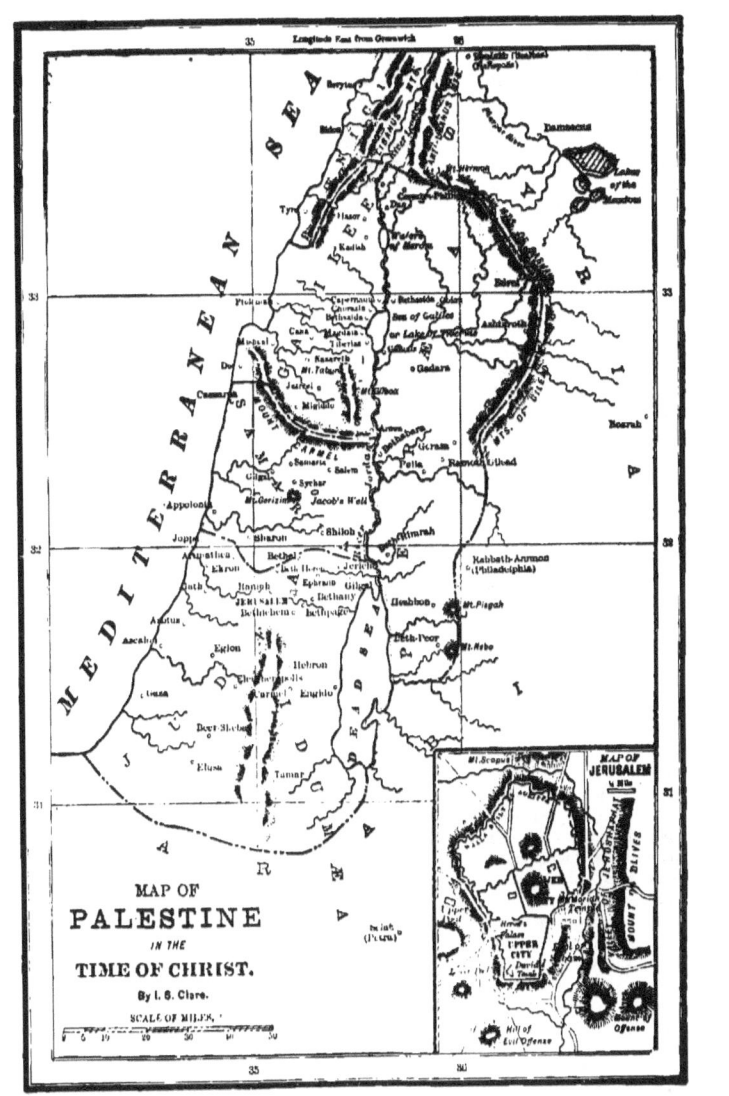

The ultimate dismemberment of Alexander's empire in consequence of the battle of Ipsus, in B. C. 301, confirmed Palestine and Cœle-Syria as portions of the Egyptian kingdom of the Ptolemies. Under the dominion of the first three Ptolemies, Judæa was allowed considerable local self-government; and so long as the Jews paid their tribute regularly, Ptolemies Soter, Philadelphus and Euérgetes seldom attempted to interfere in the religious or civil affairs of the Jewish nation. The High-Priest was the civil head of the Jewish people, as well as the chief of their national religion; and the reigns of the first three Ptolemies constituted a period of peace and prosperity for Judæa. The translation of the Hebrew Scriptures into the Greek language—known as the *Séptuagint* version—under the auspices of Ptolemy Philadelphus, has already been noticed. This was an important event in the history of the Jews and of the world, as the appearance of the Jewish sacred writings in a widely-spread language made these writings accessible to the whole civilized world, thus exercising an important influence upon the times, and particularly upon the Jews themselves. This translation made the Hebrew Scriptures known to the ancient world, and prepared the way for the spread of Christianity.

Ptolemy Philópator, the fourth of that dynasty, was a weak and licentious monarch, and mortally offended the Jews by attempting to violate the sanctity of the Holy Temple at Jerusalem by entering it in B. C. 217. This attempt at profanation was thwarted, and Ptolemy Philópator avenged himself by outrages upon the Alexandrian Jews, who had not done him any harm whatever. The Jews were so disgusted and alarmed by his conduct that they sought protection from Antíochus the Great of Syria, and voluntarily transferred their allegiance to that monarch, thus making Judæa a part of the Syrian Empire of the Seleúcidæ. Aided by the Jews, Antíochus the Great made himself master of all the coast between Upper Syria and the Desert of Sinai; and the battle of Páneas, B. C. 198, in which the Egyptians were defeated, established the power of the Seleúcidæ over Judæa, which Antíochus the Great thus wrested from Ptolemy Epíphanes, the successor of Ptolemy Philópator, after a series of bloody wars.

The Jews soon had reason to regret their change of masters, as they were more oppressed by the Seleúcidæ after the death of Antíochus the Great than they had been by the Ptolemies. Antíochus the Great allowed the Jews to manage their own religious and civil affairs, but his successor, Seleucus Philópator attempted to Hellenize them. Simon, the governor of the Temple, who had been expelled by Onías, the High-Priest, found refuge among the Syrians and informed them that there were vast treasures preserved in the sanctuary of Jerusalem. For the purpose of appropriating the sacred treasures of the Temple to his own pressing necessities and bringing them to Antioch, Seleucus Philópator sent his treasurer, Heliodórus, to Jerusalem. The Jewish tradition states that three angels made their appearance to defend the sanctuary. One of these angels was said to have been seated on a terrible horse, which trampled Heliodórus under his feet, while the other two scourged him to death, but the prayers of the High-Priest restored him to life, and the treasures of the Temple remained unmolested.

Antíochus Epíphanes, the brother and successor of Seleucus Philópator, committed greater sacrilege and cruelly persecuted the Jews. Soon after his accession, Antíochus Epíphanes was bribed to deprive Onías of the High-Priesthood. He sold the sacred office to Jason, who had already so far conformed to Greek customs as to relinquish his original Jewish name, Jesus. Under Jason's administration the Jewish nation became infected with a general apostasy, the temple service to Jehovah was neglected, academies on the Greek model were opened at Jerusalem, and the High-Priest himself publicly sent an offering to the Tyrian Hercules. Antíochus Epíphanes deprived Jason of the High-Priesthood by selling the office to Jason's brother, Menelaüs, who plundered the Temple of all its rich ornaments to pay the large bribe which he had promised to the king. Onías, who had lived at Antioch since his deposition, remonstrated against this sacrilege, whereupon the wicked Menelaüs, in great alarm, caused the worthy priest to be assassinated, but even the apostates from Jehovah lamented his death. Menelaüs then pursued his iniquitous policy with impunity until the masses, unable to endure his exactions any longer, excited a formidable riot in Jerusalem and killed the captain of the Syrian guard, who had been brought there to protect the High-Priest. The tumult was allayed by the *Sánhedrim*, or Jewish council, which sent three deputies to inform King Antíochus Epíphanes of the condition of affairs and to expose the crimes of Menelaüs. The wily priest, however, won the royal favorites by large bribes; and, at their instigation, the deputies were executed after they had presented themselves before the king. The Tyrians gave the bodies of the unfortunate deputies an honorable burial.

While Antíochus Epíphanes was invading Egypt, in B. C. 170, a rumor that he had been killed before Alexandria spread through Syria and Judæa. Thereupon Jason raised a small army to recover the High-Priesthood, marched to Jerusalem, entered the city, and massacred all who opposed his pretensions; but when Antíochus Epíphanes returned to Egypt, Jason fled from Jerusalem and wandered from one city to another as an exile, an object of universal scorn, as a traitor to his country and an inhuman monster.

Antíochus Epíphanes was greatly incensed at Jason's rebellion and at the public rejoicings of the Jews when they had heard the report of his death. He led a Syrian army into Judæa, took Jerusalem by storm, pillaged the city, massacred forty thousand of its inhabitants in three days, sold as many more into slavery among the neighboring nations, and plundered the Temple of its treasures to the amount of eighteen hundred talents (B. C. 170). Two years afterward (B. C. 168), he profaned the Temple by offering unclean animals upon the altar of burnt-offerings, polluting the entire edifice by sprinkling it with water in which flesh had been boiled, dedicating the Temple itself to Zeus, and erecting the statue of that Olympian deity on the altar of Jehovah in the inner court of the Temple, with daily sacrifices of swine's flesh. This is regarded as "the abomination of desolation," referred to by the prophet Daniel.

The tyrannical monarch strenuously endeavored to force the Grecian polytheism upon the monotheistic Jews, and sought to Hellenize them by forcible means, beginning one of the most cruel persecutions recorded in history. He issued an edict forbidding the Jews to observe any longer the Mosaic law regarding the sabbath and the rite of circumcision; and two women who were found guilty of circumcising their male children on the eighth day, according to the Law of Moses, were led around the city with the infants hung from their necks, and then cast headlong from the highest pinnacle of the city walls. To escape their atrocious cruelties, multitudes of Jews fled to the craggy rocks and caverns abounding in Palestine, living upon wild roots and herbs, to avoid the perils of death or the disgrace of apostasy. Even in these desolate places of refuge the persecuted Jews were pursued by the emissaries of the cruel monarch, and in one cave more than a thousand Jews, who had assembled to celebrate the sabbath, were massacred by the soldiers of the provincial governor. The noble constancy and heroic fortitude exhibited by many Jewish martyrs, of every age, sex and condition, often obliged their idolatrous persecutors to yield them involuntary admiration; and many of the Syrian officers secretly evaded the orders of their tyrannical sovereign, and endeavored to win the Jews by gentleness and persuasion, instead of by persecution and torture.

Mattathías, the head of the Asmonæan family, which was the first in the classes of the hereditary priesthood, was unable to endure the scenes of cruelty and profaneness displayed at Jerusalem, and therefore he retired to his native village of Modin, where he was allowed for some time to follow the religion of his fathers. At length a Syrian officer, who was sent to this remote place, assembled the people and offered the king's favor and protection as a reward for apostasy. Some miserable wretches yielded; but as one of them was about to offer sacrifice to the image of Zeus, Mattathías killed the renegade on the spot. His heroic sons, imitating their father's example, overthrew the altar and broke the idol. But as they knew that their conduct would be considered treason, they retired from their village and sought refuge in the "Wilderness of Judæa," whither they were soon followed by bands of heroic followers, resolved to vindicate the Mosaic laws at all hazards. Mattathías restored the worship of Jehovah in several of the cities from which he had expelled the Syrian garrisons, but he died before being able to recover Jerusalem (B. C. 166). In his last moments he appointed his son Judas to lead the army of the faithful, and exhorted all his sons to persevere in their heroic endeavors to restore the worship of Jehovah and the Mosaic laws to their original purity.

The struggle between the Hellenized Syrians and the Jewish rebels now assumed the character and importance of a regular war. The sons of Mattathías were called *Maccabees*, because they engraved on their standards the four Hebrew letters which were the initials of the words of the eleventh verse of the fifteenth chapter of Exodus, *Mi Kamoka B'elohím Jehovah*. JUDAS MACCABÆUS gained several great victories over the Syrian armies and reduced some of the strongest fortresses in Judæa. The most signal of his achievements was the defeat of the Syrians at Beth-horon, where the Syrian general Nicánor was slain and his whole army cut to pieces. The Maccabees recovered Jerusalem and its Temple without encountering any opposition, the Syrian garrison having evacuated the city on their approach. When the triumphant Jews came to Mount Zion and observed the desolation of the city and the Temple, they rent their clothes and vented their grief in loud lamentations. After the first emotions of sorrow had subsided, Judas Maccæbus secured the city by sufficient guards, and then employed his men in purifying the Temple and restoring its ruined altars. The holy place was thus restored three years after its profanation, and the feasts of its dedication were celebrated with all possible solemnity.

Judas Maccabæus exerted himself to maintain the independence of the Jewish nation by securing the frontiers of his country by fortresses. He repulsed many successive Syrian invasions, and signally defeated the Idumæans, the allies of the Seleúcidæ. Having finally engaged the Syrian army under Bacchídes against terrible odds, the valiant Judas was abandoned by his followers and slain, after many Syrians had fallen beneath his powerful arm (B. C. 161.) His countrymen recovered his body and buried it in his father's sepulcher at Modin. The Jews universally mourned his death, and, as they conveyed his remains to the tomb, they sang a funeral hymn in imitation of that composed by David on Jonathan's death, exclaiming: "How is the mighty fallen! How is the preserver of Israel slain!"

The Syrian army under Bacchídes recovered Jerusalem with ease, and then marched against the remnant of the revolted Jewish army under JONATHAN MACCABÆUS, the brother of the heroic Judas. Several indecisive conflicts were followed by a treaty of peace, and Jonathan Maccabæus was raised to the High-Priesthood by Alexander Balas, the competitor of Demétrius for the Syrian crown. Under Jonathan's administration, Judæa rapidly rose to be a flourishing and powerful state, and formed an alliance with the Romans and the Spartans, while Jonathan won the friendship of the Seleúcidæ by his unshaken fidelity. He was finally assassinated treacherously by the Syrian king Antíochus Tryphon, who feared that Jonathan would oppose his usurpation of the Syrian throne (B. C. 143).

SIMON MACCABÆUS, the last surviving brother of Judas and Jonathan, succeeded to the sovereignty and High-Priesthood, and obtained from the Syrian monarch the privilege of coining money, which in the East is considered an acknowledgment of independence. One of his coins has been preserved. It has an inscription in the old Samaritan character, signifying "the fourth year," and on the reverse "from the deliverance of Jerusalem." Thus, after a series of sanguinary wars, Judæa was freed from the oppressive yoke of the Seleúcidæ and became an independent kingdom under the Maccabees, or Asmonæan dynasty (B. C. 135).

After a glorious administration of eight years, Simon Maccabæus and his two sons were treacherously assassinated by his son-in-law Ptolemy, the governor of Jericho (B. C. 135). JOHN HYRCANUS, his younger son, escaped, and was immediately recognized as sovereign and High-Priest. At the beginning of his reign, the Syrian king, Antíochus Sidétes, besieged Jerusalem for two years (B. C. 135–133), destroying its restored walls, and again reducing the Jews to tribute. But after the death of Antíochus Sidétes, John Hyrcanus finally freed Judæa from the Syrian yoke. He also captured Samaria and destroyed the Samaritan Temple on Mount Gerizim. He conquered Edom, or Idumæa, and incorporated it with Judæa, and made the Jewish state as powerful as the Syrian kingdom of the Seleúcidæ, which had now become a petty state. John Hyrcanus was a zealous friend of the Pharisees in the early part of his reign, and that sect in turn exalted him as the only prince who had ever held the three offices of sovereign, High-Priest and prophet; but toward the end of his reign he quarreled with that haughty sect, and was consequently subjected to so many annoyances that he died of sheer vexation (B. C. 106). He was succeeded by his son, ARISTOBULUS I., the first of the Maccabees to assume the title of king. Aristobúlus I. was a weak and imbecile ruler, and his death was caused by remorse for having put his brother to death on a groundless suspicion (B. C. 105).

The next King and High-Priest of Judæa was ALEXANDER JANNÆUS, a Sadducee; and the Pharisees raised an insurrection against him while he was officiating as High-Priest in the Feast of Tabernacles, but Alexander severely punished this rising, slaughtering six thousand of the mob. He was a brave and able warrior, and gained victories over the Moabites and over the Arabs of Gilead, but in a subsequent war with the latter he suffered a great defeat; whereupon the Pharisees again rebelled, thus causing a civil war of six years in Judæa. Alexander Jannæus was driven to the mountains for a time, but he finally recovered the ascendency and revenged himself upon the rebels with terrible cruelty. He was given to licentious pleasures; and fatigues and debauches hastened his death (B. C. 79). He bequeathed the regency to his widow, Alexandra, and the crown to whichever of his two sons, Hyrcanus and Aristobúlus, she should find most worthy of the succession.

Alexandra was entirely under the control of the Pharisees, and soon established her authority through the influence of that sect. Her desire to retain power induced her to bestow the High-Priesthood on her eldest son, HYRCANUS II., because he was not of so enterprising a character as his brother, Aristobúlus, whom she kept carefully secluded in private life. But no sooner had his mother died than ARISTOBULUS II., in spite of the Pharisees, deposed his brother, Hyrcanus II., who was unambitious and acquiesced in his brother's usurpation. But Antípater, an Idumæan proselyte, thinking that he could easily rule in the name of Hyrcanus II., conveyed that prince to Petra, the Idumæan capital, and, having raised a large army of Arabs, invaded Judæa and besieged Aristobúlus II. in Jerusalem. Aristobúlus II. solicited the aid of the Romans, who had now extended their dominion into Asia; and both parties consented that the succession in Judea should be decided by the triumphant Pompey, who had just conquered Mithridátes the Great of Pontus.

Fearing that Pompey would decide in favor of Hyrcanus II., Aristobúlus II. fortified Jerusalem, which he resolved to defend against the Roman general. Getting alarmed at the advance of the Romans, he proceeded to Pompey's camp as a suppliant; but during his absence the Jews closed the gates of Jerusalem and refused to admit a Roman garrison, whereupon Pompey ordered Aristobúlus II. to be kept in chains and at once besieged the Holy City. The Roman general took Jerusalem by storm, after a siege of three months, and slew twelve thousand of its inhabitants. He destroyed the walls and fortifications of the city, but spared the Temple and its treasures.

Hyrcanus II. was now established on the throne of Judæa and reigned six years in peace (B. C. 63-57). In the latter year Aristobúlus II. escaped from Rome, where he had been held a prisoner, and, being joined by many of his partisans, renewed the civil war with his brother; but he was besieged in Machærus by the Roman Proconsul, who also deposed Hyrcanus II., and established a kind of oligarchy in Jerusalem. The Roman expedition under Crassus, on its way to invade the Parthian Empire, pillaged the Temple of Jerusalem of its treasures. After an interval of ten years (B. C. 57-47), Hyrcanus II. was restored to the High-Priesthood by the Romans, who, however, appointed his friend, Antípater, the Idumæan, to the office of Procurator, or civil governor, of Judæa.

Antípater, who was a cunning politician, supported Pompey in his war with Julius Cæsar, and after Pompey's defeat and death he won Cæsar's favor by affording him effective assistance when he was blockaded in Alexandria by the forces of the last Ptolemy. As a reward for these services, Cæsar appointed Antípater's second son, Herod, to the office of governor of Galilee, in which capacity the latter distinguished himself by exterminating the banditti that infested the country. After Cæsar's death Judæa was distracted by civil wars. Antípater was poisoned; his eldest son, Phásael, was put to death; and Herod was driven into exile. But through the influence of the Roman general, Mark Antony, HEROD, surnamed *the Great*, was restored to his former power by the Roman Senate and even made *Tetrarch*, or tributary King of Judæa, under the suzerainty of the Romans (B. C. 40). Herod the Great, however, had to conquer his kingdom; as the Jews submitted with reluctance to an Idumæan, and Herod's marriage with Mariámne, a Maccabæan princess, failed to conciliate them to his rule. In the very year of his accession (B. C. 40) ANTÍGONUS, son of Aristobúlus II., aided by a Parthian force, took Jerusalem, and reigned three years, as the last of the Asmonæan princes (B. C. 40-37).

After returning to Judæa from Rome, whither he had gone on Antípater's death, Herod conquered Galilee and marched against Jerusalem, which he only captured after a siege of several years, as the Jews made a heroic resistance, being firmly attached to Antígonus, and resenting the interference of the Romans and the reign of an Edomite prince. After a desperate defense, the walls of Jerusalem were taken by Herod's army, and Antígonus was executed like a common criminal (B. C. 37). Thus ended the dynasty of the Maccabees, and thus began the Idumæan dynasty of the Herods.

Herod, the first Idumæan King of Judæa under the suzerainty of the Romans, was deservedly surnamed *the Great*, because of his abilities and the grandeur of his enterprises, though he was a cruel tyrant. He caused all who opposed him to be massacred, at the very beginning of his reign. Particularly those whose wealth would enable him to reward his Roman benefactors fell victims to his sanguinary cruelty. He rebuilt the Temple, which had been almost destroyed in the frequent sieges to which it had been subjected for several centuries, and its splendor now rivaled its magnificence in the glorious days of Solomon one thousand years before. He relieved the sufferers from famine in Judæa and the adjacent countries at his own expense, buying vast quantities of corn in Egypt to feed the whole people, and supplying several provinces with seed for the ensuing harvest.

Herod the Great affected Roman tastes.

He erected a circus and amphitheater in a suburb of Jerusalem, where games and combats of wild beasts were celebrated in honor of the Emperor Augustus. He rebuilt the Samaritan Temple on Mount Gerizim, and founded Cæsaréa, adorning that new and magnificent city with imposing shrines of the Roman gods. But his universal toleration of all religions was displeasing to his Jewish subjects, and he was obliged to maintain a countless number of spies and to surround Jerusalem with a chain of fortresses, in order to keep down the rebellious inclinations of the people.

The only two surviving members of the Asmonæan or Maccabæan family were Mariámne and Aristobúlus, grand-children of Hyrcanus II. Herod married Mariámne and elevated Aristobúlus to the office of High-Priest; but he became jealous of the great popularity of Aristobúlus, and caused him to be secretly assassinated. Herod was devotedly attached to Mariámne, but he twice ordered her to be put to death in case of his own decease, while he was leading perilous expeditions from Jerusalem. When these cruel orders became known to the queen, her aversion for Herod, caused by the base murder of her grand-father and her brother, increased. She was too high-spirited to seek safety in concealment. She was brought to trial, and her inveterate enemies persuaded Herod to agree to her execution. But so intense was his grief and remorse that he was almost driven to insanity, and a violent fever nearly terminated his life. His temper now became furious, and his best friends were ordered to execution on the slightest suspicion. Three of his sons were put to death on charges of conspiracy.

While Herod the Great was in constant fear of being driven from his throne by his disaffected Jewish subjects, we are told "there came wise men from the East to Jerusalem, saying, Where is he that is born King of the Jews? for we have seen his star in the East, and are come to worship him." Herod was so greatly alarmed by this announcement that he assembled the chief-priests and the scribes, and inquired of them where Christ should be born. Being informed that the little village of Bethlehem, David's birth-place, about five miles from Jerusalem, was the place foretold by the prophets, Herod sent thither the wise men, "and said, Go and search diligently for the young child; and when ye have found him, bring me word again, that I may come and worship him also."

We are told that the infant Jesus Christ, whose birth was thus announced, was saved from the wrath of the cruel tyrant; as the wise men, "being warned of God in a dream that they should not return to Herod, they departed into their own country another way. And when they were departed, behold, the angel of the Lord appeareth to Joseph in a dream, saying, Arise and take the young child and his mother, and flee into Egypt, and be thou there until I bring thee word; for Herod will seek the young child to destroy him. When he arose, he took the young child and his mother by night, and departed into Egypt; and was there until the death of Herod." When Herod discovered that the wise men did not return, he was exceeding "wroth, and sent forth, and slew all the children that were in Bethlehem, and in all the coasts thereof, from two years old and under, according to the time which he had diligently inquired of the wise men."

Herod the Great had issued this cruel order from his death-bed, and he died in the seventieth year of his age, in the very year in which the infant Jesus of Nazareth was born, which has been discovered to have occurred four years earlier than the date from which our chronology is reckoned, or B. C. 4.

The death of Herod the Great caused great joy among all his subjects. His dominions, except Abilênê in Syria, were divided among his three sons, Archelaüs receiving Judæa and Samaria, Herod Antipas obtaining Galilee, and Philip being assigned Trachonítis. Archelaüs, however, proved to be so unworthy a governor that the Emperor Augustus Cæsar, tired of the complaints against him, deposed him from his office and banished him to Gaul; and Judæa formally became a Roman Province and was subjected to taxation. We are told that about this time Jesus Christ, then twelve years old, was brought by his parents, Joseph and Mary, to celebrate the Passover, in accordance with the Jewish custom, which required all male children who had reached that age to repair to the temple on the three great festivals, known as the Pentecost, the Passover, and Tabernacles.

The Jews very reluctantly submitted to Roman taxation, and frequently offered armed resistance to the publicans, or tax-gatherers; but when Pontius Pilate became the Roman governor of Judæa (A. D. 20), the Jews were still more alarmed for their religion, as Pilate brought with him to Jerusalem the Roman standards, which, on account of the images borne upon them, were regarded by the Jews as idols.

The Jews succeeded, after great difficulty, in inducing Pilate to remove the obnoxious ensigns, but his attempt to plunder the Temple provoked the Jews to another serious riot in Jerusalem. He ordered his Roman soldiers to attack the mob that resisted the attempt at plunder, and many innocent persons lost their lives in the tumult. Under Pilate's administration the state of society in Judæa became very corrupt, no class being free from the demoralizing effects of profligate government and popular discontent.

At this time John the Baptist, a prophet, the forerunner of the Messiah, appeared in the Wilderness of Judæa, "preaching the necessity of repentance, and announcing that the kingdom of heaven was at hand." His austere life and his novel doctrines caused many to become his disciples, and these were "baptized of him in Jordan, confessing their sins"(A. D. 26). Many considered him the Messiah; and the Evangelist tells us that "the people were in expectation, and all men mused in their hearts of John, whether he were the Christ or not. John answered, saying unto them all, I indeed baptize you with water; but one mightier than I cometh, the latchet of whose shoes I am not worthy to unloose; he shall baptize you with the Holy Ghost and with fire; whose fan is in his hand, and he will thoroughly purge his floor, and will gather the wheat into his garner; but the chaff he will burn with fire unquenchable."

The preaching of John the Baptist was only the prelude to that of a greater teacher. After Jesus Christ had reached his thirtieth year, he presented himself to John the Baptist to be baptized. After his baptism Christ at once entered upon his mission, "preaching the gospel of the kingdom, and healing all manner of sickness and all manner of disease among the people." He preached his doctrines to his disciples in his famous sermon on the Mount of Olives. But the greater part of the Jews disbelieved in his mission and plotted against his life.

Herod Antipas was meanwhile ruling in Galilee (B. C. 4—A. D. 39), while Philip held the government of Trachonitis (B. C. 4—A. D. 37). Herod Antipas was married to the daughter of an Arabian; while Philip was married to his own niece, Heródias. Herod Antipas sent away his own wife and married his sister-in-law, though she had children by his brother, thus violating the Mosaic law. The entire Jewish nation exclaimed against this incestuous marriage. John the Baptist, particularly, was sufficiently courageous to reprove both the king and his paramour in the strongest possible language. Heródias was so stung by John's reproaches that she induced her husband to imprison him, and afterwards, by means of her daughter, procured an order for John's execution. John the Baptist was accordingly beheaded in prison, but his disciples gave his remains an honorable burial, and the entire Jewish nation mourned his cruel death.

When Jesus Christ had fulfilled the object of his mission he was basely betrayed by Judas Iscariot, one of his twelve disciples, for thirty pieces of silver, and was delivered into the hands of his enemies, who put him to a cruel death on the cross. The Jews falsely accused him before Pontius Pilate, the Roman Procurator of Judæa, of a design to subvert the government

Pilate, though repeatedly declaring his belief that Jesus was innocent, finally yielded to the determined purpose of the Jewish accusers and pronounced the sentence of condemnation against the Nazarene; and Jesus Christ was crucified between two thieves on Mount Calvary (A. D. 31). The traitor Judas Iscariot hanged himself.

The crucifixion of Christ did not prevent the spread of his doctrines. On the day of Pentecost three thousand persons were converted by the preaching of the apostle Peter, and the church received fresh accessions each day. The conduct of the followers of Christ afforded a remarkable example of purity, harmony and self denial, in the wicked and distracted condition of Jewish society. Says the received account: "The multitude of them that believed were of one heart and of one soul; neither said any of them that aught of the things which he possessed was his own; but they had all things common." This fact demonstrates the communistic character of the early Christian community, and the similarity of its doctrines to those of the Essénes, one of the three sects of Judæa in the times of the Maccabees and the Herods.

The great increase of the church of Christ led to the appointment of seven deacons to take charge of "the daily ministration." The most remarkable of these was Stephen. The rulers of the synagogue, unable to confute him, accused him before the Sánhedrim, or council, of having blasphemed Moses and Jehovah. False witnesses were suborned to support the accusation, and Stephen was subjected to the mockery of a trial. He easily refuted the charges brought against him, but when he repeated his belief that Jesus was the Messiah, his enemies were overcome with rage. "They cried out with a loud voice, and stopped their ears, and ran upon him with one accord, and cast him out of the city, and stoned him; and the witnesses laid down their clothes at a young man's feet, whose name was Saul. And they stoned Stephen, calling upon God, and saying, Lord Jesus, receive my spirit. And he kneeled down, and cried with a loud voice, Lord, lay not this sin to their charge. And when he had said this, he fell asleep."

Saul, who was a native of Tarsus, in Cilicia, had consented to Stephen's death, and was so violent a persecutor that he obtained a commission to search after Christ's followers who sought refuge in Damascus. It is said that while Saul was on his way to that city he was stricken to the earth and suddenly converted to the new faith. He was thenceforth a zealous apostle of the new religion, and was called Paul. He at once became an ardent missionary, and traveled through Palestine, Asia Minor and Greece, everywhere making many proselytes. At Antioch, in Syria, the disciples of Christ were first called *Christians*. The persecution of Christ's disciples at Jerusalem was the means of propagating the gospel; because when the disciples were dispersed they carried their doctrines into every city in which the Jews had synagogues.

In the meantime Pontius Pilate was dismissed from the government of Judæa and sent to Rome to answer charges of tyranny and misgovernment before the Emperor Tiberius. His defense was unsatisfactory, and he was accordingly banished to Gaul, where he committed suicide with his own sword, as he was no longer able to bear the remorse of a guilty conscience.

HEROD AGRIPPA, the grandson of Herod the Great, had been kept in prison during the reign of the Emperor Tiberius, but was released under Calígula, the next Emperor, and obtained the provinces of Galilee and Trachonítis with the title of king (A. D. 37 and 39). Through the influence of Herod Agrippa, the Emperor Calígula was induced to recall his edict for desecrating the Temple of Jerusalem by erecting his own statue in it, and to pardon the Jews for resisting his imperious decrees. In the reign of the next Emperor, Claudius, Herod Agrippa also obtained the government of Samaria and Judæa, and for three years his dominions embraced all the territories ruled by his grandfather, Herod the Great (A. D. 41–44). He returned to Jerusalem, where he exhibited an extraordinary attachment

THE KINGDOM OF JUDÆA.

to the Jewish religion. To gratify the Pharisees, he began to persecute the Christians in the year A. D. 44. St. James, the brother of John, sometimes called St. James the Less, to distinguish him from St. James, the first Bishop of Jerusalem, was beheaded, and St. Peter was cast into prison; but soon after Peter's deliverance Herod Agrippa died in great misery from a painful and loathsome disease, whereupon Judæa was again placed under the government of Roman Procurators (A. D. 44).

The cruelty and rapacity of these Procurators, or provincial governors, filled Judaea with misery. Banditti infested the roads and even ventured to attack the towns. Certain pretended zealots, called *Sicarii*, or assassins, perpetrated the most atrocious murders in the name of religion and liberty; while false prophets and false messiahs excited frequent insurrections, which were punished with frightful severity.

Under the administration of Felix all these evils were aggravated. Felix was extremely avaricious, and was always ready to perpetrate any crime which would enable him to gratify his depraved passions. The apostle Paul was brought before this wicked governor when the Jews falsely accused him of disturbing the public peace. Nothing was proven against the apostle on his public trial, but Felix detained him in custody. At length the governor privately sent for Paul to hear him concerning the faith in Christ, "and as he reasoned of righteousness, temperance, and judgment to come, Felix trembled, and answered, Go thy way for this time; when I have a convenient season I will call for thee. He hoped also that money should have been given him of Paul, that he might loose him; wherefore he sent for him the oftener, and communed with him. But after two years Porcius Festus came into Felix's room; and Felix, willing to show the Jews a pleasure, left Paul bound."

When Porcius Festus became governor of Judæa he found the Jewish priests at war with each other concerning their shares of the tithes. Their rancor arose to such a height that the rival parties hired troops of assassins, and these carried massacre and carnage through Judæa, even the temples being stained with blood; while the country was also distracted by frequent seditions against the Romans, and by the lawlessness of bands of robbers, who plundered and massacred everywhere. At length St. Paul was brought before Festus for trial, but perceiving the vindictive spirit of the Jews, and having little faith in the firmness or justice of Festus, he appealed to the Emperor, and was sent to Rome, where he perished during the reign of Nero.

The next Roman governor of Judæa after Festus was Albinus, who was succeeded by Gessius Florus, the last and worst of these rulers (A. D. 64). Florus was a cruel and crafty tyrant. He shared the plunder of highway robbers, which he allowed and even encouraged. He twice excited riots in Jerusalem, sacrificing thousands of lives, for the sole purpose of pillaging the Temple in the midst of the tumult. He had made up his mind to drive the Jews into rebellion, with the design of preventing any inquiry into his countless oppressions. The unfortunate nation took up arms to expel the Syrians from Cæsarea, and raised seditions in nearly every city in which they were settled. The zealots ultimately attacked the Romans in the fortresses which had been erected to secure Jerusalem, and massacred all who opposed them, including even the garrisons that surrendered. The Roman governor of Syria marched into Judæa to punish these disorders, but was driven back.

The atrocities of Florus now drove the Jews into open rebellion against the Roman power, and they determined to set the whole force of the Empire at defiance (A. D. 67). The Christians of Jerusalem retired to Pella, beyond the Jordan, where they escaped the miseries of the war, while several of the higher classes of Jews also withdrew thither. The Emperor Nero sent Vespasian to command the Roman army employed against the revolted Jews. Vespasian was fiercely resisted by the Jews, and he halted his army at Cæsaréa, until the Jews, by their internal quarrels, would be reduced to such weakness as would enable him to obtain an easy triumph (A. D. 70). His expectation was realized. The zealots, who had fled from the Romans, now collected in Jerusalem, under the leadership of a vile demagogue, John of Gíschala, and being joined by the Idumæans, perpetrated the most atrocious massacres, and polluted the Temple with the most frightful assassinations. Another party was headed by Simon, the son of Gorías, whose sanguinary deeds in the country equaled those of John of Gíschala in the city. Simon was invited into the Holy City to check the violence of John and the zealots, but he soon proved himself the greater scourge of the two. A third faction was led by Eleázar, who seized the upper portion of the Temple; and thus, while the Romans were marching against the devoted city, the Jews comprising the garrison and inhabitants of the city were engaged in mutual slaughter.

In the meantime Vespasian was made Emperor of Rome, whereupon he assigned the command of his army in Judæa to his son Titus. Titus entered Judæa with a large and powerful army, and marched against Jerusalem, encountering no resistance in the open country, thus being led to believe that the Jews had repented of their rebellion and were preparing to submit. This mistaken inference led Titus to expose himself carelessly in the narrow valley of Jehoshaphat, where he became separated from his cavalry, in which perilous situation he was attacked by the Jews, and was exposed to the utmost danger, from which he rescued himself with difficulty. Titus laid siege to Jerusalem during the Feast of the Passover, when the city was filled with people from every part of Judæa. The Jews obstinately defended the Holy City with an army of six hundred thousand men. After the siege had formally commenced, the Jews, shut up in the city, suffered dreadfully from famine and pestilence; but in the midst of these horrors, and while the Roman battering-rams were destroying the walls of the city, the Jewish factions were waging a fierce civil war against each other in the streets of Jerusalem and filling the city with massacre and carnage. The horrors of the siege are beyond the power of language to describe. Reduced to the brink of starvation, the besieged Jews were obliged to use the most revolting and unnatural substances for food; while the zealots fiendishly laughed at the miseries and groans of their starving countrymen, and even went so far as to cruelly sheathe their swords on these poor wretches, under the pretense of testing their sharpness.

When the walls of the city were battered down, the Romans besieged the Temple, where the desperate Jewish factions still maintained the most obstinate resistance. Titus very much desired to spare the sacred structure, but one of his soldiers cast a lighted brand into one of the windows, and the entire edifice was soon in flames.' A terrible massacre followed. The Romans gave no quarter, and many thousands of Jews perished by fire and sword, or by suicide in casting themselves headlong from the battlements. This scene of slaughter lasted several days, until the Holy City was left entirely desolate. Ninety-seven thousand Jews were made prisoners, and eleven thousand of these were starved to death. Josephus states that during the five months of the siege there perished at Jerusalem, by famine, pestilence and the sword, more than a million of Jews and proselytes.

When the victorious Romans had finished their destructive work of burning and slaughter, Titus ordered that the whole city should be leveled with the ground, excepting a part of the western wall and three towers, which he left as memorials of his conquest. His orders were so promptly executed that, with the exception of these few structures, nothing but shapeless ruins remained to indicate the site of the renowned capital and metropolis of the Jewish nation. The Jews who had not perished were reduced to slavery and divided among the triumphant Romans as prizes. Large numbers were transported into the heart of Germany and Italy, and the golden vessels of

ROMAN SOLDIERS FIRING THE TEMPLE AT JERUSALEM.

the Temple adorned the triumphal procession of Titus at Rome. Mount Zion was plowed as a field and sown with salt, and the Temple was leveled with the ground. The victory of Titus was celebrated at Rome by a splendid triumph. A triumphal arch, which yet remains, was erected to commemorate the event, and a medal was struck, in which the conquered land of Judæa was represented as a disconsolate female sitting beneath a palm-tree, a soldier, who was standing by, laughing at her misery and mocking at her calamity. The Jews have ever since been dispersed among all nations, and are now found in every part of the civilized world. Thus ended the history of the Jewish nation. Judæa was then annexed to the Roman province of Syria (A. D. 70).

KINGS AND ROMAN GOVERNORS OF JUDÆA.

B. C.	THE MACCABEES.	B. C.	UNDER ROMAN RULE.
166	JUDAS MACCABÆUS.	37	HEROD THE GREAT, *King*.
161	JONATHAN MACCABÆUS.	4	ARCHELAUS, HEROD ANTIPAS and
143	SIMON MACCABÆUS.	A. D.	PHILIP, *Kings*.
135	JOHN HYRCANUS.		
106	ARISTOBULUS I.	20	PONTIUS PILATE, *Governor*.
105	ALEXANDER JANNÆUS.	37	HEROD AGRIPPA, *King*.
79	HYRCANUS II., (deposed).	44	FELIX, *Governor*.
69	ARISTOBULUS II.		FESTUS, *Governor*.
63	HYRCANUS II., (restored).		ALBINUS, *Governor*.
40	ANTIGONUS (to B. C. 37).	64	FLORUS, *Governor*.

SECTION XXV.—EDOM, OR IDUMÆA.

HE country called *Edom* in Scripture, and *Idumæa* by the Greeks, geographically constitutes a part of Arabia, but historically it is connected with Palestine, or Judæa, and for a long time it formed a part of the Jewish kingdom. Its study is interesting. Its former splendor is attested by its magnificent ruins now secluded in almost pathless deserts.

Edom derived its name from Jacob's brother Edom, or Esau, who settled among the Horites, in the region of Mount Seir, about eighty miles south-east from Jerusalem. There, within a narrow place, was Edom proper of the Scriptures, but the Edomites extended their dominion so as to embrace most of the country from Palestine to the Red Sea. In this extended sense Edom was the scene of some of the most extraordinary events recorded in the Hebrew Scriptures, and excites great interest in connection with the kindred land of Judæa.

The sacred Mount Sinai; the rock of Horeb, with its burning bush, and its caves that sheltered Elijah when he fled from Jezebel's persecution; the pastoral solitudes where Moses tended the flocks of Jethro, the priest of Midian; Shur and Paran, with the bitter wells of Marah, and the smitten rock that was said to have yielded water; the land of Uz, the scene of the wealth and woes of Job—these are all included within the domain of Edom.

The general physical features of this land are rocks, deserts and mountains, but many fertile oases are scattered amidst this barren region. The name of *Arabia Petræa*, or *Arabia the Stony*, has been assigned to a part of the country, because of its stony character. The peninsula of Sinai is of particular interest, as it has been more minutely explored and more elaborately described than any other portion of Idumæa. Its general aspect is peculiarly wild. A recent traveler has described it as a "sea of desolation."

He remarks that it appears as if Arabia Petræa had once been an ocean of lava, and that while its waves were reaching to the heights of mountains, it was ordered to suddenly stand still. This entire wilderness is a series of naked rocks and craggy precipices, interspersed with narrow defiles and sandy vales which are seldom refreshed with rain or adorned with vegetation. The mountain ridges, designated as *Seir* and *Hor* in the Hebrew Scriptures, extend from the Sinaitic peninsula to the Dead Sea. A long valley extends along the western side, and that valley is to this day the route of caravans, as it was the path of the Israelites in their forty years' "Wanderings in the Wilderness."

The mountain-group of Sinai is located near the center of the peninsula. The upper region of this group forms a circle thirty or forty miles in diameter. The summit of Sinai is one of the most desolate on the face of the earth, nothing being seen but huge peaks and crags of naked granite, constituting a wilderness of steep and broken rocks and valleys destitute of verdure, as far as the eye can behold. Nevertheless, water and small spots of soil producing fruit-trees are seen in the most elevated parts. Mount Sinai comprises two elevations now known as *Gebel Mousa* and *Gebel Katerin*, which are usually identified with Sinai and Horeb.

The first historical notices of Edom are found in the Hebrew Scriptures. While the Israelites were held in bondage in Egypt, the Edomites, or descendants of Esau, grew into a rich and powerful nation. The princes of Edom, as we are informed by the Book of Genesis, were celebrated long before any king reigned over Israel, and they refused to allow Moses a passage through their country to the Land of Canaan. As already related, the Edomites first settled in the rocky fastnesses of Mount Seir, which commanded the great roads traversed by the commercial caravans of the early ages.

The capital of Edom was the great commercial city called Bozrah in the Old Testament and Petra by the Greeks. This famous city was located at the foot of Mount Hor, in a deep valley. The only means of access to the city was through a narrow defile, partly natural, and partly cut through the solid rock which hung over the passage and in many places obstructed the view of the heavens. The path is so narrow that two horsemen can barely ride abreast, while near the entrance an arch thrown across at a great height connects the opposite cliffs. The pass gradually slopes downward for about two miles, while the mountain-ridge still retains its level, until at the close of the dark perspective numerous columns, statues and graceful cornices are seen, even now retaining their forms and colors as little injured by time and exposure as if they had just come from the chisel. The sides of the rocky ridges are covered with numerous excavations, some of which are private dwellings, others sepulchers. The prophet Jeremiah probably alluded to this extraordinary peculiarity in his denunciation of Jehovah's vengeance against Edom, in the following language: "Thy terribleness hath deceived thee, and the pride of thine heart. O thou that dwellest in the clefts of the rock, that holdest the height of the hill. Though thou shouldst make thy nest as high as the eagle, I will bring thee down from thence, saith the Lord."

The Edomites long maintained their distinct national existence, and successively withstood the attacks of the Egyptians, the Ethiopians, the Hebrews, the Assyrians, the Greeks and the Romans. Diodorus Siculus states that the great Egyptian king, Sesostris (Rameses the Great), was so harassed by the wars carried on against him by the Edomites that he was obliged to erect a line of defense across the Isthmus of Suez, from Heliopolis to Pelusium, to protect his dominions against their inroads. He says that it was exceedingly difficult to attack or subdue these people, because they retired to their deserts, where, if an army dared to follow them, it was certain to perish from thirst and fatigue, as the wells and springs were only known to the natives.

When David became King of Israel, the

Edomites had greatly extended their dominions. They were in possession of the ports of Elath and Ezion-Geber, on the northern point of the Red Sea (the Gulf of Akaba), and through these places they had opened a flourishing commerce with India and Ethiopia. They also maintained an extensive traffic with Phœnicia, Egypt and Babylonia. But the Hebrew armies, under Abishai, David's general, invaded Edom, routed the Edomites with terrific slaughter in the valley of salt, and forced them to receive Hebrew garrisons at Elath and Ezion-Geber. David perhaps began the trade with Ophir, which was afterwards pursued so extensively by Solomon and Hiram.

During Solomon's reign an Edomite prince named Hadad, who had sought refuge in Egypt when his native land was conquered by David, returned to Edom and led a revolt against the Hebrew supremacy. The only account which we possess concerning Hadad is that given in the First Book of Kings, as follows: "God stirred up an adversary unto Solomon, Hadad the Edomite. He was of the king's seed in Edom. For it came to pass, when David was in Edom, and Joab the captain of the host was gone up to bury the slain, after he had smitten every male in Edom (for six months did Joab remain there with all Israel, until he had cut off every male in Edom); that Hadad fled, and certain Edomites of his father's servants with him, to go into Egypt; Hadad being yet a little child. And they arose out of Midian, and came to Paran; and they took men with them out of Paran, and they came to Egypt, unto Pharaoh, King of Egypt; which gave him a house, and appointed him victuals, and gave him land. And Hadad found great favor in the sight of Pharaoh, so that he gave him to wife the sister of his own wife, the sister of Tahpénes the queen. And the sister of Tahpénes bare him Génubath his son, whom Tahpénes weaned in Pharaoh's house: and Génubath was in Pharaoh's household among the sons of Pharaoh. And when Hadad heard in Egypt that David slept with his fathers, and that Joab the captain of the host was dead, Hadad said to Pharaoh, Let me depart, that I may go to mine own country. Then Pharaoh said unto him, But what hast thou lacked with me, that, behold, thou seekest to go to thine own country? And he answered, Nothing; howbeit let me go in any wise."

The native traditions of the country preserve the memory of Hadad's reign in some degree, as one of the ruined edifices at Petra is yet called by the Arabs "the Palace of Pharaoh's daughter."

Hadad's efforts for the independence of his country were apparently only partially successful, as the Edomites remained subject to the Kings of Judah for about a century, until the reign of Jehoram (B. C. 888). Says the Hebrew account: "In his days, Edom revolted from under the hand of Judah, and made a king over themselves. So Joram went over to Zair, and all the chariots with him; and he rose by night, and smote the Edomites which compassed him about, and the captains of the chariots; and the people fled into their tents. Yet Edom revolted from under the hand of Judah unto this day. Then Libnah revolted at the same time."

Libnah was one of the cities of refuge belonging to the Kingdom of Judah, and its alliance with Edom had a tendency to perpetuate the hereditary animosity between the Hebrews and the Edomites. During the reign of Jehoram in Judah, the Edomites recovered their independence, and maintained it for eighty years. Amaziah, King of Judah, severely chastised the hostility of the Edomites. The Book of Chronicles says that "Amaziah strengthened himself, and led forth his people, and went to the valley of salt, and smote of the children of Seir ten thousand. And other ten thousand left alive did the children of Judah carry away captive, and brought them unto the top of the rock, and cast them down from the top of the rock, that they were all broken in pieces."

Azariah, or Uzziah, the son and successor of Amaziah in Judah, reconquered the Edomites. More than two centuries afterward they were subjected by Nebuchadnezzar of Babylon, and aided him in his siege and capture of Jerusalem, thus taking an active part in all the calamities inflicted upon the Jews. The prophet Obadiah declares that Edom "stood on the other side in the day that the strangers carried away captive Judah's forces, and foreigners entered into his gates and cast lots upon Jerusalem. Edom rejoiced over the children of Judah in the day of their destruction, spoke proudly in the day of their distress, and laid hands on their substance in the day of their calamity." The Edomites also "stood in the crossway, to cut off those that did escape, and to deliver up those that remained." The prophet Amos says that Edom "did pursue his brother with the sword, and did cast off all pity, and his anger did tear perpetually, and he kept his wrath forever."

During the flourishing period of the Assyrian and Babylonian Empires, which overthrew the Kingdoms of Israel and Judah, the wild freebooters of Edom remained either wholly independent or acknowledged a temporary alliance with their foes. When Babylon fell before the conquering arms of Cyrus the Great of Persia, and when Cambyses and Darius Hystaspes led the Persian armies to Egypt and Europe, these conquerors found it necessary to maintain a friendly understanding with the desert tribes, in order to obtain a passage through their territories and supplies of water and provisions for their armies. Herodotus states that on this account they were exempted from paying tribute, while the neighboring princes were heavily taxed. During the captivity of the Jews in Babylon, the Edomites conquered the southern part of Palestine and seized the city of Hebron. Thenceforth those Edomites who occupied the southern frontiers of Palestine were called *Idumæans*, while those who remained at Petra were named *Nabathæans*, as some believe, from Nebaioth, a son of Ishmael.

During the wars between the successors of Alexander the Great, Athenæus, the general of Antígonus, was sent against the Nabathæans, who ravaged the territories of Antígonus and refused him permission to collect bitumen from the Dead Sea. When Athenæus marched against them, most of them were absent from their homes, having gone to a neighboring fair, where they were in the habit of bartering the woolen goods which they obtained from the Tyrians for the spices brought from the East by the caravans. As the passes of the country had been left only slightly guarded, Athenæus easily obtained possession of Petra, surprising its magazines, and returned to the Syrian frontier richly laden with plunder. The Nabathæans, enraged at the news of this misfortune, assembled their forces, and urging their dromedaries with indescribable speed, overtook Athenæus near Gaza and almost entirely cut his army to pieces. Demétrius Poliorcétes, the son of Antígonus, hastened to avenge this disaster, but the Arabian deserts and fastnesses baffled all his efforts. An Arab chief harangued the Greek general from the top of a rock, and so vigorously portrayed to him the perils of his enterprise that Demétrius, convinced of the great hazards of his undertaking, at once returned to Syria.

Ptolemy Euérgetes, King of Egypt, seized the Arabian ports on the Red Sea, but penetrated no farther into the country. From about B. C. 200 to the beginning of the Christian era several Arab chieftains distinguished themselves in the wars of the Jews, sometimes allying themselves with the Seleúcidæ of Syria, and sometimes with the Ptolemies of Egypt. Antíochus the Great reduced a portion of the Northern Arab tribes to submission, and his son Hyrcanus was engaged for several years in chastising their incursions and depredations. About B. C. 170 the Nabathæans were ruled by a prince named Hareth, called Aretas by the Greeks. His dominions reached to the frontiers of Palestine and included the country of the Ammonites. Having made peace with the Jews, they allowed Judas Maccabæus and his brother Jonathan a passage through their territories; but notwithstanding the friendly relations existing between them, the Nabathæans were unable to resist the temptation to plunder even their friends when an opportunity presented itself; and they accordingly attacked a detachment of Jews on their march, seized their carriages, and plundered their baggage.

During the wars of the Maccabees in Judæa, the Idumæans who had settled in that country displayed the old aversion of their race toward the Jews. Judas Maccabæus severely punished them, taking and sacking their chief city, Hebron, destroying more than forty thousand of their soldiers, and leveling their strongholds with the ground. The Idumæans were thoroughly subdued by the Jews under John Hyrcanus about B. C. 130, and were only allowed to remain in Judæa on condition of accepting the Jewish religion, whereupon they adopted the laws of Moses, submitted to circumcision, and soon became incorporated with the Jews. Upon the extinction of the Maccabees, the Idumæan Herod the Great became tributary king, or Tetrarch, of Judæa, under the suzeraintly of the Romans. The name Idumæan gradually fell into disuse, until, in the first century of the Christian era, it became entirely obsolete.

The Nabathæans maintained their independence for a much longer period than did the Idumæans. When Alexander Balas, King of Syria, was defeated by Ptolemy Philométor, King of Egypt (B. C. 146), a Nabathæan prince named Zabdiel offered protection to the vanquished monarch, but was afterwards bribed with money to violate the laws of hospitality by delivering up the royal fugitive. Josephus mentions another Nabathæan prince, named Obodas, who defeated the Jews by enticing them into an ambuscade, where he cut them to pieces (B. C. 92). Josephus also states that Hareth, or Aretas, the sovereign of Arabia Petræa, overthrew Antiochus Dionysius, King of Damascus, and led an army of fifty thousand men into India.

The constant Arab incursions into Syria finally aroused the hostility of the Romans, whose dominions extended as far east as the Euphrates. The successive Roman Proconsuls of Syria—Lucullus, Pompey, Scaurus, Gabinius and Marcellínus—undertook expeditions against the marauding Arab tribes, but gained no other advantage than the payment of a tribute or a temporary suspension of hostilities. The Emperor Augustus Cæsar claimed the right to impose a king upon the Nabathæans, but they elected a sovereign of their own, who assumed the name of Aretes and remained at peace with the Romans during his entire reign, which ended with his death A. D. 40.

During the reign of the Emperor Trajan, Arabia Petræa was made a Roman province, under the name of *Palestina Tertia*, or *Salutaris* (A. D. 106). The fluctuating condition of the Roman power in the East prevented this province from being held in a condition of absolute dependence. Nevertheless, Trajan put an end to the dynasty of the ancient Nabathæan kings, and besieged Petra with a large Roman army, but its strong position and the heroic defense of its garrison baffled all his efforts for the reduction of the city. In one of the assaults headed by Trajan in person, the Emperor narrowly escaped being slain, his horse being wounded and a soldier being killed by his side; as the Arabs, notwithstanding his disguise, discovered him by his gray hairs and his majestic mien. The Romans were forced to relinquish the siege of Petra. The historians of the time ascribe this Roman repulse to the violent tempests of wind and hail, the dreadful flashes of lightning, and the swarms of flies that infested the camp of the besiegers. The Roman repulse from Petra seems to be the last military event recorded in the history of the Nabathæans.

The foundation of the Edomite city of Petra appears to have been coeval with the origin of Eastern commerce, and there is evidence that it was a flourishing commercial emporium seventeen centuries before Christ. It was the original seat of all the commerce of the North of Arabia, and there the first merchants of the world stored the costly commodities of the East. It constituted the great emporium of mercantile trade between Palestine, Syria and Egypt. The celebrated soothsayer Balaam was a native of Petra, and in his time its inhabitants were famous for their learning, their oracular temple, and their skill in augury. During the entire period of its history, Petra seems to have been a seat of wealth and commerce. In the time of Christ, Strabo described it from the account of his friend, Athenodórus, the philosopher, who spoke highly of the civilized manners of its inhabitants, of the crowds of Roman and foreign merchants found there, and of the excellent government of its sovereigns. He represented the city as surrounded with precipitous cliffs, but rich in gardens, and supplied with an abundant spring, which rendered it the most important fortress in the desert. Pliny afterwards described it as a city almost two miles in extent, having a river running through the midst of it, and situated in a valley inclosed with steep mountains, which cut off all natural access to it.

The name of Petra almost vanishes from history with the decline and fall of the Roman power in the East. The city sunk into gradual decay when the commerce which had caused its prosperity was directed into other channels. Ancient Edom was so thoroughly cut off from the rest of the world that the very existence of the once-flourishing city of Petra fell iuto oblivion; and its discovery by the German traveler Burckhardt, in 1812, in the loneliness of its desolation, seemed as if the dead had risen from their graves. No human habitation is in or near the site of this famous ancient city, and the terrible denunciation of the Jewish prophet Isaiah is literally fulfilled.

The following is the language of this prophet: "The cormorant and the bittern shall possess it; the owl also and the raven shall dwell in it; and he shall stretch out upon it the line of confusion, and the stones of emptiness. They shall call the nobles thereof to the kingdom, but none shall be there, and all her princes shall be nothing. And thorns shall come up in her palaces, nettles and brambles in the fortresses thereof; and it shall be a habitation of dragons, and a court for owls. The wild beasts of the desert shall also meet with the wild beasts of the island, and the satyr shall cry to his fellow; the screech-owl also shall rest there, and find for herself a place of rest. There shall the great owl make her nest, and lay, and hatch, and gather under her shadow; there shall the vultures also be gathered, every one with her mate."

SECTION XXVI.—LATER GREEK SCIENCE AND LITERATURE.

 DURING the period following the dissolution of the empire of Alexander the Great, the Hellenic race produced many eminent scientists, poets and historians; but these mainly flourished in Sicily, and at Alexandria, in Egypt. Under the Ptolemies, Alexandria took the place formerly held by Athens as the seat of Grecian learning and literature.

The Greeks outside of the mother country itself, especially those of Alexandria, now cultivated the mathematical and physical sciences to the highest degree of perfection known to the ancients, and learned grammarians and critics collected and arranged the works of the older Greek writers.

The most famous of these grammarians and critics who had schools at Alexandria were ARISTOPHANES and ARISTÁRCHUS, the former being the chief librarian during the reigns of Ptolemies Philadelphus and Euérgetes.

EUCLID, the eminent Greek mathematician and the father of mathematical science, flourished at Alexandria about B. C. 300, and composed a text-book on geometry used thereafter for centuries. This work immortalized his name, and in it he digested all the propositions of the eminent geometricians who preceded him, such as Tháles, Pythágoras and others. King Ptolemy Soter became Euclid's pupil, and his school was so famous that Alexandria continued to be the great resort of mathematicians for centuries. Euclid's *Elements* have been translated into most languages, and have remained for two thousand years as the basis of geometrical knowledge wherever science has cast its light. APOLLONIUS, the successor of Euclid, was also a famous Greek mathematician at Alexandria, and wrote on the conic sections.

ARCHIMÉDES, the most renowned ancient mathematician and a great scientist, was a native of Syracuse, in Sicily, where he flourished in the third century before Christ. He gained an immortal fame by his discoveries in mechanical and physical science. He was renowned alike for his skill in astronomy, geometry, mechanics, hydrostatics and optics. He invented the combination of pulleys to raise enormous weights, the endless screw, a sphere to represent the motions of the celestial bodies, etc. His knowledge of the principle of specific gravities enabled him to detect the fraudulent mixture of silver in the golden crown of Hiero II., King of Syracuse, by comparing the quantity of water displaced by equal weights of silver and gold. While he was in the bath, the thought occurred to him, upon observing that he displaced a bulk of water equal to his own body. It is said that he was so intensely excited by his discovery that he ran naked out of the bath, exclaiming: "Eureka!" (I have found it.) His knowledge of the power of the lever is indicated by his celebrated declaration to King Hiero II.: "Give me where I may stand, and I will move the world." His genius for invention was signally displayed in the defense of Syracuse against the besieging Roman army under Marcellus, when he is said to have fired the Roman fleet by means of immense reflecting mirrors, by which the heated rays of the sun were concentrated on one point. But the city was finally taken by storm, and Archimédes was slain by a Roman soldier in the seventy-fourth year of his age (B. C. 212). Nine of the many works composed by Archimédes have been transmitted to us.

ERATOSTHENES, a renowned Greek astronomer, antiquarian and scholar, flourished at Alexandria in the third century before Christ. He was, next to Aristotle, the most illustrious of Greek scholars, and was particularly distinguished as the first and greatest critical investigator of Egyptian antiquity. His researches were undertaken by command of King Ptolemy Soter, and therefore with all the advantages that royal patronage could obtain for the investigation from the Egyptian priests. Georgius Syncellus, Vice-Patriarch of Constantinople (A. D. 800), has given us an epitome of the list of Pharaohs as prepared by Eratósthenes.

Two great astronomers afterwards flourished at Alexandria—HIPPARCHUS, in the second century before Christ, and PTOLEMY, in the second century after Christ. Ptolemy was equally celebrated as an astronomer and a geographer. His theory that the earth is the center of the universe and motionless was accepted for fourteen centuries, and his great work on geography was an authority during the same period. Ptolemy's *Syntax of Astronomy*, usually styled the *Almagest*, the name given it by the Arabian scholars, explains his theories, including that of the central position and stability of the earth, and that of *epicycles* to explain the movements of the other celestial bodies. This work is to this day valued on account of its catalogue of stars, corrected from the earlier one of Hipparchus. Ptolemy's work on geography mainly consists of lists of places in various countries, with latitudes and longitudes and some notices of objects of interest. This work was only superseded by the great geographical discoveries of the sixteenth century of the Christian era.

HIPPOCRATES, a Greek of Asia Minor, who lived in the time of Socrates and Plato, was the "Father of Medicine." GALEN, a Greek born at Pérgamus, but who studied at Alexandria, Corinth and Smyrna, was the most eminent physician and medical writer of antiquity, and lived in the second century after Christ (A. D. 131-200). He settled at Rome where he acquired an immense practice, but was driven from that city by the intrigues of his jealous rivals, who ascribed his wonderful success to magic. He was recalled to Rome by the Emperor Marcus Aurelius, who confided to him the care of the health of his son Cómmodus. Only a part of his many writings remain, but even these form five folio volumes and furnish abundant evidence of his practical and theoretical skill. Says Liebig: "The system of Galen, in regard to the cause of disease and the action of remedies, was regarded during thirteen centuries as impregnable truth, and had acquired the entire infallibility of the articles of a religious creed. Their authority only ceased when chemical science, advancing, made them no longer tenable. Soon after Luther burned the papal bulls, Paracelsus burned at Basle the works of Galen."

Grecian poetry had greatly declined during the Macedonian period, and only one distinguished dramatist flourished in this age of Greek literature. This was MENANDER, the last great Athenian comic poet, who flourished about B. C. 300. He was born at Athens, B. C. 342. He composed one hundred and eight comedies, all of which have perished. A few fragments of his writings only yet remain. The high praises heaped upon him by his contemporaries are good evidence that he must have been a dramatist of the highest order.

Pastoral poetry predominated at this period. THEOCRITUS, a native of Syracuse, in Sicily, was the greatest of Grecian pastoral poets, and flourished about B. C. 270. These facts, and also the names of his parents, may be partly learned from his writings. Theócritus, in his *Idyls*, describes a pastoral life full of innocence and simplicity. His sixteenth Idyl shows that he remained at Syracuse for some time after the beginning of his poetic career. He afterwards resided at Alexandria, where, at the court of Ptolemy Philadelphus, he was classed as one of the seven celebrated men, called the *Pléiades*, or "seven stars." He stands at the head of pastoral poets. The great Roman poet, Virgil, called him "master," and in his pastorals invoked the muse of Theócritus, under the name of the Sicilian or Syracusan muse. Virgil generally imitates, and often adopts and refines, the ideas of Theócritus. In some instances, according to a custom of ancient writers, and which would in our day be considered literary theft, he translates the very words of Theócritus, incorporating them with his own.

BION and MOSCHUS were pastoral poets, and contemporaries of Theócritus, and both flourished in Sicily. Bion was born at Smyrna, in Asia Minor, but spent most of his life in Sicily. Moschus was a native of Syracuse. The pastorals of these two poets are very graceful and beautiful. Moschus acknowledged Bion as his friend and his preceptor in pastoral poetry. Bion's works consist of a few elegant and simple pastorals. Bion was a wealthy man, and one of the Idyls of Moschus informs us that he died by poison administered by a powerful enemy. That Moschus was a Syracusan and a contemporary of Theócritus is seen in one of his own pastorals.

Besides Theócritus, four other Greek poets flourished at Alexandria in the third century before Christ. These were the elegiac poets LYCOPHRON and CALLIMACHUS, the epic poet APOLLONIUS, and ARÁTUS. Lycóphron was a native of Chalcis, in Euboea, but was attracted to Alexandria by the patronage of King Ptolemy Philadelphus, who assigned him a position in the poetical constellation. Lycóphron wrote several essays on criticism and twelve tragedies, as well as numerous other poems, some of which were flattering anagrams on the illustrious names which adorned the court of Ptolemy Philadelphus. But the *Cassándra* is Lycóphron's only poem which has escaped oblivion.

Callímachus was born at Cyrênê, and received the surname of Battíades, from Battis, the king and founder of that city, whose descendant he claimed to be. He was one of the seven contemporary poets who flourished at the court of Ptolemy Philadelphus.

His works are said to have been exceedingly voluminous, and consisted of elegies, hymns and epigrams, numbering eight hundred; but only a few of his short poems have been preserved. Apollonius was a native of Alexandria, being born there in the time of Ptolemy Philadelphus. In his early youth he wrote the *Argonautica*, an epic founded on the fable of the Argonautic Expedition and the Golden Fleece. Milton, in *Paradise Lost*, made many allusions to the great epic of Apollonius.

Arátus was born at Soli, afterwards named Pompeiopolis, in Cilicia. He was the disciple of Dionysius of Heracléa, and followed his master's example in adopting the principles of the Stoic philosophy. The name of Arátus appears as one of the Pléiades of Alexandria, and his friendship with Theócritus is indicated by the sixth and seventh Idyls of that illustrious pastoral poet.

Early in the third century before Christ also flourished the Egyptian priest MANETHO, who wrote his famous History of Egypt in Greek, and who adorned the court of Ptolemy Philadelphus. Contemporary with Manetho lived BEROSUS, the Babylonian priest who wrote a complete History of Early Chaldæa and Later Babylonia in Greek, only fragments of which have been transmitted to us by APOLLODORUS and POLYHISTOR, two Greek writers.

A number of distinguished Greek historians flourished during this later period of antiquity. POLYBIUS, the most eminent Greek historian after Xenophon, flourished in the second century before Christ, and was a native of Greece itself, being born at Megalopolis, in Arcadia, B. C. 204. He was one of the thousand Achæans carried captive to Italy by the Romans in B. C. 168, on the charge of not having aided the Romans against Pérseus, King of Macedon. He resided in the house of Æmilius Paulus, the Roman general who vanquished Pérseus at Pydna. He became the intimate friend of Scipio, the son of Æmilius Paulus, and accompanied him to the siege of Carthage. The great work of Polybius is a general history of the affairs of Greece and Rome from B. C. 220 to B. C. 146, preceded by a brief view of early Roman history. This work consisted of forty books, only five of which now remain. But these are among the most valuable literary remains of antiquity, as Polybius exerted himself to learn facts, studied and traveled extensively, was thoroughly versed in war and politics, and possessed a clear insight into the relations of things. His aim being didactive, a great portion of his history consists of disquisitions. His residence at Rome and his acquaintance with the prominent men of his time enabled him to give his history a comprehensive range and render it a work of great value by his accuracy and impartiality. His account of the campaigns of Hannibal and others has made his history the delight of military leaders in all subsequent ages. His style lacks the charm of eloquence, but is clear, simple and well-sustained. Polybius reached the great age of eighty-two years. His Arcadian countrymen erected statues to his memory in all their principal cities.

DIODORUS SICULUS, another distinguished Greek historian, was a native of Sicily (hence the name Siculus), and was born about the middle of the first century before Christ. He left his native city of Agyrium in his youth and spent many years in his travels through the greater part of civilized Europe and Asia, and also through Egypt. In his journeys he gathered materials for a historical work, in the composition of which he was engaged for a period of thirty years. This universal history, which Diodorus called his *Bibliotheca Historica*, comprised forty books, of which only fifteen yet remain, the first five and the second ten. The annals of Diodorus constitute the principal remaining authority upon the subject of Egyptian, Assyrian and Babylonian antiquities, and they are accordingly very curious and valuable. Though his history was of great merit, Diodorus was neither so elegantly perspicuous as Xenophon, nor so scrupulously accurate as Polybius. He resided at Rome in the time of Julius and Augustus Cæsar, when the Greek language had become corrupted, and for this reason he cannot rival his predecessors in beauty of style and diction. Nevertheless, the language of Diodorus nearly equals the best ancient standards.

DIONYSIUS HALICARNASSEUS, so named because he was a native of Halicarnássus, in Asia Minor, was another illustrious Greek historian and a contemporary of Diodorus Siculus. He came to Rome about the time when Augustus Cæsar founded the Roman Empire. After residing in Rome twenty-two years, Dionysius wrote a history of the Roman power, for which he had long made diligent preparation and gathered many materials. His work consisted of twenty books, of which only the first eleven yet remain.

STRABO, a celebrated Greek historian and geographer, was born at Amasia, in Cappadocia, about B. C. 50, and flourished in the time of Christ. He traveled through Greece, Italy, Egypt and Asia, seeking the most reliable information concerning the geography, the statistics and the political condition of the countries which he visited. He is supposed to have died after A. D. 20. His great work, in seventeen books, besides describing various countries, gives the principal particulars of their history, notices of distinguished men, and accounts of the customs and manners of the people. It embraces almost the entire history of knowledge from the time of Homer to that of Augustus Cæsar. There is an English translation of Strabo's works in Bohn's Classical Library.

FLAVIUS JOSEPHUS, a renowned Jewish historian, who flourished in the first century of the Christian era, wrote a history of the Jewish race in Greek. Josephus was taken prisoner by the Romans at the capture and destruction of Jerusalem in A. D. 70. He has given us a most graphic and elaborate account of that famous event, and of the calamities which had befallen his countrymen.

PLUTARCH, the eminent biographer of antiquity, and a native of Greece itself, lived in the first and second centuries of the Christian era, and achieved an immortal fame by his *Lives* of the great warriors and statesmen of Greece and Rome. Plutarch was born A. D. 46, at Chæronéa, in Bœotia, the scene of the great victory of Philip the Great of Macedon over the Athenians and Thebans, which prostrated the liberties of Greece. Plutarch belonged to one of the most ancient and respectable families of his native place, and all its members were attached to the pursuits of philosophy. His tastes were early directed in the same channel, and he had received an excellent education under Ammonius, an Egyptian, who had established a famous school at Athens. Plutarch afterwards visited Egypt to store his mind with additional knowledge. After returning to his native land, he traveled through all its chief cities, and at length went to Rome, where he resided about forty years. At the close of this period he returned to Chæronéa, to spend the last years of his life in his native city. During his residence in Rome he lectured on philosophy, as early as the reign of Domitian. In his retirement at Chæronéa he completed the great work upon which his fame rests, consisting of biographies of forty-six illustrious Greeks and Romans, arranged in pairs, each pair being compared in their characters. These biographies are written with a moral purpose, and besides orderly narrative of events, they give us portraitures of their characters, presented in a graphic and vigorous style, and with much good sense, honesty and generosity.

Plutarch's Lives constitute one of the most charming productions transmitted to us from antiquity. This work has to this day been regarded as a model of biographical composition, and so deserves to be, because of the impartial, cautious, manly, and honest style in which it is written. Plutarch's morals and piety merit as much commendation as those of any other pagan writer. Altogether, though morally defective, Plutarch's Lives have done more toward inciting youth to virtuous and exalted deeds than any other Greek or Roman production. As tested by modern criticism,

Plutarch's Lives are not historical authorities; as they were written, not with a critical, but with a practical aim. They present to us the most famous types of Greek and Roman character as they appeared to the careful, scholarly, imaginative and philosophical biographer. They were Shakspeare's chief authority in the preparation of his great classical dramas. Not many ancient or modern works have been so widely read or so generally admired as Plutarch's Lives.

Several of Plutarch's other works have been lost, but there yet remain such small treatises as his *Symposiacs*, or Table Conversations, and his *Morals*, which maintain his reputation for ability and piety. The people of his native city honored him with the office of chief-magistrate, and he died among his countrymen and friends in the seventy-fifth year of his age, A. D. 120.

ARRIAN, a Greek of Asia Minor, was a historian who flourished in the early part of the second century of the Christian era. Arrian was a native of Nicomedia, in Bithynia, and came to Rome when quite young, and there studied under the famous Greek philosopher, Epictétus, whose Stoical opinions he afterwards gave to the world in two treatises, which have ever since been ranked among the finest expositions of ancient morality.

APPIAN, another Greek historian who flourished in the early part of the second century of the Christian era, contemporary with Arrian, was a descendant of one of the leading families of Alexandria. He came to Rome during the reign of the Emperor Trajan, and began to practice law in the Roman courts. He achieved such distinction as a pleader that he became one of the imperial Procurators; and, under Trajan's successors, Adrian and Antoninus Pius, he was invested with the dignity of provincial governor. Appian wrote a regular history of Rome from the times of the legendary Æneas to the times of the Empire. He also wrote various separate and extended accounts of particular civil and foreign wars in the history of the Roman people. Some of these fragmentary writings are all that now remain of his works.

DIOGENES LAERTIUS, a Greek historian who is supposed to have flourished about A. D. 200, wrote the *Lives of the Philosophers* in ten books, a work mainly valuable for the fragments which it contains of earlier writings which have perished.

HERODIAN was a Greek historian who lived in the third century after Christ. He gave an accurate narrative of the events of the Roman Empire from the reign of Marcus Aurelius Antoninus, who died A. D. 180, to the accession of Gordian III., A. D. 244, embracing a period of about seventy years. Herodian personally witnessed the principal events which signalized this period, and had the best opportunities for accurate observation, because he had long been attached to the court of the Roman Emperors. Herodian's history is in eight books, and embraces the reigns of more than twelve Emperors. This work gives us the most authentic knowledge of this stirring epoch. Herodian wrote in a style of dignity and sweetness, and his comments upon the events recorded by him are pertinent and instructive.

LUCIAN, a renowned Greek writer, was a native of Samosata, and flourished in the second century after Christ. He was of humble origin, and while young was placed with an uncle to study sculpture, but his failure in his first efforts induced him to go to Antioch and devote himself to literature and forensic rhetoric. The Roman Emperor Marcus Aurelius made him Procurator of Egypt. He died at the age of ninety. Lucian's works are chiefly in the form of dialogues, and many have been transmitted to us. The most popular are those in which he ridiculed the pagan mythology and the philosophical sects. Many of them are tainted with profanity and indecency, though written in an elegant style and abounding in wit.

LONGINUS was an illustrious Greek critic and philosopher of the third century after Christ. In his youth he traveled to Rome, Athens and Alexandria, for improvement, attending all the celebrated masters in philosophy and eloquence. At length he made his residence at Athens, where he taught philosophy and published his *Treatises on the Sublime*. His vast fund of knowledge caused him to be called "the living library." When Zenobia, Queen of Palmyra, heard of his fame she invited him to her court, intrusted him with the education of her two sons and took his advice on political matters. But this honor caused his ruin and destruction, as the Roman Emperor Aurelian, after reducing Palmyra, put him to death because he had counseled Zenobia to resist the Romans and had composed the spirited letter which that queen had addressed to the Emperor. His execution occurred A. D. 273. He encountered his fate with resignation and fortitude, saying: "The world is but a prison; happy therefore is he who gets soonest out of it, and gains his liberty."

We have already alluded to the translation of the Old Testament into Greek. The Gospels and most of the other books of the New Testament were written in Greek, so that this language was the medium through which Christ's teachings and doctrines were made known to mankind in the first few centuries of the Christian era. Many of the Fathers of the Christian Church—such as JUSTIN MARTYR, CLEMENT of Alexandria, ORIGEN, ST. ATHANASIUS, and ST. CHRYSOSTOM—also wrote in the Greek language; as did PORPHYRY, the bitter foe of Christianity, and EUSEBIUS, the historian of the early Christian Church.

In the meantime the Grecian polytheistic religion had sunk beneath the attacks of the philosophers, and no system had taken its place, so that the Greeks lived literally "without God in the world," because they perceived the absurdity of the faith of their fathers, but as yet knew of no better creed, and erected altars to "The Unknown God."

Amidst this practical infidelity the seeds were sown for a radical change throughout the whole Greek and Latin world. About the middle of the first century of the Christian era, the apostle Paul, after preaching the Gospel of Christ at Ephesus and other Greek cities of Asia Minor, passed over into Macedonia and there preached Christianity, making many converts, especially at Thessalonica, where he established a church. Driven by persecution to Athens, St. Paul preached the new faith to the assembled Athenians on Mars' Hill. The great apostle passed on to Corinth and there established a church. Christianity spread rapidly to other parts of Greece, and its growth was steady, in spite of the persecutions by which the Roman authorities endeavored to check its progress, and in spite of the charms with which the effete polytheism was surrounded. The preaching of Christianity produced a wonderful change, and its steady progress gradually affected the character of the Greek nation. Many carried into the new religion those habits of fanciful speculation which had for so long a time characterized their philosophy, and mingling some of their old theories and doctrines with the new faith, they introduced most of those peculiar beliefs which infected the early Christian Church. The Alexandrian philosophers were chiefly instrumental in producing this result, as they combined Plato's philosophy with Christ's simple teachings.

The day of great masters in Grecian art had passed, and little remains to be said upon this topic. In the third century before Christ, Queen Artemisia erected the stately *Mausoléum* at Halicarnássus, in Asia Minor, to the memory of her departed husband, Mausôlus. The entire structure was adorned with magnificent sculptures. This remarkable edifice was one of the Seven Wonders of the World, as was also the gigantic *Colossus* of Rhodes, an immense image of Apollo, which the Rhodians had erected to commemorate their gallant and successful defense against the forces of Demétrius Poliorcétes, B. C. 306. This colossal statue was so placed as to bestride the entrance to the harbor. The Colossus was more than one hundred feet high, and its thumb was so large that a man was not able to clasp it with his arms. After lying on the ground for centuries this gigantic figure was removed, when the metal of which it was composed loaded nine hundred camels.

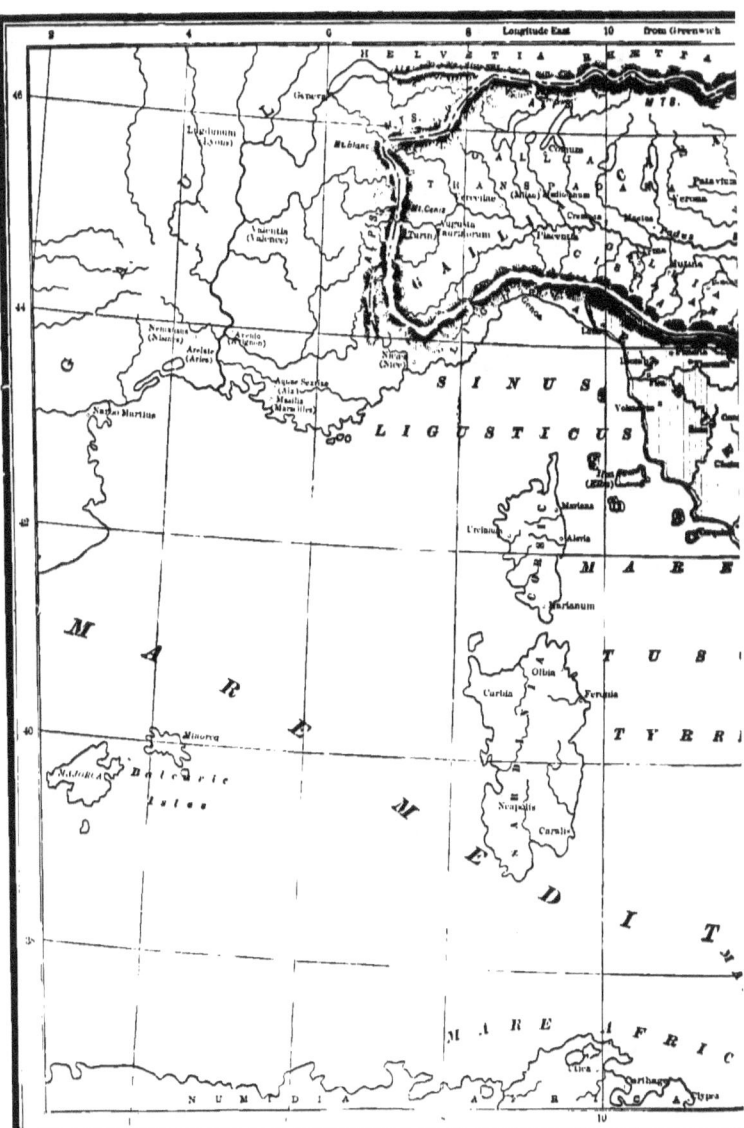

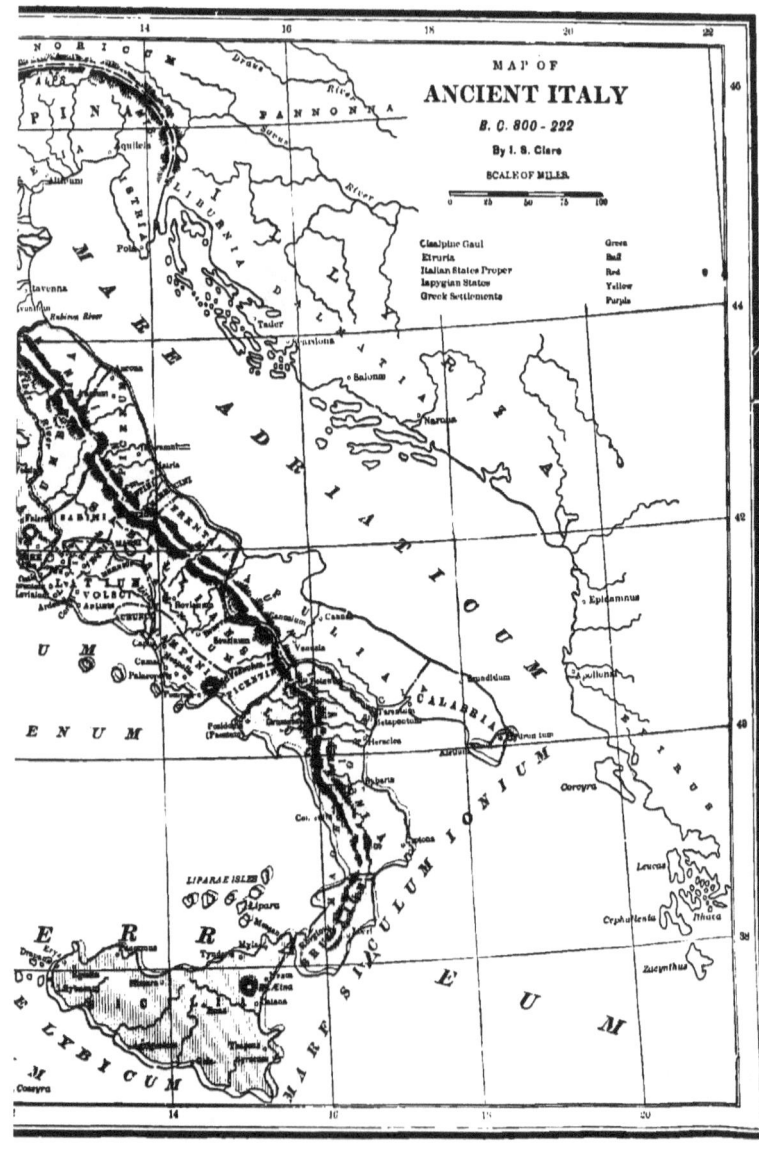

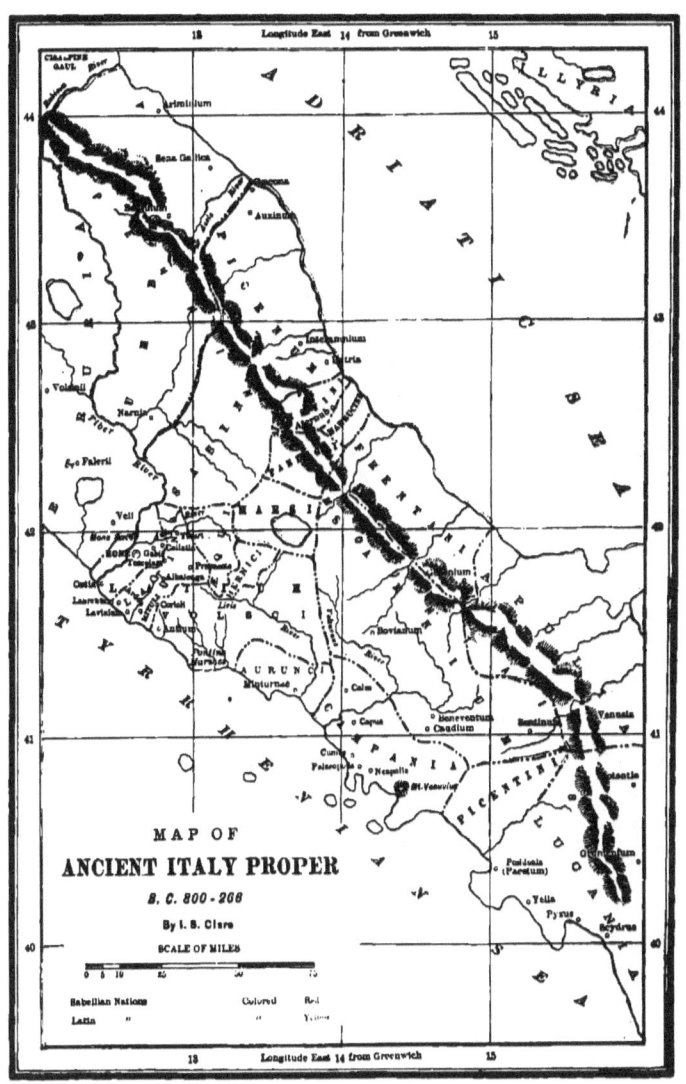

MAP OF
ANCIENT ITALY PROPER
B. C. 800-266
By I. S. Clare

CHAPTER XIV.

ANCIENT ROME.

SECTION I.—GEOGRAPHY OF ANCIENT ITALY.

ITALY is the middle one of the three peninsulas of Southern Europe, whose shores are washed by the Mediterranean sea. It is seven hundred and twenty miles long from the Alps on the north-west to Cape Spartivento on the south-east. Its greatest breadth is in the north, between the Little St. Bernard and the hills north of Trieste, which is three hundred and thirty miles. But its ordinary width is only one hundred miles. The entire area, even including the littoral islands, is not much over one hundred and ten thousand square miles. Italy is bounded on the north and north-west by the Alps, on the east by the Adriatic, on the south and west by the Mediterranean.

In proportion to its area, the littoral extent of Italy is very considerable, mainly because of the length and narrowness of the peninsula; as the principal coasts are only slightly indented. A moderate number of shallow gulfs or bays make the western coast-line somewhat irregular; but the headland of Gargano and the bay of Manfredonia are the only important breaks in the regularity of the eastern coast-line. On the southern coast are two large indentations, the deep Gulf of Taranto and the shallow one of Squillace. The Italian islands—Sicily, Sardinia and Corsica—have a similar character to the mainland. Therefore the Italian people did not have so distinct and pronounced a nautical tendency as their neighbors, the Greeks.

Italy has two famous mountain-chains, the Alps and the Apennines. The Alps bound Italy along the whole of its northern and a portion of its western side, and constitute a lofty barrier naturally isolating the region from the rest of Europe. The Alps are nowhere less than four thousand feet high along the whole boundary-line, and vary from that minimum to a maximum of fifteen thousand feet. This celebrated mountain-range is penetrated by only ten or twelve difficult passes, even in our own day. The general direction of the Alps is from east to west, or, more properly speaking, from north-east by east to south-west by west; but at Mont Blanc, the highest peak in the Alpine system, the chain suddenly changes its course, and runs almost directly north and south. From Mont Blanc southward to the Mediterranean coast the chain is about one hundred and fifty miles long, and from Mont Blanc eastward the Italian Alps are about three hundred and thirty miles long; so that this great mountain barrier forms the boundary-line between Italy and the rest of Europe on the west and north, and guards the peninsula for a distance of four hundred and eighty miles. In ancient times this huge barrier constituted a rampart which was scaled with great difficulty.

The Apennines branch off from the Alps at the point where the chain of the Alps running southward from Mont Blanc most nearly reaches the Mediterranean. From this point the Apennines run eastward nearly parallel with the shore to about the longitude of Cremona, almost ten degrees east of Greenwich, from which point the chain trends south of east across about three-fourths of the peninsula, and then runs in a direction almost south-east, parallel to the eastern and western coasts of the peninsula, along its whole length. This chain is the Apennines proper. In modern geography its more western portion is called the *Maritime Alps*. In Northern Italy the Apennines consist of but a single chain, from both sides of which twisted spurs branch off. In Central Italy the character of the range is more complicated. Below Lake Fucínus the chain forks into two branches; one range extending in a south-easterly direction; the other, of smaller elevation, branching off to the south, and approaching the southern coast very nearly in the vicinity of Salerno, curving round and rejoining the principal chain near Compsa. The range then proceeds in a single line to Venusia, where it again divides, one branch extending almost due east to the extreme promontory of Iapygia, the other running nearly due south to Reggio.

The prominent characteristic of the geography of Italy is the strong contrast between Northern Italy and Southern Italy. Northern Italy is nearly all plain; Southern Italy nearly all mountain. The conformation of the mountain ranges in the north leaves a vast plain between the parallel chains of the Swiss Alps and the Upper Apennines. This plain, through which the river Po flows from west to east, is from one hundred to one hundred and fifty miles wide. In Southern Italy, or the peninsula proper, there are few plains of more than a few miles in extent The Apennines, with their twisted spurs, spread widely over the country and constitute a continuous mountain region covering at least one half of the surface; and in Etruria, Latium and Campania separate systems of volcanic hills and mountains exist. In Apulia is an extensive plain about the Candelaro, Cervaro and Ofanto rivers.

There are only two of the many rivers of Italy of any considerable size. The largest river is the Po, the ancient Padus, which rises at the foot of Monte Viso, drains nearly the entire great northern plain, receiving more than a hundred tributaries, and having a course of over four hundred miles, because of its many windings. The principal tributaries of the Po are the Doria-Baltea (the ancient Duria), the Ticino (the ancient Ticínus), the Adda (the ancient Addua), the Oglio (the ancient Ollíus), and the Mincio (the ancient Mincíus), from the north; and the Tanaro (the ancient Tanarus), the Trebbia (the ancient Trebia), the Taro (the ancient Tarus), the Secchia (the ancient Secia), the Panaro (the ancient Scultenna) and the Reno (the ancient Rhenus), from the south. The next most important river of Italy is the Adige, or Athesis, which rises in the Tyrolean Alps, flows southward almost to Verona, and then curves round and runs parallel with the Po into the Adriatic sea. The Po and the Adige are both beyond the limits of the peninsula proper. The principal streams of the peninsula proper are the Arno, or Arnus, the Tiber, the Liris, the Vulturnus and the Silarus, on the western side of the Apennines, and the Æsis, the Alternus, the Tifernus, the Frento, the Cerbalus and the Aufidus, on the eastern side of those mountains.

Italy has a number of lakes, most of which are in the north, on the skirts of the Alps, at the point where the mountains sink into the plain. The principal lakes are the Lago di Garda, or Benacus, between Lombardy and Venetia; the Lago d' Iseo, or Sevnius; the Lago di Como, or Larius; the Lago di Lugano, or Ceresius; the Lago Maggiore, or Verbanus, and the Lago d' Orta. The only important lake in the Central Apennine region is the Lacus Fucínus. In Etruria are the Lago di Perugia, or Trasiménus; the Lago di Bolsena, or Volsiniensis; and the Lago di Bracciano, or Sabbatínus. There are also many lagoons on the sea-coast, especially in the vicinity of Venice, and several small mountain tarns.

The Italian islands are peculiarly important on account of their size, fertility and mineral treasures, and constitute almost one-

GEOGRAPHY OF ANCIENT ITALY.

fourth of the entire area of the country. Sicily is extremely productive in corn and an excellent quality of wine. Sardinia and Corsica are rich in minerals. Even the small island of Elba, the ancient Ilva, is valuable for its iron. Sicily and the Lipari Isles yield an abundance of sulphur.

Italy is naturally divided into Northern and Southern; the former embracing the plain of the Po and the mountains enclosing it; the latter comprising the peninsula proper. The peninsula proper is, however, generally divided into two portions by a line drawn across it from the mouth of the Silarus to the mouth of the Tifernus. In this manner we have a three-fold division of the country into Northern, Central and Southern Italy.

In the most ancient times Northern Italy contained three countries—Liguria, Upper Etruria and Venetia. Afterwards a portion of Liguria and nearly the whole of Upper Etruria were occupied by Gallic immigrants; and, although the boundary-lines were somewhat changed, there were still only three countries in this large and important region—Liguria, Venetia and Gallia Cisalpína (Cisalpine Gaul); the last-named having taken the place of Upper Etruria.

Liguria was the region in the extreme west of northern Italy. After the Gallic invasion it was regarded as bounded on the north by the Po, on the west by the Alps from Monte Viso (the ancient Vesulus) southward, on the south by the Mediterranean, and on the east by the river Macra. This region is almost wholly mountainous, as spurs from the Alps and the Apennines cover the entire region between the mountain-ranges and the river Po. Liguria was so named from its inhabitants, the Ligúres, or Ligyes, who at one time occupied the whole coast from below the mouth of the Arno to Massilia, in Gaul. The principal towns of Liguria were Genua (now Genoa), Nicæ (now Nice), and Asta (now Asti).

Venetia was in the extreme east of Northern Italy. From the most ancient period the Etruscans encroached upon the territories of the Veneti, as did the Gauls afterward, until only a corner of Northern Italy yet remained in their possession. This corner was located between Istria and the Lesser Menduacus, and between the Alps and the Adriatic. Venetia was mostly very flat, well watered by streams flowing from the Alps, and also fertile. The principal ancient Venetian city was Patavium, on the Lesser Menduacus, but Aquileia afterwards became the chief city.

The Etruscan confederacy of twelve cities, which was conquered by the Gauls, was situated in a region extending from the Ticínus on the west to the Adriatic and the mouths of the Po on the east. Some of its cities were Melpum, Mediolanum (Milan), Mantua, Verona, Hatria and Felsína, or Bononia. Before the Gallic invasion the Etruscan state was bounded on the north by the Alps, and on the south by the Apennines and the course of the Utis. After the Gallic conquest Gallia Cisalpína was more extensive than North Etruria had been, as the Gauls had seized all of Liguria north of the Po, and probably some of that country south of the river about Parma and Placentia, encroached upon Venetia on the east and advanced southward into Umbria. Gallia Cisalpína was bounded on the north and west by the Alps, on the east by the Adriatic and Venetia, and on the south by Liguria, the principal chain of the Apennines and the Æsis river. The entire region was exceedingly fertile, excepting some marshy districts. Gallia Cisalpína had few cities before its conquest by the Romans. The Gauls lived in open unwalled villages and allowed most of the Etruscan towns to fall into decay. Melpum and other cities ceased to exist. Mantua and Verona remained Etruscan in a state of semi-independence. Under Roman dominion Gallia Cisalpína was occupied by many important cities, founded by Roman colonies; such as Placentia, Parma, Mutína (now Modena), Bononia (now Bologna), Ravenna and Ariminium (now Rimini), south of the Po, and Augusta-Taurinorum (now Turin), Ticínum (now Pavia), Mediolanum (now Milan), Brixia (now Brescia), Cremona, Mantua, Verona and Vincentia (now Vicenza), north of the Po.

Central Italy embraced six countries— Etruria, Latium and Campania in the west, and Umbria, Picenum and the Sabine territory in the east. Etruria, Latium and the Sabine territory were the most important countries of ancient Italy.

Etruria—called Tyrrhenia by the Greeks, and now named Tuscany—was the region immediately south and west of the Northern Apennines, lying between that chain and the Mediterranean. It was bounded on the north by Liguria and Gallia Cisalpína, on the east by Umbria and the Sabine country, on the south by Latium, and on the west by the Mediterranean sea. Etruria was separated from the rest of Italy by natural boundaries, such as the Apennine mountain chain and the river Tiber. It was mainly mountainous, consisting, in its northern and eastern portions, of strong spurs branching off from the Apennines, and in its southern and western portions, of a separate system of rocky hills, of irregular ramifications, and extending from the valleys of the Arnus and the Clanis almost to the coast. The little level land contained therein lay along the courses of the rivers and near the seashore. The soil is mostly rich, but swampy in some places. Etruria contained three important lakes—Trasiménus, Volsiniensis and Sabbatínus. The original Etrurian state consisted of a confederacy of twelve cities, among which were Volsinii, Tarquinii, Vetulonium, Perusia and Clusium; and perhaps also Volaterræ, Arretium, Rusellæ, Veii, and Agylla, or Cære. Other important towns were Pisæ (now Pisa) and Fæsulæ (now Fiesole), north of the Arnus; Populonia and Cosa, on the coast between the Arnus and the Tiber; Cortona, in the Clanis valley; and Falerii, near the Tiber, about eighteen miles north of Veii.

Latium lay south of Etruria, on the left bank of the Tiber. It was bounded on the north by the Tiber, the Anio, and the Upper Liris rivers; on the east by the Lower Liris and a spur of the Apennines; on the south and west by the Mediterranean. These were the later limits of Latium. Originally many non-Latin tribes occupied parts of the country. The Volsci inhabited the isolated range of hills extending from near Præneste to the coast at Tarracína, or Anxur. The Æqui possessed the Mons Algidus and the mountain-range between Præneste and the Anio. The Hernici were settled in the valley of the Trerus, a tributary of the Liris. The Ausones occupied the country on the Lower Liris. The Latin nation embraced a confederacy of thirty cities, Alba Longa being originally preëminent. The most important of these cities were Tibur, Gabii, Præneste, Tusculum, Velitræ, Aricia, Lanuvium, Laurentum, Lavinium, Ardea, Antium, Circeii, Anxur or Tarracína, Setia, Norba and Satricum. Latium was mainly a low plain, but was diversified in the north by spurs from the Apennines; in the center and in the south by two important ranges of hills. One of these ranges, called the Volscian range, extends in a continuous line from Præneste to Tarracína; the other, which is separate and detached, rises out of the plain between the Volscian range and the Tiber, and is called the Alban range, or the *Mons Algidus*. Both these ranges are in the western part of Latium. The eastern part of the country is comparatively flat. In this section were Anagnia, the old capital of the Hernici, Arpínum, Fregellæ, Aquínum, Interamna and Lirim. On the coast of Latium were Lantulæ, Fundi, Formiæ, Minturnæ and Vescia.

Campania resembled Latium in its general character, but the isolated volcanic hills which here diversified the plain were loftier and situated nearer to the coast. In the extreme southern part of the country a strong spur branched off from the Apennines, ending in the promontory of Minerva, on the south side of the Bay of Naples. Campania extended along the coast from the Liris to the Silarus, and inland to the more southern of the two Apennine mountain chains, which divide a little below Lake Fucínus and reunite at Compsa. The Campanian plain was rich and fertile, especially about Capua. Among the leading

Campanian cities were Capua, the capital, Nola and Teanum, in the interior; and Sinuessa, Cumæ, Puteoli, Parthenopé, or Neapolis (now Naples), Herculaneum, Pompeii, Surrentum, Salernum (now Salerno), and Picentia, on the coast.

Umbria lay east of Etruria, from which it was separated by the Apennine range and the river Tiber. It was bounded on the north by Gallia Cisalpína, on the east and south-east by Picenum and the Sabine country, on the south-west and west by Etruria. Before the Gallic invasion Umbria extended as far north as the river Rubicon, and included the Adriatic coast between that stream and the Æsis; but after the Gallic conquest this region was separated from Umbria, which was thus deprived of its sea-coast. The Umbrian territory was chiefly mountainous, as it consisted mainly of the principal chain of the Apennines, with spurs branching off from both sides of the chain, from the source of the Tiber to the junction of the Nar with the Tiber. There were, however, some fertile plains in the Tiber and Lower Nar valleys. The principal towns of Umbria were Iguvium, noted for its inscriptions; Sentinum, famous for the great battle in which the Romans defeated the Gauls and the Samnites; Spoletium (now Spoleto); Interamna (now Terni); and Narnia (now Narni); which, though situated on the left bank of the Nar, was regarded as belonging to Umbria. Picenum extended along the coast of the Adriatic from the river Æsis to the river Matrínus (now Piomba). It consisted principally of spurs from the Apennines, but contained some flat and fertile country along the coast. The leading towns of Picenum were Ancona, on the coast, and Firmum (now Fermo), Asculum-Picenum (now Ascoli), and Adria (now Atri), in the interior.

The Sabine country was the most extensive and the most advantageously located country of Central Italy. It was over two hundred miles long, from the Mons Fiscellus (now Monte Rotondo) to the Mons Vultur (now Monte Vulture). In width it extended almost from sea to sea, bordering the Adriatic from the river Matrínus to the river Tifernus, and nearly approaching the Mediterranean in the vicinity of Salernum. In the north the Sabine territory embraced all the valleys of the Upper Nar and its tributaries, with a part of the valley of the Tiber, the plain south and east of Lake Fucínus, and the valleys of the Suinus and Alternus rivers. In the center it comprised the valleys of the Sagrus, Trinius and Tifernus rivers, with the mountain-ranges between them. In the south it included all of the great Samnite upland drained by the Vulturnus and its tributaries. The Sabine country consisted of a number of distinct political divisions. The north-western tract, about the Nar and Tiber rivers, extended from the principal Apennine chain to the river Anio, and was the territory of the old Sabines, or Sabini, the only people to which ancient writers applied that name. East and south-east of this region, the district about Lake Fucínus, and the valleys of the Suinus and Aternus rivers, were occupied by the League of the Four Cantons—the Marsi, the Marrucini, the Peligni, and the Vestini—who are believed to have been Sabine races. Still farther eastward, the valleys of the Sagrus and the Trinius, and the coast region from Ortona to the Tifernus, comprised the territory of the Frentani. South-east of this territory was Samnium, embracing the elevated upland, the principal chain of the Apennines, and the eastern flank of that chain for some distance. The principal Sabine towns were Reate, on the Velínus, a tributary of the Nar; Teate and Aternum, on the Aternus; Marribium, on Lake Fucínus; and Beneventum (now Benevento) and Bovianum, in Samnium.

Southern Italy, the region south of the Tifernus and Silarus rivers, embraced four countries—Lucania and Bruttium in the west, and Apulia and Calabria in the east. Calabria is sometimes called Messapia, and also Iapygia. Thus there were altogether thirteen distinct countries in ancient Italy.

Lucania extended along the western coast of Southern Italy from the river Silarus to the river Laüs. Its boundary on the north was formed by the Silarus, the Apennine mountain-chain from Compsa to the Mons Vultur and the course of the Bradanus (now Brandano). On the east Lucania was bordered by the Tarentine Gulf. On the south it was bounded by Bruttium, the line of demarcation running from the Lower Laüs across the mountains to the Crathis, or river of Thurium. The country was both picturesque and fertile, diversified by many mountain spurs from the Apennine range, and drained by many rivers. There were few important native cities in Lucania, but the coasts were densely settled with famous Grecian colonies, such as Posidonia or Pæstum, Elea or Velia, Pyxus or Buxentum, and Laüs, on the western coast; and Metapontum, Heracléa, Pandosia, Siris, Sybaris and Thurium, on the eastern coast.

Bruttium was bordered on the north by Lucania, and on every other side by the sea, being separated from Sicily by the Strait of Messana. The principal native city of Bruttium was Consentia, in the interior, near the sources of the Crathis river. The Greek towns of Bruttium were Temesa, Terina, Hipponium and Rhegium, on the western coast; and Croton, or Crotona, Caulonia and Locri, on the eastern coast.

Apulia lay wholly on the eastern coast of Southern Italy, adjoining Samnium on the west, and separated from the territory of the Frentani by the Tifernus river. The Apennine mountain-chain, extending from the Mons Vultur eastward for some distance, separated Apulia from Calabria. Apulia, unlike all the other countries of the Italian peninsula proper, was entirely a plain. Only in the north-western corner of the country do any important spurs branch off from the Apennines, but a rich and level tract extends from the base of the chain. This tract is from twenty to forty miles wide, intersected by many streams, and diversified in the east by many lakes. This plain is particularly adapted to the grazing of cattle. Some of its rivers are the Aufidus, on whose banks Hannibal won his great victory of Cannæ over the Romans, the Cerbalus and the Arpi. The only mountainous portion of Apulia is in the north and north-west, where the Apennines throw off toward the coast two strongly-marked spurs, one between the Tifernus and the Frento rivers, and a more important range east of the Frento, running in a north-easterly direction to the coast and forming the well-known rocky promontory of Garganum. The leading cities of Apulia were Larínum, near the Tifernus; Luceria, Sipontum and Arpi, north of the Cerbalus; Salapia, between the Cerbalus and the Aufidus; and Canusium, Cannæ and Venusia, south of the Aufidus. The north-western division of Apulia was called Daunia, the south-eastern Peucetia.

Calabria—also called Messapia, or Iapygia—lay south-east of Apulia, embracing the whole long promontory called "the heel of Italy," and a triangular tract between the eastern Apennine chain and the river Bradanus. In the east Calabria was low and flat, with many small lakes and no important rivers. In the west the country was diversified by many ranges of hills, spurs from the Apulian Apennines, which protected it upon the north and rendered it one of the softest and most luxurious of the ancient Italian countries. The chief city of Calabria was Taras, or Tarentum, the celebrated Spartan colony. Other Greek cities of Calabria were Callipolis (now Gallipoli), and Hydrus, or Hydruntum (now Otranto). The principal native town was Brundusium (now Brindisi).

Having described the mainland of ancient Italy, we will now proceed to give a geographical account of the three chief Italian islands—Sicily, Sardinia and Corsica. There were besides many islets along the western coast, and several off the eastern shore, which will be briefly noticed.

Sicily is estimated to contain about ten thousand square miles, and is an irregular triangle, the sides of which face respectively the north, the east and the south-west. The coasts are but little indented, but the northern has the most prominent bays and headlands, such as the gulfs of Castel-a-mare, Palérmo, Patti and Milazzo, and the headlands of Trapani (Drepanum), Capo St. Vito,

GEOGRAPHY OF ANCIENT ITALY.

Capo di Gallo, Capo Zaffarana, Capo Orlando, Capo Calava and Capo Bianco. The southwestern coast, and most of the eastern, run in smooth lines; but there is a fair degree of indentation towards the extreme south-east of the island. There are many good harbors, the most remarkable being those of Messana and Syracuse. The first of these is protected by a curious curved strip of land resembling a sickle, from which circumstance it received the old name of Zanclé. Syracuse was rendered secure in all winds by the headland of strong spur, which strikes south-east and ends in Cape Pachynus (now Passaro). Thus the island is divided by its mountain system into three regions of comparative lowland—a narrow district facing northward between the principal chain and the northern coast; a long and wide region facing the south-west, bounded on the north by the western half of the principal chain, and on the east by the spur; and a wide but comparatively short district facing the east, bounded on the west by the spur, and on

MOUNT ETNA.

Plemmyrium and the natural breakwater of Ortygia. There are likewise excellent ports at Lilybæum and Panormus (now Palérmo).

The mountain system of Sicily includes a main chain, the continuation of the Bruttian Apennines, the Aspromonte, which traverses the island from east to west, commencing near Messina (now Messana) and ending at Cape Drepanum. The principal chain, having different names in its various parts, throws off, about midway in its course, a the north by the eastern half of the principal chain. There is, however, no really very flat country in any of these lowlands. Towards the north and the south-west the principal chain and the spur throw off many branches into the tracts between the rivers; and towards the east, in the region where only there are any extensive plains, is the separate volcano of Mount Etna, which, with its wide-spreading roots, occupies nearly a third of what would otherwise be lowland.

Thus Sicily consists almost wholly of mountain and valley, with the exception of the district between Mount Etna and Syracuse, where the celebrated Piano di Catania extends itself; and is a strong and difficult country in a military point of view. Its principal rivers are the Simæthus on the east, which drains almost the entire great plain; the Himera and the Halycus on the south; and the Hypsa, near the exreme south-western corner. The only important native Sicilian town was Enna, near the center of the island. All the other important cities of the island were settled by foreign colonies. The Trojans founded Eryx and Egesta, or Segesta. The Carthaginians settled Lilybæum, Motya, Panormus and Soloeis, or Soluntum. The Greeks colonized Himera, Messana, Tauromonium, Naxos, Cátana, Mégara, Hyblæa, Syracuse, Camarína, Gela, Agrigentum, and Selinus. The history of the Greek settlements in Sicily has already been given, and need not be repeated here.

Sardinia is larger than Sicily, and has an area of about eleven thousand square miles. Its shape is that of an oblong parallelogram, with its sides facing the four cardinal points of the compass; but the south side slightly inclines towards the east, while the north side inclines still more strongly towards the west. Sardinia is not so mountainous as Sicily or Corsica, but is traversed by an important chain running parallel with the eastern and western shores, but nearer the eastern, from Cape Lungo-Sardo on the north to Cape Carbonara at the extreme south of the island. Many short branch ranges extend from each side of this chain, and cover almost the entire eastern half of the island. The western half has three separate mountain-clusters of its own. The smallest is at the extreme north-western corner of the island, between the gulfs of Asinara and Alghero. Another, three or four times larger, fills the south-western corner, and extends from Cape Spartivento to the Gulf of Oristano. The third and largest cluster is between the other two, and occupies the entire region extending northward from the Gulf of Oristano and the river Tirso to the coast between the Turnlano and Coguinas rivers. These mountain-clusters, along with the principal range, cover most of the island. But there are important plains, such as the plain of Campidano on the south, which extends across from the Gulf of Cagliari to the Gulf of Oristano; the plain of Ozieri on the north, on the upper course of the Coguinas; and the plain of Sassari in the north-west, extending across the isthmus from Alghero to Porto Torres. Sardinia is moderately fertile, but has ever been malarious. Its principal river is the Tirso, the ancient Thyrsus. The chief cities were anciently Caralis (now Cagliari), on the southern coast, in the bay of the same name; Sulci, at the extreme south-west of the island, opposite the Insula Plumbaria; Neapolis, in the Gulf of Asinara; and Olbia, towards the north-eastern extremity of the island. There was no important city in the interior.

Corsica lies directly to the north of Sardinia, and is more mountainous and rugged than Sicily or Sardinia. The island is traversed from north to south by a strong mountain-chain culminating near the center in the Monte Rotondo, the ancient Mons Antæus. Many branch ranges intersect the country on each side of the principal chain, so that the whole region consists of mountain and valley. There are many streams, but the island is too narrow for them to reach any considerable size. The principal town of ancient Corsica was Alalia, afterwards called Aleria, which was a Phocæan colony. The only other important towns were Mariaua, on the eastern coast, above Alalia; Centurimum (now Centuri), on the western side of the northern promontory; Urcinium (now Ajaccio), on the western coast; and Talcinum (now Corte), in the interior.

The smaller islands adjacent to Italy are Elba (the ancient Ilva), between the northern part of Corsica and the mainland of Italy; Giglio, (the ancient Igilium) and Giannuti (the ancient Dianium), opposite the Mons Argentarius, in Etruria; Palmaria, Pontia, Sinonia and Pandataria, off Anxur; Ischia, (the ancient Pithecussa), Procida (the ancient Prochyta), and Capri (the ancient Capreæ), in the Bay of Naples; Stromboli (the ancient Strongyle), Panaria (the ancient Euonymus), Lipari (the ancient Lipara), Volcano (the ancient Vulcania), Salína (the ancient Didymé), Felicudi (the ancient Phœnicussa), Alicudi (the ancient Ericussa), and Ustica, off the northern coast of Sicily; the Ægates Insulæ, off the western point of Sicily; the Chœrades Insulæ, off Tarentum; and Tremiti (the ancient Trimetus), in the Adriatic, north of the Mons Garganus. These islets are of no historical importance.

SECTION II.—ANCIENT RACES OF ITALY.

NCIENT Italy, in the earliest times of which we have any account, was occupied by five leading races—the Ligurians, the Venetians, the Etruscans, the Italians proper and the Iapygians. The Ligurians and the Venetians were weak and unimportant nations, inhabiting the narrow regions in the North of Italy, and exerted no influence on the general history of Italy. We will therefore devote our attention to the other three races of ancient Italy.

The Iapygians occupied the heel of Italy in the south-eastern part of the peninsula, and are believed to have been of Hellenic origin, having crossed the narrow sea from Greece to Italy and having occupied most of the foot of Italy. The Iapygian language remains in many inscriptions which have been discovered in the Terra di Otranto, and which indicates the early relation of the Iapygians with the Greeks. Other circumstances showing their early connection with the Greeks are their worship of the Grecian gods and goddesses, and the readiness with which they really became Hellenized at a later period. Thus it is apparent that a race kindred with the Greeks occupied most of Southern Italy in early times, and that that portion of the Italian peninsula was prepared for the subsequent more-actually Hellenic colonies. The Iapygian race embraced the Messapians, the Peucetians, the Œnotrians, the Chaones, or Chones, and probably the Daunii.

The Italians proper, consisting of many tribes, occupied all of Central Italy in the historical times; and seem to have immigrated into the peninsula later than the Iapygians, also to have come from the north, and to have heavily borne upon the semi-Greek population of Southern Italy. They comprised four chief subordinate races—the Umbrians, the Sabines, the Oscans and the Latins. The Umbrians and the Oscans were the most closely connected of these Italian races. The Latins were quite distinct. The Sabines are believed to have been closely related to the Umbrians and the Oscans. The Sabines included many sub-divisions, such as the Sabines proper, the Samnites, the Picentes, the Marsi, the Peligni, the Vestini, the Frentani, the Campani and the Lucani. The Samnites were also subdivided into the Caraceni, the Pentri and the Herpini. The Oscan tribes were the Volsci, the Æqui, the Hernici, the Aurunci, the Ausones and the Apuli.

The Etruscans, or Tuscans, a powerful nation of early historical Italy, were entirely different in race, language, appearance and character from all the other nations of Italy; and their origin is shrouded in the deepest mystery. Some scholars believe that they were Turanians, instead of Aryans like the other nations of Italy, and that they were thus related to the Lapps, the Finns and the Esthonians of Northern Europe, and the Basques of Spain; while others regard the mass of the people as Pelasgians, like the primitive inhabitants of Greece, and thus Aryans, like the other Italian nations, but believe them to have been absorbed and enslaved by a more powerful race from the north, who called themselves Rásena, while others called them Etruscans.

So far as can be traced, the original home of the Etruscans appears to have been in Rhætia, the country about the head-streams of the Adige, the Danube and the Rhine. At a very remote period these people occupied the plain of the Po, from the Ticínus to beyond the Adige, where they are said to have formed a confederacy of twelve cities. After flourishing for an indefinite length of time in that region, they crossed the Apennine mountain-chain to the south, ocupying the region between the Northern Apennines and the Tiber, and forming there a second confederacy of twelve cities. They afterwards crossed the Tiber and established a temporary dominion in Campania, founding in that country the cities of Capua and Nola.

Physically, the Etruscans were a brawny, stout race, short in stature, with large heads and thick arms, thus forming a strong contrast to the graceful and slender Italians. Their religious ideas were gloomy and strange. They delighted in the mystical handling of numbers. They sought to learn the will of their gods by auguries drawn from thunder and lightning, from the flight of birds, or from the entrails of slain beasts; and endeavored to avert their wrath by sacrifices prescribed and regulated by an extremely-minute and elaborate ritual. A great part·of a young Etruscan noble's education consisted in learning these rites.

The Etruscans were evidently a wealthy and luxurious race, and had made considerable progress in the arts, as shown by their castings in bronze, their terra-cotta figures, their vases, gold chains, bracelets and other ornaments. Their massive Cyclopéan walls of unhammered stone attest their skill in architecture. They were the earliest of the races of Italy to engage in maritime enterprises, and the only one that exhibited a special fondness for such pursuits. Etruscan pirates roamed over the Western Mediterranean from a very early period, and Agylla carried on an important commerce before B. C. 550.

As we have said, all the Italian races, except perhaps the Etruscans, were pure Aryans, and were therefore closely related with the Hindoos, the Medes and Persians, and the Greeks; all of whom belonged to the Aryan, or Indo-European branch of the Caucasian race.

SECTION III.—EARLY LEGENDS AND TRADITIONS OF ROME.

HE early history of Rome, based on legends and traditions, is so interwoven with fable that little reliance can be placed upon its annals for three hundred and sixty years; the early records having been destroyed when the Gauls burned the city (B. C. 390). The native sources of Roman history are the *Fasti Capitolini*, discovered at Rome partly in 1547, and partly in 1817 and 1818. These records are in fragments, but they contain a list of the Roman magistrates and triumphs from the beginning of the Republic to the close of the reign of Augustus Cæsar. The knowledge which we possess of this monumental record is derived chiefly from the works of ancient historians, such as the fragments of the early annalists, especially of Quintius Fabius Piƈtor, many of which are preserved by Dionysius Halicarnasseus. The most elaborate Roman historian concerning this early period is Livy, who describes it in his First Book. Other ancient Roman authorities were Cicero, who sketched the constitutional history of the early Roman period in his treatise *De Republica*, and Florus, who has briefly condensed this history. The works of poets and grammarians, as Ovid's *Fasti* and Virgil's *Æneid*, and other works, allude to this period. The Greek writers—such as Diodorus Siculus, Dionysius Halicarnasseus and Plutarch—give us fuller accounts of the early Roman period than do the native Roman writers themselves. The most diametrically oppo-

EARLY LEGENDS AND TRADITIONS.

site opinions have prevailed for more than a century concerning the authenticity of these ancient sources of Roman history. During the present century, the renowned German historians, Niebuhr and Schwegler, and the famous Englishmen, Thomas Arnold and Sir George Cornwall Lewis, have rejected much that was previously accepted. On the other side of the question in our century are such historians as the eminent German, Mommsen, the celebrated French writer, Ampère, and a host of English authors, such as Dyer, Newman, Keightly, Liddell and others.

Lavinium. After slaying in battle Latínus, King of Latium, Æneas united the Latins with his own followers; and thereafter the united people were called *Latins*. Thirty years afterwards the Latins removed to the Alban Mount, where they built the city of Alba Longa.

It is immaterial whether the Trojan immigration ascribed to Æneas occurred or not, as it certainly exercised no influence upon the ethnic character of the Roman people. The Romans belonged to the pure Latin race, as is proven by the fact that they spoke the Latin language, and that early

FLIGHT OF ÆNEAS FROM TROY.

The Romans belonged to the Latin branch of the Italian race, and were for twelve centuries the ruling race of Italy and the ancient civilized world. In later times they gave credence to a tradition connecting them with a body of Trojan immigrants into Italy five centuries before the founding of Rome. According to this Roman legend, Æneas, a famous Trojan warrior, left his native country immediately after the fall of Troy, and made his way to the western shores of Italy where he founded the city of

traditions connected them specially with the cities of Lavinium and Alba Longa, which all accounts recognize as two of the thirty Latin towns. Though the Romans were to some extent a mixed people, they were preeminently and essentially a Latin nation.

We will now proceed with the narration of the early legends and traditions respecting the origin of Rome. Several centuries after the time of Æneas there reigned at Alba Longa a king named Procas, who had two sons, Numitor and Amulius. When Procas died, Numitor was to succeed to the throne of Alba Longa; but Amulius seized the throne and made himself king, and afterwards caused the son of Numitor to be slain, and made his daughter Sylvia become a Vestal Virgin. Sylvia married Mars, the god of war, with whom she had twin sons, Romulus and Remus. Amulius ordered the two infants to be drowned in the Tiber, but the basket which contained them floated to the foot of the Palatine Hill, where they were found by a she-wolf, which carried them to her den and nursed them as her own offspring. Some time afterward the two children were taken to the house of a shepherd on the Palatine Hill, where they were brought up. At length Remus was taken to Alba Longa and brought before Amulius. Romulus and his friends went to Alba Longa and rescued Remus, killed Amulius, and placed Numitor on the throne of Alba Longa.

Romulus and Remus prepared to return to the Palatine Hill, where they resolved to build a city, and they inquired of the gods by divination which should give his name to the city. They watched the heavens for one day and one night; and at sunrise Remus saw six vultures, and soon afterwards Romulus saw twelve. It was decided that the favor of the gods was on the side of Romulus, who accordingly began to build a city on the Palatine Hill. When Remus, who was mortified and angry, saw the low wall and the ditch which inclosed the space for the new city, he scornfully leaped over and exclaimed: "Will this keep out an enemy?" Upon this insulting conduct, Remus was slain, either by Romulus or by one of his followers. The city, which was named *Rome*, in honor of Romulus, is said to have been founded in the year B. C. 753. Rome at first contained a thousand dwellings; and its population was rapidly increased by exiles, criminals, fugitives from justice, and desperate characters of all sorts, who fled to the new city for refuge.

ROMULUS was chosen the first King of Rome, and a Senate of one hundred members was established. But the Romans, as the inhabitants of the new city were called, were without wives; and as the neighboring people refused to give their daughters in marriage to such desperate characters, Romulus determined upon securing by stratagem what he could not obtain by force. He therefore arranged some games and shows at Rome, and invited the neighboring people to attend. The Sabines and the Latins came in great numbers, bringing their wives and daughters with them. When the shows began, Romulus gave a signal, whereupon the Roman youth rushed upon the unsuspecting strangers, seized the most beautiful maidens, and carried them off for wives.

THE CAPITOLINE WOLF.

The outrage just mentioned led to a war between the Romans and the Sabines. A large army under Titus Tatius, the Sabine king, laid siege to Rome. The Romans garrisoned and fortified the Capitoline Hill. Tarpeia, the daughter of the Roman commander, agreed to open the gates of the fortress to the Sabines if they would give her the golden bracelets which they wore on their arms. She accordingly opened the gates; but as soon as the Sabines entered the fortress, they killed the traitress with their brazen shields. Having gained possession of the Capitoline Hill, the Sabines were able to defy the Romans for a long time.

Many battles were fought between the Romans and the Sabines in the valleys which divide the Capitoline and Palatine Hills. At length, when the Sabines advanced near the city, the Romans retired inside the city walls and shut the gates. As the Sabines were about to enter

RAPE OF THE SABINE WOMEN.

the city the gates flew open. The Romans again shut them, but they opened a second time. A mighty stream of water burst forth from the Temple of Janus and swept away the Sabines who had entered the city. Ever afterward the gates of the Temple of Janus stood open when Rome was at war, that the gods might come out to aid the Romans; but in times of peace the gates were always closed.

The Romans made great efforts to retake the Capitoline Hill. At length, while the armies were combating, the Sabine wives of the Romans rushed between the contending forces, and, by their earnest entreaties and supplications, induced both parties to suspend hostilities. A treaty of peace followed, by which the Romans and the Sabines were to be united as one nation, and Romulus and Titus Tatius were to reign jointly at Rome. Soon afterward Titus Tatius was killed at Lavinium, and Romulus thereafter reigned alone.

After a reign of thirty-seven-years, Romulus came to his death in an unknown manner (B. C. 716). The Roman legend states that, while he was present at a public meeting in the Field of Mars, there arose a great tempest and whirlwind, while at the same time the sun was eclipsed and it was as dark as night. The furious storm, the thunder and lightning, and the solar eclipse, so terrified the people that they fled to their homes. When the storm was over, and the light of the sun returned, Romulus was not to be found. The Romans mourned for him, but believed that his father, Mars, the god of war, had carried him to heaven in a fiery chariot. Some time afterward, a Roman, while returning to the city by night from Alba Longa, saw the ghost of Romulus in more than mortal beauty. The ghost addressed this Roman thus: "Go tell my people to weep no more for me; bid them be brave and warlike, and they shall make my city the greatest upon earth." The phantom then vanished. The Romans built a temple to Romulus, offered sacrifices to him, and worshiped him as a god by the name of *Quirinus*

After an interregnum of one year the Roman people chose the wise and good Sabine, NUMA POMPILIUS, for their second king (B. C. 715). Numa Pompilius was the *first religious lawgiver* of the Romans. He regulated the religious affairs of Rome, and established the Roman religion on a firm basis, giving it the distinctive characteristics by which it is known. He professed to have obtained his directions from the nymph Egeria in his interviews with her in her sacred grove "by the spring that welled out from the rock." He embodied these counsels in his laws. He taught his subjects habits of industry and peace, and sought to educate them in the principles and love of right and justice. His entire reign was peaceful; the gates of the Temple of Janus being never opened, as the Romans had no foes to confront. The wise and good king encouraged agriculture, reformed the calendar, and built temples. After his peaceful and prosperous reign of forty-two years, Numa Pompilius died at the age of eighty (B. C. 672). He was buried under Mount Janiculum, on the opposite side of the Tiber, and the books of his sacred laws and ordinances were buried near him in a separate tomb.

After an interregnum of a year after the death of the peaceful Numa Pompilius, the warlike TULLUS HOSTILIUS became the third King of Rome (B. C. 672). During the reign of Tullus Hostilius the Romans engaged in a war with the Albans, the people of Alba Longa. Hostilities were brought on by the robberies committed on both sides of the boundary between the Roman and the Alban territory. The Albans advanced within five miles of Rome, and there pitched their camp. The armies of the two nations, regarding themselves as of a common descent, were for some time unwilling to engage in conflict. They finally agreed to have the contest decided by a combat to be fought by six champions, three from each side; and the defeated nation was to become subject to the victorious one. In the Roman army there were three brothers, born at one birth, called Horatii; and in the

Alban army there were three brothers, also born at one birth, named Curiatii. These, being fixed upon as the champions, took their places between the two armies and engaged in combat. After two of the Horatii had fallen, the other Horatius began to flee; but suddenly turning, he fell upon the three wounded Curiatii, and killed them in succession. When the victorious Horatius returned to Rome, he met his sister Horatia, who had been betrothed to one of the Curiatii. Horatia shrieked aloud, and reproached her brother for having slain her lover. This so enraged Horatius that he plunged a knife into his sister's heart, and she fell dead. For this crime Horatius was condemned to death; but he was afterwards pardoned, because, by his victory over the Curiatii, he had saved the Romans from slavery. In accordance with the terms of the agreement made just before the combat, the Albans became subject to the Romans, whose army marched home in triumph.

In a war with the Fidenates the Alban general Mettius Fuffetius kept his army aloof, instead of joining the Romans in battle, intending to take the side of the conquerors. After gaining the victory, the Romans resolved to punish the Alban general for his treachery. They seized Mettius Fuffetius and bound him between two chariots, after which they drove the horses in opposite directions, thus tearing him asunder. They then proceeded to Alba Longa and destroyed the city, compelling the inhabitants to emigrate to Rome.

Tullus Hostilius reigned thirty-three years, and was killed by lightning, which struck his house and destroyed it with his whole family. Thus ends the purely legendary and fabulous history of primeval Rome.

THE HORATII GOING TO BATTLE.

SECTION IV.—ROME UNDER THE KINGS.

WITH Tullus Hostilius, the third King of Rome and the builder of the Senate-House, the authentic history of primitive Rome under the kings begins. We will now glance at the history of early Rome as it is viewed by modern historians. The received chronology represents Rome as founded B. C. 753. Modern writers, led by the eminent German historian, Dr. Mommsen, regard several tribes, such as the Ramnes, the Tities and the Luceres, dwelling together in the vicinity of Rome, as having a common stronghold on the seven hills of Rome, and tilling their fields from the neighboring villages, while a city gradually arose around this stronghold. Says Mommsen: "The founding of a city in the strict sense, such as the legend assumes, is of course to be reckoned altogether out of the question. Rome was not built in a day." The legends of Romulus and Numa Pompilius are therefore discarded as being mystical rather than historical, and the period of certainty only begins with the reign of Tullus Hostilius, the third king, though the tradition of the struggle between the Horatii and the Curiatii is also classed as belonging to the domain of fiction and fable. The leading events of the reign of Tullus Hostilius are regarded as facts. The date of his accession, according to the received chronology, is B. C. 672.

Tullus Hostilius conquered Alba Longa, destroyed the city, and transferred its inhabitants to the Cælian Hill in Rome. Rome thus became protectress of the Latin League, with the right of presiding at the annual festival, though Rome was not a member of the Latin League, like Alba Longa had been, but a distinct power in alliance with the League. The federal army was commanded alternately by a Roman and a Latin general, and all the territories conquered in the wars of the League were divided equally between Rome and the Latin League, thus giving Rome a share equal to that of the League.

The early Roman government was a monarchy, the king being elective and called *Rex*, meaning *ruler* or *director*. He exercised great but not absolute power over his subjects. The death of the king was followed by an interregnum, during which the government was administered by the Senate or Council, whose ten chief men, called Decem Primi, exercised the royal authority, each in his turn, for five days. The Senate elected the king, and the people confirmed their choice. Next to the king were the hereditary nobility called *patricii*, or *patricians*, who derived their rank from their descent from a noble ancestry. There were originally one hundred of these noble houses, or families, called *gentes*, but they were afterwards augmented to two hundred by the union of the Roman nobles, Ramnes, and the Sabine nobles, Tities. Each of these noble houses, or families, was represented by its chief, who, by virtue of his position, was a member of the Senate or Council of the king. All the members of a noble family had a single clan-name; all might participate in certain sacred rites, and all possessed certain rights of property in common. All males of full age of the noble rank possessed the right to attend the public assembly, *Comitia Curiata* (Assembly of the Curiæ). In this assembly they were divided into ten *Curiæ*, each of which consisted of members of ten families. Each *Curia* had its chief, styled *Curio*. The chief of the ten *Curiones* presided over the Comitia Curiata, and was called *Curio Maximus*. No change of law could be effected without the consent of both the Senate and the Comitia Curiata. The Senate could both discuss and vote upon public measures; but the Comitia Curiata could only vote upon them. The Comitia Curiata also had the privilege of deciding upon peace or war; and was a court of appeal, for any of its members, from the decisions of the king or of a judge.

Besides the patricians there were two other classes in the Roman state—the *clients* and the *slaves*. The clients were the dependents of the nobles or patricians, and thus constituted the poorer class. They were allowed to choose a patron from the nobles, and bore his clan-name. They possessed no civil or political rights, though personally free. They generally tilled the lands of their patrons, or carried on a trade under their protection. They very much resembled the *retainers* of the Middle Ages. They followed their patron to war, contributed to his ransom, or to that of his children, in the event of their captivity, and aided in defraying the costs of any law-suit in which they might become involved, or the expenses of his service in any of the honorable public offices. The patron was in turn bound to protect the interests of his clients at the legal tribunals, if necessary. The relations of patron and client descended from father to son; and it was regarded as a great distinction for a noble house to have a large clientage, and to extend that which it had inherited from its ancestry. The slaves were not numerous in the Roman state in the time of the kings, but were in the same condition as those of other countries.

By adding the Albans to his subjects, Tullus Hostilius increased the number of patricians by uniting with them the Alban nobles, Luceres; thus creating three tribes, embracing thirty *curiæ* consisting of three hundred *gentes*, or noble houses. The Senate consisted of only two hundred members for some time longer, as the Alban gentes were not at first vested with the privilege of constituting a part of it. Tullus Hostilius also increased the Vestal Virgins from four to six, because Rome had now become the dwelling-place of the Albans; but this was the only change effected in the religious organization of Rome.

The fourth King of Rome was ANCUS MARTIUS, the *second religious lawgiver*, reputed to have been a grandson of the legendary Numa Pompilius; therefore being one of the Sabines, or Tities. He ascended the throne B. C. 640, according to the received chronology, and is said to have reigned twenty-four years (B. C. 640–616). Ancus Martius carried on successful wars against the Latin towns, conquering several of them and transporting their inhabitants to Rome, thus greatly augmenting the power and importance of that rising state. Many of the new Latin colonists became clients of the noble houses, but the wealthier and more independent class refused to take this position, and at length these became so numerous that it was found necessary to assign them some definite place in the state. Ancus Martius is said to have accordingly organized them into a distinct class of freemen, dependent on the king's protection. This is regarded as the origin of that class, afterwards known as *plebs*, or *plebeians*, or *commons*. They embraced several elements: 1. Free settlers; either political refugees, mercenary soldiers or merchants. 2. Forced settlers, comprising the conquered people transported to Rome, excepting those who were admitted into the patrician order, or who became clients of a noble house. 3. Clients who had been deprived of their patrons by the extinction of the gens to which they had been formerly attached. 4. The issue of marriages of inequality, or the children of patricians by wives of a lower grade with whom their marriages were illegal, and who were unable to attain the rank of their fathers. The rapid growth of Rome had necessitated a formal recognition of the plebeian class of freemen at this early period. Ancus Martius settled them upon the Aventine Hill, but we have no knowledge of the regulations which he established for their government, as they were superseded by subsequent arrangements of his second successor.

Rome made rapid advances toward civilization and power during the reign of Ancus Martius, who extended the Roman territory to the sea on the west; founded the port of Ostia at the mouth of the Tiber; established salt works in its vicinity; constructed a bridge of piles, the *pons sublicius*, across the Tiber; strongly fortified the Hill Janiculum;

drained the low lands about the seven hills of Rome by means of the *Fossa Quiritium*; and erected the Mamertine, the first Roman prison.

The fifth King of Rome was LUCIUS TARQUINIUS PRISCUS, or Tarquin the Elder, who ascended the throne in B. C. 616, according to the received chronology, and reigned thirty-eight years (B. C. 616–578). There are different accounts respecting his origin. By some his parents are said to have been of Grecian descent; by others he is regarded as of Etruscan extraction. His name was derived from the Etruscan town of Tarquinii, where he was born.

Tarquin the Elder carried on important wars. He repulsed a fierce attack of the Sabines, who had crossed the Anio and threatened Rome itself. He next attacked the Latin towns on the Upper Tiber and in the angle between the Tiber and the Anio, and reduced all of them except Nomentum, thus conquering Antemnæ, Crustumerium, Ficulea or Ficulnea, Medullia, Cænína, Corniculum and Cameria. Near the end of his reign he invaded the country of the Etruscans and gained some important advantages over them. By these conquests Tarquin the Elder very greatly enlarged the population and dominion of Rome.

Tarquin the Elder also improved Rome with many public works. He is said to have built the great sewer, called the *Cloaca Maxima*, the most remarkable monument of regal Rome yet remaining—a grand and massive construction. He is also regarded as the builder of the strong and solid quay of massive masonry along the left bank of the Tiber, which restrained the natural tendency of the river to overflow that bank and inundate the marshy valley between the Palatine and Capitoline Hills. This king erected the *Forum*, with the rows of porticos and shops surrounding it. For the entertainment of the people, he constructed the race-course known as the *Circus Maximus*, between the Palatine and Aventine Hills. He likewise designed and commenced the great Temple of Jupiter on the Capitoline Hill, but the work was completed by his son and second successor, Tarquin the Proud, the last King of Rome.

Tarquin the Elder is regarded as the author of two important constitutional changes. 1. He increased the number of members of the Senate from two hundred to three hundred, by adding to it the representatives of the *Gentes Minores*, or *Younger Houses*, who are regarded as the *houses* adopted in the patrician order from the Alban nobility when they were removed from Rome. 2. He "doubled the equestrian centuries," or, in other words, doubled the actual number of patrician *houses*, which had dwindled to only one hundred and fifty. From the noblest of the conquered people, Tarquin formed three half-tribes of fifty *houses* each, and attached them to the Ramnes, the Tities and the Luceres, but on inferior conditions.

Tarquin the Elder was assassinated B. C. 578 by hired agents of the sons of Ancus Martius, who endeavored to obtain the crown for themselves by this means. But their hopes were doomed to disappointment, as Tarquin's son-in-law, SERVIUS TULLIUS, an Etruscan general, succeeded to the throne as the sixth King of Rome. After gaining some important successes over the Etruscans, Servius Tullius determined upon effecting a thorough change of the Roman constitution, and he is known as the *civil lawgiver*.

Before the reign of Servius Tullius the patricians alone were invested with civil and political rights. That class only held all magisterial offices, all the higher orders of the priesthood, the ownership of the public lands, and the privilege of using a family name. The patricians were the only *populus*, or people, in a political sense. Servius Tullius invested all classes of Roman freemen with the franchise, thus giving the plebeians a share in the government. On the basis of the existing organization of the army, he established a new popular assembly, called the *Comitia Centuriata* (Assembly of the Centuries), in which every free Roman, patrician and plebeian, voted alike. He divided the whole body of Roman citizens into *classes*, in proportion to their wealth, and subdivided these classes into *centuries*, in proportion to the whole amount of property owned by the class. To each century, whatever the number of persons composing it, he gave only a single vote in the assembly. In consequence of this arrangement, the richer classes were clothed with decidedly preponderating power; but if they differed among themselves, the poorer classes came in and decided the question in dispute.

Wealth now acquired some portion of the power previously reserved for rank. Each citizen possessing property was obliged to serve in the army, and his military position was accurately graded by his rank in life, or, in other words, according to his wealth. The highest class were the *Equites*, or horsemen; which were divided into eighteen centuries, of which the first six—two for each of the original tribes—were patricians, while the remaining twelve comprised the wealthier and more powerful plebeians.

Excepting the Equites, the Roman soldiers fought on foot. The mass of the Roman people composing the infantry were divided into five classes. The first class was composed of eighty centuries, and embraced those who were able to equip themselves in complete brazen armor and fought in the front rank of the phalanx. Forty of these centuries consisted of young men from seventeen to forty-five years of age, constituting the flower of the Roman infantry. The remaining forty centuries were formed of men between the ages of forty-five and sixty, and were generally retained as a garrison for the city. The second, third and fourth classes were each composed of twenty centuries, but the fifth class consisted of thirty centuries. The second class fought immediately behind the first, and wore no coat of mail, while their shields were made of wood instead of brass. The third class wore no greaves, and the fourth carried no shields. The fifth and lowest military class did not constitute any portion of the phalanx, but served as light-armed infantry, and was armed with darts, or javelins, and slings. All these military classes were required to equip themselves for war. Below them were the poorest people, who were called out and armed at the public expense in great emergencies; or they followed the army as supernumeraries, and were ready to take the weapons and places of those who fell in battle.

Hitherto the only Roman tribes were the three of the patrician order—the Ramnes, the Tities and the Luceres. Servius Tullius divided the city into four tribes and the country into twenty-six, each tribe composed of land-owners regardless of rank. The whole thirty tribes met in a new popular assembly, the *Comitia Tributa* (Assembly of the Tribes), in the Forum at Rome; while the Comitia Centuriata (Assembly of the Centuries) convened outside the city-walls on the field of Mars. The tribes assembled in the Forum had all the powers of self-government, electing their own respective *Tribunes, Ædiles* and *Judex* (Judges). Thus Servius Tullius invested the plebeians with the right of self-government, and also provided for the proper assessment and collection of the land-tax, which the Tribunes were obliged to levy, collect and pay into the public treasury. He provided for the needy plebeians by making to them an allotment of the public lands on the Etruscan side of the Tiber, which had been acquired in his early wars, and which were assigned to these plebeians in full ownership. The patricians were highly exasperated at the act of Servius Tullius, as they had previously leased these lands from the state for the pasturage of their cattle and flocks, and therefore were reluctant to yield them.

Some authors tell us that it was during the reign of Servius Tullius that Rome acquired externally a new and most important position, being acknowledged as the actual head of the Latin League, or, at any rate, of all but a few recalcitrant towns, such as Gabii. There is no doubt but that Rome occupied that position at the end of the regal period, and it may have been first assumed during the reign of Servius Tullius. Rome's position was not exactly like that which had been occupied by Alba Longa, the latter city having been one of the thirty cities, exercising a presidency over her sister states, thus giving her a superiority of rank and dignity but no real control over the league. Rome was never one of the cities of the Latin League; but her position was that of a separate state confronting the league on terms of equality or even superiority to it in power, and when accepted as a close ally necessarily exercising a protectorate. Equality between Rome and Latium was jealously insisted upon by the terms of the alliance, but Rome was practically supreme and directed the policy of the league at will.

Servius Tullius likewise extended the limits of the city of Rome. The original "Roma Quadrata" was built on the Palatine Hill, but suburban settlements now covered the Esquiline, the Cælian and the Aventine Hills, while the Capitoline, the Quirinal and the Viminal Hills were occupied by the Sabines. Servius Tullius inclosed the Seven Hills, *Septimuntium*, and a large space between and around them, within a new wall, which remained the city wall without change for more than eight centuries, until the time of the Emperor Aurelian.

Servius Tullius reigned forty-eight years, from B. C. 578 to B. C. 534. As his greatest desire was for the continuance of his reformed institutions, he had resolved to abdicate the throne, after causing the Roman people assembled in the Comitia Centuriata to choose, by their free votes, two chief-magistrates who should administer the government for only one year, and who were to provide for the election of their successors in like manner before the end of their term of office. But Rome was not destined to pass so easily by a bloodless revolution from royalty to a popular government; as the patricians, disgusted by his infringement of their exclusive privileges, revolted under the leadership of Tarquin, son of Tarquin the Elder and son-in-law of Servius Tullius, assassinated the beneficent Servius in the Senate-House, and placed Tarquin upon the throne (B. C. 534). According to an old Roman legend, the wicked Tullia, daughter of the murdered Servius Tullius, and wife of Tarquin, his successor, in her haste to congratulate her wicked husband, drove her chariot over her father's corpse, which lay in the street.

LUCIUS TARQUINIUS SUPERBUS, or Tarquin the Proud, the seventh and last King of Rome, soon proved himself to be an unscrupulous tyrant. He commenced his reign by setting aside all the popular laws of the good Servius Tullius, and restoring the privileges of the patricians; but as soon as he felt secure in his power, he oppressed both patricians and plebeians, so that all classes of Romans felt his severity. He forced the poorer classes to toil upon the public works which his father had commenced, and upon those which had been begun by himself. Such were the permanent stone seats of the Circus Maximus, a new system of sewers, and the great Temple of Jupiter on the Capitoline Hill.

By wars or intrigues, Tarquin the Proud conquered the Volscians and other nations and made himself supreme throughout Latium. He concluded a treaty of commerce and friendship with Carthage, and otherwise attested his capacity for government; but his tyranny increased each year, and his insolence disgusted the patricians. He deprived Roman citizens of their property without consulting the Senate, and imposed upon all classes civil and military burdens beyond what the law allowed. As he became suspicious of the patricians he caused charges to be preferred against some of that order, and took cognizance of the accusations himself, sentencing some of the accused to death, and others to banishment without the right of appeal.

Finally the vile act of Tarquin's son Sextus produced a revolt which ended kingly government in Rome. According to the old Roman tradition, while the Romans were besieging the town of Ardea, Tarquin's sons, Sextus, Titus and Aruns, and their cousin Collatínus, got into a dispute about the good qualities of their wives, and all agreed to visit their homes by surprise. They found the wives of Sextus, Titus and

Aruns feasting and making merry, while Lucretia, the wife of Collatinus, was found working at her loom. They all agreed that Lucretia was the worthiest lady. Sextus fell into a violent passion for Lucretia, and shortly afterwards he behaved towards her in such a manner that she committed suicide. Lucius Junius Brutus, a relative of the royal family, bound himself by an oath to avenge the wicked act of Sextus. The outrage of Sextus aroused the indignation of the Roman people; and Brutus, showing them the bloody corpse of Lucretia and haranguing them, induced them to expel the royal family from the throne of Rome, and to abolish monarchy altogether. Tarquin the Proud and his family, finding themselves abandoned, retired into voluntary exile (B. C. 508).

Some modern historians have doubted the charges of tyranny which the Roman historians brought against Tarquin the Proud; but, as Mommsen truly asserts, they are in general proven "by the formal vow which they (the Romans) made, man by man, for themselves and for their posterity, that henceforth they would never tolerate a king;" and "by the blind hatred with which the name of king was ever afterwards regarded at Rome." Even Julius Cæsar, centuries afterward, did not dare to assume the kingly title, notwithstanding that it was thrice offered to him; and Augustus, in formally setting up an empire, found himself obliged to avoid the outward appearance of a revival of royalty. Nevertheless the king had been assigned the duty of offering certain sacrifices, and therefore the name was retained in the office of the "king for offering sacrifice." It was decreed that this "king"—"whom they considered it their duty to create that the gods might not miss their accustomed mediator—should be disqualified from holding any further office, so that this official was at once the first in rank, and the least in power of all the Roman magistrates."

KINGS OF ROME.

B. C.	KINGS.	CHARACTER.
753	ROMULUS.	The Founder.
715	NUMA POMPILIUS.	The First Religious Lawgiver.
672	TULLUS HOSTILIUS.	The Conqueror.
640	ANCUS MARTIUS.	The Second Religious Lawgiver.
616	TARQUINIUS PRISCUS.	The Builder.
578	SERVIUS TULLIUS.	The Civil Lawgiver.
534	TARQUINIUS SUPERBUS (to B. C. 508).	The Tyrant.

SECTION V.—ROMAN RELIGION.

THE Roman religion, like the Grecian, was a polytheism. The Romans had no images of their gods for the first one hundred and seventy years after the founding of the city. In every nation idolatry has perhaps been a later corruption of an earlier and more spiritual system. The Roman religion was not so beautiful and varied in its conceptions as the Grecian. It furnished little inspiration to poetry or art, but it kept alive the simple domestic virtues, and regulated the transactions of the farm, the forum and the shop, by a series of principles pure in themselves and derived from a higher range of being.

The chief gods of the Romans were Jupiter and Mars. Jupiter was regarded as the supreme deity, but Mars was the special deity of this warlike people during their early history. March, the first month of the Roman year, was named after and conse-

MASK OF THE JUPITER OTRICOLI.

JUNO.

crated to Mars. The great war festival occupied a large part of this month; and during its first few days the twelve *Salii*, or Leapers, priests of Mars, who were selected from the noblest families, marched through the streets singing, dancing, and beating their rods upon their brazen shields. This festival began with horse-racing on the 27th of February, and its principal days were known as the day of the shield-forger (March 14th), the day of the armed dance at the Comitium (March 19th), and of the consecration of trumpets (March 25th). Wars were commenced with this festival, and the end of the campaign was followed in the autumn by a second festival in honor of Mars, called the consecration of arms (October 19th). Quirinus, under whose name Romulus was worshiped, was only a duplicate Mars, produced by the combination of the Roman and Sabine mythologies. Quirinus likewise had his twelve leapers, and his festival, the Quirinalia, which was celebrated on the 17th of February with similar ceremonies.

All the days of the full moon were sacred to Jupiter, as were all the wine festivals and various other days. The next important festivals were those relating to corn and wine, and marked the several periods of the farmer's year. On April 15th sacrifices were offered to Telles, the nourishing earth; on April 19th to Ceres, the goddess of germination and growth; on April 21st to Páles, the patroness of flocks; on April 23d to Jupiter, as the protector of the vines and the vats of the vintage of the preceding year, which were opened on this day for the first time; and on April 25th a deprecatory offering was made to Rust, the bad enemy of the crops. In May the twelve priests known as the Arval Brothers held their festival of three days in honor of Dea Dia, invoking her blessing in maintaining the earth's fertility and granting prosperity to Rome's entire territory. The harvest festivals were celebrated in August. The wine celebrations in honor of Jupiter occurred in October. The two thanksgivings—one in gratitude for the full granaries; the other the Saturnalia, or seed-sowing festival—occurred in December, the latter on the 17th. A third celebration was held in December, in honor of the shortest day of the year (December 21st), which brought back the new sun. At the close of the ceremonial year occurred the strange festival called the Lupercalia, or wolf-festival, during which a certain class of priests ran about the city, girdled with goat-skins and leaping like wolves, scourging the spectators with knotted thongs; and also the Terminalia, or boundary-stone festival in honor of Terminus, the god of boundaries or landmarks.

One of the most perfectly Roman deities was Janus, the double-faced god of beginnings. All gates and doors, the morning, the opening of all solemnities, and the month of January, were sacred to Janus, who was always invoked before any other god. January, which was originally the eleventh month of the Roman year, was dedicated to Janus because the labors of the husbandman in Southern Italy began anew in that month. Sacrifices were offered to Janus on twelve altars, as well as prayers every morning. The first of March—the Roman New Year's Day—was especially sacred to Janus. That day was regarded as giving tone to the entire year. Accordingly, people were careful that their thoughts, words and actions on that day should be pure, beneficent and just. They greeted each other with gifts and good wishes, and generally commenced some work which they had designed to perform during the year, while they were very much discouraged if any trifling accident occurred. The Temple of Janus was located at the foot of the Capitoline Hill, between the Palatine and Quirinal Hills, or between the original Roman and Sabine cities. Armies leaving the city marched out through the gates of this temple, and returning passed through them into the city; and therefore these gates stood open when Rome was at war, so that the god might come out to aid the Romans, while in time of peace the gates were always closed, as already stated.

Vulcan, the god of fire and of the forge, was another of the chief gods of Rome, and

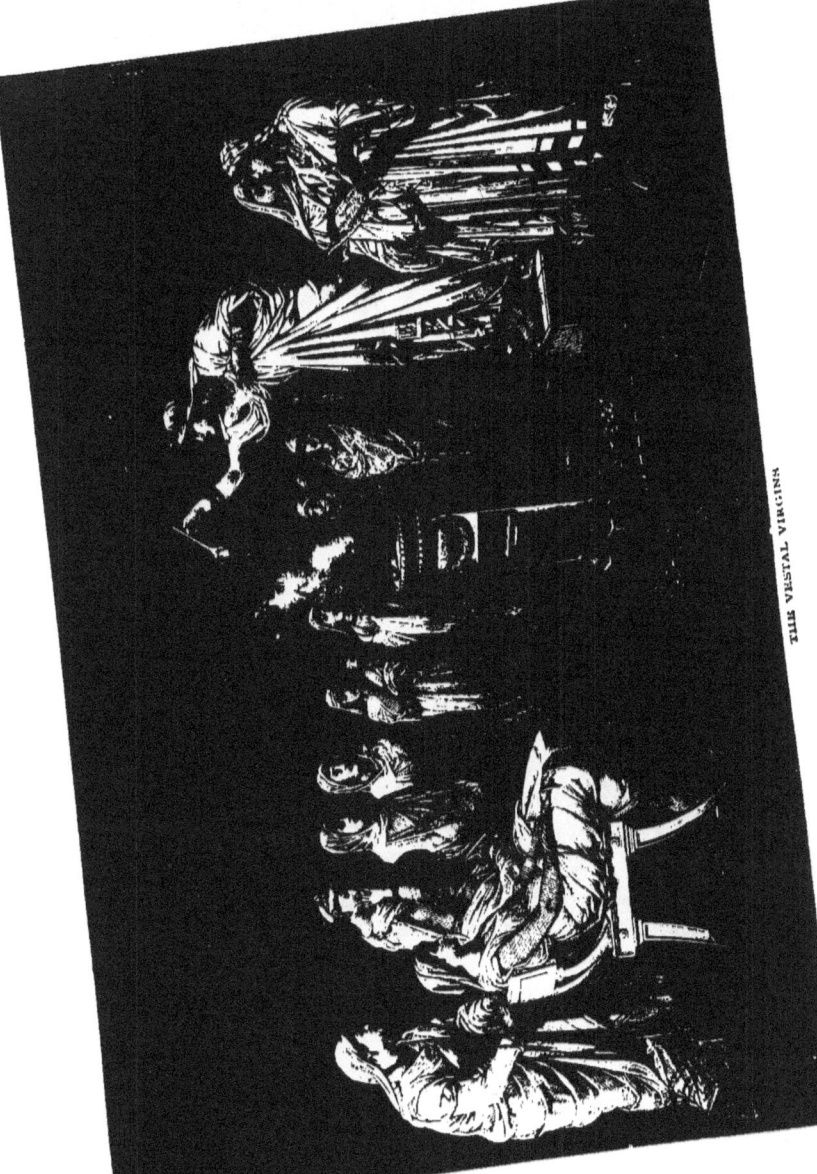

THE VESTAL VIRGINS

A HARUSPEX OFFICIATING.

TEMPLE OF NEPTUNE, PAESTUM.

was honored with two festivals, the consecration of trumpets in May, and the Volcanalia in August.

The gods of the domestic hearth, or the household, and of the store-room, and those of the forest and the field were the dearest to the Romans of all their deities, though of inferior rank to the divinities already named. Vesta, the household goddess, was near and dear to all Romans, who regarded her as the source of all their domestic prosperity and happiness. Every Roman hearthstone was a temple to Vesta, and every meal was a sacrifice in her honor. The great temple to this goddess was the hearthstone of the city. In that temple six maidens, called the *Vestal Virgins*, daughters of the most illustrious families, guarded the sacred fire, the symbol of the goddess, by day and by night. The Vestal fire was believed to be mysteriously connected with the origin of all things. The Vestal Virgins were highly reverenced, and their intercession was of peculiar efficacy in imploring pardon.

The Vestal Virgins did not live in seclusion, as did the nuns of monkish times, but were permitted to make their appearance in public, and even to be present at the sports and games. When one of these virgins died, her place was difficult to supply, as there was a great repugnance among young maidens to become Vestals, in consequence of the dreadful punishment inflicted for a violation of the Vestal's vows of chastity, the unfortunate delinquent being buried for her offense; but few suffered for a long succession of ages. In consequence of the reluctance of young females to become Vestals, the chief priest was usually under the necessity of seizing upon some maiden by violence and compelling her to assume the office of a Vestal.

Over the main entrance of every house was a little chapel of the Láres, the spirits of good men and of the ancestors of the family, to whom the father paid his devotions whenever he entered his dwelling upon returning home from a journey There were public Láres, or protecting divinities, in each city under Roman sway, and these were worshiped in a temple and in numerous chapels, usually located at the street crossings. Their names were kept secret, as the Romans intensely cherished the "belief that the name of the proper tutelary spirit of the community ought to remain forever unpronounced, lest an enemy should come to learn it and calling the god by his name should entice him beyond the bounds." Rural Láres and Láres Viáles were worshiped by travelers.

In the course of time the Romans incorporated the Grecian and other mythologies into their own religious system, so that they finally had an indefinite number of gods and goddesses. After their intercourse with the Greeks had commenced, the Romans regularly consulted the Delphic oracle and highly valued its utterances. After the capture of Veii the Romans presented the Delphic shrine with a tenth of the spoils. The only oracle possessed by Rome was that of Faunus, the favoring god, on the Aventine Hill. There were a number of oracles of Fortune, Faunus and Mars in Latium, but none of them gave any audible responses by the mouth of inspired persons, like the one at Delphi. At Albúnea, near Tibur, Faunus was consulted by the sacrifice of a sheep. The skin of the sheep was spread upon the ground, and the person seeking direction slept upon it, believing that he ascertained the will of the god by visions and dreams. The Romans often had recourse to the Greek oracles in Southern Italy; and the most acceptable gift which the inhabitants of Magna Græcia were able to offer to their friends in Rome was a palm-leaf inscribed with some utterances of the Cumæan sibyl, a priestess of Apollo at Cumæ, near Naples. The Romans usually learned the will of their gods by augury.

The Sibylline Books, which constituted one of the most highly cherished possessions of the Romans, were believed to have been purchased by one of the Tarquins from a mysterious woman who brought them to Rome, asking an exorbitant price for nine volumes. The king having refused to purchase them, the Sibyl went away and destroyed three of the books. She then returned with the remaining six and demanded the same price for these which she had asked for the original nine. As Tarquin again declined to purchase them, she again departed and destroyed three more books. She appeared a third time before Tarquin and asked as much for the remaining three as she had at first wanted for the whole nine. The woman's strange conduct excited Tarquin's curiosity, and he bought the three books, which were found to contain important revelations regarding the future destiny of Rome. They were given in charge of one of the four sacred colleges, and were kept in a stone chest under the temple of Jupiter Capitolinus. They were consulted only by order of the Senate on occasions of great public calamity.

The Romans are believed to have learned their different methods of divination from the Etruscans, such as the interpretation of signs in the heavens, of thunder and lightning, of the flight or voice of birds, of the appearance of sacrifices, and of dreams. The legends ascribed to the first Tarquin the introduction of Etruscan divinities and methods of worship into Rome. At a later period the Roman Senate specially decreed the cultivation of "Etruscan discipline" by young men of the noblest birth, lest a science of such importance to the state should be corrupted by coming into the hands of low and mercenary persons.

The four sacred colleges of the Romans were those of the *augurs*, the *pontiffs*, the *heralds*, and the *keepers of the Sibylline Books*. The augurs were gradually increased in number from three to sixteen, being distinguished by a sacred dress and a curved staff, and being held in the highest honor. They were charged with the duty of ascertaining the will of the gods from the flight of birds and from the appearance of the entrails of victims. Any public act of any kind—such as the holding of elections, the passage of laws, the declaring of war—could only be performed after "taking the auguries;" as in theory the gods were the rulers of the state, the magistrates being only their deputies. In case an augur declared, in the midst of the Comitia, that it thundered, even if falsely, the assembly at once dispersed. The augurs frequently made an unfair use of their great power in the political struggle between the patricians and the plebeians. The plebeians, having originally been foreigners, were regarded as having no share in the Roman gods, who thus became the exclusive patrons of the patricians. When plebeians were at length elected to high offices, in consequence of a change in the Roman constitution, the augurs declared the elections null and void in several instances, on the pretext that the auspices had been irregular; and no one having the right to appeal from their decision, their veto was absolute.

The pontiffs, or *pontifices*—"Bridge Builders"—as constituting one of the four sacred colleges, was the most famous of the religious institutions attributed to the good king Numa Pompilius. The pontiffs superintended all public worship according to their sacred books, and were obliged to give instruction to all such as applied for it, respecting the ceremonies with which the gods could be approached. Whenever sacred officers were to be appointed, or wills were to be read, the pontiffs convoked the Comitia. They only could judge of certain cases of sacrilegious crime, and in very early times only they possessed both the civil and religious law of the Romans, as the scribes did among the Hebrews. The highest magistrates submitted to their decrees, as well as did private individuals, provided three members of the college agreed in the decision. The pontiffs alone knew what days and hours might be used to transact public business. They were assigned the keeping of the calendar; and as these august and reverend dignitaries were only men, they sometimes made use of their power to prolong the yearly office of a favorite Consul, or to cut short the term of one of whom they disapproved. The Roman Emperors adopted the title of *Pontifex Maximus*, or Supreme Pontiff, and transmitted it to the Popes, or Bishops of modern Rome.

The heralds, or *fetiáles*, were the guardians of the public faith of the Romans in all their dealings with other nations. In case war was to be declared by Rome against another nation, it was a herald's duty to enter the enemy's territory, and four times to set forth the causes of complaint, once on each side of the Roman boundary, then to the first citizen whom he happened to meet, and, finally, to the magistrates at the seat of government; and solemnly to invoke Jupiter to give victory to those having a just cause.

The *flamens*, or kindlers, were the priests of particular gods, as one of their chief duties was to offer sacrifices by fire. The principal one of them all was the *Flamen Dialis*, or priest of Jupiter. The next were the priests of Mars and Quirinus. The priests were allowed to hold civil offices, but the purity and dignity of the priestly life were guarded by many curious laws. However, a priest was not allowed to mount a horse, to look upon an army outside the walls, or, in early times, to leave the city for even but one night.

After the good king Servius Tullius had completed his census, he performed a solemn purification of the city of Rome and the Roman people, by means of prayers and sacrifices, to avert the anger of the gods. During the continuance of the Roman Republic this ceremony was repeated after every general registration, which occurred once every five years. Sacrifices of a pig, a sheep and an ox were offered; while water was sprinkled from olive-branches, and certain substances were burned, whose smoke was believed to have a cleansing effect. Farmers, in like manner, purified their fields, shepherds their flocks, generals their armies, and admirals their fleets, to guard against disasters which the gods might send as a punishment for some secret or open act of impiety. An army or a fleet always underwent lustration before undertaking any enterprise. In the case of the fleet altars were erected on the shore near which the ships were enclosed. The sacrifices were carried around the fleet three times in a small boat by the generals and priests, prayers being offered aloud for the success of the expedition.

SECTION VI.—THE ROMAN REPUBLIC'S EARLY STRUGGLES.

THE Roman Republic, which was established upon the expulsion of Tarquin the Proud, B. C. 508, lasted four hundred and eighty years, and embraced four distinct periods. The first period was characterized by a struggle for existence against external foes, and by a constitutional development in the long and bitter contest between the patricians and the plebeians within the state. During this entire period the main interest centers upon the struggle between the two orders and the growth of the Roman constitution and laws; the foreign wars of the young republic being only of secondary importance, no extensive conquests having yet been made. The only wars of importance during this early period were the First Latin War, the war with Veii, and the defensive war against the Gauls.

Upon the establishment of the Roman Republic, the leaders of the revolution which overthrew Tarquin the Proud restored the constitution of the good Servius Tullius and improved it. In place of the king, two magistrates, called *Consuls*, were to be elected annually by the Comitia Centuriata, and during their terms of office they possessed all the power and dignity of kings. They were preceded in public by a guard of twelve *lictors*, bearing *faces*, or bundles of rods, as emblems of authority. Out of the city, when the Consul was engaged in military command, an ax was bound up with the rods, in token of his absolute power over life and death.

The first Consuls were Lucius Junius Brutus and Lucius Tarquinius Collatínus, the founders of the Republic. Brutus was a plebeian; but Collatínus, the husband of Lucretia, was a patrician.

The Senate, which had fallen away during the tyrannical reign of Tarquin the Proud, was again raised to the ideal number of three hundred by the addition of one hundred and sixty-four life-members of the order of Equites, many of whom were plebeians. The right of appeal, which Tarquin the Proud had suspended, was now restored and extended to all freemen. These arrangements produced a spirit of harmony between the different orders of the state. But the patricians were dissatisfied. Their hatred and fear of the tyrannical Tarquin had rendered it necessary on their part to conciliate the plebeians for the purpose of obtaining their powerful assistance in the revolution which rid Rome of the tyrant; but no sooner had the revolution been effected than the patricians endeavored to recall the concessions which they had never intended should be granted to the plebeians as permanent privileges.

Lucius Junius Brutus—known as the Elder Brutus—whom we have noticed as the founder, and one of the first two Consuls, of the Roman Republic, was one of the most celebrated characters of this early period, and many beautiful legends are connected with his name. Brutus was a nephew of Tarquin the Proud. Seeing his relatives put to death by order of that jealous tyrant, Brutus is said to have feigned idiocy, in order to appear to be of no consequence. After the outrage of Sextus and the consequent suicide of Lucretia, he threw off the mask, and by his bold and earnest eloquence he instigated the Roman people to expel the tyrannical king and his family from Rome.

The following is another legend concerning Brutus. On one occasion King Tarquin the Proud was terribly frightened by a strange omen. A serpent glided from beneath the altar at the time of sacrifice, and devoured the entrails of the victim. The king, greatly alarmed, determined to send his two sons and his idiotic nephew, Brutus, to Delphi to seek from the famous oracle at that place for an explanation of the dreadful portent. When the two princes had presented their offerings, they laughed at the half-witted Brutus, who offered only his staff; but they were unaware that the pretended idiot had hollowed out the staff and filled it with gold. In answer to the inquiry as to who should reign in Rome after Tarquin the Proud, the Delphic oracle said: "He of you who shall first kiss his mother." Thereupon the two princes agreed to draw lots for the privilege; but Brutus understood the oracle better, and fell as if by accident upon taking his departure from the famous temple, and kissed his mother earth.

The following circumstance in connection with the legendary history of Brutus illustrates the stern virtue and indomitable patriotism of this wonderful man. After his expulsion, Tarquin the Proud sent to Rome to ask for all the goods that had belonged to him; and after some time the Senate ordered that his goods should be restored to him. But those whom he had sent to Rome to ask for his goods conspired with many young patricians and the sons of Brutus to restore the deposed and exiled king to his throne. A slave accidentally overheard them talking together, and when he had ascertained that the letters were to be given to the messengers of Tarquin, he went to Brutus and told him all that he had heard. Brutus defeated the plot by causing the young conspirators to be seized and obtaining possession of their letters. Brutus then ordered the lictors to bind his own two sons, Titus and Tiberius, along with the other conspirators, and to scourge them with rods, in accordance with the law. The stern Brutus, in his judgement-seat in the Forum, from feelings of patriotism, which made him forget the father in the judge, then ordered the execution of his sons. Accordingly, the lictors struck off their heads with their axes before their father's eyes. Brutus did not stir from his seat, nor turn his eyes away from the sight. But the spectators saw that the stern father and patriot was inwardly

THE REPUBLIC'S EARLY STRUGGLES.

grieving over his children. "Then they marveled at him, because he had loved justice more than his own blood, and had not spared his own children when they had been false to their country and had offended against the law."

The young Republic was involved in wars with the Etruscans, the Latins and other neighboring Italian nations, which endeavored to restore the banished Tarquin the Proud. The Romans were so preoccupied with their internal affairs for a long time that they had no time left to maintain their supremacy in Latium, and consequently Rome fell from the highest to the very lowest position among the nations of Central Italy, thus losing her power and prestige as the immediate result of the change from a monarchy to a republic.

The Latins threw off the Roman supremacy, and the Etruscans waged war against Rome. Lars Porsena, king of the Etruscan city of Clusium, seems to have actually conquered Rome and to have held the city in subjection for some years, receiving from the Roman Senate an ivory throne, a golden crown, a scepter and a triumphal robe, in token of homage. In pursuing their attacks upon Latium the Etruscans were defeated, and Rome recovered its independence, but with the loss of her territories west of the Tiber. The hostile Latins, the Sabines and the Oscans ravaged the other lands of the Romans without opposition, carrying away the crops and the farm-buildings, as well as the cattle. These losses greatly impoverished the Romans, the main suffering naturally falling upon the poorer people, whose small farms constituted their only possessions and their only means of support.

With these early foreign wars of the Roman Republic are connected some of the most interesting legends of early Roman history. In a battle with the Etruscans, Aruns, a son of the exiled Tarquin the Proud, observing Brutus at the head of the Roman cavalry, spurred his horse very furiously to the charge upon his antagonist, each running his spear through his adversary, so that both fell mortally wounded. The Roman women mourned tor Brutus a whole year, because they honored him as the avenger of the wrongs of Lucretia, the victim of the foul crime of Sextus Tarquinius.

One of the most famous legends of this Etruscan war was that of Horatius Cocles. When Lars Porsena, King of Clusium, had reached the Hill Janiculum, just across the Tiber from Rome, the city was in the most imminent danger of capture, as the Etruscans could have entered it by crossing the Sublician bridge. But in this dire extremity the city was saved by the valor of Horatius Cocles, who, with almost superhuman strength, kept the whole Etruscan army at bay, while his two comrades broke down the bridge behind him. Then fervently praying: "O Father Tiber, take me into thy charge and bear me up!" he plunged into the stream, and, amid a shower of darts from the enemy, he swam to the opposite shore in safety. The state honored him with a statue and bestowed upon him as much land as he was able to plow round in one day. Few Roman legends are more celebrated than this gallant deed of Horatius Cocles, and Roman historians in later ages loved to relate it. Macaulay, in one of his *Lays of Ancient Rome*, speaks of this legend in the following lines:

"When the goodman mends his armor,
 And trims his helmet plume;
When the goodwife's shuttle merrily
 Goes flashing through the loom;
With weeping and with laughter
 Still is the story told,
How well Horatius kept the bridge
 In the brave days of old."

Another well-known legend of this Etruscan war was that of Mucius Scævola. While Lars Porsena was besieging Rome, a young Roman patrician, named Mucius, penetrated into the Etruscan camp for the purpose of assassinating Porsena, but by mistake he killed one of the attendants of the Clusian king. Thereupon he was seized and brought into the presence of Porsena, who threatened him with torture unless he made a confession. But Mucius thrust his right hand into a fire that was burning close by and kept it there until it was burnt off, to show Porsena that no torture could induce him to betray the plans of his countrymen. Porsena, admiring such fortitude and patriotism, gave Mucius his liberty; whereupon the heroic young Roman, in gratitude, warned the Clusian king to raise the siege of Rome and make peace, as three hundred young Romans had sworn to take his life, and that he had been chosen by lot to make the first attempt. Porsena, alarmed for his life, immediately made peace with the Romans and marched home. The Romans ever afterward held Mucius in high honor and bestowed upon him the surname of Scævola, the *Left-Handed*.

Still another legend of this Etruscan war was that of the battle of Lake Regillus. As a final effort to recover his throne, the exiled Tarquin applied for aid to his son-in-law, Octavius Mamilius, King of Tusculum; and the Latins at once espoused his cause. A protracted and sanguinary battle was fought at Lake Regillus, during which it at one time appeared as if the Roman army was about to give way; whereupon Aulus Postumius offered a prayer to the twin deities, Castor and Pollux, vowing to erect a temple in their honor if they would come to the aid of the Romans. But a short time had passed,

"When he was aware of a princely pair,
That rode at his right hand.
So like they were, no mortal
Might one from the other know;
White as snow their armor was,
Their steeds were white as snow."

Another charge being made under this more than mortal leadership, the Latins fled. That same evening two young men rode into Rome on white steeds, and announced the victory of the Roman arms. They were seen washing their steeds at the spring Juturna, in the Forum, after which they vanished.

"And all the people trembled,
And pale grew every cheek;
And Sergius the High Pontiff
Alone found voice to speak:
'The Gods who live forever
Have fought for Rome to-day!
These be the great Twin Brethren
To whom the Dorians pray.'"

During these early wars of the Roman Republic, according to Livy, the first *Dictator* was appointed. The Dictator was an absolute and irresponsible master of the state, superior to the Consuls, the Senate and the Comitia, and even above the laws themselves. Thereafter, in times of great public danger, a Dictator was always appointed. The first Dictator must have been appointed by the Senate, according to Livy; but in after-times the Senate, though claiming the right to nominate, practically usually selected the Consul who should nominate.

Although monarchy was abolished, Rome was not by any means under a free government. As soon as the Republic was relieved from the hostility of foreign foes, it began to be distracted by domestic troubles. As already stated, the patricians intended to revoke the concessions which they had granted to the plebeians in a moment of necessity, when the first opportunity presented itself; and as external dangers had now passed, they began to grievously oppress the plebs.

The greater part of the first period of the Republic is absorbed in struggles between the two great orders in the state. This period is not as attractive as the romantic legends of the regal period, or as interesting as the stirring events of the subsequent period of conquest. Nevertheless, the stages by which this great ancient people won their freedom and eventually established a perfectly pure democracy must ever be of the highest importance to the student or reader of history.

Rome had hitherto mainly derived her wealth from the products of the soil. The loss of the lands west of the Tiber, and the ravages of the hostile nations in the Roman territory after the establishment of the Republic, had reduced the Roman masses to general poverty. At the same time, in consequence of the necessities and losses of the government, the taxes were vastly increased; and these were levied upon the scale of former assessments, and not upon the reduced value of property prevailing at the time. In addition to this, the state required the immediate payment of the taxes for five years.

The patricians having possession of all the offices, exempted themselves from the payment of tithes, and soon became immensely wealthy; while the plebeians were compelled to pay taxes for the little farms in their possession, and to perform military service without pay. In time of war the lands of the plebeians were left untilled, and their dwellings were often burned by the enemy. The plebeians consequently became very poor, and incurred debts with the patricians which it was impossible to discharge, under the existing circumstances, as they were required to pay exorbitant rates of interest for the money thus borrowed. The patricians took full advantage of the cruel Roman laws concerning debt, enforcing those harsh laws to the fullest extent; and the sufferings of the insolvent plebeians became intolerable. According to the Roman law, if a debtor failed to discharge his obligations when they became due, his estate was seized; and he and his whole family became slaves to his creditor, or were thrown into prison and maltreated. Many plebeians sold themselves as slaves to their patrician creditors to discharge their debts. Those plebeian debtors who refused thus to sign away their own and their children's liberty were frequently cast into prison, loaded with chains, and starved or tortured by the cruelty of their creditors. The patrician castles commanding the hills of Rome contained gloomy dungeons, in which were perpetrated untold atrocities upon those who were so unfortunate as to incur the wrath of their owners.

Patrician tyranny at length produced a general insurrection of the plebeians. According to a legend, an old man, covered with rags, pale and emaciated, having escaped from his creditor's prison, rushed into the Forum and implored the aid of the people. He showed them the scars of the wounds which he had received in twenty-eight battles with the enemies of Rome. He was immediately recognized as a brave old captain in the army. He related to them that his house had been burned by the enemy in the Etruscan war, and that his taxes had been nevertheless rigorously exacted from him. He had been obliged to borrow money, and finally he had lost all his property; and when it had become impossible for him to discharge his debts, he and his two sons were enslaved by his creditor. He also showed them the marks of the stripes which had been inflicted upon him by his creditor. The plebeians could not now restrain their rage and indignation. They demanded relief. At this instant, news reached Rome that the Volscians had taken up arms against the Romans. The plebeians rejoiced at this intelligence. They refused to enlist in the army, and told the patricians to fight their own battles. As the plebeians could not be compelled to enlist, the Consuls promised them relief, and conceded their demand for the release of the imprisoned debtors, whereupon many plebeians joined the military ranks; but no sooner had the Volscians been defeated than the debtors were ordered back to their prisons.

Fourteen years after the founding of the Republic (B. C. 494), the plebeians, driven to despair by patrician tyranny, withdrew from Rome in a body and retired to Mons Sacer (the Sacred Mount), on the opposite side of the Tiber, about three miles from the city, where they announced their intention to found a new city, where they might live and govern themselves by more just and equal laws.

Seeing that they could not afford to lose the services of so large and useful a class as the plebeians, the patricians dispached ten Senators, with Menenius Agrippa at their head, to treat with the plebeians, and to induce them to return to Rome. According to an old Roman legend, Agrippa represented to them the disadvantages of dissensions in a state, and related to them the fable of the quarrel between the stomach and the members. The members, complaining that the stomach remained idle and enjoyed itself, refused to labor for it any longer; the hands refused to put food to the mouth; the mouth refused to open, and the teeth refused to chew; but while they thus attempted to starve the stomach, they starved themselves; and at last they discovered that the stomach was as useful to the body as they were themselves. The plebeians understood the moral of the fable, and they agreed to a treaty with the patricians.

The patricians were obliged to yield, and the seceded plebeians were induced to return to Rome, being allowed to dictate their own terms. These conditions were the cancellation of all claims against insolvent debtors; the release of all imprisoned or enslaved debtors; and the annual election, by the people, of two magistrates, called *Tribuni Plebis*, or *Tribunes of the Plebs*, whose persons should be sacred, and whose duty it was to defend and protect the interests and rights of the plebeians, and to prevent, by the word *veto* (I forbid it), any measure which endangered the rights and liberties of the plebeians. The Tribunes were afterwards increased to five, and still later to ten in number. Two plebeian *Ædiles* were likewise appointed, and their duties were to superintend the streets, buildings, markets and public lands, as well as the public games and festivals, and the general order and peace of the city. These Ædiles were judges in minor cases, like those of modern police courts; and they were subsequently the guardians of the decrees of the Senate, which the patrician magistrates had sometimes tampered with. After winning this great victory for popular rights, the plebeians returned to their old homes at Rome (B. C. 494). The scene of this decisive triumph of the commons was consecrated to Jupiter, and was known in after years as *Mons Sacer* (the Sacred Mount). Thenceforth the plebeians of Rome had an important part in the affairs of the Republic. This victory was the prelude to other popular constitutional triumphs, which the plebeians wrested from the patricians during a long series of struggles.

In this connection comes another celebrated legend of the early days of the Roman Republic (B. C. 488). The haughty patrician Caius Marcius—who had received the surname of Coriolánus, from his valor at the capture of the Volscian town of Corioli—was hated by the plebeians, who refused him the Consulate. This so exasperated Coriolánus that when, during a famine in Rome, a supply of corn arrived from Sicily, he advised the Senate not to distribute any to the plebeians unless they consented to the abolition of the office of Tribunes. This insolent proposal so incensed the plebeians that they would have torn the haughty patrician to pieces had not the Tribunes summoned him before the Comitia Tributa. Coriolánus himself boldly defied his political enemies, and his relatives and friends vainly interceded for him. He was sentenced to banishment from Rome. Enraged at this treatment, Coriolánus went over to the Volscians, the inveterate enemies of the Romans, and offered to lead their armies against his own countrymen. The Volscian king induced his people to intrust Coriolánus with the command of their forces, and he accordingly led a Volscian army against Rome, sweeping everything before him and taking town after town. He advanced within five miles of Rome, ravaging the lands of the plebeians, but sparing those of the patricians. Despair reigned in the city. The ten leading Senators were sent to entreat him to spare his native city, but he received them with the utmost sternness, and told them he would not relent until he had reduced the city to absolute submission. The next day the pontiffs, the augurs, the flamens and all the priests came in their official robes and vainly entreated him not to ruin his country, but Coriolánus was still inexorable. There seemed to be no hope for the city, which would soon have fallen into the patrician traitor's hands; but the next morning the noblest Roman matrons, headed by Veturia, the aged mother of Coriolánus, and by his wife, Volumnia, leading his little children by the hand, came to his tent. Their lamentations and appeals turned him from his revengeful purpose. Yielding to the solicitations of his mother, Coriolánus burst into tears, exclaiming: "Mother, you have saved Rome, but you have ruined your son!" He then raised the siege of Rome and led the Volscians home. It is said that the Volscians, enraged at his retreat from Rome, put him to death; but a tradition states that he lived to a great age, in exile among the Volscians, and that he was frequently heard to exclaim: "How miserable is the condition of an old man in banishment!"

In B. C. 485 Spurius Cassius, one of the two Consuls for that year, proposed the *First Agrarian Law*, providing for a division of a certain portion of the public lands among the plebeians to prevent future suffering. He likewise proposed that the plebeians when serving in the army should be paid for their services, and that the tithe of produce levied by the state upon the lands leased by the patricians should be strictly collected and thus applied. The other Consul opposed the law, and charged Spurius Cassius with seeking to win popular favor for the purpose of making himself king. Notwithstanding this opposition, the First Agrarian Law was passed. After the expiration of his year of the Consulate, Spurius Cassius was brought to trial, through the powerful influence of the patricians, and was condemned as a traitor. He was scourged and beheaded, and his house was razed to the ground (B. C. 485). Thus Spurius Cassius died the death of a martyr to the cause of the poor.

Having thus gotten rid of the popular leader, the patricians threw off the mask, and proceeded to deprive the plebeians of all the advantage of the new law. They demanded the exclusive right to elect both Consuls, only requiring the plebeians in the popular assemblies to ratify their choice. The patrician Consuls refused to enforce the Agrarian Law, thus preventing a division of the public lands. The only resource of the plebeians then was to refuse to perform military service, and the Tribunes now made their power felt by protecting the commons in their refusal to enlist. The Consuls thwarted their purpose by holding their re-recruiting stations outside of the city walls, where the Tribunes had no jurisdiction. Though a plebeian might keep himself safe under the protection of the Tribunes within the city, his lands could be laid waste, his buildings burnt, and his cattle confiscated, by order of the patrician authorities. The plebeians still had one last expedient. Though the Consuls could thus force them to enlist, the plebeian soldiers could not be compelled to win a victory, and thus they soon gratified their revenge. Considering the patricians as worse enemies than the foreign foes whom they encountered in the field, the plebeians allowed themselves to be defeated by the Veientians.

The noble family of the Fabii, the most devoted champions of the patricians, had been in possession of the Consulate for six successive years. This aristocratic family now perceived the danger to the state from further opposition to the popular will; and when Kæso Fabius became Consul, in B. C. 479, he insisted upon the execution of the Agrarian Law of Spurius Cassius. The patricians haughtily resisted his demand, and the Fabii at once retired from Rome in disgust, founded a little colony in Etruria, on the little river Crémera, a few miles from Rome, settling there with their hundreds of clients, their families, and a few patricians who were attached to them from friendship and sympathy. They promised to still remain loyal and valiant defenders of Roman interests, and to maintain this advanced post with their own resources in the war which Rome was then waging against Veii. Two years after this migration, the Fabian settlement was surprised by the Veientians, every man being put to death (B. C. 477).

As the Consuls still refused to execute the Agrarian Law, they were impeached at the expiration of their official term by Genucius, one of the Tribunes of the plebeians. On the morning of the day assigned for the trial, Genucius was found murdered in his bed (B. C. 473). This treacherous crime was caused by the patricians, who were alarmed at the danger by which they were menaced. The popular indignation was immensely increasd by this dastardly deed, but the plebeians were paralyzed for the moment, and the Consul proceeded with the enlistment of soldiers. The centurion Vólero Publilius, a strong and active plebeian, refused to be enrolled, and appealed to the Tribunes for protection. Alarmed by the fate of Genucius, the Tribunes hesitated, and Vólero Publilius called upon the plebeians to aid him in upholding his rights. In the tumult which ensued the Consuls and all their retinue were driven from the Forum.

The next year (B. C. 471), Vólero Publilius was chosen Tribune. He proposed a law that the Tribunes should thenceforth be elected by the plebeians only in the Comitia Tributa in the Forum, instead of by the entire people in the Comitia Centuriata. This measure was intended to avoid the overwhelming vote of the clients of the great patrician families, who were obliged to conform to the decrees of their patrons, and who frequently controlled the action of the whole people in the Comitia Centuriata. The patricians managed for a year, by various delays, to prevent the passage of the bill. Appius Claudius, one of the Consuls, stationed himself in the Forum with an armed force to oppose its passage; and it was only after the plebeians, imitating the patricians in resorting to force, had seized the Capitol and held possession of it for some time under military guard, that the famous *Publilian Law* was passed (B. C. 471). This has been called the "Second Great Charter of Roman Liberties," and it conferred upon the tribes assembled in the Comitia Tributa the power to elect their own Tribunes and Ædiles, as well as the right to discuss all questions concerning the whole Roman people. It was a long stride in the direction of equal rights in Rome.

While the aristocracy and the commonalty were thus contending for power within Rome, the Æqui and the Volsci, the two Oscan nations which had conquered a considerable portion of Latium, and which had advanced to within a short distance of Rome itself, were waging war against the Romans. After taking advantage of the changes in the Latin League to extend their power to the Alban Mount and over the southern plain of Latium, the Æqui and the Volsci extended their forays to the very gates of Rome, forcing the rural population to seek refuge, with their cattle, within the walls, where a plague which was then raging contributed the horrors of pestilence to those of war. In the meantime the Veientians, or the people of Veii, an Etruscan nation, had advanced to the opposite side of the Tiber and had threatened the Hill Janiculum.

The civil struggles in Rome had led to the exile of many Roman citizens, and in most instances these exiles joined the hostile nations. Rome was the champion of oligarchy among the cities of Italy, as Sparta was among those of Greece. Party spirit was frequently stronger than patriotism, and the sympathy between Roman and foreign aristocrats was greater than that between patricians and plebeians at home. Thus an exiled noble was willing to undertake the task of ruining his country; and the legend of Coriolánus fully illustrates the condition of the Roman Republic at that early period.

In the meantime another visitation of pestilence carried off thousands of the people of Rome. The Æquians and the Volscians ravaged the country to the very walls of the city, and the crowded multitude were threatened with the horrors of famine. During all this time the patricians maintained their pretensions with unabated vigor, while the plebeians watched with great eagerness for an opportunity to establish their rights on a firm foundation. These internal disorders so greatly wasted the strength of Rome that she was scarcely able to maintain herself against the attacks of external foes. It was very evident that a thorough and radical reform was necessary to redress the civil grievances of the commons.

In B. C. 462 Terentilius Harsa, one of the Tribunes of the plebs, proposed the appointment of a board of ten commissioners, five patricians and five plebeians, to revise the Roman constitution, to define the duties and powers of Consuls and Tribunes, and to frame a code of laws from the vast mass of decisions and precedents. The struggle over the passage of the *Terentilian Laws* lasted ten years (B. C. 462-452), during which Rome was on the brink of ruin. During the progress of this internal struggle the Volscians several times came near gaining possession of the city. During these troubles many Roman citizens became exiles. The chief of these was Kæso Quinctius, the son of the great patrician Lucius Quinctius, surnamed Cincinnátus, meaning *curly-head*.

Kæso Quinctius had been exiled for raising riots in the Forum to prevent the passage of the Terentilian Laws, but he afterwards returned with a band of Roman exiles, headed by a Sabine leader named Appius Herdonius, who occupied the city and seized the Capitol, and demanded the recall and reënfranchisement of all banished Roman citizens. The whole band of exiles was defeated and slain by the citizens.

In revenge for his son's death, Cincinnátus, who was then one of the Consuls, declared that the Terentilian Laws should never pass during his term of office, and that he would immediately lead the entire citizen-soldiery out against the enemy, thus preventing a meeting of the tribes in the Comitia Tributa. The augurs were even to accompany him and consecrate the ground of the encampment, so that a lawful assembly might be held under the power of the Consuls, and repeal every law which had thus far been enacted at Rome under the authority of the Tribunes. At the end of his official term, Cincinnátus declared his intention of appointing a Dictator, whose authority would supersede that of all other officers, patrician or plebeian. All these things could be done under the strict forms of the Roman constitution; but the Senate and the more prudent of the patricians perceived that such an exercise of the Consul's power might tax the patience of the plebeians too far, and persuaded Cincinnátus to desist. At the expiration of his official year, Cincinnátus retired to his farm, which he himself cultivated.

War went on between the Romans and the Æquians, and treaties were only made to be broken. In B. C. 458 the Æquians invaded the Roman territory and formed an intrenched camp on Mount Algidus, one of the Alban hills. The Roman Senate sent ambassadors to Gracchus, the Æquian commander, to complain of this violation of the peace. Gracchus, who was a vain-glorious and haughty man, received the Roman ambassadors in his tent, which was pitched under the shade of an oak. He answered all their remonstrances with mockery, saying: "I am busy, and cannot hear; tell your message to this oak tree." One of the Roman ambassadors instantly replied: "Yea, let this sacred oak hear, and let all the gods hear, how treacherously you have broken the peace!" The ambassadors returned to Rome, and war was declared against the Æquians.

When the Roman army marched out, the crafty Gracchus retreated before them, and the Romans followed him heedlessly until he had lured them into a narrow valley with high and steep hills on each side. He then seized and guarded the defiles in front and rear, and covered the hills on both sides with his troops. The Romans thus found themselves decoyed into a trap, in which they could neither advance nor retreat. They were in imminent peril of starvation, as there was neither food for the men nor grass for the horses in the narrow valley. To their good fortune, five horsemen had broken out of the valley through one defile before the rear was quite closed up, and these succeeded in making their escape to the city with the intelligence of the perilous situation of the entrapped Roman army.

Upon the reception of this astounding news, the Roman Senate unanimously exclaimed: "There is only one man who can save us. Cincinnátus must be Dictator." The honest patrician farmer was thereupon invested with that high office. When the deputies of the Senate came to inform Cincinnátus of his appointment, they found him plowing his own fields across the Tiber, clad only in his tunic, or shirt. They bade him clothe himself in order to hear the decree of the Senate creating him Dictator.

His wife brought him his toga, which he immediately put on. They then informed him of the dangerous situation of the Roman army, and announced to him that he had been appointed to the Dictatorship. The next morning before dawn he appeared in the Forum and ordered every man to close his shop; stopped the courts of law; gave directions that no man should attend to his private affairs until the entrapped army was delivered; and ordered every citizen of age to bear arms to appear in the Field of Mars before sunset, with provisions for five days, and a dozen stout stakes, which were also used by the Roman soldiers in pitching their camp. The city was all astir with the din of military preparations, and the citizens in all quarters were felling trees and dressing food.

All was ready at sunset and the newly-levied army left Rome, reaching Mount Algidus by midnight. Cincinnátus ordered his soldiers to cast their baggage in a pile, but to keep the stakes. He then formed them into a long column, with which he completely surrounded the enemy on the mountain. This was no sooner done than his whole army sent up a tremendous shout. The sound echoed through the camp of the astonished foe, filling them with utter consternation. The entrapped Romans in the valley also heard the shout, and said to each other: "Our people have come to help us, for it is a Roman hurrah!" So they shouted back and commenced to attack the enemy. In the meantime the Roman army of deliverance under Cincinnátus was engaged in digging a vast trench around the mountain, and fencing it with a rampart of stakes and turf. At dawn the next morning the Æquians were surprised and amazed to find themselves thoroughly inclosed. As they were unable to escape, they offered to surrender to Cincinnátus on his own terms; and the victorious Romans stripped their enemies of their arms, baggage and valuables, after which they marched home in triumph.

Unbounded joy reigned in Rome. The tables were set out at every door laden with food and drink, and the soldiers and the citizens feasted together. Cincinnátus, who had returned to Rome a conqueror only twenty-four hours after he had quitted the city, was hailed as the father and protector of his countrymen, and they honored him with a golden crown. After holding the Dictatorship a fortnight, he resigned it and returned to his plow.

The passage of the Terentilian Laws was delayed six years longer; but ultimately, in B. C. 452, the patricians yielded the main point, and the *Decemvirs*, or ten commissioners to revise the constitution, were chosen. Though the Decemvirs were all patricians, they were men of known moderation and integrity, and enjoyed the confidence and regard of both patricians and plebeians. For the time they were entrusted with all the powers of the state, constituent, legislative and executive; thus superseding both Consuls and Tribunes. During the deliberation upon their work, commissioners had been sent to Greece to study the laws of the Hellenic states. These commissioners now returned to Rome, bringing with them an Ionian sophist, Hermodórus of Ephesus, who gave such valuable aid to the Decemvirs in explaining whatever was obscure in the notes of the commissioners that he was honored with a statue in the Comitium.

The result of the labor of the Decemvirs was the *Laws of the Twelve Tables*, which became the "source of all public and private right" at Rome for many centuries. The existing offices of the state were abolished, and a new government was established instead of the old, consisting of Decemvirs or Ten Men, five of whom were patricians and five plebeians, and these were invested with the executive power of the state. The Decemvirs were elected for one year by the entire body of Roman citizens in the Comitia Centuriata, and confirmed by the patricians in the Comitia Curiata.

The provisions of the new code of laws extended to every department of life. The old Roman laws gave the father absolute right of property in his family. He was allowed to sell his wife, his son, or his daughter. Although the religious law denounced the selling of a wife by her husband as impious, no penalty was attached to it; the persons guilty of such an act being merely marked by the curse of the chief pontiff for the wrathful judgments of the gods. If a father desired to free his son, the process was more difficult than the emancipation of a slave; as the latter, if sold to another master, might be liberated at once, but a son sold into slavery and liberated returned to his father's possession. This subjection of the son could only end with the father's death, though the son himself might then be an old man.

The Laws of the Twelve Tables provided that, in case a father had sold his son three times, he was deprived of all further control over him; but a son emancipated in this manner was regarded as severed from all relationship with his father, and lost all right of inheritance in his father's property. Women were regarded as minors and wards during all their lives. In case of their father's death, unmarried women passed under the control of their brothers; while married females were the absolute property of their husbands. A widow might become the ward of her own son. Marriages between patricians and plebeians were declared illegal, and children born of such marriages could not inherit any of their fathers' possessions.

The Laws of the Twelve Tables punished the defamation of character with the severest penalties; and their definition of libel was so stringent that no poet or historian dared speak of the living except in terms of praise. This circumstance renders it more difficult to obtain a correct idea of the public men of Rome than of those of Greece, as the Greek historians dwelt with conscientious impartiality upon public men and measures, and the license of the comic poets of Greece, though frequently employed with insolent injustice, still show us all the weak points of character, and discloses to us the man as actually viewed by his contemporaries. Even while writing about the past, the Roman historians could often draw their materials only from funeral orations, or from the flattering verses of dependent poets, treasured up among the records of illustrious families.

During their appointed official year, the Decemvirs completed ten tables of laws; and, in accordance with the Roman idea, these were so just and so acceptable that the public assemblies readily consented to renew the Decemvirate for another year, in order to enable these ten lawgivers to complete their code. The patrician Appius Claudius was reëlected as a member of the new Decemvirate, and his unscrupulous character fully displayed itself in the tyrannical nature of the government. The Roman people discovered that they had simply created ten Consuls instead of two, and that they had deprived themselves of the protection formerly afforded them by the popular Tribunes.

A vile outrage committed by Appius Claudius led to the overthrow of the Decemvirate. Appius had conceived a strong passion for the beautiful Virginia, the fifteen-year-old daughter of the plebeian Virginius, who was a distinguished centurion in the army. Appius Claudius had seen the charming maiden going daily to school in the Forum, attended by her nurse, and he determined to get her into his possession. He caused her to be seized in the Forum, and declared that she was the slave of one of his clients, that she had been born of a slave woman in his house, and sold to the wife of Virginius, who had no children of her own. The friends of Virginia and of the plebeians denounced this atrocious falsehood with indignation, and rallied in such numbers for her rescue that the Decemvir's lictors were obliged to release the maiden under bonds to appear the next day before the judgment-seat of Appius Claudius, where it would be shown that she was the daughter of Virginius.

Virginius, who was with the Roman army before Tusculum, was hastily summoned, and, after riding all night, reached the city early the next morning. In the character of a suppliant he appeared in the Forum with his daughter and a host of matrons and friends. But his plea was not heard. To his utter amazement and indignation, Appius Claudius decided that the maiden should be considered a slave until her freedom could be proved, in spite of the existence of a law proposed by himself the previous year, that no one should be regarded as a slave until proven such. Seeing that justice was denied him before such a tribunal, Virginius requested one last word with the Forum, mounted his horse at the city gate, and rode to the army before Tusculum.

His plebeian comrades in the army at Tusculum arose at his appeal and hastened to Rome to avenge his wrong. They entered the city and marched through the streets to the Aventine, calling upon the plebeians to elect ten Tribunes to defend their rights. Icilius, the betrothed lover of Virginia, roused the other Roman army near Fidénæ. The plebeians in the army under Icilius over-

DEATH OF VIRGINIA.

his daughter; and, drawing her aside with her nurse into one of the stalls of the Forum, he seized a butcher's knife and plunged it into her heart, exclaiming: "Thus only, my child, can I keep thee free!" Then turning to Appius Claudius, he cried: "On thy head be the curse of this innocent blood!" The Decemvir ordered the instant arrest of Virginius, but not a hand was raised to seize him. With the bloody knife in his hand, he rushed through the multitude in threw the Decemvirs who were with them, and also chose ten Tribunes and marched to Rome, where they joined their comrades. The twenty Tribunes chose two of their number to act for the rest, and placed a strong garrison in the Aventine; after which the whole plebeian class, accompanied by the army, withdrew from the city and retired to the Sacred Mount a second time, and there commenced the building of a new plebeian city (B. C. 449).

THE REPUBLIC'S EARLY STRUGGLES.

The Senate had thus far refused to take any action against the Decemvirs, but this second secession of the plebs to the Sacred Mount forced them to act. Rome was thus a house divided against itself, and could not in this condition expect to resist her foreign foes. The Senate clearly saw that the revolution was successful, and that the demands of the popular party must be conceded. The Senate accordingly yielded, and the plebeians consented to return to Rome on condition of the abolition of the Decemvirate (B. C. 449).

Appius Claudius and the other Decemvirs were accordingly removed. Appius and one of his colleagues were cast into prison, where Appius himself committed suicide. The other Decemvirs fled from Rome, and their property was confiscated. The Decemvirate was thus abolished, and was superseded by a government composed of two Consuls, who were freely elected by the whole body of the free citizens in the Comitia Centuriata. The Tribunate of the plebeians was restored as it had existed before the establishment of the Decemvirate, the number of Tribunes being increased to ten. The people were allowed the right of appeal to the Comitia Centuriata from the sentence of the Consuls. The Ædiles were entrusted with the decrees of the Senate, in order to prevent their being ignored or falsified by the magistrates. It was also distinctly enacted that the Tribunes should be invested with the right to initiate legislation by consulting the tribes assembled in the Comitia Tributa on important matters.

The first Consuls chosen under this new arrangement were Valerius and Horatius, both of whom were patricians, but possessed the confidence and respect of the plebeians. Their first act was to lead an army against the Sabines, who, encouraged by the internal dissensions of Rome, had invaded the territory of the Republic. The two Consuls gained so signal a victory over the invaders that the Sabines ceased their incursions upon the Roman territory for a century and a half. Upon returning to Rome, the victorious Consuls were denied a triumphal entry, which Roman law and custom entitled them to, by the Senate, because they were the friends of the plebeians. Thereupon the plebs, in the Comitia Tributa, decreed a *triumph* to the Consuls in spite of the Senate, which was thus again forced to yield to the popular will.

A strong reaction now set in in favor of the aristocracy, who opposed the new laws with such vigor and determination that the plebs seceded a third time, seizing the Hill Janiculum, west of the Tiber and opposite Rome (B. C. 444). Again a compromise was effected, by which the plebs once more returned to Rome. Finally a law was passed legalizing marriages between patricians and plebeians, and providing that the children of such unions should inherit their father's rank. The plebeians were still excluded from the Consulate, and it was agreed to divide its powers and dignities among five officers—two *Censors* and three *Military Tribunes*. The Censors were to be chosen, for five years, only from the patricians, but by a free vote of the tribes in the Comitia Tributa; while the three Military Tribunes might be chosen from either the patricians or the plebeians for only one year.

The patricians did not at once relinquish their opposition to the interests of the plebeians. Under the pretense that the auspices were irregular, the aristocracy contrived to prevent the election of Military Tribunes for six years, choosing Consuls in their places as before; while Censors alone were regularly elected. For the first time Military Tribunes were chosen in B. C. 438, and the people only secured their election with great difficulty; but in the three following years Consuls were again chosen, the people's rights thus being utterly ignored, although conceded to them by law. An important law enacted through the efforts of Æmilius, the Dictator, in B. C. 433, limited the Censors' official term to eighteen months, thus leaving that office vacant most of the time, as the Censors were only elected once in five years.

The Censors were invested with truly royal splendor and extraordinary powers. They took a census of the citizens and their property once in five years, immediately after their election. After this general registration came a ceremonial purification of the people, called a *lustration*. For this reason each period of five years between the takings of two censuses was called a *lustrum*. The Censors were the guardians of the public morals, and their power extended to many matters that could scarcely be reached by the general operation of law. They were empowered to erase from the registry the name of any citizen they chose, with no other restriction on their action than their convictions of duty. They were expected to erase only the names of the unworthy, and they likewise were authorized to add the names of such as they believed deserved that honor. They were the sole judges of the evidence presented to them in such cases. The citizen who was tyrannical to his wife or children, or cruel to his slaves, or neglected his land, or wasted his fortune, or pursued a dishonorable occupation, was punished by being degraded from his rank, whatever that might be. If the citizen so offending was a Senator or a knight, he was deprived of his gold ring and his purple-striped tunic; if only a private citizen, he was expelled from the tribes and disfranchised. The Censor's powers were designed for the public good, but the abuse of these powers afterward was hurtful.

A period of tranquillity followed the changes just mentioned, until a famine occasioned fresh troubles to the state. Spurius Mælius, a wealthy merchant, for the purpose of ingratiating himself with the masses, purchased a quantity of corn in Etruria and distributed it among the poor of Rome. He thus acquired such wonderful popularity and influence that he aspired to the sovereign power, and planned a conspiracy to this effect among his followers, but the plot was discovered in due season to defeat its purpose. In this crisis of the Republic, the venerable Cincinnátus, then eighty years of age, was appointed Dictator for the third time. He ordered Spurius Mælius to appear before him; and when the latter disregarded this command, the Dictator sent an officer, who killed him on the spot. The house of Mælius was demolished, and all his property was bestowed on the poor.

The constant hostilities with the surrounding nations rendered it necessary for Rome to keep a standing army, which soon became an essential part of the Roman power, and also obliged the patricians to study the interests of the plebeians. It was now agreed to have the soldiers regularly paid out of the money raised by the collection of the rents for public lands. The number of Military Tribunes was increased from three to six. Their chief, the Præfect of the city, was a patrician, and was chosen by his order, but the other five were elected from either or both classes, by a free vote of the entire body of citizens in the Comitia Centuriata.

The Etruscan city of Veii had long been one of the most formidable enemies of the Roman Republic; and when the Veientians had murdered the Roman ambassadors and refused to give satisfaction for the outrage, the Romans resolved upon the subjugation of the hostile city. They accordingly laid siege to Veii in B. C. 402; but the place was so exceedingly strong both by nature and art that it was able to defy all the efforts of the Romans for ten years. During the summer of the seventh year of the siege there was a great drought, and the springs and rivers were almost dry. But suddenly the waters of the Alban Lake, located about twelve miles from Rome, embosomed in lofty hills, began to rise. They overflowed the banks of the lake and covered the fields and houses, till they reached the hill-tops, and, overflowing, poured down a torrent into the plains below. Seeing their fields and country-seats thus devastated, the Romans offered prayers to their gods, whom they endeavored to propitiate by sacrifices. But as these proved unavailing, they sent to Greece to consult the oracle of Apollo at Delphi. The people of Veii heard of this catastrophe; and one day an old Veientian was talking from the walls of the besieged city with a Roman sentinel. The latter boasted that his countrymen would soon capture the city, whereupon the old Veientian laughed, saying: "You will never take it till the Lake of Alba is empty." This answer produced much consternation among the Romans, as they considered the venerable Veientian a prophet. They enticed him out of the beleaguered city and held him as a captive. When closely questioned he declared that what he had said was written in the book of fate.

When the messengers sent to Delphi returned to Rome, they brought with them a response corresponding with the old Veientian's assertion. The Romans were now thoroughly convinced that their success was dependent upon the draining of the Alban Lake. Accordingly, they sent workmen, who excavated a tunnel through the rocky hills around the lake, thus emptying the lake of its superfluous waters. This remarkable work, a mile in length, can be seen at the present day. The Romans, now believing that the fates were on their side, appointed the patrician, Furius Camillus, Dictator, and pressed the siege of Veii more closely than ever. Camillus ordered a mine to be dug under the wall, into the very citadel of Veii. When these operations were completed, but before the farther end of the mine had been broken through, Camillus sent to Rome, directing all who desired to share in the plunder of Veii to repair to the army. When all was ready, and the besieged were wholly unaware of what was in progress underground, Camillus ordered a general assault upon the walls of the city, to divert attention from his stratagem. The King of Veii was then in the temple of Juno, in the citadel, offering a sacrifice for the deliverance of the city. When the soothsayer standing by him saw the animal killed, he cried: "This is an accepted offering, for victory is certain to him who lays the victim upon the altar." The Romans heard these words underground, and suddenly burst into the citadel, seized the sacrificial victim, and laid it upon the altar. Veii was thus taken, after a siege of ten years, and its inhabitants were reduced to slavery (B. C. 392).

Great rejoicings occurred at Rome in consequence of this great victory. Camillus entered the city in triumph, riding in a chariot drawn by four horses. Some men thought him too proud of his exploit, and predicted that his pride would have a fall. Camillus afterwards laid siege to the Etruscan city of Falerii. A Falerian schoolmaster, who had the care of the sons of the leading citizens of Falerii, embraced the opportunity, when he was walking with his boys outside the wall, to lead them into the Roman camp and deliver them into the hands of the besiegers. Indignant at this treacherous act, Camillus ordered the schoolmaster's hands to be tied behind his back, and then bade the boys flog him back to the city; as he said: "The Romans never make war upon children." Won by the generosity of Camillus, the Falerians surrendered at discretion.

On the very day of the capture of Veii by the Romans, it is said that the Gauls reduced the Etruscan stronghold of Melpum, in Northern Etruria. The loss of these two frontier fortresses was the commencement of the speedy decline of the Etruscan power. The Romans commemorated their joy by their long-continued custom of ending every festal game with a mock auction called the *Sale of Veientes.* The Romans also conquered Capéna, Népete and Sunium with their lands. Within half a century the Gauls conquered all the Etruscan possessions in Campania and north of the Apennines; while the Romans reduced all the Etruscan territories between the Ciminian forests and the Tiber. The Etruscan nation had already been weakened through excessive luxury; the nobles being very rich, while the masses were poor and enslaved.

Notwithstanding his signal achievements, Camillus soon experienced the ingratitude of his countrymen. He had incurred the hatred of the plebeians by his unequal distribution of the plunder of Veii when that city was taken, and various charges were now preferred against him. He was unwilling to subject himself to the ignominy of a public trial, and therefore he withdrew from Rome and retired into exile. It is said that, as he was passing out at the gate, he turned around and prayed to the gods that his countrymen might one day be made sensible of his innocence and their own ingratitude. This desire on his part was soon realized, as we shall presently see.

The Gauls were a branch of the great race known as Celts, or Kelts, who in ancient times inhabited all Western Europe, as embraced in the modern countries of Portugal, Spain, France, Belgium and the British Isles, or, in other words, all that part of Europe west of the North Sea, the Rhine and the Alps. They were at the time now referred to in a condition of utter barbarism, being but slightly acquainted with agriculture or commerce, and subsisting on the milk and flesh of their cattle. They were turbulent and brutal in their manners, and easily excited, but lacked energy and perseverance.

About the time of the last war between Rome and Veii, some unknown causes produced a migratory movement among the Gauls, who had occupied the whole territory of modern France, Belgium and Western Switzerland from the earliest times. Their country was called Gaul. One portion of the Gauls crossed the Alps about B. C. 400, and quickly made themselves masters of the whole plain of the Po; and in consequence of their conquest and occupation of this region Northern Italy was named Cisalpine Gaul, meaning Gaul this side of the Alps. They soon crossed the Apennines and overran Etruria, finally laying siege to Clusium, a city of Southern Etruria.

According to tradition, a Clusian citizen, named Aruns, was the cause of this Gallic invasion. Aruns had been the guardian of a Lucumo, or chief man of Clusium, and having suffered injury from him and being refused redress by the magistrates of the city, he resolved to have revenge on his country. Accordingly, he crossed the Alps into Gaul, taking with him a large quantity of the wines and fruits of Italy, conveying them on the backs of mules. Seeing that the barbarian Gauls were highly delighted with these presents, the injured Clusian invited them to go with him into Italy and take possession of the country which produced these delicacies, at the same time assuring them that the country could be easily conquered. Immediately an immense horde of Gauls, taking with them their women and children, crossed the Alps into Italy. Guided by Aruns, they marched to Clusium and laid siege to that city.

The Clusians applied to the Romans for aid, whereupon the Roman Senate sent three of the Fabian family as ambassadors to induce the Gauls to withdraw from Italy and not to molest the Clusians, who were allies of the Romans. The Gauls replied that they wanted land and that the Clusians must divide their territory with them. The Fabii, angry at the failure of their mission, entered Clusium and joined the Clusians in an attack on the besieging Gauls. By this act they degraded their sacred character as ambassadors, and violated the Roman law which forbade any citizen bearing arms against a foe before war had been formally declared and before he had taken the military oath. In a sally from Clusium, one of the Roman ambassadors killed a Gallic chief; and while he was stripping him of his armor, he was recognized by the Gauls. Brennus, the king of the Gauls, immediately sounded a retreat, and then selected his stoutest warriors and sent them to Rome, complaining of the violation of the laws of nations by the Roman ambassadors, and demanding that they be given up to justice. Most of the Roman Senators acknowledged the wrong, but were unwilling to deliver up men of noble birth to the vengeance of a barbarian foe. They therefore referred the matter to the Roman people, who instantly elected the offending ambassadors to the office of Military Tribunes, and then informed the Gallic envoys that nothing could be done with them until the expiration of their official terms. When Brennus received this reply from the Romans, he gave the word to his followers: "For Rome!" With seventy thousand of his followers, Brennus took up his march directly for Rome, threatening vengeance against the violators of international justice. The Gauls over-

SENATOR PAPIRIUS AND THE GAUL.

spread the plains, but did not molest the property of the husbandman, nor plunder the towns.

The Gauls crossed the Tiber and advanced to the banks of the little river Allia, eleven miles from Rome. The Roman legend states that the barbarians were prevented from surprising Rome by a supernatural warning to the Romans. This legend states that as a plebeian named Cædicius was passing along the foot of the Palatine Hill at night he heard a voice more than human from the neighboring grove of Vesta calling him by name. He turned to see who had spoken to him, but saw no one. He heard the voice a second time, ordering him to go to the magistrates in the morning and inform them that the Gauls were approaching. Upon the reception of this news at Rome, an army was quickly levied and led against the barbarian invaders on the Allia.

In the fatal battle of the Allia, which followed, the Romans had only forty thousand men to confront the seventy thousand Gauls on the opposite side of the Allia. The Roman left wing rested on the Tiber, while the right occupied some broken ground. Brennus attacked the Roman right wing and quickly routed it; whereupon the Roman left was panic-stricken at being out-flanked, and broke ranks, fleeing in dismay towards the river. The Gauls attacked the fugitives on all sides. Great numbers of Romans were slain; many were drowned; and the survivors, mostly without arms, fled in consternation to Veii. The survivors of the right wing fled across the hills to Rome, bringing the tidings of their dreadful defeat. Before night the Gallic cavalry appeared before the walls of the city, but made no attack. During the night and the next day the Gauls were occupied in plundering and rioting outside the walls of Rome, and alarming the inhabitants within the walls by singing and shouting.

The Roman defeat on the Allia rendered it impossible to defend the city; but about a thousand Romans under the valiant patrician Marcus Manlius garrisoned the Capitol, which they resolved to defend to the last extremity, with a supply of provisions; while most of the inhabitants fled for refuge to the neighboring towns, or dispersed themselves over the country. A part of the sacred objects used in worship were hidden under ground. The Vestal Virgins fled with the remaining portion to Cære. About eighty priests and patricians, resolving not to survive the ruin of their city, clothed themselves in their long robes of state, and having devoted themselves with solemn ceremonies to the cause of the Republic, they sat on their ivory seats in the Forum, awaiting death.

On the second day after the battle on the Allia the Gauls entered Rome, and, as a death-like silence prevailed and they at first saw no person, the city appeared deserted; but when they entered the Forum, they saw the walls of the Capitol covered with armed men, and the aged Senators seated in order in the space beneath, in profound silence and as immovable as statues. The barbarian invaders were struck with superstitious awe at the first sight of these venerable men, whom they imagined to be divinities. At length one of the Gauls rudely seized hold of the long white beard of Marcus Papirius, one of the Senators. The old man, incensed at this indignity, struck the insolent barbarian over the head with his ivory staff; but that blow was a costly one for Rome. The Gauls immediately massacred all the Senators, plundered the city and set it on fire. All Rome, with the exception of the Capitol and a few houses on the Palatine Hill, was totally reduced to ashes (B. C. 390).

The Gauls then summoned the garrison in the Capitol to surrender, but the garrison made a gallant defense. When Brennus found it impossible to capture the place by assault, he blockaded it closely, hoping thus to starve the garrison into a surrender. In the meantime some Etruscans, taking advantage of the unfortunate situation of the Romans, ravaged the Veientian territory, where the Roman peasantry had found refuge, with such property as they had been able to save. But the Romans at Veii attacked these marauders in the night and dispersed them. Having thus procured a supply of arms, which they so much needed, these Romans prepared to act against the Gauls. A brave Roman youth, named Pontius Cominius, swam on corks down the Tiber one night, eluded the vigilance of the Gauls, and clambered up the steep ascent of the Capitol. After giving the requisite information to the garrison, this daring youth returned by the way he came.

The next day the Gauls observed a bush on the side of the hill which had given way as Cominius had grasped it in climbing up. They also saw that the grass was trodden down in different places, thus showing that the rock was accessible, and they resolved to scale it. Accordingly, at midnight a select body of Gauls moved silently to the spot and began to climb the steep ascent, feeling their way slowly and cautiously. No noise was made. The Romans were sound in slumber, and their sentinels were negligent or sleepy. All proceeded successfully, and the foremost Gaul had just reached the top when the sacred geese in the Temple of Juno awoke and began to flap their wings and scream, thus awaking Marcus Manlius, whose house was near the spot. He ran to the edge of the cliff which the Gauls were ascending, and threw the foremost Gaul headlong down the cliff; and this one in his fall knocked down all the others. The garrison were now aroused, and they repelled the assailants.

The sentinel whose negligence had thus imperiled the Capitol and its garrison was thrown headlong down the rock with his hands tied behind him; and every man of the garrison gave Marcus Manlius half a pound of corn and a quarter of a flask of wine, as a reward for his vigilance. In memory of this occurrence, a goose was afterwards annually carried in triumph at Rome on a soft and finely-adorned litter.

After the siege and blockade of the Capitol had lasted seven months, famine began to prey upon the garrison. The valiant little band of Romans had already exhausted their store of provisions. In the meantime a pestilence broke out among the Gauls, in consequence of the non-burial of the bodies of the Romans whom they had massacred and whose decomposing bodies polluted the atmosphere in the summer heat, and the ranks of the besiegers were being rapidly reduced. Thus both parties, weary of the siege, came to an agreement; Brennus, the Gallic king, agreeing to retire from Rome and its territory on condition of receiving a thousand pounds of gold. When both parties had sanctioned this treaty, the Romans produced the gold; but in weighing it, the Gauls attempted to defraud them, and when the Romans complained of this, the Gallic leader threw his sword into the scale, exclaiming: "Woe to the vanquished!"

The Romans thus saw that they were at the mercy of the barbarians; but, says the Roman legend, while the dispute over the gold was in progress, the banished patrician Camillus arrived at the gates of the city with a large army for the relief of the garrison. He soon made his appearance among the contending parties, and inquired about the cause of the controversy. On ascertaining the condition of affairs, Camillus ordered the gold to be returned to the Capitol, saying: "It has ever been the custom with us Romans to ransom our country, not with gold, but with iron. I only am the man to make peace, as being the Dictator of Rome; and my sword alone shall purchase it."

Each side then again appealed to arms, and a battle was fought amid the ruins of Rome, in which the Gauls were defeated. A second Roman victory, on the Gabine road, annihilated the Gallic army. Camillus entered Rome in triumph, leading Brennus captive. This much dreaded barbarian leader was put to death, and the only response to his remonstrances was given in his own words: "Woe to the vanquished!"

Such is the account of the capture and deliverance of Rome, as generally current among the Roman historians. But there is reason to believe that the part relating to the raising of the siege and the withdrawal of the Gauls has been falsified by the national vanity of the Romans; as more impartial

ROME PLUNDERED BY THE GAULS.

and trustworthy sources inform us that the Gauls retired peacefully, carrying away with them the entire ransom of a thousand pounds of gold. The reason thus assigned for the withdrawal of the Gauls from Rome is that they were recalled to defend their new acquisitions in Northern Italy, or Cisalpine Gaul, against the Venetians.

The Gauls were followed some distance by Camillus, who had been recalled and again made Dictator. He cut off straggling parties of the enemy, and appears to have recovered some of the rich booty which the barbarians had carried away with them, but the stories of his great victories over them are fictions. The Gauls had not only crippled Rome, but had first crushed the Etruscans, thus relieving Rome from any danger from that nation, and had then extended their ravages to the Umbrians, the Sabines, the Latins, the Æqui and the Volsci, all of whom had suffered almost as much as Rome. The enemies of the Roman Republic were therefore not in a condition to profit by its momentary weakness.

The retreat of the Gauls from Rome was followed by a wide-spread and general distress. The farms, which furnished subsistence for so many of the Roman people, had been laid waste; their fruit-trees, buildings, implements, stock and stores, even the seed-corn required for the next year's sowing, had been burned.

The city of Rome was now a heap of ruins, in which the course of the former streets could no longer be traced, and the government did not take any measures to lay out others. The state's haste to rebuild the city was productive of great confusion. "Men built houses where they could, where the ground was most clear of rubbish, or where old materials were most easy to be got. Hence, when these houses came to be joined together by others so as to form streets, these streets were narrow and crooked, and, what was still worse, were often built across the lines of the ancient sewers, so that there was now no good and effectual drainage. This irregularity continued till Rome was again rebuilt after the great fire in the time of the Emperor Nero."

The government furnished roofing materials and allowed the people to take wood and stone from the public forests and quarries, on condition that every individual thus assisted would furnish security to complete his building within the year. But the pledges were frequently forfeited; and to defray the expense of rebuilding, as well as to pay the excessive taxes for restoring the fortress and the temples, the poor were again under the necessity of borrowing money at exorbitant rates of interest from the rich. Thus the poor were again at the mercy of the rich; and insolvent debtors were dragged from their homes, to toil as slaves in the shops or fields of their merciless creditors.

Many of the plebeians preferred to stay in the Etruscan towns in which they had found refuge, and even to remain at Veii, where they might live in freedom from the arrogant domination of the patricians, and form a privileged class themselves. A general secession of the plebeians to Veii was prevented by Camillus, who appealed to their patriotism, exhorting them not to abandon the spot which had been chosen by Romulus. While the subject was under deliberation, a fortunate omen induced most of them to remain and rebuild their city. Just as a Senator was rising to speak, a centurion, marching with his company to relieve guard, gave the usual word of command: "Halt! here is the best place to stay." The Senators exclaimed: "A happy omen! The Gods have spoken—we obey." The multitude were seized with the enthusiasm, and cried with one voice: "Rome forever!" Still so many plebeians remained at Veii that the population of Rome was greatly diminished, and a large mass of the conquered Etruscans were brought into Rome to supply the deficiency. The new settlers were furnished with Roman lands, were organized into four new tribes, and were invested with the full civil and political rights of Roman citizens. The "new people" constituted more than one-sixth of the entire population of the restored city.

MARCUS CURTIUS LEAPING INTO THE GULF.

THE REPUBLIC'S EARLY STRUGGLES.

The patrician Marcus Manlius—whose gallant defense of the Capitol against the besieging Gauls had acquired for him the surname of Capitolinus—espoused the cause of the oppressed plebeians and came forward as their champion. His aims were not wholly disinterested, as he felt deeply mortified at the elevation of Camillus, and himself aspired to be the foremost man in Rome. With his aims of individual aggrandizement, he sought to ingratiate himself with the plebeians. He sold the best portion of his own lands and employed the proceeds to the payment of the debts of the poor, thus delivering them from imprisonment and maltreatment. He thus won the unbounded gratitude of the plebeians, who constantly thronged his house, and to whom he denounced the selfish cruelty of the patricians, in relieving themselves of the whole burden of the public calamity by shifting that burden on the shoulders of the plebs. He even accused the patrician class of embezzling the vast sums raised to replace the treasures of the temples, which had been borrowed to bribe the Gauls into their retreat from Rome.

Marcus Manlius was cast into prison for making this charge, and the plebeians now began to look upon him as a martyr to their cause. After his release he denounced the patricians with his former vehemence. He fortified his house on the Capitoline Hill, and, supported by the plebeians, he held the whole height in defiance of the government. His treason was so manifest that even the Tribunes of the plebs united with the patricians against him, and the valiant defender of the Capitol was brought before the Comitia Centuriata for trial.

Manlius appeared, followed by several comrades whose lives had been saved by him in battle, and also by four hundred debtors whom he had rescued from their prisons. He exhibited the spoils of thirty foes whom he himself had slain, and forty crowns or other honorary rewards bestowed upon him by his generals. He appealed to the gods, whose temples he had saved from desecration, and bade the people to look at the Capitol, the scene of his greatest glory, ere they pronounced judgment against him. There was no possibility of convicting such an offender in such a presence, as the very spot on the Capitol where Manlius had stood single-handed against the besieging Gauls could be seen from the Forum. He was subsequently condemned for treason, and was thrown headlong from the Tarpeian Rock, the rocky cliff of the Capitoline Hill, facing the Tiber. Thus the spot which had been the scene of his glory became that of his punishment and infamy. His house, in which his plots had been carried on, and which had been built for him as a reward for his valor, was ordered to be razed to the ground, while his family were ever afterward forbidden to bear the name of Manlius.

Shortly after the execution of Marcus Manlius the plague broke out at Rome. The disaffected people ascribed it to the anger of the gods because of the destruction of the hero who had saved their temples from pollution. But the patricians, in consequence of their triumph over Manlius, and their steady opposition to the popular claims, had developed such strength that the plebeians became overawed and no longer exhibited the spirit and courage which they previously displayed in their struggles with the aristocracy.

The Romans submitted to the orders and requisitions of their priests with implicit obedience, even encountering death itself at their command, as illustrated in the case of Marcus Curtius. During an earthquake a great gulf opened in the Forum, and the augurs declared that it would not close until the most precious things in Rome were cast into it. Curtius arrayed himself in complete armor, mounted his horse, and boldly leaped into the yawning abyss, declaring that nothing was more truly precious than patriotism and military virtue. The Roman historians tell us that the gulf immediately closed upon him, and he was no more seen.

The rash attempt of Marcus Manlius to overthrow the power of the patricians only confirmed that power. The suffering continued increasing for seven years. The plebeians were hopelessly discouraged, and their old men would no longer accept public office. But in this crisis Rome was rescued from its miserable oligarchy by two remarkable men—Lucius Sextius Lateranus and Caius Licinius Stolo—Tribunes of the plebs. Licinius belonged to one of the oldest and wealthiest plebeian families, connected with the patrician class by many intermarriages. Having become Tribune along with his friend, Lucius Sextius Lateranus, in B. C. 376, Licinius proposed three laws for the relief of the plebeians from the general poverty which weighed them down so hopelessly, and from the political inequality under which they were suffering, and his measures are known as the *Licinian Laws*.

The first of these laws, designed to relieve immediate distress, provided that the enormous interest already paid upon debts should be reckoned as so much defrayed of the principal, and, therefore, should be deducted from the sum still due; and that the balance should only be paid in installments spread over a period of three years. The second law, intended to prevent future poverty, provided that the public lands, which the patricians had hitherto absorbed in great measure, should be thrown open equally to the plebeians; that no person should be allowed to hold more than five hundred *jugera* (about three hundred English acres) of the public lands, or pasture more than one hundred oxen or five hundred sheep upon the undivided portion; and that each landowner should employ a certain amount of free labor in the cultivation of his farm. The third law, a remedy for political inequality, restored the Consulate, with the provision that one of the Consuls for each year should be a plebeian; and to make the gain of the commons yet more secure, provision was made for increasing the keepers of the Sibylline Books to ten, five of them to be plebeians.

The patricians resisted the passage of the Licinian Laws for nine years, but these beneficent measures were formally accepted and ratified by the Senate and the Comitia Curiata in B. C. 367; while at the same time the office of *Prætor* was instituted and confined exclusively to the patricians, most of the civil and judicial functions hitherto exercised by the Consuls devolving thereafter upon this new office, but the Consuls retained the absolute military power. Upon the termination of the long struggle between the patricians and the plebeians, Camillus dedicated the newly-built Temple of Concord on the Capitoline Hill (B. C. 367). The first plebeian Consul under the Licinian Laws was Lucius Sextius Lateranus. In less than half a century both the Prætorship and the Dictatorship were opened to the plebeians.

The friends of the plebs had hoped that their rights had been fairly secured to them, but the patricians unlawfully ignored the Licinian constitution, and practically usurped the chief political power by managing for twenty years to elect patricians almost exclusively to the Consulate. In fourteen years of this period there were twenty-one patrician and seven plebeian Consuls. The plebeians very naturally considered themselves as defrauded of their rights. The patricians were fully aware that the plebeians might rise to claim their constitutional rights. They therefore sought to avert the threatened storm by making peace with all the neighboring nations, and thus avoiding the necessity of calling out the army; but their ambition could not always be so easily restrained, and when Rome became involved in a war with the Samnites the plebeians took advantage of the opportunity to claim their rights, as we shall presently see.

The restless and turbulent Gauls again invaded Latium, in B. C. 367, the year of the passage of the Licinian Laws. They were defeated by the aged general Camillus, who had been six times Military Tribune and five times Dictator. During their second invasion of Latium, the Gauls encamped within five miles of Rome, and struck consternation into the hearts of those who remembered the Gallic devastations thirty years before; but they at length broke up their camp without fighting and marched into Campania. While returning through Latium the barbarians were disastrously defeated. They encamped upon the Alban Mount during the winter of B. C. 350, and joined the Greek pirates on the coast in ravaging the country, until they were driven away by Lucius Furius Camillus, a son of the great general of that name.

In B. C. 346 the Gauls entered into a treaty with the Romans, and never again invaded Latium. They remained the dominant race between the Alps and the Northern Apennines, and along the Adriatic southward to Abruzzi. Mediolanum (now Milan) and many other towns were held by the Etruscans in a kind of independence, while the Gauls resided in unwalled villages. The Gauls learned letters and the arts of civilized life from their Etruscan subjects, and were the means of spreading this knowledge to all the hitherto-barbarous nations of the Alpine region.

SECTION VII.—SAMNITE WARS AND CONQUEST OF ITALY.

THE political struggles which developed the Roman constitution were followed by a series of foreign wars between Rome and her most powerful Italian rival, the Samnites being, for the supremacy of Southern Italy. The Samnites were a Sabine race, settled in the Oscan territory as conquerors. Their possessions were mainly inland, and embraced the snow-covered mountain range separating the Apulian plain from the Campanian, but they reached to the coast between Naples and Pæstum, where they included the once-celebrated cities of Herculaneum and Pompeii.

The Samnites ranked with the Latins as the most warlike races of Italy, but the Samnite conquests were far more brilliant and extensive at this period than were those of the Latins. While the Greek and Etruscan power was declining in Southern Italy, the Samnites became masters of the entire southern portion of the Italian peninsula, except a few Greek colonies like Tarentum and Neapolis (now Naples). Nevertheless, Latium, under the Roman leadership, had advanced slowly but surely, securing each advantage by the establishment of Roman colonies, united with the parent city by the strongest ties of obedience; while the Samnite nation was without any definite policy or any regularly constituted head. Each new settlement divided and weakened them.

After conquering Cumæ and Capua, the Samnites adopted the luxurious habits of the Greeks and the Etruscans, whom they had superseded, but with whom they still maintained cordial relations. The inhabitants along the shores who were very friendly toward the Greeks had a great dread of their rude countrymen of the mountains, almost as intense as had the cultured Hellenes themselves, thus furnishing the basis of a division in the Samnite race. The civilized and Hellenized Samnites sought the assistance of the Romans against the plundering hordes of their own race, who were constantly descending from the Samnian hills to devastate the fields. The Romans agreed to render the desired aid on condition that their supremacy should be acknowledged throughout Campania, thus breaking their former treaty with Samnium.

The wars between Rome and Samnium are known as the *Samnite Wars*, and there were three of these struggles. The First Samnite War opened when two Roman armies marched into Campania, while the Latin allies of the Romans invaded the territory of the Peligni on the north. The Roman arms were crowned with success, and both Consuls were honored with a triumph. At the request of the Campanians, the Romans left a large force to guard the cities of Campania during the winter. The plebeian soldiers were still suffering under the weight of poverty, and their protracted absence from their farms caused great distress among their families.

In the second year of the war the disaffection in the Roman army culminated in a mutiny of the plebeian soldiers, who now resolved to settle the long quarrel between their class and that of the patricians. . The two Consuls endeavored to disband the army gradually before the mutiny came to an open outbreak, but the army thwarted the execution of this purpose by rising in open rebellion at once and marching to Rome, where the mutinous troops formally demanded a redress of popular grievances. On the way they released all slaves for debt whom they found working in the fields of their creditors, formed a fortified camp on the slope of the Alban Hills, and were joined by a large number of the oppressed plebeians from the city.

The government hastily levied another army to oppose the mutinous troops, and placed it under the command of Valerius, who had been appointed Dictator in this emergency. The family of Valerius had always been the faithful friends of the commons, and Valerius himself was highly esteemed by all classes for his generous character, as well as for his military glory. When the two armies, which were both composed of plebeians, met each other, they refused to fight. The army under Valerius would not oppose their mutinous plebeian brethren, who had simply risen to right the wrongs of their class, and not from any disloyalty to their country; while the mutinous troops would not fight their fellow plebeians and the defenders of their common country. The two armies simply stood facing each other, until remorse on one side and pity on the other had overcome all mutual resentment between patricians and plebeians, when both rushed forward and grasped each other's hands or threw themselves into each other's arms with tears and requests for forgiveness. The Senate was thus unable to reduce the mutineers to submission, and was obliged to concede all just demands, along with an amnesty for the irregular and revolutionary proceedings of the mutinous troops; and this strange military rising ended in a permanent internal peace between the two orders in the Republic.

After long negotiations, Genucius, a Tribune of the plebs, secured the enactment of a series of laws which both classes accepted as the basis of a reconciliation. The Licinian Laws were practically restored, and the patricians were punished for their long disregard of them, by a provision that both Consuls could not be selected from the patrician order, while both might be plebeians. A law was likewise enacted that no plebeian should hold the same office twice within ten years, or two offices within one year. In order to relieve the general distress, all outstanding debts were canceled, and the taking of interest for money loaned was prohibited.

In the meantime, while these internal events occupied the attention of the Romans, the Latins had been left to carry on the war against the Samnites without Roman assistance. The Latins were so encouraged by their repeated successes over the Samnites that they declared their independence of Rome. The Romans therefore made peace with Samnium and entered into an alliance with the Marsian League, a confederation of Sabine towns (B. C. 341), and two years later turned their arms against the Latins, who had secured the alliance of their recent foes, the Campanians, the Sidicinians and the Volscians. The Samnites remained neutral in this struggle, known as the *Great Latin War*, which began B. C. 339.

The two Roman Consuls led their armies into Campania and encamped in the plain of Capua, opposite the combined army of the Latins and their allies. As the Romans and the Latins were so much alike in their language, dress, arms, etc., that it was difficult to distinguish friends from foes in an engagement, the Roman Consul Manlius gave stringent orders that no soldier in his army should leave his ranks; threatening punishment by death for any disobedience of this order. When both armies were drawn up in face of each other, ready for battle, Metius, the Latin general, pushed forward in front of his lines and challenged any Roman knight to meet him in single combat. There was a general pause for some time, no Roman daring to disobey orders, until Titus Manlius, the son of the Roman commander who had issued the order against any one in his army leaving his ranks, burning with humiliation at seeing the entire Roman army intimidated, boldly rode forward and faced the Latin challenger. The soldiers of both armies stood still to witness the personal combat. The two champions drove their horses against each other with a tremendous shock. Metius wounded his antagonist in the neck, but Titus Manlius killed his adversary's horse. The Latin general, thus thrown to the ground, endeavored for a while to support himself upon his shield; but his Roman opponent followed up his blows and laid Metius dead as he was attempting to rise.

Titus Manlius returned to his ranks in triumph, laying the spoils of his victory at his father's feet. The stern Roman Consul addressed his son in these words: "Titus Manlius, as thou hast regarded neither the dignity of the Consulate nor the commands of thy father—as thou hast destroyed military discipline and set an example of disobedience, thou hast reduced me to the deplorable extremity of sacrificing either my son or my country. Lictor, bind his hands, and let his death be an example to the Romans in the future." The whole Roman army was struck with astonishment at this cruel mandate, and stood in silent surprise. But when the young champion's head was struck off, and his blood was streaming on the ground, a scream of horror ran through the Roman ranks. The dead body of Titus Manlius was carried forth outside the camp amid the wailings of the Roman soldiery, and was buried with military honors. "Manlius, the father, was forever regarded with horror, but Manlius, the Consul and general, was strictly obeyed as long as he commanded the armies of Rome."

The decisive battle between the Romans and the Latins was fought at the foot of Mount Vesuvius. Just before the battle, the augurs, having taken the auspices as usual, declared that Fate demanded the sacrifice of a general on one side and an army on the other. It was accordingly understood among the Roman officers that whichever portion of the army should begin to give away, the Consul commanding in that quarter would devote himself as a sacrifice to the gods for his country, so that the Latin army might be the one that must perish. Manlius, the patrician Consul, led the right wing of the Roman army. Publius Decius, the plebeian Consul, was in command of the left. The battle commenced with great fury, and as the two armies had frequently marched under the same leaders, they fought with all the animosity of a civil war. Both armies fought with equal courage, but at length the Latin right wing prevailed, and the Roman left began to yield. Decius now perceived that the moment had arrived for him to devote himself to his country's cause. He therefore instantly called the chief pontiff, and bade him dictate the form of words in which he must devote himself to the gods and the grave; as he himself, as a plebeian, was unacquainted with the ceremonies by which the gods must be addressed. In accordance with the pontiff's direction, Decius wrapped his toga around his face, set his feet upon a javelin, and repeated the imprecation, which was in the following words: "Thou Janus, thou Jupiter, thou Mars our father, thou Quirinus, thou Bellona; ye Lares, ye the nine gods, ye the gods of our fathers' land, ye whose power disposes both of us and of our enemies, and ye also, gods of the dead, I pray you, I humbly beseech you * * * * * that ye would prosper the people of Rome and the Quirites with all might and victory, and that ye would visit the enemies of the people of Rome * * * * * with terror, dismay and death. And according to these words which I have now spoken, so do I now, on behalf of the commonwealth of the Roman people * * * * * on behalf of the army, both of the legions and the foreign aids * * * * * devote the legions and the foreign aids of our enemies, along with myself, to the gods of the dead and to the grave." It was considered an act of impiety to ask the gods for victory without making a sacrifice, as Nemesis avenged unmingled prosperity as well as crime.

Decius then sent his guard of twelve lictors to Manlius to announce his fate, armed himself and mounted his horse, plunged into the midst of the enemy, carrying confusion and terror into the Latin ranks, and finally fell covered with wounds. The Latins, struck with superstitious awe, began to give way, but fought with still greater obstinacy, like men struggling against fate. They were pressed on every side by the Romans and were finally utterly overthrown. The main forces of the two armies were so equally matched that Manlius won the victory finally by bringing on his poorer supernumeraries, whom he had armed to form a double reserve. The carnage was so great that almost three-fourths of the Latin army perished.

The Romans won a second victory over the Latins much more easily, and the Latins were too much exhausted to rally for a third battle. The Latin League was completely broken up, and Roman law was established throughout Latium and Campania. Some of the Latin cities even became Roman colonies. The Romans and the Latins being kindred in race and language, their transient hostility gave place to a close and permanent alliance. The battle of Mount Vesuvius was one of the most important in the history of Rome, because, by giving the sovereignty of Latium to Rome, it opened the way to the Roman conquest of the ancient world.

The Romans were unable to undertake any great foreign war for the next twelve years, in consequence of the invasion of Southern Italy in B. C. 332 by Alexander of Epirus, uncle of Alexander the Great. This Grecian invader had come to Italy to war with the Samnites. The Romans entered into a treaty with him, but they were also ready to take the field against him if he ventured to encroach upon their territories, as he would certainly have done had he conquered the Samnites. He was, however, defeated and slain in battle in B. C. 326.

Rome being now mistress of Latium and Campania, and having secured her northern frontier by a treaty with the Etruscans, felt herself sufficiently strong to attempt the conquest of Samnium, her only powerful rival for the dominion of Southern Italy. The second contest between Rome and Samnium—known as the *Second Samnite War*—began in B. C. 326 and continued twenty-two years (B. C. 326–304). The war was commenced by Roman aggressions upon the Samnite territory, and the real object of the Romans was the dominion of the entire Italian peninsula. Rome and Samnium fought as principals in the war for the sovereignty of Italy, and almost all the Italian nations were the allies on one side or the other.

The chief allies of the Samnites were the Lucanians and the Tarentines, who had become alarmed at the rising greatness of Rome. The Roman Senate, in this emergency, appointed Papirius Cursor Dictator. During the first five years of the war the advantage was generally on the side of the Romans, and their foes begged for a truce, which the Romans granted. The Samnites wreaked their anger at their ill success on their leader, Brutulus, whom they held responsible for the war. They accordingly resolved to deliver him up to the Romans, but the noble Samnite leader committed suicide to avoid this disgrace. Nevertheless his corpse was sent to Rome, the prisoners whom the Samnites had taken in battle were released and sent home, and gold was carried to Rome to ransom the Samnite captives. Nothing, however, could move the arrogance of the haughty Roman Senate, who were resolved to reduce the Samnites to complete subjection.

Rather than surrender their national independence, the Samnites determined to dare and endure everything. They placed Pontius, an able general, at the head of their army, and bade defiance to the Roman power. The Roman Consuls, Veturius and Postumius, at once led a large army into Samnium, B. C. 321. The crafty Pontius resorted to a well-contrived stratagem. He

SAMNITE WARS AND CONQUEST OF ITALY.

sent ten of his soldiers, disguised as shepherds, to throw themselves in the way of the Roman army. The Romans met these pretended shepherds and asked them what route the Samnite forces had taken, and were told indifferently that they had marched to Luceria, a town in Apulia, and were then actually besieging the town. Fully crediting this false intelligence, the Roman Consuls advanced boldly and incautiously with their combined forces, and near the town of Caudium, between Naples and Beneventum, they reached a narrow defile between two woody mountains, known as the *Caudine Forks*. The Romans entered this passage; but when the van of their army reached the farther end of the defile, they found their way obstructed by trunks of trees and rocks. They then faced to the right about, and endeavored to return by the way they came, but found the entrance closed in the same manner, and also observed the woods and hills occupied by the Samnite soldiery. To their utter consternation, the Romans perceived that they were caught in a trap, and were unable to advance or retreat.

The entrapped Roman army endeavored to fight its way out, and a most sanguinary struggle ensued, the Romans being utterly defeated in their efforts, and half their number being slain. The Samnite general, Pontius, seeing that he had the Roman army entirely in his power, forced the two Consuls to terms. The remainder of the Roman army were surrendered as prisoners, but were generously spared by Pontius on condition that an honorable peace should be signed by the two Consuls and the two Tribunes of the people who were present with the Roman army, and that the Roman troops should retire from the Samnite territory. The Roman army was thus obliged to submit to the ignominy of "passing under the yoke." This was done by setting up two spears, with a third across the top; under which every man of the Roman army passed, after being deprived of all his arms and clothes except a single garment. Disarmed, half-naked, and burning with shame at this humiliation, the discomfited Romans were then allowed to march away toward Rome; but Pontius retained six hundred Roman knights as hostages for the fulfillment of the treaty stipulations.

When the Romans reached home they found their countrymen overwhelmed with grief, indignation and humiliation. All business was suspended and a new army was instantly levied. The unfortunate Consuls resigned their offices, and new ones were elected. The soldiers who had just returned from their disastrous campaign slunk out of sight in their houses, or dispersed themselves over the country. The Roman Senate repudiated the treaty, and sent the two Consuls who had signed it, stripped and bound, to the Samnite general, that he might wreak his vengeance upon them for deceiving him. But Pontius, refusing to punish the innocent for the guilty, declined to receive the two Consuls, and vainly demanded that the treaty be faithfully observed, or that the whole Roman army which he had captured and released be restored to him again as prisoners. With unusual magnanimity, Pontius restored the six hundred hostages to their freedom.

Hostilities were accordingly renewed, and for six years the war went on without any event of much importance; but in B. C. 315, the Samnites gained another great victory at Lautulæ, in consequence of which the cause of Rome seemed so hopeless that almost all of her allies deserted her. Campania revolted against Rome, and the Ausonians and the Volscians entered into an alliance with Samnium. But the following year (B. C. 314), the tide of war turned in favor of the Romans, who, by an extraordinary effort, placed a large army in the field, and this army defeated the Samnites so disastrously in the decisive battle of Cinna that their power was crushed beyond all hope of recovery.

Notwithstanding this terrible Samnite defeat, the war continued ten years longer, in consequence of the efforts of the Etruscans, the Oscans and the Umbrians to preserve the balance of power in Italy by preventing the Romans from becoming supreme in the peninsula. But as these foes of Rome did not act in unison, the Romans were able to defeat their forces, one by one, until B. C. 304, when the Samnites were reduced to subjection to Rome, and all the nations engaged in the war made peace. Rome was now the first nation in Italy. The conquered Samnites were, however, far superior to their Roman conquerors in intellectual culture, as the former had been subject to the refining influences of Grecian civilization. Pontius, the Samnite general, was well versed in Greek philosophy, and far surpassed the proudest Romans of his time in the elevation of his character.

In the second year of the war the discontents of the Latins broke out into open hostilities. The Romans adopted a conciliatory policy, and the discontented portion of Latium was incorporated with Rome. To show that this was not merely a nominal union, the Romans elected Lucius Fulvius, the leader of the Latin rebels, Consul for the year. These wise measures thoroughly identified Latium with Rome, and put an end to the troubles between the Latins and the Romans.

Near the end of the Second Samnite War the Æqui, who had been for eighty years in a state of neutrality, took up arms against the Romans; and in B. C. 304, after the peace of that year between the Romans and the Samnites had left Rome free to act, the Roman Consuls marched at the head of forty thousand men into the Æquian territory. In a sharp and severe struggle of fifty days, the Romans captured and destroyed forty-one Æquian towns. A large portion of the captive Æquians were sold into slavery, and the remainder were made subject to the Roman authority. A few years later, however, they were clothed with the rights of Roman citizenship, were enrolled in the tribes, and served in the Roman ranks in the wars with the Samnites.

For six years after the close of the Second Samnite War the Samnites were busily engaged in organizing the *Italian League*, a confederation of Italian states, against Rome. In this league the Etruscans, the Umbrians and the Cisalpine Gauls in the North of Italy were allied with the Samnites, the Lucanians, the Apulians and most of the Greek cities of the South; all the allies being animated and united together by a common hatred and jealousy of the rising power of Rome. Rome had the advantage in wealth, in numbers and in compactness. Her own and her allies' territory extended across Italy from the Mediterranean to the Adriatic, thus dividing the states of her enemies.

In B. C. 298 the *Third Samnite War* began with the invasion of both Samnium on the south and Etruria on the north by Roman armies. The Romans defeated the Etruscans at Volaterra, and about the same time they captured Bovianum and Aufidena in the North of Samnium. The next year (B. C. 297) the Roman Consul Fabius defeated the Samnites; and Decius, the other Consul, defeated the Apulians and compelled Lucania to submit to the power of Rome. In B. C. 295 the combined forces of the Cisalpine Gauls, the Etruscans, the Umbrians and the Samnites advanced toward Rome. The boldness and sagacity of the Roman Consuls saved the Republic in this emergency. They retained one army at home to meet the invasion, and sent another into Etruria. This movement exposed the weakness of the league, as the Etruscans and the Umbrians, deserting their allies, recalled their forces to defend their own territories. The Samnites and the Cisalpine Gauls then retreated across the Apennines to Sentinum, where they were overtaken and attacked by the Second Roman army, which had closely pursued them. A sanguinary conflict ensued, in which the Gallic war-chariots had almost driven the Roman legions under the Consul Decius from the field; but Decius, imitating the example of his father, Publius Decius, in the battle of Vesuvius, solemnly devoted himself to the powers of death for the deliverance of his country. The Roman legions finally won the victory, and twenty-five thousand of their enemies lay dead upon the bloody field (B. C. 295).

The battle of Sentinum really decided the

war, as it dissolved the league against Rome. The Cisalpine Gauls retired to their own country in Northern Italy, and took no further part in the struggle. Rome now prosecuted the war separately in Etruria and Samnium. The Samnites resisted bravely and obstinately; and in B. C. 292, twenty-eight years after his great victory at the Caudine Forks, the venerable Samnite general, Pontius, defeated the Roman army under the Consul Fabius Gurges. The Romans had been confident of victory, and were so exasperated by this defeat that they would have deprived Fabius of his command had not his aged father, Fabius Maximus, offered to serve as his lieutenant.

The next year (B. C. 291) the Romans gained a great victory, breaking the power of the Samnites and taking Pontius prisoner. The aged Samnite general was made to walk, loaded with chains, in the triumph of the victorious Roman Consul. When the triumphal procession reached the ascent to the Capitol, Pontius was led aside and beheaded in the Mamertine prison. This was the ungrateful treatment which the Roman Senate meted out to the Samnite general who thirty years before had magnanimously spared the lives and liberties of two Roman armies, and even released the Roman Consuls who had been given over to his vengeance. This base conduct toward a gallant foe has been called the greatest blemish in the annals of Rome. The Third Samnite War ended with the unconditional submission of Samnium to the power of Rome. A part of the Samnite territory was annexed to Rome, and Samnium became a subject ally of the great military Republic. The Romans established a colony of twenty-five thousand people at Venusia, to hold the conquered territory in awe (B. C. 290).

In the same year (B. C. 290), the Roman Consul Curius Dentatus began and ended another war with the Sabines, who had espoused the cause of their kinsmen, the Samnites. The Sabines were subdued, and their extensive country, rich in oil, wine, and forests of oak, came into the possession of Rome.

Notwithstanding the success of the Romans in these wars, the plebeians suffered greatly from the burdens occasioned thereby. Their farms had been neglected during their absence with the army, thus bringing the agricultural population to the verge of ruin; while those who were so unfortunate as to have been taken prisoners had to be ransomed at ruinous sacrifices by their relatives.

Curius Dentatus, the conqueror of the Sabines, sought to relieve the general distress by proposing a second agrarian law for the division of the Sabine lands among the poor. The patricians opposed this measure so bitterly that the life of Curius Dentatus was in extreme peril, notwithstanding his great services. As the aristocratic opposition increased, the popular demands rose higher, and finally the plebeians again seceded from Rome and established themselves on Mount Janiculum. The patricians even then refused to yield, until a threatened foreign invasion obliged the Senate to grant the demands of the plebs, and to appoint Hortensius, a plebeian of ancient family, Dictator. His wise and conciliatory counsels restored internal tranquillity to the Republic. He convened all the Roman people in a grove of oaks outside the city walls, and proposed the famous *Hortensian Laws*, which were ratified by solemn oaths by the vote of the entire assembled people (B. C. 286). The Hortensian Laws either abolished or largely reduced all outstanding debts, allotted seven *jugera* (almost four and a half English acres) of land to every citizen, deprived the Senate of its veto, and declared the Roman people assembled in the Comitia Tributa to be the supreme legislative power in the Republic. Thus ended the civil strife of Rome for a century and a half.

No sooner was this internal trouble ended than a new external danger menaced Rome. The Romans had rewarded the Lucanians for their services by ceding to them the Greek cities in their territory; but when the Lucanians, in alliance with the Bruttians, endeavored to reduce these cities, the inhabitants of Thurium appealed to Rome for protection. The Romans granted the request of the Thurians, forbidding the Lucanians and the Bruttians to secure the spoil promised them. The inhabitants of the Greek city of Tarentum had long been jealous of the Roman power, and had been for some time engaged in organizing a new and powerful coalition against the Republic. The Tarentines took full advantage of the anger of the Lucanians and the Bruttians at being deprived of their prey, to induce them to join an alliance with themselves, and succeeded. The Tarentines also induced nearly every nation of Italy to join the league against Rome; and in B. C. 283 the storm gathered simultaneously and swiftly from all quarters; the Romans being thus threatened by the Samnites, the Lucanians and the Bruttians from the south, and by the Etruscans, the Umbrians and the Cisalpine Gauls from the north.

Arretium remained faithful to its alliance with Rome, and was besieged by an army of Etruscans and Gauls. The Roman Consul Metellus marched to the relief of the besieged Arretians, but was defeated with the loss of his entire army. Roman ambassadors who were sent to remonstrate with the Senonian Gauls for their violation of their treaty with Rome were murdered, and their bodies were hewn to pieces and cast out without burial. This atrocious outrage, which the laws of even the rudest savages pronounced sacrilege, provoked a speedy and terrible vengeance from the Romans. The Roman Consul Dollabella led an army into the Gallic territory, and ravaged the country frightfully with fire and sword, reducing every village to ashes, massacring all the men, and carrying all the women and children into slavery; thus literally extinguishing this Gallic tribe.

The Bonian Gauls, alarmed and exasperated by the fate of their kinsmen, now took the field to avenge them, and joined their forces to those of the Etruscans. Their united armies marched immediately toward Rome, but were defeated by the Romans with frightful loss at their passage of the Tiber, near the little Lake Vadimo, very few escaping from the field.

In the South of Italy the Roman army had maintained itself in Thurium with great difficulty. In B. C. 282 the Roman Consul Gaius Fabricius Luscinus compelled the Lucanians to raise the siege of that city and defeated them in an important battle, after which he gained several victories over the Samnites and the Bruttians; thus breaking up the coalition against the Romans in the South, and collecting so large an amount of spoil as to enable him to defray all the expenses of the war for the year, besides allowing every one of his soldiers a liberal share, and leaving in the Roman treasury a surplus equal to half a million dollars of our money.

Tarentum, which had instigated the war against Rome, had never taken any part therein, but had managed to throw all its burdens and losses upon her allies. To punish Tarentum for her passive but mischievous policy, a Roman fleet was sent to cruise around the eastern and southern coasts of Italy to watch the Tarentines. In sailing to the Adriatic this fleet anchored in the harbor of Tarentum, which was still nominally at peace with Rome. The Tarentines were unable to longer restrain their pent-up hostility, and they proceeded in a mob to the harbor, attacked the Romans, who did not suspect any danger, and sunk their whole fleet. The Tarentines then marched to Thurium, expelled the Roman garrison, and severely punished the Thurians because they had submitted to the Roman power. With remarkable moderation, the Romans offered to abstain from hostilities with Tarentum on condition that the Tarentines should release all the prisoners which they had taken, that they should restore Thurium, and surrender all those who had instigated the attack upon the Roman fleet. The Tarentines haughtily rejected these terms, and, in behalf of all the Greek cities of Italy, they solicited the aid of Pyrrhus, King of Epirus, the greatest general of his time, and one of the greatest of ancient times Pyrrhus, whose restless ambition never allowed him to remain quiet, and who had long desired a pretext for meddling in the affairs of Italy, gladly granted the request of the Tarentines; and in B. C. 280 he crossed the Adriatic and invaded Southern Italy with an army of twenty-two thousand five hundred infantry, three thousand cavalry, and twenty elephants—the first of those animals ever seen in Italy.

Pyrrhus had already won and lost the crown of Macedon for the first time. His army was drilled and equipped in the Macedonian style, and his personal character surpassed that of any other monarch then reigning. "He was the first Greek that met the Romans in battle. With him began those direct relations between Rome and Hellas, on which the whole subsequent development of ancient, and an essential part of modern, civilization are based. The struggle between phalanxes and cohorts, between a mercenary army and a militia, between military monarch and senatorial government, between individual talent and national vigor—this struggle was first fought out in the battles between Pyrrhus and the Roman generals; and though the defeated party often afterwards appealed anew to the arbitration of arms, every succeeding day of battle simply confirmed the decision."

The gay and self-indulgent Tarentines had supposed that the King of Epirus would fight their battles for them and leave them to enjoy the ease which they had secured during the first part of the war, and forget their promises to furnish him troops and subsidies; but Pyrrhus soon gave them to understand that they had found in him a master instead of a servant. He stopped the sports of the circus and the theater, and the banquets of the clubs, and compelled the citizens to keep under arms from morning till night to perform garrison duty. They soon became disgusted, and sought peace with Rome, but Pyrrhus fastened his grip upon them more tightly and treated Tarentum as a conquered city, sending a number of the chief citizens to Epirus as hostages.

After securing the city of Tarentum, thus providing himself with an excellent base of operations, Pyrrhus took the field against the Romans, who did all that prudence might suggest, to meet this formidable foe. The Consul Lævinus was sent with a large army to Southern Italy. Pyrrhus sent an ambassador, desiring to mediate between the Romans and the Tarentines; but Lævinus replied that he neither esteemed him as a friend nor feared him as an enemy. The two armies now advanced and soon came in sight of each other at Heracléa, on the banks of the little river Liris. Pyrrhus saw that his own force was inferior to the Roman army in numbers, and as he viewed the Roman camp he remarked that the "barbarians" appeared to display nothing of the barbarous character in their tactics. At that time the Greeks were accustomed to designate as "barbarians" all other nations but themselves.

The object of Pyrrhus was to prevent the Romans from crossing the river; but their cavalry out-maneuvered him and gained a ford higher up, thus enabling their entire army to cross the stream. Pyrrhus then led his Thessalian cavalry against the Romans, who stood their ground firmly. He next advanced with his infantry. Seven times were the troops of Pyrrhus driven from the field, and seven times did they regain it. Finally Pyrrhus brought his elephants into action, and the sight of these strange animals struck terror among the Romans, frightening their horses and their men alike, and thus breaking their ranks. The Thessalian cavalry then charged and scattered the Romans, and their rout became general. The miserable remnant of the Roman army fled to Venusia, leaving Pyrrhus complete master of the field (B. C. 280).

While viewing the sanguinary field the next day, Pyrrhus exclaimed: "Had I such soldiers as the Romans, the world would be mine; or had they such a general as I, the world would be theirs!" He ordered the bodies of the dead Romans to be burned and buried like those of his own men. Not a man of the Roman army would have escaped had not a Roman officer wounded an elephant and thus thrown the pursuing forces of Pyrrhus into confusion. The Romans altogether lost fifteen thousand men, of whom seven thousand were killed. Pyrrhus, however, bought his victory dearly, as four thousand of his best troops and several of his best officers were slain, and he did not have the advantage possessed by the Romans of being able to replace the slain. Pyrrhus had thus proven his great military ability, and he now proceeded to reap the fruits of his victory.

Many Italian cities now entered into an alliance with Pyrrhus, and nearly every one of the Greek cities joined him in the war. Some of these new allies of the Epirote king had been subjects or friends of Rome. He had endeavored to recruit his army from the prisoners he had taken in battle, and whose valor he had recognized by his generous treatment of them. He explained to them that this was a practice somewhat prevalent among the Greeks; but he was completely surprised that not a solitary Latin or Roman captive joined him. He "learned that he was fighting not with mercenaries, but with a nation." He seems to have been deeply impressed with this conviction, and with the difficulty of the enterprise which he had undertaken.

Pyrrhus therefore dropped the role of warrior and sought to achieve his object by the exercise of the astute diplomacy of which he was master. He hoped that the Romans would be so thoroughly dispirited by their first reverse that they would be disposed to accept an honorable peace; and he endeavored to secure the independence of the Greek cities of Italy, and to protect that independence by forming between them a series of states of the second and third class as independent allies of the new Greek power. In other words, he demanded, as the conditions of peace, the liberation of all the Greek towns—and, therefore, of the Campanian and Lucanian towns especially—from their subjection to Rome, and the restitution of the territory taken from the Samnites, the Daunians, the Lucanians and the Bruttians.

Pyrrhus sent his peace proposals to Rome through his friend and minister Cineas, the Thessalian orator. This person was so skillful a negotiator that Phyrrus often said that he had won more victories by the eloquence of Cineas than by the swords of his soldiers. Cineas performed his task with consummate skill, and, by improving every opportunity of impressing the Romans with his admiration for their military bravery, he induced many to listen to his proposals of "peace, friendship and alliance." At this juncture Appius Claudius—who had been Censor thirty years before, and who was now a blind old man—was informed in his house of the mission of Cineas, and of his success in inducing the Senate to make peace with a victorious foe still upon the soil of Italy. Filled with patriotic indignation at the very thought of such a proposal, the blind old man caused his attendants to convey him in a litter into the Senate-House, where he gave vent to such an outburst of eloquent and indignant denunciations of the proposals of the King of Epirus that the Senate rose to its true dignity, and answered Cineas that Rome would never consent to a peace so long as a foreign army remained on the soil of Italy. The Senate also voted that Cineas should leave the city that day. When Cineas returned to the camp of Pyrrhus, he informed his master that Rome looked like a great temple, and the Senate like an assembly of kings.

The war then went on; Pyrrhus fighting for glory, and the Romans for existence. It was a struggle between the genius of Pyrrhus and the unconquerable will of the Romans. While the peace negotiations were in progress, Pyrrhus had moved into Campania. When he received the Roman Senate's answer to his peace proposals, he marched towards Rome, with the design of acting in concert with the Etruscans. He was greatly surprised when he found the Roman Consul Publius Lævinus with a fresh army prepared to resist him. The Roman commander protected Capua against the Epirote king, and thwarted his efforts to open communication with Neapolis. Rome's attitude was so firm that none of her important allies, except the Greek cities of Southern Italy, ventured to desert her. Pyrrhus encountered no army on his march toward Rome, but all the Latin cities closed their gates against him. He was astonished at the flourishing condition of the country, and he obtained a better knowledge of the resources of Rome than he had at any time before.

One Roman army under the Consul Lævinus followed Pyrrhus closely, watching for a favorable moment to attack him; and another Roman army under the Consul Tiberius Cornucanius, who had just made a treaty of peace with the Etruscans, hastened from the north to oppose the Epirote king; while a third army was organizing in Rome itself. After advancing to within forty miles of Rome, Pyrrhus retreated back to Tarentum, and there went into winter-quarters. The Romans likewise returned into winter-quarters.

During the winter an embassy was sent from Rome to negotiate with Pyrrhus for an exchange of prisoners. At the head of this embassy was Fabricius, a Roman Senator, who had long been a model to his countrymen for his contentment amid poverty. Pyrrhus received the embassy very kindly, and offered the venerable Senator costly gifts, in order to test his integrity; but Fabricius was proof against such temptation. The next day Pyrrhus ordered one of his largest elephants to be placed behind a curtain, which was drawn at a signal, and discovered the animal raising his trunk over the old Senator's head in a threatening manner. Fabricius stood unterrified, and then turning to the Epirote king, said: "Neither your gold yesterday nor your big beast to-day can move *me*." Pyrrhus was highly pleased to discover so much integrity and firmness in a "barbarian." Pyrrhus, however, refused to consent to an exchange of prisoners, but generously allowed all his captives to return to Rome to take part in the winter holidays—the Saturnalia—on their simple word of honor to return to captivity after the holidays if the Roman Senate refused to make peace. The Senate refused, and every man returned, according to his promise.

In his second campaign (B. C. 279), Pyrrhus gained a second brilliant victory over the Romans and their allies at Asculum, in Apulia. Besides his Greek troops, Pyrrhus brought more than fifty-thousand Italian allies into the field. The Romans, after a desperate resistance, were forced to give way, leaving six thousand dead upon the field. Pyrrhus, however, had himself suffered such loss in this engagement that he is said to have exclaimed: "Another such victory, and I am undone!"

The next year (B. C. 278), while the two armies were preparing for a third great battle, a letter was brought to Fabricius, the honest Roman Senator, from the physician of Pyrrhus, offering, for a large bribe, to poison the King of Epirus. The honest old Roman was fired with genuine indignation at this treacherous proposal, and he immediately proposed in the Senate that Pyrrhus should be informed of the base conduct of his physician, which was accordingly done. When Pyrrhus received the message, he exclaimed, in amazement at the magnanimity of his enemies: "Admirable Fabricius, it would be as easy to turn the sun from his course as thee from the path of honor!" In gratitude for the noble conduct of Fabricius and the Roman Senate, Pyrrhus immediately sent Cineas to Rome with his thanks, and at once released all the Romans whom he had taken prisoners, and sent them home rich with presents.

The Romans, nevertheless, still firmly refused to make peace unless Pyrrhus would retire from Italy. It was very evident to Pyrrhus that every victory which he might gain would diminish his forces, while the Romans would constantly be able to recruit their armies with fresh levies; so that the more victories he would gain, the weaker he would finally become. The courage and patience of the Romans were obstacles which he would be utterly unable to overcome. The Samnites were his only Italian allies who were of any use to him, and he despised all the others. Yet his military honor would not permit him to abandon the contest until a favorable opportunity presented itself as a pretext to withdraw from

Italy, but his utter disgust for the results of the war induced him to embrace that much desired opportunity when it arrived.

The wife of Pyrrhus was the daughter of Agáthocles, the tyrant of Syracuse, and his son was the grandson of Agáthocles, both being thus the natural heirs of that monarch. Agáthocles was murdered, and Syracuse was hard pressed by the Carthaginians, wherefore the Syracusans solicited the aid of Pyrrhus. They reasoned that if Syracuse must lose her independence, she might, under the King of Epirus, become the capital of a great Hellenic empire in the West. Pyrrhus willingly granted the request of the Syracusans, and withdrew from Italy in B. C. 278, leaving garrisons in Locri and Tarentum, and landed with his army in Sicily.

Before Pyrrhus arrived in Sicily the Carthaginians had concluded an offensive and defensive alliance with the Roman Republic; and just before he retired from Italy, Pyrrhus made another unsuccessful effort to obtain a peace with Rome. After landing in Sicily, he drove all before him for a time, capturing the strong town of Eryx, where he himself was the first to mount the scaling-ladders. He reduced the Carthaginians to such extremities that they offered to make peace, notwithstanding their alliance with the Romans, offering to furnish him the ships and the money which he so much needed. Pyrrhus haughtily rejected their offer, but his victorious career was terminated by his disastrous defeat at Lilybæum. He remained in Sicily about two years, and at one time he seemed to be on a fair way to succeed in his plans; but his old restlessness and the complaints of his Italian allies, who accused him of deserting them, caused him to indiscreetly return to Italy near the end of B. C. 276.

His fleet was pursued and defeated by the Carthaginian fleet with the loss of seventy ships, and his Sicilian conquests were at once lost by rebellion. On landing in Italy he defeated a body of Mamertines who had crossed the straits from Sicily, but was himself defeated in an attempt to take Rhegium. He, however, seized Locri, which had massacred his Epirote garrison during his absence in Sicily. He severely chastised the inhabitants of that city, and plundered the rich treasury of the temple of Proserpine to replenish his own exhausted military chest. He then marched to Tarentum, and when he arrived there he had twenty thousand infantry and three thousand cavalry. These were chiefly Italian mercenaries, who would only serve as long as they were sure of pay and plunder; his experienced Epirote veterans having all perished in his wars. The money taken from the Locrian temple was sent to Tarentum in a ship, which was driven back by a storm upon the coast of Locri. Believing that he had incurred the vengeance of the goddess Proserpine by his sacrilege, Pyrrhus restored the treasure to the temple, and put to death those who had instigated him to perpetrate the deed.

The Roman army under the Consul Curius Dentatus was encamped near Beneventum in a strong position on a height, where he intended to await the arrival of the other Consul, Lentulus. Pyrrhus had intended to attack the Roman army at daybreak, but was terrified by a dream, so that he desired to abandon the project. His officers represented the impolicy of allowing the two Roman armies to unite, and he accordingly ordered an attack. In order to reach the heights in the rear of the Roman camp, the troops of Pyrrhus were obliged to march by a circuitous route through a dense forest, by torchlight. They lost their way in the wood, their torches burned out, and they did not reach the spot where they were to assail the Romans until broad daylight.

In the battle which followed, the troops of Pyrrhus, exhausted by their long march, were unable to stand against the fresh Romans. The Consul Curius Dentatus descended into the plain to engage the main army and routed one wing, but before the other wing the Romans were driven back to their camp by the elephants. There, however, the tide of victory was turned in favor of the Romans. Having discovered that nothing terrified the elephants so much as fire, the Romans had provided an abundance of arrows headed with tow, and balls compounded of tar, wax and rosin. These were showered in a blaze upon the huge animals, so that they turned affrighted upon their own ranks and threw them all into disorder. The rout was complete, and the camp of Pyrrhus was taken (B. C. 275).

The Romans profited by the lesson of this victory, and were ever on the watch for improvement. They had previously pitched their tents without order, but this new venture taught them to measure out the ground and fortify the whole of it with a trench, so that many of their subsequent victories are attributable to their improved method of encamping. Pyrrhus now utterly despaired of being able to withstand the Romans, wherefore he abandoned the war in Italy and returned to Epirus, leaving a garrison in Tarentum (B. C. 275).

During the first invasion of Italy by Pyrrhus, the Eighth Legion, stationed at Rhegium, and chiefly composed of Campanian mercenaries, had thrown off their allegiance, as the Mamertines had done in Sicily, massacred the Greek inhabitants, and held the town as an independent military post. They were now reduced to submission, and most of the garrison were put to the sword; the remainder, consisting of the original soldiers of the legion, being tried at Rome, were scourged and beheaded.

The Romans quickly established their supremacy over both Central and Southern Italy. In Southern Italy they took Tarentum, the original cause of the war, and forced Lucania and Bruttium to submit, in B. C. 272; took Rhegium by storm, in B. C. 270; and conquered all Southern Italy by the end of B. C. 265. In Central Italy they conquered Picenum, and forcibly removed half the inhabitants to the shores of the Gulf of Salerno; reduced Umbria in B. C. 266, and then the chief cities of Etruria. Rome was now supreme mistress of the Italian peninsula from the Macra and the Rubicon on the north to Tarentum and Rhegium on the south.

Hitherto the Romans, like the Spartans, had prided themselves upon the simplicity and homeliness of their manners. When the Samnites sent envoys to Marcus Curius to induce him to use his influence with the Senate and offer him a gift of gold, they found the ex-Consul seated by his fire roasting turnips in the ashes, with a wooden platter before him. He replied respecting their proffered gift thus: "I count it my glory not to possess gold myself, but to have power over those who do."

The eleven years succeeding the departure of Pyrrhus from Italy were a period of the greatest prosperity which the commons of Rome ever enjoyed, and the wealth resulting from the conquest of Italy materially changed the Roman style of living. Every Roman freeman received from the Senate a sum of money, or a fresh grant of seven *jugera* (about four and a half English acres) of land. The state property of the conquered nations went to the Roman state, which thus came into the possession of valuable forests, mines, quarries, fisheries and public lands. A largely-increased number of officials was required for the administration of the public revenues, and rich and poor alike profited by the results of the war.

Rome planted her new territories with colonies, for the purpose of securing them permanently. This system is said to have been commenced as early as the times of the Tarquins, but it now received a powerful impetus by the rapid development of the Roman power. Several centuries after this period the Roman colonies extended from the Atlantic coast on the west to the river Euphrates on the east. These colonies were of two kinds—*Roman* and *Latin*. The most favored of the colonies were those of *Roman citizens*, in which the inhabitants retained all their rights as citizens of Rome, voting in the public assemblies, and being eligible to any public office to which they could be chosen if residents of Rome. The colonies with a *Latin franchise* were those in which the inhabitants lost their rights as citizens of Rome, the right of voting and of holding office, but retained the remainder of their citizenship. The colonies were planted thickly throughout the Italian peninsula; and their interests being more nearly related with Rome than with the country in which they were settled, they constituted the great bulwarks of Roman power in Italy.

The Roman colonies were connected with the city of Rome itself by a system of roads, the first of which was the celebrated *Appian Way*, which, when completed, was three hundred and sixty miles long, extending from Rome to Brundusium. It was paved the entire distance with square blocks of stone, and was of such durable construction that much of it remains to the present day. It left Rome by the Porta Capena, or Gate of Capua, passing through Aricia, Velitræ, Setia, Tarracína, Minturnæ, Sinuessa and Casilinum, and first terminating at Capua, from which it was continued to Venusia about B. C. 291, and afterwards to Brundusium. It was constructed at the instance of Appius Claudius "the Blind" as far as Capua, between the years B. C. 310 and B. C. 306, during his term of office as Censor; hence its name, the Appian Way. Other roads afterwards constructed connected every portion of Italy, and united all parts of that country with Rome as a common center. Wherever Rome extended her power, a well-built road was constructed with some center from which communication could be maintained with Rome; wherefore it was commonly said that "All roads lead to Rome." The great aqueducts to supply the city of Rome with water—whose extensive and durable remains strike the eye of the modern traveler with wonder—were also begun by Appius Claudius "the Blind."

The system by which the Romans maintained their authority over the conquered states of Italy was exceedingly complex. Rome granted her colonies the right of self-government. These colonies elected their own officers and administered their own internal affairs. Every foreign city under the dominion of Rome was considered a separate state, being placed on a certain definite footing in relation to the central community. The most highly favored of these cities were those known as the *fœderatæ civitates*, which were states that had submitted to Rome upon conditions, varying in different cases, but in all cases implying the exclusive management of their own domestic concerns, the appointment of their own governors, and the administration of their own laws. The next to these in the advantage of position were the *muncipia*, foreign states which had received some or all of the rights of Roman citizenship, along with all of its burdens. Lastly were the *dediticii*, who were natives of communities which had surrendered themselves to Rome absolutely, and which had all of the burdens, and none of the rights, of Roman citizens. Rome appointed a governor to administer Roman law in these communities.

Rome reserved to herself certain rights which she considered sufficient to protect her sovereignty. She retained the sole power to make war or peace. She only might receive embassies from foreign powers, conclude treaties or coin money. She likewise claimed and exercised the right to demand of her subject allies such troops, and the money to equip and support them, as she needed in time of war. As has already been noticed, the property of the conquered states passed to her. By B. C. 267 the public domain had increased so largely that it was found necessary to appoint four *Italian Quæstors* to collect the revenue therefrom. These Italian Quæstors were the first Roman functionaries who had a residence and a district outside of Rome assigned to them by law.

During this period the last vestiges of patrician supremacy received their deathblow, and the plebeians were admitted to complete political equality with the aristocracy. In B. C. 339 a law proposed by Pullilius Philo had admitted the plebeians to one place in the Censorship and also to the Prætorship. A law proposed by Ovinius—of uncertain date—conferred upon all ex-Consuls, Prætors and Curule Ædiles the right to sit in the Senate. In B. C. 300 the Ogulnian Law increased the number of pontiffs and augurs, and provided that half of each should be plebeians. These changes were in full operation at this period and exerted a marked influence upon the prosperity of the Roman people, who, united and contented at home, were in a position to present a solid front to Pyrrhus, and finally to triumph over him, and to extend their dominion and supremacy over all Italy. The Censors were actually obliged to exert their efforts to check the power of the commons. About B. C. 312 Appius Claudius "the Blind" had extended the right of suffrage—which had previously depended upon the double qualification of free birth and the ownership of a tract of freehold land—to freedmen and non-landowners. These two numerous classes were thus enrolled among the tribes as voters; and instead of assigning them to the tribes of the city, where they belonged almost exclusively, Appius Claudius distributed them through all or nearly all the tribes, so that they might be able to control elections. To rescue Rome from the threatened danger of mob rule, the successors of Appius Claudius in the Censorship confined these new voters to the city of Rome itself, thus giving them the control only of four tribes out of thirty-one, and so averting the danger which had menaced the state. This matter had been arranged by the first years of the third century before Christ. In this century also the Romans first used a silver currency, their coins having previously been copper.

Thus now for the first time this powerful ancient state was changed from an aristocratic republic to a pure democracy; so that Rome had now become truly a government of the people, by the people and for the people.

Something like literature and oratory began to make its appearance at this early time. Brief dry chronicles of public events were kept. The funeral orations delivered on men of rank were preserved in their families. It appears to have been the custom to sing the praises of illustrious men at feasts and banquets. Ballads of Romulus and Remus constituted the entertainment of the common people. None of these old poems have been preserved, but it is believed that Livy incorporated many of them in his History of Rome.

About this period Cneius Flavius achieved immense popularity by two acts highly beneficial to the people. The *dies fasti*, or days on which the courts sat and administered justice, had been thus divided in a very perplexing manner through the year, and people were only able to ascertain them by consulting the pontiffs. Flavius constructed a calendar in which the nature of each day was marked. He hung it up in the Forum, thus saving the common people much trouble and loss of time. He likewise drew up and published a collection of all the legal forms in civil actions, thus greatly simplifying the business of law-suits.

During the period of the conquest of Italy, and during the period of the Punic Wars which followed, the Romans exhibited their sterling patriotism, their probity, and their political tact in its highest degree. Their conquests and their political organization were the two things that they thus far only accomplished; and their genius mainly appeared in the art of governing mankind, in which they were without a parallel among the nations of antiquity; but in art, science, philosophy and literature this great military people had as yet done absolutely nothing.

SECTION VIII.—PUNIC WARS AND FOREIGN CONQUESTS.

 HAVING conquered all their rivals in Italy, the Romans now cast longing eyes beyond the limits of the peninsula. The Carthaginians were in possession of a portion of Sicily, and, like the Romans, they only desired an opportunity to embroil the various states of that island in hostilities with one another for the purpose of grasping the whole of the island. The meddling of the two powerful republics of Rome and Carthage in the affairs of Sicily gave rise to the three long and bloody wars between these rival powers, known as the *Punic Wars*, which covered a period of more than a century, and which ended in the destruction of Carthage and in making Rome mistress of the civilized world.

The earlier wars of Rome had reduced her citizens to pecuniary distress. The war with Pyrrhus and the succeeding wars with Carthage and other foreign states actually augmented the wealth of the Roman people. They began to consider war a means of profit, and after their conquest of Italy they sought a new quarrel with the deliberate design of adding to their riches. Carthage, by her great wealth, derived from her immense commerce, seemed to open the most promising field for plunder, and a pretext was only wanting to begin the struggle, but this was presently found.

In B. C. 264 Híero II., King of Syracuse, secured the alliance of the Carthaginians in a war against the Mamertines, "Sons of Mars," a powerful band of Italian mercenaries, who, by fraud and injustice, had seized the city of Messana and other fortresses in the North-east of Sicily, massacred the inhabitants and rendered themselves independent. The Mamertines, on the other hand, had placed themselves under the protection of Rome. The Romans at first hesitated to acknowledge their disreputable allies, and had themselves but recently chastised the Mamertines of Rhegium for precisely the same crime which the "Sons of Mars" had perpetrated at Messana; but when the Carthaginians had gotten possession of the citadel of Messana, the Romans willingly accepted the alliance of the freebooters and resolved to afford them military aid.

The first war between Rome and Carthage—the *First Punic War*—commenced in the year B. C. 263, when a Roman army of twenty thousand men under the Consul Claudius landed in Sicily, thus successfully eluding the vigilance of the Carthaginian fleet.

The Roman Consul Claudius seized the Carthaginian admiral Hanno in a public assembly in Messana; and Hanno, in order to obtain his release, removed the Carthaginian garrison from the citadel, surrendered the citadel to the Romans, and evacuated Messana with his fleet. Upon returning to Carthage, Hanno was crucified by order of the Carthaginian government, and another officer, also named Hanno, was assigned to the command of the Carthaginian fleet. Carthage at the same time issued a formal declaration of war against Rome.

The united Syracusan and Carthaginian armies besieged the Roman army under Claudius in Messana, but were defeated; and the successive Roman victories soon procured other allies for the Romans among the Sicilian states, and encouraged them with the hope of acquiring possession of the entire island. Híero II., King of Syracuse, now became distrustful of his allies, the Carthaginians, and returned home. The next year he made peace with the Romans, and remained their faithful friend and ally during the rest of his life, embracing a period of almost half a century. Most of the Greek cities of Sicily followed his example.

The Carthaginians, who regarded Sicily as rightfully their own, were filled with the most intense rage at the intrusion of the Romans. They hired a large number of

BATTLE OF MYLAE.

mercenaries from Spain, Gaul and Liguria, and formed a grand military and naval station at the city of Agrigentum, in Sicily. The Carthaginians were reduced to great extremities; and the Carthaginian general, Hannibal, son of Gisco—not the great Hannibal—unable any longer to meet the Romans in the open field, shut himself up in Agrigentum, which he fortified very strongly. The Romans, eager to obtain possession of the Carthaginian magazines, immediately laid siege to Agrigentum, notwithstanding its great natural and artificial strength, and defeated a large Carthaginian army which had been sent to its relief. The Carthaginian garrison, in despair, evacuated the city, leaving it and all its valuable stores to fall into the possession of the Romans (B. C. 262).

Several towns in the interior of Sicily now surrendered to the Romans, but those upon the coast were prevented from following their example by dread of the Carthaginian fleet. While the Romans were thus making themselves masters of Sicily, a Carthaginian fleet under Hannibal, who had escaped from Panormus (now Palermo) with most of his troops, carried on the war by sea, where the Carthaginians were supreme, and ravaged the coasts of Italy with a fleet of sixty ships (B. C. 262). The next year (B. C. 261) a Carthaginian naval detachment under Boödes, the lieutenant of Hannibal, captured the Roman squadron under the Consul Scipio at the Lipara Isles. Hannibal again set out with fifty ships to ravage the Italian coasts once more.

Seeing that the Carthaginians had complete command of the sea, the Romans were strongly impressed with the necessity of creating a powerful navy, but they themselves did not know how to build ships. A people as indomitable as the Romans were not discouraged or intimidated under such circumstances. They determined upon the construction of a navy, and an accident at this moment came to their aid. A Carthaginian quinquereme (a vessel with five rows of oars) was driven in a gale to the southern coast of Italy, and this served for a model. In sixty days the Romans, who had hitherto had no vessels greater than triremes, built a fleet of one hundred and sixty first-class war-vessels. While the building of the ships was in progress, stages had been erected, on the shore, on which the sailors, the rowers, and the fighting men were taught the maneuvers to be practiced on shipboard; and every obstacle was surmounted by perseverance. But the Romans were fully conscious of their want of naval experience, and aware that their main chance of success on the sea was in fighting hand to hand, as on shore. To accomplish this purpose, they invented a machine called a *crow*, for grappling the enemy's vessels with their own, and thus enabling them to board the enemy's ships and fight as on land. In the fore part of each ship they erected a mast with a pulley-wheel at the top, by which was suspended a long ladder, furnished with a sharp iron hook at the outer end. This ladder was to be raised on approaching the enemy's ship, and let fall upon her deck. As the two vessels would thus be grappled fast, the Romans could rush from deck to deck by the ladder, and thus meet the Carthaginian seamen in a hand-to-hand struggle.

The Consul Duilius was the commander of this first great Roman fleet. When the Carthaginians saw him, they put to sea with a hundred and thirty ships, with every confidence of victory. They so heartily despised the Romans that they even took no pains to form in line of battle. They were somewhat perplexed at the sight of the *crows*, but they soon advanced and attacked this new Roman fleet off Mylæ, B. C. 260. The Romans approached and dropped the *crows*, and boarded the Carthaginian ships before their enemies had time to comprehend this new method of naval warfare. Forty-four Carthaginian ships were taken or sunk. Three thousand Carthaginians were killed, and seven thousand were taken prisoners. The tidings of this unexpected victory produced unbounded rejoicings at Rome. A column, decked with the *rostra*, or beaks of the captured Carthaginian ships, was erected in the Forum; and Duilius was permitted, thereafter as long as he lived, to have a torch carried in front of him, and to be preceded by a flute-player, whenever he returned home from a feast.

Other great Roman naval victories followed that off Mylæ. In B. C. 259 the Roman navy attacked Sardinia and Corsica, possessions of Carthage, and took the town of Aleria, in the latter island. There was an indecisive naval fight off Cape Tyndaris, in B. C. 257. In the meantime the Carthaginians assembled at Lilybæum a fleet of three hundred and fifty ships, carrying a hundred and fifty thousand men—probably the greatest naval armament of ancient times. The Romans collected at Messana a fleet of three hundred and thirty ships, carrying a hundred and thirty-nine thousand men. These two gigantic naval armaments encountered each other off Ecnomus, on the coast of Sicily, in B. C. 256. The Romans were commanded by the Consuls Regulus and Manlius, the Carthaginians by Hanno and Hamilcar; and the Romans were again victorious, sinking thirty of the Carthaginian vessels and capturing sixty.

In B. C. 255 the Romans under the Consuls Regulus and Manlius invaded Africa, determined to carry the war into the enemy's country. As the Carthaginian fleet was too weak to oppose them, Regulus and Manlius landed their armies safely near Cape Bon, and captured and fortified the town of Clypea, which they made their headquarters. The country between that place and the city of Carthage was like a garden, abounding in cornfields, vineyards, and beautiful country-seats of the wealthy citizens of Carthage. The Romans pillaged and devastated this lovely region, laying it waste with fire and sword. The beautiful villas of the Carthaginian nobles and merchants afforded valuable spoils; and twenty thousand persons, many of whom were of high rank and accustomed to all the refinements of wealth, were carried away into slavery.

The devastation of their country to the walls of Carthage alarmed the Carthaginians, who had in the meantime recalled Hamilcar from Sicily. In the winter Manlius returned to Rome with half the Roman army and all the plunder taken from the Carthaginians, thus leaving Regulus alone to prosecute the war in Africa. While the armies of Regulus and Hamilcar lay encamped near the river Bagrada, that of Regulus is said to have encountered a gigantic serpent, one hundred and twenty feet long, which drove the Roman soldiers away when they went to the river for water. The Romans found it necessary to use the balista and other military engines against the huge reptile, and thus finally killed him. The skin and jaw-bones were sent to Rome, where they were preserved in one of the temples for many years.

A battle between the two armies ended in a disastrous defeat for the Carthaginians, with the loss of seventeen thousand men killed, and five thousand men and eighteen elephants taken. Regulus quickly followed up his victory, overrunning and ravaging the country in every quarter around Carthage, and taking more than three hundred walled towns or villages. Vainly did the judges and nobles of Carthage cast their children as a sacrifice into the brazen arms of Moloch, from which they rolled into the fiery furnace which was always burning before the image. This horrible sacrifice did not appease the hideous idol, and defeat continued to attend the Carthaginian arms. In great alarm the Carthaginians sued for peace, but, as the conditions of the inexorable Regulus were too humiliating for them, they resolved to still rely on the arbitrament of arms, and so the bloody war continued.

The Numidian allies of Carthage, taking advantage of the distress of the Carthaginians, revolted; and all the country people fled into the city, which soon began to experience the horrors of famine. In their distressful situation, the Carthaginians, destitute of able generals among their own countrymen, sent to Sparta to solicit the services of the able and experienced Spartan general Xanthippus, whom they offered to place at the head of their armies. Xanthippus consented to give the Carthaginians his services, and brought four thousand Greek mercenaries with him. Upon his arrival at Carthage, he gave the magistrates instructions for levying their troops, assuring them that their armies had been beaten by the ignorance of their own officers, and not by the strength of the Romans.

By the exertions of Xanthippus, the Carthaginians were aroused from their despondency and inspired with confidence, and a respectable army was soon raised and placed in the field. Xanthippus made the most skillful disposition of his forces, placing his cavalry on the wings, and the elephants at proper intervals back of the line of the heavy armed infantry. He then brought up the light-armed troops in front, and directed them to discharge their missiles and retire through the line of the infantry. In this manner Xanthippus engaged the Romans, and in a terrible battle with them he utterly defeated them with terrific slaughter, their army being thoroughly annihilated, and the greater part of it destroyed, only two thousand Romans escaping from the field, and Regulus himself being taken prisoner (B. C. 255).

Other misfortunes befell the Romans at this time. A terrible disaster overtook their fleet which had been sent to bring away the shattered remnants of the once-splendid army of Regulus from Africa. A violent storm came on, and this fleet was totally wrecked off the southern coast of Sicily, which was strewn with the remains of two hundred and sixty ships and one hundred thousand men; while the enormous spoils obtained by the plunder of the Carthaginian territory were swallowed up by the waves (B. C. 255). In Sicily the Carthaginian general, Carthalo, recovered Agrigentum.

The Romans were almost driven to despair by these repeated losses, but their indomitable will never allowed them to relax their exertions. They equipped a new fleet, which took the important town of Panormus (now Palermo) in Sicily, in B. C. 254. This newly-built fleet, consisting of one hundred and fifty ships, shared the same fate as its predecessor, being wrecked in a storm in B. C. 253, every vessel being swallowed up by the waves. But in Sicily, in B. C. 250, the Roman Proconsul Metellus defeated the Carthaginians in a great battle near Panormus; twenty thousand Carthaginians being killed and more than one hundred elephants being captured, these latter being exhibited in the triumph of Metellus. This brilliant Roman victory tended to restore the equilibrium between the contending forces.

Soon after the battle of Panormus, the Carthaginians, weary of the contest with Rome, took Regulus from his prison in Carthage and sent him on an embassy to Rome for the purpose of bringing about a peace, making him first swear that in case the negotiations for peace should fail he would return to his dungeon in Carthage. They had flattered themselves that Regulus, weary of his four years' imprisonment in a hostile city, would exert himself for a pacification. When the old general approached the gates of his native Rome, many of his friends came out to meet him. Their acclamations resounded through the city, but Regulus refused to enter the gates, and manifested a spirit of settled melancholy. He was vainly entreated to visit his little dwelling and participate in the joy inspired by his return. He persistently reiterated that he was now a slave, belonging to the Carthaginians, and therefore unfit to partake in the liberal honors of his country.

The Roman Senate, as usual, assembled outside the city walls, to give audience to the ambassadors. Regulus opened the business in accordance with the instructions which he had received from the Carthaginian Council, and the Carthaginian ambassadors confirmed his statements. The Senate, also weary of a war which had now lasted fourteen years, were disposed toward peace. But when Regulus was called upon for a speech, he astonished all his hearers by raising his voice in favor of a continuance of the war. The Romans manifested pity and admiration for the man who had so eloquently spoken against his own personal interest, and were therefore unwilling to decide in favor of a policy which was sure to be his individual ruin. But Regulus relieved them from their embarrassment by breaking off the negotiations abruptly; and, bound by his oath, he at once returned to Carthage with the Carthaginian ambassadors, without embracing his family or formally bidding farewell to his friends.

burning sun, and then put him into a cask set all around with sharp spikes, where he died in prolonged agony. This story is believed to have been invented by the Romans to fire their soldiers with deadly hatred against the Carthaginians, and as a pretext for their own subsequent barbarous treat-

DEPARTURE OF REGULUS FOR CARTHAGE.

The Roman historians tell us that after the return of Regulus to Carthage, the Carthaginians, wrought up to the most furious rage at his conduct in breaking off the negotiations for peace, resolved to punish him with the most cruel torture. After cutting off his eye-lids and putting him into a dungeon, they exposed his naked eyes to the

ment of the Carthaginians; and though Regulus doubtless ended his days as a prisoner at Carthage, there are good reasons for believing that he died a natural death.

Hostilities were now renewed with increased animosity on both sides, and for the next eight years the Romans were defeated in many battles, and if the Carthaginians

BATTLE OF THE ÆGUSA (PUNIC WAR).

would have possessed the steady resolution and perseverance of their enemies they would have quite effectually crushed them. A Roman fleet of a hundred and twenty-three ships, under the Consul Publius Claudius Pulcher, attacked Drepana, in Sicily. The Consul hoped to surprise the place by sailing in the night, but he did not arrive until after daybreak, thus giving the Carthaginian admiral, Adherbal, time to sail out of the harbor and meet him.

The Consul's contemptuous disregard of religious auspices had a dispiriting influence upon his men. The sacred chickens refused their food, which was considered an ill omen. The Consul ordered them to be cast into the sea, saying: "If they will not eat, let them drink." It was felt that a battle begun with what was considered an act of impiety was doomed to disaster. The Romans were totally defeated in the battle which followed, losing ninety ships, the Consul escaping with only thirty-three. Shortly afterwards the Romans lost another entire fleet in a storm, one hundred and twenty war-vessels and eight hundred transports being thus sunk. After this disaster the Roman Senate encouraged the citizens to fit out privateers.

A Carthaginian fleet under Hamilcar Barcas, the father of the great Hannibal, ravaged the coasts of Italy at his pleasure, causing the Romans severe suffering, and meeting with little resistance, as the Romans had no leader capable of opposing him successfully. But no catastrophe, caused either by the arms of the enemy or by the fury of the elements, could overcome the inflexible perseverance of the Romans; and their renewed exertions finally turned the tide of war in their favor. Fabius Buto once more showed his countrymen the path to victory by defeating a considerable Carthaginian fleet. Finally the Romans rallied all their forces to put an end to the long and weary struggle, which was becoming more and more burdensome through the devastations of the Italian coasts by Hamilcar Barcas.

As the Roman Senate scarcely made any effort to stop the ravages of Hamilcar Barcas, the wealthier Roman citizens, by one of the grandest exhibitions of patriotism in the world's annals, took the matter into their own hands. In the twenty-third year of this exhausting struggle (B. C. 242), these patriotic citizens, by private subscription, built and equipped a fleet of two hundred first-class ships, manned by sixty thousand sailors, and presented it to the state. The command of this fleet was assigned to the Consul Caius Lutatius Catulus. This commander drove the inferior Carthaginian fleet before him, reached Sicily, seized the harbors of Lilybæum and Drepana, and besieged both these cities by land and sea with vigor.

A Carthaginian fleet hastily sent to Sicily arrived off Drepana in the spring of B. C. 241. The Romans instantly sallied out to attack this fleet, and a decisive battle occurred between the two fleets off the little island of Ægusa (now Favignano), in which the Romans won a most brilliant victory, fifty Carthaginian ships being sunk, and seventy falling into the possession of the victorious Romans. This reverse so dispirited the Carthaginians that they sued for peace.

The terms which the Romans now exacted were the same as those which Regulus had offered at the gates of Carthage. The Carthaginians agreed to evacuate Sicily and all the adjacent islands; to pay to Rome one thousand talents of silver as a war-indemnity, and twenty-two hundred talents within ten years; to deliver up all prisoners and deserters without ransom; and to abstain from waging war against any of the allies of Rome, and from sending any war-ship into any portion of the Roman dominion.

Thus ended the First Punic War in B. C. 241, after a continuance of twenty-three years (B. C. 264-241), resulting in the elevation of Rome to the rank of a first-class naval power, while Carthage lost her foothold in Sicily and her supremacy in the Western Mediterranean. The Romans had suffered immense losses during the progress of this long struggle. Seven hundred Roman ships had been taken or destroyed; the population of Rome and her allies had vastly diminished; and the enormous property taxes imposed during the war caused great distress. Extensive sales of land for the purpose of raising money to defray the expenses of the war opened the door to that vast inequality in the distribution of wealth which subsequently proved so ruinous to the Republic. The gates of the Temple of Janus were now closed for the second time since the founding of Rome. As the Romans were now at peace with all nations, they found leisure to direct their attention to the arts of peace. They began to have a taste for poetry, the first liberal art that manifests itself in every civilized nation, and the first that likewise decays. The Romans had previous to this period been entertained only with rude ballads, or with the boorish drolleries known as the *Fescennine verses*. They now produced graver compositions, satirical in their nature; and after that they imitated the Greek drama. Elegiac, pastoral and didactic compositions soon began making their appearance in the Latin language.

In B. C. 238, when Carthage was embarrassed by a mutiny of her mercenary troops, Rome seized the island of Sardinia, and did not only refuse to surrender it upon the demand of Carthage, but threatened to renew the war. Carthage was in no condition to recommence hostilities, and not only consented to the cession of the island to Rome, but even paid a fine of twelve hundred talents for her remonstrance. In B. C. 227 Rome, encouraged by her successful seizure of Sardinia, also annexed Corsica to her dominion. For the purpose of governing Sicily, Sardinia and Corsica, the Romans placed these islands under the administration of *Proconsuls*, these officials exercising the functions of governor, commander-in-chief and supreme judge. A Proconsul was appointed for Sicily, and another for Sardinia and Corsica combined. This was the beginning of the system of Proconsular government, by which Rome afterwards ruled all her extensive foreign possessions. On completing their official year, the two Consuls divided the *provinces* between them by lot or agreement, each holding in his own provinces both military and civil authority, while the finances were managed by *Quæstors* responsible to the Senate. When the provinces had become numerous, most of them were governed by *Proprætors*. Rome claimed one-tenth of the entire produce of these conquered countries, and also a duty of five per cent. on all imports and exports.

The Greeks on the Adriatic coast having solicited the aid of Rome against the ravages of the Illyrian pirates, who were destroying their commerce, Rome sent three ambassadors to Teuta, the Illyrian queen, to demand the cessation of these outrages (B. C. 230). The Illyrian queen refused to put a stop to what she considered the rights of her subjects, and, seizing the ambassadors, caused two of them to be murdered, and imprisoned the third. Thereupon Rome declared war at once, and the next year (B. C. 229) sent a fleet of two hundred ships into the Adriatic, and the pirates were exterminated. The greater part of Illyria became tributary to Rome, the queen being compelled to pay an annual tribute and to keep her corsairs within stricter bounds in the future. Roman power was thus established over a portion of Illyria and Dalmatia, and a Roman protectorate was extended over the Greeks of Apollonia, Epidamnus and Corcyra. In gratitude for this important service, the Greeks admitted the Romans to equal rights with the Hellenic race in participation in the Isthmian Games and the Eleusinian Mysteries. A far more important result to Rome was that she obtained a footing on the Eastern side of the Adriatic and the right to interfere in Grecian affairs.

While thus asserting her power in Illyria and Greece, Rome was also desirous of extending her dominion to its natural limits in the Alps. At this time the Republic had become involved in difficulties with the Cisalpine Gauls and the Ligurians, who made war against Rome in B. C. 238, but were compelled to consent to peace by surrendering some of their territories two years later (B. C. 236). In B. C. 232 the Romans resolved to strike a death-blow at the power of the Cisalpine Gauls, in order to free the Republic from the danger which constantly menaced her from that quarter, and to extend her dominion, for which purpose Roman colonies were planted in the country of the Senonian Gauls. These Roman colonies were pushed so steadily forward, and became so numerous in the next seven years, that the Gauls clearly saw through the designs of the Republic, and accordingly found themselves under the necessity of taking up arms to defend their territories from Roman encroachments.

The war between the Romans and the Cisalpine Gauls commenced in B. C. 225. After taking the alarm, the Cisalpine Gauls obtained fresh forces from their kinsmen in Transalpine Gaul. Thus reinforced, they marched into Central Italy, overran Etruria as far as Clusium, and threatened the city of Rome with the same fate which it had suffered at the hands of their ancestors under Brennus. Three Roman armies were quickly put into the field to oppose the Gallic invaders. One of these armies was routed by the Gauls; but another under the Consul Æmilius, assisted by Regulus, son of the Regulus who acted so prominent a part in the First Punic War, routed the Gauls in a great and decisive battle near Telamon, in Etruria, almost destroying the entire Gallic host. The result of this great Roman victory was that all of Cisalpine Gaul was conquered and annexed to the territories of the Roman Republic (B. C. 222), after a war of three years. In order to hold this territory, the Romans planted colonies at Mediolánum (now Milan), Comun (now Como), Placentia, Parma, Modena, Mantua, Verona and Brixia. These Roman colonies were connected with Rome itself by the great military road called the *Flaminian Way*, and by its branches. Thus Rome was now mistress of all Italy, from the great mountain barrier of the Alps on the north to the southern coast of Sicily on the south.

In the meantime causes were at work which were rapidly ripening into another war between Rome and Carthage. Ever since the close of the First Punic War, Carthage, which had only yielded to Rome from necessity, and which had consented to the aggressions of her powerful and arrogant rival only because she was unable to prevent them, had been industriously and energetically endeavoring to retrieve her losses, and making preparations to renew the struggle with Rome which she intended to bring about just as soon as she was ready for it. A large majority of the citizens of Carthage were in favor of renewing hostilities with the mistress of Italy at the earliest possible moment.

For the purpose of recruiting the power and wealth of Carthage, Hamilcar Barcas had employed all his energies in the conquest of Spain, in which country the Carthaginians intended to form a province which should compensate for the loss of Sicily. Hamilcar Barcas began this task in B. C. 236. At his death, in B. C. 238, his schemes were taken up by his son-in-law, Hásdrubal, who prosecuted them with vigor and skill. These two Carthaginian commanders not only endeavored to reduce Spain under the dominion of Carthage, but at the same time diligently labored to raise that country to a condition which would render it an efficient ally. Hásdrubal organized and developed the resources of the country by building towns, encouraging commerce, teaching the native Spaniards the arts of civilization, especially agriculture, training the native tribes into efficient soldiers, and successfully working the newly-discovered silver mines. These mineral resources of Spain were fully developed, and the country enjoyed a prosperity which it had never before experienced. The revenue derived from this source not only defrayed all the expenses of the province, but yielded a vast surplus which rapidly filled up the Carthaginian treasury.

At the end of the First Punic War an important change was made in the Carthaginian system, in the appointment of Hamilcar Barcas to the chief command of the Carthaginian army for an indefinite period. and in the relinquishment to the army itself of the right to select his successor. Hamilcar

Barcas was slain in battle with the natives of Spain, in B. C. 227, whereupon his troops selected Hásdrubal, his son-in-law, to command them. Hásdrubal lost his life at the hands of an assassin in B. C. 220. The Carthaginian army in Spain thereupon chose Hannibal, the eldest son of Hamilcar Barcas, as their commander, and the home government in Carthage was obliged to ratify their choice.

When thus placed at the head of the Carthaginian army, Hannibal was still a young man, being then only twenty-eight years of age. Notwithstanding his youth, he was an experienced soldier, and his first recollections were those of war. He had accompanied his father to Sicily when a mere child, and had been a witness to the agony of that heroic commander when obliged to consent to the humiliating peace which ended the First Punic War. When nine years of age, Hannibal had accompanied his father to Spain, where the latter took his son before the altar of his country's gods and made him take a solemn oath of eternal and unrelenting enmity to Rome. This oath had never been forgotten by Hannibal. He had thus been trained to consider himself the avenger of his country's wrongs, and he had been very carefully educated for his mission.

Though most of the youth's life was passed in the camp, his education was carefully attended to. Besides the culture belonging to Phœnicians of rank in his time, Hannibal had a good knowledge of the Greek language. He was light and firmly built in his bodily frame, and was an excellent runner, a skillful rider and a good swordsman. He had remarkable powers of endurance, which enabled him to hold out against fatigue, hunger, and loss of sleep. He soon distinguished himself for his military valor, and was fighting by the side of his father when the latter was slain. His brother-in-law, Hásdrubal, assigned him the command of the cavalry; and Hannibal soon gained the confidence of the army, in consequence of his wonderful skill as a military leader and his brilliant personal valor.

When, therefore, Hásdrubal was killed, the troops instinctively looked to Hannibal as their natural leader. He was one of the worthiest, as well as one of the most talented, characters of his time; and was the greatest man that Carthage ever produced, and one of the greatest military geniuses that the world has ever brought forth. "The power which he wielded over men is shown by his incomparable control over an army of various nations and many tongues—an army which never in the worst times mutinied against him. He was a great man; wherever he went he riveted the eyes of all."

Hannibal first devoted himself to the complete establishment of the Carthaginian power in Spain, and to the training of his army for the great enterprise for which it was ultimately destined, by his wars against the native tribes, which occupied him about two years. He was fully conscious of the weakness of Carthage in a defensive war, and resolved from the start to assail Rome in her own dominions and thus prevent her from attacking the territories of Carthage at home.

Believing that the decisive moment had arrived, Hannibal deliberately sought the quarrel with Rome to which he had devoted his life. The Greek city of Saguntum, on the eastern coast of Spain, had placed itself under the protection of Rome. Hannibal laid siege to it and took it after an obstinate defense of eight months (B. C. 219), and sent the spoil of the captured city to Carthage for distribution among the citizens. The Roman Senate sent an embassy to Carthage to demand that Hannibal and his army should be delivered up for having trespassed on Roman territory and thus violated the peace. When the Carthaginian Senate rejected this unreasonable demand, the Roman embassy under Quintus Fabius declared war, which the Carthaginian Senate readily accepted (B. C. 218). Thus began the second great struggle for supremacy between the mighty republics of Rome and Carthage—the gigantic conflict known as the *Second Punic War*—which convulsed the lands of the Western Mediterranean for a period of seventeen years (B. C. 218–201).

Like his father and brother-in-law, Hannibal held the supreme command of the Carthaginian armies, both in Spain and in Africa, and the defense of both countries devolved upon him. He had resolved from the beginning to make both secure by carrying the war into Italy. His army was intensely devoted to him, and as Carthage lacked a navy sufficient to cope with that of the Romans, he resolved to invade the Roman territory from the land. The Gauls, one of the new cities founded by the Carthaginians in Spain, Hannibal committed the government and defense of Spain to his brother Hásdrubal, and marched towards the Alps with his immense forces, two-thirds of which were drawn from the African dominions of Carthage, and the remaining third from the Carthaginian territories in Spain. Hannibal placed no reliance upon his elephants, but simply took them along for the moral effect which he expected that

QUINTUS FABIUS DECLARING WAR TO THE CARTHAGINIAN SENATE.

by their frequent passages of the Alps, had taught him that that great mountain barrier could be crossed, and he determined to lead his army into Italy by way of Spain and Gaul.

Having during the winter offered solemn sacrifices and prayers for success, at the distant shrine of the Tyrian Hercules at Gades (now Cadiz), and having assembled an army of ninety thousand infantry, twelve thousand cavalry, and thirty-seven elephants, at Carthagena, or New Carthage, they would produce upon the Gauls, among whom he relied upon finding able guides to show him the most practicable route across the Alps.

In the spring of B. C. 218 Hannibal crossed the Ebro. The Spanish tribes between the Ebro and the Pyrenees resisted Hannibal's army, but were subdued, and Hannibal left a detachment of twelve thousand men to hold them in subjection. When he reached the Pyrenees, he sent a part of his army back home, having resolved to do so from the first, for the purpose of showing the remainder how much confidence he had of success in his daring enterprise. He retained fifty thousand infantry and nine thousand cavalry under his own command, and with these troops and his thirty-seven elephants he marched through the territory of the Gauls friendly to him to the Rhone.

In the meantime the Romans had been diligently preparing an expedition against Carthage. When the troops designed to take part in this expedition were in readiness, some of them were called off to suppress a rebellion against the Roman power in Cisalpine Gaul. When they returned, it was decided to send them into Spain, under the command of the Consul Publius Cornelius Scipio, to aid the allies of Rome in that country. They started for Spain by sea, but on the voyage they touched at the Greek city of Massilia (now Marseilles), in Gaul, which was in alliance with Rome. Here Scipio learned to his astonishment that Hannibal had already arrived at the banks of the Rhone. The Roman Consul therefore abandoned the expedition to Spain, and, with the aid of the Gauls of the Lower Rhone, who were friendly to Rome, he endeavored to prevent Hannibal from crossing that river.

Accordingly, when Hannibal reached the Rhone, near the site of the modern town of Orange, about twenty miles above Avignon, he found a large army of Gauls drawn up on the opposite bank of the river to dispute his passage. He was threatened with a fatal delay on account of the difficulty of transporting the elephants across the stream, as the Roman army was likewise approaching by rapid marches. By a skillful maneuver, Hannibal surmounted this difficulty. He sent a detachment to cross the river farther up in the darkness of the night with orders to assail the Gauls in the rear, at a given signal. When all was ready he gave the signal and began to cross the stream. The Gauls rushed down to oppose him, but they soon beheld the camp behind them in flames, and fled; after which Hannibal's army crossed the Rhone (B. C. 218).

As the elephants dreaded the water, they could not be compelled to enter the boats, and were therefore conveyed across the stream by a timely artifice. Floats, or rafts of timber, covered with earth, were prepared and fastened to the shore of the river. The elephants, deceived by the appearance of these earth-covered rafts, took them for solid earth, and allowed themselves to be led upon them. The floats were then loosened from the shore and towed across the river by means of boats.

After marching one hundred miles up the east bank of the Rhone, Hannibal wheeled to the right, directing his course to the foot of the Alps, over which he was to explore a new passage to Italy. True to his expectation, Hannibal found no lack of guides among the Gauls. He choose the pass now known as the Little St. Bernard, the highest and longest pass of the Alps, but the easiest of the ancient routes across those mountains, and the one permitting him to transport the baggage and stores of his army. It was almost winter when the difficult project of crossing the Alps was undertaken, and the season vastly multiplied its horrors and difficulties. The tremendous height and steepness of the mountains, capped with snow, that appeared to rest among the clouds; the mountaineers, of barbarous and fierce aspect, attired in animal skins, with long shaggy hair, presented a scene that struck terror and astonishment into every beholder.

Among the narrow defiles of the mountains, the Gauls attacked the Carthaginian army with showers of stones and rolled great rocks down upon them from the precipices. An immense number of men, horses and elephants were lost before Hannibal's army escaped these perils. On the ninth day the Carthaginian troops reached the summit of the Alps, and there they halted for a rest of two days. Here Hannibal's soldiers were disheartened by a great fall of snow and by the prospect of additional difficulties; but their leader pointed out the rich plain of the Po, and assured them of the facility with which Italy might be conquered, thus raising their spirits, and the march was resumed.

PUNIC WARS AND FOREIGN CONQUESTS.

But the difficulties in the way of Hannibal's army now increased. The newly-fallen snow had covered up the paths, so that the soldiers lost their way, and vast numbers of them fell down the precipices and were killed. At length they discovered the work of cutting a passage through this massive solid rock. They effected this by making large fires of wood on the rock until it was heated red hot, and then quenching it with vinegar. In this manner the huge solid rock was split into fragments, and a

HANNIBAL'S ARMY CROSSING THE ALPS.

their march obstructed by a massive rock, almost perpendicular, which shelved down a depth of a thousand feet. There Hannibal's soldiers pitched their camp amidst the deep snow, and the next day they began passage was opened, through which Hannibal's entire army passed and finally reached the open country on the south side of the mountains. Hannibal's passage of the Alps occupied fifteen days (B. C. 218).

Having mustered his forces, after crossing the Alps, Hannibal discovered that he had lost in the passage one half of the fifty-nine thousand men which he led across the Pyrenees. Whatever his faults may have been, his passage of the Alps, in the face of difficulties almost insurmountable, proved him to be one of the greatest generals that ever lived. The Insubrian Gauls welcomed Hannibal as a deliverer, and took advantage of the opportunity thus afforded to liberate themselves from the hated dominion of Rome.

When intelligence of Hannibal's invasion of Italy reached Rome, the Consul Publius Cornelius Scipio was sent with an army against the invaders. Hannibal advanced against Scipio, and defeated and routed his army on the banks of the river Ticinus with heavy loss, Scipio himself being wounded (B. C. 218). The Consul Tiberius Sempronius was now recalled from Sicily and sent with another Roman army against Hannibal. The armies of Scipio and Sempronius were both united, and Sempronius assumed command of the whole, as Scipio was disabled on account of his wound. The next great battle was fought on the banks of the river Trebia, in December of the same year (B. C. 218).

The crafty Carthaginian leader, well aware of the impetuosity of the Romans, sent a detachment of one thousand cavalry, each trooper carrying a foot-soldier behind him, to cross the Trebia and ravage the country. As Hannibal had foreseen and desired, this devastation provoked the Romans to battle. The Carthaginians, pretending a panic, fled hastily to the river, the Romans pursuing them across the stream, which was swollen by a heavy rain. It was a cold winter morning, and the Romans had been roused from their sleep to fight at the first alarm, without taking their breakfasts. When they had waded across the river and had become benumbed with the intense coldness of the water, they were suddenly attacked by the whole Carthaginian army, drawn up and ready to receive them. The Romans, chilled, hungry and fatigued, were unable to maintain their ground against Hannibal's fresh troops, but were completely routed. The defeated Romans lost twenty-six thousand men killed or drowned in the Trebia. Only ten thousand Romans survived; and these, finding themselves surrounded on all sides, broke through the enemy's ranks, and after fighting desperately in their retreat, finally succeeded in finding shelter in the city of Placentia. After this second great victory in Italy, Hannibal led his army into winter-quarters in Liguria, where he rested until the following spring.

Hannibal's two victories at the Ticinus and the Trebia made him master of Cisalpine Gaul, or Northern Italy; and the Cisalpine Gauls, who had thus far stood aloof from the struggle between two giant powers, now flocked to his standard in large numbers. Notwithstanding his successes, Hannibal was greatly hampered by the sufferings of his African and Spanish soldiers, who were unable to endure the unusual severity of the intensely cold winter.

Early the next spring (B. C. 217) Hannibal attempted to cross the Apennines, but was obliged to desist in consequence of a violent storm of thunder, hail, wind and rain. The Romans were defeated in a battle at Placentia. Hannibal then marched his army southward through a marshy region, consuming four days in wading amid mud and water, during which his troops suffered every hardship. Hannibal lost an eye, and nearly all his beasts of burden perished. At length he entered Etruria, where a large Roman army under the Consul Caius Flaminius lay encamped to dispute his further progress. Hannibal thus anticipated the movement of Flaminius, who had intended to dispute the passage of the Apennines with the Carthaginian general. When Flaminius failed to do this, he awaited Hannibal at Arretium. Flaminius was a vain braggart and considered himself Hannibal's superior, but the Carthaginian commander soon taught his boastful antagonist a severe lesson.

Having learned the character of Flaminius, Hannibal, instead of attacking him, marched southward past him, and laid waste the country along his route, at the same time, by his taunts, stinging the Consul into abandoning his strong position and following him. Enraged at the sight of Hannibal's devastations, Flaminius was eager to come to blows with his adversary. Hannibal retreated before the Romans until he had decoyed the army of Flaminius into a narrow defile between the two steep hills of Cortona, closed at its outlet by a high hill, and at its entrance by Lake Trasiménus.

In this position Hannibal placed his troops in ambush, so that the Romans were hemmed in between the Carthaginian army and Lake Trasiménus before they were aware of their peril. Hannibal's stratagem on this occasion was favored by an accident. When the Romans were entering the defile in the morning, a dense fog arose from the lake, filling the lower portion of the defile. The Romans were thus unable to see their enemies, or even their own men march, while Hannibal's troops on the hills were in the sunshine. This military stratagem on the part of Hannibal was never surpassed in the success of its execution. At a given signal, the Carthaginian soldiers rushed down from the hills and assailed the army of Flaminius in front, flank and rear. Not having time or space to form in line of battle, the Romans were cut down in columns, so that they speedily encountered a disastrous defeat. The Consul Flaminius himself was killed. Fifteen thousand of the Roman soldiers were killed or driven into the lake and drowned. Six thousand were taken prisoners, and ten thousand saved themselves by dispersion and flight (B. C. 217).

While this great battle was in progress, a terrible earthquake occurred, which, though it destroyed many cities and towns, overturned mountains, and stopped rivers in their courses, was unnoticed by the combatants, whose fury in the storm of battle was such that not one of them in either army perceived this great convulsion of nature. In the language of the immortal Byron, as expressed in the following forcible and beautiful lines:

"Such was the storm of battle on that day,
And such the fury whose convulsion blinds
To all save carnage, that beneath the fray
An earthquake rolled unheededly away.
None felt stern nature rocking at his feet,
And yawning forth a grave for those who lay
Upon their bucklers for a winding sheet.
Such is th' absorbing hate when warring nations meet."

The Roman disaster of Trasiménus quite overwhelmed the people of Rome, as all Etruria was in the power of Hannibal, to whose advance the road to Rome was open. The Romans broke down all the bridges over the Tiber; and the Senate, unmoved and resolute, appointed Quintus Fabius Maximus Dictator in this momentous crisis.

Hannibal did not advance upon Rome after his great victory at Lake Trasiménus, but marched into Apulia to rest and recruit his army. He endeavored to detach the Italian nations from their alliance with Rome by releasing the captives belonging to them that he had taken, and sending them away without ransom. But his efforts were useless, as the Italian towns closed their gates against him and not one espoused his cause. During the month following his victory of Trasiménus, Hannibal thoroughly reorganized his army on the Roman model. He used the arms which he had taken in battle to equip his troops, and the work of reorganization was effected in the enemy's very presence.

The Dictator Quintus Fabius Maximus, while possessed of courage, had also a proper degree of caution. He perceived that the only method by which the Romans could obtain any advantage over the enemy was by closely following them, harassing them and fatiguing them, by turning every wrong movement of theirs to his own advantage, and by avoiding decisive battles. For this purpose he always encamped upon the highest grounds, those which were inaccessible to the enemy's cavalry. Whenever they moved, he watched their movements, straitened their quarters, and cut off their provisions. By pursuing this new and cautious policy, Fabius Maximus acquired the title of *Cunctator*, or the Delayer.

STRATAGEM OF HANNIBAL.

Fabius Maximus appears to have supposed that Hannibal would not venture to advance so long as the Roman army was held intact, but he soon found himself mistaken, as the gifted Carthaginian eluded him by descending into the rich plains of Campania. Hannibal had formed connections in Capua, the Campanian capital and the second city of importance in the Roman dominion, ranking next to Rome itself. He hoped that the Campanians would revolt from their alliance with Rome and espouse his cause; but in this hope he was doomed to disappointment, and he was obliged to content himself with ravaging the country and collecting provisions to supply his army for the ensuing winter. During all this time the Roman soldiers, in consequence of the cautious policy of their new leader, were obliged to view from the hills the depredations of Hannibal's Numidian cavalry, who ravaged the country with fire and sword beneath their very eyes. The Roman troops were highly exasperated at Fabius, and clamored to be led to battle.

In pursuit of his new system of tactics, Fabius Maximus at length seized the road leading to Capua, inclosed Hannibal among the Samnian mountain-passes, and lined the heights commanding the road with his troops, thinking that it was impossible for Hannibal to escape. The skillful Carthaginian general, however, rescued himself by such a stratagem as only a man of prompt resources could invent. He obtained two thousand oxen, and fastened bundles of brushwood to their horns, set the brushwood on fire at night, and drove them towards the heights which the Romans occupied. The oxen tossed their heads and ran wildly up the heights, seeming to fill the entire forest with fire. The Roman sentinels and outposts that were to guard the mountain passes fled in consternation, at seeing such a body of flames advancing towards them. By this stratagem Hannibal succeeded in drawing off his army and escaping through the defiles, but with considerable loss to his rear-guard. Fabius immediately withdrew the force he had posted to hold the road to Capua, and followed what he thought to be Hannibal's army. As soon as Hannibal found the road clear, he led his army past the point of danger, and the next morning he extricated his light troops from their position on the heights, inflicting a considerable loss upon the Romans. He then retired into Apulia, with abundance of provisions to supply his army during the winter.

Still pursuing the same cautious policy, Fabius Maximus followed Hannibal in all his movements, but was recalled to Rome before long. Upon his departure from the army, he left strict orders to Minucius, who commanded the army during his absence, not to risk a battle. Minucius disregarded these orders by abandoning the strong position which Fabius had occupied on the hills, descending to the plains, and engaging the enemy with success in some slight actions. These advantages were highly exaggerated at Rome; and the Roman people, who were dissatisfied with the slow and cautious mode of warfare pursued by Fabius Maximus, were anxious for a great and decisive battle, and were consequently induced to pass a decree placing Minucius on an equality of command with the Dictator.

Fabius did not complain, but when he returned to the camp he divided the army with Minucius. Each general now followed his own separate plan; and Hannibal, by skillful maneuvering, was soon enabled to entice Minucius into an engagement, where the latter's troops were only saved from being cut off to a man by Fabius, who, sacrificing his private resentment to the public good, hastened to the relief of Minucius. Minucius frankly acknowledged his fault, and the entire army once more encamped together. When his official year expired, Fabius Maximus retired from the command of the Roman army; and Terentius Varro, a man of low origin, with only his wealth and his self-conceit to recommend him, was appointed his successor, being one of the Consuls for that year. Varro's associate in command was the other Consul, Æmilius Paulus, a man of quite different character, experienced in the science of war, cautious in action, and possessed with an utter contempt for his colleague.

In the spring of B. C. 216 the Roman army numbered ninety thousand men; and the two Consuls, Terentius Varro and Æmilius Paulus, resolved to hazard a great battle with Hannibal, who was then encamped at Cannæ, in Apulia. As the Romans approached, Hannibal took a position bringing the wind in his rear, knowing that the wind must greatly distress the advancing Romans, because at that season it was constantly blowing one way, and carrying vast clouds with it from the parched plains behind. Hannibal's army now numbered but sixty-thousand men, two-thirds the number of the Roman army by which it was now opposed.

On their arrival in sight of Hannibal's army, the two Roman Consuls agreed to take the command on alternate days. Æmilius Paulus commanded on the first day, and considered it prudent not to attack the enemy. But on the following day, Terentius Varro, without asking the advice of his colleague, gave the signal for battle, crossed a branch of the river Aufidus, that separated the two armies, before the little town of Cannæ, and arranged his forces in line of battle. The battle commenced with the attack by the light-armed Roman infantry. The Roman cavalry engaged next, but as they were unable to stand against Hannibal's Numidian cavalry, the Roman legions came up to support their own cavalry. The battle now became general. The Romans vainly endeavored to break the center of the Carthaginian line, where the Gauls and the Spaniards were stationed. When Hannibal observed this movement on the part of the Romans, he ordered a portion of those troops to give way, so as to allow the Romans to advance until they were surrounded, when a chosen body of African troops fell upon the Roman flanks, and as the Romans were unable to offer any effectual resistance they were cut down, in the language of the ancient historian, "like ripe corn before the reaper." The Consul Terentius Varro made a desperate effort to remedy his fatal blunder; but Hannibal's Africans, who were fresh and vigorous, maintained with ease the advantage which they had gained over Varro's wearied troops. At length the rout of the Romans became general along the whole line, and Varro's boastings ceased. The Consul Æmilius Paulus was killed while fighting bravely; while Varro escaped to Venusia with seventy horse. Such was the famous battle of Cannæ, in which the Romans suffered so frightful a defeat that the very existence of Rome was in danger (B. C. 216). The Roman loss was fifty thousand killed, among whom were so many knights that it is said that Hannibal sent to Carthage, as trophies, three bushels of rings stripped from their fingers.

This catastrophe, the greatest ever experienced by the Romans, produced consternation and grief at Rome; but the courageous Senate remained as firm and immovable as ever. By the advice of Fabius Maximus, the Senate took measures to preserve the tranquillity of the city. A general mourning of thirty days was appointed, and all public and private religious rites were suspended. Fabius Pictor, the writer of the earliest Roman history, was sent to Greece to consult the oracle of Apollo at Delphi; while recourse was also had to the Sibylline Books, and by their directions, two Greeks, a man and a woman, were buried alive in the ox-market. Such was the influence exercised by superstition in this alarming crisis of Rome's affairs.

The Senate appointed Marcus Junius Dictator. All the Roman citizens of age to bear arms were enrolled, and many of the slaves volunteered their services. The weapons and arms which the Romans had taken from their enemies in former wars, and which had been hung up as trophies in the temples and porticos, were now taken down and put to active use. Military critics have censured Hannibal for not marching to Rome immediately after his great victory at Cannæ, but his army was inadequate to the siege of the city, and the allies of the Romans would have been able to cut off his supplies.

Hannibal's great victory at Cannæ made him master of all Southern Italy. Excepting the Roman colonies and the Greek cities held by Roman garrisons, every town in that portion of the Italian peninsula surrendered to the triumphant Carthaginian general. Capua opened its gates to him and became his winter-quarters, and there Hannibal desired to repose and recruit his army, after the fatigues of three eventful years in this history of Rome and Carthage. Capua had for a long time been considered the abode of luxury and the corruption of all military virtue. A new scene of pleasure was now opened to Hannibal's barbarian soldiers, who immediately abandoned themselves to riotous living and debauchery. These corrupting influences enervated his hardy veterans, who were consequently disabled from enduring the fatigues of war when they were again called into active service in the field.

In consequence of his victory at Cannæ, Hannibal gained two important allies—King Philip V. of Macedon and Hierónymus, King of Syracuse. Thus Rome was obliged to divide her forces, in order to confront her new foes. Hannibal considered his ultimate triumph as certain. But his ungrateful country prevented this result by pursuing a selfish and ungenerous policy in her conduct towards the only man capable of defeating Rome.

Rome's conduct in this perilous emergency was worthy of her name and her past history. By the greatest exertions another large Roman army was placed in the field to confront Hannibal, while Macedon and Syracuse were too much occupied at home to be able to render any aid to the Carthaginian leader. The Greek cities and the Roman colonies of Southern Italy, undismayed by the catastrophe of Cannæ, kept their gates closed against the victorious Carthaginians; and it was very evident that Hannibal had obtained every advantage that could be acquired without a new campaign. Besides, the Roman armies were now led by new generals.

Under the leadership of such able commanders as Tiberius Sempronius Gracchus and Marcus Valerius, and, above all, by Marcus Claudius Marcellus, who became the ruling spirit of the war, the Romans were enabled during the year B. C. 215 to make a successful sally against Hannibal at Nola, which he was then besieging. The Carthaginian leader next endeavored to force the Romans to raise the siege of Capua and attacked them in their trenches, but met with a disastrous repulse in which he suffered considerable loss. He then advanced in the direction of Rome, but was obliged to retire, in consequence of finding a superior army prepared to confront him. Thus the corrupting influences of the luxurious living at Capua so enervated Hannibal's troops as to put an end to his career of victory in Italy; and he was obliged to acknowledge that he needed heavy reinforcements from Africa and Spain in order to effect the conquest of Italy.

Hásdrubal, Hannibal's brother, had been defeated by the two Scipios on the banks of the Ebro, in Spain, and was so hard pressed in that country that the troops and supplies which had been raised in Carthage for Hannibal were sent to Hásdrubal, as the security of Spain was of the first importance. While the war had been in progress in Italy, the Romans, commanded by Marcus Claudius Marcellus, were occupied in Sicily, where they were engaged in the siege of Syracuse.

In B. C. 215 Hierónymus, King of Syracuse, was killed. The city was for a long time defended by the mechanical ingenuity of the celebrated philosopher and mathematician Archimédes, who invented machines that destroyed the Roman ships, and thus baffled their efforts to capture the city. The Romans, however, were finally enabled to obtain possession of many of the outworks of the city by treachery, and thus eventually obliged the inhabitants to surrender (B. C. 212). The revenge of the Romans was terrible. The triumphant Roman soldiery pillaged Syracuse, and vast numbers of the citizens were massacred.

During the plunder of the city, a Roman soldier entered the room where Archimédes was deeply engaged in a mathematical problem, and not knowing who he was, killed him. This deed overwhelmed the triumphant Marcellus with grief, as he admired the genius of Archimédes, although it had been exercised against himself. Already there had begun to prevail at Rome a love for science, and numbers of the most distinguished citizens of the Republic were proud of their patronage of art and literature. Marcellus ordered that Archimédes be honorably buried, and that a tomb be erected to his memory. The numerous paintings, statues, and other works of art, found in Syracuse, were sent to Rome to adorn that city; and the prosperity of Syracuse was forever at an end.

Capua was besieged by several Roman legions, and, reduced by famine, was compelled to surrender in B. C. 211. Twenty-seven Capuan Senators died by their own hands, and fifty-three by the ax of the executioner; and the citizens of Capua were reduced to slavery, and the treasures of the unfortunate city were sent to Rome. In B. C. 209 Tarentum was taken by the Romans under Fabius Maximus, who reduced the citizens to slavery and took possession of the treasures of the captured city. All the towns of Southern Italy and Sicily which had revolted against the Romans soon returned to their allegiance.

In Spain, Hásdrubal gallantly defended himself against the Romans under the command of the Scipios—Cneius and Publius—who sought to wrest that vast peninsula from the Carthaginian dominion. The Scipios had by degrees succeeded in gaining the superiority over Hásdrubal, and had well-nigh driven him out of Spain, when in B. C. 212 he inflicted a terrific defeat upon the Scipios, both of whom were slain. Thereupon the Romans sent Caius Claudius Nero, an able but unpopular leader, to succeed the Scipios, with a reinforcement of twelve thousand troops. This commander was successful in restoring the prestige of the Roman arms, but he was unable to win over any allies to Rome, though he almost succeeded in capturing Hásdrubal in B. C. 210. The next year the Roman Senate sent the younger Publius Scipio, the son of the Consul Publius Scipio, to Spain to succeed Nero.

The younger Scipio was the first of a long line of great Roman commanders, and he soon exhibited his military talents by reducing Hásdrubal to extremities and taking Carthagena, the capital of the Carthaginian possessions in Spain. In B. C. 208 he defeated Hásdrubal in the South of Spain.

In the meantime Hannibal was reduced to such desperate straits in Southern Italy that the Carthaginian Senate ordered his brother Hásdrubal to proceed to his assistance with a body of forces drawn from Spain. Accordingly after his last defeat in Spain, Hásdrubal left two of his subordinates in control of the Carthaginian interests in Spain, and marched for Italy by way of Gaul. He fought his way to the North of Spain, and crossed the Pyrenees at their western extremity, into Gaul. He advanced to the Alps without encountering any opposition. Many of the Gauls joined his standard, thus largely increasing his army as he advanced. He crossed the Alps by his brother's route, and descended into Cisalpine Gaul, or Northern Italy, in the spring of B. C. 207. The Romans had not expected him in Italy so soon, and were therefore unprepared to oppose him. He might have taken Rome and thus decided the war in favor of Carthage had he advanced upon the city promptly, but he threw away all his opportunities by turning aside to lay siege to Placentia, and the letter disclosing his plans fell into the possession of the Consul Nero, thus giving the Romans due warning.

In the meantime Hannibal, who since the battle of Cannæ had been occupied with completing the conquest of Southern Italy, began moving northwards as soon as he heard that his brother had passed the Alps. Nero followed him very closely with a Roman army of forty thousand men, but it was very evident that the Carthaginian general was not hampered in his movements by this

DEATH OF ARCHIMEDES.

Roman army, as he eluded it by one of the flank marches so characteristic of him, when he felt disposed to do so.

When Hannibal arrived at Canusium he halted to await a dispatch from his brother providing for the union of their armies. The Roman outposts intercepted this letter and carried it to Nero. It disclosed Hásdrubal's purpose to proceed toward the south by the Flaminian road, and mentioned Narnia as the place where he hoped to join Hannibal. Nero instantly sent a detachment of eight thousand men from his army to Narnia to insure the safety of that place, and with a body of seven thousand select troops he left his camp and hastened to Senna Gallica, where the other Roman Consul, Marcus Livius, was awaiting Hásdrubal's advance.

Hásdrubal was ignorant of the reinforcement of the Roman army under Livius by the detachment under Nero, but his ear discerned one more trumpet note than usual at sunrise in the Roman camp, and as he rode forth to reconnoiter, he found that the horses had been over-driven and the armor of the men stained. He therefore delayed until night, when he moved to make the passage of the river Metaurus in quest of a stronger position. But he was betrayed by his guides, and at dawn the next morning his exhausted troops were yet on the nearer side of the stream, where the Roman army under the two Consuls, numbering forty-five thousand men, soon overtook Hásdrubal's force of sixty thousand men.

Hásdrubal made the best arrangements of his troops possible in this emergency, placing the ten elephants in front "like a line of moving fortresses," his veteran Spanish infantry on the right, the Ligurians in the center, and the Gauls on the left. The conflict which followed—known as the battle of the Metaurus (B. C. 207)—was most fierce and bloody. Both armies fought with the conviction that the fate of the war depended upon the issue of this struggle, and there was absolutely no hope for the vanquished. Finally the Consul, by a circuitous movement, fell upon the Spanish infantry, which had already borne the brunt of the contest. Hásdrubal himself fought bravely during the whole conflict, and, when he perceived that all was lost, he disdained to survive his defeat or to adorn a Roman triumph, and spurring his horse into the midst of a Roman cohort, he fell covered with wounds, thus bravely meeting a soldier's death. The carnage was frightful. The Carthaginian army was totally destroyed, fifty-six thousand of Hásdrubal's troops being slain.

Hannibal had long been looking impatiently at Canusium for his brother; and on the very night when he had been assured that he would arrive, the Consul Nero, with his victorious army, reached Hannibal's camp at Canusium, and ordered Hásdrubal's bloody head to be thrown into the camp over the ramparts. Thereupon Hannibal, struck with the bloody sight, exclaimed: "I see the doom of Carthage!" In this brutal manner did the Consul repay Hannibal's generosity in giving honorable burials to Æmilius Paulus, Gracchus, and Marcellus.

Hannibal was right in his interpretation of the significance of the bloody message, as his brother's terrible defeat and death had lost everything for Carthage. He abandoned his camp and retreated southward into Bruttium, resolved to act on the defensive and maintain his position in Southern Italy among the mountain fastnesses of that region, whose ports afforded him a safe exit from the country. For three years did Hannibal hold this position, but the events of his campaigns in Italy during this period were unsuccessful.

To add to the gloom of the cause of Carthage, the Romans now alarmed the Carthaginians with the prospect of a war in Africa by entering into an alliance with Massinissa, King of Numidia; and the youthful Cornelius Publius Scipio—who in a campaign of five years had established the Roman supremacy in Spain, and who upon his return to Rome was honored for his services by being made Consul—now formed a plan to invade Africa and thus make the Carthaginians tremble for their own city.

Accordingly, in B. C. 204, Scipio sailed from Italy for Africa with an army of thirty thousand men, forty ships of war, and four hundred transports. He encountered no enemy on his voyage, and effected a landing on the African coast near Utica. He found the Carthaginians supported by an army of fifty thousand Libyan infantry and ten thousand cavalry, under Syphax, a native king, and he therefore found himself obliged to confine himself to the coast.

The following year (B. C. 203) Scipio surprised the Carthaginian camp and defeated their army with frightful slaughter, forty thousand of them being slain. He then besieged Utica. The Carthaginians made great efforts to defend so important a city, and were strengthened by a reinforcement of Macedonian and Spanish auxiliaries, but were again defeated and routed by Scipio, and were pursued by the victorious Roman legions to the very walls of Carthage itself. The Carthaginians were unable to keep the field any longer in the face of these repeated defeats, and Carthage itself was exposed to the perils of a siege. Tunes (now Tunis), almost within sight of Carthage, opened its gates to the triumphant Scipio.

In this dire extremity, the Carthaginian Senate recalled Hannibal from Italy for the defense of his own country (B. C. 202). The regret and mortification of Hannibal at receiving this order was indescribable, but he obeyed with the promptness and submission of the meanest soldier. He retired from Italy with the deepest grief, after having held dominion over the finest portions of that country for sixteen years. After landing at Leptis, he took up his march for Hadrumetum, where numerous volunteers were awaiting his arrival.

The urgent requests of the citizens of Carthage induced Hannibal to advance to Zama, a town about five day's march to the west of Carthage. Upon his arrival at Zama, he sent three spies to explore the Roman camp. These were taken and brought before Scipio, who ordered them to be shown through every part of his camp, after which they were dismissed and allowed to return to Hannibal's camp in safety. Struck by this conduct of Scipio, which evinced so much confidence in his own strength, Hannibal proposed a personal interview, hoping thus to obtain favorable terms of peace from the Roman commander.

The two generals met the next day. Hannibal opened the conference by expressing the wish that one people had not gone out of Africa, or the other out of Italy, their natural dominions. He reminded Scipio of the instability of fortune, alluding to himself as a remarkable example; and concluded by offering, on the part of Carthage, to cede Spain, Sicily, Sardinia, and all the other islands in the Western Mediterranean, to the Romans. Scipio's reply was that nothing remained for Carthage except victory or unconditional submission. This ended the conference, and each general withdrew to prepare for the inevitable conflict.

Then followed the famous battle of Zama —one of the most important battles in all history—which was fought in the spring of the year B. C. 202. It was important in various particulars—as regards commanders, armies, the two contending powers, or the dominion that was at stake. Hannibal's army had the advantage of the superiority of numbers, but his troops were chiefly raw levies; only a portion of them having served in his campaigns in Italy, and being thus able to vie with the troops of Scipio in discipline and steadiness.

The battle commenced with the elephants on the Carthaginian side. At the very first onset, these huge beasts were terrified by the shouts of the Romans, and were wounded by the Roman slingers and archers. They quickly turned on their drivers, and spread confusion in the Carthaginian ranks, especially among the cavalry. The Romans followed up this advantage, and soon put the entire Carthaginian army to rout, so that Hannibal was disastrously defeated. Twenty thousand were killed on the Carthaginian side, and as many were taken prisoners. The Romans lost only two thousand men. Hannibal, who had done every-

PUNIC WARS AND FOREIGN CONQUESTS.

thing a great general could do to win the victory, fled with a few horsemen to Hadrumetum, fortune apparently delighting in confounding his experience, his genius and his valor.

After his arrival at Hadrumetum, Hannibal was summoned to Carthage by his government, and he returned to that city after an absence of thirty-six years. The battle of Zama had extinguished the last hope of Carthage, which was now absolutely at the mercy of victorious Rome, and the vanquished Carthaginians were obliged to submit to whatever conditions their Roman conquerors chose to dictate.

Accordingly, in B. C. 201, peace was concluded between the contending powers. Carthage surrendered all her territories outside of Africa to Rome, and restored to Massinissa, King of Numidia, the efficient ally of the Romans in the last campaign of the war, all the territory which she had wrested from him. Carthage also gave up her fleet and her elephants to the Romans, and agreed to pay to Rome a yearly tribute of two hundred talents, and bound herself to enter upon no war in the future without the consent of the Romans.

Thus ended the Second Punic War, after a continuance of seventeen years (B. C. 218-201), in the humiliation of Carthage, which now virtually lost her national independence and became a tributary of Rome. The victorious Scipio—thereafter surnamed *Africanus*, in memory of his conquest—was received with unbounded enthusiasm at Rome on his return to that city, and was honored with a most splendid triumph (as the magnificent pageants and processions which the Romans gave in honor of their victorious generals were called); while Hannibal was driven into exile by his ungrateful countrymen.

The *triumph* was the highest reward which a Roman general could attain; and, as Scipio's triumph was the most splendid in all Roman history, we may as well describe it in this connection.

The victorious chieftain waited outside the city walls until the Senate had decided in regard to his claim to the honor. Several conditions had to be observed. It was required that the victory must have been over foreign, and not over domestic foes; that it must not have been for the recovery of something lost, but for an actual extension of Rome's dominion; that the war must be finished and the Roman army withdrawn from the field, as the soldiers were entitled to a share in their general's triumph. The honor could only be conferred upon individuals of Consular or Prætorian rank. An officer of lower grade could only receive an *ovation*, in which he entered the city on foot; but the chariot was a mark of kingly state only to be allowed to the highest in rank.

When a triumph was decreed, a special vote of the Roman people allowed the general to retain his military command inside the city walls for the day, because he must have resigned it upon entering the city gates, without a suspension of the law. On the appointed day, the Senate and all the magistrates, in magnificent costume, met the general thus honored at the Triumphal Gate. They were placed at the head of the procession, and were followed by a band of trumpeters and by a train of wagons laden with the spoils of the conquered countries, which were indicated by tablets inscribed with their names in large letters. Models of the captured cities, in wood or ivory; pictures of mountains, rivers, or other natural features of the countries subjugated; loads of gold, silver, precious stones, vases, statues, and whatever was most costly, curious, or admired in the spoils of temples and palaces, constituted an essential portion of the display. A band of flute-players came next, and these were preceded by white oxen, destined for the sacrifice, their horns being gilded and adorned with wreaths of flowers and fillets of wool. Elephants and other strange animals from the subdued regions were followed by a train of captive princes or leaders with their families, and a multitude of captives of inferior rank, loaded with chains.

The twelve lictors of the imperator followed next in single file, their fasces being wreathed in laurel. The triumphant general himself came last, in his chariot drawn by four horses. His robes sparkled with golden embroidery. He bore a scepter, and his head was decorated with a wreath of Delphic laurel. Behind him was a slave holding a crown of Etruscan gold, who was instructed to whisper in his master's ear occasionally: "Remember that thou art but a man." The general's sons and lieutenants rode behind him; and were followed by the whole army, their spears being adorned with laurels. These either sang hymns of praise, or amused themselves and the spectators with coarse jokes and doggerel verses at the expense of their general. This rude license of speech was supposed to neutralize the effect of extravagant flattery, which the Romans were taught particularly to dread, as are the modern Italians. All the inhabitants of the city, in gala dress, thronged the streets; and all the temples and shrines in the city were adorned with flowers.

One feature of the occasion presented a horrible contrast to the joy of the day. Some of the captured leaders were led aside and put to death, just as the procession had almost completed its march to the Capitol. When the execution of these distinguished captives was announced, the sacrifices were offered in the temple of Jupiter Capitolínus. The general's laurel crown was placed in the lap of the image. A magnificent banquet was served; and the "triumphator" was escorted home, late in the evening, by a multitude of citizens carrying torches and pipes. The state presented him a site for a house; and a laurel-wreathed statue of the founder of this triumphal mansion was placed at his entrance, to commemorate his glory to his latest posterity.

By the result of the Second Punic War, Rome got rid of her most dangerous rival for the dominion of the civilized world, and became supreme over the Western Mediterranean and the lands surrounding it. A Roman protectorate was established over the native tribes of Northern Africa, and the hitherto-independent kingdom of Syracuse was annexed to the Roman province of Sicily. The principal portion of Spain was likewise annexed to the Roman dominions, and the wealth of the great military republic was now vastly increased.

The Romans severely punished the Southern Italian states for their revolt against the Roman power after the battle of Cannæ. All the native races of Italy, except those of Latium, were depressed, and a Latin dominion was extended over the entire Italian peninsula. The war between the Romans and the Cisalpine Gauls, begun during the Second Punic War, continued after the peace between Rome and Carthage; but ten years after that treaty of peace (B. C. 191) the Cisalpine Gauls were finally and thoroughly subdued, and they became Latinized with wonderful facility.

In the meantime, during the Second Punic War, the Romans had become involved in a long war with Philip V., King of Macedon. After Hannibal's great victory at Lake Trasiménus, Philip believed the power of the Roman Republic to be irretrievably ruined, and was encouraged to prosecute his designs against the Roman power on the east side of the Adriatic. Accordingly in B. C. 216 the King of Macedon began to negotiate with Hannibal for an alliance with Carthage, with a view of furthering his ambitious designs in Greece and Illyria. The Macedonian ambassadors were taken prisoners by the Romans, but the following year the negotiations between Philip and the Carthaginians were brought to a successful termination, and an alliance was concluded between Macedon and Carthage. Philip began the war against Rome in B. C. 214 by besieging Apollonia, the principal seaport of the Romans in Illyria, and capturing Oricum. But the Macedonian king soon discovered that he had seriously underestimated the power of Rome. The Romans under Marcus Valerius Lævínus raised the siege of Apollonia by surprising the Macedonian camp, and Philip was obliged to burn his ships and beat a hasty retreat. Still cherishing his designs against the power of Rome, Philip aroused the animosity of the Greeks by his insolent and arbitrary treatment of them, and caused Aratus of Sicyon, the general of the Achæan League, to be poisoned for venturing to remonstrate with him.

In B. C. 211, when the Romans had recovered from their disasters in Italy, they formed an alliance with the Ætolians, the Elians, the Spartans, the Illyrians, and Attalus I., King of Pergamus, and invaded the Macedonian dominions, reducing Philip to such desperate straits that he was obliged to solicit aid from Carthage, instead of being able to furnish assistance to that power in her gigantic struggle with Rome.

The Romans captured Zacynthus, Nesos and Œniadæ, Anticyra in Locris, and the island of Ægina, and bestowed them on the Ætolians. The first two years of the war were signalized with various success. In B. C. 209 Philopœmen, the commander of the armies of the Achæan League, defeated the Spartans, the allies of the Romans, at Mantinéa; thus enabling the King of Macedon to dictate terms of peace to the Ætolians, with whom he made a separate treaty. The Romans, desirious of devoting all their exertions to the destruction of Carthage, agreed to a treaty of peace with Macedon, on terms honorable to all parties, B. C. 205.

The unscrupulous and reckless ambition of Philip V. of Macedon soon involved him in wars with Rhodes and Pergamus, in which his fleet was defeated off Chios; but his subsequent victory of Ladé gave him possession of Thasos, Samos, Chios in Caria, and several places in Ionia. As Pergamus was an ally of Rome, Philip's attack on that kingdom involved him in another war with the Roman Republic. In B. C. 200 Rome remonstrated with the Macedonian king because of his attack on her ally and his violation of the treaty of peace in which Pergamus had been included; but Philip disregarded Rome's warning. Rome therefore declared war against the King of Macedon in the same year (B. C. 200).

In the meantime Philip was engaged in besieging Athens, but was obliged to retire when the Roman fleet arrived before the city. But before he withdrew he gratified his rage by barbarously destroying the beautiful gardens and buildings in the suburbs, including the Lyceum and the sepulchers of the Athenian heroes. He afterwards returned with a larger army and perpetrated additional outrages. Some of the Greek states were the allies of Rome in this war; some were in alliance with Macedon, while others were neutral. For several years the war was not marked by any decisive results; but in B. C. 198 the Consul Titus Quinctius Flaminius succeeded in inducing the Achæan League to join the Roman alliance, to which the Ætolian League had already become attached. At the same time Flaminius declared himself the champion of the separate independence of the Greek states, and nearly every state of Greece espoused his cause.

In B. C. 197 the Roman army commanded by Flaminius inflicted an irretrievable defeat upon King Philip V. of Macedon in the decisive battle of Cynoscéphalæ, near Scotussa, in Thessaly. The Macedonian kingdom, already menaced from the direction of Illyria by a combined army of Romans, Illyrians and Dardanians, and from the sea by the fleets of Rome, Pergamus and Rhodes, was so exhausted that Philip was under the necessity of soliciting peace. In B. C. 196 a treaty of peace was made by which the Macedonian king withdrew his garrisons from the Greek towns and acknowledged the independence of the Greek states, surrendered his fleet to the Romans, and paid a war-indemnity of one thousand talents to Rome. To gratify the national vanity of the Greeks, Flaminius, at the Isthmian Games, proclaimed the independence of Greece from the Macedonian dominion; but the Romans were as anxious to extend their supremacy over all Greece as the King of Macedon had been to maintain his ascendency over the country, and the Roman armies were not withdrawn from the Hellenic peninsula until B. C. 194.

In the final settlement of Grecian affairs, the Romans assigned smaller limits to the various Greek states than they had previously possessed, and left the Achæan and

Ætolian Leagues remain as a check upon each other. Most of the Grecian states were satisfied with the new arrangement, as the separate independence of each state was guaranteed. But the Ætolians were not contented, and sought to induce Macedon, Sparta, and the Syrian kingdom of the Seleúcidæ to assist them in subverting the new settlement. Antíochus the Great of Syria responded to the request of the Ætolians by marching into Greece with an army not sufficiently large for the task on hand; and he was defeated by the Romans at Thermopylæ in B. C. 191, and compelled to retreat into Asia Minor, whither he was pursued by the Roman army commanded by Scipio Africanus and his brother Scipio Asiaticus. After sustaining a frightful defeat in the great battle of Magnesia, near Ephesus, from the two Scipios (B. C. 190), Antíochus the Great was forced to accept a peace by which he gave up to the Romans all his territories in Europe and all those in Asia Minor except Cilicia, to pay to the Romans fifteen thousand talents, (a sum equal to about fifteen million dollars of our money), and to deliver up Hannibal, who was then living in exile at his court, and whom the Romans believed to have contributed to the war by his intrigues. The Ætolians were compelled to submit unconditionally to Rome, which deprived them of a part of their territory, and reduced them to the condition of subject allies of the Republic.

Finding the vindictive Romans determined upon his destruction, Hannibal secretly left the dominions of Antíochus the Great, and, after wandering for some time from one petty state to another, finally found refuge at the court of Prusias, King of Bithynia. But the Romans did not feel secure so long as the great Carthaginian general was living. With a mean and revengeful spirit utterly unworthy of a great nation, they sent one of their generals to Prusias to demand that Hannibal be delivered into their power. Fearing to incur the resentment of the Romans, and hoping to conciliate their friendship by this breach of hospitality, Prusias ordered a guard to be placed over Hannibal with the design of surrendering him to the Romans.

The unfortunate old Carthaginian general, thus persecuted with implacability from one country to another, and perceiving that all means of escape were cut off from him, finally committed suicide by swallowing poison, which he had for a long time carried with him for this purpose (B. C. 183). With his dying breath he reproached the Romans for their degeneracy and Prusias for betraying his guest. Hannibal's great rival and conqueror, Scipio Africanus, who, having been treated with ingratitude by his own countrymen, spent his last days in voluntary exile, died the same year.

On his return to Rome from his campaign against Antíochus the Great of Syria, Scipio Africanus was accused of having secreted some of the treasure obtained from the Syrian king; and, scorning to answer the unjust accusation, the conqueror of Hannibal retired into exile into a country village of Southern Italy, where he died shortly afterwards (B. C. 183). The instances of Hannibal and Scipio Africanus are striking illustrations of the saying that "Republics are ungrateful."

Scipio directed that his remains should not be conveyed to Rome, which had repaid his valiant services with such base ingratitude. Nevertheless, the day of his death was a day of universal sorrow in Rome, and many who had treated this great general with injustice during his life shed tears at his death. A monument was afterwards erected at the place where he died. Scipio had ordered this inscription upon his tomb: "Ungrateful country, you do not possess even my bones!" His brother, Scipio Asiaticus, was also for a time a victim of persecution, but a reaction set in before his death, and he received due honor for his eminent public services.

It is said that during their exiles from their respective countries, Hannibal and Scipio Africanus frequently met at Ephesus, in Asia Minor, where many friendly conversations occurred between them. On one of these occasions Scipio is said to have asked

Hannibal whom he considered the greatest general; to which Hannibal replied: "Alexander; because that, with a small body of men he had defeated very numerous armies, and had overrun a great part of the world." Whereupon Scipio inquired: "And who do you think deserves the next place?" To this Hannibal answered: "Pyrrhus; he first taught the method of forming a camp to the best advantage." Scipio then asked: "And whom do you place next to those?" "Myself," responded Hannibal. Upon this Scipio asked, smiling: "Where, then, would you have placed yourself if you had conquered me?" Hannibal thereupon answered: "Above Alexander, above Pyrrhus, and above all other generals."

Hannibal is unsurpassed as a general. Not a solitary military blunder can be charged against him; and the skill and address with which he contrived to keep in constant obedience an army consisting of the most discordant elements is truly wonderful. The charges of perfidy and cruelty which the Roman writers made against him are utterly groundless and are not substantiated by facts. Hannibal's character appears nowhere so great as when, after his defeat at Zama, he, with his spirit unbroken, applied the powers of his gigantic mind to the reform of political abuses among his countrymen, and to the restoration of the finances, in the hope of again elevating his country to independence. In this he manifested genuine patriotism.

The year B. C. 183—which witnessed the death of Hannibal and Scipio Africanus—was also signalized by the death of Philopœmen, the second chieftain of the Achæan League, who was compelled to drink the cup of poison during this same fatal year.

In the meantime the Romans were prosecuting four other wars in the West of Europe. They had not yet thoroughly subdued the Spanish peninsula, where the gallant resistance of the inhabitants of Lusitania (now Portugal) constantly occupied the attention of the Roman arms. The Romans likewise waged wars against the mountain tribes of Liguria, and against the natives of Sardinia and Corsica. Tiberius Sempronius Gracchus finally conquered Sardinia about B. C. 176. He carried so many Sardinian captives to Rome as slaves that the term "Sardinians for sale" became a synonym in Rome for anything cheap and worthless.

Philip V. of Macedon, the old enemy of Rome, aided that power in the war against Antíochus the Great of Syria and the Ætolians; and, in reward for this service, the Romans permitted him to extend his dominion over portions of Thrace and Thessaly. When the Romans no longer needed his assistance, they ordered him to surrender all his territories but Macedon proper. In the negotiations which followed, and which were conducted by Philip's second son, Demetrius, who had for a long time resided at Rome as a hostage, the Roman Senate somewhat relaxed its demands on account of its friendly feeling for the young prince. This induced Philip's eldest son, Perseus, to bring an accusation of treason against his brother, of whom he was jealous. Perseus forged letters to sustain his charges, and Philip caused Demetrius to be put to death. His discovery of the truth when too late caused Philip such bitter remorse as to hasten his death, which occurred in B. C. 179.

Philip V. had intended to leave the crown of Macedon to a distant relative named Antigonus, thus punishing Perseus for his crime in having caused the death of Demetrius; but Antigonus was not present at the Macedonian court when Philip died, and Perseus ascended the Macedonian throne without opposition. Philip had spent his last years in preparing for a renewal of the war with Rome, which he perceived to be inevitable, and Perseus diligently continued these military preparations. The mines were worked industriously and the Macedonian treasury was rapidly filled. The losses in the population of the kingdom were supplied by the importation of colonies from Thrace. The Macedonian army was augmented and carefully disciplined, and Perseus contracted alliances with the Illyrians, the Gauls and the Germans, whose assistance the Macedonian king expected to employ in the impending war with the Roman Republic.

For eight years Perseus continued his warlike preparations. He might have drawn all the Greeks to his standard, as there was already a large party in Hellas which preferred the supremacy of Macedon to that of Rome; but Perseus wavered, and pursued such a selfish and penurious policy that his opportunity was lost to him. In B. C. 172 Eúmenes II., King of Pergamus, formally accused Perseus before the Roman Senate of hostile aims. When Eúmenes returned home from Rome, he was murdered near Delphi; and as the Romans believed Perseus to have instigated the murder, they declared war against him.

In B. C. 171 a Roman army landed in Epirus, and during the two following months the Greeks were prevailed upon to espouse the Roman cause and to take sides against the King of Macedon. The Romans crushed the Bœotian League, which was friendly to Macedon, and induced Thessaly and Achæa to join the Roman alliance. The supporters of Perseus were crushed everywhere, and Perseus himself was induced to accept a truce during the two months. When the Romans were fully prepared, they marched into Thessaly, but were attacked and defeated by Perseus, who neglected to follow up his victory.

In B. C. 168 the Roman army under the command of Lucius Æmilius Paulus inflicted a crushing defeat upon Perseus in the decisive battle of Pydna—a battle which made Rome mistress of the civilized world. Perseus fled to the sacred island of Samothrace, but was soon obliged to surrender himself to a Roman squadron. He was carried a captive to Rome to grace the triumph of his conqueror, and was then imprisoned in a dungeon. The generous intercession of Æmilius Paulus in the fallen king's behalf obtained his release, and Perseus was permitted to pass the remainder of his life in a milder kind of captivity at Alba Longa.

The Roman victory at Pydna put an end to the Macedonian kingdom, which was divided into four states subject to Rome, and these were not permitted to hold any intercourse with each other. To compensate the Macedonians for the loss of their national independence, a tribute equal to but half of the taxes which their kings had exacted from them was required by the Romans. The four states into which the Macedonian kingdom was divided were Macedon proper, Thessaly, Epirus and Thrace.

Another result of the Roman triumph over Perseus was the subjection of the greater portion of Greece to the Roman supremacy. All the Grecian confederacies except the Achæan League were dissolved. Achæa had been the faithful friend and ally of Rome during these wars with the Kingdom of Macedon; but Rome now considered it essential that she should be without a possible rival in Greece, and that therefore Achæa should either submit to Rome unconditionally or that she must be conquered. Accordingly, in B. C. 167, the Roman Republic demanded the trial by the Achæan League of one thousand of its leading citizens on charges of having secretly afforded assistance to the King of Macedon. The Achæan assembly did not dare refuse compliance with this demand from Rome; and the thousand accused Achæan citizens, among whom was the historian Polybius, were carried captive to Italy and imprisoned in the Etruscan towns. Thus the party friendly to Rome was left in power in Achæa.

Twenty years after the overthrow of Perseus, King of Macedon (B. C. 148), an impostor named Andriscus, who pretended to be the brother of that monarch, instigated the Macedonians to revolt against the Roman dominion; but they were speedily subdued by the Roman arms, and Macedonia finally became a Roman province; and this was soon followed by the subjection of all Greece to Roman sway.

The thousand Achæan captives had been kept imprisoned in Italy for seventeen years without a hearing, with the deliberate design of exasperating their partisans in Greece; and finally, when all but three hundred of their number had died, the survivors were suddenly released and sent back to their native land, with the hope that their resentment against Rome would cause them to commit some rash act of hostility—a hope in which the Romans were not disappointed. Burning with vengeance against Rome, three of the surviving captives who had just returned came into power in Achæa; and their resentment gave the Romans what they most anxiously desired—a pretext for an armed invasion of the Achæan territory. The Achæan League took up arms to defend the independence of its territories, and war was declared in B. C. 146. But one of the Achæan leaders was disastrously defeated and slain at Thermopylæ; and another, with the remnant of the Achæan army, made a stand at Corinth, where he was defeated by the Roman army under the Consul Mummius, who took and plundered that city and reduced it to ashes. Thebes and Chalcis suffered the same fate. The statues, pictures, and other valuable effects taken by Mummius at Corinth were sent to Rome. Mummius was so ignorant of the value of works of art that he contracted with the shipmasters who conveyed his plunder to Italy that in case the statues and paintings were lost, they should furnish others as good in their stead.

With the capture and destruction of Corinth, in B. C. 146, Greece became a Roman province under the name of *Achæa;* and within a few years the land of the Hellenes was placed under Proconsular government, like the other provinces of the Roman Republic. Greece remained under Roman dominion, first under the Republic and the undivided Empire until A. D. 395, and thenceforth under the Eastern Roman Empire for over a thousand years, until the conquest of that empire by the Ottoman Turks in A. D. 1453, under whose dominion Hellas remained until it recovered its independence in A. D. 1829.

During the same year that Greece yielded to Roman sway (B. C. 146), Carthage was destroyed by the Romans. After the close of the Second Punic War the Carthaginians seemed inclined to remain at peace; but the ambition of their neighbor on their western border, Massinissa, King of Numidia, who, to their misfortune, lived to be over ninety years of age, would not permit them to remain quiet. Massinissa was constantly encroaching upon the Carthaginian territory and seizing the towns belonging to Carthage.

When the Carthaginians appealed to the Roman Senate as umpire, that body sent out commissioners, who almost invariably decided in favor of Massinissa. On one of these occasions, Marcus Porcius Cato—commonly known as Cato the Elder—acted as commissioner. When this distinguished Roman Senator beheld the beauty and fertility of the Carthaginian territory, its high state of culture, and the strength, wealth and population of the city of Carthage itself, he became apprehensive lest it might yet imperil the supremacy of Rome. His vanity, likewise, of which this venerable moralist possessed a sufficient share, was wounded because the Carthaginians, who were manifestly in the right, did not instantly acquiesce in the decision rendered by him and his colleagues; and he returned to Rome intensely embittered against them.

Thenceforth Cato made a practice of concluding all his speeches in the Senate, on whatever subject, with this sentence: "Delenda est Carthago." (Carthage must be destroyed). On one occasion he carried a number of fresh African figs to the Senate-House, and shook them out of his cloak while the attention of the other Senators was directed towards him. As the Senators admired the fruit, he exclaimed: "The country that produces these is but three days' sail from Rome!" By artful tricks of this nature, Cato kept alive among the Romans the memory of the First and Second Punic Wars, and the danger with which the existence of Carthage threatened Rome. At length the Roman Senate, pretending to regard the conduct of Carthage in defending her own territories against Massinissa as a breach of the peace, declared war.

The Carthaginians first sought to conciliate the Romans, and banished all their citizens who had incurred the resentment of their old foes. In great alarm, the Carthaginians also gave up three hundred noble Carthaginian children as hostages, at the demand of the Romans. The Roman army then crossed over into Africa. The Carthaginians were now commanded to give up all their arms and military stores. This command, hard as it was, was promptly obeyed. They brought two hundred suits of armor and weapons in wagons to the Roman camp. The Roman Consul Censorius commended them for their diligence and obedience, and then informed them of the decree of the Roman Senate. This was that the Carthaginians should abandon their city, and build another city, without walls or fortifications, not nearer to the sea-shore than ten miles, while Carthage was to be burned to the ground.

The Carthaginians gave themselves up to grief and despair at this cruel and insolent demand. They rolled themselves in the dust, tore their garments, beat their breasts, called upon their gods, and bitterly reproached the Romans for their cruelty and treachery. When they recovered from these paroxysms, they took courage from despair, set their insolent foes at defiance, and resolved to perish beneath the ruins of their city rather than submit to such humiliation. Then began the *Third Punic War* (B. C. 149) —the last of those great struggles between Rome and Carthage.

The Carthaginians made vigorous preparations for the defense of their city. The two Hásdrubals were appointed commanders. Their temples and other sacred places were turned into workshops. Public buildings were torn down to provide wood and metal, and in a remarkably brief time the walls and their defenders were again armed. Catapults for the defense of the walls, and arms and armor for the troops, were manufactured. Men and women were engaged day and night in manufacturing arms; and the women cut off their long hair to be twisted into bow-strings, and to make cords for the catapults.

During all this time the Roman army was at Utica, so that the preparations for the defense of the city were carried on before the very eyes of the insolent foe. At length the Romans advanced, expecting to find the city defenseless. To their indescribable astonishment they saw the walls armed and lined with defenders prepared to resist any attack to the death. The Romans at once perceived that an assault was impossible, and they commenced the siege of Carthage by land and sea. The Romans had not expected such an exhibition of courage and patriotism on the part of the Carthaginians, and for two years the Roman army met with some signal repulses.

In the third year of the war and of the siege, Scipio Æmilianus, the adopted son of the great Scipio Africanus, was assigned to the command of the Roman army. He formed a camp within a dart's cast of the city wall, which extended quite across the isthmus on which Carthage was situated. By this means Scipio cut off the besieged Carthaginians from the land, so that their only chance of obtaining supplies was by sea. But Scipio resolved to deprive them of this resource likewise, by blockading the mouth of the harbor. He then commenced the construction of a huge mole from shore to shore, with large stones. At first the Carthaginians mocked at the efforts of the Romans; but when they discovered how speedily the work progressed, they were seized with alarm, and at once began to dig another passage out of the port. They labored so incessantly and stealthily that the Romans were foiled in their efforts; and the Carthaginians having built a fleet of two hundred new ships out of their old materials in their blockaded port, sent a naval detachment of fifty vessels to sea by the new artificial channel. If they had taken advantage of the surprise and consternation of the Romans, who were totally unprepared for the sudden turn of affairs, they might have attacked and destroyed the Roman fleet. But they merely made a demonstration and then returned to port, and the two fleets engaged the third day afterwards. The small vessels of the Carthaginians caused

STORMING OF THE BYRSA, CARTHAGE.

the Romans considerable annoyance, but while they were returning to port they produced much confusion on their own side, of which the Romans took advantage. On the following day Scipio attacked the quay where the Carthaginian vessels were stationed; and after a terrible conflict the Romans finally effected a permanent lodgment on the place.

When spring opened the besieging Romans vigorously attacked the inner harbor. The besieged Carthaginians set fire to the buildings on one side during the preceding night, as they had expected the assault from that quarter. But a strong party of the Romans secretly approached on the opposite side, and obtained possession of the place while the attention of the defenders was directed to a different quarter. Thereupon Scipio advanced to the great market, and there kept his followers under arms during the night. The next morning he proceeded to attack the citadel, in which the greater part of the inhabitants had now sought refuge. Three streets, filled with houses six stories high, connected the citadel with the market.

As the Romans attempted to penetrate these three streets, they found themselves assailed from the roofs, whereupon they burst into the houses, and pursued the Carthaginians from roof to roof, killing them and throwing them down from the battlements. Others of the Romans, in the meantime, forced their way along the streets. Weapons flew in every direction. The air resounded with the groans of the wounded and the dying, with the shrieks of women and children, and with the shouts of the victorious Romans. The assailants at length arrived in front of the citadel.

By order of Scipio the conquered city was set on fire. A frightful scene of horror and devastation ensued. Carthage was shrouded in flames; and the miserable inhabitants, between the fire and the enemy, were destined to perish. Old men, women and children, driven from their dwellings and hiding-places by the spreading conflagration, perished by thousands; and every description of shocking misery now startled the eye.

The flames raged unabated for six days. On the seventh day the Carthaginians in the citadel offered to surrender on condition that their lives should be spared. The request was granted to all except deserters, and fifty thousand came out of the citadel. The deserters, nine hundred in number, retired with Hásdrubal to the temple of Esculapius. As this temple was built on a lofty precipitous site, they were able to defend themselves there until they were overcome with fatigue and hunger. Hásdrubal stole away from his followers and surrendered himself to Scipio, who made him sit at his feet in sight of the Carthaginians, who reproached him as a coward and a traitor, and then setting fire to the temple, all perished in the flames.

While this dreadful catastrophe was in progress, it is said that Hásdrubal's wife, whom he had left in the temple with her two little children, stepped in front of Scipio and exclaimed: "O! Roman, thou hast warred against an enemy, and hast no vengeance to fear from the gods; but may the deities of Carthage, and thou likewise, punish Hásdrubal, that traitor to me, his children, and her temples!" She then reproached her husband in the following words: "O! wretched, faithless, and most cowardly of men! these flames will consume me and my children, but what a triumph wilt thou adorn! thou, the general of mighty Carthage! and what punishment wilt thou not undergo from him before whom thou art sitting!" After she had said this, she cut the throats of her children, and cast them and herself into the flames.

While the victorious Scipio Æmilianus was viewing the ruin of this mighty city, which had stood for more than seven centuries, which had abounded in wealth, which had spread her commerce far and wide, which had subdued numerous powerful nations, and which had made Rome tremble for her own existence, he could not refrain from shedding bitter tears. In his commiseration for the sad fate of this formidable rival of his country, Scipio repeated the following lines from Homer:

"Yet, come it will; the day decreed by fates—
How my heart trembles while my tongue relates!
The day when thou, imperial Troy, must bend,
And see thy warriors fall, thy glories end!"

The Greek historian Polybius, who was present, asked Scipio as to the meaning he intended to convey. Scipio answered that his thoughts were centered on his own country, which, he foresaw, must likewise fall submissive to the vicissitudes that control human affairs.

Scipio allowed his soldiers to pillage the fallen city while it was a prey to the flames. He despatched his swiftest sailing vessel to Rome, with the account of his conquest. The unfeeling Romans gave way to the most extravagant joy on hearing of the end of Carthage. Ten commissioners were sent to Africa to aid Scipio in regulating the affairs of the conquered country.

The city was totally destroyed. A tenth part of the population only survived the destruction—about thirty thousand men and twenty-five thousand women. Most of these were sold into slavery. Only the ruins of the city were left standing, and the Roman Senate sternly commanded the triumphant Scipio to destroy even these. Scipio accordingly ordered the ruins to be set on fire, and they continued burning seventeen days, until not a vestige of the once-mighty city of Carthage remained, except the heap of ashes which marked the spot where this once-famous mistress of the Western Mediterranean had stood.

Heavy curses were pronounced on any one who should attempt to rebuild the destroyed city. All the towns which had remained faithful to Carthage were treated in the same rude manner. Those which had espoused the cause of Rome, especially Utica, were rewarded with an increase of territory. The territory of Carthage became a Roman province under the name of *Africa*, of which Utica was made the capital. This city became the resort of Roman merchants and ships, and these inherited the prosperous commerce formerly enjoyed by Carthage (B. C. 146). A poll tax was levied upon the people of the newly-conquered province, and a Proprætor was sent from Rome every year to govern it. Thus ended the Third Punic War after a continuance of only four years (B. C. 149-146).

The Romans were still engaged in constant wars with the native Celtic tribes of the Spanish peninsula. These tribes were hardy, brave, and freedom-loving; and they easily defended themselves in their own country, because of its great natural strength. In the northern and western portions of the peninsula the native tribes still continued to gallantly resist the efforts of the Romans to subdue them, and the armies of the Republic found the attempt at conquest an almost impossible task. The Lusitanians, who occupied the region embraced by the modern Kingdom of Portugal, were particularly distinguished for their unconquerable spirit. They were even able to inflict a disastrous defeat upon the Roman army commanded by the Prætor Servius Sulpicius Galba in B. C. 151. The following year (B. C. 150) Galba avenged himself by a most infamously treacherous act. He entered into a treaty with three Lusitanian tribes on the northern bank of the Tagus, and promised to remove them to better settlements. Relying upon his plighted word, the Lusitanians, seven thousand in number, came to him to obtain the proffered lands. They were separated into three divisions, disarmed, and some of them were massacred, the remainder being sold into slavery.

One of those who escaped from the treacherous Galba was Viriathus, a man of humble origin, but of wonderful courage. His countrymen now selected him as their leader. His remarkable bravery and skill won their admiration, and his simplicity and frugality, his unaffected manners, and his boundless generosity to his own countrymen excited their enthusiasm, so that he was universally recognized as their king. "It seemed as if in that prosaic age one of the Homeric heroes had appeared."

Viriathus defeated the Roman armies in seven stubbornly-fought battles, and in the last of these he forced the Roman general, Servilianus, to surrender with his entire army. He was extremely magnanimous in the hour of victory, and concluded a treaty of peace with the Roman commander by which the Lusitanians were acknowledged as an independent sovereign community, with Viriathus as king. The Romans promised to respect the Lusitanian kingdom over which Viriathus reigned; while that king promised, on his part, to be their friend and ally. The Roman Senate ratified these conditions of peace with the deliberate design of violating them, and made use of the first pretext to renew the war.

Viriathus sent trusted messengers to remonstrate with the Romans against the breaking of the treaty and to propose conditions of peace, but the Roman Consul bribed these envoys to assassinate their king, and the valiant Viriathus was stabbed while asleep by his most trusted friends. The Lusitanian soldiers honored their murdered hero with a magnificent funeral, and continued the war against the Romans, but within a year the Lusitanian army was decisively defeated and forced to surrender; whereupon Lusitania became a Roman province.

The war between the Romans and the freedom-loving Numantians, in the North of Spain, still continued. The Roman commanders supplemented the efforts of their armies with the basest treachery. The city of Numantia held out gallantly against the Roman army under Quintius Pompey. A terrible winter carried sickness and suffering into the ranks of the Roman legions, and Pompey offered favorable terms of peace to the Numantians, but disgraceful to the besiegers, according to Roman ideas. The Numantians accepted these conditions, and when they had made all their stipulated payments but the last, Pompey's successor in the Consulate arrived at the Roman camp. Being thus relieved of his command, Pompey denied ever having made a treaty with the Numantians, and persistently reiterated this falsehood before the Roman Senate.

The war continued six years; and after two large Roman armies had been utterly destroyed, Scipio Æmilianus, the conqueror of Carthage, and the greatest general of his time, besieged Numantia with an army of sixty thousand men and starved the city into surrender (B. C. 133). Great numbers of the Numantians, rather than become prisoners to an enemy whom they had so often found guilty of falsehood, destroyed their women and children, and then setting fire to their city, threw themselves into the flames and perished to a man. Scipio Æmilianus selected fifty of the most illustrious of the survivors to grace his triumph, and sold the remainder into slavery. The city was leveled with the earth, and its territory was distributed among the neighboring tribes. Excepting the northern coast, the whole Spanish peninsula was now subject to the Roman Republic, and was divided into three Roman provinces—Hispania Tarraconensis, Hispania Bœtica, and Lusitania. The Lusitanian mountains continued to be infested by brigands for a long time, and this made it necessary to build the isolated country-houses in that region like fortresses, capable of defense in case of need. Spain ultimately became the most prosperous and the best organized of all the countries under the dominion of Rome, the country being occupied by a thriving and industrious population, and being rich in corn and cattle.

About the same time the Roman dominion was enlarged by the acquisition of the Kingdom of Pergamus, by bequest from its last king, Attalus Philométer. The will was disputed by Aristonícus, whose opposition was speedily crushed, and Pergamus was organized into a Roman province under the name of *Asia*. The Greater Phrygia was detached and bestowed upon Mithridátes IV., King of Pontus, as a reward for his aid to the Romans in the war against Aristonícus. By the bequest of Attalus Philométer, the Roman Republic came into possession of most of Asia Minor.

SECTION IX.—RISE OF LATIN LITERATURE.

ATIN literature took its rise during the period of the Punic Wars. During the period of the Kings, and during the earlier ages of the Republic, nothing deserving the name of literature existed among the Romans. The Roman people during these early times were too much occupied in war, and their peculiar taste was too strongly inclined towards conquest and the enlargement of their dominion to allow them any considerable leisure or patronage to the arts of peace. But subsequently, when the Romans had attained to security and opulence, and when they had been led by their very conquests to a knowledge of the arts and sciences prevailing in the conquered countries, they commenced to patronize and cultivate these arts and sciences.

The first intercourse of the Romans with the Greeks made the Romans acquainted with the productions of Grecian taste and art, and stimulated a desire to imitate them. This was probably the origin of Latin, or Roman literature. There was, however, something more national in the first rude attempt of the Romans at dramatic composition. About the close of the fourth century from the founding of Rome, a plague broke out in the city. Having exhausted its own superstitious ceremonies without effect, the Roman Senate decreed that the *histriones*, or play-actors, should be summoned from Etruria to appease the wrath of the gods by their scenic representations. The Etruscan actors were thus called to play at Rome, their performances consisting mainly of rude dances and gesticulations, accompanied by the flute. Some kind of a story was represented by pantomimes, but there does not seem to have been any dialogue. This whimsical kind of religious expiation appears to have had at least a portion of its designed effect. The Roman multitude were amused. The fancy of the Roman youths was powerfully aroused, and they amused the Etruscan actors, improving on the entertainment by rallying each other in jocose and extempore dialogue.

About the same time the *Fescennine verses*, originally employed in Etruria at the harvest-home of the peasantry, began to be applied by the Romans to marriage ceremonies and public diversions. There were likewise songs of triumph in a rude measure, and these were sung by the soldiers at the ovations of their leaders, some of these laudatory strains being seasoned with coarse jokes and camp jests. These effusions afterwards expanded into ballads, in which the exploits of heroes and the adventures of the Roman armies were related. None of these ballads were preserved by the Romans after they had acquired a knowledge of Greek literature.

The Roman conquest of Magna Græcia, and the intercourse opened to the Romans with the Greek colonies of Sicily, were instrumental in causing a sudden improvement in the Latin language, and an equally sudden advancement in taste and literature among the Romans. In consequence of these events, the Romans could not fail to acquire a part of Grecian taste and spirit, or, at any rate, to admire the beautiful creations of Grecian fancy. Many of the Roman conquerors remained in the Greek cities of Southern Italy, while the people of these cities who were most distinguished for literary attainments established their residence in Rome.

We first find the primitive vestiges of literature among the Romans in the latter portion of the fifth century from the founding of Rome, or during the stirring epoch of the Punic Wars. This literature appeared earliest in the form of dramatic poetry. The first who attempted to establish a regular theatre at Rome was LIVIUS ANDRONICUS, a native of Magna Græcia, who was born B. C. 219. His earliest play was 1epresented about a year after the close of the First Punic War. But little remains of his pieces to the present day except their titles. Nevertheless they continued popular in Rome for a long time, and were read by the boys at school even during the reign of Augustus Cæsar. The plays of Livius Andronicus seem to have been tragedies.

NÆVIUS, the next Roman dramatic poet, was distinguished as both a tragic and a comic writer. He lampooned the elder Scipio and other illustrious Roman citizens, for which he was imprisoned, and ultimately banished from Rome. ENNIUS, the first Roman lyric poet, was born in Calabria about B. C. 240, and has generally been honored as the "Father of Roman Song." Ennius served as a soldier in the armies of the Roman Republic. The fragments of his works yet remaining indicate that Ennius vastly surpassed his predecessors in the art of versification, as well as in poetic genius. He professed to imitate Homer, and endeavored to persuade the Romans that the soul and genius of that celebrated epic poet of early Greece had revived in him through the medium of a peacock, in accordance with the process of the soul's transmigration, according to the Pythagoréan doctrine. Ennius made use of the old national ballads in the production of an epic poem called the *Annals*, which embodied the leading events of Roman history prior to his time. His versification was rugged, but he occasionally produced lines of considerable harmony and beauty, and his conceptions were frequently set forth with remarkable energy and spirit. He likewise attempted dramatic, satiric and didactic poetry; but only fragments of his works yet exist. Ennius wrote an epic on the First Punic War.

PLAUTUS, the first Roman comic poet, born B. C. 227, was a writer of great genius. He possessed a rich vein of wit, a happy invention, and great force of humorous expression. His chief models were the Greek comic writers, and he was especially successful in low comedy. It is said that he realized a considerable fortune by the popularity of his plays, and that he lost it in specula-

tion. He was thus reduced to the necessity of working as a common laborer, when the general resort to the theater at Rome was diminished by a famine. The Roman people were so captivated by the drollery and the homely wit of Plautus that his plays were yet favorite pieces on the Roman stage even after the more elegant performances of Terence began to be represented. In modern times such eminent dramatists as Molière, Shakspeare and Dryden have copied from Plautus.

TERENCE, the most celebrated of the early Roman comic poets, was a slave and was born at Carthage in B. C. 192. He was the delight and ornament of the Roman stage. After he had obtained his freedom he became the friend of Cœlius and the younger Scipio. After Terence had written six comedies at Rome, he went to Greece, and never returned to Italy. One account informs us that he lost his life at sea on his voyage back to Italy, with one hundred and eight comedies which he had translated from Menander, the last great Athenian comic poet. Other accounts state that having sent these translated comedies before him to Rome by sea, they were lost by shipwreck, and that Terence died of grief in consequence in Arcadia.

Six comedies of Terence are yet in existence, and are remarkable for the high excellence of the characters, the truth and the refinement of the dialogue, and the management of the plot. Terence possessed less invention and less comic power than Plautus, but he had more taste, a better style, and a keener knowledge of human nature. In regard to style, Terence is considered as a model of correct composition.

MARCUS PORCIUS CATO—Cato the Elder—is the earliest of the Latin prose writers whose works are extant, and was born B. C. 235. Like nearly all Roman citizens, Cato was brought up in the profession of arms. In the brief intervals of peace, he resided during his youth at a small country-house, in the Sabine territory. He was distinguished for his industry, his frugality and his fondness for agriculture. In the morning he went to the villages round about, to plead and defend the cause of such as applied to him for aid. He then returned to his fields, where he toiled with his servants until they had completed their task, wearing a plain cloak over his shoulders in winter, and being almost naked in summer. After this he sat down with them at table, eating the same bread and drinking the same wine. Thus he became the best farmer of his time. He also occupied all the more important civil and military offices of the Republic. During most of his life he exhibited the most intense aversion to Grecian learning and refinement, but in his old age he commenced the study of the Greek language.

Cato wrote history, orations, and works on morals, education, medicine, war, and other topics. All his works are lost, except a treatise on farming, and some epistles. His work on farming lacks method, but abounds in curious matter, giving rules for purchasing and cultivating land, for housekeeping, for making cakes and puddings, for fattening chickens and geese, for curing pains and disorders, etc.

History was not written among the Romans simply for the gratification of curiosity, but also to stimulate by the force of example, and to urge the citizens of the Republic to emulation in military prowess. They accordingly had annalists from the earliest period of the Republic, but the works of all the early Roman historians have perished.

Conquered Greece exerted a powerful influence upon Roman civilization, life and manners. Greek musicians, artists, schoolmasters and philosophers flocked to Rome in large numbers. A taste for Greek culture prevailed, and the young patricians were carefully instructed in the Greek language. This spirit in the Roman nation was encouraged by the Scipios, Flaminius, Marcellus and many other celebrated public men. The Greek learned men, philosophers and poets endeavored to carry the Greek spirit and language to Rome, along with the works of Grecian art. Under the protection of the Scipios, Roman poets composed verses in imitation of their Greek prototypes, as in the case of Plautus and Terence. But as the minds of the Romans were directed wholly to the practical, to the conduct of war, the government of the state, and the administration of justice, the Romans did not attain the same high rank in intellectual culture as the Greeks. The Roman people took more delight in spectacles addressed to the senses, such as rough gladiatorial combats and the contests of wild beasts, than in the productions of the mind.

As Rome extended her power, the manners of the Roman people degenerated, and they became corrupted by intercourse with the conquered nations. The stern virtue and simple manners of the earlier Romans gradually gave way before the Greek luxury and refinement; and the wealth of the Orientals flowed into Italy, producing extravagance and effeminacy among the people whose ancestors had been distinguished for their honest poverty, their stern military and civic virtue, and their republican simplicity. The Romans thus imitated the Greeks and the Orientals in the elegance and refinement of the arrangement of their dwellings, in the luxury and extravagance of their meals and dress, in their politeness and suavity in social intercourse, and in sensual enjoyments and luxurious pleasures. The conquering Romans acquired the vices and excesses of the nations which they vanquished and subdued, together with their wealth and civilization.

The elder Cato—celebrated for his stern virtue and old Roman simplicity—in his office of Censor, tried in vain to stem the tide of corruption and moral degeneracy which threatened to engulf the Roman commonwealth. By his instrumentality, the Greek philosophers and teachers were banished from Rome, and the most severe punishments were inflicted upon such of his countrymen as committed offenses against public morality. At his death, Cato declared that his countrymen were a degenerate race.

SECTION X.—CIVIL WARS AND FALL OF THE REPUBLIC.

ROME had now become mistress of the civilized world. Although Roman conquests were still made, the period upon which we are now entering was distinguished chiefly for the degeneracy of the Roman people, and for a century of civil wars which finally ended the Roman Republic. The Roman conquests brought wealth, with its attendant evils—luxury, corruption, and loss of patriotism and civic virtue. The two classes of the Roman population—the rich and the poor—began to entertain the most deadly animosity toward each other.

The old strife between patricians and plebeians had long ceased. Many plebeian families had become patrician through their members having held high offices of state; and they had their clientage, their share in the public lands, their seats in the Senate, and their right to display waxen images of their ancestors in their houses or in funeral processions, equally with the oldest patrician families. Freedmen were constantly admitted to the franchise.

The political and social condition of Rome was now such as to endanger the liberties of the citizens. The great mass of the population were extremely poor, while the majority of the nobility were immensely rich. All the land, as well as all the lucrative offices, had come into the possession of the nobles; and thus the greatest inequality in the distribution of property existed. The large plantations were cultivated by slaves; and thus the peasants, driven from their lands by unscrupulous and rapacious land-owners, were reduced to the most extreme poverty and social distress.

Rome's foreign wars now became few and unimportant, and the internal affairs of the Republic demanded the greater part of the attention of the Roman people. The old trouble of poverty now again threatened consequences fatal to the Republic. During the long period of foreign war and conquest, during the epoch of the Samnite and Punic Wars, the repeated and heavy losses in battle kept the Roman population sufficiently reduced to prevent the pressure of poverty from being felt very generally or seriously. But when the Roman dominion over Italy had been fully established by the final conquest of Liguria in B. C. 177, and these exhaustive wars of the Romans for the dominion of Italy thus ultimately ceased, the Roman population began to increase rapidly. In B. C. 173 there were only 269,015 adult male Roman citizens; but by B. C. 136 there were over 320,000; by B. C. 125 there were 390,736; and by B. C. 114 there were 394,336.

The result of this rapid increase in the Roman population was an over-supply in the labor market. No new Roman colony had been sent out since B. C. 177, and no more plunder from conquered countries remained to be distributed; and the lands of Italy being all assigned, and all the neighboring nations being subdued, there was no further relief to be expected from that source. The poverty of the Roman masses became more and more wide-spread and deeper with the rapid increase of the population. The Licinian Laws, which required the employment of a certain amount of free labor by landowners, and which limited the amount of land owned by a single proprietor, had been for a long time disregarded in both particulars. Capitalists had absorbed the public lands, which thus had come into the possession of a small class of wealthy men, who preferred to have them cultivated by the cheaper method of slave labor. It became more and more difficult every day to earn a livelihood in Rome, and the only means of acquiring wealth was by cultivating the public lands on a large scale, in farming out the revenue, or in governing the provinces. But the rich ruling class wholly controlled these sources of wealth, and they only resigned them to persons of their own class, so that the rich were gradually becoming richer and the poor poorer; and Rome thus became "a commonwealth of millionaires and beggars."

It is true that there was absolute political equality between all citizens, all having a voice in public affairs; and the franchise was constantly conferred on freedmen, so that political distinctions were ended, and Rome was a pure democracy; but the government was virtually in the hands of a wealthy oligarchy. Many plebeian families had become noble, on account of their members having held high offices of state, but the number of these formed but a small portion of the entire population, and they soon found their interests closely identical with those of the old patrician families rather than with those of the class from which they had risen, and the common bonds of riches and future gains united them in one party.

The vast hosts of slaves could be purchased at so low a price that the labor market was overcrowded and free labor was driven into beggary.

What made matters worse was that the mass of voters had become accustomed to being bribed by actual gifts of money, by the free distributions of corn, or by the exhibitions of magnificent games at the personal cost of the magistrates. Thus there was in Rome a systematic training in political corruption, which rendered the Roman populace ready to follow the bidding or the fortunes of any demagogue who promised them relief from the evils which were clearly perceived by all. It was also very evident that the troops were in sympathy with their suffering fellow-citizens rather than with the wealthy ruling class, and that the army could not be relied upon in case of a popular outbreak. If the masses should have been driven to rebellion by hunger or despair, they would have found powerful allies in the vast multitude of slaves, whose brutal treatment by their masters always kept them ready to revolt at the first opportunity. The wisest Roman leaders perceived these elements of danger which menaced the public security, but the great body of the nobles closed their eyes to the fact, and frustrated every measure proposed as a remedy for existing ills, blindly intent only upon the promotion of their own selfish interests, and having no sympathy for the masses in their distress.

A warning of the danger thus threatening the state was foreshadowed in the *First Servile War*, which broke out in Sicily in B. C. 134 and lasted two years. Two hundred thousand slaves rose in rebellion against their masters in that island, being driven to despair by the cruel treatment to which they had been subjected. The revolted slaves scourged the beautiful island of Sicily by many revengeful deeds. The rebellious slaves seized the town of Enna, and appointed one of their number named Eunus for their leader. Eunus defeated the Roman armies sent against him, took the strong city of Taurominium, and maintained a resistance of several years. The Consul Rupilius led an army against him, but only accomplished his purpose by treachery. Eunus was betrayed by one of the slaves who had been bribed by the Consul, his followers were massacred, and Eunus died in prison. Their revolt was suppressed with exceeding difficulty, and at one time it threatened to spread to the mainland of Italy. Servile outbreaks were attempted at Minturnæ, Sinuessa and several other places, but were promptly suppressed.

Among those who clearly perceived the existing evils, and most earnestly endeavored to find a remedy therefor, was a member of one of the noblest of the plebeian families, a Tribune of the people—Tiberius Sempronius Gracchus, a son of Cornelia, daughter of the great Scipio Africanus. After being elected Tribune, Tiberius proposed a series of measures in B. C. 133, by which he sought to relieve the prevailing distress among the great mass of Roman citizens, and to improve the general condition of Italy by substituting free labor for that of the slaves in the tilling of the soil, thus furnishing employment to the great body of the poor freemen. For this purpose he proposed: 1. To revive the long-neglected Licinian Laws, which prohibited any person from holding more than five hundred *jugera* (about three hundred English acres) of the public land, with a provision permitting him to hold two hundred and fifty *jugera* additional for each adult unemancipated son. 2. The appointment of a permanent commission of three members to enforce this law. 3. The division of the public lands which would become vacant by the enforcement of the Licinian Law, among the poorer citizens. 4. The compensation of the large landholders thus dispossessed for the losses which they sustained in improvements, etc., by making themselves absolute owners of the five hundred *jugera* of land assigned them. 5. The proviso making the new enactments inalienable.

In proposing these measures, Tiberius Gracchus was beyond all doubt actuated by pure patriotism and by an unselfish desire to ameliorate the condition of the wretched masses in the Roman commonwealth. But his proposed remedies for existing ills were fiercely opposed by the nobles, and the disinterested reformer was bitterly denounced as a demagogue. By disregarding the Licinian Laws, many of the Roman nobles and the richer Italians had become holders of amounts of land far exceeding the maximum limit proposed by the measures of Tiberius Gracchus. Those noble and wealthy families had been in possession of these lands for years, and had incurred great expense in erecting buildings upon them; the property having been transferred and used as though the holders were the absolute owners.

Octavius, a Tribune, the colleague of Tiberius, led the opposition to the measures which the latter proposed. When the measures were introduced before the Comitia Tributa, Octavius forbade the proceedings by interposing his veto, and thus preventing the vote of the assembly from being taken. In the excitement of the heated controversy, Tiberius Gracchus unfortunately resorting to extreme measures, appealed to the people to depose Octavius, and this measure was accordingly adopted by the vote of the assembly. The Comitia Tributa then passed the measures proposed by Gracchus, and appointed Tiberius Gracchus, his brother Caius Gracchus, and his father-in-law Appius Claudius as a commission of three to see that the new laws were enforced.

Gracchus and his colleagues then set about their new task of resuming control of the public lands and redistributing them, but the work was more difficult that its author had imagined. He was confronted with the constant and incessant hostility of the aristocracy, who declared that, though they were unable to prevent the enforcement of the laws, they would take vengeance on Gracchus; while the increasing demands of the people forced the reformer into proceedings of a more revolutionary character.

The Kingdom of Pergamus, with its well-filled treasury, had just come into the possession of the Romans by the bequest of its last sovereign. Gracchus proposed to the Roman people that the treasures of the Pergamene kingdom should be distributed among the new landholders for the purpose of furnishing them with the means to purchase implements and stock for their new lands, basing this proposition on the declaration that the citizens of Rome possessed the right to decide upon the manner in which the newly-acquired treasures should be disposed of. Gracchus is also said to have proposed to shorten the term of military service, to deprive the Senators of their exclusive right to act as civil jurymen, and to confer the privileges of Roman citizenship on the Italian allies of the Republic.

A crisis had now been reached. On the approach of the time for the election of Tribunes for the ensuing year, the aristocratic party was aroused to such fury and desperation that they determined to prevent the re-election of Tiberius Gracchus by any and all means.

While the election for Tribunes was in progress, Gracchus was addressing the people at the Capitol, but was interrupted and threatened by the nobles and their retainers. He vainly begged to be heard, and finally raised his hand to his head to signify that his life was in danger. His opponent instantly raised the false cry that Gracchus had demanded a crown, thus producing a universal uproar in the city. A large body of Senators accompanied by their retainers, armed with clubs, and headed by Scipio Nasíca, thereupon proceeded to the Capitol, knocking down every one who ventured to oppose them. Perceiving his danger, Gracchus attempted to flee, throwing away his toga to expedite his movements, and endeavoring to force his way through the vast multitude. But happening to stumble over a person lying on the ground, Satureius, one of the Tribunes who belonged to the aristocratic faction, killed him with a blow from the broken piece of a seat (B. C. 132). Three hundred of the partisans of Gracchus were likewise slain. The vengeance of the Senate did not relent here; as many of the supporters of the murdered Gracchus were banished without any process of law, and nothing was left undone to inspire the Roman people with abhorrence of his pretended crimes. Scipio Nasíca, who was quite a wealthy Senator and a large landholder, was the leader of the Senatorial faction in all these proceedings, which caused civil bloodshed in Rome for the first time in several centuries. The enemies of Tiberius Sempronius Gracchus would not allow his remains an honorable burial, but cast his body into the Tiber.

As in most cases, so in this, political assassination did not accomplish its object. The people were horror-stricken at the open murder of one of their Tribunes. Never before had so bold an outrage been committed by Roman nobles. So great was the odium which fell upon Scipio Nasíca that the Senate, in order to screen him from the popular resentment, was obliged to send him to Asia, on the pretext of public business, but really as a sort of honorable exile. He died there in the course of several months, a victim of mortification and remorse.

The murder of their valiant champion only made the people more resolute in their determination to prosecute the work begun by Tiberius Gracchus. The party in the Senate favorable to the reforms now came into power in that body; and, in accordance with a decree of the Senate, the work of re-distributing the lands was resumed.

In B. C. 129 the great general, Scipio Æmilianus, the conqueror of Carthage and Numantia—who had been one of the first to perceive the need of reform, and who was a sincere friend of the people—seeing that the agrarian commission were too extreme in these measures, to secure the success of the laws of Gracchus, and that the commission was inciting fresh discontents, proposed a measure which he carried, depriving the commission of the power of distributing the public lands, and conferring that power upon the two Consuls. But this effort to control the reform cost the great hero his life. He was basely assassinated in his bed on the morning of the day which he had appointed for an oration before the Senate concerning the rights of the Latins in the distribution of the public lands.

There is no doubt but that the murder of Scipio Æmilianus was committed by some member of the Gracchan party. The murder was an unwise act, as the dead hero was a true friend of the people, his only desire being to secure the triumph of the popular cause by curbing the revolutionary spirit of the supporters of Gracchus. The popular party opposed any investigation of the assassination; and the aristocracy, who considered the murdered general as their enemy rather than their friend, were just as willing to let the matter drop.

In the murder of Scipio Æmilianus, Rome sustained a very great loss. He was "the first statesman and the first general of his age," and was also "one of the purest and most disinterested public men the Republic ever produced." Sustained by the indignation of the more moderate citizens at the assassination of the general, the Senate now suspended the operation of the law of Gracchus; but as the lands had already been almost all distributed, this action of the Senate amounted to very little.

The claims of the Latins and other Italians

to the Roman franchise now produced fresh troubles. Some of the leaders of the popular party advocated these claims, believing that such an accession to the tribes would enable them to control the Senate more effectually. These claims were presented to the Senate in the form of a law, the Senate's assent being asked by Quintius Fabius Flaccus, who was one of the Consuls in B. C. 125. The Senate managed to avoid the necessity of taking action on the measure by sending Flaccus on a foreign mission. The town of Fregellæ, disappointed at the action of the Senate in this matter, broke out in open revolt. The Romans suppressed the outbreak, destroyed the walls of the city, deprived the city of all its privileges, and reduced it to the rank of a mere village. The other Italian towns were frightened into submission by this severe punishment.

Meanwhile Caius Sempronius Gracchus, younger brother of the murdered Tiberius Gracchus, made his appearance in Rome. The government had detained him in Sardinia as Quæstor, but had recalled him on the charge of being one of those who instigated the revolt of Fregellæ. Being triumphantly acquitted of this charge, he received an enthusiastic greeting from the popular party, by whom he was chosen Tribune by an unusually large vote.

Caius Gracchus was the ablest leader that the people had in many years. He was his brother's superior in every respect, and though his measures were more revolutionary than those of Tiberius, they were also more statesmanlike, and were better calculated to remedy the evils at which they were aimed.

The objects of Caius Gracchus were to relieve the poorer classes, to humble the Senate, to advance the interests of his supporters, and to avenge himself on his foes. His measures were: 1. A renewal of the agrarian law of his brother, somewhat modified. Caius reduced the size of the allotment, and provided that the landholders should be considered the owners of the lands which they held, on condition of paying a yearly quit-rent to the state; while good character was made a necessary requisite to the right of holding lands. 2. The state was required to sell corn to such citizens as applied for it, at half the ordinary price. This measure was justified by the circumstances of the case, as there was an urgent necessity to relieve the prevailing distress. 3. The minimum age of enlistment for the army was fixed at seventeen years, while the state was required to furnish the soldier's equipment which had hitherto been deducted from his pay. 4. The exclusive privilege of furnishing juries was conferred on the Equites, or knights, who thus became a distinct order. 5. The Senate was required to determine the Consular provinces, and to allow the Consuls to decide among themselves, by lot or by agreement, which provinces each of them should govern. 6. The Roman Censors were assigned the assessment of the taxes of the new Roman province of Asia. 7. The Tribunes of the people were entrusted with the management of the public roads of Italy. 8. The establishment of Roman colonies at Capua, Tarentum and other places in Italy, and also at Carthage and in Gaul. This last measure was designed as an outlet for the overcrowded population of the city of Rome. A Roman colony of six thousand persons was thus sent to erect a city on the site of the famous metropolis destroyed by Scipio Æmilianus. Another Roman colony was sent to Aquæ Sextiæ (now Aix), in the South-east of Gaul. Thus Caius Gracchus extended the colonial system of Rome into the provinces, that system having hitherto been confined to Italy.

The second measure of Caius Gracchus did not produce such happy results, although it seemed justified by the prevailing distress. The law restricted the distribution of grain to residents of the city of Rome itself. To meet the demand which set in, an immense series of storehouses, called the *Sempronian Granaries*, was erected. This law likewise induced all the poor and incapable people of the country around Rome to flock to the city and to become residents thereof. Caius had contrived this for the purpose of increas-

CIVIL WARS AND FALL OF THE REPUBLIC. 949

ing the number of his partisans and of being able to control the elections. He succeeded in this object; but the measure had a more far-reaching result, as it caused Rome to be filled with an idle, restless, dangerous pauper class; which proved a source of actual peril to the city for centuries.

By investing the Censors with the right to tax the new Roman province of Asia, it became necessary to farm out the revenues of that province to a new class which now arose to supply the need for it. The privilege of collecting the taxes was sold to the highest bidder; and the class which was thus assigned this collection made itself disagreeably prominent in the subsequent history of Rome under the title of *Publicans*.

Caius Gracchus wished to clothe all free Italians with the rights of Roman citizenship, and would have done so if he had dared, but the mere proposal of such a measure destroyed his influence. Both the aristocracy and the commons of the city of Rome were unwilling to grant this extension of the Roman franchise, and the commons were so alarmed by the proposal that they listened to all the charges which the aristocracy made to influence them against Caius. The Senate encouraged Livius Drusus, another Tribune of the people, and the colleague of Caius, to supplant him in the favor of the fickle multitude by proposing measures even more popular, which the Senate, however, never intended should be adopted. Drusus accordingly proposed that the landholders should be released from the quit-rent which Caius had imposed upon them, and that twelve Italian colonies should be established, each consisting of three thousand colonists, the people being allowed to select suitable men to plant these colonies. The people ratified these laws of Drusus as readily as they had those of Caius Gracchus; and Drusus, by these measures and by grants of money and remissions of taxes to the people, soon contrived to supplant Caius in the favor of the fickle populace. Caius Gracchus was a candidate for the Tribunate for a third term in B. C. 121, and Drusus was the opposing candidate. Caius was deprived of the office through a false return which the election officers had been bribed to make. Opimius, the most violent aristocratic leader, was then chosen Consul.

In December, B. C. 121, Caius Gracchus ceased to be a Tribune of the people by the expiration of his term of office. He was bitterly opposed by the new Consuls, and the aristocracy were resolved to get him out of their way as speedily and as summarily as they had rid themselves of his brother. They therefore commenced by attacking his establishment of the colony of Junonia on the site of Carthage, the wisest of his measures, though the most unpopular. The assertion was now made that the newly planted boundary stones of the colony had been dug up by the African hyenas. The augurs, upon being consulted, declared that such signs ought to be a solemn warning against endeavoring to erect a city on a site which the gods had accursed. The Senate accordingly forbade the establishment of the Junonian colony.

Caius Gracchus sought to defeat this law in the assembly which had been convened to confirm it. A crisis was brought on by an accident. While the auguries were being taken, and the Consul Opimius was performing the usual morning sacrifice, one of his lictors, while carrying away the entrails of the victim, said contemptuously to the friends of Caius: "Make way there, ye worthless fellows, for honest men!" This insult so incensed the persons to whom it was addressed that they stabbed him to the heart with their sharp writing styles. This violent act gave Opimius the opportunity which he had so eagerly sought. The Senate assembled hastily, and passed a vote requiring the Consul to "take care that the republic receive no detriment;" thus investing him with Dictatorial power. Opimius instantly issued a proclamation offering that any person who should bring him the head of Caius Gracchus, or of his colleague, Fulvius Flaccus, should receive a reward of its weight in gold.

The Forum and the Senate-House were occupied by the aristocratic party, who were armed, the next day; while the Cretan mercenaries of the army occupied the Capitol. Perceiving that a bloody conflict was inevitable, Caius Gracchus and his followers retired to the Aventine Hill, the old stronghold of the plebeians, and proposed to come to terms with the Senate and the Consuls; but the latter, fully conscious of the superior strength of their party, were resolved to crush Caius. The Consul Opimius offered pardon to all who should abandon Caius, and this offer had the desired effect, so that the younger Gracchus found his forces much diminished by desertion.

Thirsting for vengeance against Caius and his adherents, the Consul Opimius led the forces of the Senate to the Aventine and attacked Caius Gracchus and his followers, who had been reduced by the Consul's threats and promises to two hundred and fifty men, of humble rank. The Senatorial party, consisting of the nobles, the Cretan mercenaries and a number of slaves, massacred the little band which still adhered to Gracchus on the Aventine. Gracchus and his former colleague, Fulvius Flaccus, endeavored to cross a bridge leading from the city, but were pursued so closely that they were forced to seek refuge in a grove near the Tiber, long dedicated to the Furies, where they were overtaken and murdered. The bloodthirsty foes of Gracchus then cut off his head and stuck it on the point of a spear as a trophy. Septimuleius, an intimate friend of Gracchus, obtained possession of the head and carried it to his home, where he took out the brain and filled the cavity with lead to increase its weight. He then carried it to the Consul Opimius, who gave him seventeen pounds of gold as his recompense. The aristocrats then avenged themselves on the partisans of Caius Gracchus by causing three thousand of them to be strangled in prison by order of the Senate.

Thus perished Caius Sempronius Gracchus, in B. C. 121. The memory of the Gracchi was officially proscribed; and Cornelia, their worthy mother, was not allowed to wear mourning for the last and noblest of her two illustrious sons. But the people disregarded the mandate of the government, as they honored the memory of the two brothers with statues, and offered sacrifices on the sacred ground where they had fallen, in spite of all the precautions of the police.

Cornelia, the mother of the Gracchi and the daughter of Scipio Africanus, was an illustrious Roman lady. After the early death of her husband, Cornelia devoted herself to the education of her sons, and was rewarded for her care by their constant esteem and affection. After the murder of Caius, she retired to Misenum, where her house became the resort of all the talented and learned men of the age. Cornelia spoke her own language with elegance, and was well versed in Greek literature. Her letters to her distinguished sons are regarded as the purest specimens of Latin prose. She lived to a good old age, and the Roman people honored her memory with a statue bearing the inscription: "Cornelia, the mother of the Gracchi."

With the fall of the Gracchi ended the freedom of the Roman people. Thenceforth an insolent and corrupt aristocracy ruled the Roman Republic. The Tribunes, who had hitherto been the guardians of popular rights, becoming rich themselves, now concurred with the nobles in oppressing the people; while the old Roman virtue was dead.

The Republic had for a long time been verging to its fall, and no human means could have saved it. The Roman Senate was now essentially different from that venerable assembly which braved the fury of the invading Gauls, and which overthrew such great generals as Pyrrhus and Hannibal, as much by their virtues as by their arms. The men who at this time constituted this illustrious body could only be distinguished from the rest of the Roman people by their luxurious habits. They ruled the commonwealth by the prestige of an influence and power won from wealth and mercenary dependents.

The removal of the check of popular control left the aristocracy full freedom to give

CIVIL WARS AND FALL OF THE REPUBLIC. 951

unrestricted vent to their profligacy and corruption, which increased daily. But their very excesses gradually weakened the power which they had gained by such iniquitous means. Seeing what success had followed the resort to violence and armed tumult on the part of the aristocrats, the commons before long employed these very means against the aristocracy. Both classes, however, were equally corrupt; and while foreign princes bought their crowns from the Roman nobles, these nobles bought their offices from the Roman people. The Roman masses were so corrupt that they were willing to sell their votes to any noble or aristocrat who paid their price therefor. Driven to want and despair by their poverty and their inability to procure the means of subsistence in an honorable way, the people endeavored to supply their necessities by selling their manhood.

The venality and corruption of the Roman Senate were clearly made manifest in their disgraceful conduct in connection with the events which led to the *Jugurthine War*, which commenced in B. C. 111. The Romans had rewarded Massinissa, King of Numidia, their ally in the Second Punic War, for his services in that struggle, by bestowing upon him the greater portion of the Carthaginian territory, thus making his kingdom embrace the country comprised in modern Algeria.

Massinissa's son and successor, Micipsa, absorbed in the study of Greek philosophy, cared very little for power and dominion, and resigned the government of his kingdom to his nephew Jugurtha, whom he elevated to a position of equality with his own sons Adherbal and Hiempsal. On his death-bed, Micipsa divided all civil and military offices in his kingdom between his sons and his nephew. None of the parties to the inheritance was satisfied with this will. The two sons of Micipsa disputed the claim of Jugurtha, who was of illegitimate birth, to any share in the government; while Jugurtha himself had the audacity to claim the whole.

During the controversy Jugurtha procured the assassination of Hiempsal. A civil war then ensued between Jugurtha and Adherbal, in which Jugurtha was victorious over his cousin, whom he drove from the kingdom. Jugurtha was a brilliant and able leader, and was a complete master in the art of intrigue, which he had learned during his service in the Roman army. Adherbal escaped to Rome and appealed to the Roman Senate to reinstate him in his authority.

The Senate at first appeared inclined to punish the usurper; but Jugurtha, well aware that every Roman Senator now had his price, sent envoys to Rome and furnished them liberally with gold to bribe the Senators. These envoys used this gold so well that the Roman Senate refused to grant Adherbal's request to be put in Jugurtha's place, and even blamed him for the assassination of his brother. Roman commissioners, appointed by the Senate for the purpose, decreed that the Kingdom of Numidia should be divided between Jugurtha and Adherbal, assigning the western or better portion to Jugurtha; while Cirta, the capital of a sandy region, was bestowed on Adherbal.

Dissatisfied with this arrangement, and stimulated by his previous success to fresh iniquities, Jugurtha made war upon his cousin, wrested his territory from him, gained possession of his person by a capitulation, put him to death in violation of a treaty, and massacred the inhabitants of Cirta, of whom many were Italians. Rome instantly declared war against Jugurtha, and sent an army into Numidia, and the many Roman successes finally drove Jugurtha into a peace. He used his gold very effectually among the Romans. He was required to surrender unconditionally, but his kingdom was restored to him on the payment of a small bribe.

The indignation of the Roman people forced the Roman authorities to investigate the manner in which the peace had been obtained. Memmius, one of the Tribunes of the people, exposed the profligate venality of the Roman aristocracy before the assembled Roman people in the Comitia Tributa.

In consequence of this exposure, Cassius

Longinus was sent to Africa as Prætor, with orders to bring Jugurtha to Rome, for the purpose of convicting those who had accepted bribes from the usurper. Jugurtha was brought before the Comitia Tributa and questioned by Memmius; but Bæbius, another Tribune, forbade the Numidian king to reply, having been bribed for that purpose. The assembled people were aroused to the most intense indignation; but the corrupt Tribune, Bæbius, paid no heed to their wishes or feelings. Encouraged by his success, Jugurtha ventured on another atrocity. His cousin Massiva had taken advantage of Jugurtha's presence in Rome to advance his own claims to the Numidian crown; and Jugurtha, seeing that he was likely to succeed in obtaining the support of the Romans, resolved to put him out of the way. Assassins were easily procured, and Massiva was secretly murdered in Rome itself, Jugurtha assisting the murderer to escape. The Romans were unable to endure such an insult, and the Senate was aroused to such indignation that it at once canceled the peace, and ordered Jugurtha to depart from Rome instantly. It is said that as Jugurtha went out of the city gate, he looked back, and, gazing at Rome, exclaimed sarcastically: "If I had gold enough, I would buy the city itself."

The war between the Romans and Jugurtha was then renewed. The Consul Albanus was sent with a Roman army to follow Jugurtha to Africa, but Albanus assigned the direction of the war to his brother, Aulus, an incompetent commander; while Jugurtha's gold corrupted the Roman commanders, as it had previously corrupted the Roman Senators; and the Roman generals thus allowed themselves to be defeated, and, after their army had been obliged to pass under the yoke, they made a peace with Jugurtha, agreeing to evacuate Numidia within ten days.

When intelligence of this catastrophe reached Rome, the city was filled with grief and mortification. The Roman authorities rejected the treaty which their venal commanders had negotiated with the Numidian King, and banished those commanders. The native African tribes, believing that they had found a deliverer from the Roman dominion, rallied to Jugurtha's standard in great force.

But the Romans were now thoroughly in earnest in prosecuting the war, and assigned the conduct of the military operations in Africa to Quintus Metellus, a brave, able and determined commander, who was also a man of a high order of talents, of spotless integrity, and pure morals; his only defect being pride, which Sallust, the Roman historian who recorded these events, called "the common failing of the nobility." On arriving in Africa, Metellus found the Roman army completely disorganized; but, by diligently attending to his duties, he soon placed it on an efficient footing. Among the officers commanding under Metellus was Caius Marius, the son of a Latin farmer, who had passed his early life in the labors of the field. His manners were rude, his countenance was frightful, and his stature was gigantic, but his talents and his valor had raised him to a high position in the military service.

Metellus found Jugurtha to be an able antagonist; and the indecisive operations, which so far produced no result, caused a suspicion among the Roman people that Metellus had also been bribed by the Numidian king's gold. Marius took advantage of this unjust suspicion to gratify his own boundless ambition and to advance his own personal interests. When Metellus was obliged to solicit at Rome for a continuance of his command, according to custom, Marius resolved to obtain the office for himself, and thus acquire all the credit of putting an end to the war. With this object in view, Marius privately traduced Metellus, by his emissaries, whom he sent to Rome; and after he had succeeded in arousing a spirit of discontent against his superior, Marius obtained a leave of absence and returned to Rome to stand as a candidate for the Consulate—the great object of all his ambition.

But the Consulate was an office which had hitherto been in the exclusive possession of the nobility. Marius, however, had the sagacity to perceive that the times had changed, and that the people would gladly embrace an opportunity to humble the insolent and corrupt aristocracy. On his return to Rome, Marius was received with high favor by the people, while Metellus was abused by them. Metellus was a noble, while Marius was from the ranks of the people themselves. When the elections approached, the Tribunes harangued, and the peasants and the workmen of the city quit their business to support Marius. The nobility were beaten, and Marius was chosen Consul (B. C. 107). He was then invested with the supreme power to prosecute the war against Jugurtha, and Metellus was recalled from Africa. But Marius did not make any further progress in reducing Jugurtha than Metellus had made.

The war still went on; and Jugurtha, convinced that he must ultimately succumb to the Romans if left alone to continue the war, induced his father-in-law, Bocchus, King of Mauritania, to enter into an alliance, by promising him one-third of his kingdom. The united armies of the two kings attacked the Roman camp at night, gaining considerable advantage. But this success was soon followed by reverses. The Romans won two victories, in one of which they slew ninety thousand of the allied Numidians and Mauritanians.

Finding the Romans too strong for him, Bocchus sought peace for himself. The Roman Senate haughtily received his ambassadors, and reminded him that Jugurtha must be delivered into their power. The pride of the Mauritanian king struggled against such a demand; but the artful negotiations of the crafty Cornelius Sulla, a young noble who commanded under Marius, finally induced Bocchus to betray his son-in-law. The wily Numidian king, who had for so long a time defied the power of Rome, was lured to a conference and delivered into the power of Sulla, who commanded the Roman army during the absence of Marius (B. C. 105).

The captive Jugurtha was loaded with chains and sent to Rome, and furnished a melancholy illustration of fallen greatness and disappointed ambition. After gracing the triumph of Marius, with his two sons, he was cast into the Tullian dungeon, at the foot of the Capitol. As he entered, he said, with affected gayety: "Hercules! what a cold bath you have!" Here he was starved to death (B. C. 106).

The Roman people regarded Marius as Jugurtha's conqueror; and, in spite of the prohibition by the law, he was reëlected Consul in B. C. 104, and held the office for five consecutive years.

Rome was now menaced by a great danger. Two powerful tribes of barbarians— the Cimbri and the Teutones—who were partially Celtic and partially German, had for some unknown reason been driven from their own homes beyond the Rhine and the Danube, and were pressing upon the Roman frontier, having moved down and overrun the region between those rivers and the Alps. As early as B. C. 113 a horde of the Cimbri crossed the Alps into Istria, and defeated the Roman army under the Consul Papirius Carbo. The Cimbri then turned back, and, after being joined by the Teutones, made an irruption into South-eastern Gaul, and demanded that they receive lands. The Roman Consul Marcus Junius Silanus replied to this demand by attacking them, but was disastrously defeated with the loss of his camp. The Cimbri did not follow up their victory, but devoted themselves to the work of conquering the neighboring tribes. A Roman army under the Consul Marcus Aurelius Scaurus was sent against the barbarians in B. C. 107, but was also defeated with great slaughter. In B. C. 105 a Roman army under the Consul Lucius Cassius Longinus was defeated and slain by the Tigurinians, a Helvetic people, who had joined the Cimbri; and the remnant of his army only escaped destruction by passing under the yoke. A Roman army of eighty thousand men was also defeated with heavy loss the same year, near the modern town of Orange on the Rhone, thus leaving Italy exposed to barbarian invasion, only the

Alps being between the Cimbri and the Roman territory.

Marius, who was now made Consul for the third time, contrary to the law, applied himself to the task of restoring the discipline of the army. Sulla, who was his legate the first year, and a Tribune the second year, exhibited great diplomatic skill in Gaul, as he had previously done in Numidia, thus increasing the jealousy and the animosity with which the rude and ferocious Marius regarded him. The other Consul died just before the elections, whereupon Marius proceeded to Rome to hold them; and his friend, the Tribune Lucius Apuleius Saturninus proposed Marius for Consul the fourth time, in accordance with an arrangement just made between them. Marius affected to decline the honor; whereupon Saturninus called him a traitor to his country if he refused to serve her in so dangerous a crisis of barbarian invasion. Both acted their respective parts in the scene very well, and Marius and Quintus Lutatius Catulus were made Consuls for that year. Both Consuls were assigned the province of Gaul.

In B. C. 104 the Cimbri turned aside into Spain, but the Celtiberians drove them across the Pyrenees. They then returned to Gaul and quickly overran the western portion of that country in the direction of the Seine. The Teutones, a kindred nation, from the Baltic region, and the Helvetii from the Swiss Alps, joined the Cimbri in B. C. 103. The combined tribes then planned a systematic invasion of Italy. The Teutones endeavored to invade Italy by way of Provence, and the western passes of the Alps; while the Cimbri made an inroad into Helvetia (now Switzerland), and attempted to enter Italy by way of the eastern Alpine passes, with which they were familiar.

It was absolutely essential to defeat the barbarian hordes in detail, so as to prevent them from combining their forces. In order to raise the courage of his men, and to accustom them to the sight of the gigantic bodies and the ferocious manner of the barbarians, Marius crossed the Alps into Gaul and fortified a strong camp on the banks of the Rhone. He declined all challenges to fight, contenting himself with repelling the assaults of the barbarians, who finally gave up all hopes of forcing him into an engagement, and determined to cross the Alps into Italy, leaving Marius behind them. It is said that they spent six days in marching past the Roman camp, and that as they passed they jeeringly asked the Roman soldiers if they had any messages to send to their wives.

Marius then broke up his camp and followed the Teutones, keeping on the high grounds until he arrived at Aquæ Sextiæ (now Aix), where he selected for his camp an eminence where there was no water; and when his soldiers complained, he pointed to a stream running by the camp of the enemy, and told them that they must purchase that stream with their blood. Thereupon his men exclaimed: "Lead us on then at once, while our blood is warm!" To this request, the Consul coolly replied: "We must secure our camp."

The camp-servants, carrying axes, hatchets, and some swords and spears, for their defense, went down to the stream to water their beasts, and they drove away all of the barbarians whom they met. The noise aroused the Ambrons, who were then at dinner. They put on their armor and crossed the stream. The Ligurians advanced to battle, some more Roman soldiers followed, and the Ambrons were driven back to their wagons with some loss. This repulse enraged the barbarians exceedingly, and the Romans passed the night in great anxiety, fearing an attack.

In the morning Marius, after sending the legate Claudius Marcellus, at the head of three thousand men, to occupy a woody hill in the rear of the enemy, made ready to offer battle. The barbarians impatiently charged up the hill. The Romans, having the advantage of the ground, drove back the enemy. Marcellus attacked the barbarians in the rear, and they were completely routed. In this great battle—fought in the summer of B. C. 102—the Teutones were entirely

GERMAN WOMEN DEFENDING THEIR WAGON CASTLES AGAINST THE ROMANS.

destroyed as a nation; one hundred and fifty thousand men and a large number of women were killed, and ninety thousand were taken captive and sold into slavery. This great Roman victory freed Gaul from barbarian invasion. While Marius, after the battle, stood with a torch, about to set fire to a pile of the arms of the barbarians, messengers arrived with intelligence that he had been chosen Consul for the fifth time.

The other Consul, Catulus, had not been so fortunate in the meantime. Fearing that he could not safely divide his forces to defend the passes of the Alps, Catulus retired behind the Atesis, securing the fords, and having a bridge in front of his position to communicate with the country on the other side. But when the Cimbri descended from the Alps into Italy by the Brenner Pass, and were beginning to fill up the river channel, the troops of Catulus became alarmed, and as the Consul was not able to retain them he led them back, leaving the plain of the Poe to the barbarians.

The next year Catulus was retained in his command as Proconsul; but his deficiency as a general was supplied by the military talents of Sulla, who had left the army under Marius to join him. Marius, who was then at Rome, summoned his soldiers from Gaul, and hastened to join them with the troops under Catulus, hoping to earn the glory of a second great victory over vast barbarian hordes. Thus in July, B. C. 101, the united armies of Marius and Catulus fought a great battle with the Cimbri at Vercellæ. Marius stationed his own troops on the wings, and those of Catulus in the center, which he threw back, for the purpose of allowing them no more share in the engagement than possible.

But this maneuver utterly failed, as an immense cloud of dust, which arose, prevented the troops from seeing each other.

Marius in his charge left the enemy on one side, while the brunt of the battle fell upon the troops under Catulus. The Romans were favored by the dust, because it prevented them from seeing the number of their enemies. The barbarians were exhausted by the excessive heat of the weather, and they were obliged to yield. They could not escape, as their front ranks had bound themselves together with chains from their waists. A dreadful spectacle met the eye when the Romans drove the Cimbri to their line of wagons. Their women rushed out, fell on the fugitives, and then killed themselves and their children. The men also took their own lives in different ways. The Cimbri were thus as decisively annihilated as a nation in the valley of the Po. in Cisalpine Gaul, as the Teutones had been the previous year in Transalpine Gaul. One hundred and forty thousand of the Cimbri were thus slain, and the remaining sixty thousand were made captives and sold as slaves.

Marius and Catulus together were honored with the most magnificent triumphs. Marius had done little toward gaining the victory; but it was ascribed to him because of his rank and the fame of his former achievements. The multitude hailed Marius as the "Savior of his Country." He was also called the "Third Founder of Rome," being thus compared with Romulus and Camillus; while the populace poured out libations to him with the gods at their meals.

Italy was thus saved from barbarian inundation. "The human avalanche which for thirteen years had alarmed the nations from the Danube to the Ebro, from the Seine to the Po, rested beneath the sod or toiled under the yoke of slavery."

One great evil resulting from the struggle with the Cimbri and the Teutones was the immense number of slaves which it dispersed over the Roman dominions. In B. C. 102 the *Second Servile War* broke out in Sicily, and lasted three years. The slaves, again driven to despair by the cruelty with which they had been treated, took up arms a second time against their masters, whom they outnumbered. Led by a slave named Selvius, who assumed the name of Trypho and the dignity of king, the revolted slaves defeated the Roman armies. In another portion of the island the slaves made a Cilician named Athenio their king, but he submitted to Trypho, after whose death he held the chief command. Finally the Consul Marcus Aquilius killed Athenio in battle with his own hand, and suppressed the rebellion (B. C. 99).

The cruel use which the nobility had made of their victory over the Gracchi, and the scandalous corruption and profligacy which they had manifested in the case of Jugurtha, had intensely exasperated the people against them, and had alienated from them the affections of all who prized justice and honor. Ambitious and revengeful men took advantage of this condition of public feeling, to have themselves elected Tribunes, and to obtain the enactment of laws injurious to the nobles collectively and individually.

Marius was elected Consul for the sixth consecutive time, in violation of law; and it is said that by means of both bribery and intrigue he prevented Metellus from being his colleague, and that he thus caused Lucius Valerius Flaccus, on whom he could depend, to be chosen Consul with him. His most intimate friends and counselors were Glaucia and Saturninus, two unprincipled demagogues, both of whom were deadly enemies of Metellus, who, while he was Censor, would have degraded them for their scandalous lives had it not been for Marius, who interposed his power and influence in their interest.

Glaucia, as Prætor, presided when Saturninus was a candidate for the Tribunate the second time. Nevertheless, Saturninus was defeated, and Nonius, a bitter enemy of both Glaucia and Saturninus, was elected; but when the newly-elected Tribune left the Comitia Tributa, these two unscrupulous partisans of Marius sent a body of their satellites after him, and these assassinated him; and the next morning Glaucia, without waiting for the people, made his worthless adherents appoint Saturnínus in his place, no one venturing even to complain.

A series of popular measures was now introduced. By one of these laws, the land which had been recovered from the Cimbri beyond the Po was to be treated as conquered land, regardless of the rights of the Cisalpine Gauls who held it, and was to be divided among Roman citizens and soldiers. One hundred acres was to be assigned to each of the veterans in Africa; colonies were to be sent to Sicily, Achæa and Macedonia; and the prize gold was to be used in purchasing the lands to be divided. By another law, corn was to be distributed gratis to the Roman people every month. The law for dividing the lands of Cisalpine Gaul also provided that, in case of its passage, the Senate must swear to it within five days, and that any one refusing to do so should be expelled from the Senate and fined five hundred thousand sesterces.

The laws respecting the division of the lands were not all satisfactory to the town population, who perceived that Rome's subject Italian allies would be mostly benefited by the advantages resulting therefrom. The originators of these laws were therefore careful to bring into Rome from the country vast numbers of such as had served under Marius, for the purpose of overawing and outvoting the people of the city. To frustrate these plans, the people of the city cried out that it thundered; and, according to the Roman superstition, this would have rendered the vote illegal. But Saturnínus did not heed this cry, and urged the passage of his proposed law. The people of the city then girt their clothes about them, seized whatever they could lay their hands on, and attacked the country people, who returned the attack, at the instigation of Saturnínus, drove them off, and then passed the law.

As Consul, Marius laid the matter before the Senate, declaring that he for one would never take the oath, thus affecting to be opposed to the law, in this manner laying a trap for Metellus, who was thus ensnared into making a similar declaration. After the other Senators had expressed their approbation, Marius adjourned the Senate. He hastily convened the Senators again five days later, and informed them that the people were very determined that the measure should be adopted, that he saw no other alternative but for the Senators to swear to it as far as it was law, and that when the country people had returned to their homes the Senate might easily show that it was not law, because it had been carried by force and when it thundered. Marius himself and his partisans then swore to the measure; and the other Senators were induced by fear to do the same, although they then clearly saw through the trick.

Metellus was the only one who refused to swear to the measure. The next day Saturnínus caused him to be dragged from the Senate-House; and when the other Tribunes defended Metellus, Glaucia and Saturnínus ran to the country people and told them that they had no chance of receiving any land if Metellus was permitted to stay in Rome. Saturnínus then proposed that the two Consuls should be directed to interdict him from fire, water and lodging. The city people armed themselves and were determined to defend Metellus; but the latter, thanking them for their zeal in his behalf, said that he would not have his country endangered on his account, and retired into voluntary exile in the island of Rhodes. Saturnínus then procured the passage of his bill against Metellus, and Marius proclaimed it with intense satisfaction.

When the elections were again held, Saturnínus caused himself to be re-chosen; and a freedman named Lucius Equitius Firmo, whom Saturnínus represented to be a son of Tiberius Gracchus, with the design of gaining for him the popular favor, was elected a Tribune at the same time, through the machinations of Saturnínus. But the great object of Saturnínus and his faction was to get Glaucia into the Consulate—a matter of some difficulty; as Marcus Antonius, the eminent orator, had already been chosen as one of the Consuls, and Caius Memmius, a man of high character and exceedingly popular, was the candidate for the other place in the Consulate.

Saturnínus and his adherents, however, were not to be thwarted in this way. They accordingly caused some of their satellites, armed with sticks, to attack Memmius and beat him to death, in open day, in the midst of the election and before all the people. The Comitia Tributa was dispersed; and the next morning Saturnínus, who had summoned his partisans from the country, occupied the Capitol, with Glaucia, the Quæstor Caius Saufeius and some others.

The Senate, which had assembled in the meantime, declared them public enemies, and directed the Consuls to provide for the safety of the state. Marius then very reluctantly took up arms against his supporters. While he hesitated, some of the more determined of the opposite party cut the pipes which supplied the Capitol with water. When the thirst had become intolerable, Saufeius proposed to burn the Capitol; but the others, relying on Marius, agreed to surrender on the public faith.

There was a general demand that they be put to death; but Marius shut them up in the Senate-House, for the purpose of saving them from the fury of their enemies, and under the pretext of proceeding against them in a more legal manner. The people, however, refused to be frustrated in their vengeance. They accordingly stripped off the roof, and flung the tiles down on Saturnínus and his companions and killed them. Many of their supporters, among whom was the false Gracchus, were likewise slain. The Senate, and the assembled people in the Comitia Tributa, then joyfully passed a decree for the recall of Metellus from exile.

After a few years of tranquillity another reformer arose to give trouble to Rome. This was Marcus Livius Drusus, the son of the Drusus who had opposed Caius Gracchus. He was a young man of good intentions, but of little talents; of many estimable qualities, but of great haughtiness and arrogance. Being elected Tribune in B. C. 91, Drusus proposed a series of measures by which he designed to remedy the evils of the state and restore the authority of the Senate. He sought to reconcile the Senatorial and Equestrian orders at Rome, and to do justice to the Latins. He proposed to deprive the Equites, or knights, of the judicial power which they had abused, to restore that power to the Senate, and to admit all the Italians to the franchise, thus giving them the rights of Roman citizenship. He procured the passage of a law dividing the right to furnish *judex*, or *judices* (judges), between the knights and the Senate. To gain the support of the common people at Rome, Drusus proposed that the Roman colonies in Italy and Sicily, which had been voted a long time before, should be formed; and that the Sempronian Law, providing for the free distribution of corn, should be retained.

Drusus carried on his measures with some violence, and his bill proposing the admission of the Italians to the Roman franchise was obstinately resisted. One evening, when he returned home from the Forum, followed by an immense crowd, as usual, and was in his hall dismissing them, he cried out that he was wounded. A shoemaker's knife was found sticking in one of his thighs, but the assassin was not discovered. As Drusus lay dying, he asked: "Ah! my friends and relations, will the Republic ever have such a citizen as I?" The assassination of Drusus was not judicially investigated, and all his laws were abrogated. Thus the aristocracy again resorted to assassination, their usual method of warfare, but this time they struck the blow at one of their own order (B. C. 91).

The knights determined to push their success to the uttermost, and to break down the authority of the Senate. With this design they proposed a law providing for the punishment of all who openly or secretly assisted the Italians in their designs against the state. As many of the leading Senators had favored the claims of the Italians, the knights intended to drive such Senators from the city in this manner. The Tribunes interposed their veto, but the knights stood around them brandishing their naked daggers, and procured the passage of their proposed law; while prosecutions were instantly instituted against the principal Senators, many of whom were condemned, and others retiring into voluntary exile.

In the meantime the assassination of Drusus was the signal for the civil war which he had sought to avert. With his death ended all hopes which the Italians may have entertained of obtaining justice from Rome. The Italians therefore determined on an appeal to arms to obtain their just rights.

The Italian allies began secretly making the requisite combinations among themselves. The Romans were aware of what they were meditating, and sent spies to the various Italian towns. One of these Roman spies observing a youth led as a hostage from the town of Asculum, in Picenum, to another town, informed the Roman Proconsul Quintius Servilius, who hastened thither and severely reproved the Asculians for their action; but they attacked him and killed him and his legate, Fonteius, after which they massacred all the Romans in the town and plundered their dwellings.

Before the Italian allies began hostilities, they sent envoys to Rome to demand that they be admitted to participate in the honors and benefits of that state to whose greatness they had so largely contributed. The Roman Senate replied that if they repented of what they had done they might send a deputation; otherwise not. The allies then determined to risk the hazards of war. They formed their army from the contingents of the several states constituting the Italian League, and it consisted of one hundred thousand men, exclusive of the domestic forces of each state.

All the Sabellian nations except the Sabines, who had long since become Roman citizens, participated in this war against Rome—namely, the Marsi, the Marrucini, the Peligni, the Vestini, the Picentini, the Samnites, the Apuli and the Lucani. They entered into a close alliance, formed a federal republic which they called *Italia*; and selected Corfinium, the principal town of the Pelignians, for their capital, changing its name to *Italica*. They appointed a Senate of five hundred members, two Consuls and twelve Prætors. The first two Consuls of this new Italian Republic were Pompædius and Papius. Rome was obliged to struggle for her own existence against foes whose armies equaled her own in numbers, discipline and valor, and whose commanders were as talented and as skillful as any which she could bring into the field to oppose them. Thus arose the *Social War*, which convulsed Italy with its horrors for two years (B. C. 90-88), and which cost about three hundred thousand lives.

For a time it appeared as though the allies would be successful, as all the advantages of the Social War were at first on their side. They defeated the Roman army under the Consul Lucius Cæsar, and took the town of Æsernia, in Samnium. They also seized Venafrum by treachery, and destroyed two Roman cohorts there. They likewise defeated a Roman force of ten thousand men under the legate Perperna, killing four thousand of them, overran Campania and took Minturnæ, Nola Stabiæ and Salernum. In Campania they destroyed the Roman army under the Consul Cæpio.

The Roman armies under the Consuls Marius and Rutilius advanced to the river Liris, and threw two bridges over that stream close to each other. Vettius Scato, the Marsic commander, who was encamped opposite Marius, went and lay in ambush during the night near the force under Rutilius; and when the Romans crossed the river in the morning, he drove them back with the loss of eight thousand men, Rutilius himself being fatally wounded in the head. But in the meantime Marius had crossed the stream and captured the camp of Vettius, thus forcing the Marsic leader to retreat. When the dead bodies of the Consul Rutilius and others of rank were brought to Rome for burial, the people were so dispirited that the Senate passed a decree requiring that all who fell on the field in the future should be buried on the spot; and the Italians, upon hearing of this action of the Roman Senate, made a similar decree respecting their own dead.

When the Marsians attacked Marius they were driven back into some vineyards, but he did not venture to pursue them thither. Sulla, however, who was encamped behind the vineyards, upon hearing the noise, surprised and attacked the fleeing Marsians, who lost six thousand men. The conduct of Marius in this war was little worthy of his previous military renown. Either his advanced age, or a nervous disorder with which he was afflicted, as he said himself, caused him to act with timidity and irresolution, shutting himself up in an intrenched camp, permitting the foe to insult him, and finally resigning his command.

The first year of the struggle was now near its end. The Roman Senate had found itself under the necessity of permitting the freedmen to enlist in the legions, while the Etruscans and the Umbrians manifested symptoms of a disposition to participate in the revolt of the allies, negotiations having been opened between those nations and the allied states, so that Rome was menaced with a revolt of all the subject allied states of Italy.

In this perilous emergency the opponents of the claims of the allies were obliged to yield; and Rome, perceiving her inability to subdue the revolt, averted the threatened danger to her Italian dominion by a timely concession. The Consul Julius procured the passage of a law conferring the Roman franchise upon the Latins and upon all the other Italians who had not revolted, and finally upon all the allies who should recede from the Italian league and lay down their arms. The *Julian Law*—as this prudent measure was called—at once quieted the Etruscans, and prevented them from joining in the revolt, as it did the other Italian states that still remained faithful in their allegiance to the Roman Republic. Thus this adroit measure saved Rome in a most dangerous crisis, by preventing further accessions to the ranks of the revolted allies, and by raising up a powerful peace party in Rome itself which clamored for an acceptance of the conciliatory Julian Law. One after another of the allied states withdrew from the Italian league and returned to their allegiance upon the conditions of Roman citizenship granted by the Julian Law.

The two Roman Consuls for the year B.

C. 89 were Cneius Pompeius Strabo and Marcus Porcius Cato. As the Italian league grew weaker by the secession of state after state, the Romans recovered their lost military superiority. The Consul Strabo defeated a force of fifteen thousand of the Italian allies who were marching toward Etruria, five thousand of them being killed; and as it was winter more than half of those who escaped perished from hunger and cold.

The Romans laid siege to Asculum, whereupon Judacilius, a native of that town, advanced to its relief with eight cohorts, sending word to the inhabitants to make a sally when they saw him. But they failed to do so, and he forced his way into the town. Seeing that the defense of the place was hopeless, he determined that those who had turned the people against him should not escape, and accordingly seized them and put them to death. He then raised a funeral pyre in a temple, placed a couch upon it, feasted with his friends, swallowed poison, then lay down upon the couch, directing his friends to set fire to the pyre, and thus perished in the flames.

Fortune was now everywhere averse to the allies, who had lost their best commanders one by one. The spirit of resistance gradually grew fainter. The Roman armies under Sulla and the elder Pompey recovered Campania, while the capital of the Italian league was taken. Finally all the allies, except the Samnites and the Lucanians, submitted, and received the Roman franchise; and thus, after the Social War had lasted two years, that sanguinary civil struggle was ended in B. C. 88, by Rome granting the very concessions which the allies at first demanded, and which, if granted then, would have obviated the contest.

Before the close of the Social War, a bloody war broke out in Asia between the Romans and Mithridátes the Great, King of Pontus. This powerful monarch, who was also a good linguist, had conquered several Asiatic states and annexed them to his dominions, thus awakening the jealousy of the Romans, who were now aiming at supreme sovereignty in Asia. Mithridátes caused eighty thousand Romans and Italians to be massacred in one night, defeated two powerful Roman armies which had been sent against him, and made himself master of all Asia Minor and Greece.

The slow policy of Marius during the Social War, whose first year had been so disastrous to Rome, had weakened his prestige and popularity; while the merits of Cornelius Sulla, who carried off all the honors of the war in the campaigns of B. C. 89 and 88, were so generally recognized that he was raised to the Consulate for the year B. C. 88, along with Quintus Pompeius Rufus, and the management of the war against Mithridátes the Great, King of Pontus, was assigned to him. The old friendship between Marius and Sulla had long before given place to mutual jealousy. The appointment of Sulla to the conduct of the *First Mithridatic War* aroused the envy and resentment of Marius to the highest degree; and he determined, if possible, to deprive Sulla of his command, and to neutralize the action of the Senate in the matter.

In the furtherance of his schemes, Marius leagued himself with Publius Sulpicius Rufus, a Tribune of the people, a man of talent, of daring character, and deeply immersed in debt. These two accordingly projected a scheme to obtain a popular majority in the Comitia Tributa. As this could not be accomplished as the tribes were then constituted, Sulpicius introduced a bill providing for the distribution of the new citizens created by the Julian Law among all the tribes. As the new citizens were highly dissatisfied with their existing condition, Marius reckoned that they would give their votes to those who would relieve them of that condition. But the old Roman citizens were not so willing to surrender their own monopoly of political power and influence by admitting the newly enfranchised Italians to places among the tribes of the Roman commonwealth. The proposed scheme of Marius and Sulpicius would enable these new citizens to outnumber and outvote the old citizens; and they would naturally support Marius as their champion

CIVIL WARS AND FALL OF THE REPUBLIC.

and benefactor. The two Consuls sought to defeat the measure; but as the day of voting approached, Sulpicius enjoined his partisans to come to the Forum with concealed daggers, and to follow his directions. A tumult ensued; the adherents of Marius and Sulpicius drew and brandished their daggers, and the Consuls threatened. Pompeius fled, and Sulla withdrew to consult the Senate. In Sulla's absence, the party of Sulpicius and Marius attacked and murdered the son of Pompeius, simply because he had spoken his mind freely. Sulla, being unable to resist, started to take command of his army, then at Nola, in Campania. Sulpicius then procured the passage of his bill forthwith, and the management of the Mithridatic War was by violence transferred from Sulla to Marius.

Sulla was not the man to submit quietly to such an outrage, and by being able to appear as the champion of the law he had an immense advantage over his adversaries. He at once assembled his troops, informing them of what had transpired at Rome; and, as they had great expectations of plunder in the East, and were also suspicious that Marius might have other troops and other officers, they requested Sulla to lead them to Rome immediately. Sulla very willingly complied with their wishes, and marched to Rome at the head of six legions. Sulla's soldiers stoned the Tribunes who had been sent by Marius to assume command. Marius forced the Senate to send two Prætors to forbid Sulla's advance to the city, but they narrowly escaped with their lives from the soldiery.

Other embassies were sent to Sulla, imploring him not to approach Rome any nearer than where he was then, at the fifth milestone, Marius desiring to have sufficient time to prepare for defense. Sulla clearly penetrated this design of his antagonist, but gave the promise. Nevertheless he followed closely after the envoys when they set out on their return to the city. Sulla himself, with one legion, seized the Cælian Gate; while Pompeius, with another legion, secured the Colline Gate. A third legion went round to the bridge; a fourth remained outside; and Sulla led the remaining two legions into the city. The people commenced to hurl missiles and tiles on them from the roofs of the houses; but they desisted when Sulla threatened to set fire to the houses. Marius and his followers gave battle to Sulla's troops at the Æsquiline Hill, but were defeated; and after vainly seeking to incite an outbreak of the slaves, Marius and Sulpicius both fled out of the city (B. C. 88).

On the following day Sulla convened the people of Rome; and after deploring the condition in which the Roman constitution had been brought by the actions and the violence of wicked men, he proposed a return to the former wholesome condition of affairs, as the only remedy. He proposed that no measure should be brought before the people until it had been examined and approved by the Senate; and that the voting should be by the classes, in accordance with the arrangement of King Servius Tullius, and not by the tribes assembled in the Comitia Tributa. As the Senate was then so much reduced, Sulla selected three hundred of the most respectable men to increase its number. All the recent measures of Sulpicius were declared illegal; and Sulpicius and Marius, and the latter's son and about twelve other Senators who adhered to the Marian party, were outlawed, and their property was confiscated. Thus Sulla placed the government of the Republic in the hands of the aristocracy by depriving the people of their power.

Sulpicius was betrayed to Sulla by a slave, and was put to death. Marius escaped in the night to Ostia, where one of his friends had a vessel ready for him. After embarking in this ship, a storm appeared, and Marius was obliged to land near Circeii, where, as he and his companions were rambling about, some herdsmen, who knew him, told him that some cavalry had just been in quest of him, and got him into a wood, where they remained during the night without food.

The next morning Marius and his companions started for Minturnæ, but as they were turning around, they saw a troop of horsemen in pursuit of them. Two ships happened then to lie near the shore, and they ran and boarded them. The horsemen came to the shore, and called out to the crews to put Marius out of the vessel; but moved by his entreaties, the crews refused to deliver him up, and sailed away. Afterwards they reflected on the danger they were incurring to themselves, and persuaded him to land at the mouth of the Liris to get some food and rest; and while he was lying asleep in the grass, they got aboard the vessels and set sail, leaving Marius to his fate.

Marius rambled about the marshes until he came to the lonely hut of an old man, whose compassion he implored. The old man led him away into a marsh near the river, and, inducing him to lie down in a hollow spot, covered him with sedge and rushes. Marius soon heard at the hut the voices, of the cavalry in pursuit of him; and, fearful that the old man might betray him, got up and went into the marsh, where he stood in mud and water up to his neck. But he was discovered, dragged out, naked as he was at the time, and led to Minturnæ, where he was closely confined.

The authorities at Minturnæ decided to put him to death, and sent a Gallic horseman to kill him. When this Gaul approached the spot in the dark room where Marius was lying, he was appalled by the fiery glare of the venerable hero's eyes, when Marius arose and cried with a tremendous voice: "Dost thou dare to kill Caius Marius?" The Gaul rushed out, saying: "I cannot kill Caius Marius." The magistrates then resolved not to be responsible for the death of so great a man; and, releasing Marius, led him to the coast, where they placed him aboard a vessel to sail to Africa.

Marius landed at Carthage; but soon a messenger arrived from Caius Sextilius, the Roman Proprætor of that province, commanding him to depart. Marius long sat in silence, sternly looking at the envoy; and when the envoy asked him what reply he should make to the Proprætor, the old warrior groaned and said: "Tell him you saw Caius Marius sitting an exile amidst the ruins of Carthage." Marius then retired to the isle of Cercina, where his son and several of his older friends joined him, all watching the course of events.

After the flight of Marius, Sulla quitted Rome to take the field against Mithridátes the Great of Pontus. His departure was the signal for civil war. The people of Rome elected Cinna, a partisan of Marius, Consul, and called upon Sulla to answer for his crimes. Cinna sought to restore the laws of Sulpicius; but the aristocracy rose in arms in the interest of Sulla, and the Senate expelled Cinna from the city. Cinna appealed to the army, and, supported by the troops and by the great mass of the Italians, he invited Marius to return from Africa (B. C. 87).

When Marius, on his return, landed in Italy, he was surrounded by men of ruined fortunes and by slaves, and these constituted a formidable army. Cinna, after his expulsion from Rome, raised another army among the Italian states. Sertorius, another partisan of Marius, raised a third army; and Papirius Carbo raised a fourth. All these armies marched upon Rome. After a vain effort at resistance, the Senate opened the gates of the city to the combined armies of Marius (B. C. 87).

Upon entering Rome, Marius was elected Consul, as the associate of Cinna. He breathed vengeance against his enemies, and organized a guard of slaves to execute his work of proscription. These received orders to massacre every person whose salute Marius did not return as he walked about the streets of the city, and these bloody instructions were executed without scruple. These ruffians, thus privileged to massacre by wholesale, at once abandoned themselves to every frightful atrocity; and very soon Cinna and Sertorius decided to put all their foes to the sword.

Marius, Cinna and Carbo now entered into a league to massacre all the Senators who were obnoxious to the popular party. A dreadful slaughter followed. The heads of the murdered Senators were stuck upon poles, and their bodies were dragged to the

MARIUS AMONG THE RUINS OF CARTHAGE.

CIVIL WARS AND FALL OF THE REPUBLIC. 963

Forum and left a prey to the dogs and the vultures. Sulla was declared a public enemy, and his house was demolished. Lists were daily made out of all whom it was desirable to butcher, and the assassins had orders to murder all nobles named in the lists. The houses of these were pillaged, and their families were given to dishonor. Every species of enormity was perpetrated to gratify the vengeance of Marius and his colleagues, and a perfect reign of terror prevailed in the city.

After desolating the city, the soldiers were dispersed over the neighboring towns and villages, where they perpetrated the same frightful atrocities, their deeds of cruelty being unsurpassed in the darkest periods of the world's history. After thus wreaking their vengeance upon the nobility, and thus glutting their thirst for the blood of their enemies, Marius and Cinna, in utter contempt for the Roman constitution and laws, declared themselves Consuls for the year B. C. 86, without going through the formality of an election.

Marius was intensely superstitious by nature, and he had now fulfilled the prediction of the oracle which had told him that he would be Consul seven times; but he did not live long to enjoy the power which he had acquired by such sanguinary means. He died sixteen days after entering upon his seventh Consular term, from the effects of intemperance and debauchery, and from remorse at the crimes he had committed against his countrymen (B. C. 86).

After his death, his assassins attempted to continue their bloody work. Sertorius assembled them under pretense of giving them their pay; and when he had surrounded them with his troops, he caused them to be cut down to a man, more than four thousand thus falling victims to massacre. By the death of Marius, Cinna was left as sole Consul, which position he held until the return of Sulla in B. C. 84, nominating himself and associating with him whomsoever he chose.

In the meantime, while these bloody transactions were occurring in Rome, Sulla had been triumphantly prosecuting the war in the East against Mithridátes. With only a small force, he defeated a Pontic army of one hundred and twenty thousand men at Chærónéa, in Greece, where Philip the Great of Macedon had crushed the liberties of Hellas. This great victory of Sulla struck terror into his enemies at Rome. The Senate sent the Consul Flaccus, and Fimbria, an experienced general, with an army to attack Mithridátes, and to turn their arms against Sulla if they found him disaffected towards the Senate, thus outlawing Sulla.

In the meantime Sulla encountered two more armies of Mithridátes in Greece, and defeated them with terrible slaughter. In the last of these battles twenty thousand Pontic soldiers were driven into a river and drowned, and twenty thousand others were cut to pieces in a marsh. Plutarch says that the marshes were dyed with blood, that the course of the river was stopped by the dead bodies, and that in his own time, two centuries after the battle, the swords, bows, helmets, and coats of mail were found buried in the sand. Sulla also took Athens by storm.

After Flaccus and Fimbria had arrived in Asia Minor they quarreled. Fimbria won the soldiery to his side, attacked Flaccus and put him to death; after which he assumed the command and marched against Mithridátes, whose son he defeated and compelled to seek refuge in Pergamus, where his father resided. Fimbria pursued him day and night, and entered Pergamus. Mithridátes and his son fled a few hours before to Pitané, where the Romans at once besieged them. Having no ships to blockade the town by sea, Fimbria ordered Lucullus, the Roman admiral, to sail to Pitané with his fleet at once; but Lucullus refused, from motives of private spite, thus enabling Mithridátes to escape with his ships to the island of Lesbos. But Fimbria successfully prosecuted the war in Asia Minor, reducing most of the large cities, while Lucullus was finally induced to attack the fleet of Mithridátes, who was completely defeated and obliged to accept the terms of peace dictated by the Romans, who thus recovered Greece and Asia Minor.

Having carried everything before him in Greece and Asia Minor, Sulla now turned his arms against his rival, Fimbria. The latter found himself too weak to prevail by force, and so he conspired to murder his antagonist, but his plot miscarried and he committed suicide.

After being thus freed from all his enemies in Asia, Sulla raised enormous contributions from the provinces which he had subdued, thus amassing an immense treasure. He then directed his course toward Rome, first transmitting by letter to the Senate a full account of his victories in the East, accompanied with a declaration of his decision to take full revenge upon his enemies at home, but that he would protect the new citizens in their rights. This announcement of Sulla spread consternation throughout Italy. Cinna was frightened into inaction by this letter. The Senate raised an army to oppose Sulla, but all the troops deserted to him. The people of Rome hated Cinna and Carbo, who were the two Consuls after the death of Marius, and who had incurred the popular odium in consequence of their oppression and misgovernment. The people therefore flocked in crowds to Sulla's standard. The Senate, having everything now to fear from Sulla, appealed to his compassion; but Sulla reiterated his determination that his enemies at home must perish by the sword or by the ax of the executioner.

Sulla returned to Rome with the prestige of great victories, with the vast treasures amassed by plunder in the East, and with an army enthusiastically devoted to him. He was without doubt then the greatest living general, and his soldiers were accustomed to victory. Yet, although confident of victory, he did not underestimate his domestic foes; well knowing the formidable character of the Marian faction, and justly appreciating the power of the newly-enfranchised Italians, who constituted the main strength of the Marian party. He, however, fully despised the Roman mob; and his declaration that he intended to respect the rights of the Italians secured the neutrality of that powerful element at the very beginning of the struggle.

Sulla landed at Brundusium (now Brindisi), in Southern Italy, in B. C. 83; and Italy became a prey to the horrors of civil war, but Sulla defeated every army sent against him. Soon after landing at Brundusium, Sulla was joined by Metellus, Pius, Crassus and Pompey. Sulla defeated the army of the Consul Norbanus near Capua, and won the troops of Scipio over to his cause. He then retired into winter-quarters in Central Italy, and passed the season in strengthening his cause. In the spring of B. C. 82 the Marian party had placed an army of two hundred thousand men in the field against him, commanded by the Consuls for that year, Papirius Carbo and the younger Marius, the son of the old rival of Sulla; Cinna having been killed in a tumult in Rome. Carbo took his position at Clusium, in Etruria, because that region was friendly to the Marian party.

Sulla attacked and defeated the younger Marius in the great battle of Angiportus, and compelled him to retreat to Præneste, where he was closely besieged by a detachment which Sulla left there for that purpose. The younger Marius succeeded in inducing the Samnites and the Lucanians to come to his rescue; and Telesínus, an experienced Samnite general, raised an army of forty thousand men, and advanced toward Præneste under the pretense of raising the blockade and relieving Marius.

In the meantime Sulla marched to Rome and entered the city without opposition, and then marched against Carbo and attacked him in his intrenched position at Clusium, but was repulsed. Carbo was afterwards beaten repeatedly. After making a pretense of going to the relief of Marius at Præneste, Telesínus, the Samnite general, marched by night toward Rome, and at dawn the next morning he was within a few miles of the city, threatening to put every man to the sword, without exception. A sally against Telesínus was repulsed, Sulla himself being driven back to his camp.

Rome was now on the brink of ruin. Telesínus advanced with one wing of his army to storm the walls; but in this critical emergency a Roman detachment commanded by Crassus attacked and routed the Samnite general's other wing; whereupon Telesínus was assailed in front and flank, and utterly defeated by the troops under Sulla and Crassus in a desperate battle at the Colline Gate, which saved the city from destruction and decided the civil war in favor of Sulla (B. C. 82).

Sulla was now master of Rome and of all Italy; and the aristocratic faction, which he represented, was completely triumphant. He made a sanguinary use of his victory, and, like Marius, he determined to slaughter all his enemies; and all Italy was filled with massacre. The four thousand prisoners whom he captured in the battle at the Colline Gate were put to death by his orders in the Campus Martius, as were also eight thousand whom he had taken on his march to the city.

In Rome a general proscription of Sulla's enemies resulted in heaping up the streets with the dead bodies of the massacred partisans of Marius; and when a grave Senator, in affright at these horrible atrocities, ventured to ask the bloodthirsty tyrant when he intended to cease from the slaughter of his countrymen, he replied, with amazing coolness, that he would take the subject into consideration. Cato the Younger—afterwards so renowned in Roman history on account of his opposition to Julius Cæsar—was at this time about thirteen years of age. One day, upon seeing the heads of several noble Romans exposed to the public gaze, after having been cut off by order of Sulla, he was aroused to such indignation at the horrible sight that he cried out to his teacher and demanded a sword for the purpose of killing the tyrant.

It is said that almost five thousand of the most wealthy and distinguished men of Rome were massacred by Sulla's orders. All the relatives of Marius, as far as they could be found, were put to death. Lists of the "proscribed" were made out, and any friend of Sulla was authorized to add to the number. As the wealth of the victim usually went to the accuser, avarice often prompted the accusation. The proscriptive policy of Sulla was not confined to Rome, but was extended to every part of Italy, as the Italians had generally sided with Marius and his party in the civil war, because they regarded that party as their champions and benefactors. Twelve thousand persons are said to have perished at Præneste, and numbers almost as large in all the other Italian towns which had favored the Marians. Thus Sulla's atrocities surpassed those of Marius by great odds.

When Sulla had glutted his revenge, he caused himself to be proclaimed *Perpetual Dictator*, with absolute power (B. C. 80). Having thus become unlimited sovereign of Rome, he annulled every law which stood in his way, and governed entirely by his own will. He made numerous radical alterations in the Roman constitution, or, more properly, he introduced and enforced a new constitution, framed in accordance with his own peculiar views, and intended to strengthen his own aristocratic order.

Sulla's private character was notoriously bad, he being abandoned to intemperance and every species of vice, although his manners were polished, he differing in this particular from the rude and boorish Marius. Notwithstanding his own dissolute character, Sulla recognized the utter corruption of the Roman people as the real source of all the troubles and disorders which afflicted the state. He accordingly engaged in the hopeless task of reforming his countrymen by means of a series of severe enactments directed against luxury and crime, but these laws were utterly disregarded from the start.

Concerning the government, Sulla began by degrading the office of Tribune of the people by depriving it of all its powers except that of protecting the persons of citizens against the other magistrates, and by disqualifying the Tribunes for the Consulate. The exclusive right of initiating legislation was conferred on the Senate, and that famous body was once more clothed with the sole judicial power. The practice of electing any one to the office of pontiff or augur was abolished; and it was ordained that all candidates for the most exalted positions should be required to pass through the lower grades in regular succession, and with fixed periods of time intervening between them. The Senate was reorganized by adding three hundred of Sulla's most zealous partisans. The tribes were "purified" by excluding all the Italians who had aided the Marian cause, and ten thousand slaves were emancipated and enfranchised. The confiscated lands of the Marians were distributed among Sulla's veterans, in numerous instances to the injury of the industry of the country.

After holding the supreme Dictatorship for two years, Sulla, to the surprise of everybody, resigned his power and retired to his country-seat at Puteoli (B. C. 79). He passed the remainder of his days in recreation and the preparation of his memoirs. Thus, after a career of the most horrible tyranny and cruelty, this monster was permitted to spend the rest of his life undisturbed. It is said that one day a young man followed him home, cursing and reviling him, and that Sulla bore it with patience, only remarking: "Your conduct will teach another Dictator not to lay down his office so readily." He afterwards retired to Cumæ, where he passed his time in writing his memoirs, in hunting, fishing, drinking, and reveling with players and musicians. Here he died soon afterward of a loathesome disease, occasioned by intemperance and debauchery (B. C. 78); and was honored with the most magnificent funeral ever seen in Italy.

Sulla composed his own epitaph, the substance of which was that no man ever surpassed him in serving his friends or injuring his foes. He was undoubtedly a man of great abilities as a general and a statesman, but never was there a more heartless monster. He was cruel, more from a calm contempt of human nature than from natural ferocity. He utterly despised the human race, and was therefore an aristocrat.

The Roman Senate might well mourn for Sulla, as he had restored the rule of the nobility by destroying popular government in the Roman Republic. Nevertheless the aristocracy found his radical changes too great for them. The abolition of the election of pontiffs and augurs, and the law of succession in the offices of state, were insurmountable obstacles in the way of the ambition of the nobles, who coveted these exalted stations and did not take kindly to the slow method by which they were now attainable. The Consul Lepidus sought to procure the abolition of Sulla's laws in the year of the ex-Dictator's death, but was unsuccessful in the effort, as the time for the complete reaction in favor of the people had not yet arrived.

The death of both Marius and Sulla did not put an end to the civil wars occasioned by their ambitions and rivalries, as some of the provinces continued to be disturbed by the jealousies of the leaders of the contending factions, although tranquillity appeared to be restored to Rome and Italy for the time. The youthful Cneius Pompey—afterwards so renowned as the rival of Julius Cæsar—was one of Sulla's partisans, and crushed the Marian factions in Sicily and Africa during the life of Sulla. In B. C. 77 Pompey was sent into Spain as Proconsul to suppress the revolt of the Marian faction in that country under Sertorius, one of the ablest and most upright of the Marian leaders, and who had been assigned the command in Spain by Cinna mainly to get him out of the way of his own ambition in Italy. During the period of the Sullan proscription, many of the Marians who fled from Italy to escape Sulla's vengeance found refuge in Spain, and entered the service of Sertorius.

Sulla's Proconsul, Annius, drove Sertorius out of Spain, whereupon he fled to Africa. Invited by the Lusitanians, Sertorius returned to Spain in B. C. 81, at the head of an army consisting of Libyans and Moors, and made himself master of the country by defeating Sulla's forces on the Guadalquivir. When Pompey arrived in Spain, Sertorius had wrested almost the whole peninsula from the Sullan party.

CIVIL WARS AND FALL OF THE REPUBLIC.

Pompey, too, was defeated by him, and the war lasted five years longer. Finally, in B. C. 72, Sertorius was assassinated by Perpenna, one of his own officers, who assumed the command of his army. Pompey defeated Perperna in the first battle which ensued, and took him prisoner. Sertorius had designed the restoration of the Marians to power at Rome, and Perperna sought to save his own life by betraying the plans of his party in Rome, but in this he failed, as Pompey put him to death. With Sertorius perished the Marian cause in Spain, and tranquillity was soon restored in that remote Roman province.

While the civil war in Spain was still in progress, a dangerous rebellion of the slaves, headed by the gladiator Spartacus, broke out in Italy. Spartacus was originally a Thracian shepherd, and had been brought to Rome as a captive and was there trained to be a gladiator. A favorite sport of the Romans was to see these gladiators—who were captives taken in war—fight with wild beasts, or slay each other in the amphitheater. Spartacus, with thirty other gladiators, had escaped from his place of confinement at Capua and taken to the highway in the mountains of Campania. Having been joined by slaves, fugitives from justice, and desperadoes of every sort, Spartacus soon had one hundred and twenty thousand men under his command. Spartacus defeated five large Roman armies under the two Consuls, two Prætors, and the governor of Cisalpine Gaul; but at last he was defeated by the Prætor Marcus Crassus. Spartacus fought at the head of his followers until he fell covered with wounds and expired upon a heap of Romans who had fallen beneath his powerful arm. When he had first been wounded in his legs, he fought on his knees, wielding his sword in one hand and his buckler in the other, until he was overpowered and exhausted. Twelve thousand of his followers were put to the sword, and the remainder were finally subdued by Pompey, who was now the growing rival of the wealthy Crassus, (B. C. 70).

When Pompey and Crassus returned to Rome, both demanded the Consulate as the reward of their services to the Republic. The Sullan constitution forbade their election, because they had not passed through the requisite grades; but as their services were too eminent, and as they were too powerful to be refused their demand, the laws of Sulla were dispensed with in their case, and both were accordingly made Consuls for the year B. C. 70. Hitherto they had been among the most devoted followers of Sulla. As soon as they were elevated to the Consulate both changed their politics, apparently becoming convinced that so purely an oligarchical constitution as that of Sulla could not be maintained, and also seeing that their own political interests demanded its abrogation. They accordingly resolved to secure the support of the middle class of the Roman population, who brought along with them the support of the lower orders, thus enabling these two rising public men to crush the power of the aristocracy.

Pompey was most admired for his character, but Crassus was the richest man in Rome. He entertained the people at one thousand tables, distributed corn to the poor, and fed most of the citizens for almost three months. After becoming Consuls, Pompey and Crassus proceeded to reform the Sullan constitution. They restored the former power of the Tribunes, which Sulla had taken away. They again divided the judicial power equally between the Senate, the knights, and the Tribunes of the treasury; the latter a class of rich men who collected the revenues and paid the wages of the troops. The government was purified of its worst corruptions, partially by prosecutions, and partially by a restoration of the office of Censor, which had also been abolished by Sulla. They purged the Senate by expelling sixty-four of its members. They carried all these measures, notwithstanding the stubborn opposition of the Senate and the nobility. The two Cousuls were supported in their reform movements by the illustrious orator, Marcus Tullius Cicero, who arose to distinction in the prosecution of Verres for misgovernment in Sicily. By his indefatigable energy and his wonderful eloquence, Verres was found guilty of the charges brought against him, and was driven into exile. Cicero exposed the corrupt condition of the entire system of Roman provincial government so thoroughly that the Senatorial party were unable to make any defense, and were consequently obliged to submit.

When his term of office in the Consulate expired, Pompey declined to accept the government of a province, as was the usual custom with the retiring Consuls; but remained for the time at Rome retired from public life, quietly awaiting the course of events. He did not, however, remain in retirement for any considerable length of time, as his services were soon required to suppress the Cilician pirates, who had been the masters of the Mediterranean since the destruction of the naval power of Carthage, Egypt and Syria. At this time the Mediterranean swarmed with pirates, whose fastnesses and strongholds were in the mountainous country of Cilicia, in Asia Minor. The pirates would capture towns and villages, and carry off the inhabitants and sell them into slavery. They swept all merchant vessels from the Mediterranean, ravaged the Italian coasts and plundered the Italian ports, even extending their depredations in Italy as far inland as the Appian Way. Many Roman nobles and Senators were taken captive by them, and only obtained their freedom by the payment of a heavy ransom. The interruption of commerce by these piracies threatened Rome with famine. In this emergency Pompey was invested with the supreme command over all the coasts and islands of the Mediterranean. Powerful Roman fleets were sent against the pirates, and in less than three months they were driven from the seas and forced to seek refuge in their Cilician fortresses, where they were subdued by Pompey, who distributed them as colonists in the various cities and towns of Asia Minor (B. C. 67).

In the year B. C. 74 the Roman Republic became involved in another war with Mithridátes the Great, the powerful King of Pontus. After the Roman general Lucullus had defeated Mithridátes and driven him into Armenia, Mithridátes was aided by his son-in-law, Tigránes, the powerful King of Armenia; but Lucullus defeated the Armenian king's two hundred thousand men at Tigranocérta, the Armenian capital (B. C. 69), and gained another victory over Tigránes the next year (B. C. 68). The Roman troops having mutined, Lucullus was defeated by Mithridátes.

On motion of Manlius and Cicero, the Roman Senate then invested Pompey with the chief command of the Roman army in Asia, and gave him absolute powers (B. C. 67.) In B. C. 66 Pompey inflicted a crushing defeat upon Mithridátes on the banks of the Euphrates, overthrew Tigránes, and made Pontus a Roman province (B. C. 66). Three years afterwards, Mithridátes, abandoned by his followers and having lost all his dominions, poisoned himself (B. C. 63). The year after his victory over Mithridátes (B. C. 65), Pompey subverted the Syrian Empire of the Seleúcidæ, and Syria became a Roman province.

About this time the throne of Judæa was claimed by two brothers, John Hyrcanus II. and Aristobúlus II. Each applied for aid to Pompey, who decided in favor of Hyrcanus. Aristobúlus prepared to resist the Romans, and shut himself up in Jerusalem, which was taken by Pompey after a three months' siege (B. C. 63). Hyrcanus was seated on the Jewish throne, but was required to pay tribute to the Romans. Aristobúlus was carried a prisoner to Rome to grace the triumph of Pompey.

While Pompey was winning laurels in Asia, the Roman Republic was brought to the very brink of destruction by a conspiracy headed by Lucius Sergius Catiline, a noble who was singularly constituted, both by art and nature, for intrigues and conspiracies. He possessed courage equal to the most desperate attempts, and his eloquence gave specious color to the most dangerous ambition. His ruined fortunes, his profligate manners, his vigilance and perseverance in the pursuit of his aims, made him insatiable after wealth, simply with the design of lavishing it on his abandoned pleasures. Having involved himself in immense debts by his dissipations and extravagances, Catiline determined to extricate himself by any means, however iniquitous.

He had collected about him a large number of individuals of desperate fortunes, either involved in bankruptcy or dreading the punishment which their infamous crimes deserved—in fact, all who had anything to expect from a revolution. He endeavored by every means to inveigle young men of noble birth, and for this purpose he spared no expense in gratifying their vices. Among his associates were some of the leading men of Rome—magistrates, Senators, knights, and several women of rank. He was stimulated in his efforts to make himself master of the Republic by the recent examples of Marius and Sulla. Catiline expected to be supported by all the disaffected Italians, and by criminals, slaves and gladiators, and calculated on the tacit acquiescence of the Marian party.

Catiline assembled a meeting of his most trustworthy associates, and disclosed his plans to them. He represented them as the most oppressed and wretched of men, and their rulers as the most merciless tyrants. He promised them that the success of his plans would be followed by the abolition of debts, the proscription of the wealthy, and rapine and plunder for all his accomplices. The conspiracy was accordingly decided upon, and we are told that the conspirators bound themselves by a solemn oath before they separated, drinking human blood mingled with wine.

Catiline and his accomplices had planned a general insurrection throughout Italy, assigning different portions of that country to different leaders. Rome was to be set on fire in several places at once; and Catiline, in command of the army which the conspirators were to raise in Etruria, was to seize possession of the city amid the general confusion, and massacre all the Senators.

Léntulus, one of his profligate associates in the plot, who had been a magistrate in the city, was to preside in their general councils. Cethégus, a man of rank and influence, but actuated by the desire to gratify his revenge against Cicero, was to direct the massacre in the city; and Cassius was to order the firing of the houses.

As the great obstacle to the success of the plot was the vigilance of the great orator, Marcus Tullius Cicero, one of the two Consuls for that year, and who had won that high office by his consummate eloquence and his recognized statesmanship, the conspirators resolved to murder him. Two of them ventured upon this task on the morning following the secret conference. But Cicero had previously obtained a knowledge of the designs of the conspirators, through the instrumentality of a woman named Fulvia, by bribing her lover, Curius, one of the conspirators; and the attempt to assassinate the Consul was thus frustrated.

While the entire city was thrown into alarm and consternation by rumors of the danger by which it was menaced, Catiline had the audacity to make his appearance in the Senate-House, when Cicero unmasked the designs of the conspirators. Cicero, aroused to indignation at the sight of Catiline, poured forth such a torrent of invective upon the head of the daring conspirator that he was overwhelmed with terror and confusion and was unable to reply. The whole Senate denounced the arch conspirator as a public enemy and a parricide; whereupon Catiline threw off the mask, and exclaimed in a furious manner that he would quench the flames raised around him by the ruin of his country; after which he departed from the Senate-House.

After a short conference with Léntulus and Cethégus, Catiline quitted Rome in the night with a small retinue, and proceeded to Etruria, where Manlius, one of the conspirators, was collecting a large army to support the conspiracy. In the meantime Cicero took proper measures to secure the safety of the city. Catiline's accomplices endeavored to form an alliance with the

Allobroges, a people of Gaul, who had sent ambassadors to petition the Roman Senate for some relief from oppressive taxation. These Gallic ambassadors betrayed the negotiations to Cicero, who managed the matter so skillfully that he arrested the leading conspirators with the proofs of guilt on their persons.

After an animated debate, the Senate resolved to put the conspirators to death. Caius Julius Cæsar—a man destined to occupy the most prominent place in Roman history—was now rapidly rising into notice as the leader of the popular party; and was the only one who protested against the dangerous precedent of violating the Porcian Law, which forbade the infliction of capital punishment on a Roman citizen. Léntulus, Cethégus and Cassius, with several other conspirators, were instantly taken to the Mamertine prison, where they were strangled.

In the meantime Catiline had collected an army of twelve thousand men in Etruria, but only a fourth part of these were thoroughly armed, the other three-fourths having been supplied with such weapons as they could obtain—clubs, darts and lances. At first Catiline refused to enlist the slaves, who flocked to him in vast numbers, but relied on the strength of the conspiracy in the city. However, on the approach of the Proconsul Antonius, who was sent with an army against the arch conspirator, and on hearing that his accomplices in Rome had been put to death, Catiline became convinced that his cause was doomed.

He now endeavored to save himself by rapid marches in the direction of Gaul, but the passes of the Apennines were closely guarded to prevent his escape. The Proconsular army approached, and Catiline was hemmed in on every side. Perceiving that his escape was cut off, he resolved to offer battle to Antonius, and the two armies encountered each other near Pistoria. The conspirators, with Catiline at their head, fought with the courage of desperation, until every one of their number had been slain (B. C. 62)

In saving Rome by defeating this infamous conspiracy, Cicero, as Consul, had performed the most glorious act of his life. His vigilance and patriotism were duly appreciated by his grateful countrymen, who unanimously declared that he had saved the Republic; and the Senate conferred upon him the glorious title of "Father of his Country."

The Senate and the aristocratic party were alarmed by the return of Pompey from Asia with the prestige of a conqueror, immediately after the overthrow of Catiline. The Senate and the aristocracy feared that the returned general would follow the example of Sulla, but he dispelled their anxieties by disbanding his army as soon as he entered Italy, and by proceeding to Rome with only a few friends. He was accorded a most splendid triumph in honor of his Asiatic conquests, the procession occupying three days in marching through the city, though the army did not take any part in it.

When Pompey demanded the Consulate a second time for himself, allotments of land for his veterans, and the confirmation of his proceedings during his campaigns in Asia, the Senate bluntly refused his request. The aristocratic party had resolved to punish him for obtaining the command of the Roman forces in the East in opposition to their wishes, but their short-sighted course only involved themselves in ruin.

A new leader had risen to prominence in Rome during Pompey's absence in Asia; and the direction of public affairs had fallen into the power of four men—Marcus Tullius Cicero, Marcus Porcius Cato, Marcus Crassus and Caius Julius Cæsar. Cicero—the greatest of Roman orators and a bold and daring statesman—was the chief of the oligarchical faction, to which Pompey belonged. Cato—a descendant of the famous Censor, Cato the Elder, and therefore called Cato the Younger—was a man of the same old republican stamp as his illustrious ancestor, and was the leader of the Senatorial party. Crassus—the richest man in Rome and famed for his wealth, but indolent and without great talents—was the leader of the

THE CATILINARIAN CONSPIRATORS BEFORE THE SENATE.

Roman Lady—Slave.

Inhabitant of Germany at the Beginning of Our Era.

Julius Cæsar.

Prætorian Guard.

ROME, BEGINNING OF CHRISTIAN ERA.

CIVIL WARS AND FALL OF THE REPUBLIC. 971

aristocratic party. Cæsar was the recognized chief of the Marian party, or the democratic or popular party, and was therefore regarded as the champion of the masses.

Cæsar was the nephew of Marius and the son-in-law of Cinna. His talents had been recognized by Sulla, who had been persuaded with great difficulty to exempt him from the list of the proscribed during the reign of massacre and blood by which he had overthrown the Marian party. In granting Cæsar's pardon, Sulla remarked: "That boy will some day be the ruin of the aristocracy, for I see in him many Marii." Cæsar was born in B. C. 100, and was therefore at this time more than thirty years old. He had identified himself with the party of the people since he was seventeen years of age. Besides being of noble birth, he prided himself upon being the nephew of Marius by the marriage of his aunt Julia to that famous leader.

Cæsar's first service in the army was at the siege of Mitylênê. He had won a civic crown for saving a citizen. Upon his return to Rome, he won distinction by his speeches against Dolabella, whom he indicted for extortion in Macedonia. He next went to Rhodes to receive instruction in eloquence under Molo, Cicero's tutor. He was captured by Cilician pirates on his way there, but was redeemed by the payment of a heavy ransom; whereupon he collected a few ships, attacked his captors, took them captive, and crucified them. When, about B. C. 74, he heard that he had been chosen pontiff, he returned to Rome, where he passed the next seven years, without taking any part in politics, but gaining many friends by his winning manners.

In B. C. 67, when Pompey led a Roman fleet against the Cilician pirates, Cæsar was made Quæstor. His aunt Julia, the widow of Marius, died the same year. Cæsar delivered a noble funeral oration over her remains, and carried a waxen image of Marius in the funeral procession in defiance of the law. In B. C. 65 he was created Curule Ædile, and added to his popularity by the magnificence with which he celebrated the public games. He rendered still more substantial service as Curator of the Appian Way by repairing that famous road at his own expense.

The Cimbrian trophies and the statues of Marius had been removed through the instrumentality of Sulla, so that the Republic had lost her memorials of the services of that great general. Cæsar now undertook to restore these memorials in a single night. The citizens went to look at them the following morning, and the aged veterans of Marius wept for joy at the sight. Cæsar not having actually violated the law, the Senate was unable to prosecute him for this proceeding; and thenceforth the people idolized him as their leader, while honors were accorded him in rapid succession.

In B. C. 63 Cæsar became *Pontifex Maximus*, or religious superintendent; in B. C. 62 he was made Prætor; and in B. C. 61 he was appointed Proconsul of Hispania Bœtica (Farther Spain). In this latter capacity he displayed his remarkable military talents by the final conquest of Lusitania, and won the enthusiastic devotion of his soldiers. Cæsar's influence in Rome was not diminished by his absence from the city, and the movements of his party remained under his direction. His Proconsulate in Spain likewise supplied him with the means to pay a large portion of his debts.

Cæsar was then (B. C. 61) thirty-nine years old, and his great career had now dawned upon Roman history. He was a model of manly beauty. He was conscious of his personal attractions, and his enemies accused him of dandyism. He had retained a perfect bodily vigor in spite of all his early dissipations, and he had now adopted temperate habits. He was skillful in fencing, riding and swimming, and possessed wonderful capacity for performing sudden tiresome journeys. He generally traveled by night, in order to gain time. His vigor of mind was equal to that of his body. He possessed surprising power of intuition. He had a wonderfully retentive memory, never forgetting anything.

Cæsar's warm, generous heart, which

never forsook a friend, but which ever remained faithful through prosperity and adversity, endeared him to his friends and followers above everything else. Nor were his motives interested in this particular. Cæsar had genuine attachment for his friends. He never gave any of his partisans cause to complain of coldness or ingratitude on his part; and their affection for him was clearly demonstrated by their manifestation of intense grief at his assassination. He regarded his mother with the purest veneration while she lived, and he bestowed an honorable affection upon his wives and his daughter Julia, which received their due reward.

Like all men of genius, Cæsar was capable of great anger, but he kept his temper under perfect control. He was essentially a practical man, not a theorist, and usually succeeded in finding the best and most suitable measures in conducting his operations. He never tried to hasten events, but calmly awaited the proper time to execute his designs. Everything undertaken by him indicated clearness of judgment, unwavering determination, and an absolute independence of action, which could not be swayed by any favorite or mistress. As a military commander, he displayed a quickness of conception and execution, an unerring genius in detecting the weak points of an enemy, and the happy quality of being able to strike every blow in its right place. He magnanimously shared in the dangers and hardships of his troops, and was their generous friend and companion, no less than their inflexible commander. It is therefore not surprising that victory followed Cæsar's footsteps.

As a necessary consequence, the possessor of such admirable qualities was a statesman. "From his early youth Cæsar was a statesman in the deepest sense of the term, and his aim was the highest which man is allowed to propose to himself—the political, military, intellectual and moral regeneration of his own deeply decayed nation, and of the still more deeply decayed Hellenic nation, intimately akin to his own."

His measures were taken with reference to the remote future, while also affecting the present. He lifted the world up out of its degradation, making it greater and better for his having lived in it, though he was ruthlessly cut down at the very threshold of his great mission. This great, grand character stands out in bold relief, amid all the gloom enveloping the history of this period—the most renowned warrior, the most talented statesman, the most perfect leader in the history of Rome, and in the history of all antiquity.

In his military command in Spain, Cæsar acquired wealth for himself and his soldiers, and reputation by subduing the Lusitanian mountaineers. When he returned to Rome, he desired both a triumph and the Consulate; but he could only obtain the former after it was decreed by the Senate, and the latter by being personally present at the approaching election. He therefore relinquished the showy for the solid advantage; and accordingly Cæsar and Bibulus, the latter a mere instrument of the Senate, were chosen Consuls for the year B. C. 59.

Such was the man to whom Pompey looked for support when the Senate denied him his just reward for his valuable and important services to the Republic. For some time Cæsar had been endeavoring to detach Pompey from the aristocratic party; while Pompey, whose feelings were stung with the treatment accorded him by the Senate, readily accepted Cæsar's offer. Cæsar sought at the same time to turn the mutual jealousies of Pompey and Crassus to his own advantage. With consummate skill, he applied himself to the task of reconciling these two jealous rivals, well aware that the result would be favorable to the advancement of his own political interests. In this undertaking Cæsar succeeded so well that he persuaded both Pompey and Crassus to forget all their old jealousies and rivalries, and to unite with himself in a project for taking upon themselves the management of the destinies of the Republic.

Accordingly these three men—Cæsar,

A DRUIDICAL SACRIFICE.

Pompey and Crassus—effected a private arrangement among themselves by which they agreed that nothing should be done without their mutual concurrence. The union of these three men for one common object—which would in modern times be called a *ring*—is designated as the *First Triumvirate* (meaning a league of three men), and was effected in the year B. C. 59. By this political partnership these three men took upon themselves the government of the Republic, and practically usurped the authority of the Senate. The Triumvirs divided the dominions of the Republic among themselves—Pompey receiving Italy, Spain and Africa; the wealthy Crassus, whose avarice was unbounded, chose Syria, which was famed for its wealth; and Cæsar obtained Gaul, the complete conquest of which was intrusted to him. The power of Crassus was due to his immense wealth; that of Pompey to his distinguished military services; and that of Cæsar to his overshadowing genius and his boundless popularity.

The united influence of the Triumvirs was soon felt in all Cæsar's official acts. He introduced an agrarian law providing for the distribution of the rich public lands of Campania among the poorest citizens and Pompey's veterans. This measure was passed against the violent opposition of the other Consul, Bibulus, and the Senate; and the lands were accordingly divided. A commission of twenty, headed by Pompey and Crassus, was appointed to divide the lands; and the poor and the veterans accordingly obtained their respective claims.

The defeated Consul, Bibulus, who had declared that he would rather die than yield, now secluded himself in his house, and did not again show himself in public until after the expiration of his official year. Cæsar caused all of Pompey's proceedings in Asia to be ratified; and likewise attached the Equites, or knights, to his order, by conceding them more favorable terms in farming the provincial revenues. The bond between the Triumvirs was strengthened by Pompey's marriage with Cæsar's daughter Julia. Cæsar, whose wife Cornelia had been dead for some years, married Calpurnia, the daughter of Piso.

The Triumvirs were supported in their schemes by Clodius, a man of profligate character, but possessing considerable influence with the people. His main object on this occasion was to wreak his vengeance on Cicero, who had given testimony against him in a criminal trial. In order to do this more effectually, Clodius caused himself to be transferred from the patrician to the plebeian order. He then became a candidate for the Tribunate, and was elected with little opposition. Through the exertions of Clodius, the Senate was deprived of its leaders by the banishment of Cicero and the appointment of Cato the Younger to the command of an expedition sent to deprive Egypt of Cyprus; but Cicero was recalled at the expiration of a year, and was restored to his dignity and estates.

At the expiration of his Consulate, or more properly his Dictatorship, Cæsar obtained the government of Illyricum and of both Cisalpine and Transalpine Gaul, for a period of five years, with a commission to "protect the friends and allies of the Roman people." He selected this post because it enabled him to acquire a great military renown, to win to him the army more completely, and to be sufficiently near to Rome to take full advantage of all the circumstances that might arise there in his favor. He was at this time forty years of age.

The ancient countries of Britain (now England), Gaul (now France and Belgium), Helvetia (now Switzerland) and Spain were inhabited by many tribes, which were united by the bonds of a common race and religion. The ancient Gauls and Britons held their priests, or *Druids*, in great veneration, and regarded the oak as a sacred tree, while they also looked upon the mistletoe with reverence. The religious and race ties of the inhabitants of all these countries of Western Europe were sufficient to unite them occasionally in resistance to their common foes, the Germans on the North-east and the Romans on the South-east; but were not strong enough to prevent rivalries among themselves. The Roman possessions in Transalpine Gaul—founded in B. C. 121, when the colony which settled Aquæ Sextiæ had been sent out through the exertions of Caius Gracchus—now extended northward along the Rhone as far as Geneva; while vast hordes of Germans had occupied the country west of the Rhine, from the vicinity of the modern Strasburg to the North Sea.

Cæsar's victorious career in Gaul lasted eight years. During his first summer in that country (B. C. 58), by the wonderful celerity of his movements, Cæsar conquered two nations and established the Roman supremacy in the center of the country. The Helvetii, who occupied the western portion of the present Switzerland, found their narrow country too small for them, and accordingly determined to emigrate and conquer new lands to the westward. They burned twelve towns and four hundred villages; and assembled at Geneva, to the number of three hundred and sixty-eight thousand persons, men, women and children, with the design of crossing the Roman province into the West of Gaul. Cæsar prevented the Helvetii from crossing the Rhone at that point by the construction of a wall nineteen miles long, along the east bank of the river. He brought three legions from Italy, and followed the Helvetii along their second route farther north, and defeated them near Bibráte, killing over two hundred thousand of them. The remnant of the Helvetic nation—less than a third of the number with which they had started on their migration—were forced back to their native mountains.

Immediately after Cæsar's great victory over the Helvetii, the Séquani, a Celtic tribe occupying the country north of the Helvetii, had called in the aid of Ariovístus, the most powerful of the German chiefs, against a rival tribe called the Ædui, who were designated as the allies and kinsmen of the Romans. After subduing the Ædui, Ariovístus attacked his recent allies, the Séquani, and demanded two-thirds of their lands in payment for his services in their behalf. All the Gauls implored Cæsar's assistance, and Cæsar encountered Ariovístus near the Rhine, in the region of the modern Alsace. This famous German chieftain was regarded as invincible; and his followers, who had not slept under a roof for fourteen years, were of such gigantic stature that the Roman soldiers became panic-stricken at the prospect of fighting them. Cæsar had to exert all his powerful genius to restore the confidence of his troops; and, although he shamed them out of their cowardice by telling them that if they deserted him he would fight the enemy with the Tenth Legion only, every man made his will before the battle commenced. A desperate battle ensued near Basle, in which the vast German host was totally destroyed, losing eighty thousand men, Ariovístus himself making his escape across the Rhine in a little boat.

In his second year in Gaul (B. C. 57), Cæsar invaded the country of the Belgæ, north of the Seine, conquering it after a stubborn campaign; the Belgæ receiving so terrible an overthrow that the rivers and marshes were choked and heaped up with the bodies of the slain. The Roman Senate decreed Cæsar a public thanksgiving of fifteen days for the conquest of Gaul. The next year (B. C. 58) his lieutenant, Decimus Brutus, fought the first naval battle on the Atlantic, with the high-built sailing vessels of the Gauls; while Cæsar conquered Brittany and crushed the revolt of the maritime tribes. Cæsar had thus conquered the whole of Gaul, from the Rhine and the Jura on the east to the Atlantic on the west; and, with the exception of a few brief rebellions, the whole country remained under the dominion of Rome.

In one of the battles in Gaul, the Romans were in extreme danger of being utterly routed, when Cæsar, hastily snatching up a buckler, rushed through his ranks into the midst of the foe, and thus turned the tide of battle in his favor, the barbarians being routed with frightful carnage. Cæsar passed his winters at his head-quarters in Cisalpine Gaul, whence he was able to control the affairs of his party in Italy.

CIVIL WARS AND FALL OF THE REPUBLIC.

In the winter of B. C. 56 he was obliged to reconcile Pompey and Crassus, who were about taking up arms against each other. He succeeded in settling the quarrels of these two jealous rivals in personal interviews which he held with them in his camp at Lucca and Ravenna, and arranged a plan of future operations for the Triumvirate. It was here agreed between the three that Pompey and Crassus should be Consuls the next year (B. C. 55), and that, after the expiration of their Consular term, Pompey should be Proconsul of Spain, and Crassus Pronconsul of Asia, while Cæsar was to be Proconsul of Gaul for a second and prolonged term of five years.

In choosing Gaul, Cæsar selected the most arduous and the least lucrative province for himself; but he desired to commence the execution of his great project for civilizing the West, and organizing the entire Roman dominion into one compact state.

2—62.-U. H.

The political and social revolution begun by the Gracchi had not yet been completed, and it was very evident that the struggle of parties must again lead to a conflict of arms, as it did in the time of Marius and Sulla. In such an event, Cæsar desired to be near Italy, and to have a disciplined and devoted army upon whose loyalty he could rely.

In B. C. 55 the Germans again crossed the Rhine into Gaul in large force. Cæsar defeated them on the west bank of that river,

ANCIENT GAULS.

and then threw a bridge over the stream near Coblenz, and there crossed the river into Germany, and inflicted a severe chastisement upon the tribes of that region. Late in the autumn of the same year (B. C. 55), Cæsar undertook a reconnoitering expedition into Britain, on the pretext that the Britons had furnished supplies to the Gauls during his recent wars with those people; but a report of the pearl fishery on the British coast is believed to have furnished a stronger motive.

On approaching the British coast, near Dover cliffs, Cæsar found the shore covered with armed natives, whereupon he sailed along a few miles farther, and landed at Deal, in spite of the fierce resistance of the Britons. At length the Britons were so terrified by Cæsar's power that they sued for peace. The Britons gave some hostages for the faithful observance of the treaty then made, when a spring tide suddenly damaged the Roman fleet, and the Britons determined to hazard a battle. They therefore attacked one of the Roman legions while it was foraging, and Cæsar experienced some difficulty in saving it. The Britons then assailed the Roman camp, but were repulsed. Having neither cavalry nor provisions, Cæsar considered it advisable to return to Gaul, and readily concluded peace with the Britons. He then retired from Britain, and wrote a letter to the Roman Senate, recounting what he styled his victory in Britain. The Senate, in recognition of his services, decreed a thanksgiving of twenty days, in spite of the opposition of Cato the Younger and other enemies of Cæsar. Cato stoutly insisted that Cæsar ought to be delivered to the vengeance of the barbarians, to avert the wrath of the gods for his having seized the German ambassadors.

The next year (B. C. 54), Cæsar invaded Britain a second time, this time taking with him five legions. He fought several battles with the Britons, defeating their king, Cassivelaúnus, crossing the Thames, and capturing his chief town. But the Britons were far less civilized than the Gauls; and their towns were simply fortresses in the forests, without walls, while their houses were nothing more than wigwams. After imposing tributes upon the conquered tribes and taking hostages, but leaving no garrisons in Britain to hold the natives in subjection, Cæsar returned to Gaul.

The next year (B. C. 53) a formidable revolt broke out among the Gauls, who defeated a strong Roman detachment, and menaced another, under Quintus Cicero, the renowned orator's brother, with a similar fate. Cæsar instantly hastened to Cicero's relief, defeated sixty thousand Gauls, and restored tranquillity to the country. As the Germans had assisted the Gauls in their revolt, Cæsar crossed the Rhine a second time, near Coblenz, in the summer of B. C. 53. But the Germans had such a widespread dread of his arms that they fled to their wooded hills, without offering any resistance.

The following year (B. C. 52) all Gaul was in revolt against Cæsar; and this campaign was the most difficult, as well as the most brilliant, of all Cæsar's military operations. Vercingétorix, King of the Arvérni, and the ablest of the Gallic chieftains, instigated a revolt of all the Gallic tribes, and almost liberated the entire country from the Roman dominion.

While Cæsar was besieging this chief in Alesia, a Gallic army of more than two hundred and fifty thousand men encamped around the Romans and besieged them in turn. But the genius of the renowned Proconsul was equal to the emergency. He kept down every effort at sorties from the Gallic garrison within, while he defeated the outer Gallic army; after which he compelled the garrison to surrender the town, and took Vercingétorix prisoner. Six years afterward the Gallic chieftain adorned Cæsar's triumph, after which he was executed in the Mamertine prison, at the foot of the Capitol. The Gauls were now convinced that resistance was hopeless. Cæsar's firm and skillful management in pacifying Gaul, and organizing the Roman government in the country, finished the task for which his splendid victory had led the way; and by the year B. C. 50 Gaul was tranquilized.

The military talents displayed by Cæsar in his conquest of Gaul rank him as one of the greatest generals of all time. While in Gaul, he is said to have conquered three hundred nations, subdued three millions of people, killed one million, and reduced another million to slavery. Cæsar gave an account of his campaigns in Gaul in his *Commentaries*, which he wrote while conducting those campaigns.

In the meantime, while Cæsar was thus pursuing his conquering career in the West,

VERCINGETORIX SURRENDERS GAUL TO CAESAR.

another of the Triumvirs, Crassus, was not so fortunate in the East. After taking possession of Syria, Crassus, in the year B. C. 54, led an expedition into the Parthian Empire for purposes of conquest and plunder, hoping thus to increase his vast wealth. He crossed the Euphrates with his army, and commenced to ravage Mesopotamia. Several of the Greek towns in that region submitted without offering any resistance; but, instead of pushing his conquests without delay, Crassus returned to Syria to pass the winter, thus affording the Parthians sufficient time to concentrate their forces.

Crassus spent the winter in accumulating more money. A Parthian embassy was sent to Syria to meet him and to complain of his aggression in invading their dominions, as they had afforded the Romans no just cause for war. Crassus boastfully told the Parthian ambassadors that he would give his answer in Seleucia, a city on the west side of the Tigris, opposite Ctesiphon, the capital of the Parthian Empire. One of the ambassadors laughed, and, showing the palm of his hand, said: "Crassus, hairs will grow there before you see Seleucia."

When the Roman soldiers ascertained the numbers of the Parthians, and their method of fighting, they were dispirited. The augurs announced evil signs in the victims. The officers of Crassus advised him to pause before engaging in this perilous enterprise, but all to no purpose. The Armenian prince, Artabazus, counseled him to march through the mountainous country of Armenia, which was unfavorable to cavalry, in which the strength of the Parthians consisted; but Crassus paid no heed to his advice. His reply was that he would march through Mesopotamia, where he had left many heroic Romans in garrisons.

The Armenian prince, who had brought six thousand cavalry to join Crassus, and had promised as many more, perceived the desperate character of the enterprise, and withdrew. Crassus crossed the Euphrates at Zeugma. The roaring of the thunder, the flashing of the lightning, and other ominous signs, according to the Roman superstition, had no effect upon the rash and reckless Roman general. He marched along the eastern bank of the river. No enemy could be seen; and Cassius, one of the officers of Crassus, advised him to keep on the borders of the stream until they should arrive at the point nearest Seleucia; but Akbar, an Arab emir, who had been on friendly terms with the Romans when Pompey was in that part of Asia, joined Crassus, assuring him that the Parthians were collecting their most valuable property with the design of fleeing to Hyrcania and Scythia, and for this reason he urged the Roman general to hasten forward as rapidly as possible.

The account given by the Arab emir was false, and was intended to hurry Crassus and his army to their destruction. But Crassus, relying upon the advice and intelligence of the treacherous Arab, left the river and entered the broad plain of Mesopotamia. The Arab led the way; and when he had brought the Roman army to the place which he had agreed upon with the Parthians, he rode off, giving Crassus every assurance that what he had done was for his advantage.

When too late, the Romans discovered that their leader had been duped, as a party of Roman cavalry sent to reconnoiter the same day were met and attacked by the Parthians, and were almost all slain. Crassus was perplexed, but still he continued his advance, drawing up his infantry in a square, flanked on each side by his cavalry. The army arrived at a stream, where the Roman officers desired their leader to rest for the night and endeavor to hear further tidings, but he persisted in marching on, and finally came in sight of the Parthians. But the Parthian general kept most of his army out of view, and those of his troops who appeared had their armor covered to deceive the Romans.

At a given signal the Parthians commenced beating their kettle-drums; and when they supposed that this unusual sound had filled the Romans with terror, they flung off their coverings, and appeared glittering in helmets and steel corslets. They then poured in multitudes round the solid mass of the Roman army, and discharged showers of arrows upon them, fresh supplies of missiles being at hand on the backs of camels. The Roman light troops vainly endeavored to drive them off, and Crassus ordered his son to charge them with a force of cavalry. The Parthians retired and drew the Roman cavalry on; but when they had gotten them a sufficient distance from the Roman main army, they turned upon their pursuers, riding around and around, raising so much dust that the Romans were unable to see to defend themselves, and many of them were slain.

Finally the young Crassus broke through the Parthian lines with a party of cavalry and arrived at the summit of a hill. There he was surrounded by the Parthians; and at last, being wounded, and perceiving no hope of escape, he caused his shield-bearer to kill him. The Parthians cut off his head and stuck it on the point of a spear. Crassus was marching to his son's relief, when he heard the roll of the Parthian drums, and presently beheld the foe with that son's bloody head held aloft. Consternation filled the Roman ranks at this sight, and Crassus endeavored in vain to encourage his troops, exclaiming that the loss was his, not theirs. The Parthians hung upon the Roman front and flanks all day, raining showers of arrows upon them. The Romans retreated at night, and Crassus gave way to despair. He held a council of war with his officers, and it was decided to retreat under cover of the darkness. This decision was instantly carried into effect, but the Parthians discovered the movement through the wailings of the sick and wounded Romans, who were left behind. But, as the Parthians were not accustomed to fight by night, they waited until morning.

The Parthians took possession of the deserted Roman camp the next morning, and massacred four thousand men whom they found there; after which they pursued the retreating army of Crassus and cut off stragglers. The Romans reached the town of Carrhæ, where they had a garrison. In order to gain time, the Parthian general made proposals of peace; but the Romans soon discovered his insincerity, and Crassus retreated from Carrhæ in the night, under the guidance of a Greek. This Greek guide treacherously led the Roman army into a place full of marshes and ditches. Cassius had distrusted this false guide in season, and turned back and saved himself with about five hundred cavalry. Octavius, the second in command, had faithful guides; and was thus enabled to secure a position among some hills, with his division of five thousand men, so that Crassus was able to escape from the marshes, after the Parthians had assailed him while he was in that perilous situation.

The Parthians were now apprehensive that the Romans would escape during the night, and they therefore released some of their prisoners, declaring that their king did not desire to push matters to extremities. In order to further promote this stratagem, the Parthian commander and some of his officers rode to the hill where Crassus was stationed, with their bows unbent; and the Parthian general held out his hand, calling Crassus to come down and meet him. The Roman soldiers were overcome with joy at these indications of good will, but Crassus utterly distrusted them. Finally, after urging and pressing, the Parthian commander and officers commenced abusing and menacing Crassus. The Roman general then took his officers to see the force by which he was threatened, after which he went down, accompanied by Octavius and other officers.

The Parthians at first affected to receive Crassus with respect, and brought a horse for him to mount; but it was not very long before they quarreled with their prisoners and put them all to death. The Parthians then offered quarter to the Roman troops, most of whom at once surrendered. In this disastrous expedition, which Crassus undertook from motives of ambition and avarice, without a shadow of justice, twenty thousand Romans were slain, and ten thousand were taken prisoners. It is said that the triumphant Parthians, in reproach of the insatiate avarice of Crassus, poured melted gold down his throat, after cutting off his head.

When intelligence of the defeat and death of Crassus reached Rome, the city was plunged into grief and mortification because of the humiliating disaster to the Roman arms. The loss of Crassus gave the people no concern, but his removal was a great misfortune, as he only was able to keep up the friendship between Pompey and Cæsar. The death of Crassus left Pompey and Cæsar as the only two masters of the Roman world. But these two great generals, being jealous of each other's fame, soon became rivals and enemies. A civil war was, therefore, inevitable, in which the two parties should range themselves in opposition under these two illustrious leaders.

Pompey at first favored all of Cæsar's projects, and procured him a prolongation of his command and supplies of troops; but he soon grew envious of exploits that obscured his own fame. His partisans began to detract from the brilliant character of Cæsar's victories, and many of the official letters of the illustrious Proconsul of Gaul were suppressed by the Senate. It soon became evident that the jealousies between these two great rivals could only be settled on the battle-field, and events were rapidly hurrying matters to a crisis. The death of Pompey's wife Julia, Cæsar's daughter, destroyed the last tie of friendship between the two rivals; and Pompey allied himself closely with the aristocratic party, and was therefore warmly supported by the Senate. Pompey remained in Rome to promote his individual political interests, governing Spain through his legates.

When Cæsar was informed of the proceedings against him, he demanded permission to hold the Consular office in his absence, along with a prolongation of his Proconsulate in Gaul. This demand was made by Cæsar for the purpose of seeing whether Pompey would make any open opposition to him. Pompey remained apparently inactive, but secretly engaged two of his partisans to maintain in the Senate that the laws did not permit any one in his absence from Rome to stand as a candidate for the Consulate; and the Senate accordingly passed a decree requiring him to relinquish his Proconsular power and to return to Rome before becoming a candidate for the Consulate a second time. Cæsar was very well aware that the only safety for himself was at the head of his army, as Cato the Younger and other Senators had already threatened to impeach him for illegal acts of which it was alleged that he had been guilty while Consul.

Cæsar therefore determined to remain in Gaul until matters had more nearly approached a crisis. It was not to be expected in these latter days of political degeneracy in the Roman Republic that the conqueror of Gaul would give up his devoted legions and all the treasures of his province to place himself unreservedly in the power of his political foes. Such virtue had been common in the days of Marcus Curtius, but self-sacrifice for the good of the state was now a thing of the past. At the same time Cæsar very well knew that the sacrifice of his life would not promote the public interests. In these degenerate days of the Republic, Rome required a master; and his own schemes for building up a great empire from the scattered portions of the Roman provinces, by extending equal civil and political rights to all the conquered nations, were undoubtedly the broadest and the most practical that had thus far been contrived. Cæsar believed that the great interests of the Roman state and his own individual interests were identical.

Cæsar's enemies at Rome now embraced every opportunity to deprive him of his resources. Under the pretext of a war with Parthia to avenge the fate of Crassus, Pompey and Cæsar were each required to furnish one legion to be sent into Asia. Pompey had formerly lent a legion to Cæsar, and now demanded its return. Cæsar dismissed the two legions, attaching both officers and private soldiers to his interests by giving to each of them his share of the treasure which was to be distributed at his approaching triumph. At the same time Cæsar wrote to the Senate, which was now fully committed to the interests of Pompey, offering to resign his command if Pompey would do the same, but not otherwise. The two legions which Cæsar dismissed were kept in Italy, being stationed at Capua, within Pompey's immediate reach.

Cæsar further strengthened his party at Rome by the great profusion in which he lavished bribes, particularly on Caius Curio, a Tribune of the people, who possessed great political influence, as well as on Mark Antony and Quintus Cassius, also Tribunes of the people. The Senate now passed a decree recalling Cæsar from his government. But Curio placed an unexpected obstacle in the way of this movement by proposing that both Pompey and Cæsar should relinquish their respective Proconsulates. The apparent fairness and impartiality of this proposal involved Pompey and his adherents in great perplexity, and considerable time was spent in debates and negotiations.

Pompey was as eager for civil war as Cæsar could possibly be. The joy which the people manifested upon his recovery from a severe illness gave an exaggerated idea of his influence over the masses. He was likewise thoroughly misled by the accounts which had been furnished him concerning the disaffection of Cæsar's army toward their general, as well as the discontent of Cæsar's province with his Proconsulate. Accordingly, Pompey derided the fears of his friends, who dreaded Cæsar's power; and when it was asserted that there were no troops in Italy to oppose Cæsar, Pompey replied: "Wherever I stamp my foot, legions will spring up."

After a violent debate, the Senate passed a decree demanding that Cæsar should unconditionally relinquish his command and disband his army by a certain day, under penalty of being declared a public enemy in the event of refusal. The Tribunes Antony and Cassius vetoed the measure, but their veto was ignored; and believing their lives in danger, both left Rome secretly, disguised as slaves, and fled to Cæsar's camp at Ravenna, in Cisalpine Gaul, or Northern Italy. The Senate now resolved that troops should be raised in every portion of Italy, and that Pompey should be furnished with funds from the public treasury, so that war was practically declared against Cæsar.

Cæsar's foes thus forced him to take a decisive step, and he now saw no other alternative than to accept the challenge which Pompey and the Senate had thus flung into his face. He knew that if he submitted he would place his country in the power of incompetent men. The Roman Republic was now rotten to the core, and free government existed only in name. The very men who outlawed Cæsar were faithless to the spirit of the laws and the better republicanism of an earlier period, and were destitute of all civic virtue and patriotism, seeking only their selfish personal interests. Cæsar was the real friend of the Roman masses, and the champion of Roman freedom; and the very existence of the Roman state depended upon his decision.

Accordingly, Cæsar assembled the officers and soldiers of the Thirteenth Legion, and informed them of the treatment which he had received and the state of affairs at Rome. Says Professor Mommsen: "There spoke the energetic and consistent statesman, who had now for nine and twenty years defended the cause of freedom in good and evil times; who had braved for it the daggers of assassins and the executioners of the aristocracy, the swords of the Germans, and the waves of the unknown ocean, without ever yielding or wavering; who had torn to pieces the Sullan Constitution, had overthrown the rule of the Senate, and had furnished the defenseless and unarmed democracy with protection and with arms by means of the struggle beyond the Alps. And he spoke, not to the Clodian public whose republican enthusiasm had been long burnt down to ashes and dross, but to the young men from the towns and villages of Northern Italy, who still felt freshly and purely the mighty influence of the thought of civic freedom; who were still capable of fighting and of dying for ideals; who had themselves received for their country in a revolutionary way from Cæsar the burgess rights which the government refused to them; whom Cæsar's fall would leave once more at the mercy of the fasces, and who already possessed practical proofs of the inexorable use which the oligarchy proposed to make of these against the Transpadanes."

Feeling the force and justice of Cæsar's appeal, the Thirteenth Legion, which were all the troops that he had with him at Ravenna, declared their determination to

audacity of his enterprise. If he crossed the stream with hostile designs, he transgressed the laws of his country. He accordingly pondered for some time in settled melancholy, looking earnestly at the stream, and questioning himself, whether he should venture to profane it by crossing it with hostile views. Said he to himself: "If I pass this river, what miseries shall I bring upon my country! And if I stop short, I am undone!" At last yielding to a sudden impulse, he exclaimed: "Let the die be cast!"

CÆSAR CROSSING THE RUBICON.

stand by their general in the impending crisis. He therefore sent orders to his legates in Gaul to join him by forced marches with all their troops, after which he started on his march for Rome with the Thirteenth Legion. When he arrived at the Rubicon, a small stream flowing east into the Adriatic, near the modern city of Rimini, he halted. The Romans had always been taught to consider this little river the sacred boundary of Italy proper; and Cæsar hesitated upon its banks, under an impression of terror at the

Instantly he spurred his horse into the stream, and led his troops across (B. C. 48).

When tidings of Cæsar's passage of the Rubicon reached Rome, the city was thrown into the utmost consternation, as it was feared that the conqueror of Gaul intended a general massacre of his enemies. The citizens fled into the country for safety, while the country people sought refuge in the city. Pompey was utterly overwhelmed with confusion. Favonius, a Senator, sarcastically asked him: "Where is now the army that was to rise out of the earth at your bidding? Let us see if it will appear at the stamp of your foot." Pompey was completely deceived in his expectations of the support of the people in his behalf. His troops were all deserting to Cæsar. The lower classes were either in sympathy with Cæsar, or desired a change; and it was evident that his progress in Italy could not be stayed. Therefore the Senate and Pompey and all their partisans fled from Rome, leaving back the public treasury with all its immense sum (B. C. 48).

Cæsar subdued all Italy within sixty days, and Pompey sailed from Brundusium with twenty-five thousand men for Greece, abandoning his country to his rival. Sicily and Sardinia speedily followed the fate of the Italian mainland. After pursuing Pompey to Brundusium, Cæsar was so elated by his success that he returned to Rome, where the Tribune Metellus remonstrated against his proceedings as contrary to the laws. But Cæsar told him that this was no time to talk about laws, and that all must obey him. Cæsar then went to the public treasury, and, not finding the keys, sent for a smith to break open the door. Metellus again interposed his objections, whereupon Cæsar threatened to put him to death, saying: "Know, young man, that it is easier to do than to say." After breaking open the treasury, Cæsar took out all the money, and even the most sacred deposits.

Cæsar's enemies were astonished at his moderation and the justice of his course. He respected the property of his absent foes, compelled his soldiers to behave themselves as fellow-citizens of the Romans and Italians; and he soon won the mass of the population, and particularly the wealthy class, to his cause by his wise policy.

After remaining in Rome about a week, Cæsar started for Spain to attack Pompey's legates, who had seven legions in that Roman province. He encountered an unexpected resistance from the city of Massilia (now Marseilles), in South-eastern Gaul; but, leaving a detachment to besiege the town, he continued his march to Ilerda, in Spain, where he found his enemies posted under the command of Afranius and Petreius. After an indecisive battle at Ilerda, Cæsar took advantage of the incapacity of his foes, and soon reduced them to such desperate extremities that they were obliged to surrender at discretion. After reducing the remainder of Spain, Cæsar returned to complete the siege of Massilia. He soon compelled the city to surrender, sparing the lives of the citizens, but forcing them to give up all their arms, magazines and money (B. C. 49).

During Cæsar's absence in Spain and Gaul, he had been made Dictator, a post which he accepted upon his return, but only held it for eleven days. During this period he was again elected Consul, and obtained the passage of laws for the recall of all the exiles banished by Sulla except Milo, and for the relief of debtors. He inaugurated a great project for the consolidation of the Roman provinces by extending the full privileges of Roman citizenship to the Gauls.

While Cæsar was thus employed in Italy and the Western Roman provinces, Pompey was making active preparations in Greece to oppose the arms of his rival, and to end the civil war with a decisive conflict. All the Eastern monarchs in alliance with the Roman Republic had pronounced in favor of Pompey and had sent him large supplies. Pompey had attacked Cæsar's forces in the East under Antony and Dolabella, and had defeated them, taking Dolabella prisoner. Multitudes of the most eminent Roman citizens and nobles came daily to join Pompey. At one time he had more than two hundred Senators in his camp, among whom were Cicero and Cato the Younger, whose approbation of his cause was considered equivalent to an army.

Cæsar determined to pursue Pompey into Greece, but his inferior naval force exposed his army to great perils and hardships in their passage across the Adriatic from Brundusium to Dyrrachium (now Durazzo). After Cæsar himself had crossed with a part of his army, and had found the remainder much delayed in their passage, he recrossed the sea in an open fishing-boat. The fisherman, not knowing who his passenger was, was alarmed at the turbulence of the waves, but the Dictator encouraged him with the memorable words: "Fear nothing; you carry Cæsar and his fortunes."

Both armies being now in the field, they marched and countermarched through a wearisome campaign, in which both leaders exhibited equal reluctance to risk a battle. From Epirus the two armies moved into Thessaly, and at last encountered each other at Pharsalia, to contend for the dominion of the Roman world. Pompey's army was composed of forty-five thousand infantry and seven thousand cavalry, besides light troops. Cæsar's force consisted of only twenty-two thousand infantry and one thousand cavalry. But Cæsar's inferior numbers were balanced by their superior qualities, his soldiers being mainly hardy veterans, accustomed to victory, and inspired with the fullest confidence in themselves and their leader; while Pompey's troops were chiefly raw levies.

When Pompey's officers saw the inferior numbers of Cæsar's troops, their confidence was raised to the highest degree, and they regarded victory as certain. They even disputed about dividing the spoils before the battle was fought, and disposed of all dignities and offices in the Republic, assigning the Consuls for several succeeding years. Scipio, Spinther and Domitius engaged in an angry controversy as to which of them should be rewarded with the dignity of Pontifex Maximus, then held by Cæsar. Others sent to Rome to engage houses suitable to the offices which they expected to enjoy after the victory to which they looked forward so confidently. Pompey, being naturally superstitious, had been very much encouraged by favorable signs in the entrails of the victims at the taking of the auspices by the augurs on this occasion; and he accordingly determined to hazard an engagement on the 9th of August, B. C. 48.

On that day was fought the famous battle of Pharsalia. Cæsar's army was divided into three bodies; the center being commanded by Domitius Calvinus, the left wing by Mark Antony, and the right wing by Cæsar himself. This last wing consisted of Cæsar's favorite Tenth Legion, and was to confront Pompey himself. The appearance of Pompey's cavalry at one place indicated his designs so clearly that his adversary readily perceived them. Cæsar therefore drew six cohorts from his rear and concealed them behind his right, directing them to wait until Pompey's cavalry approached, and then to aim their spears in the faces of the horsemen, who, being of the young nobility of Rome, dreaded a scratch in the face much more than the severest wound in the body. Cæsar then placed his own handful of cavalry on the right of the Tenth Legion.

When the signal for battle was given, Cæsar's line advanced, while Pompey's line awaited the assault without moving from its position. When Cæsar's troops saw their foe motionless, they came to a sudden halt. After a short pause, during which both parties gazed at each other in a kind of amazement, Cæsar's soldiers dashed forward, darting their javelins and drawing their swords. Thereupon Pompey ordered his cavalry to charge. Cæsar's troops fell back, but his reserve of six cohorts then advanced and struck at the faces of their enemies, soon producing the effect which had been anticipated. The effeminate young Roman nobles, valuing themselves upon their beauty, were intimidated by the ugly wounds which they saw inflicted upon their comrades, and thought only of saving themselves. They were soon utterly routed, fleeing in disorder, and leaving the archers and the slingers to be cut to pieces.

Cæsar's successful cohorts now advanced against the flank and rear of Pompey's line, which resisted gallantly until Cæsar's third line assailed them in front and drove them back to their camp. The auxiliaries had fled while Pompey's right wing was fighting bravely. Seeing that the result of the battle was no longer doubtful, Cæsar called upon his troops to pursue the auxiliaries, but to spare the Romans, in Pompey's army. Pompey's auxiliary troops were accordingly slaughtered in vast numbers, but his Romans laid down their arms and received quarter. Although Pompey's army was now overthrown, Cæsar regarded his victory as incomplete until he was in possession of Pompey's camp. Pompey's cohorts and the Thracians, who guarded his camp, resisted with great obstinacy, but were driven from the trenches and put to flight.

Cæsar's victory being thus won, the conqueror took a view of the sanguinary field, which he saw covered with the dead bodies of his countrymen. He felt, or affected to feel, a deep distress at the sight, mournfully exclaiming: "They would have it so!" Cæsar treated his vanquished foes with great humanity; and by the clemency and moderation which he manifested in his subsequent conduct, he soon added to the glory of the honors which he had achieved as a conqueror. Fifteen thousand of Pompey's soldiers were slain. Twenty thousand surrendered the next morning, and enlisted in Cæsar's army.

As soon as Pompey perceived that his soldiers gave way, he lost all presence of mind. He fled from the bloody field, and rode with about thirty followers to the gates of Larissa, but would not enter the town, fearing that the inhabitants would incur his victorious rival's wrath. He then proceeded to the Vale of Tempe, and boarded a merchant vessel which he found lying at the mouth of the Penéus, whence he sailed to the mouth of the Strymon. Having obtained some money from his friends at Amphipolis, he proceeded to the island of Lesbos, where he took on board his wife Cornelia and his son Sextus. After collecting a few vessels he sailed to Cilicia, and thence to Cyprus.

It is said that Pompey consulted with his friends whether he should seek refuge with the King of Parthia, or with King Juba of Numidia, or with the young Ptolemy XIII. of Egypt, whose father had been restored to the Egyptian throne through Pompey's influence some years before. He finally decided upon fleeing to the court of the latter, and accordingly sailed to Egypt. When Pompey arrived at Pelusium, he was informed that the young king of Egypt was at that city with an army, being then at war with his sister-wife Cleopatra, whom their father had made joint heir to the Egyptian throne. Pompey sent a request to Ptolemy for his protection. The young Egyptian king's ministers, either suspecting Pompey's designs, or despising his fallen greatness, determined upon putting him to death; and the young king was persuaded to this course by a young Roman in his army named Septimius, in order to gain the favor of the victorious Cæsar.

Ptolemy's ministers sent Achilles, a captain of the guard, and the young Roman Septimius, just alluded to, who had been a centurion, along with some others, in a small boat, to invite the fallen Pompey to land. They requested him to come into the boat, as the shore was too shallow to be approached by a ship. He consented, and, after embracing his wife Cornelia, he entered the boat; reciting the following lines from Sóphocles:

"He who unto a prince's house repairs,
Becomes his slave though he go thither free!"

They rowed toward the shore for some time without a word being spoken. At last Pompey turned to Septimius, saying: "If I mistake not, you and I have been fellow soldiers." Septimius simply nodded in reply, and Pompey commenced reading over a speech which he had written in Greek, to deliver before the young King Ptolemy XIII. As the boat was nearing the shore, Pompey rose from his seat to prepare to land, whereupon Septimius stabbed him in the back. Achilles and the others then struck the fallen general; and Pompey, seeing the fate that inevitably awaited him at the treacherous hands of those upon whose hospitality he had so innocently relied, drew his toga over his face, fell back and expired. His head was then cut off, and the body was cast upon the beach, where it remained until two of his friends burned it on a funeral pyre made out of the wreck of a fishing-boat.

FLIGHT OF POMPEIUS FROM PHARSALIA.

Such was the melancholy end of Pompey the Great, a man of commanding genius, of remarkably pure private morals, and of a most highly amiable character. While he possessed these virtues, he was vain and ambitious, and unable to brook a rival. He did not possess his rival's energy for restraining the violence of his followers; and Cicero had good reasons for his fears that if Pompey were to be victorious in the struggle, there would be more sanguinary violence than in case of Cæsar's success.

Intelligence of Pompey's assassination caused fresh divisions among his partisans. Many who were personally friendly to him, and who held out in hopes of again being under his leadership, resolved to avail themselves of the triumphant Cæsar's clemency. Pompey's widow, Cornelia, returned to Italy, well aware that she had nothing to fear from Cæsar. Cato the Younger and Pompey's two sons, Cneius and Sextus, hastened to join Juba, King of Numidia.

Immediately after his victory at Pharsalia, Cæsar closely pursued Pompey to Egypt, and was not informed of his death until he arrived at Alexandria, when messengers from King Ptolemy XIII. brought him Pompey's bloody head and signet-ring. The conqueror wept bitterly, and turned away in disgust at the sight of these relics; and ordered the head of his unfortunate rival to be interred with due honors, and bestowed rewards and favors on Pompey's most faithful adherents. To show his disapproval of the treachery of the Egyptians in the assassination of Pompey, Cæsar caused a temple to be erected near Pompey's tomb, dedicated to Némesis, the goddess of vengeance. He also ordered the assassins to be put to death.

Cæsar remained at Alexandria for about five months, regulating the affairs of Egypt and arranging the disputed succession to the Egyptian crown. The young Ptolemy XIII. was greatly disappointed when Cæsar, captivated by the charms of Cleopatra, dedecided in favor of her claims to the throne of Egypt. Ptolemy's adherents then arose against Cæsar, who, having taken only a few troops with him to Alexandria, was soon involved in the greatest peril by this sudden outburst of insurrection. A desperate battle was fought in the streets of Alexandria. Cæsar set fire to the Egyptian fleet, but unfortunately the flames extended to the great library established by Ptolemies Soter and Philadelphus, and the greater portion of this magnificent collection of the most valuable literary works of antiquity fell a prey to the flames. Cæsar succeeded in making his escape from the city. After the struggle had been prolonged for some time, Cæsar received reinforcements from Syria, which enabled him to overthrow the army of Ptolemy XIII., who, after the battle, was drowned in the Nile (B. C. 48). In a naval battle in this war, Cæsar was obliged to save his life by swimming from ship to ship, holding his sword in his teeth, and the manuscript of his *Commentaries upon the Gallic Wars* in one hand over his head.

After thus establishing Cleopatra upon the throne of Egypt, Cæsar marched hastily into Asia Minor against Phárnaces, son of Mithridátes the Great of Pontus, who was endeavoring to recover his father's dominions, and who had defeated the Romans at Nicopolis with heavy loss. In a short campaign of five days (B. C. 47), Cæsar won a decisive victory over Phárnaces at Ziela, defeating him so easily that he sent to the Roman Senate his memorable despatch announcing his victory, in three words: "Veni, vidi, vici" (I came, I saw, I conquered).

Having thus settled the affairs of the East, Cæsar returned to Rome, where he found matters in great confusion in consequence of the quarrels between Antony and Dolabella. Cæsar reconciled these two leaders with difficulty; after which he proceeded to Africa, where his enemies, Cato the younger and the sons of Pompey, had collected an army as large as that which Cæsar had conquered at Pharsalia. The Pompeians had established a Senate at Utica and threatened to prolong the civil war.

In his effort to begin military operations against the Pompeian party in Africa, Cæsar encountered an unexpected obstacle in a mutiny of his veterans in Southern Italy. Wearied with the extraordinary hardships of their last campaigns, and fancying that their leader could not do without them, they refused to embark for Sicily, and began their His ears were greeted with cries of "Discharge!" Instantly taking them at their word, he addressed them as "citizens," not as "soldiers," promising them, at his coming triumph, their full share in the treasure and

CÆSAR AT THE GRAVE OF ALEXANDER THE GREAT.

march toward Rome. After providing for the safety of the city, Cæsar suddenly made his appearance among the mutinous legions and demanded to know what they wanted. lands which he had intended for his faithful followers, though allowing them no part in the triumph itself. Cæsar's presence and his voice had the effect of reviving the old affection of the mutinous legionaries, and they stood in silence and shame at the sudden break of the tie which had been their sole glory in the past. At length they commenced imploring, even with tears, that they might be restored to their leader's favor, and be honored once more with the name of "Cæsar's soldiers." Their humble request was granted after some delay; the ring-leaders being only punished by a reduction of one-third in their triumphal presents. Thus the mutiny was ended.

Upon arriving in Africa, Cæsar found the Pompeians very much more formidable than he had expected. They were well supplied with cavalry and elephants, and were able to fight on the fields of their own selection. They won a victory near Rúspina (B. C. 47); but the next year, in the greater and far more decisive battle of Thapsus, Cæsar gained a complete victory (B. C. 46). Cæsar's soldiers disregarded his orders to spare their fellow-citizens, as they were resolved to obtain rest from the hardships of war at any sacrifice of Roman lives; and fifty thousand Pompeians were left dead upon the battle-field.

By his victory at Thapsus, Cæsar became master of the whole Roman province of Africa. Leaving a strong detachment of his army to besiege the town of Thapsus, Cæsar advanced to Utica, which was garrisoned by Cato the Younger, who had from the first been actuated by the most inflexible hostility to Cæsar. Cato's Senate at Utica consisted of three hundred of the Roman traders who resided in that city. Upon receiving tidings of the defeat of his partisans at Thapsus, Cato convened his Senate and endeavored to inspire its members with courage and resolution; but when he discovered that they were inclined to throw themselves on Cæsar's clemency, he resigned all hopes of defending the city. A detachment of the Pompeian cavalry, which had fled from the defeat of Thapsus, arrived at Utica at this juncture; and Cato endeavored to induce them to remain for the defense of the city; but while he was absent from the Senate, that body decided upon surrender.

Thereupon Cato prepared for suicide. He arranged his accounts, and commended his children to the care of a friend. In the evening he bathed and supped with his family as usual, discussing philosophical subjects. He took a walk after supper, after which he retired to his chamber, where he passed the time in reading over Plato's Dialogue on the Immortality of the Soul. He then lay down and slept soundly for several hours. He arose towards morning and stabbed himself with his sword. Hearing the sound of his fall, his friends rushed into the room, and a surgeon endeavored to bind up his wound; but Cato thrust every one from him, tore open his bowels, and expired. Cato did not wish to survive the Roman Republic, which he saw had virtually approached its end. Cato's death put an end to the civil war in Africa; and after giving orders for the rebuilding of Carthage, the conquering Cæsar returned to Rome in possession of absolute power.

When Cæsar arrived in Rome on his return from Africa, the obsequious Senate decreed to him honors of every kind. That body had already ordered a thanksgiving of forty days for his victory in Africa, granted him the Dictatorship for ten years, and decreed that his chariot should be placed in the Capitol opposite the statue of Jupiter, with the Dictator's statue standing on a globe of brass, inscribed with the words: "Cæsar the Demigod." Instead of the proscriptions which had marked the alternate triumphs of Marius and Sulla, Cæsar proclaimed universal amnesty, and endeavored to avail himself of the wisdom of all parties in the work of civil reorganization.

After addressing the Senate and the people, assuring them of his clemency and his regard for the Republic, Cæsar prepared to celebrate his triumphs for his various foreign conquests. Four of these triumphs were celebrated in one month; the first being for Gaul, the second for Egypt, the third for Pontus, and the fourth for Numidia. These triumphs were only for the conquest of foreign foes, as it was considered unbecoming to triumph over Roman citizens. The first triumph was the most magnificent; but as the procession was approaching the Capitol, the axle of the triumphal chariot broke, and Cæsar found himself obliged to mount another, thus giving occasion to much delay. In the second triumph were pictures of battles, the Pharos of Alexandria on fire, etc. The third triumph displayed a tablet with Cæsar's laconic despatch at the close of his Pontic campaign: "Veni, vidi, vici." There were two thousand eight hundred and twenty-two golden crowns borne in triumph. Cæsar feasted the people of Rome at twenty thousand tables spread in the streets and public squares of the city; and to one hundred and fifty thousand citizens he presented ten pecks of corn, ten pounds of oil, and four hundred sesterces in money apiece. While he was returning home from the banquet, lights were borne on each side of him by forty elephants.

Cæsar afterwards entertained the people of Rome with all kinds of games, shamfights, chariot-races and horse-races, huntings of wild beasts, etc. He rewarded his veteran soldiers by presenting twenty-four thousand sesterces to each private, forty-eight thousand to each centurion, and ninety-six thousand to each Tribune. In addition to this pay, they all received donations of land.

Cæsar then directed his attention to regulating the disorders of the Republic; and the benefit of one of his provisions is felt in our own day—namely the rectifying of the calendar. Through the negligence of the pontiffs, the reckoning of time had fallen into hopeless confusion; so that harvest festivals were celebrated in spring, and those of the late vintage occurred in mid-summer. As Pontifex Maximus, Cæsar reformed the calendar, by adding ninety days to the current year; after which, with the assistance of an Alexandrian astronomer, he adapted the reckoning to the sun's course. He made the Roman year consist of three hundred and sixty-five days, and added a day every fourth year. The *Julian Calendar*—as rectified by Pope Gregory XIII. in A. D. 1582—is the reckoning which Christian nations now follow. In recognition of Cæsar's services in this matter, the Roman Senate ordered his clan-name to be given to his birth month —*July*.

The civil war was not yet fully closed in the Roman provinces, as the Pompeians were still in arms in Spain. Cæsar proceeded to that province, and overthrew Pompey's sons in the desperate and decisive battle of Munda (March 17, B. C. 45); Cneius Pompey being killed; but Sextus making his escape, and soon afterwards submitting to Cæsar and receiving his father's estates.

After thus settling the affairs of Spain, Cæsar returned to Rome for the fourth time; and the servile Senate created him Dictator and Censor for life, with the title of *Imperator*, and invested him with all the powers of an absolute monarch, although the name and outward forms of the Republic were allowed to remain. Cæsar was invested with the power of making peace or war without consulting either the Senate or the people. As Imperator, he was allowed to name his successor. His person was declared sacred, and all the Senators bound themselves by a solemn oath to watch over his safety, so that it was treason to plot against him. His statues were ordered to be placed in all the temples, and his name in civil oaths was associated with the names of the gods.

Cæsar now laid aside the sword and cultivated the arts of peace, altered the laws, and corrected many abuses. Turning his thoughts to legislation, he increased the Senate to nine hundred members, and chose the Senators from the provinces as well as from Rome itself. He confined the judicial power to the Senate and the knights. To perpetuate his power, he reserved to himself the appointment of one-half of those who were to be elected to offices in the state; and at the approaching elections he always informed the people as to whom he desired to have chosen to the remaining places. He granted the full privileges of Roman citizenship to the whole population of Cisalpine Gaul, and to many communities in Transalpine Gaul, in Spain, and in other Roman provinces; and in every possible way sought

CAESAR REFUSING THE CROWN.

to obliterate the distinctions between Rome and her provinces, so as to make the entire Roman world a homogeneous whole, thus substituting a great Mediterranean empire for the mere city government which for more than a century had swayed the destinies of Italy and the world.

Cæsar atoned for the narrow policy of municipal Rome by rebuilding the two great commercial cities, Carthage and Corinth, which the jealousy of the Roman Republic had destroyed. He rewarded his veterans with lands beyond the sea, and sent eighty thousand of the poorer inhabitants of the over-crowded city of Rome into the Roman provinces in Europe, Asia and Africa as colonists. His projects embraced the varied interests of all classes and all nations within the Roman dominion; and were designed, by uniting all, to attain a higher civilization than any one of them had reached alone. The Greek schoolmaster and the Jewish trader followed the Roman soldier into the most inhospitable regions of Germany, Dalmatia, or Spain.

Cæsar caused the Romans laws to be digested into a code—a much needed reform. He arranged a settlement between the debtor and creditor classes on a basis acknowledged by both as liberal and just, and "which left financial honesty untouched." He restored the Licinian Law which required the employment of a certain amount of free labor in the tilling of the lands. He encouraged the increase of the free population by granting exemptions to such as had no less than three children. He granted the freedom of the city to all physicians and professors of the liberal sciences; and sought to advance the cause of education in every portion of the Roman dominions, and to civilize mankind by the power of learning rather than by force. He collected a Greek and Latin library on the model of that founded by the Ptolemies at Alexandria.

Cæsar proposed a plan for changing the course of the Tiber, so as to drain the Pontine marshes, and thus add to the city an extensive tract of land available for building. He also proposed to connect Rome with Tarracina, a larger and more convenient port than that of Ostia. He likewise planned the erection of a new theater and a magnificent temple to Mars.

Though Cæsar occupied the highest rank as a general, he was more of a statesman than a warrior; and desired to found his government upon the popular confidence, and not upon military power. When he first assumed command of an army, he was already in his fortieth year. He executed all his great works as a ruler during the short intervals of military affairs. Seven important military campaigns occupied five and a half years following his accession to power; and while he was planning an expedition against Parthia to avenge the fate of Crassus, his career was ended forever by a violent death.

All the genius of Cæsar, and all the wisdom and clemency which distinguished his exercise of the supreme power, could not compensate, in the minds of many of his countrymen, for the crime of elevating himself to power on the ruins of the Republic. It was rumored that, before starting on his Parthian expedition, he designed to assume the title of king. Although he already exercised the full power of a monarch, the name *king* was still intolerably odious to the Roman people. Whether he ever really intended to assume that empty honor, must forever remain a secret. At the Feast of the Lupercalia, February 15, B. C. 44, Mark Antony, his colleague in the Consulate, offered him a crown in the full presence of the Roman people. It was believed that this was done at the secret instigation of the Dictator, but the popular disapprobation of the act obliged Cæsar to refuse the title and emblem of royalty.

Still it was suspected that the Dictator was aiming at a kingly dignity; and at length a conspiracy was formed by about sixty Senators for the assassination of Cæsar, most of whom were among his partisans during the civil war between him and Pompey. At the head of the conspirators were the Prætor Marcus Cassius, who hated Cæsar, and Marcus Junius Brutus, a sincere friend of liberty and a republican of the old stamp, but also a firm friend of Cæsar, who had bestowed upon him many distinguished honors. This Brutus prided himself upon being a descendant of the famous Lucius Junius Brutus, the founder of the Roman Republic; so that the love of freedom appeared to be transmitted to him with the blood of an illustrious ancestry.

The Ides (15th) of March, B. C. 44, was the day fixed upon for the assassination to take place. The augurs had foretold that this day would be fatal to Cæsar. His wife Calpurnia dreamed on the night previous that she saw him assassinated. He was so influenced by these omens that he felt disposed to postpone going to the Senate-House on that day; but one of the conspirators, who called upon him in the morning, represented to him the absurdity of his absence from the Senate on account of his wife's unlucky dreams. Cæsar was thus prevailed upon to be present at the Senate on that day, and the conspiracy was almost detected. While he was passing through the streets, a slave who knew of the plot endeavored to approach him and give information, but was prevented from doing so by the crowd. Artemidórus, a Greek philosopher, who had become aware of the plot, put a paper giving an account of it into Cæsar's hand; but the Dictator, supposing the paper to be an ordinary matter of business, handed it to a secretary along with other papers, without reading it, in accordance with his custom.

When Cæsar entered the Senate-House, where the conspirators were ready to receive him, he met an augur named Spurnia, who had foretold his danger. Cæsar said to him smiling: "Well, the Ides of March are come." Thereupon the augur replied: "True, but they are not yet passed." When Cæsar had taken his seat in the Senate-House, the conspirators approached him under the pretense of saluting him. One of them, named Cimber, in a suppliant attitude, pretended to implore for the pardon of his brother, who had been banished by the Dictator. The others zealously seconded him. Cimber, affecting extraordinary earnestness, seized hold of the bottom of Cæsar's toga, thus preventing the Dictator from rising. This was the preconcerted signal for the attack, and all the conspirators instantly rushed upon Cæsar with their daggers. Casca, who was behind, first stabbed the Dictator in the shoulder. Cæsar turned upon this assailant with his stylus, or steel writing-rod, and wounded him in the arm.

The Dictator now received thrusts of daggers from every side. He defended himself vigorously, rushing upon his assailants and throwing down such as opposed him, until he saw his dear friend Brutus among the conspirators, when he ceased all resistance, covered his face with his toga, and exclaimed: "Et tu Brute" (And thou too, Brutus). He then fell down at the base of Pompey's statue, pierced with twenty-three wounds, and expired. As soon as the bloody work of the conspirators was accomplished, Brutus, brandishing his dagger, addressed Cicero thus: "Rejoice, father of our country, Rome is free!" The majority of the Senators, seized with fear and astonishment, fled from the Senate-House and hid themselves in their houses. Thus perished the greatest man that Rome —some say the greatest man that the world— ever produced. He was a great warrior, statesman, orator and historian.

The rejoicings of Brutus and his fellow-conspirators at Cæsar's death were totally unfounded, as Roman liberty had virtually perished with the Gracchi. Cæsar understood the times better than his assassins, well knowing that the Republic was beyond the power of resurrection. In killing Cæsar, the conspirators removed the only man who was capable of governing the Roman people with clear insight, firmness and beneficence; and thus plunged the state once more into the horrors of civil war, making Rome an easy prey for a less able and less liberal tyrant and usurper. If Brutus and his fellow-conspirators would have been able to restore to their countrymen of that generation the simple and self-denying virtues of their ancestors, Rome would indeed have been free.

COLOSSAL STATUE OF JULIUS CÆSAR AT NAPLES.

The death of one man could not change the character of the nation, whose corruption had gradually eaten away the vitality of the Republic. The conspirators had stricken down the strong arm that was needed to guide the Roman state through this crisis.

The Senatorial conspirators had seriously miscalculated in their expectations that the Roman people would come to their support in this emergency, as all classes were thrown into consternation by the assassination, fearing that this great tragedy would be followed by a return of proscription and revenge. Cæsar's partisans now had an opportunity to gratify their ambition under the pretense of upholding justice. Of these, Mark Antony distinguished himself above all others. He was a man of but moderate abilities, disgraced by habits of vice, and only ambitious of power because it furnished a broader field for his immoralities. He was, nevertheless, a skillful general, having had experience in military life from his youth.

Antony was Consul in the year of Cæsar's assassination; and along with Lepidus, a man like himself, fond of commotions and intrigues, he contrived a plan to seize the chief power in the state. In pursuance of this project, Lepidus took possession of the Forum with a select body of troops. Antony's next move was to gain possession of Cæsar's papers and money. The Senate was then convened to declare whether Cæsar had been a legal magistrate or a tyrannical usurper. This question caused great embarrassment to many of the Senators, who had received all their offices from Cæsar, and had obtained vast fortunes by serving him. Therefore to pronounce him a usurper would imperil their property, while to declare him innocent might endanger the state.

In this dilemma the Senate endeavored to reconcile the two contradictory opinions, by sanctioning all of Cæsar's acts, but granting a pardon to his assassins. This decree did not satisfy Antony, because it granted security to many men who were the avowed enemies of tyranny, and who, he foresaw, would actively oppose his plans for restoring absolute power. Therefore when Antony saw that the Senate had ratified all of Cæsar's acts, without distinction, he contrived a scheme to make the murdered Dictator rule after his death. Having gained possession of Cæsar's account books and papers, Antony bribed his secretary to insert in them whatever he thought proper. By this project vast sums of Cæsar's money were distributed so as to favor Antony's schemes.

Antony obtained a decree from the Senate for the performance of Cæsar's funeral obsequies. On the day of the funeral, the body of the murdered Dictator was taken into the Forum with the greatest solemnity; and Antony, having assigned himself these last duties of friendship, arose before the assembled multitude to deliver the funeral oration. He first read Cæsar's will, in which the Dictator made Octavius, his sister's grandson, his heir, authorizing him to assume the name of Cæsar, with three-fourths of his private fortune. The gardens which Cæsar possessed on the other side of the Tiber were left to the Roman people; and three hundred sesterces (about eleven and a fourth dollars of our money) were left to each citizen.

After reading Cæsar's will, Anthony proceeded with the funeral oration. He began artfully to excite the passions of the multitude by enumerating the brilliant exploits and the noble acts of the murdered Cæsar. He then lifted Cæsar's bloody toga, pierced by the daggers of the assassins, and showed the number of stabs in it. Antony also showed the people an image of wax representing Cæsar's body all covered with wounds. The people, becoming so excited that they could no longer restrain their indignation against the assassins, stormed the Senate-House, tore up the benches to make a funeral pile, and ran through the streets with lighted brands to set fire to the houses of Brutus, Cassius and the other conspirators. These individuals were, however, well guarded, and repulsed the assaults of the mob with ease; but seeing that they were no longer safe in Rome, Brutus and Cassius fled from the city.

Antony was for a time the most popular

CIVIL WARS AND FALL OF THE REPUBLIC.

MARK ANTONY DELIVERING THE FUNERAL ORATION OVER THE DEAD BODY OF CÆSAR.

man in Rome, and he proceeded in his work of preventing Cæsar's assassins from profiting by their crime. Having succeeded in accomplishing his first purpose, he went on with his chief design with the same cunning. He assumed an appearance of moderation, and affected an anxiety to obtain an act of amnesty. He soon threw off the mask, and proposed extraordinary honors to Cæsar's memory, with a religious supplication to him as a divinity. Brutus and Cassius soon discovered that Antony meditated civil war, and their cause was becoming more desperate every day; wherefore they retired from Italy, seeking refuge in the Eastern Roman provinces, where they determined to make a stand in their own defense and in the cause of the Republic.

Antony soon found a powerful rival in the youthful Octavius Cæsar, the grandson of the murdered Dictator's sister Julia, and his adopted son and principal heir. This young man had been educated with great care under the eye of his adopted father. He now made his appearance at Rome, having come from the camp at Appolonia to claim his inheritance, out of which he carefully distributed the legacies to the soldiers and the citizens. Cicero was induced to regard Octavius as the hope of the state; and in his third great series of orations, called the *Philippics*, the renowned orator destroyed Antony's popularity and his influence with the Senate. Antony thereupon retired into Cisalpine Gaul, levied an army of veterans, and besieged Mutína, (now Modena), thus inaugurating a new civil war. The Senate then declared Antony a public enemy, and sent an army under the two Consuls for the year B. C. 43, Hirtius and Pansa, against him. At Cicero's instance, Octavius was made Prætor and associated with the two Consuls in the command. Two of Antony's legions deserted to Octavius, and Antony was routed in two battles near Mutína and driven across the Alps, but the victorious Consuls were both slain in the last battle.

The Senate now also antagonized Octavius and refused him the Consulate, whereupon Octavius led his legions to Rome and forced the Senate to confer upon him the supreme power, although he was but nineteen years old. He compelled the people to elect himself and Quintus Pedius as Consuls for the year B. C. 42. He also caused the Senate to confirm his adoption by his grand-uncle, and to indict Cæsar's assassins. All these having fled from Rome at his approach, he caused them to be condemned in their absence, and also a similar sentence to be passed upon Sextus Pompey. Octavius was made sole commander of the armies of the Republic, and invested with power to make war or peace with Antony, who was now descending from the Alps with seventeen legions, having been in the meantime joined by Lepidus, who had been master of the horse to Julius Cæsar. But the Senate now dreaded the power of Octavius as much as it had just feared that of Antony, and revoked the sentence of outlawry against the latter.

Disgusted with the vacillation of the Senate, and desiring the assistance of Antony and Lepidus to overthrow Brutus and Cassius, who had by this time raised a large republican army in the East, Octavius opened negotiations with his two rivals. Accordingly Octavius, Antony and Lepidus met on a small island in the little river Reno, near Bononia (now Bologna), in Cisalpine Gaul, and formed a league called the *Second Triumvirate*, by which these three leaders took upon themselves the government of the Roman world for five years (B. C. 43). In their conference of three days on this occasion the three Triumvirs partitioned the territories of the Republic and determined the fate of thousands, thus making a cruel and tyrannical use of their power by causing all of their most powerful opponents to be put to death, each Triumvir abandoning his best friends to the vengeance of his colleagues. Antony obtained the government of Gaul; Lepidus that of Spain; and Octavius that of Africa and the isles of the Mediterranean. The Triumvirs agreed to hold Italy and the Eastern provinces in common until they had subdued all their enemies.

The Triumvirs at once commenced their

CIVIL WARS AND FALL OF THE REPUBLIC. 995

bloody work of proscription and massacre as agreed upon, and the noblest citizens of Rome were sacrificed to the political enmity and the ignoble ambition of the Triumvirs. Lepidus yielded his brother to the vengeance of his colleagues; Antony sacrificed his uncle; and Octavius, to his eternal shame, allowed Cicero to be abandoned to the wrath of Antony, whose relentless animosity the illustrious orator had incurred in consequence of his severe and eloquent invectives.

CICERO.

Antony sent in pursuit of the great orator a band of assassins, headed by a Tribune whose life Cicero had saved by defending him in a capital trial. The assassins murdered Cicero near his own villa at Formiæ, on the road from Rome to Naples. His head and right hand were nailed to the rostrum at Rome, from which he had so many times discoursed of the sacred rights of Roman citizens. Altogether, two thousand knights and three hundred Senators fell victims to the sanguinary hatred of the Triumvirs. Those who were able to make their escape found refuge with Sextus Pompey in Sicily, or with Brutus and Cassius in Greece.

In the meantime Brutus and Cassius had raised an army of more than a hundred thousand men in the Eastern Roman provinces. Both had persuaded the Roman students at Athens to declare for the cause of freedom and the Republic. Brutus raised a large army in Macedonia, while Cassius collected a formidable force in Syria. Both these armies were united at Smyrna, and the spirit of the Roman patriots began to revive at the sight of so formidable a military force.

Brutus and Cassius first marched against the Rhodians and the Lycians, who had refused their customary contributions to Rome. After they had reduced these people to submission, Brutus and Cassius again met at Sardis, where they decided to hold a private conference. They accordingly shut themselves up in a room together, ordering that no person be admitted. Brutus commenced by reproaching Cassius for selling offices for money, and oppressing the tributary states by over-taxation. Cassius bitterly resented the imputation of avarice; and the controversy became animated, until, after considerable loud talking, both burst into tears. Their friends who listened at the door overheard the increasing vehemence of their voices, and began trembling for the results, until one of them, named Favonius, who prided himself upon his unrestrained cynical boldness, entered the room and calmed their animosity.

After this noisy interview, Cassius invited Brutus to an entertainment, where for a time political cares and anxieties gave way to freedom and cheerfulness. It was believed that Brutus, as he was retiring from the feast to his tent, saw a specter which predicted to him his future fate. Plutarch tells us that in the dead of night, when the entire camp was perfectly quiet, Brutus, having been awakened from his sleep, was engaged in reading by the light of a lamp, as was his usual custom. He suddenly heard a noise as if somebody was entering the tent. As he was looking toward the door, he saw it open, and a huge figure of frightful aspect standing in his presence. After silently watching the specter sternly gazing at him for several moments, Brutus asked: "Art thou a demon or a mortal, and why comest thou to me?" Thereupon the specter answered: "I am thy evil genius, Brutus; thou shalt see me again at Philippi." To this, Brutus coolly responded: "Well, then, we shall meet again." Thereupon the phantom vanished; and Brutus called his servants and asked them if they had seen anything. They replied that they had not, and Brutus resumed his reading. Impressed with the extraordinary circumstance, he related it to Cassius, who attributed it to an imagination disordered by watchfulness and anxiety.

As soon as Octavius and Antony had finished their bloody work of proscription and massacre in Rome, they raised an army of more than one hundred thousand men, with which they crossed the Adriatic into Greece. Brutus and Cassius advanced to meet them by way of Thrace. The Roman world awaited in breathless suspense the impending conflict, upon the issue of which depended the fate of the great Republic which had reduced the civilized world under its dominion. The triumph of Brutus and Cassius would be a victory for freedom and the Republic. The success of Octavius and Antony would bring a sovereign with absolute authority on the ruins of the Republic. Brutus was the only man who calmly awaited these coming events. His indifference regarding success, and his satisfaction with having discharged his duty, are forcibly indicated in the following remark, which he made to one of his friends: "If I am victorious, I shall restore liberty to my country; if not, by dying I shall myself be delivered from slavery; my condition is fixed; I run no hazards."

The republican army numbered eighty thousand infantry and twenty thousand cavalry. The army of the Triumvirs amounted to one hundred thousand infantry and thirteen thousand cavalry. The two armies encountered each other at Phillippi, in Macedonia, in November, B. C. 42. Cassius desired to know what Brutus intended to do in case of defeat. Brutus replied thus: "Formerly, in my writings, I condemned the death of Cato, and maintained that to avoid calamities by suicide is an insolent attempt against Heaven which sends them. But I have since altered my opinion. I have given up my life to my country, and I think I have a right to my own way of ending it. I am resolved, therefore, to exchange a miserable being here for a better hereafter, should fortune turn against me." When Brutus had given this answer, Cassius embraced him, saying: "My friend, now we may venture to face the enemy, for either we shall be conquerors or we shall have no cause to fear those that are so."

The first battle of Philippi then commenced. Antony assumed the sole command of the army of the Triumvirate; Octavius being sick, or pretending to be so. The latter's courage was never manifest in the hour of battle. Antony furiously assailed the lines of Cassius, while Brutus on the other hand assaulted the forces which Octavius should have commanded. Brutus penetrated the enemy's ranks to their camp, routing and dispersing the troops of Octavius. But while the soldiers of Brutus abandoned themselves to plunder, the lines of Cassius were forced and his cavalry put to flight. Cassius made every possible effort to rally his infantry, staying those who fled, and seizing the standards with his own hand. But the valor of Cassius was not equal to the task of inspiring his fleeing troops with courage; and finally, in despair, he retired to his tent, where he was soon afterwards found dead. It was generally believed that he committed suicide; but many were convinced that he was treacherously assassinated by his freedman Pindarus, as his head was found severed from his body.

Brutus, now the sole commander of the republican army, assembled the dispersed troops of Cassius, and encouraged them with fresh hopes of victory. His design was to starve the Triumvirate army, which was now suffering from want of provisions, as a result of the loss of their fleet. But his purpose was overruled by his followers, whose confidence in their own strength, and arrogance toward their general, increased daily.

Finally, after a rest of twenty days, Brutus was obliged to hazard the fate of another conflict; and the second battle of Philippi was accordingly fought. The two armies were drawn out, and they remained in sight

CIVIL WARS AND FALL OF THE REPUBLIC.

of each other for some time without venturing upon an engagement. It was believed that Brutus himself lacked his former ardor, by having seen a second time, or imagining to have seen, the specter during the previous night. Nevertheless, he encouraged his troops, and gave the signal for battle. He again had the advantage where he commanded personally, as usual, cutting into the enemy's ranks at the head of his infantry, and producing great slaughter among them. But a panic seized the troops formerly commanded by Cassius, and their terror being communicated to the rest, caused the route of the entire army.

Surrounded by his most valiant officers, Brutus fought with the most astonishing valor for a long time. The son of Cato the Younger and the brother of Cassius were slain in fighting at his side. Finally he was forced to yield to superior numbers, and fled from the field. The Triumvirs, feeling certain of victory, had given orders that Brutus should not be permitted to escape by any means; but his friend, Lucilius, determined to save him from peril at the risk of his own life. Observing a detachment of Thracian cavalry closely pursuing Brutus, Lucilius threw himself in their way, telling them that he was Brutus. The Thracians instantly made him a prisoner, and informed Antony of their capture; and that Triumvir at once hastened to meet his distinguished captive, for the purpose of insulting his misfortunes. The stratagem so abated the ardor of the pursuit that Brutus escaped from his enemies with a number of his most faithful followers.

On the approach of night, he sat down under the shelter of a rock. After sitting for some time to take breath, he repeated a line from Euripides, expressing a wish to the gods that guilt should not escape punishment in this life. He added this line from the same poet: "O virtue! I have worshiped thee as a real god; but thou art an empty name, and the slave of fortune!" With great tenderness he then called to mind those whom he had seen perishing in battle. He despatched a friend to ascertain all about those who were still remaining; but this individual never returned, having been slain by a detachment of the enemy's cavalry. Judging correctly concerning this person's fate, Brutus now determined to die also, and implored those standing about him to give him their last aid; but every one of them declined to gratify his melancholy wish. He then retired aside with his friend Strato, entreating him to perform this act as a last deed of friendship. When Strato refused his request, Brutus ordered one of his slaves to execute what he so ardently desired. Thereupon Strato exclaimed that it should never be said that Brutus needed a slave for want of a friend in his last extremity; and, turning his head aside with these words, he presented the point of his sword. Brutus threw himself upon the pointed weapon, which penetrated his body, causing instant death.

Philippi was the grave of the Republic, and the lost hopes of Roman liberty expired with Brutus. Thus the Roman Republic, which was founded in B. C. 508 by Lucius Junius Brutus, the first renowned Roman patriot, perished in B. C. 42 with his no less illustrious and patriotic descendant, Marcus Junius Brutus, after an existence of almost five centuries; or, briefly stated, Roman freedom and republican government began with a Brutus and ended with a Brutus.

The Triumvirs made a cruel use of their victory, putting to death their political opponents without the least shadow of mercy. The leading men of Rome either fell victims to assassination, or committed suicide to escape the insults of the hired assassins sent to murder them. A Senator and his son being ordered to cast lots for their lives, both refused. The father voluntarily surrendered himself to the executioner, and the son committed suicide by stabbing himself in the executioner's presence. Another begged for the favor of the rites of burial after his death, to which Octavius replied that he would soon find a grave in the vultures that would devour him. The head of Brutus was sent to Rome and cast at the foot of Cæsar's statue. His wife Porcia, the daughter of Cato the Younger, claimed his ashes; and followed the example of her father and her husband by committing suicide, which she did by swallowing coals of fire.

After the Triumvirs had thus established their power on the ruins of the Republic, they began thinking of enjoying the homage of the people whom they had subjected. Antony went to Greece to receive the flattery of the refined Athenians. He passed some time at Athens, conversing with the philosophers and being present at their disputations. Thence he crossed over into Asia Minor, where all the Eastern monarchs who acknowledged the Roman supremacy came to pay him homage, while the fairest princesses sought to win his favor by the value of their presents or by the charms of their beauty. In this manner Antony passed from kingdom to kingdom, attended by a succession of sovereigns, exacting contributions, bestowing favors, and giving away crowns at his pleasure. He conferred the Kingdom of Cappadocia upon Sysenes, because he admired his mother's beauty; and he bestowed the Kingdom of Judæa upon Herod the Great.

Cleopatra, the beautiful but wicked Queen of Egypt, surpassed all other princesses in the arts by which she strove to allure Antony. Serápion, her governor in Cyprus, had furnished aid to Cassius. Antony summoned her to give an account of her course, and she promptly and willingly complied, relying upon her powers of fascination. Antony was at Tarsus, in Cilicia, when Cleopatra determined to personally attend his court. She sailed down the river Cydnus to meet him, with the most magnificent ceremony; the stern of her galley being covered with gold, its sails being of purple silk, and its oars of silver, while the rowers were keeping time to the sound of flutes and cymbals. Cleopatra exhibited herself reclining on a couch spangled with stars of gold, and such other ornaments as are generally ascribed to Venus by poets and painters. On each side of her were boys like Cupids, fanning her by turns; and charming nymphs, attired like Nereids and Graces, were stationed at suitable places around her. As she was passing, the banks of the river were perfumed by the incense burning on board her galley; and multitudes of people delightedly and admiringly gazed upon the spectacle.

Antony was soon captivated by her beauty, and was utterly unable to withstand that passion which ultimately proved the cause of his ruin. After thus securing her power, Cleopatra started on her return to Egypt; while Antony hastily followed her. After his arrival at Alexandria, Antony abandoned himself to indolence, luxury and vice, equally regardless of the calls of honor, interest or ambition. He found ample means for the gratification of his vicious indulgences among the luxurious Alexandrians.

While Antony was thus wasting his time in Egypt, Octavius undertook to lead the veteran soldiers back to Italy and settle them in that country, and was diligently engaged in providing for their support. He had promised them lands in Italy in payment for their past services, but they could only obtain their grants by expelling the original owners. As a result of this, vast numbers of women, with children on their arms, whose tender years and innocence aroused universal compassion, daily filled the streets and the temples with their lamentations. Multitudes of husbandmen and shepherds came to implore the conqueror to allow them to retain their property. Among this number was the celebrated Roman poet Virgil, to whom the human race is more indebted than to a thousand conquerors. He most humbly begged to be allowed to retain his patrimonial farm. Octavius granted Virgil's request; but his unfortunate neighbors, the countrymen of Mantua and Cremona, were unceremoniously deprived of their landed possessions.

Rome and Italy now endured great suffering. The insolent soldiery pillaged at their pleasure; while Sextus Pompey, the enemy of the Triumvirs, was master of the sea, and used his power to cut off Rome from all foreign intercourse, thus preventing the importation of the usual supplies of corn. In addition to these miseries, Italy suffered from the horrors of a new civil war. Lucius, the brother, and Fulvia, the wife of Antony, incited a rebellion against Octavius concerning the division of the lands. Lucius placed himself at the head of an army; but Octavius, with a superior force, hemmed him in between two armies, and forced him to retreat to Perusia, where he was besieged and starved into a surrender. On this occasion, Octavius was guilty of great cruelty to his vanquished foes. He caused three hundred nobles of Perusia to be sacrificed on an altar erected to the memory of Julius Cæsar, on the anniversary of the famous Dictator's assassination, March 15, B. C. 40.

When Antony heard of his brother's overthrow, he left Egypt and hastened back to Italy. At Athens he met his wife, Fulvia, whom he blamed for instigating the recent disturbances in Italy, and treated her with great contempt. Leaving her on her deathbed, he crossed the Adriatic into Italy, meeting the army of Octavius at Brundusium. A bloody struggle was expected; but the two rival Triumvirs opened negotiations, which were soon followed by a treaty of peace, in which all offenses and insults were mutually forgiven. To cement the union Antony married Octavia, the sister of Octavius. A new division of the Roman world followed; the West being assigned to Octavius, the East to Antony, and Africa to Lepidus. The next year Sextus Pompey, whose fleets, having complete command of the sea, threatened Rome with famine, was also admitted into the political partnership; being allowed to hold the islands of Sicily, Sardinia and Corsica, together with the Peloponnesus, on condition of supplying Rome with grain.

Mutual jealousies rendered the peace of short duration. Sextus Pompey never fulfilled the conditions under which he had been admitted to the partnership, in consequence of which a two years' civil war followed between him and Octavius, which was ended by the great sea-fight off Naúlochus, in B. C. 36, in which Agrippa, Cæsar's intimate friend, routed the forces of Sextus Pompey, who fled in despair to Asia, where he was slain the next year by one of Antony's lieutenants. Pompey's land forces, deserted by their leader, prevailed upon Lepidus to take command of them and to declare war against Octavius. But the young Cæsar behaved with a boldness worthy of his name. Going unarmed and almost unaccompanied into the camp of Lepidus, he, by his eloquence, induced the troops to desert their unworthy general and to follow him.

After Lepidus had been thus degraded, Octavius and Antony remained at the head of affairs for three years. Antony was now the only obstacle in the way of the ambition of Octavius, who was anxious to make himself sole master of the Roman world. He began by making Antony's character as contemptible as possible in the minds of the Roman people, and in this purpose he was aided by the follies of Antony himself. Antony had in the meantime led an unsuccessful expedition against the Parthians; after which he returned to Egypt, where he again plunged into luxury and dissipation, and allowed himself to be enslaved by the charms of Cleopatra, who studied every art to increase his passion and vary his amusements.

Not satisfied with sharing with the Egyptian queen all the delights which her kingdom afforded, Antony now determined to enlarge his sphere of luxury by bestowing upon her some of the kingdoms under the Roman dominion. He therefore gave her all of Phœnicia, Cœle-Syria and Cypress, and also a large portion of Cilicia, Arabia and Judæa. He had no right to bestow these territories, but he foolishly pretended to grant them in imitation of Hercules. This combination of vice and folly, Antony's debaucheries, and his utter enslavement to the caprices of an abandoned woman, thoroughly disgusted his Egyptian friends, many of whom deserted him and carried such accounts of his foolish and disgraceful conduct to Rome that all his partisans in that city abandoned him; and a decree was passed depriving him of his office of Consul.

Octavius fully profited by the folly of his rival. Observing that the Roman people were sufficiently exasperated at Antony, Octavius sent his sister Octavia, Antony's second wife, ostensibly to reclaim her husband, but in reality to furnish a sufficient pretext to come to an open rupture with him; being confident that Antony would dismiss her with contempt. When Antony heard of his wife's approach, he was at Leucopolis, in Caria, absorbed in his revels with Cleopatra. Octavia's arrival was distasteful to both Antony and Cleopatra. The Egyptian queen, fearing the charms of Antony's wife, endeavored to convince Antony of the strength of her passion by a well-feigned melancholy. Cleopatra's artifices, along with the endless flattery and importunity of her partisans, had such effect upon Antony's weakness that he sent orders for Octavia to return to Rome, without seeing her. This insult on the part of Antony was soon followed by his determination to marry Cleopatra.

In accordance with this intention, when Antony and Cleopatra returned to Alexandria, the former assembled the inhabitants of that city in the public theater, where he caused an alcove of silver to be erected, under which two thrones of gold were placed, one for himself and the other for the queen. On one of the thrones he took his seat, dressed as Bacchus; while Cleopatra occupied the other throne, clothed in the ornaments and attributes of Isis. On this occasion Antony proclaimed Cleopatra Queen of all the Roman provinces which he had formerly granted to her; and associated Cæsario, her son by Julius Cæsar, as partner in the government. He conferred the title of King of Kings on the two children which she had borne to himself, assigning them very large dominions. To cap the climax of his follies, he then sent a detailed account of his proceedings to the Consuls at Rome.

Antony's desertion of Octavia, his intended marriage with Cleopatra, and his bestowal of several Roman provinces in Asia upon the dissolute queen, brought matters to the crisis which Octavius desired, and rendered civil war between the two rivals inevitable. Octavius accordingly declared war against Antony, and both sides were making earnest preparations for the struggle which was to make one of them sole master of the Roman world. Their armies were suitable to the magnitude of the purpose for which they were called forth. Antony had the largest forces, embracing all the military strength of the East; his army numbering one hundred thousand infantry and twelve thousand cavalry, and his fleet amounting to five hundred ships of war. The forces of Octavius were better disciplined than those of Antony, and his cavalry were as numerous; but his infantry consisted of only eighty thousand men, and his fleet of only two hundred and fifty ships, though the latter were better built and manned than those of Antony.

The rival fleets and armies were at length assembled on the opposite shores of the Gulf of Ambracia, near the city of Actium, in Epirus. They remained in view of each other for several months, without coming to action. Finally Antony was influenced by Cleopatra to hazard a naval engagement on September 2d, B. C. 31. He arranged his fleet before the mouth of the gulf; and Octavius, or more properly Agrippa, who commanded in his name, drew up his fleet in opposition. The two armies on the opposite sides of the gulf constituted themselves spectators of the conflict, and encouraged the fleets, by their shouts, to engage.

Both sides commenced the battle in the usual manner. The prows of the ships were armed with brazen peaks, with which it was the custom to drive with great fury against each other. As Antony's vessels were large, unwieldy and ill-manned, they were incapable of the essential swiftness; while the ships of Octavius were unable to stand the rude encounter, on account of the lightness of their construction. Consequently, the conflict assumed the character of a land battle; the ships running along-

CLEOPATRA DURING THE BATTLE OF ACTIUM.

side of each other, and the men fighting hand to hand with great ardor for a long time.

The victory was in doubt until Cleopatra suddenly turned the fortune of the day in favor of Octavius. Suddenly seized with a panic, she tacked about with her Egyptian squadron of sixty vessels, and fled from the engagement. Antony, leaving his fleet and army to take care of themselves, immediately followed after her, thus deserting the men who had gallantly risked their lives in his cause. Nevertheless the battle lasted until evening, when Antony's forces were partially beaten by the skill of Agrippa, and partially induced to submission by the liberal promises of Octavius.

The troops of Antony, not believing that their general had fled, held out for a week, expecting him to return to lead them; but as they received no tidings concerning him, and as they were deserted by their allies, they made terms with the victorious Octavius. When Cleopatra fled from the battle, Antony followed after her in a single ship. When he came up with her vessel, he entered it, but did not manifest any desire to see her. She was in the stern, and he went to the prow and there remained silent and melancholy. He thus passed three days, during which he did not see or speak to Cleopatra, either from shame or indignation. But the queen's female attendants afterwards effected a reconciliation between them, and they lived in friendly intercourse as formerly.

Supposing that his army remained loyal to him, Antony sent orders to lead it into Asia. But when he arrived in Egypt, he was informed that it had joined the army of Octavius. This intelligence so enraged him that it was with great difficulty that he was restrained from committing suicide. Cleopatra manifested more resolution than her lover. As she had amassed a vast amount of treasure, she conceived a plan to convey her fleet across the Isthmus of Suez into the Red Sea, and thus make her escape to some remote region beyond the power of the triumphant Octavius.

Her scheme was partially executed, and a number of vessels were launched in the Red Sea; but these were attacked and burned by the Arabs, and the Egyptian queen was therefore obliged to relinquish a design so full of difficulties. She then began to fortify the approaches to her kingdom, and prepared for a defensive war. She likewise negotiated for foreign aid from the princes in alliance with Antony. While Cleopatra was thus occupied, Antony displayed the most deplorable weakness. He first pretended to imitate Timon the misanthrope, and shut himself up in utter solitude. But his temper would not permit him to remain long in this condition. He therefore abandoned his cell, giving himself up to feasting and all sorts of extravagance.

Meanwhile the forces of Octavius advanced on each side of Egypt. Cornelius Gallus occupied Paretonium, the key of the Egyptian kingdom on the west. Antony hastened with the Egyptian fleet and army to check his progress, but was forced to retreat with heavy loss. Pelusium, the principal Egyptian fortress on the eastern side, surrendered to Octavius at the first summons; whereupon Octavius advanced upon Alexandria. Antony stationed the Egyptian army upon an elevated ground close to the city, whence he sent orders to his fleet to engage the enemy. He waited to view the conflict, and finally he was gratified at seeing his galleys advance in good order. But his joy soon gave way to rage when he saw them salute the ships of Octavius, and both fleets uniting and entering the harbor of Alexandria together.

At the same time the Egyptian cavalry deserted Antony. He endeavored to lead on the Egyptian infantry, but these were vanquished with little difficulty, and Antony was obliged to return to Alexandria. Overcome with rage and fury, he ran about wildly accusing Cleopatra of having betrayed him, when he had sacrificed his interests for her sake only. He was not deceived in this suspicion, as it was by the secret orders of the Egyptian queen that her fleet had deserted to the enemy.

CIVIL WARS AND FALL OF THE REPUBLIC.

For a long time Cleopatra had dreaded the effects of Antony's jealousy, and had studied how to secure herself against it. She had erected a structure near the temple of Isis, apparently intending it for a sepulcher. She removed her most valuable treasures to this place, covering them with torches, fagots and other combustible materials. This retreat she designed for the twofold purpose of escaping from the sudden resentment of Antony and of defending herself against Octavius by threatening to burn all her treasures unless he granted her favorable terms of capitulation. She now retired to this place, closed the gates, and gave orders to spread rumors that she was dead.

These rumors soon reached the ears of Antony, arousing all his former passion for Cleopatra. In paroxysms of grief, he exclaimed: "Miserable man that I am! what is there now worth living for, since all that could soothe or soften my cares is departed? O Cleopatra! our separation does not so much afflict me as the disgrace I suffer in permitting a woman to instruct me how to die!" He then called one of his freedmen, named Eros, whom he had engaged by oath to put him to death whenever he should be driven to this final resource by the evil hand of fortune. He therefore now ordered this freedman to execute his sworn promise. The faithful Eros accordingly drew his sword as though he were about striking a blow, when he suddenly turned his face and plunged the weapon into his own bosom, dropping dead at his master's feet. For a moment Antony paused over his faithful servant's body, in admiration of this sign of attachment. He snatched the sword and stabbed himself, falling backward on a couch. The wound which he thus inflicted upon himself was fatal; yet, as the blood stopped, he partially recovered his spirits, and implored those who rushed to his aid to put an end to his life; but, seized with astonishment and terror, they all fled.

In this wretched condition Antony remained until he was informed that Cleopatra was still living, and that she desired to have him brought to the monument in which she had sought refuge. He was therefore taken to that place. Cleopatra, who was accompanied only by two of her women, did not dare to open the gate; but she threw down cords from the window, and with these Antony was drawn up. Bathed in blood, he extended his hand to the queen, and faintly tried to raise himself from the couch on which he had been laid. Cleopatra abandoned herself to grief, tore her clothes, beat her breasts, kissed the mortal wound of Antony, and called him her husband and lord. Antony begged her to moderate her transports of grief and to preserve her life if that could be done with honor. Said he: "As for me, lament not my misfortunes, but congratulate me upon the happiness which I have enjoyed. I have lived the greatest and most powerful of men, and though I fall, my fate is not ignominious. A Roman myself, it is by a Roman I am at last overcome!" When he had said this, he expired.

By command of Octavius, who had heard of Antony's desperate behavior, Proculeius now made his appearance. He was sent to use every means to get Cleopatra into his power. Octavius had a twofold motive for his solicitude on this occasion. He was anxious to prevent her from destroying the treasures in the monument, and to preserve her person as an ornament to grace his triumph. But the queen was upon her guard, and declined holding any intercourse with Proculeius except through the gate, which was well secured. Finally an entrance was effected through the window by means of a ladder; and Cleopatra, seeing that she was a prisoner, attempted to stab herself with a poniard, but the weapon was wrested from her. Octavius gave orders that she must be treated in every respect with the deference and submission to which her rank entitled her. Cleopatra appears to have entertained some hope of acquiring the same influence over Octavius that she had wielded over Antony, but she found herself utterly unable to captivate him by her charms.

At last Cleopatra was secretly informed

that within three days she was to be sent with her children to Rome to grace the triumph of her conqueror. She accordingly resolved upon suicide. First throwing herself upon Antony's coffin, she bewailed her captivity, and reiterated her determination not to survive her lover. After bathing, and ordering a sumptuous banquet, she attired herself in the most magnificent style. After she had partaken of the banquet, she ordered every one except her two women to leave the apartment. Meanwhile she had managed to have an asp secretly brought to her in a basket of figs; after which she wrote to Octavius, informing him of her desperate intention, and desiring to be laid in the same tomb with Antony.

Upon receiving this letter, Octavius at once sent messengers, in hopes of thwarting the queen's purpose, but they did not arrive in time. When they entered the chamber, they saw Cleopatra lying dead upon her couch, attired in her royal robes. Iras, one of her faithful attendants, was stretched lifeless at the feet of her mistress; while Charmion, the other attendant, barely alive, was putting the crown on the queen's head. One of the messengers sent by Octavius exclaimed: "Alas! is this well done, Charmion?" Charmion replied: "Yes, it is well done. Such a death is becoming a glorious queen, descended from a race of glorious ancestors!" When Charmion had uttered these words, she fell and expired.

Thus died Cleopatra, the last of the famous dynasty of the Ptolemies; and with her death Egypt became a Roman province (B. C. 30). The immense wealth which had been amassed by the Ptolemies was seized by the triumphant Octavius and conveyed to Rome. The submission of Egypt to Rome was followed by a universal peace; and when Octavius returned to Rome the next year (B. C. 29), he celebrated a threefold triumph, and the gates of the temple of Janus were closed for the third time.

The battle of Actium made Octavius sole master of the Roman world. Roman liberty was now gone forever; and the Roman people, who had lost all the virtues and republican spirit of their ancestors, made no attempt to restore the republican constitution. The most illustrious citizens besought Octavius to take the government into his own hands; and the people, tired of the oppression of the aristocracy, gladly placed themselves under the sway of a single master. The Roman Republic ended, and the *Roman Empire* began, in the year B. C. 27, when the Roman Senate conferred upon Octavius sovereign powers with the titles of Augustus (the Divine) and Imperator (Emperor); and thenceforth he was called Augustus, instead of Octavius. We will give a full account of the establishment of the empire in a subsequent section.

The city of Rome was now inhabited by a motley population, gathered from all portions of the Roman world; and this population, being deficient in patriotic sentiment and principles, was better fitted for a monarchy than for a republic. It was a remarkable circumstance that during the violent internal dissensions which had caused the subversion of the old republican government, and amid all the devastation and bloodshed of civil war, the Roman state was constantly growing more powerful and formidable, and was able to subdue every nation that ventured to take up arms against it.

LICTOR—ROMAN EMPEROR—ROMAN NOBLE.

HERMAN (ARMINIUS).

ROMAN WARRIORS.

STANDARD BEARER (GERMAN)—ROMAN GENERAL.

ROME.

SECTION XI.—PROVINCES OF THE ROMAN EMPIRE.

WE HAVE now reached a point at which we must take a survey of the Roman Empire, whose history was now the history of the ancient civilized world. All the countries of Europe, Asia and Africa surrounding the Mediterranean had now become absorbed in the dominion of the seven-hilled city on the Tiber. The only rival of this grand and magnificent empire was the Parthian Empire on its eastern border. "The very name of Rome reminds us of every image of grandeur, power and magnificence; and every association connected with it serves to concentrate around the Eternal City a halo of splendor and glory."

From the reign of Augustus to that of Constantine the Great—embracing a period of about three and a half centuries—the vast Roman Empire was bounded by almost the same frontiers. This permanence of her imperial limits may partly be attributed to the sagacity with which the Roman leaders, at the time of Rome's greatest power, voluntarily stopped short in their career of conquest where they discovered the best military frontiers. The Roman Empire was mainly enclosed within natural boundaries, such as great rivers, mountain ridges, deserts, seas and the vast ocean. Though great rivers afford but little obstacles to the armies of civilized nations, they are usually formidable barriers to the inroads of barbarian and savage hordes. On the west this vast empire was bounded by the Atlantic Ocean; on the south by the great African desert; on the north by the Scotch Highlands, the German Ocean or North Sea, the rivers Rhine and Danube, and the Euxine or Black Sea; and on the east by the Armenian mountains, the historic river Euphrates and the Syro-Arabian desert.

Thus the Roman Empire embraced all Southern and Western Europe, Western Asia and Northern Africa, comprising the entire basin of the Mediterranean; and that vast sea had become a Roman lake. The Empire was almost three thousand miles in extent from east to west, and about one thousand miles from north to south; and embraced the territory occupied by the modern countries of Portugal, Spain, France, Belgium, Western Holland, England, Wales, the Scotch Lowlands, Rhenish Prussia, part of Baden, Wurtemberg, nearly the whole of Bavaria, Switzerland, Italy, the Tyrol, Austria proper, Western Hungary, Croatia, Slavonia, Servia, Bulgaria, Montenegro, European Turkey, Greece, Asia Minor, Syria, Palestine, Egypt, Barca, Tripoli, Tunis, Algeria and Morocco.

The Roman Empire exclusive of Italy was divided into *provinces*, which may be classed under three heads—the Western, or European; the Eastern, or Asiatic; and the Southern, or African. The Western, or European provinces, were Spain, Gaul, Britain, Vindelicia, Rhætia, Noricum, Pannonia, Mœsia, Illyricum, Macedonia, Thrace, Achæa, Sicily, and Sardinia including Corsica. The Eastern, or Asiatic provinces, were Asia proper, Bithynia, Galatia, Pamphylia, Cappadocia, Cilicia, Syria and Palestine. The Southern, or African provinces, were Egypt, Cyrenaica including Crete, Africa proper, Numidia and Mauritania.

Spain—called Hispania by the Romans, and Iberia by the Greeks—was the most western of Rome's European provinces, and embraced the entire Spanish peninsula; whose boundaries were fixed by nature, being washed on all sides by the Atlantic and the Mediterranean, except on the north-east, where it was separated from Gaul by the Pyrenees. This vast province was subdivided into three portions, usually administered by three different governors—namely Lusitania, or the country of Lusitani, corresponding almost to the modern Portugal; Bætica, or the country about the Bætis (now Guadalquivir), corresponding to the modern

Andalusia; and Tarraconensis, embracing the remainder of the peninsula.

Three principal nations inhabited Lusitania—the Gallæci in the north, the region of the modern Gallicia; the Lusitani in the center; and the Turdetani in the south. Lusitania had three great rivers, the Durius (now Douro), the Tagus, and the Anas (now Guadiana). The principal towns of the province were Augusta Emerita (now Merida), on the Anas, and Olisipo (now Lisbon), on the Tagus. Bætica was occupied by the watered by the Ibérus (now Ebro), the Turia, the Sucro (now Jucar) and the Tader (now Segura) rivers. It was occupied toward the north by the Astúres, the Cántabri, the Vaccæi, the Vascónes and other nations; in the central part by the Carpetani, the Celtibéri and the Ilergetes; and along the eastern coast by the Indigetes, the Ausetani, the Ilercavónes, the Suessetani, the Contestani, the Cosetani and other nations.

The chief cities of Tarraconensis were Tarraco (now Tarragona), the capital, on

ROMAN AQUEDUCT IN SEGOVIA, SPAIN.

Turduli towards the north, and the Bastuli towards the south. The Bætis was the only important river of Bætica; and the only important towns of the country were Corduba (now Cordova) and Hispalis (now Seville), in the interior, and Gades (now Cadiz), on the southern coast.

Tarraconensis was by far the most extensive of the three subdivisions of the Spanish peninsula, and embraced the upper courses of the Durius, the Tagus and the Anas rivers, along with the whole region the eastern coast; Carthágo Nova (now Carthagena); Cæsar-Augusta (now Saragossa), on the Ibérus; Tolétum (now Toledo) on the Upper Tagus; and Ilerda (now Lérida). The Balearic Isles—Major (now Majorca), Minor (now Minorca), and the Pityusæ, Ebusus (now Ivica) and Ophiusa (now Formentera)—were also included in Tarraconensis.

Spain was the first country outside of Italy that yielded to the Roman arms, but its ultimate subjection baffled the efforts of

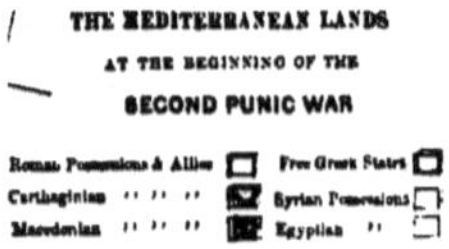

THE MEDITERRANEAN LANDS
AT THE BEGINNING OF THE
SECOND PUNIC WAR

Roman Possessions & Allies ☐   Free Greek States ☐
Carthaginian   "   "   " ☒   Syrian Possessions ☐
Macedonian   "   "   " ▨   Egyptian   "   ☐

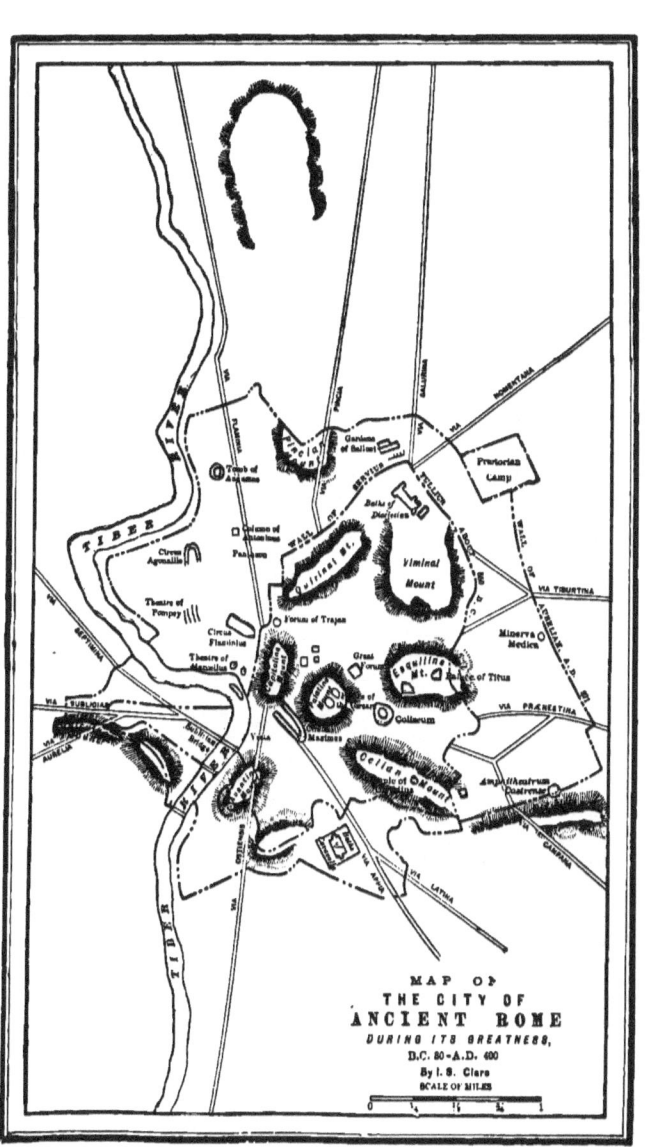

the most skillful Roman generals for near y half a century. This country was celebrated for its silver, which was so abundant that the most ordinary implements were made from it. While the Romans held the country in subjection, they employed forty thousand men in the mines, and erected many fine cities. A magnificent aqueduct at Segovia yet remains, being one of the best preserved of the Roman structures still existing.

Gaul—called Gallia by the Romans—embraced the territory occupied by the modern France, Belgium and Western Switzerland. It was bounded on the north and west by the Atlantic Ocean; on the east by Roman Germany, which is sometimes included in Gaul, Rhætia and Cisalpine Gaul; and on the south by the Mediterranean and Spain, being separated from the latter by the Pyrenees mountain chain. The five chief rivers of Gaul were the Scaldis (now Scheldt) and the Sequana (now Seine) in the north; the Liger (now Loire) and the Garumna (now Garonne) towards the west; and the Rhódanus (now Rhone) in the south.

Augustus subdivided Gaul into four districts—Aquitania, the country of the Aquitani, towards the south-west, from the Pyrenees to the Loire; Lugdunensis, to the north-west, extending from the British Channel to Lugdunum (now Lyons), the capital; Narbonensis, towards the south-east, between Aquitania and the Maritime Alps; and Belgica, towards the north-east, extending from the British Channel to Lake Geneva.

Aquitania embraced the valleys of the Garumna (now Garonne), Duranius (now Dordogne), Carantonus (now Charente), and half the valley of the Liger (now Loire). The principal tribes of Aquitania were the Aquitani in the south; the Santónes and the Pictónes towards the north-west; the Bituriges towards the north-east, in the region around Bourges; and the Arverni to the south-east, in Auvergne. The chief cities of Aquitania were Climberris and Burdigala (now Bordeaux).

Lugdunensis comprised the territory between the Loire and the Seine, along with the tongue of land extending along the Saone to a little below Lyons. The principal tribes of Lugdunensis were the Ædui in the south; the Senónes, the Parisii, the Carnútes, and the Cadurci in the interior; the Veneti, the Osismii, the Curiosolítæ, the Unelli and the Lexovii upon the coast. Lugdunum (now Lyons), the capital, was located in the extreme south-east of the province. The other chief towns were Lutetia Parisiorum (now Paris), Genabum (now Orleans), and Juliómagus (now Angers).

Narbonensis extended from the Upper Garonne on the west to the Var on the east, lying along the Pyrenees and the Mediterranean, and reaching inland to the Cevennes, the middle Rhone and Lake Geneva. The principal tribes occupying this region were the Volcæ in the west, the Allobroges in the country between the Rhone and the Isere (Isara), the Vocontii between the Isere and the Durance, and the Salluvii on the coast near Massilia. The chief cities of Narbonensis were Narbo (now Narbonne), the capital, on the Mediterranean; Tolosa (now Toulouse), Vienna (now Vienne), Nemausus (now Nismes), Geneva and Massilia (now Marseilles).

Belgica extended from the Seine to the Scheldt, and southward from the Burnese Alps and the northern shore of Lake Geneva. It was bounded on the east by Roman Germany and Rhætia, on the west by Gallia Lugdunensis, and on the south by Gallia Narbonensis and Gallia Cisalpína. The principal tribes inhabiting Belgica were the Caletes, the Ambiani, the Bellovaci, the Atrebates, the Morini and the Nervi in the north; the Suessiones, the Remi, the Treviri, the Leuci and the Lingones in the central region; and the Séquani and the Helvetii towards the south. The principal towns of Belgica were Noviodunum (now Soissons), Durocortorum (now Rheims), Augusta-Trevirorum (now Trêves), Divodurum (now Metz), Vesontio (now Besançon), and Aventicum (now Avenches in Switzerland).

The four great divisions of Gaul—Aquitania, Lugdunensis, Narbonensis and Belgica—differed considerably in language, manners and customs; but the inhabitants of all four belonged to the Celtic race. The religion of the Gauls was like that of the ancient Britons, and the priests of both peoples were called *Druids*. The Gauls worshiped a supreme god called Hésus, or Æsar, to whom they believed the oak to be sacred, particularly if the parasitical plant called mistletoe was seen growing upon it. Their religious rites were bloody. Human victims were sacrificed in their groves and stone circles, and we are told that their nobles occasionally volunteered to offer themselves upon the national altars. Temples were not built in Gaul until after its conquest by the Romans; but long previous to that event the worship of a multitude of inferior deities had been introduced.

The various Gallic tribes were generally independent of each other; but on great occasions a general council of the whole Gallic nation was summoned, especially when preparations were made for any of the great migrations which proved so disastrous to Italy and Greece. The superior valor of the Gauls made them formidable foes to all the nations of Southern Europe. It was usually said that the Romans fought with other nations for conquest, but with the Gauls for existence. However, from the time that Julius Cæsar conquered their country, the Gauls seemed to lose their courage along with their liberty. They only revolted when the extortions of their Roman rulers became insufferable, and their efforts were neither well-directed nor vigorous.

Roman civilization produced equally as great effects in Gaul as in any other Roman province. Many public works of gigantic size and of great utility were constructed in this country. Roads were opened and paved with stone, durable bridges were erected, and aqueducts were formed to supply the cities with water. Remains of these stupendous works can still be seen, and these excite the wonder and admiration of the beholder.

Britain—called Britannia by the Romans, and Albion by the Greeks—comprised that part of the present island of Great Britain embraced by modern England, Wales and the lowlands of Scotland. After their conquest of Britain, the Romans divided the count y into five districts—Britannia Prima in the south; Flavia Cæsariensis, north of the preceding division; Maxima Cæsariensis, north of the latter; Valentia, farthest north; and Britannia Secunda (now Wales).

Britannia Prima embraced all that portion of England south of the Thames river and Bristol Channel. Its principal towns were Durovernum (now Canterbury), Calleva Atrebatum (since Silchester), Venta Belgarum (now Winchester), Aquæ Solis (now Bath). The isle of Vectis (now Wight) was included in this division. Flavia Cæsariensis included all that part of modern England extending northward from the Thames to a line drawn from the mouth of the Humber to the mouth of the Mersey, in the vicinity of the present city of Liverpool. The principal towns of this region were Londinium (now London), on the Thames, the capital; Lindum (now Lincoln), Camulodunum (since Maldon), Venta Icenorum (since Caistor), Ratæ (now Leicester), Verulamium (now St. Albans), and Deva (now Chester). Maxima Cæsariensis extended northward from the district just mentioned to Adrian's Wall, which extended from the mouth of the river Tyne westward to Solway Frith. Its chief towns were Eborácum (now York), the capital of the district, and also the capital of the entire province of Britain; Mancunrum (now Manchester), Luguvallium (now Carlisle), Pons Ælii (now Newcastle on Tyne), and Longovicum (now Lancaster). The Isle of Mona or Monœda (now Man) belonged to this district.

Valentia included all that portion of Northern England and Southern Scotland extending from the Wall of Adrian to the Wall of Antonínus Pius; the latter wall extending from the Frith of Forth on the east to the Frith of Clyde on the west. The principal towns of Valentia were Alata Castra (now Edinburgh), the capital; Lindum (now Linlithgow), Tuessis (now Berwick), Colonia (now Lanark), Carbantorigum (now Kirkcudbright) and Randvara (now Renfrew).

Britannia Secunda included the whole of modern Wales and the small portion of modern England west of the Sabrína (now Severn) and the Antona (now Avon) rivers. The chief towns of this section were Isca Silurum (now Caerleon), Conovium (since Caer Rhun), Segontium (now Caernarvon), Menapia (now St. David), Gobannium (now Abergavenny), Magnæ (since Kentchester), and Bravinnium (since Leintwardine). The isle of Mona (now Anglesey) was included in this section.

Britain was not reduced to the condition of a Roman province until long after the time of Julius Cæsar; but as that famous conqueror nominally subjected the country to the Roman dominion, it will be better to give a description of its ancient condition in this connection than to interrupt the political history of the Empire as given in a subsequent section. The name of Britain was first applied to the group of islands in the Atlantic now known as British, the largest of the islands being called Albion. The southern portion of Albion—now named England—was first settled from Gaul. The savage and barbarous tribes that occupied the north and east of that portion of the island are said to have been of German origin; and there is a prevailing tradition that the Scots in the north-west of the island originally came from Ireland.

That portion of Britain now comprised in England and Wales was in ancient times divided among seventeen tribes, to whom some tribes of inferior importance were perhaps subject. The principality of Wales— formerly including the entire territory west of the Severn—was occupied in Roman times by the Silúres, the Démetæ and the Ordovíces. The last-mentioned tribe inhabited North Wales, and in their mountain fastnesses they defied the Roman power for a long time. The island of Mona (now Anglesey)—famous as the ancient seat of the Druids—was held by the Ordovíces. The inhabitants of the region north of the Friths of Forth and Solway were called Metæ and Caledonii, but were subsequently known as Picts and Scots. Hibernia, or Juverna—the modern Ireland—was know to the Romans only by name.

The most important tribes in that part of Britain embraced in modern England were the Cantii, in Kent; the Trinobantes, in Essex; the Iceni, in Norfolk and Suffolk; the Catyeuchlani, the Dobuni and the Cornavii, in the midland counties; the Regni, in Sussex, Surry and Hampshire; the Belgæ, in Somersetshire and Wiltshire; the Damnonii in Devonshire and Cornwall; the Brigantes, in Yorkshire, Lancashire, Cumberland, Westmoreland and Durhamshire; and the Coritani, in Lincolnshire and Nottinghamshire. The most important tribes in the region of the Scotch Lowlands were the Damnii, the Sélgovæ, the Otadeni, the Gadeni and the Novantæ.

The Roman Emperors Antonínus Pius and Septimius Sevérus successively erected three walls to check the destructive inroads of the Picts and Scots. According to Camden, the last wall was the most important; that authority having very carefully traced it. That wall extended from Blatobulgium (now Bulness), on the Irish Sea, along the side of Solway Frith by Burgh-upon-sands, to Lugovallum (now Carlisle), thence passing into Itúna (Eden), whence it extended on over the little rivers Cambeck, Living and Poltrose, into the hills of Northumberland, along which it passed on to the German Ocean (now North Sea). This wall was about eight feet in thickness, and was protected by a ditch twelve yards wide.

When the Romans first visited Britain, the inhabitants of that country had made considerable progress in civilization. The country was densely populated and well supplied with cattle. The houses of the Britons were as good as those of their southern neighbors, the Gauls. They used plates of iron and copper for money. They did not make much use of clothing, as they painted and tattooed their bodies instead.

In war they used scythed chariots; the scythes, or blades, being fastened to the axle-trees. They drove these scythed chariots at full speed against the enemy's ranks. The principal traffic of the Britons was with the Gauls and the Phœnicians, who came to the Cassitérides (the Scilly Isles) for tin.

We know little regarding the religion of the ancient Britons, except that they were held in mental bondage by the priest-caste known as *Druids*, and that they offered human sacrifices to their gods. Each tribe of Britons had its own king; but in certain emergencies all the tribes elected a common chief, who, however, exercised but little more than nominal authority. The most remarkable monument of the Druids still existing is Stonehenge, in Wiltshire, and consists of a circular structure of immense stones, which is believed to have been a national temple. The Romans abandoned Britain early in the fifth century A. D.

Roman Germany—sometimes included in Gaul—was subdivided into Lower or Inferior Germany and Upper or Superior Germany. Lower Germany lay upon the coast of the German Ocean, or North Sea, between the mouth of the Scheldt and the mouth of the Rhine. It embraced Eastern Belgium, Western Holland, and Rhenish Prussia as far south as the Ahr. The principal tribes of this region were the Batavi and the Menapii in the north; the Ubii on the Rhine near Cologne; the Eburónes and the Condrusi on the river Mosa (now Meuse); and the Segni in the Ardennes. The chief towns were Noviómagus (now Nimeguen), Colonia Agrippinensis (now Cologne) and Bonna (now Bon).

Upper Germany was a narrow strip of territory along the course of the Rhine from Remagen, at the opening of the Ahr valley to the mouth of the Ahr river. This region was occupied by the Carácates, the Vangiónes, the Nemetes, the Triboci and the Rauraci. The chief cities were Ad Confluentes (now Coblenz), Mogontiacum (now Mayence), Borbetómagus (now Worms), Argentoratum (now Strasburg), and Augusta Rauracorum (now Basle).

Vindelicia lay between the Danube and the Bavarian Alps; thus corresponding almost with that portion of Modern Bavaria lying south of the Danube, but including a corner between the Rhine and the Upper Danube, now belonging to Wurtemberg and Baden. It was occupied by the Vindelici towards the north, and by the Brigantes towards the south. The chief towns were Augusta Vindelicorum (now Augsburg) and Brigantia (now Bregenz) on Lake Constance.

Rhætia lay south of Vindelicia and east of Helvetia, thus including the modern Tyrol, the Vorarlberg, and the present Swiss canton of Grisons. It was inhabited by such tribes as the Rhæti, the Venostes, the Vennónes, the Brixentes, the Tridentini, the Medoaci, etc. Its chief cities were Veldidena (now Wilten, near Innsprück). Curia (now Chur or Coire) and Tridentum (now Trent).

Noricum lay east of Vindelicia and Rhætia, extending along the Danube from the junction of that great river with the Inn to a point a short distance above Vienna. It embraced Styria, Carinthia, and most of Austria proper. The principal cities were Juvavia (now Salzburg) and Boiodurum (now Passau).

Pannonia lay east and partly south of Noricum, being bounded on the north and east by the Danube, which in this portion of its course makes the great bend by which its lower course is thrown three degrees south of its upper course. On the west Pannonia was divided from Noricum by an imaginary boundary line. On the south it was separated from Illyricum by the mountains directly south of the valley of the Save. Pannonia thus embraced all of modern Hungary south of the Danube, along with Slavonia and portions of Austria proper, of Styria, Croatia and Bosnia. It was divided into Upper Pannonia and Lower Pannonia.

Upper Pannonia bordered on Noricum, extending along the Danube from a little above Vienna to the mouth of the Arrabo (now Raab). The principal tribes occupying this region were the Boii in the north; the Latovici, the Jassii and the Colapini in the south, along the course of the Save. The chief cities were Vindobona (now Vienna) and Carnuntum, on the Danube; Siscia (now Zissek), on the Save; and Æmona (now Laybach), between the Save and the Julian Alps.

Lower Pannonia lay along the Danube from the mouth of the Arrabo (now Raab) to the mouth of the Save. The leading cities were Acincum (now Buda-Pesth) and Acimincum (now Peterwardein), on the Danube; Mursa (now Eszeck) on the Drave; and Sirmium (now Zabatz, or Alt-Schabaaz) and Taurunum (now Semlin) on the Save.

Mœsia was the most eastern of the Roman provinces on the Danube; and it was bounded on the north by that stream from its junction with the Save to its own mouth, on the east by the Euxine (now Black Sea), on the south by the Balkan mountain range, and on the west by the river Drinus (now Drina), which separated it from Illyricum. Thus Mœsia embraced the territory comprised in modern Servia and Bulgaria. It was divided into Upper Mœsia and Lower Mœsia.

Upper Mœsia extended from the Drinus and the mouth of the Save to the little river Cebrus, or Ciabrus (now Ischia), from which a line drawn southward separated it from Lower Mœsia. This region therefore embraced Servia and a portion of Western Bulgaria. The principal towns were Singidunum (now Belgrade) and Naissus (now Nissa).

Lower Mœsia was a longer and narrower tract, and extended from the Ciabrus to the mouth of the Danube, thus embracing about nine-tenths of the modern Bulgaria, along with a small part of Roumelia. The principal towns were Dorostolum (now Silistria) and Axiopolis (now Rassova), on the Danube; and Odessus (now Varna), Tomi (now Tomisvar) and Istrus (now Kustendji), on the Euxine coast.

The portion of Lower Mœsia bordering on the Euxine was frequently called Pontus. For that reason Tomi, the place of the poet Ovid's exile, is called a city of Pontus, though it did not belong to the kingdom called Pontus, which, as we have already seen, was in the North-east of Asia Minor. Tomi is said to have been so named from Medea having cut her brother Absyrtus to pieces in that place, so that her father's pursuit of her might be delayed; while he collected his child's scattered limbs. In a familiar distich, Ovid alludes to this circumstance, thus:

"Tomi its name from horrid murder bore,
For there a brother's limbs a sister tore."

Illyricum lay along the western coast of the Adriatic from the peninsula of Istria to Aulon (now Avlona), in Epirus. This province therefore comprised the present Montenegro, the Herzegovina, and most of Albania. The northern part of Illyricum was known as Dalmatia, and the southern part as Illyria proper. Among the chief tribes occupying Illyricum were the Iápydes and the Liburni, in the north; the Breuci, the Mazæi, the Dæsitiátæ and the Deimates, in the central region; and the Autariátæ, the Parthini and the Taulantii, in the south. The chief cities were Scardona (still retaining its ancient name); Narona (now Narenta), on the Naro; Epidaurus, on the Gulf of Cattaro; Scodra (now Scutari, on the Bojana); Lissus (now Lesch, or Allessio, on the Drinus); Dyrrhachium (now Durazzo) and Apollonia (now Pollina). All these towns were located on or near the coast. The Illyrians were remarkable for their skill in naval architecture, and infamous for their inveterate piracy.

Macedonia lay south of Illyricum and Upper Mœsia, and extended across the peninsula from the Adriatic to the Ægean. This province was bounded on the east by Thrace, from which it was separated by the river Nestus. On the south it was divided from Achæa by an imaginary line extending from the Ambracian Gulf on the west to the Maliac Gulf on the east. In addition to the ancient Macedon, it included most of Epirus and all of Thessaly. Its leading cities were Nicopolis, on the Gulf of Ambracia, founded by Augustus to celebrate his victory of Actium, and Edessa, Pella, Berœa, Thessalonica and Philippi.

Thrace was south of Lower Mœsia and east of Macedonia. This country continued to retain a semi-independent position under the first Cæsars, being governed by its own kings, Rhescúporis and others, who were allowed to rule on condition of acknowledging the Roman supremacy; but the Emperor Claudius reduced it to the condition of a full province of the Empire. The chief Thracian tribes in Roman times were the Odrysæ, the Bessi and the Cœletæ. The principal cities were Byzantium (now Constantinople) and Apollonia (now Sizeboli), in the east; and Philippopolis and afterwards Adrianople, in the interior.

Achæa lay directly south of Macedonia, corresponding very nearly with the modern Kingdom of Greece. This province included the Ionian Isles and the Cyclades, but not Crete, which was attached to the province of Cyrenaïca. The leading cities of Achæa were Patræ (now Patras), Corinth and Athens.

We will now briefly describe the Eastern, or Asiatic provinces—Asia proper, Bithynia, Galatia, Pamphylia, Cappadocia, Cilicia, Syria and Palestine.

Asia proper included the ancient Mysia, Lydia and Caria; and therefore comprised the entire western coast of Asia Minor, extending from the Cianian Gulf in the Propontis to Caunus on the Sea of Rhodes. It extended inland toward the east as far as the thirty-second meridian of east longtitude, where it bordered on Galatia and Cappadocia. It was bounded on the north by Bithynia, and on the south by Pamphylia. Ephesus was the Roman capital of Asia; but Smyrna, Pergamus, Sardis, Apaméa Cibotus and Synnada were towns of almost equal importance.

Bithynia lay north-east of Asia proper, and had nearly its old dimensions; extending along the coasts of the Propontis, the Bosphorus and the Euxine, from the mouth of the Macestus on the west to the mouth of the Parthenius on the east. It extended inland a little south of the fortieth parallel of north latitude, being bounded towards the south-east by the upper course of the Sangarius (now Sakkariyeh) river, which separated it from Asia proper and Galatia. The Roman capital of Bithynia was Nicomedía (now Ismid), in the inner recess of the Gulf of Astacus. The other important cities were Nicæa, or Nice (now Iznik), Chalcedon (now Scutari) and Heracléa (now Eregli).

Galatia was east of Bithynia, and included the ancient Paphlagonia, North-eastern Phrygia, and a portion of Western Cappadocia. The southern portion of the province, lying on both sides of the Halys, was Galatia proper; and was occupied by three tribes—the Tolistoboii, the Tectosages and the Trocmi. The principal city of Galatia was Ancyra (now Angora), on the Sangarius river. The other chief towns were Pessínus, on the western border, in the country of the Tolistoboii; Tavia, east of the Halys, in the country of the Trocmi; and Sinôpé, on the Euxine.

Pamphylia was south of Asia proper; and comprised Pamphylia proper, the territory originally bearing the name, along with Lycia, Pisidia and Isauria. This province extended along the southern coast of Asia Minor from Caunus to Coracésium, and inland to Lakes Bei-Shehr and Egerdir. The chief city was Perga, in Pamphylia proper. The other noted towns were Xanthus, in Lycia; Etenna and Antioch, in Pisidia; and Oroanda and Isaura, in Isauria.

Cappadocia was east of Galatia and Pamphylia, and included four subdivisions— Lycaonia, the most western, adjoining Isauria and Asia proper; Cappadocia proper, east of Lycaonia, on both sides of the river Halys; Pontus, north of Cappadocia proper, between it and the Euxine; and Lesser Armenia, south-east of Pontus, a rugged mountain region lying along the Upper Euphrates. The principal city of Cappadocia was Cæsaréa Mázaca (now Kaisariyeh), between Mount Argæus and the river Halys. The other important towns were Iconium (now Koniyeh), in Lycaonia; Tyana and Melitêné (now Malatiyeh), in Cappadocia proper; and Amisus, Trápezus (now Trebizond), Amasía, Sebastía and Nicopolis, in Pontus.

PROVINCES OF THE ROMAN EMPIRE. 1017

Cilicia was east of Pamphylia and south of Cappadocia, and extended along the southern coast of Asia Minor from Coracésium to Alexandria (now Iskanderoun). The eastern part of the province was called Campestris, while the western portion was named Montana, or Aspera. Tarsus, on the river Cydnus, was the capital. The other important towns were Issus, in the pass of that name; Mopsuestia, on the Pyramus; and Seleucia, on the Calycadnus, near its mouth.

The provinces of Asia Minor were in general the most tranquil part of the entire Roman Empire; and the most peaceful, if not the happiest, period in the history of Asia Minor was that during which it was under the Roman dominion. A sufficient evidence of the wealth attained by individuals in this portion of the Empire is found in the sepulchers of private persons, like that of Icesius, discovered by Mr. Ainsworth, which was not surpassed by the tombs of the Pontic kings.

Syria adjoined Cappadocia and Cilicia, and extended from about the thirty-eighth parallel of north latitude on the north to Mount Carmel on the south, a distance of almost four hundred miles; being bounded on the east by the Euphrates as far as Thapsacus and then by the waterless Syrian desert, and on the south by Palestine. This province was subdivided into ten principal regions. 1. Commagêné, towards the north, between Cilicia and Armenia; its chief city being Samosata (now Sumeïsat), on the Euphrates. 2. Cyrrhestica, south of Commagêné, between Cilicia and Mesopotamia; its chief cities being Cirrhus, Zeugma (now Rum-kaleh), and Bambycé, or Hierapolis (now Bambuk). 3. Seleucis, on the Mediterranean coast, south of Cilicia and southwest of Cyrrhestica; its chief city being Antioch, with its suburb, Daphné, and its port, Seleucia. 4. Casíotis, south of Seleucis, so called from the Mons Casius, extending along the Mediterranean shore from the foot of that mountain to the river Eleútherus (now Nahr-el-Kebir); its principal cities being Laodicéa and Marathus. 5. Phœnicia, a narrow strip of territory along the Mediterranean coast, south of Casíotis, extending from the river Eleútherus to Mount Carmel; its leading towns being Antaradus, Berytus (now Beyreut), Sidon, Tyre and Ptolemais (now Acre). 6. Chalybonítis, south of Cyrrhestica and east of Seleucis, lying between Seleucis and the Euphrates; its leading city being Chalybon (now Aleppo). 7. Chalcis, or Chalcidicé, south of Chalybonítis; its principal city being Chalcis, on the lake into which the river Aleppo empties. 8. Apamêné, south of Chalcidicé and east of Casíotis, embracing a large part of the Orontes valley and the country east of that valley; its chief city being Apaméa, and other important towns being Epiphanéa (now Hamah) and Emesa (now Homs). 9. Cœle-Syria, south of Apamêné and east of Phœnicia, comprising the valley between the Lebanon and the Anti-Lebanon mountains, together with the Anti-Lebanon itself and the fertile region at its eastern base towards Damascus; its chief cities being Damascus, Abila and Heliopolis (now Baalbec). 10. Palmyrêné, the desert region south of Chalybonítis and east of Chalcidicé and Apamêné, embracing some fertile oases, the chief of which contained the celebrated Tadmor or Palmyra, "the city of Palms." The capital of the whole Roman province of Syria was Antioch, on the Orontes. Damascus and Emesa were the other most important Syrian cities in Roman times.

Palestine lay south of Syria, and was subdivided into a number of districts, the five principal ones being Galilee, Samaria, Judæa, Idumæa and Peræa; the last including Ituræa, Trachonítis, Auranítis, Batanæa, etc. Galilee was wholly an inland country, being cut off from the coast by Phœnicia. It extended from Mount Hermon on the north to the plain of Esdraelon and the valley of Beth-shan on the south. The most important cities of Galilee were Cæsaréa Philippi, near the site of the ancient Dan; Tiberias, on Lake Tiberias; Capernaum and Jotapata.

Samaria lay south of Galilee; and extended from the plain of Esdraelon on the north to the hill-country of Benjamin on the south, and from the Mediterranean coast on the west to the river Jordan on the east, including the rich plain of Sharon and the hill-country of Manasseh and Ephraim. The principal cities of Samaria in Roman times were Cæsaréa, on the Mediterranean coast; Sebasté (the ancient Samaria), Neapolis (the ancient Shechem, now Nablus), and Shiloh, in the interior.

Judæa was south of Samaria, and lay along the Mediterranean coast from a little north of Joppa (now Jaffa) to Raphia (now Rafah); being bounded on the east by the river Jordan and the Dead Sea, and on the south by Idumæa, or Edom. This region contained the hill-country of Judah and Benjamin, the desert towards the Dead Sea, and the rich Sheffélah, or plain of Philistia. The principal cities of Judæa were Jerusalem, Hebron and Joppa (now Jaffa). Idumæa, or Roman Arabia, was the district between Judæa and Egypt; comprising Idumæa proper, the peninsula of Sinai, and a narrow tract along the eastern coast of the Red Sea, extending southward to the twenty-fourth parallel of north latitude. The principal city of Idumæa was Petra.

Peræa was the tract east of the Jordan, comprising the whole habitable region between that river and the Syrian desert. The more northern portions of this district were called Iturœa and Trachonítis. South of these were Auranítis (the ancient Hauran), Galadítis (the ancient Gilead), Ammonítis (the ancient Ammon), and Moabítis (the ancient Moab). The chief cities of Peræa were Gérasa (the ancient Jerash) and Gádara.

Some of the states of Asia Minor, Syria and Palestine were at first allowed to retain a qualified independence, but before the end of the first century of the Christian era they were all absorbed in the Empire.

The Southern, or African provinces, as we have already seen, were five in number—Egypt, Cyrenaica with Crete, Africa proper, Numidia and Mauritania. Egypt was by far the most important of all Rome's African provinces, as it was the granary of the Empire.

Egypt under the Roman dominion comprised the Delta, the Nile valley, the whole region between the Nile and the Red Sea, the northern coast of Africa from the western mouth of the Nile as far as Paretonium, and the oases of the Lybian desert as far west as the twenty-eighth meridian of longitude east from Greenwich. The province extended as far south as Assouan. Egypt proper, or the Nile valley and the Delta, comprehended three regions—Ægyptus Inferior, or the Delta, containing thirty-five nomes; Heptánomis, or Middle Egypt, containing seven nomes; and Ægyptus Superior, or the Thebaid, containing fifteen nomes. Alexandria was the capital of Roman Egypt, as it had been the seat of government of the Ptolemaïc kingdom. The other important Egyptian cities were Pelusium, Sais and Heliopolis, in Ægyptus Inferior; Arsinoë, Heracleopolis, Antinoë and Hermopolis Magna, in the Heptánomis; and Thebes, Panopolis, Abydos, Ombos and Syêné, in Ægyptus Superior. Alexandria continued to be the seat of learning and refinement under the Roman dominion, as it had been under the Ptolemies.

Cyrenaica lay west of Egypt, and extended along the Mediterranean coast between meridians nineteen and twenty-seven east longitude from Greenwich. It was a considerably wide district, extending far enough inland to include the oasis of Ammon, and probably that of Aujilah. The principal towns of this province were Berenicé (now Benghazi), Arsinoë (now Teuchira), Ptolemaïs (now Dolmeta), near Barca, and Cyrêné (now Grennah). In the island of Crete, which belonged to Cyrenaica, the most important towns were Gnossus, on the northern coast, and Gortyna, in the interior.

Africa proper embraced the territory now included in the two Beyliks of Tunis and Tripoli. This province extended along the Mediterranean coast from Automalax, on the Greater Syrtis, to the river Tusca (now Wady-ez-zain), which separated it from Numidia. Africa proper consisted of two very different regions—a narrow strip of flat coast corresponding to the modern Tripoli; and a wide, hilly, and exceedingly fertile tract corresponding to the present Tunis. The principal towns in the hill district were Utica, the capital of the province of Africa, and Carthage, Hadrumetum and Hippo Zarítus. The chief towns in the low eastern region were Tacapé and Leptis Magna, or Neapolis.

Numidia, as a Roman province, was only a small district; its sea-coast extending only from the Tusca to the Ampsaga, a distance of about one hundred and fifty miles; and reaching inland as far south as the Atlas mountains, while it was bounded on the east by Africa proper and on the west by Mauritania. This province thus embraced the territory now comprised in the eastern part of the French province of Algeria. The chief town of Numidia was Hippo Regius, the modern Bona.

Mauritania—the country of the Mauri, or Moors—lay west of Numidia, from which it was divided by the river Ampsaga, and extended along the shores of the Mediterranean and the Atlantic as far west as Cape Ghir; thus including the territory of the present Empire of Morocco, except the extreme western part, and that of the modern Algeria, except the extreme eastern portion, which constituted the province of Numidia. The province of Mauritania was divided at first into two portions by the river Mulucha (now Mulwia). Tingitana, the western division, was named from its capital, Tingis (now Tangier). The chief cities of Cæsariensis, the eastern division, were Cæsaréa and Igilgilis; both of which w:re situated on the Mediterranean coast. In the later days of the Empire, Mauritania was divided into three districts—Tingitana in the west, Mauritania Cæsariensis in the middle, and Mauritania Sitifensis in the east. The capital of Mauritania Cæsariensis was Cæsaréa; and that of Mauritania Sitifensis was Sitifi, in the interior.

We have now given the extent and described the provinces of the Roman Empire in the time of Augustus. But during the first and second centuries of its existence, several large provinces were added to the Empire by conquest, but these were afterwards relinquished. So we have described what may be classed as the permanent provinces of the Empire, or those provinces which constituted parts of it during the whole or the greater portion of the period of its existence. Those provinces which temporarily formed parts of the Empire were conquered between the years A. D. 14 and A. D. 114. The most important of these were the Agri Decumates and Dacia, in Europe; and Armenia, Mesopotamia and Assyria, in Asia.

The Agri Decumates came under the Roman protection near the end of the reign of Augustus, but were not incorporated into the Empire until about A. D. 100. These territories included a region between the Upper Danube and the Middle Rhine, extending from about Ingolstadt, on the Danube, to the mouth of the Lahn, on the Rhine; and thus embracing most of Wurtemberg and Baden, along with a part of South-western Prussia. The most important city of this section was Sumalocenna, on the Upper Main.

Dacia was conquered and annexed to the Empire by the Emperor Trajan, in A. D. 114. This province embraced all of the present Hungary east of the Theiss, along with the territory of the present Kingdom of Roumania. It was separated on the west by the Theiss from the Jazyges Metanastæ, who occupied the tongue of land lying between the Danube and Theiss rivers. Dacia was bounded on the north by the Carpathian mountains. It extended eastward to the Hierasus, which is either the Sereth or the Pruth. On the south it was separated from Mœsia by the Danube. The native capital of the country was Zermizegethusa, which the Romans named Ulpia Trajana. Other important Dacian towns were Tibiscum (now Temesvar), Apulum (now Carloburg) and Napoca (now Neumarkt). Dacia remained a province of the Roman Empire until A. D. 272, when the Emperor Aurelian, unable to defend it any longer against the invading Goths, ceded the province to that warlike race of barbarians; so that the Danube again became the northern boundary of the Empire in that quarter.

The Emperor Trajan—who, by adding Dacia to the Roman Empire, gave that Empire its greatest extent in Europe—also enlarged the Roman dominions to their greatest territorial limits in Asia, by the conquest of Armenia, Mesopotamia and Assyria, a few years after the subjugation and annexation of Dacia, or in A. D. 114. But these three Asiatic countries were relinquished by Trajan's successor, Adrian, who reëstablished the Euphrates as the eastern boundary of the Roman dominions.

Armenia lay east of Cappadocia, and extended eastward to the Caspian Sea. It was bounded on the north by the river Cyrus, or Kur; on the south by the Mons Masius; and on the south-east by the lofty mountain range between Lakes Van and Urumiyeh, and by the river Araxes (now Aras). The principal cities of Armenia were Artáxata, on the Araxes; Amida (now Diarbekr), in the upper valley of the Tigris; and Tigranocérta, on the flanks of the Niphates mountains.

Mesopotamia lay south of Armenia, and extended from the crest of the Mons Masius near to the shores of the Persian Gulf, embracing the entire region between the Euphrates and Tigris rivers. The principal regions of Armenia were Osrhoëné and Mygdonia, in the north; and Babylonia and Mesêné, in the south. Seleucia, on the Tigris, was an important city of Mesopotamia in Roman times. Other important Mesopotamian cities were Edessa and Carrhæ (the Haran of Abraham's time), in Osrhoëné; Nísibis in Mygdonia; Circésium, near the mouth of the Khabour; and Hatra, in the desert between the Khabour and the Tigris.

Assyria lay east of the Tigris, between that stream and the Zagros mountain chain, and extended southward to the Lesser Zab, or probably to the Diyaleh. Arbéla—where Alexander the Great inflicted the death-blow upon the Medo-Persian Empire—was the only important Assyrian town in Roman times. Assyria was twice conquered by the Romans—both times in the second century of the Christian era—first by the Emperor Trajan, and afterwards by Septimius Sevérus; but was soon relinquished each time.

Having described the provinces of the Roman Empire, we will next proceed to give a brief account of the inhabitants of this immense domain. The Roman Empire contained a population of about one hundred and twenty millions. Three civilizations prevailed in this vast dominion—the Latin, the Greek and the Oriental. The Latin civilization prevailed in Italy and Western Europe; the Greek civilization in Eastern Europe and Asia Minor; and the Oriental civilization in Egypt, Syria and the other Asiatic provinces. Throughout this vast assemblage of races and nationalities, national recollections and national feelings were obliterated and sunk in imperial Rome. These recollections and feelings were replaced by two distinctions between the inhabitants of the Empire—that of language and that of rank.

The Latin language was spoken where the Latin civilization prevailed—in Italy, Gaul, Spain and Africa, and among the Roman colonies in Britain and in the other provinces of Western Europe. From the time of the Roman conquest of these countries, the Romans gradually diffused the Latin civilization and language among the native populations. Especially in Gaul, Spain and Africa did the Latin language become firmly rooted; and the customs and manners, and, in fact, the entire civilization of those countries, became thoroughly Roman.

The Greek language was the tongue in those countries which had become permeated with Hellenic civilization and Hellenic influences—in Greece and in other European lands east of the Adriatic and south of the Danube, and also in Asia Minor, and partially in Syria and Palestine. These countries had been Hellenized by Grecian colonists or by the Macedonian conquerors;

and under the Roman dominion they retained the Greek manners, customs, language and culture, while they were politically Roman.

The lands in which the Oriental civilization existed—especially Egypt, Syria and Palestine—had become somewhat Hellenized under the rule of Alexander the Great and his successors; but this Grecian influence was merely superficial, as the native populations of these Oriental lands had never given up their own languages, or their own religious ideas or habits of thought. Neither did these Orientals become Latinized under the Roman dominion—they did not adopt the Roman language and civilization; although their political destinies were swayed from Rome. Syriac was spoken in Syria, Armenian in Armenia, and Coptic in Egypt.

The great mass of the rural populations in all the conquered countries preserved their own provincial languages and habits. The Celtic language was spoken in Britain and in the North of Gaul, while Illyrian was spoken in Illyricum. Where the native inhabitants were most enslaved, they made the greatest exertions to acquire the language of their masters. The Romans, on the other hand, were obliged to make the advances where the conquered people were the most numerous and powerful. There was, however, a constant shifting of population throughout the Empire, in consequence of the immense traffic in slaves, the military service, and the exercise of civil functions. From these causes, every Roman province exhibited in its lower classes a strange commingling of dialects.

The period of the Empire was distinguished by six classes of the people: 1. The Senatorial families, proprietors of immense lands and enormous wealth. 2. The inhabitants of large towns, a mixture of artisans and freedmen, who subsisted on the luxury of the rich, and shared in their corruption. 3. The inhabitants of small towns, who were poor, despised and oppressed. 4. Husbandmen, who tilled the soil. 5. Slaves, who constituted one-half of the inhabitants of the Empire. 6. Banditti, who escaped oppression by taking to the woods and the mountains, and living by brigandage.

The peasantry throughout the Empire were rigorously deprived of arms, and were incapacitated from contributing to the defense of the country. The free cultivators were allowed but little personal liberty, except the name. They toiled upon the land for certain fixed wages, usually paid in produce; but they were separated from their masters, the landholders, by an impassable distance. They were immediately dependent on some favorite slave or freedman, and were the victims of every kind of oppression.

The slaves lived in huts, under the eyes of overseers, as did the negro slaves on an American plantation before the late civil war. These wretched creatures were worked almost continually with chains to their feet, and were shut up every night in holes underground. The appalling sufferings of so great a proportion of the people of the Empire, and their inveterate hatred toward their oppressors, produced their natural results in the process of time—servile insurrections, conspiracies, assassinations and poisonings.

Among even the free population of sixty millions in the Empire, only the small proportion inhabiting Italy, under the envied name of Roman citizens (*civis Romanus*), possessed political independence, or had the smallest share in the government. The provinces were, however, left in possession of their independent municipal constitutions and functionaries.

SECTION XII.—NEIGHBORS OF THE ROMANS.

THE Romans loosely assigned the name *Germany* to all the countries east of the Rhine and north of the Danube as far as the modern Poland. They called the countries now known as Poland and the western portion of modern Russia by the general name of *Sarmatia*. They named the greater portion of the vast domain now included in the Russian Empire in Europe and Asia, *Scythia*, which was almost wholly an unknown region. The Romans did not discover, or at least did not explore, the countries about the Sínus Codánus (now Baltic sea); though these lands had been visited in very early times by the Phœnicians.

The Romans were never distinguished for any great zeal in maritime discovery. They appear to have considered Scandinavia, or Scandia (now Sweden), Nerígen (now Norway), and Eringia, or Furningia (now Finland) as isles in the German Ocean (now North Sea). The Orcades (now Orkney isles) were discovered when Britain was circumnavigated; but previous to that time some indistinct account of a distant island named Thúle had been received. Many believe this island to have been one of the Zetland group, while others think it was Iceland.

The Germans were always very formidable foes of the Romans, and belonged to the Aryan branch of the Caucasian race. They took their name from their own language—Ghar-mans, meaning *War-men*, or warriors; as they chiefly prided themselves upon their military virtues, as do most savage and barbarous nations. The Romans called them Cimbri and Teutones in the earliest ages. The Cimbri gave their name to the Chersonésus Címbrica (now Jutland). The modern names *Deutschen* and *Dutch* have been derived from the Teutones. A confederation of German tribes in the third century of the Christian era took the name of *Allemanni*, or *All-mans*, meaning *complete men;* for which reason the French still call Germany *Allemagne*.

Among the most important of the German tribes were the Cimbri and the Saxons; the former being the most remarkable in ancient times, and the latter during the middle ages. These tribes occupied the country on the east bank of the Albis (now Elbe) river as far eastward as the Vistula. West of the Albis as far as the Visurgis (now Weser) were the Upper Chauci; and west of the Visurgis as far as the river Amásia (now Erus) were the Lower Chauci. West of the latter were the Frisii, whose territory in Eastern Holland still bears the name of *Friesland*. The Marcomanni anciently occupied the region between the sources of the Rhínus (now Rhine) and the Ister, or Danubius (now Danube); but they subsequently established themselves in the territory of the modern Bohemia and Moravia, and likewise in a portion of Gaul, driving the Boii before them.

The Hercynian forests and mountains—as all the unexplored portion of Eastern Germany was called by the Romans—seem to have been the original home of the Quadi, the Suevi and the Hermandúri, who became very formidable enemies to the Romans in the age of the Antonines. The original seat of the Longobardi (men with long beards)—afterwards famous in Italy under the name of *Lombards*—was in the upper region of the Elbe. The Gepidæ were located near the mouth of the Vistula; and it is believed that thé original home of the warlike Burgundians was on the same river; but they and the Semnónes had migrated westward as far as the Elbe in the first century of the Christian era. The Æstui, famous for their traffic in amber, were located on the Baltic coast.

In addition to the Hercynian forest, Germany contained Sylva Melibóca (the Hartz mountains), Sylva Barcénia (the Black Forest), and Sylva Cæsia (the Teutoberger Forest). The Rhínus (now Rhine) formed the boundary between Germany and Gaul. Other rivers besides those already mentioned were the Isela (now Isel), separating the Bructéri from the Frisii; the Lúpias (now Lippe), in the territory of the Marsi; and the Viádrus (now Oder), near the source of which many authors consider to have been the original seat of the Burgundians.

In considering the condition of ancient Germany, or *Germania*, as it was called by the Romans, we must bear in mind that the tribes of that country frequently migrated from one section to another, particularly in the second century after Christ, and that the name of one chief tribe was often assigned to a large confederation of tribes. Especially is this the case with the Franks (*free men*), who were a union of several hordes resolved to preserve their national independence, rather than a single tribe.

We will now proceed to a description of the prominent national characteristics of the ancestors of the modern Germans. Our chief authority on this point is the great Roman historian Tacitus, who wrote his *Germania* in A. D. 98.

The larger portion of Germany was originally covered with forests, in which wild animals and game were abundant. The climate was damp and foggy, and the winters were longer and colder than they now are. The soil was mostly fertile, but marshy in a number of places. The Germans were distinguished from the races of Southern Europe by their large and robust physical frames, their greater daring and activity, their respect for the honor of their women, and by "a sense they called honor, which led them to sacrifice their life rather than their word."

The numerous tribes constituting the German nation were grouped into the confederations already named. The different tribes —except the Saxons, who had no kings except in time of war, when the nobles elected one of their number as a leader—had each a royal family which was believed to have been descended from Odin, the chief deity of the Northern nations of ancient Europe. The king of each tribe was chosen from this royal family by the free votes of his comrades.

The ancient Germans were an agricultural people, but war and the chase were their favorite pursuits. Men unable to bear arms and women were assigned the tilling of the soil and other peaceful occupations. The Germans possessed the virtues of bravery, simplicity, hospitality and truthfulness; but they were frequently fierce and cruel, and indulged in gambling, drunkenness and indolence. They celebrated the great exploits of their ancestors in their songs, and were always willing to yield their lives in defense of their freedom.

The ancient Germans were divided into two classes—the nobles and the common freemen. The nobles were usually wealthier than the freemen, but owed their influence more to their personal characteristics than to their riches. They were the recognized leaders of the people in peace and war. The freemen were all equals, and comprised the bulk of the nation. Both nobles and freemen held slaves, who were captives taken in war and their children, and persons condemned to slavery in punishment for crime. The slaves were the absolute property of their masters, and were denied all redress against injustice, but were generally well treated.

The Germans had few laws. Most all crimes perpetrated by nobles or freemen were punished by fines, the amounts of these differing among the various tribes. Family ties were very strong among this ancient people. Marriages only occurred after the contracting parties had thoroughly developed their powers of mind and body. The wife occupied a position of honor and influence, though she was in a certain sense purchased by her husband. She was her husband's companion and friend, and accompanied him on distant mi'itary expeditions. She was brave and virtuous, and was trained to the use of arms.

Children were under the supreme authority of their father. A freeman's orphan children were under the protection of their relatives until they were able to take care of themselves. The quarrels of a freeman were espoused by his relatives; and in case of his murder they were bound to see that the *Wergeld*, or price of his blood, which was distributed among the members of his family, was exacted and paid.

Ancient Germany had no cities. The free inhabitants usually resided in villages, in which the huts or family dwellings were all separated from each other, each being surrounded by a patch of land. The lands around the villages were at first held in common, but in the process of time they were divided among individual owners. An indefinite number of villages constituted a *hundred*. Each village and hundred had its own chief, who was chosen by the votes of the freemen. The chiefs of the hundreds were under the chiefs of the tribes.

Some of the German tribes had kings, who, as already remarked, were elected from certain noble families who were believed to have been descended from the gods. The chiefs of the hundreds were the princes of the tribes, and formed the council of the king or principal chief. The princes vied with each other in the number of their followers, each of whom took a solemn oath to be faithful to his lord, and it was considered the worst crime possible to violate this oath. The chief furnished his followers with war-horses, and with armor and food, in return for their services.

Notwithstanding the importance of the station of the chiefs in ancient Germany, they possessed but comparatively limited authority. The *meetings of the people* were above all the chiefs. The village even had its meetings; but the meetings of the hundred and those of the tribe were the really important ones. These meetings were not representative, like modern parliaments and legislatures. All freemen were entitled to the right of attending them. The meetings of the village and those of the hundred did not concern themselves with the affairs of the tribe.

All matters relating to the tribe came before the meeting of the entire people. In this general meeting the king or other chiefs of the tribe and the chiefs of the various hundreds were elected. In these general meetings also the young freeman obtained from his father, or from some prince, the arms which were the emblem that he had acquired a position of independence in the tribe. All difficult cases of justice were decided by the meeting of the tribe. This meeting likewise was vested with the power of declaring war and concluding peace, and also sanctioned the occasional expeditions of the chiefs with their followers to distant lands.

When questions of more than ordinary gravity were to be presented at the meeting, they were previously discussed by the king or other chief and by the princes of the tribe; but the final decision rested with the people themselves. The common freemen seldom took a prominent part in the deliberations of the meeting. The chiefs submitted their proposals to the people in clear terms, presenting the arguments on each side of the question. If the freemen disagreed with their chiefs, they expressed their opinions by cries of disapproval; and they signified their assent to a proposition by clashing their armor.

The religion of the ancient Germans was in consonance with their habits. Odin, or Woden, was their supreme god; and Freya was his wife. Thor, or Donar, their son, was the god of thunder and a very powerful deity. Baldur, the sun-god, was likewise a deity of considerable importance. The Germans erected no temples in honor of their gods, but worshiped them in sacred groves, and occasionally offered sacrifices of human beings to appease the wrath of these deities. The Germans paid great attention to oracles and old prophetesses; and ascertained the will of their gods by means of lots, the flight of birds, and the neighing of sacred horses.

The Germans believed that their gods took a direct interest in the affairs of mortals. Their idea of happiness in a future life was to sit forever in the presence of Odin, drinking beer from the skulls of their enemies, feasting on the flesh of the wild boar, and engaging in terrific combats for amusement. Only such as died in battle were admitted to a participation in such joys. Cowards and those who ended their life peacefully by dying a natural death were excluded. This opinion is forcibly expressd in the death-song sung by Lodbrog for himself in the Edda, as seen in the following lines:

> "With flashing swords our might we proved;
> But this my hearty laughter moved,
> That bliss eternal shall be mine
> Where the halls of Odin shine;
> To him, great sire, my deeds are known,
> For me he has prepared a throne,
> Where richest ale incessant flows
> In the hollow skulls of foes.
> The brave man never shrinks at death,
> Gladly I resign my breath;
> No regrets my soul appal
> As I haste to Odin's hall."

This is clearly the creed of a savage race of warriors, such as the ancient Germans were. Their only delight was in military exercises and in the use of weapons. They were always armed when they attended any public assembly or festival. The sacredness with which they regarded the sword is clearly shown by the circumstance that they took their most solemn oath in kissing the naked blade of the weapon.

The name of Odin, or Woden, is preserved in our Wednesday, meaning Woden's day. Thor's name is commemorated in Thursday, or Thor's day. Freya's name has given Friday its designation.

In Britain, the savage Picts and Scots of Caledonia, as the Scotch Highlands were called, successfully resisted all attempts of the Romans to conquer them; and the Emperors Adrian and Septimius Severus were obliged to protect the southern portion of the island from the incursions of these savage tribes by erecting walls across the island from sea to sea in order to shut them in among the Caledonian highlands.

On the frontiers of the Roman Empire in Asia were the wild tribes of the Caucasus in the north-east—the Iberians and the Albanians—who maintained their independence. On the east, beyond the provinces or Cappadocia and Syria, were the Kingdom of Armenia and the Parthian Empire. Armenia alternately submitted to the Romans, the Parthians, and the successors of the latter, the New Persians. On the south of the provinces of Syria and Palestine were the unconquered Arab tribes, who defied every effort made by the Romans to subdue them; though in Trajan's reign Arabia Petræa paid nominal allegiance to Rome, but was abandoned by Trajan's successor, Adrian.

Beyond the southern confines of the Roman Empire, in the great African desert—known anciently as Libya—were the Gætulians, who first became known to the Romans during the Jugurthine War. These people were never subdued by the Roman armies, but in later years they paid homage to the Roman Proconsul or Prefect of the province of Africa.

Though the Romans by their conquests succeeded to the great commercial marts of the Phœnicians, the Greeks and the Egyptians in Asia, and the trading stations of the Carthaginians in Africa, they made no effort to encourage traffic and opened no new routes for trade; and under their dominion many of the ancient highways of commerce, especially in Asia, fell into disuse.

The Romans became acquainted with India after their conquest of Egypt; and in the reigns of the later Emperors some efforts were made to establish an extensive commerce with that distant Eastern land by the route of the Red Sea. India was then divided into India proper, or India within the Ganges, whose western coast (now called Malabar), was well known; and India beyond the Ganges, which embraced Burmah and the peninsula of Malacca. The Carnatic coast was also known. The Romans knew of Malacca as the Chersonésus Aúrea, meaning the *golden peninsula*. They knew the island of Ceylon by the name of Taprobáne, or Salice, and the island of Sumatra as Labodii, or Hordei.

ANCIENT HISTORY.—ROME.

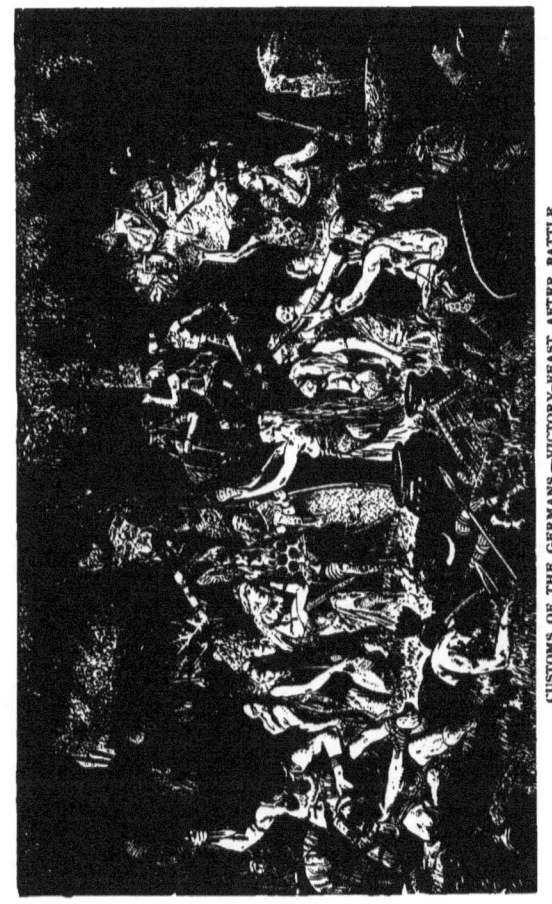

CUSTOMS OF THE GERMANS.—VICTORY-FEAST AFTER BATTLE.

SECTION XIII.—THE CITY OF ROME.

OME was originally built in the form of a square, on the Palatine Hill, for which reason it was called *Roma Quadrata*. After the founding of the city, and after its enlargement at any subsequent period, the first care was to mark out the *Pomœrium*, a consecrated space around the city walls on which it was unlawful to erect any edifice. This custom was the evident outcome of the necessity of preventing besiegers from finding shelter near the fortifications of the city. In this, as in innumerable other instances, the early Roman legislators gave utility the sanction of superstition.

The prescribed form for marking the Pomœrium was as follows: A bullock and a heifer were yoked to a bronze or copper plowshare, and the course of the future wall was marked by a furrow. The plow was so guided that the sods fell to the inside; and if any went in an opposite direction, great care was exercised to turn them in the right way. The plow being sacred, the ground would have been profaned by anything impure passing over it after it had once been touched by the plow. As things unclean, as well as things clean, cannot always be kept from passing into a city, when the plow reached a place where the builders intended to put a gate, it was taken up and carried to the place where the wall was resumed. For this reason the Latins called a gate *porta*, from the verb *portare*, signifying *to carry*.

The *Comitium*, or place of public assembly, was then consecrated. The most remarkable feature of this ceremony was the preparation of a vault, called *mundas*, in which were placed the first fruits of all things used to sustain life, and a part of the native earth of each colonist. Many superstitious notions were attached to this structure. It was believed to be the entrance to the invisible world; and it was opened three times yearly, with many solemnities, to admit the spirits of the departed.

The first extension of the Pomœrium may have been occasioned by inclosing the Quirinal Hill for the Sabines, when they united themselves with the Romans in the early years of the city. Next was added the Cælian Hill, on which the followers of Cælus Vibenna, the mythical Etruscan adventurer, are said to have erected their habitation. The Viminal Hill was inclosed by Tullus Hostilius after he had destroyed Alba Longa; and Ancus Martius added the Aventine Hill, which was considered the special habitation of the plebeians. Tarquin the Elder enlarged the city by the addition of the Esquiline and the Capitoline Hills, which completed the number of the seven hills for which the city was famous. The Pincian and Vatican Mounts were annexed to the city at a very much later period, as was also the Janiculum Mount on the northern side of the Tiber, thus making the number of hills ten.

The city was first fortified with outworks by Ancus Martius, especially by raising a castle and a garrison on Mount Janiculum, which was connected with the city by a wooden bridge, called *pons sublicius*. But Tarquin the Elder was the first to embellish the city with magnificent edifices, of utility as well as of ornament. The great sewer by which the city was drained, and whose immense proportions are still admired, is usually ascribed to that king.

Rome began to be regularly rebuilt after the Gauls had destroyed the city; and numerous magnificent structures, both public and private, were erected when wealth was so enormously increased after the conquest of Carthage and Western Asia. When the Consul Mummius conquered Greece, the Romans knew so little about the fine arts that they destroyed many beautiful pieces of statuary for the sake of the materials of which they were constructed. But thenceforth Roman taste was improved by a more constant intercourse with the Greeks, particularly when Athens became the university of the Roman Empire; though the long civil wars between the aristocratic and democratic factions frustrated the development of these improvements until after the establishment of the Empire on the ruins of the Republic by the Emperor Augustus.

The most remarkable buildings of Rome were the *Circus Maximus*, the *Capitol* with its temples, the *Senate-House*, the *Forum*, the *Campus Martius* and the *Flavian Amphitheater*. The Circus Maximus—which was erected by Tarquin the Elder, but which was so enlarged by subsequent additions that it was capable of containing two hundred thousand spectators—was a most magnificent structure; and was reserved for public games, races and shows. The Circus Maximus was the first Roman amphitheater; in the arena of which were exhibited the cruel fights of the gladiators, which the Romans viewed with savage delight, together with races and combats of wild beasts.

The Capitol was began on the Saturnian Hill, which was named *Capitoline*, because a human head was found by the laborers who dug the foundation during the reign of Tarquin the Elder. The great structure was built on the northern summit of the hill. The rocky eminence on the southern side was called the *Tarpeian Rock*, in commemoration of the treason of Tarpeia in the legendary days of primeval Rome. Public criminals were frequently executed by being thrown headlong from the peak of this cliff.

The Temple of Jupiter Capitolinus, one of the buildings of the Capitol, was generally considered the national sanctuary of the Romans. It was commenced by Tarquin the Elder and completed by Tarquin the Proud; and was annually improved by the valuable presents which victorious generals and foreign princes, desirous of conciliating the Roman people, offered as votive gifts. The Emperor Augustus alone presented gold and jewels valued at more than five thousand pounds.

This magnificent edifice was burned to the ground during the civil war between Marius and Sulla, but was rebuilt with increased splendor; and Cicero tells us that the statue of Jupiter Capitolinus was erected on the pedestal at the very time of the discovery of the conspiracy of Catiline. This splendid temple was again destroyed twice during the reigns of the Emperors Vespasian and Domitian, but was restored each time with additional splendor.

The Sibylline Books, and other oracles supposed to contain important revelations regarding the fate of the city, were preserved in the sanctuary, under the care of fifteen persons of the highest rank, called the *Quindecémviri;* while the chronological archives of Rome were likewise preserved there. The chief magistrate yearly drove a nail into the temple—a custom which is believed to have been the first rude method of marking the progress of time.

There were several other temples on the Capitoline Hill, the most remarkable being that of Jupiter Feretrius—said to have been built by the legendary Romulus—where the *spolia optima* were deposited. The *spolia optima* were the trophies presented by a Roman general who had slain the enemy's leader with his own hand. These trophies are said to have been only offered three times—by Romulus, Cossus and Marcellus. The deity to whom these offerings were presented was called Feretrius, from the *feretrum*, or bier, on which these spoils were conveyed to the temple.

The Capitol was the citadel of Rome, except in the reign of Numa Pompilius, the second king, when the Quirínal was selected as the strongest place. This fact tends vastly to sustain Niebuhr's theory that an ancient Sabine town named Quirium stood on that hill, which modern writers confound with Cúres. It is believed that the double-faced Janus, whose temple was closed when Rome was at peace, was the emblem of the united cities of the Romans and the Sabines, and that the opening of the temple gates in time of war was to enable the inhabitants of one of the cities to aid the other.

THE CIRCUS MAXIMUS (RESTORED).

THE FORUM, ROME.

The Forum, or place of public assembly, and of the great market, was in the valley between the Palatine and Capitoline Hills. This place was surrounded with temples; with halls for the administration of justice, called *basilicæ;* and with public offices. It was likewise adorned with statues of eminent Roman warriors and statesmen, and with trophies from the conquered nations. Among these memorials of conquest were several *rostra*, or prows of ships, taken from the Carthaginians at Antium. These were utilized as ornaments to adorn the pulpits from which the magistrates and public orators harangued the general assemblies of the Roman people. This custom gave rise to the phrase "to mount the rostrum." In

CIRCUS MAXIMUS.

the middle of the Forum was the drained marsh called the *Curtian Lake*, connected with the celebrated legend of Marcus Curtius, which we have related on page 891.

In the Forum was the famous Temple of Janus, constructed wholly of bronze, and believed to have been erected during the reign of Numa Pompilius. So incessantly were the Romans at war that the gates of this temple were closed but three times in eight centuries. At no great distance from this temple was the celebrated Temple of Concord, in which the Senate quite frequently assembled. Storks were encouraged to build in the roof of the structure, because of the social instincts ascribed to those birds. In the same vicinity was the Temple of Vesta, where the constant fire was kept burning by the Vestal Virgins. In this temple was preserved, it is said, the *Palladium*, or sacred image of Minerva, on which depended the fate of Troy, and other relics which were consecrated by superstition.

The Senate-House—the grand legislative hall of the Roman nation—was above the pulpits belonging to the public orators. This splendid edifice is said to have been erected by Tullus Hostilius, the third King of Rome; but the Senate had several other places of meeting, often holding their sessions in the temples. The Senate-House was likewise decorated with the statues of renowned Roman warriors and statesmen.

Close to the Senate-House was the *Comitium*, or court in which the patrician *Curiæ* were assembled. This space was not roofed until the close of the Second Punic War, soon after which the Comitia Curiata gradually fell into disuse. Before this space was covered with a roof, it was called a temple; the word *templum* properly signifying not simply a building, but an inclosure consecrated by the augurs. In the vicinity of the Senate-House were the principal theaters and baths.

The Campus Martius was the place for the elections of magistrates, the reviews of troops, and the registration of citizens. This was the favorite place of exercise for the young nobles. It was at first a large common, which had constituted a portion of the estate of Tarquin the Proud, and was confiscated after the banishment of that tyrannical king; after which it was dedicated to Mars, the god of war, because the Romans considered that deity the father of Romulus.

The Campus Martius remained unimproved for a long time; but in the reign of the Emperor Augustus it began to be surrounded with several magnificent buildings. In different portions were planted shrubs and ornamental trees, and porticos were erected, under which the citizens might continue their exercises in rainy weather. Most of these improvements are attributable to Marcus Agrippa, the ablest general and wisest statesman in the court of the Emperor Augustus.

Near the Campus Martius, this Marcus Agrippa erected the famous *Pantheon*, or Temple of all the Gods—the most perfect and the grandest monument of ancient Rome that has survived the ravages of centuries. This celebrated edifice is now used as a Christian church; and its circular form, and the beautiful dome forming its roof, excite universal admiration. The Colosséum in Regent's Park, London, is modeled after the Roman Pantheon.

The Flavian Amphitheater—which was erected during the reign of the Emperor Vespasian, in the latter half of the first century of the Christian era, and whose ruins are known as the *Colosséum*—could seat almost a hundred thousand persons. Theaters and public baths, and buildings for the exhibition of *maumachiæ*, or naval combats, were erected by the Emperors to compensate the people for the loss of liberty.

Among the most remarkable public constructions of ancient Rome were the numerous aqueducts to supply the city with water. Pure streams were sought at a great distance, and were conveyed in these artificial channels, supported by arches, many of them over a hundred feet in height, across steep mountains, deep valleys and dangerous morasses, which architects of less enterprise would have regarded as insurmountable obstacles. The first aqueduct was erected during the Censorship of Appius Claudius "the Blind," about four centuries after the founding of Rome. Under the Emperors no less than twenty of these stupendous works of public utility were erected, thus bringing so abundant a supply of water to the city that rivers appeared to flow through the streets and sewers. Even in our own day, when but three of these aqueducts remain, after the lapse of all these centuries, notwithstanding the barbarian ravages and governmental neglect, Rome has as good a supply of wholesome water as any other city.

THE COLOSSEUM AT ROME.

ROMAN GAMES.

THE CITY OF ROME.

Commerce and industry flourished, and Augustus could truly boast that he "found Rome of brick and left it of marble." The city, during the prosperous days of the Empire, contained a population of over four millions. The city was inclosed by walls twenty miles in circumference, and the walls are said to have been pierced by thirty-eight gates. The most remarkable of these gates were the Tergéminal, the Carmental, the Triumphal, the Naval and the Capéna; the last being near the great aqueduct. There were also extensive suburbs.

convenience; some being large enough to accommodate three thousand bathers at once. Innumerable fountains were supplied from the aqueducts, and many of these were of wonderful architectural beauty.

There were innumerable porticos, or piazzas, covered with colonnades, adorned with statues, and which were intended as places for the citizens to meet for business or walk for pleasure. They were sometimes separate structures, and sometimes connected with other edifices. The most splendid of these porticos was that of the Temple of

PLAN OF ROME—TIME OF AUGUSTUS.

During the period of the Empire, the city of Rome was unrivaled for magnificence, wealth and luxury. It was enriched by its conquering generals with the plunder of hundreds of nations, and the treasures of the most powerful monarchs were emptied into its coffers. In the zenith of its splendor and glory, "the Eternal City" contained four hundred and twenty temples, five regular theatres, two amphitheatres, and seven extensive circuses. The city had sixteen public baths, constructed of marble, and furnished with every desirable

Apollo, on the Palatine Hill. The largest one was named *Milliaria*, because it had a thousand columns. There were numberless palaces, public halls, columns and obelisks. The city was also adorned with a number of triumphal arches, having statues and various sculptured ornaments. Some of the arches were of wonderful splendor; being built of the finest marble, in the form of a square, with a large arched passage in the middle and a small one at each side.

Thirty-one roads centered in Rome. These issued from the Forum, traversing Italy, pervading the provinces, and ending at the frontiers of the Empire. Augustus erected a gilt pillar in the middle of the Forum, called the *Milliarium aureum*, from which were reckoned the distances on the various roads. This remarkable monument was discovered so recently as 1823. The Tiber was crossed by eight bridges.

Rome was surpassed by Athens in architectural beauty, but was far superior to it in works of public utility. Every succeeding Emperor considered it necessary to improve and enlarge the structures that had been erected for the comfort and convenience of the citizens. The ruins of the ancient structures of this magnificent capital and metropolis of the Roman world strike the eye of the modern beholder with wonder and amazement, and have excited admiration in all ages.

SECTION XIV.—AUGUSTAN AGE OF LATIN LITERATURE.

THE later years of the Republic were noted for several eminent writers who flourished during that period. Among poets were LUCRETIUS and CATULLUS. Lucretius was the most remarkable of Roman poets, as he combined the exactness of the philosopher with the enthusiasm and imagination of the bard. While he appears to have no perfect model among the Greeks, he has left a production unsurpassed by anything of the kind in later ages.

Lucretius was born about B. C. 95. He lived in a period prolific of important events, but appears to have kept himself retired from public affairs. He was sent in accordance with the custom of that time, with other young Romans of rank, to study at Athens, where he attended on the instructions of Zeno and Phædrus. Cicero was one of his fellow-students.

Lucretius is said to have committed suicide in a fit of insanity when he was in his forty-fourth year. His great work is a philosophical and didactic poem, entitled *On the Nature of Things*, and embraces a complete exposition of the theological, physical and moral system of Epicurus. It is a composition unsurpassed in energy and richness of language, and in genuine sublimity. Nothing appears more remarkable than the slight mention of Lucretius by succeeding Latin authors, which may be ascribed to the spirit of free-thinking which pervaded his writings, thus rendering it unsafe to extol his poetical genius.

Catullus was born B. C. 86. Beyond his intimacy with Cicero, little is known of his life. He wrote odes, songs, satires, elegies and epigrams. He ranked above all the other Latin poets, except Virgil and Horace, in literary merit. His productions are very refined in feeling and graceful in expression. Catullus was not free from the influence of the growing corrupt taste of the age.

The most ancient Roman historical writings yet extant are those of SALLUST, who was born B. C. 85, and took part in politics early in his life. In the civil wars between Cæsar and Pompey, he sided with Cæsar, and was made Proconsul of Numidia, where he enriched himself by plundering the province. Upon returning to Rome, Sallust erected a splendid palace in the suburbs, which was surrounded by the most delightful pleasure-grounds, and these were long afterwards famous as the *Gardens of Sallust*. This place became the residence of several Roman Emperors, and was burned to the ground when the city was taken by the Goths under Alaric, A. D. 410.

Sallust wrote a History of Rome from the death of Sulla to the conspiracy of Catiline, which, with the exception of a few fragments, has utterly perished. But two other works of his are yet extant—his *History of the Conspiracy of Catiline* and his *History of the Jugurthine War*. Sallust adopted Thucydides as his model, and his chief characteristics are a noble brevity and a vivid manner of representing events. The reflections accompanying his narrative are so just and pointed that some have regarded him as the father of philosophical history. The characters which he drew have been considered master-pieces in all ages. He has seized the delicate shades no less than the prominent features, and has thrown over them the most lively and appropriate coloring. Sallust died B. C. 34.

The most celebrated Roman writer of the republican epoch was CICERO, who excelled equally as a statesman, as an orator and as a philosophical writer. He was born at Arpinum, in Southern Italy, B. C. 106. He was instructed in oratory by Apollonius Molo, of Rhodes, and likewise studied at Athens. After returning to Rome, Cicero was appointed Quæstor and afterwards Consul. It was while he held the latter office that he rendered the Republic such valuable service by defeating the conspiracy of Catiline. But he was soon afterwards banished from Rome, through the influence of the profligate Tribune Clodius. He voluntarily retired from Italy to Greece, and was soon recalled to Rome in the most honorable manner. In the civil war between Pompey and Cæsar, Cicero sided with Pompey, but was reconciled to Cæsar after the battle of Pharsalia. Mark Antony was Cicero's inveterate enemy; and during the Second Triumvirate, the illustrious orator was proscribed through Antony's influence, and was murdered by one of his emissaries, B. C. 43.

Cicero was amiable in disposition, and upright in principle. His faults were vanity and infirmity of purpose; but he was, taken altogether, one of the brightest characters of ancient times. He was a voluminous writer. A great portion of his literary productions have perished, but sufficient remain to give us an exalted opinion of his literary and oratorical talents. His works consist of orations, letters, rhetorical treatises and philosophical dissertations.

Cicero was the greatest of Roman orators; but he likewise surpassed all other orators, of any age or nation, in a general and discursive acquaintance with philosophy and literature, along with a wonderful facility in communicating the results of his labors in the most copious, perspicuous and attractive manner. Cicero was an admirer of Plato, but in questions of morality he adopted the principles of the Stoics. In his philosophical writings he exhibited the opinions of all the different sects. His great aim was to explain to his fellow-citizens, in their own language, all that the Grecian sages had taught on the most important subjects, for the purpose of enlarging the minds and reforming the morals of his countrymen. His literary productions are a most valuable collection, and have been a great source of information to all subsequent ages.

JULIUS CÆSAR was also one of the Latin writers in the last years of republican Rome. We have already seen the prominent figure which his life and character played in the political history of his country. His great literary works are his *Commentaries on the Gallic and Civil Wars*, which comprehend but a short period of time, but include events of the greatest importance, and detail the greatest military operations, probably, in all ancient history.

The military genius of Rome is clearly presented through the pages of Cæsar's writings, which comprehend all the varieties offered to our interest and admiration by warfare—battles, sieges, defenses, encampments, retreats, marches through woods and over mountains, passages of rivers, and those yet more interesting accounts of the spirit and discipline of the enemy's soldiers and the talents of their commanders. Cæsar's style is remarkably clear and easy, and is characterized by a simplicity more truly noble than the pomp of words. He never alludes to himself with affectation or arrogance. Excepting the false colors in which he disguises his ambitious schemes against his country's liberties, he relates everything with fidelity and candor. Cæsar's other writings have perished.

Another Roman writer during the later

years of the Republic was VARRO, who was renowned for his learning, and wrote on agriculture, grammar, antiquities and numerous other subjects. Varro's works are said to have included five hundred volumes.

The literature of the Roman Republic and that of the Roman Empire are not separated by any great period of time, yet their difference in spirit can be very readily distinguished. Cicero died during the lifetime of Augustus, but his genius breathes only the spirit of the Republic. Virgil and Horace were born citizens of the Republic, but their writings bear the impress of monarchical influence.

Augustus was a great patron of literature and the arts, and his reign was the golden age of Roman literature. So many writers flourished at this time that the most brilliant period of any nation's literature has since been called its *Augustan Age.* Thus the Augustan Age of Rome became proverbial in history. At no other time were men of learning and genius so liberally rewarded and encouraged by statesmen, politicians and military leaders as that which a grateful and appreciative posterity has stamped with the name of the first Roman Emperor.

Among the various arts by which the Emperor Augustus endeavored to interest the Roman people and to make them forget their freedom, the most remarkable was his encouragement of learning and literature, and the patronage which he bestowed on men of learning and letters. From his infancy everything contributed to give him a taste for learning and a respect for scholars. After he became firmly established in the imperial power, without a competitor, Augustus continued the pursuit of his private studies with unceasing diligence. When he read a Greek or Latin author, he dwelt mainly on what might be a lesson or an example in the administration of the affairs of state, or in his own personal conduct.

The literary taste of Augustus is apparent from the number of his Greek secretaries, his superintendents for the care of his collection of statues and pictures, his copyists and his librarians. When he was unable to sleep at night, he had a reader or a story-teller, like the Oriental monarchs, who sat by him; and he frequently listened to them until he fell asleep. Among the many embellishments which he bestowed on the city of Rome were two public libraries—the Octavian, which stood in the portico of Octavia; and the Palatine, on the hill of that name, near the Temple of Apollo.

Augustus erected at the Palatine library, from his own share of the spoils of the conquered towns in Dalmatia, a magnificent colonnade, with double rows of pillars, adorned with statues and paintings by the principal Greek artists. This edifice was open below, but comprehended a large and curious library above, with retiring-rooms for private reading, public halls for recitation, schools for teaching, and every other possible allurement and aid to study. Delightful walks, suitable for exercise or meditation, were all around this structure, some under shade and others exposed to the sun, for summer or winter. A gigantic statue of Apollo, in bronze and of Etruscan workmanship, presided as the genius of the place.

Augustus also provided means for the careful education of the Roman youth. He bestowed liberal gifts of money on literary men in general, along with that attentive and respectful regard which they all desired, and which animated their exertions by elevating their station in society. The beginning of the political career of Augustus had been indeed somewhat inauspicious to the rising poets of Rome. Virgil, Tibullus and Propertius all mourned the losses which they had endured during the period of the Second Triumvirate. But no sooner had Virgil exhibited his genius than his lands were restored to him, and crowns were assigned or statues erected to other poets.

During the last days of his life, when he was incapable of attending to public affairs, Augustus was conveyed in his litter to Præneste, Tibur or Baiæ, through beautiful alleys leading to the sea, or among fragrant groves which he had planted with myrtles and laurels, the shade of which was then considered conducive to health. While on these journeys he read the works of the poets whose genius he had fostered, and he was continually attended by philosophers, whose conversation afforded him his chief solace. Even when he was on his death-bed at Nola, Augustus passed his moments in philosophic conversations on the vanity and emptiness of all human affairs. Augustus was likewise a good judge of literary composition and a true critic in poetry, and thus he never misplaced his patronage, or lavished it on the persons whose writings might have had a tendency toward corrupting instead of improving the taste and learning of the time.

VIRGIL was the most eminent Roman poet of the Augustan Age, and the greatest of all the Latin poets. He was born in the village of Andes, now called Pietola, near Mantua, B. C. 70. He studied at Cremona at an early age, but received most of his education at Naples. His paternal farm was taken from him by one of the soldiers of Octavius during the rule of the Second Triumvirate, but it was restored to him through the favor of Octavius. Having become acquainted with the poetical genius of Virgil, Octavius, upon becoming the Emperor Augustus, and all the learned men at the imperial court, honored the poet with their friendship. He visited Athens near the end of his life, but was soon obliged to return to Italy on account of ill health, and died at Brundusium a few days after landing, B. C. 19. At his own request, he was buried at Naples, and travelers are still shown his tomb on the hill of Posilippo.

Virgil's great epic poem, the *Æneid*, is an imitation of Homer's Iliad in many important points; but is a work of genius and refined taste. His diction is more finished, and better adapted to a highly cultivated age, than that of his illustrious Greek master; but the latter surpasses him in invention and sublimity of thought. Virgil was likewise the author of four books of *Georgics*, which treat of agriculture, the planting of trees, the training of animals, and the keeping of bees. He also wrote pastorals, in imitation of those of Theócritus, the Sicilian poet. Virgil's style and versification, throughout all his works, display the highest degree of excellence.

HORACE, the Latin poet usually ranked as next to Virgil, was the greatest Roman lyric poet. He was born at Venusia, in Apulia, B. C. 65. At an early age he went to Rome for his education, and visited Athens when he was twenty-one to finish his studies. When Brutus and Cassius endeavored to restore the Republic, Horace and other Roman youths then at Athens joined their standard. Horace was at the battle of Phillippi, and in one of his poems he frankly acknowledged that he threw away his shield and fled with his defeated comrades. He had a kind friend in Virgil, who recommended him to notice at Rome, so that he was admitted to the society of the Emperor Augustus and the leading men of his court.

The fame of Horace rests mainly on his lyrics. His lyrical genius is unsurpassed in variety and versatility of talent. His chief characteristics are elegance and correctness of thought, and felicity of expression. Besides his numerous odes, Horace wrote satires and epistles in verse, which exhibit a noble earnestness seasoned with the most refined humor and pleasantry. His style is inimitable and defies every effort at translation, for which reason his writings seem flat and do not excite any taste when they are read in any other language.

OVID, the third great Roman poet of the Augustan Age, was born at Sulmo, B. C. 43. He was taken to Rome by his father in early youth to be educated for the law, but his taste for poetry and literature prevailed over every other inclination. He visited Athens and the principal cities of Asia Minor. After he had taken up his residence in Rome, he devoted his time to the Muses, and became a favorite with the leading men of the age. When Ovid was fifty-one years of age, Augustus banished him to Tomi, in the wild and barbarous province of Mœsia, on the shores of the Euxine sea. No explanation of this proceeding on the part of the Emperor has ever been discovered, but it has caused much controversy among scholars. Ovid betrayed much weakness of character under his misfortune, and endeavored by means of all the arts of entreaty and adulation to prevail upon the Emperor to recall him, but all to no purpose. Tiberius, the second Emperor, was just as inexorable as Augustus had been, and Ovid died in exile, A. D. 18.

Ovid is renowned as a poet of very fertile imagination, a lively, blooming wit, and a luxuriance of thought and expression; but the latter qualities are carried to excess. His largest and most beautiful poems are the *Metamorphoses*, or mythological stories; the subjects of which were derived from Greek writings which have perished. Ovid's work is thus highly valuable as a record of ancient mythology. He likewise wrote elegiac, didactic and other poems.

TIBULLUS and PROPERTIUS were distinguished elegiac poets. Tibullus was born about B. C. 30. The Roman critic, Quintilian, assigns him the first rank among the Latin elegiac poets. His poems display a combination of soft, tender feelings with a noble and accurate expression. His invention is rich, and is not disfigured with unnatural ornaments. Tibullus wrote four books of elegies. Propertius was born B. C. 15, was the friend of Virgil and Tibullus. His elegies, likewise consisting of four books, display a rich poetical expression and a correct style.

LIVY (Titus Livius)—the greatest of Roman historians—was the most celebrated of the prose writers of the Augustan Age, and was born at Padua, B. C. 58. He passed most of his early life at Rome, where he spent twenty years in the preparation of his excellent work, the *History of Rome*, from the founding of the city to his own time. This achievement gave him so high a reputation, even during his own lifetime, that a story is related concerning a person who traveled from Gades (now Cadiz), in Spain, to Rome, just to see the illustrious historian. Livy's historical work consisted of one hundred and forty-two books, of which only thirty-five remain. The loss of the others is mainly attributable to Pope Gregory I., who ordered every copy to be burned that could be found, because the work contained stories about pagan miracles.

Livy's great merit is his masterly style, which excels that of any other historian in clearness, liveliness and finished elegance. All readers have been delighted with the spirit and beauty of his narrative, the eloquence of his harangues, and the picturesque touches which set off his descriptions. Livy has been charged with credulity, because he relates the prodigies and the portents which he found recorded in the old annals, and which we know are mythical. But we must remember that the historian introduces these subjects into his work as characteristics of the age, and with a reminder to the reader that he does not vouch for the truth of all that he relates.

Another famous Latin prose writer of the Augustan Age was Livy's great contemporary, CORNELIUS NEPOS, the celebrated biographer. The names here given are but a portion of the eminent writers who adorned the golden age of Roman literature. In this auspicious period, which ended the rancor of civil war and restored peace to Rome, with the enjoyments of society, the example of a few distinguished poets tended to incite all to emulation. One bard caught the spirit from the genius of another, and as everything contributed to the diffusion and the promotion of the flame of literary ardor, the national spirit of poetry triumphed completely.

Though these eminent Latin writers devoted their talents to the cultivation of the same department of literature, they were so entirely free from being tainted with the jealousy with which men of genius and learning have been so frequently infected that they did not only pass their lives in habits of the closest friendship, but entertained and expressed the most sincere admiration for each other's literary works. Their example was followed by their contemporaries, and was humanized and improved by the temper of the times. No class of literary works produced at one period ever gained the admiration of mankind so strongly as did those of the Augustan Age of Rome. The blaze of poetic genius which illumined the court of Augustus was not outshone by the splendors of the age of Pericles in Athens.

The Greeks gave the first impulse to poetry. The Romans impressed the traces of it more deeply upon the world. The works of Roman genius only were accessible to imitation when Europe first awoke from its long sleep of barbarism and ignorance. For this reason the most beautiful parts of modern poetry have been formed on the classical models of the Augustan Age of Latin literature. There is scarcely a famous poetical production that has no traces of the sentiments, the character, the imagery, or the diction of those Latin poets.

We find no Latin writer on philosophical topics in the Augustan Age. The Romans had been engaged in wars and political conflicts for seven centuries, and these entirely absorbed their thoughts. Thus their language and ideas became copious in everything concerning the operations of war or politics, and well adapted to the demands of history or oratory. But the Romans did not have any exact terms for metaphysical ideas, nor a sufficient number of subjects in their minds for the purposes of philosophical illustration.

There were also so large a number of Greek schools of philosophy that the Romans had very little motive or incentive to originate any new systems; as any one might find, in the doctrines of one or another Grecian sect, tenets which might be sufficiently accommodated to his own taste and station. The Roman youth of aristocratic birth attended the schools of Athens, Rhodes and Alexandria for the purpose of learning rhetoric and philosophy. The Greek philosophers were also patronized at Rome. The respect shown by Augustus for these Greek sages was a wise measure, and exceedingly popular with the whole Roman people.

SECTION XV.—GENERAL VIEW OF ROMAN CIVILIZATION.

THE architectural art was skillfully practiced by the Romans in the very earliest period of their history. They were indebted for their primitive skill in this art to the Etruscans. Their most ancient temples were crowned with steeples, as they seem to have had a taste for both circular and elliptical forms. The original walls of Rome were constructed principally of earth, but the first Tarquin commenced the erection of a stone wall, which was finished by Servius Tullius, who added battlements and a fosse to the work. Tarquin the Proud completed the Capitol, which had been founded by his father, and both of these are credited with the construction of the *cloaca*, or drains of the city. These were so skillfully and substantially formed that they have excited the wonder and admiration of after times. We have already described the great public edifices of the city of Rome.

Sculpture was introduced into Rome from Etruria in the earliest ages of the city; but for a long time only statues of the gods were formed, and these were made only of wood or clay. Afterwards representations of warriors were exhibited, but the Romans did not possess skill in the fabrication of these figures. The first brazen statue at Rome was set up in the Temple of Ceres, and the cost of it was defrayed out of the property of Cassius, who was condemned on the charge of aspiring to arbitrary power.

The vanity of Cassius caused him to display his own image in front of the altar of Vesta, but the Censors would not permit it to remain, and they ordained that no statue of any citizen, however renowned, should be erected by private gratitude or respect; but this restriction was subsequently removed, and Rome abounded with statues.

The Romans made some efforts at painting, but with only partial success. A citizen named Fabius derived the appellation of *Pictor*, or "painter," from his performance in this department of the fine arts, before the Punic Wars; but we know nothing of his skill. Valerius Messala publicly exhibited a picture of a battle in which he had defeated the Carthaginians, but the name of the battle is not mentioned. Scipio Asiaticus, with as much ostentation, displayed in the Capitol a pictorial representation of his victories over Antiochus the Great of Syria. Lucius Mancinus obtained the Consulate by pointing out the beauties of a picture illustrating his achievements to the admiring citizens.

When the conquest of Greece had excited a general taste for refined works of art, many of the Romans imitated the Grecian productions which they were unable to excel. Julius Cæsar expended vast sums in purchasing pictures of the famous Greek painters. Augustus patronized this fine art, and specially encouraged portrait painters.

In early times all Romans lived in humble dwellings; but in later times the wealthy occupied splendid mansions, called *villas*, the floors of which were inlaid with stone or marble in mosaic, the walls and ceilings gilded and ornamented, the roofs terraced and covered with artificial gardens, and the furniture glittering with tortoise shell and ivory. The chief apartments were on the ground floor, and were entered through the *atrium*, or great entrance-room, in which the nobles ranged the images of their ancestors, hung the family portraits, and received their clients. The windows were at first mere openings with shutters, but in the time of the Empire they were closed with glass obtained at great expense from the East. Artificial heat was supplied by braziers.

The walls and ceilings of Roman dwellings were painted in colors, or frescoed with representations of mythological groups, landscapes, or scenes from daily life. Roman furniture consisted of tables, chairs, dinner-couches, lamps, vases, mirrors, urns, incense-burners, etc. The floors were covered with many-colored carpets from Eastern looms. Houses were heated by means of fire-places or portable furnaces; sometimes by admitting air heated by a furnace beneath. Beautifully-formed oil-lamps were used for lighting. The lamps were supported upon a beautiful candelabra.

The early Romans lived mostly on bread and pot-herbs; but when conquests brought wealth, all ranks indulged in luxuries, so that in the degenerate ages of Rome eating the most delicious food was the great end of life to many Romans. The Romans had three meals—*jentaculum*, taken soon after rising; *prandium*, the middle meal; and *cœna*, taken about three o'clock. Cœna, the last and principal meal, was in later times served with great magnificence. For this meal particularly, the guest-chambers or eating-halls were constructed. The table, being either quadrangular or rounded, had three couches on each side, each couch having three pillows on which to support the arm in reclining. Nine persons were accordingly accommodated at a table; the post of honor being the middle place, and all reclining on the left arm.

At the entertainments of early and frugal times, only the ordinary dress was used; but with the advance of luxury, a peculiar habit, light and easy, became the custom at convivial meetings. Sitting was the attitude at meals in primitive times; but couches were subsequently brought into use, first for the men only, but afterwards for both sexes. Various meats and vegetables were eaten. Pure wine, and wine mixed with honey (*mulsum*), and with water (*calda*), were drunk at feasts by the guests crowned with chaplets. Falernian wine was of bright amber tint. While eating, the Romans reclined on their low couches around the table, instead of sitting upright. There were at first no table-cloths. Instead of knives and forks, two spoons (*cochlear* and *lingula*) were used. On the table were oil-lamps. The dishes were brought and removed by slaves.

At the principal meal of the rich there were usually three courses. The first consisted of eggs, salad, radishes, etc., to excite the appetite; with which they generally drank mead or mulsum. The second course constituted the essential portion of the meal. The third was the dessert, consisting of fruits, pastry and confectionery. It was the custom at social banquets to appoint a master of the feast, who appears to have been selected by a throw of the dice. Healths were drunk, the memory of the gods and heroes being generally honored in the first place. Social games or plays were practiced, after and during the meal, between the courses and dishes.

During the period of the Republic it was the custom for a patron to invite at times all his clients to a common supper in his halls. In the time of the Empire it became customary to give the clients a small basket of food, instead of a supper. Wine was the beverage which the Romans mainly used, and there were very many varieties. The most celebrated of Italian wines were the Falernian, already alluded to, and the Marsic. Of the foreign wines, the Lesbian and Chian had the preference. One of the most important things in the eyes of a wealthy Roman was to have a good supply of choice and approved wines for his domestic comfort and happiness. For this reason, great attention was bestowed on the culture of the vine, even though other branches of agriculture were to be neglected. The wine was kept in *amphoræ*, or earthen jars, ranged around the walls of the cellar, partially sunk in sand; each jar having a mark to denote the name of the Consul in office when the wine was made. The villa of Diomedes, in Pompeii, has a very large cellar, which extends around and under the entire garden, and is ventilated and lighted by port-holes from above. Some of the wine-jars are yet standing as they were packed and labeled more than eighteen centuries ago.

The Romans remained a temperate and frugal people until their armies marched into Asia. After their triumph over Antiochus the Great of Syria, the various pleasures and the dissolute indulgences of Ionia, Lydia and Syria enticed the stern and hardy conquerors to imitation; and thenceforth successive relaxations of the old method of discipline and manners were introduced. Every kind of voluptuous indulgence came into vogue. But luxury only attained its full height, and the decline of morals proceeded to the utmost extreme of depravity, after the death of the Emperor Augustus, whose Censorial authority and powerful influence checked the progress of degeneracy for a time. Augustus was not

ROMAN CITIZEN IN TOGA.

himself a model of purity, but he watched over the preservation of good morals with apparent anxiety. Most of his successors were less vigilant in that regard. An innocent species of luxury was that dependent upon dress and personal ornament. After the establishment of the Empire, the simplicity of attire gave way to fondness for gorgeous apparel among the higher classes.

Roman garments were made of wool until the second century after Christ, when linen was introduced. The Roman inner-dress consisted of tunics, or short under-garments with sleeves. The most remarkable dress of the men was the *toga*, or loose robe, wrapped around the body so as to cover the left arm and leave the right nearly bare. This woolen toga, full for the rich and scanty for the poor, had early become the distinctive dress of the Roman nation. In later times its use in the streets was exchanged for the *pallium*, or *lacerna*, a mantle of warm cloth, which was also at first sleeveless and short, like a waistcoat, but

ROMAN LADY IN STOLA.

was gradually lengthened, and afterwards received the addition of sleeves and was fastened by a belt. When a Roman was running for office he marked his toga with chalk, thus making it white, in Latin *candida*, whence our word *candidate*. Boys wore a toga with a broad purple hem until the age of sixteen, when they put on the manly toga.

The distinctive dress of the Roman women was the *stola*, or loose frock, fastened about the person with a double girdle. The *palla*, or gay-colored mantle, was worn out of doors. The hair, encircled with a garland of roses, was fastened with a gold pin; while pearls and gold adorned the neck and arms. In the progress of refinement females had three garments. The stola, being the outer one, was richly ornamented with embroidery and clasps of gold. The three garments were intended to be worn together, but the poor had frequently only one. This palla for the women extended down to the feet, while the lacerna for the men reached only to the knees.

Romans of both sexes went with their heads uncovered, except when on journeys, when dark-colored hoods were worn. At sacrifices, festivals and games, or in a long journey, many wore a woolen or leather cap. When a slave became a freedman, he was permitted the constant use of the *pileus*, or Phrygian cap, as a mark of liberty. In the house *soleæ* were strapped to the bare feet, but out of doors the *calceus*, or shoe, was worn. On the ring-finger—the fourth of the left hand—every Roman of rank had a massive signet-ring. Fops loaded every finger with jewels.

Senators were distinguished by a tunic having broad studs or knobs worked into it. The knights had narrow studs, and the common people none at all. The kings of early Rome wore a white toga, with a broad purple border, and protuberances of scarlet. The Roman Emperors wore a toga entirely of purple when in public. Triumphant generals wore a toga adorned with various representations in embroidery, resembling the work of the pencil, and for that reason call *toga picta*.

The Roman ensigns of royalty were borrowed from the Etruscans, and consisted of a golden crown, an ivory chair, an ivory scepter surmounted by an eagle, a white toga with purple embroidery or borderings, and a body of twelve lictors, who went before the king, each carrying a *fasces*, or bundle of rods with an axe in the middle. After the abolition of kingly government,

ROMAN CHARIOT RACE.

GENERAL VIEW OF CIVILIZATION.

the use of lictors was continued; the Consuls being accompanied by twelve of them, bearing their fasces, which has become emblematical of a republic.

The Romans spent much time in their splendid baths. The luxurious patricians of the Empire bathed seven or eight times a day. The edifices designed for public baths were of extraordinary size and magnificence. They were erected among extensive gardens and walks, and were surrounded by porticos. marble, and three thousand persons could be seated in them at one time. The baths of the Emperor Diocletian surpassed all others in size and sumptuous decoration. One of its halls is now used as a church by the Carthusians, and is among the largest and the most magnificent of modern Rome.

The chief public amusements of the Romans were the *circus*, the *theater* and the *amphitheater*. At the circus they bet on their favorite horses and charioteers. At

ROMAN LADY AT HER TOILET.

The main edifice contained spacious halls for swimming and bathing, others for various athletic exercises, and others for the declamations of poets and the lectures of philosophers, or for all kinds of polite and manly diversion. Architecture, sculpture and painting were made to exhaust their refinements on these establishments, which were compared to cities, on account of their vast extent. The baths of the Emperor Caracalla were ornamented with two hundred pillars and sixteen hundred seats of the theater they witnessed tragedies and comedies. At the amphitheater they beheld with delight the bloody combats of gladiators. The last was the most brutal pastime of the Romans. The gladiators were slaves, captives, condemned criminals and hired ruffians. They fought in the arena, with each other, or with lions, tigers, leopards and elephants. The victor, if a captive or a slave, obtained his freedom; while a freeman obtained a pecuniary recompense. The vanquished were put to death, unless the spec-

2—66.-U. H.

tators, by an upward movement of the thumb, signified their wish to spare the life of the unfortunate wretch. Games were exhibited by the Emperors and wealthy Romans for weeks, and thousands of wild beasts and gladiators would be killed, to the great delight of all classes of Romans, including even ladies of rank.

Julius Cæsar gratified the people with a combat between five hundred men and twenty elephants. On another occasion he exhibited a thousand combatants, on horseback and on foot, against twenty elephants, each with a tower on his back containing sixty warriors. The Emperor Cómmodus himself fought with the gladiators in the amphitheater, where he conquered seven hundred and fifty times, and consequently styled himself "Conqueror of a Thousand Gladiators."

After acquiring some naval skill, the Romans added sea-fights to their other amusements. An extensive edifice was erected surrounding a channel large enough for the evolutions of a large number of galleys. Sometimes the exhibitions were simply trials of speed; but at other times they were regular naval engagements, in which there was bloodshed merely for the gratification of the hard-hearted spectators.

The brutality which ever characterized the Romans, even in the progress of refinement, was clearly evinced by the institution and continuance of gladiatorial combats. Such exhibitions could only entertain a people having a strong tincture of ferocity in their nature. It has been supposed that the custom of killing slaves at the funerals of princes and heroes, or of forcing them to fight with each other, was the origin of the practice of gladiatorial combats. But the Roman fondness for war was doubtless the chief cause.

Two citizens named Brutus are mentioned as the first who exhibited gladiators at Rome, and this exhibition was at their father's funeral. The example which they set was followed by citizens and magistrates alike. At first criminals, captives or slaves were employed on these occasions. Even trivial offenses were considered sufficient to justify an exposure of a fellow-creature to the risk of death. Afterwards, citizens who had not been guilty of any crime, but who desired to display their courage, were induced to enter the lists; and regular schools of gladiators were instituted.

The gladiators did not all fight with the same weapons, or in the same manner. Some were completely armed, while others had merely a trident and a net for entangling adversaries. These combats were sometimes introduced at social gatherings to enliven the festivities. Guests who could thus be entertained may well be regarded as but little above cannibals.

The private amusements of the Romans display the national characteristics in many instances. They had various methods of ball-playing. One method depended on the triangular position of three persons who threw the ball to each other, the first who let it fall being the loser. The quoit was often thrown for private diversion, and boys and young men were fond of playing with a hoop furnished with rings. A game which resembled chess, and required as much skill, was likewise played. The Romans were especially fond of games of risk; dice being shaken and thrown out in a body, as in modern times. The Emperor Augustus was much addicted to this pastime, notwithstanding that it was forbidden by law.

As already observed, the manners of the early Romans were marked with simplicity. As they were not ashamed of their sentiments or their conduct, they avoided all artifice and dissimulation as degrading. They were attentive to decorum and respectful to their superiors, but not servilely submissive. They were not wholly without friendship, but they were destitute of the warmth of attachment and the tenderness of sympathy. In their paternal relations they were not so kind and acquiescent as they were stern and haughty. In the relations of husband and master they were inclined to be arbitrary and impetuous. The hardihood generated by their political zeal gradually entered into their social nature

and marked their portrait with harsh lines. The Romans preserved this rigidity of character for ages, and it was even found in their women, who were thus in a considerable degree devoid of that softness which ought to characterize the female sex. Altogether, the early Romans possessed the characteristics which distinguished the Spartans; both these nations having cultivated the military virtues, which they prized above all else.

Roman books were rolls of papyrus bark, or parchment, written upon with a reed pen, dipped in lamp-black, or sepia. The back of the sheet was often stained with saffron, and its edges were smoothed and blackened; while the ends of the stick on which it was rolled were adorned with ivory or gilt wood, whence our word *volume*, a roll. Writing was done with a sharp instrument, or *stylus*, upon thin wooden tablets coated with wax. These were then tied up with linen thread, the knot being sealed with wax and stamped with a ring.

The Roman mother took charge of the early education of her children; after which the father assumed that duty, and his authority over his sons lasted until his death, unless he resigned it, or the son became a flamen of Jupiter. Elementary schools for boys and girls existed at Rome from an early period; but for centuries only reading, writing and arithmetic were taught. In later ages the Greek language and literature were taught. School punishments were severe and flogging was frequent.

The household work of the Romans was all done by slaves. In early times there were a few slaves to each household, but in the time of the Empire there were slaves for every kind of work. There were born slaves and bought slaves. The born slaves were the children of persons who had been reduced to slavery by being taken captive in war. The common sort of slaves were sold like cattle in the slave-market, but the more beautiful and valuable were disposed of by private bargain in the taverns. Prices varied from twenty dollars to four thousand dollars.

Roman marriages were always preceded by a solemn affiance or betrothment, which often occurred many years previous to the wedding, and even during the childhood of the parties. The Romans had three forms of marriage. The highest was called *confarreatio*. The bride, dressed in a white robe with purple fringe, which was bound around the waist by a marriage girdle, and her face covered with a bright yellow veil, was taken forcibly, as it were, from the arms of her mother or nearest relative, and was escorted by torchlight to her future home. A cake (*far*) was carried before her, and she carried a distaff and spindle with wool.

When she arrived at the flower-wreathed portal, she was lifted over the threshold, lest she might stumble upon it—a mishap which would be an evil omen. She was supported by two youths, one on each side; while another preceded her with a lighted torch or flambeau; and sometimes a fourth followed, carrying the bride's little furniture in a covered vase. She bound the door-posts of her new residence with white woolen fillets, and anointed them with the fat of wolves. She then stepped upon a sheepskin spread before the entrance, and called aloud for the bridegroom, who instantly came and offered her the key of the house, which she handed to the chief servant. Her husband also brought fire and water, which both he and his bride then touched, as a symbol of purity and fidelity. Music, singing and feasting followed. The ceremony ended with a marriage supper, after which the husband scattered nuts among the boys.

Like the Greeks, the Romans believed that the souls of the unburied dead wandered about without rest, not being admitted into Hades. When a Roman died, the body was laid out on a bier and placed in the atrium of the house for some days, with the images of the ancestors of the deceased persons; and a branch of cypress or pine was placed before the dwelling, as an emblem of death. Children and youth were buried at night, with lighted torches and without attendants; but adults were interred by day, and with a certain degree of ceremony, according to rank. The funeral of a distinguished individual was announced in the city previously by a herald.

On the day of burial, the corpse was taken to the Forum, accompanied by a funeral procession, in which the musicians and women hired as mourners advanced first, uttering lamentations and singing the funeral song. Next in the procession came those who bore the images of the ancestors of the deceased; followed by the relatives, all dressed in black. Then came players, mimics and dancers, one of them imitating the words and actions of the deceased; after which came the corpse, supported by bearers, and followed by a numerous train of both sexes.

At the Forum an address was delivered by a relative, eulogizing the deeds of the deceased and those of his ancestry. The procession then moved to a place beyond the walls, where the body was buried, or, in later times, burned. When a corpse was to be burned, it was laid on a funeral pile, and sprinkled with spices, or anointed with oil; after which the nearest relatives applied the torch, with averted faces. Weapons, clothing, and other articles belonging to the deceased, were thrown upon the pile; and when the whole was consumed, the embers were quenched with wine. The bones and ashes were afterwards collected and put into an urn, sometimes with a small phial of tears. The urn was solemnly laid in the earth or in a tomb. Nine days after the funeral, articles of food were placed beside the tomb, which was beautifully decorated with wreaths; and beside the niches were placed lamps and an inscription.

The Roman army was divided into legions, consisting of infantry and cavalry. The legion originally consisted of three thousand infantry and three hundred cavalry, but afterwards it contained from five thousand to six thousand men. Before the time of

ROMAN ARMOR.

Marius and Sulla all Roman citizens were subject to military duty; but from that time a soldier remained constantly with the army for twenty years. The legion then consisted of ten cohorts of six hundred men each, all under pay; and the army was then composed of legionaries and auxiliaries sent from the provinces or from the allied states. Under Augustus the legion consisted of seven thousand men. There were also mercenaries, as slingers from the Balearic Isles and bowmen from Crete.

A Roman legion was drawn up in three ranks, designated respectively as the *Hastati*, the *Principes* and the *Triarii*. There were also *velites*, or light troops, who detached themselves from the main body of the army at the beginning of a battle, and skirmished with missiles. The Hastati were young men in the bloom of life and occupied the front rank. The Principes were men in the full vigor of middle age and composed the second rank. The Triarii were veterans and constituted the rear rank. The legion was divided into *maniples*, or companies, of a hundred men each; each company being commanded by a *centurion*, or captain, and having its own standard, consisting of a silver eagle on a pole.

The Roman legionaries wore a coat-of-mail formed of metal or hide and worked over with little iron bands, an iron or brazen helmet, and greaves for the legs plated with iron; carried a large round shield, made of wood, leather and iron; and were armed with a short but stiff and pointed sword, worn on the right side, and with two *pilums*, or javelins. The Roman knights, or cavalry, wore the same kind of coats-of-mail, helmets and greaves, carried the same kind of shields, and were armed with a pilum and a sword. The mercenaries wore a leather helmet, carried a small round shield, and were armed with a pilum and with bows and slings.

The only instruments of martial music were horns and trumpets. No one could be a soldier under seventeen years of age. All between the ages of seventeen and forty-five were liable to service. Those over forty-five were exempt. Sixteen years was the regular term of service for the infantry, and ten for the cavalry. Persons without property were not enrolled for service, because they were not supposed to have sufficient bravery and patriotism, as they had nothing to lose.

For three centuries after the founding of the city, the Roman soldiers received no pay; but afterwards they were allowed a stipend of two bushels of wheat per month and three ounces of brass per day; this pay being subsequently increased. Those who distinguished themselves for their valor in battle were honored with various extraordinary rewards. Among the most common were golden and gilded crowns, such as the camp-crown for those who first entered the enemy's intrenchments; the mural crown for those who first scaled the walls of a city; and the naval crown for those who captured a ship of war. Wreaths and crowns formed of leaves and blossoms were also general, such as the civic crown of oak-leaves for rescuing a citizen from death or captivity; the obsidional crown of grass for relieving a besieged city; and the triumphal crown of laurel, worn by the general at his triumph.

When a Roman army took the field, it marched in the following order. First came the light-armed troops; followed by the heavy-armed, both infantry and cavalry; after which came the pioneers; next the baggage of the general and his horses, guarded by cavalry; then the general himself; then the Tribunes; then the standards; then the choice men of the army; and lastly the servants and drivers of beasts.

No part of Roman discipline was more admirable than the encampment of the army. The camp was regularly measured out and fortified by a ditch before any soldier was allowed sleep or refreshment, no matter how fatigued the troops might have been by a long march or a severe battle. The Roman camp was an exact square of four hundred feet, with a rampart of earth and stakes three feet high, surrounded by a ditch nine feet wide and seven feet deep. Careful watch was kept over the camp at night, and pickets were frequently sent out to guard against a surprise and to see that the sentinels were vigilant. The arrangements in every Roman camp being the same, a Roman soldier always knew where he properly belonged, and was easily able to find the rallying point of his division in case of an alarm.

In the discipline of the Roman camp, the soldiers were occupied with various exercises, from which an army was called *exercitus* in Latin. These exercises included walking and running while being completely armed, leaping, swimming, vaulting upon wooden horses, shooting arrows, hurling javelins, carrying weights, attacking the wooden image of a man as an enemy, etc. The comfort of a Roman soldier made it necessary that he should be able to walk or run in complete armor with perfect ease. On ordinary marches he was under the necessity of carrying a load weighing sixty pounds and consisting of his provisions and usual implements, along with his weapons and armor.

Catapults to discharge darts, and the ballista to hurl stones, were used to attack walls. Walls were also assailed with a battering-ram, a long beam with an iron head, which was driven against the masonry by a body of men till a breach was made. Besieging-towers of several stories were also used; and on them were soldiers, who cleared the walls by means of their missiles, or

THE ROMAN FORUM

made a direct attack by the drawbridges. The besiegers protected themselves while scaling or undermining walls by joining their shields together so as to form a *testudo* (tortoise); while the garrison showered their arrows and javelins, and hurled great rocks upon their assailants, and tried to turn aside or grapple the battering-ram.

The Romans had three kinds of ships— the war-galley, the transport and the ship of burden. The war-galley was mainly propelled by oars. The transport was often towed by the war-galley. The ship of burden was moved by sails. Roman ships of burden were usually much inferior in size to modern merchant vessels, although some of enormous length are mentioned. In the reign of the Emperor Caracalla, a great obelisk was transported from Egypt to Rome, in a ship which must have been of more than a thousand tons burden.

Roman ships of war sometimes had five rows of oars. Some had turrets for soldiers and warlike engines. Others had sharp prows covered with brass for the purpose of dashing against the vessels of their enemies. Ancient naval tactics were very simple. The ships came at once to close action, and the battle was a combat between single vessels. For this reason the personal valor of the Romans was more than a match for the naval skill of the Carthaginians; thus enabling them to acquire the supremacy of the seas as well as the ascendency on land.

As we have already seen, the Roman *triumph* was a grand military pageant in honor to a victorious general. It consisted of a grand procession along the Via Sacra (Sacred Street) to the Capitol, where a bull or an ox was sacrificed to Jupiter. It was an occasion of general rejoicing. The temples were thrown open and adorned with flowers; and the people crowded the streets, or occupied balconies or temporary scaffoldings, to gaze on the spectacle. The victorious commander entered the city by the gate of triumph, in a chariot drawn by four horses, and was met by the Senate and the magistrates. The procession then passed on, consisting of the civil officers; the spoils of the vanquished foe; the priests with the victims for sacrifice; captives of all ranks in chains; the lictors with their fasces; the victor with a laurel bough in his right hand and a scepter in his left, and with a laurel wreath on his head; while the victorious army brought up the rear.

The description which Plutarch gives of the splendid triumph with which Æmilius Paulus was honored for his glorious termination of the war with Perseus, King of Macedon, by his great victory at Pydna, will give the reader an adequate idea of the magnificence which the Romans displayed on these festive occasions.

The people erected scaffolds in the Forum and in the Circus Maximus, and in every other quarter of the city where they were best able to view the pomp. The spectators were attired in white apparel. All the temples were open, and full of garlands and perfumes. The ways were cleared and cleansed by a great number of officers, who drove away all who thronged the passage or straggled up and down.

The triumph continued three days. On the first day, which was almost too short for the sight, were to be seen the statues, pictures, and images of an extraordinary size, taken from the vanquished foe, drawn upon seven hundred and fifty chariots. On the second day the fairest and richest armor of the Macedonians, both of brass and steel, all newly-furbished and glittering, was conveyed in a vast train of wagons. This armor appeared to be tumbled carelessly on heaps and by chance, although piled up with the greatest art and order. Helmets were thrown on shields, and coats of mail upon greaves; Cretan targets and Thracian bucklers, and quivers of arrows, lay huddled among the horses' bits; while the points of naked swords, intermixed with long spears, appeared through this mass of arms and equipments. All these arms were tied together with such ease that they struck against one another as they were drawn along, and made so harsh and terrible a noise that the very spoils of the con-

GENERAL VIEW OF CIVILIZATION.

quered enemy could not be viewed without dread. After these wagons loaded with armor, followed three thousand men, carrying the coined silver in three hundred and fifty vessels, each weighing three talents and being carried by four men. Others brought silver bowls, goblets and cups, all arranged in such order as to make the best show, and all as valuable for their size as for the thickness of their engraved work.

On the third day, early in the morning, first came the trumpeters, who did not sound as they were accustomed to do in a procession or solemn entry, but such a charge as the Romans used when they encouraged their soldiers to fight. Next followed young men, girt about with girdles curiously wrought, leading one hundred and twenty stalled oxen to the sacrifice, with their horns gilded and their heads adorned with ribands and garlands; and with these were boys carrying dishes of silver and gold.

After these was brought the gold coin, divided into seventy-seven vessels weighing three talents each, resembling the vessels containing the silver. Next followed those bringing the consecrated bowl, which Æmilius Paulus caused to be made, and which weighed ten talents and was adorned with precious stones. The cups of Antigonus and Seleucus were next exposed to view, along with those made after the fashion invented by Thericles, and with all the gold plate used at the table of Perseus.

Then came the chariot of Perseus, carrying his armor, with his diadem thereon. After a short interval the vanquished king's children were led captives, and with them were a train of nurses, masters and governors, all of whom wept and extended their hands to the spectators, and taught the little infants to implore their compassion. There were two sons and a daughter of the fallen monarch, who, on account of their tender age, were wholly insensible of the magnitude of their misery. This insensibility of their condition made it much more deplorable, because Perseus himself was little regarded as he passed along, while the Romans looked with pity upon the infants, and many of them were unable to refrain from shedding tears. All viewed the scene with a mingling of sorrow and joy until the children had passed.

After the children and the attendants followed Perseus himself, attired in black and wearing slippers, in accordance with the Macedonian custom. He looked like a person wholly astonished and devoid of reason, because of the magnitude of the catastrophe which had befallen him. Then came a large company of his friends and familiars, with their countenances disfigured with grief, and who manifested their sorrow for their king's misfortune, and their total disregard for their own, by their tears and constant looking upon Perseus.

After these were carried four hundred gold crowns, which had been sent to Æmilius Paulus as a reward for his valor, from the cities by their respective ambassadors. Then came Æmilius Paulus himself, seated on a chariot magnificently adorned, attired in a garment of purple interwoven with gold, and carrying a laurel branch in his right hand. This victorious general was a man worthy to be beheld even without these ensigns of power. After the chariot of the triumphant commander followed his entire army, the soldiers each also carrying laurel boughs in their hands, and all arranged into bands and companies; some singing odes, in accordance with the usual custom, mingled with raillery; others singing songs of triumph and the praises of their general, whom all men admired and considered happy, but whom the good did not envy.

SECTION XVI.—FLOURISHING PERIOD OF THE EMPIRE.

FROM the battle of Actium, the Roman Empire may be said to have really dated, as Octavius then became sole master of the Roman world (B. C. 31); though it was a few years later (B. C. 27) when the Roman Senate conferred upon him all the powers of sovereignty with the titles of *Augustus* (the *Divine*) and *Imperator*, or *Emperor* (chief commander); and gave his name to the sixth (now eighth) month, as the name of Julius Cæsar had been given to the fifth (now seventh) month. Octavius himself dated his Empire from the battle of Actium, when he was thirty-two years of age. Dating from that event, his reign lasted forty-five years. No sooner had he thus become master of the Roman world than he at once proceeded to establish an imperial monarchy under republican forms upon the ruins of the Republic.

During his long reign he was enabled to establish the Empire on secure foundations, and to settle it so firmly that it continued to survive for centuries, notwithstanding the great trials to which it was subjected. His prudence and sagacity made it possible for him to avoid the errors of his grand-uncle, Julius Cæsar, and to secure the supreme power into his own hands, while seeming to conform strictly to the forms of law. In this manner he conciliated the republicans, who fancied that they saw the Republic revived under his rule, while the monarchists were delighted upon beholding their most cherished wishes thus realized under the young Cæsar.

Augustus prudently refrained from assuming the title of Dictator, or the rank or state of a king. He lived as a wealthy Senator in his mansion on the Palatine Hill, and he always went abroad without the pomp or the retinue of a monarch. Notwithstanding all his apparent regard for republican forms, Augustus was absolute master of the Empire, attaining this end by personally assuming the most important civil offices, which had previously been held by different individuals. His most general title was that of Imperator, which had been formerly held by the Consular commanders during their terms of office.

As Imperator, or chief commander, Augustus held the *proconsulare imperium*, or command of all the provinces. As *Princeps Senatus* (Prince of the Senate), which he became in B. C. 28, he had the right to propose laws to that famous body, which it ratified with the readiest subserviency. As *Perpetual Tribune of the People*, involved in the *tribunicia potestas*, which title he obtained in B. C. 23, his person was rendered sacred. As *Perpetual Consul*, involved in the *consularis potestas*, and *Perpetual Censor*, involved in the *potestas censoria*, both of which titles he obtained in B. C. 19, he possessed all the powers belonging to those offices. As *Pontifex Maximus* (religious superintendent), which office he assumed upon the death of Lepidus, in B. C. 12, he was supreme in all religious affairs. The agnomen of *Augustus* and the honorary title of *Pater Patriæ* were simple distinctions which conferred no rights or powers.

The Senate continued to exist nominally, as a check upon Augustus, but really as a body subservient to his wishes. All the bolder leaders had perished in the recent civil wars, and those who survived cared more for the Emperor's favor than for their own rights or independence. There were six hundred Senators, who were such persons as Augustus, when Censor, had permitted to remain, and such as he now appointed to the Senatorial office. The Senate was composed, not only of Romans and Italians, but also of provincials to some extent. These provincial Senators were, however, required to reside in Italy, and in later ages they were obliged to be landholders in that country. No one could be a Senator without possessing a property qualification,

COLOSSAL STATUE OF AUGUSTUS.

first placed by Augustus at four hundred thousand sesterces, and gradually raised to twelve hundred thousand sesterces.

The Senate nominally remained in possession of its former powers and privileges. In theory the Emperor obtained his authority from that body, which was recognized as the ultimate seat of the civil power and authority; and Augustus always affected the most scrupulous desire to obtain its assent to his measures—a very easy task, because all the Senators were wholly subservient to him. At a subsequent period the Senate dwindled to utter insignificance, while the Emperors became as absolute despots as Oriental potentates.

Augustus wisely left to the Roman people some remnants of their former privileges. The Emperor nominated the Consuls and one-half of the other magistrates, while the remaining magistrates were elected by the people from among the candidates approved by the Emperor. The old course of legislation remained undisturbed, and the whole series of *Leges Juliæ*, enacted under Augustus, were sanctioned by both the Senate and the Comitia Centuriata. Only the judicial rights of the Roman people were wholly extinguished at this time, the place of the *provocatio ad populum* giving way to the prerogative of pardon assumed by the Emperor. The Empire, however, naturally tended to encroach gradually more and more upon the remaining popular rights; and after the death of Augustus the Roman people practically ceased possessing any real political power or privilege, though the great assemblies of the people maintained a certain show of election and a certain title to a share in legislation to the very end of the existence of the Empire.

Thus, though Augustus had gained the sovereign power by his army, he resolved to govern the Empire with the aid of the Senate; which body, though so greatly fallen from its former splendor, he knew was the best constituted, and the most remarkable for wisdom and justice, of all the different orders of the Roman state. He therefore shared with the Senate the chief power in the administration of his government, while he secured the loyalty of the people and the army by donations and acts of favor. In this way the Emperor caused the odium of severity to fall upon the Senate, while he solely retained the popularity of pardon.

By thus restoring the splendor of the Senate to a certain extent, and discountenancing corruption, Augustus pretended to reserve to himself a very moderate share of authority, to which no one could object— simply, the power to compel all ranks of Romans to do their duty. This was practically retaining the absolute control of the state in his own hands; though the ignorant masses viewed his seeming moderation with astonishment, believing themselves restored to their political freedom; while the Senate fancied its former power reëstablished in every respect but the tendency to injustice. It was even asserted that by such a government the Romans did not lose any of the happiness which could be secured to them by liberty, while they were thus exempt from all the evils occasioned by liberty.

The great extent of the Empire and the multiplicity of its affairs rendered it necessary for the Emperor to have the aid of others in the government. He accordingly established a regularly-constituted Council of State to assist him. This Council of State discussed and prepared all important public affairs and all measures of legislation, and consisted of the chief annual magistrates and fifteen Senators chosen by the Senate for a term of six months.

The old offices were continued and new ones were created. The most important of the new offices were the Præfect of the city and the commander of the Prætorian Guard. The City Cohorts, an armed police force, kept order in Rome; and the ten thousand Prætorian Guards protected the Emperor's person. The multitude in the city were also kept in order by a succession of splendid games and shows, and by liberal supplies of corn, wine and oil.

The provinces of the Roman Empire were ruled by the Emperor and the Senate jointly. Those which were securely at peace were called *Senatorial Provinces*, and were governed by Proconsuls appointed by the Senate. Those which required the presence of an army were called *Imperial Provinces*, and were managed by the Emperor or his legates. The standing army which kept this dominion in subjection numbered three hundred and fifty thousand men; one-half consisting of twenty-five Italian legions, each legion numbering nearly seven thousand men, and the other half embracing the provincial auxiliaries. Augustus maintained seventeen legions in Europe—eight on the Rhine, four on the Danube, three in Spain, and two in Dalmatia. He kept eight more in Asia and Africa. Two powerful fleets were stationed on the Italian coasts—one at Ravenna to guard the Adriatic; and the other at Misenum, near Naples, to protect the western portion of the Mediterranean.

Thus, although the Roman Empire was a monarchy, the old forms of the Republic were faithfully preserved. The Consuls were elected every year in the usual manner, and the Senate discussed matters of state as if the legislative power was still vested in that body. As the name of king still continued odious to Roman ears, Augustus was obliged to content himself with the title of Imperator, which had been borne by the commanders of Roman armies in the best days of the Republic; thus showing to what extent mankind are influenced by names.

Upon assuming the supreme power, Augustus underwent an entire change of character. He became distinguished for his clemency and moderation; and endeavored, by a beneficent and paternal administration, to obliterate the remembrance of the cruelties of which he had been guilty as one of the Triumvirs. By a cool and calculating policy, he was thus transformed into a mild and merciful ruler, really desirous of promoting the welfare and happiness of his subjects.

Some writers tell us that Augustus at first desired to resign his power, as did Sulla, but that he was dissuaded from such a course by his friends, Agrippa and Mecænas, who truly represented to him that the Roman state could not be governed any longer by its old constitution, and that he would merely retire to make room for another master. Nevertheless, Augustus went through the form of an abdication in the Senate, but resumed his authority, on the urgent request of that body. To still further display his moderation, he consented only to hold the sovereign power for ten years—an example which was followed by all his successors. This gave rise to the *Sacra decennalia*, or the festival celebrated at each renewal of the imperial authority.

Amid all the adulations of the Senate and the people, Augustus still remembered that he was indebted to the army for his elevation. He accordingly exerted himself diligently to attach the soldiers to his interest, dispersing his veterans over Italy in thirty-two colonies, dispossessing the inhabitants in many places to make room for these new settlers.

It is computed that the revenues of the Roman Empire under Augustus amounted to two hundred million dollars; but this vast sum was only about sufficient to defray the expenses of the civil, military and naval establishments, and of the public works undertaken to adorn the metropolis.

By assuming the title of Pontifex Maximus upon the death of Lepidus, B. C. 12, Augustus became the head of the state religion, like the ancient kings; thus acquiring more power than he had previously exercised as a sovereign. The title of Imperator, or Emperor, as conferred on Julius Cæsar, was simply a military one, and merely had reference to his command over the Roman armies; but with regard to Augustus and his successors, this title likewise implied the sovereignty of the Empire; and in this sense it has been transmitted to modern times. The titles of Augustus, Cæsar, and Imperator, or Emperor, were borne by all the successors of this Emperor. The title *Kaiser*, the German for *Cæsar*, has been borne by all the sovereign rulers of the German and Austrian Empires since the fall of Rome. The title *Czar*, as borne by the absolute ruler of the Russian Empire for the last three centuries, also means *Cæsar*.

As long as the Roman Empire lasted, it was customary to speak of the Roman sovereign as *Imperator* (or *Emperor*), when alluding to his military capacity, and to call him *Cæsar* when referring to his civil authority. Formerly, any general invested with the title of Imperator was distinguished by a purple robe; but from this time the purple was an ensign of imperial dignity.

Augustus exercised his supreme authority by excluding a number of ignorant and unfit individuals from the Senate, by this means reducing that body to six hundred members. He recalled many who had been banished for political offenses, and restored their estates. He likewise organized an efficient and vigilant police, which freed Italy from the molestation of the banditti which had infested the country and the provincial towns during the civil wars, and which even had annoyed Rome itself.

Augustus also repaired the great Italian roads, which had been allowed to lapse into a bad condition. The public roads were among the most valuable, no less than the most durable, monuments of the power and greatness of the Roman nation. Some of these roads extended from the center of the city of Rome to the most distant provinces of the Roman Empire. The portions of the roads outside the city were paved with stone. The roads through the open country were at first overlaid with gravel, but were afterwards paved on a bed of composition, as may still be seen in the remains of Roman roads in Britain.

The Censors had care of the public roads of Rome at an early period; but Augustus appointed *Curatores Viarum* (surveyors of the roads), who were empowered to enforce statute labor to keep the roads in repair, exemption from which labor might be purchased with money. The construction of new roads was paid for out of the revenues of the government, when not indebted to the munificence of public-spirited persons.

These new roads were made by the military, who were accustomed to labor four hours daily at some useful employment in the open air, to keep up their health and strength and to fit them for military duty.

The greatest works performed in the time of Augustus were those by which Rome was converted from a very plain city into the most magnificent capital in the ancient world. It was a favorite boast of the Emperor that he found Rome a city of brick, but left it a city of marble; and this he truly did, as the splendid edifices which he erected were constructed principally of the latter material.

The Roman people were not taxed or oppressed in any manner for these improvements, which were made at the personal expense of the Emperor and the wealthy nobles, the latter being stimulated by the example of the former. Among these wealthy nobles was the Emperor's son-in-law, Agrippa, one of the greatest men of the time, who held a distinguished rank in the Empire, being next in authority and dignity to Augustus himself. Agrippa was a great soldier and engineer, an eminent statesman, and a liberal patron of the arts. He expended large amounts in public works, the greatest being the Pantheon.

The works of Augustus were directed towards the general embellishment of the city rather than the erection of any particular edifice. The Campus Martius, which had hitherto been an open space, began to be covered with elegant structures; but there was no royal palace, the Emperor residing in a private mansion on the Palatine Hill, and his mode of living being similar to that of the wealthy Senators and the rich citizens.

Roman civilization was now rapidly spreading throughout the Empire. Learning was cultivated; the country was improved; new towns were built; villas and ornamental gardens were constructed; roads were made; and the people were instructed in many useful arts, of which they had hitherto been ignorant. Wherever the Roman dominion was established, many opulent families fixed their residence; and as they were the superior people, the higher classes of the natives adopted the Roman dress, language and manners.

These opulent Romans were the means of improving the agriculture and horticulture of Europe by introducing into the Roman provinces the flowers and fruits of the East, and the cultivation of flax from Egypt. It was during the reign of Augustus, after Egypt had become a Roman province, that the Romans commenced using linen, a manufacture for which the Egyptians were especially famous. Glass was likewise manufactured at Alexandria and sent to Rome, which was the great market of the time for the richest productions of all lands.

The Roman manufactures were mainly carried on by slaves. One of these manufactures was paper, made from the papyrus plant obtained from Egypt. The papyrus plant grows in marshy places, as high as ten feet. Paper was made from the thin coats or inner rind, by joining them together. A layer thus prepared was laid on a board, and another layer was laid over it crosswise. These two layers being thus pressed together and dried in the sun formed a sheet of paper. A book was made by pasting the sheets together in a length and rolling them on a stick; and the writing was in columns, with a blank space between them. These rolls were called volumes, and were kept in cases in the libraries. There were many booksellers at Rome, and most of them employed persons in making copies of the works which they had for sale, a list of which was generally hung up on the shop door.

The people of Rome were generally abundantly supplied with the luxuries, as well as the necessaries of life, from various portions of the Empire. Ice and excellent cheese were sent from the regions of the Alps. Pork, geese and salt were sent from Gaul in large quantities. Spices, perfumes, precious stones and many beautiful manufactured articles were brought from the East. The Romans also received an abundance of gold, silver and iron, as tribute from different nations.

Many manufactures were carried on in different portions of Italy; tapestry being made at Padua, and all kinds of steel goods at Como. The principal trade was in grain and other provisions for use in Rome itself. This important branch of commerce was under the immediate direction of the Emperor, one of whose titles was Commissary-General of Corn. A kind of wood sent to Rome from Mauritania was used for making large tables, which were often inlaid with ivory and sold for such immense prices that the Roman ladies were accustomed to saying that they had a right to be extravagant in pearls and jewels while their husbands spent so much money for such costly tables.

One of the commodities which the Romans obtained from remote quarters of the globe was manufactured silk, which they purchased from a people who visited the eastern part of the Roman dominions from some unknown land farther east; but it is uncertain whether these strangers were Tartars, Chinese or Hindoos.

The Romans were wholly ignorant of the nature of silk, not knowing how or where it was produced, but they were willing to pay any price for it because it was scarce and beautiful. It was sold at Rome for its weight in gold, so that only ladies of the highest rank were able to procure it. It was also so scarce that they made their slaves unweave the thick Eastern silks to manufacture slighter ones, in order that they might have several yards instead of one.

Silk was worn at this period by females; but in the process of time the fine Roman gentlemen used silk in their dress, either in the form of a toga or a scarf, or sometimes in another kind of loose robe, as the toga now began to be left off, except by clients when they waited on their patrons. But silk remained so expensive that its use was frequently restricted by sumptuary laws, and it was usually interwoven with cotton or wool. It is mentioned as an illustration of the extravagance of the Emperor Heliogábalus that he had a robe of pure silk.

The Romans, however, mainly displayed their luxury in cookery. Their tables were

FLOURISHING PERIOD OF THE EMPIRE.

furnished with the most costly viands and the choicest wines, in such abundance that the supper of a Roman citizen when entertaining his friends might have served for a royal banquet. The dishes were frequently of embossed silver, and were so large that a boar might be brought whole to the table. About this time table-cloths began to be used. In going home from a supper, gentlemen were generally attended by slaves carrying torches; and when a man of rank made his appearance in public, several slaves usually preceded him to clear the way.

At this period the Romans appeared to have all the luxuries that could be procured by wealth; but they had become a people quite different from what their ancestors had been; and the power of the Roman Empire, in consequence of its vast extent, now depended upon keeping up a large military force.

The reign of Augustus was mainly one of peace and prosperity, and was the great era of learning and the fine arts. Every Roman of rank had a library. This was the golden age of Latin literature, adorned by the poets Virgil, Horace and Ovid, and the great historian, Livy; all of whom were patronized by Augustus, and Virgil being so great a favorite that he died a very wealthy man.

The Romans were not originally in the habit of treating their Emperors with much outward ceremony, as shown by numerous anecdotes related of Augustus, of which we will mention one as an illustration. One of the sovereign's official duties was that of calling the citizens to account for any impropriety in their behavior, as the Censors had been authorized to do in previous times. Absurd as it may appear in such an age as that of Augustus, persons were sometimes brought before a tribunal on a charge of waste or extravagance; and the Emperor, as Censor, was obliged to notice the accusation.

On one occasion a certain knight was summoned before the Emperor to answer to a charge of having squandered his patrimony; but when his defense came to be heard, it was ascertained that he had augmented his fortune, instead of having wasted it; whereupon Augustus told the knight that he was acquitted. The knight replied: "Another time before you listen to a charge against an honest man, take care that your informer is honest."

Some disturbances in Gaul and Spain induced the Emperor to cross the Alps and the Pyrenees (B. C. 27). He reduced the Cantabrians, who occupied the province now known as Biscay, and the Asturians. In order to restrain these tribes in the future, Augustus founded several cities and provided them with strong fortifications. While resting in Spain from the fatigues of his campaign, Augustus received ambassadors from the Scythians, the Sarmatians, the Hindoos, and even from the Seres, who are believed to have been the Chinese.

It was on his recovery from a fit of illness, which spread universal joy throughout the Empire, that the Senate conferred the Tribunate upon Augustus for life. thus rendering his person *sacro sancl*. This dignity was thenceforth united with the imperial office, and therefore all attempts against the sovereign's life became high-treason. It was upon entering his tenth Consulate that the Senate by oath approved all the acts of Augustus, and set him entirely above the power of the laws. Some time afterward the Senate offered to swear to all the laws which he had already proposed, and even to such as he should propose thereafter.

Notwithstanding the concentration of authority in his person, Augustus admitted every one to familiarity with him, and was distinguished for his affability and condescension. Although he could condemn or acquit whomsoever he pleased by his own sole word, he allowed the laws to take their proper course, and even pleaded personally for individuals whom he wished to protect.

The following incidents are related of Augustus. When one of his veteran soldiers entreated his aid, the Emperor bade him to apply to an advocate; whereupon the soldier replied: "Ah ! it was not by proxy that I served you at the battle of Actium."

This answer pleased the Emperor so highly that he pleaded the soldier's cause, and gained it for him. On another occasion a petitioner approached Augustus in so awe-struck a manner as to excite the Emperor's displeasure, which he expressed thus: "Friend, remember that I am a man, and not an elephant. Be bolder." At another time, while Augustus was sitting in judgment, Mecænas, observing that the Emperor was disposed to be severe, and not being able to approach him, threw a paper into his bosom, on which was written: "Arise, butcher!" Augustus read the paper without giving any evidence of displeasure, and, instantly rising from the judgment-seat, he pardoned the criminals whom he was about to condemn.

The reign of Augustus, though generally one of peace, was disturbed by a few wars. Ælius Gallus failed in an attempt to conquer Arabia, B. C. 24. Agrippa and Carisius subdued the Cantabrians and other tribes of Northern and North-western Spain about B. C. 19. Tiberius and Drusus, the Emperor's step-sons, and others, reduced the tribes inhabiting the Alpine countries of Rhætia and Vindelicia and the Danubian countries of Noricum, Pannonia and Mœsia, during twenty-five years of almost uninterrupted warfare (B. C. 16–A. D. 9); and all these countries were formally annexed to the Roman Empire.

Two other tribes besides the Vindelici and the Brigantes are mentioned by Horace in his ode celebrating the conquest of this country by Tiberius and Drusus, addressed to Augustus in the following lines:

"Of late the Vindelicians knew
Thy skill in arms, and felt thy sword,
When Drusus the Genauni slew,
And Brenni swift, a lawless horde.
The towers which covered all around
The rugged Alps' enormous height,
By him were leveled with the ground,
And more than once confessed his might."

The most important of the wars of the reign of Augustus were those with the Germans. In B. C. 12 the Emperor began a series of attacks upon the German tribes east of the Rhine and north of the Danube, for the purpose of effecting the entire subjection of those races and extending the Roman dominion over the whole of Germany. The Roman armies invading Germany were commanded by Drusus until B. C. 9, but after the death of that prince the command devolved on Tiberius. Large Roman armies overran Germany, while Roman fleets subdued the German coasts and the banks of navigable German rivers. The Romans erected forts to hold the conquered country in subjection, and the Roman language and laws were introduced. Augustus supposed that his armies had reduced Germany to complete subjection.

The Germans, however, only submitted to the Roman dominion in name, their spirit being unsubdued, while they waited patiently for a favorable opportunity to recover their independence. From A. D. 4 to A. D. 8 the Germans remained quiet and seemingly submissive. Near the end of this period Tiberius was superseded in the command of the Roman legions on the German frontier by Quintilius Varus, who had been Proconsul of Syria. The new Roman commander discontinued hostile operations, applying himself to the organization of his new province, but forgetting the difference between the freedom-loving Germans and the servile Syrians, the latter of whom he had governed with an iron hand. His harsh and oppressive measures caused the Germans to rise in armed rebellion (A. D. 9).

The revolted Germans were under the leadership of the valiant Hermann, whom the Romans called Arminius. Hermann was a prince of the German tribe of the Cherusci. He had been educated at Rome, and was familiar with Roman tactics. He had been made a Roman citizen and a knight. Nevertheless, his German patriotism was as strong as ever, and he had for a long time meditated the recovery of his country's independence. When Hermann had fully matured all his plans, he caused Varus to be informed that a certain tribe in the North of Germany had revolted from the Roman power. Varus was then in the country of the Cherusci, near the Weser, and he instantly led a large army against the rebels.

Hermann permitted the Roman commander to penetrate with his legions far into the Teutoberger Wald, the difficulties of which were increased by the marshy nature of the ground, caused by heavy rains. After Varus had been thus enticed with his legions into the depths of the German forests, he found his way suddenly blocked by barricades of fallen trees; and in a narrow valley his legions were unexpectedly assailed by a shower of javelins from the German hosts under Hermann, which had by this time completely surrounded the astonished Roman legions. The Germans occupied the wooded heights on all sides, and all avenues of escape were cut off from the army under Varus.

The battle was renewed the following day, and the Roman army was literally cut to pieces, three legions being totally destroyed, and all the captives being sacrificed upon the altars of the German gods. Varus himself was wounded, and committed suicide in despair at his defeat and to escape captivity. This was one of the most terrible defeats that had ever attended the Roman arms, and put an end to the Roman power in Germany. The Roman garrisons throughout Germany were speedily overpowered and massacred, and within a few weeks not a living Roman was to be found on German territory. This great victory of Hermann reëstablished the independence of Germany (A. D. 9), and the Romans never thereafter obtained a foothold in the country. In recent years the Germans have honored Hermann with a colossal statue on the site of his great victory.

The intelligence of this great catastrophe to the Roman arms produced consternation and grief at Rome; and the loss of this army was a terrible blow to the Emperor Augustus, who, in paroxysms of grief, exclaimed: "Quintilius Varus! restore me my legions!" The superstitious believed that supernatural portents had accompanied the disaster; as the Temple of Mars was struck by a thunderbolt, comets blazed in the heavens, and fiery spears darted from the northward into the camp of the Prætorian Guards. A statue of Victory, which had stood on the northern frontier of Italy, facing in the direction of Germany, was said to have turned of its own accord, looking toward Rome.

Though the Romans renewed the war the following year, and Roman legions were led against the Germans by Tiberius, they did no more than make retaliatory raids across the Rhine. Between the years A. D. 12 and 14, Germanicus, another Roman commander, pursued a similar policy, but made no attempt at conquest or occupation. By the will of Augustus, which was adopted as the policy of his successors, the Rhine was regarded as the frontier between the Roman dominions and the German territories in this quarter, and so remained for almost five centuries, until the tide of German conquest swept over it and engulfed the Roman Empire, laying upon its ruins the foundations of the modern states of Europe.

While Augustus was peacefully ruling over a hundred and twenty million pagans and polytheists, there occurred within the Eastern limits of his Empire an event destined to work a wonderful change in the future condition of the world. This event was the birth of JESUS CHRIST—the founder of a great monotheistic religion, which was eventually to displace the pagan and polytheistic religions of the Roman world, and to become the universal religion of the Aryan races inhabiting Europe. Jesus Christ was born in the year B. C. 4—according to our common era—in the little village of Bethlehem, in Judæa, about five miles from Jerusalem; during the reign of Herod the Great, the Idumæan whom Mark Antony had made Tetrarch, or tributary king, of Judæa under the Romans. It has been discovered that Jesus was born four years earlier than the date originally assigned as that of his birth; but as a change of reckoning dates would now cause great confusion, time is still computed from the originally-assigned date of his birth.

In the midst of unparalleled power and

prosperity, Augustus was assailed by domestic troubles. He suffered personally from ill health for the greater portion of his life. He ardently wished to be succeeded by an heir of his own blood; but, though married three times, his only child was his daughter Julia, whose conduct was so abandoned and disgraceful, and caused her father such affliction, that he once resolved to put her to death, but was finally induced to spare her life and to banish her to an island on the Italian coast. His last wife, Livia, formerly the wife of Tiberius Nero, was an imperious woman, who, conscious of the strong attachment of her husband, controlled him at her pleasure. She had two sons by her former husband, Tiberius and Drusus; the former of whom was of so obstinate and turbulent a temper that Augustus exiled him to Rhodes for five years.

The connections from whom Augustus would have selected his successor were all removed by death, so that he was obliged to appoint his obnoxious step-son Tiberius as his heir. He required Tiberius to adopt as his heir the young Germanicus, the son of Drusus, the brother of Tiberius; and bestowed upon Germanicus the hand of his grand-daughter Agrippina in marriage. A son was born to this union during the lifetime of Augustus, and afterward became the Emperor Caligula.

In his seventy-fourth year, Augustus began thinking of withdrawing from the fatigues of government, and of making Tiberius his partner in the imperial office. He accordingly invested his step-son with almost as much authority as he himself had exercised. He then made his will, intrusting it to the care of the Vestal Virgins; after which he ordered the census of the Roman people to be taken, showing the city to contain a population of four millions one hundred and thirty-seven thousand.

Shortly afterward, Augustus, having accompanied Tiberius in his march into Illyria, was taken ill at Naples. Hastening toward Rome, the illness assumed a fatal character at Nola, in Campania, and the Emperor was unable to proceed any farther.

A few hours before he died, he ordered a mirror to be brought to him, and his hair to be combed and arranged with more than usual care ; after which he addressed his friends who stood around him, and asked them whether he had acted his part in life well. All having replied that he had, he said: "Then give me your applause." Upon uttering these words, he expired (A. D. 14); after a reign of forty-five years from the battle of Actium, B. C. 31.

The death of Augustus caused sincere and universal grief throughout the whole Roman Empire. There was a suspicion that he had been poisoned by his wife Livia, in order to obtain the succession more speedily for Tiberius. She was very careful to conceal his death for a time, until measures were proposed to transmit the imperial authority to her son; and when all was in readiness, she caused the death of her imperial husband to be made known, with the announcement of his appointment of Tiberius as his successor.

The honors paid to the memory of Augustus exceeded all bounds. Temples were erected to his name, and divine worship was offered to him. A Senator named Numerius Atticus contrived to turn the extravagant adulation of the people to his own benefit, by swearing that he saw Augustus ascend to heaven; and for this oath he received a large sum of money. After this proceeding no one uttered any doubt concerning the departed Emperor's divinity.

Upon the death of Augustus, in the year A. D. 14, his step-son, TIBERIUS, at once became Emperor with the consent of the Roman Senate and people; and his accession was hailed with the most extravagant joy by the Senators and the knights. Tiberius had lived in a state of profound dissimulation under Augustus, and was not sufficiently hardy to exhibit his real character, although he was now fifty-six years of age. He met the adulation of the Roman nobility with a duplicity equal to that which they themselves had manifested, affecting to decline the sovereign power; but, after long debates, he accepted the imperial dignity.

In the beginning of his reign, Tiberius displayed only generosity, clemency and prudence. Having bound himself by oath to adhere to his illustrious predecessor's policy, he aspired to gain the affections or remove the suspicions of the virtuous Germanicus, whom Augustus had forced him to adopt as his heir. But the jealousies of Tiberius were intensely aggravated by a mutiny of the Roman legions on the German frontier, which offered to elevate the idolized Germanicus to the imperial purple; but that prince, either from generosity or lack of ambition, declined to sanction the treason, and thus secured the quiet accession of his uncle. Nevertheless, Tiberius chose to consider Germanicus as a rival, and repaid that prince's fidelity with so apparent a hostility that the courtiers soon discovered that the quickest way to secure the Emperor's favor was to injure Germanicus either by word or deed; and thenceforth the Emperor was resolved upon the young prince's destruction.

During the early years of the reign of Tiberius, Germanicus prosecuted the war against Hermann in Germany, and after several defeats he achieved some successes over the German chieftain. The glory which Germanicus thus acquired aroused the jealousy of Tiberius to the highest degree; and the prince was accordingly recalled to Rome in A. D. 17, under the pretense of rewarding him with a triumph, but in reality to put an end to his success. A multitude of Roman citizens thronged out to meet Germanicus at a distance of twenty miles from Rome. This evidence of the wonderful popularity of the young prince so alarmed the Emperor that he became anxious to remove from the city a person whose mildness and virtue were so strongly contrasted with his own tyranny and debauchery.

Tiberius accordingly removed Germanicus from his command in Germany, and appointed him to the government of the Roman provinces of Asia and to the direction of the war in the East; but at the same time he sent Piso, with his infamous wife, Plancina, into Syria, giving them secret instructions to take off Germanicus by poison. Notwithstanding all the efforts of the unscrupulous Piso to thwart Germanicus and to bring him into disgrace, the young prince succeeded in settling the affairs of Armenia, and in organizing Cappadocia and Commogêné as Roman provinces. Germanicus finally died near Antioch, in Syria, A. D. 19; having been poisoned by Piso, who thus accomplished the atrocious task for which he had been sent out. The grief at Rome for the death of Germanicus was so intense, and the suspicions which fell upon Piso were so strong, that he was arraigned for the murder, and only escaped the vengeance of the law by committing suicide.

Tiberius was thoroughly conscious of his utter unfitness for the exalted station which he occupied, but he was so jealous of all the members of the Julian house and of his own relatives that he was afraid to ask the aid of any of them in the difficult task of governing the Empire. Tiberius as much distrusted all the great patricians, each of whom he suspected of being a rival. He therefore abolished the Council of State established by Augustus, and gave way to the native cruelty of his disposition, causing many of the most eminent nobles to be put to death for high-treason.

As Tiberius found the sole management of the affairs of the Empire too great a task for him, he called to his aid an assistant whose abilities he believed would make him useful, while his position would never render him a dangerous rival because of his insignificance. This imperial assistant or minister was a Volsinian knight named Ælius Sejanus. The Emperor made this minister Prætorian Prefect, and placed such reliance upon him that Sejanus soon acquired the most complete influence over his sovereign. This individual, whom the Emperor considered too obscure to be dangerous, was as depraved as his master, so that his name has passed into a proverb.

No sooner did Sejanus become the Emperor's prime minister than he secretly aspired to wear the imperial purple himself, and sought to win the favor of the Prætorian

Guards, as a step in the accomplishment of the object of his ambition. His next move was to seduce Livilla, the wife of Drusus, the son of Tiberius; and, with her aid, he removed Drusus by poison, A. D. 23. His success in preventing the discovery of his crime made him sufficiently audacious to ask the Emperor's permission to marry Livilla. This bold request opened the Emperor's eyes to the ambition of his favorite, but Tiberius allowed himself to be influenced by Sejanus, though refusing to permit the marriage which had been requested. The most successful scheme of Sejanus was the removal of Tiberius from Rome. By the most artful temptations, Sejanus induced the Emperor to relinquish the cares of government to his favorite, and to retire to the beautiful island of Capreæ, near Naples, where he abandoned himself to every kind of luxury and vice.

Having thus the entire administration of the Empire in his hands, Sejanus employed multitudes of spies and informers to rid himself of every obstacle in the way of his ambitious designs. He caused many of the most eminent Romans to be put to death, after obliging them to submit to the useless mockery of a trial. In this manner he proceeded, removing every one who seemed to stand between him and the imperial dignity, every day increasing his influence with Tiberius, and his power with the Senate. He first sought the destruction of the remaining members of the family of Augustus. By intrigue and falsehood he induced the Emperor to consent to the arrest and imprisonment of Agrippina, the widow of Germanicus, and her sons, Nero and Drusus. By his persistence he induced Tiberius to consent to his marriage with Livilla, and was formally betrothed to her, at the same time being created associate Consul with the Emperor. The number of statues of Sejanus set up in Rome exceeded even those of the Emperor; and people swore by his fortune in the same manner as they would have done if he had been raised to the imperial purple, and he was more dreaded than even the tyrannical Emperor himself.

But the rapid rise of Sejanus appeared simply preparatory to the greatness of his fall. The Emperor now suddenly changed his policy toward his favorite, whose ambition alarmed him and caused him to cease bestowing favors upon him. Sejanus soon detected the evidences of his master's altered feelings toward him; and, to secure his own safety, he organized a plot for the assassination of the Emperor. Tiberius received secret warnings of the plot of his favorite, and sent a messenger to Rome with a letter to the Senate, instructing him to inform Sejanus that it contained an earnest recommendation to have him invested with the power of Tribune.

Deceived by this hope, Sejanus hastily convened the Senate; and when he presented himself to that body, he was surrounded with a multitude of flatterers, who congratulated him upon his new dignity. But when the fatal letter was read, in which he was charged with treason, and in which were given the orders for his arrest, the Senators at once abandoned him. Those who had been most servile in their flatteries of the ambitious minister now became the loudest in their invectives and execrations. The Senate quickly passed a decree condemning Sejanus to death. This decree was executed the very same day, and a general massacre of his friends and relatives at once followed. His innocent children, regardless of their tender ages, were put to death with circumstances of the utmost barbarity; and the fickle multitude broke to pieces the many statues which had been erected in his honor (A. D. 31).

The treachery of the one man whom he had trusted had the effect of making Tiberius a' thorough misanthrope. His embitterment toward all mankind made him more suspicious than ever before. Hearing for the first time of the murder of his son Drusus, he was seized with alarm for his own security; and actuated by a desire for vengeance, no less than by a wish to remove every one whom he regarded as dangerous to himself, he inaugurated such a reign of terror in Rome as the city had never before

FLOURISHING PERIOD OF THE EMPIRE. 1061

witnessed. Remaining in his beautiful retreat in the island of Capreæ, his rage was continually inflamed for further executions; and he gave orders that whoever was accused should be put to death without trial, so that the entire city was filled with slaughter and mourning.

Livilla, the betrothed wife of Sejanus, Agrippina, Nero, Drusus, and all the relatives of Germanicus were executed. Hundreds of wealthy Romans of both sexes were massacred, and even innocent children fell victims to the cruelty of the tyrant. A man named Carnulius committed suicide to avoid the torture designed for him, whereupon Tiberius exclaimed: "Ah! how has that man been able to escape me!" When a prisoner earnestly implored to be executed speedily, the tyrannical Emperor replied: "Know that I am not sufficiently your friend to shorten your torments." In this manner lived Tiberius, odious to mankind and a burden to himself. At length, in the twenty-second year of his reign, his appetite left him.

In the reign of Tiberius the last remnants of Roman freedom disappeared. The Emperor deprived the Comitia Tributa of the power to appoint magistrates, and thereafter all these officials were appointed by the sovereign. Tiberius also extended the penalties of treason to words, and even to thoughts. Augustus had scrupulously observed the requirements of the criminal laws in removing such as were obnoxious to him; but Tiberius abolished the right of trial at one blow, his victims being executed solely upon his order. He quartered the Prætorian Guards in a camp just outside the walls of Rome, to overawe the citizens into submission to his tyranny.

It was during the reign of Tiberius that Jesus Christ grew up to manhood, began his public ministry at the age of thirty (A. D. 27), and was finally crucified on Mount Calvary, under the Prætorship of Pontius Pilate, the Roman governor of Judæa (A. D. 31). In the latter years of the reign of Tiberius the first missionaries of Christ's doctrines commenced their labors, going out from Jerusalem to the surrounding country, and laying the foundations of that great moral and religious revolution which was eventually to conquer the Roman Empire itself. In the year of the death of Tiberius, Saul of Tarsus, while on his way to Damascus to persecute the followers of Jesus Christ, was suddenly converted to the new religion, of which he, under the name of Paul, was the great apostle and missionary during the remainder of his life.

After teaching the new faith at Antioch, where the disciples of Christ were first called Christians, St. Paul carried the gospel through Asia Minor and Greece; and Christianity rapidly spread among the Jews, and also among the Eastern, or Greek, and the Western, or Latin Gentiles. The commingling of the Hebrew, Greek and Latin civilizations—the result of the conquests of Alexander the Great and the Romans—brought about the propagation and final triumph of this beneficent monotheistic religion. Christianity was powerfully aided by the existence of the Roman Empire—the union of many polytheistic nations under one government.

Tiberius finally fixed his residence at Misenum, where he became a victim of fainting-fits, which all considered fatal. Caius Cæsar, the son of Germanicus, supposing the Emperor to be dead, caused himself to be proclaimed Emperor by the Prætorian Guards, and went forth from the apartments of Tiberius amid the applauses of the multitude; but suddenly he was informed that Tiberius had revived. This unexpected intelligence alarmed the entire court; and every one who had before given evidence of his joy now affected sorrow and abandoned the new Emperor, through a pretended solicitude for the fate of the old one.

Caius Cæsar appeared stricken with dismay and sat in gloomy silence, expecting instant death instead of the imperial dignity to which he had aspired. Macro, the commander of the Prætorian Guards, averted this danger by smothering Tiberius with bed-clothes, under the pretense of keeping him warm. Thus died the Emperor Tiberius, A. D. 37, in the seventy-eighth year of his age, and the twenty-third of his reign. During the reign of Tiberius the forms of the Roman constitution were retained, but its spirit and substance were thoroughly altered; and the government degenerated into a despotism as complete as that of an Oriental monarchy, the Senate simply remaining in existence to register the Emperor's edicts.

Upon the death of Tiberius, the Roman Senate, army and people hailed Caius Cæsar as Emperor with the utmost enthusiasm, expecting great benefits from this son of the worthy Germanicus and his wife Agrippína. Caius Cæsar is better known as CALIGULA, a nickname given him in his childhood by the Roman legions in Germany, whose pet he was, on account of his little military boots, called *caligæ*, which he wore to please them. He was twenty-six years of age at his accession to the imperial office, and all considered him a young man of an amiable and generous disposition.

Caligula commenced his reign by liberating all the state prisoners, recalling all exiles, dismissing the entire multitude of spies and informers who had been encouraged by his tyrannical predecessor, and restoring the regular magistrates and the popular assemblies. By these and other similar acts of magnanimity, he acquired such popularity that when he was stricken with illness the whole Empire was filled with sorrow, and sacrifices were offered in every temple for his recovery. It is probable that this attack of sickness disordered his brain, as the savage conduct which he thenceforth displayed was only worthy of a madman; and his character underwent an entire change, as he degenerated into a cruel and capricious tyrant.

At the accession of Caligula the imperial treasury contained a surplus amounting to more than a hundred million dollars of our money, but he squandered this vast sum in the course of several months; and to supply his necessities he resorted to the most oppressive taxation and to an arbitrary use of the laws respecting treason. The estates of the attainted persons being forfeited to the Emperor, it soon became evident that to be a traitor in the Emperor's eyes it was only necessary to be possessed of wealth. Executions and suicides were of frequent occurrence, and the Emperor's cruelty and wantonness increased with every additional victim.

Caligula had a singular habit of nodding with his head or pointing with his finger at such persons as he desired to have put to death; and his executioners instantly seized and despatched the victims. He kept a box of poisonous compound, which he offered to the more distinguished personages whom he desired to deprive of their lives. He expected them to use the poison in the same manner that snuff is taken. Those who took a pinch of the drug died from its effects; while those who refused were executed for treason. This profligate imperial monster lived in open incest with his sister Drusilla until her death in A. D. 38.

Caligula ordered all the prisoners in Rome to be thrown to wild beasts without trial; and he took a fiendish delight in witnessing the sufferings of his victims and in protracting their tortures, in order, as he said, that they might feel themselves dying. Seeing that none had the courage to oppose his sanguinary whims, he began to consider himself as more than a mortal being and to claim divine honors. He accordingly erected a temple to himself as a god by the name of Jupiter Latiaris, and instituted a college of priests to superintend the worship of himself. The patricians of Rome had now sunk so low that they contended for the privilege of ministering at this shrine.

His reverence for his favorite horse Incitatus is shown by the circumstance that he built a stable of marble and a manger of ivory for the animal; and whenever the beast was to run a race, the Emperor stationed sentinels on the preceding night to prevent the slumbers of his favorite steed being disturbed by any noises. He also frequently invited the horse to the imperial table, where the animal was fed with gilded oats and drank the most expensive wines from jeweled goblets; and only his death prevented him from raising the beast to the office of Consul.

While Rome was scandalized by the foolish and outrageous conduct of Caligula, the city was suddenly astounded at the news that the Emperor had determined to lead an expedition against the Germans. The grandest preparations were made for this expedition, and Caligula conducted his army to the sea-coast in Gaul, where he disposed his engines and warlike machines with great display, drew up his ranks in line of battle, went on board a galley and coasted along the shore, and commanded his trumpets to sound and the signal to be given as if for battle. He then ordered his soldiers to collect shells from the beach and to put them into their helmets. These were called "spoils of the ocean." The Emperor called his army together, as would a conquering general after a victory, and harangued them, extolling their exploits. In commemoration of this wonderful achievement, Caligula ordered a stately tower to be constructed on the site.

After this mockery of a triumph, Caligula returned to Rome, where he resumed his career of extravagances. He made use of a number of contrivances to imitate thunder, and frequently exclaimed in defiance of Jupiter: "Do you conquer me, or do I conquer you!" He affected to hold conversations in whispers with the statue of that deity, and generally appeared incensed at its answers, threatening to send it back to Greece, whence it had been brought to Rome.

The cruelties of Caligula increased every day. He caused many Senators to be put to death, after which he summoned them to appear. He caused many old and infirm men to be cast to wild beasts to rid the state from such unserviceable citizens. Every tenth day he sent off numbers of victims to his menagerie, which he spoke of as "clearing his accounts." When the supply of criminals was exhausted at the public games, he caused spectators to be seized at random from the multitude and to be thrown to the wild beasts, first ordering their tongues to be cut out, in order that they might not shock him with their dying curses.

On one occasion, when Caligula was angry at the citizens, he expressed a wish that the whole Roman people had but one head, in order that he might chop it off at one blow. Finding the Senate more reluctant in their adulations than he had expected, the Emperor resolved to massacre the entire body. But the Romans had by this time grown tired of this wicked and contemptible monster, and a plot was formed for the assassination of the Emperor. The leader of this conspiracy was Cherea, the commander of the Prætorian Guards, whom Caligula had for a long time treated with insult.

As the Palatine Games, which continued four days, were now at hand, the opportunity was considered favorable for accomplishing the designs of the conspirators. The first three days were permitted to pass; and Cherea selected the fourth day, when the Emperor would have occasion to retire through a private gallery to the baths near the palace, after the conclusion of the games. The fourth day of these games exceeded any of the first three days in splendor; and Caligula appeared more sprightly and condescending than usual, enjoying the amusement of seeing the people scramble for the fruits and other things thrown among them by his order, being wholly unsuspicious of any conspiracy against him.

In the meantime, however, some news of the plot began circulating among the multitude, and the tyrant would certainly have discovered it if he would have had any friends remaining. A Senator standing near the Emperor inquired of an acquaintance whether he had heard anything new, and was answered in the negative. Thereupon the Senator responded: "Then you must know that this day will be represented a piece called the 'Death of a Tyrant.'" The person addressed thus comprehended the meaning of this reply, and counseled the Senator to be cautious.

The conspirators waited very anxiously

for many hours, and the Emperor appeared determined to pass the entire day without taking any refreshment. Cherea was exasperated at this unexpected delay, and would have attacked the Emperor in the midst of the whole multitude had he not been restrained. While the arch conspirator was thus hesitating, one of Caligula's attendants persuaded the Emperor to go into the bath and take some slight refreshment, in order that he might be better able to enjoy the remainder of the entertainment. When Caligula arose, the conspirators used every precaution to keep off the crowd and to surround him, on pretense of looking after his comfort.

When the Emperor had entered a little vaulted gallery leading to the bath, Cherea assailed him with a dagger, striking him to the ground and exclaiming: "Tyrant, think upon this!" The other conspirators surrounded the wounded Emperor, who was resisting and exclaiming that he was not dead; whereupon they killed him with thirty wounds (A. D. 41). Such was the deserved fate of Caligula, who had reigned not quite four years (A. D. 37-41). Seneca summed up his character thus: "Nature seems to have produced him for the purpose of showing what michief can be effected by the greatest vices supported by the highest authority."

The Senate claimed the right to name the successor to the imperial purple; but wasted so much time in discussing the proper course to be pursued that the Prætorian Guards took upon themselves the task of giving the Empire a new sovereign, and accordingly proclaimed CLAUDIUS, the brother of Germanicus and uncle of Caligula, as the next Emperor; and the Senate was obliged to ratify their choice. This bold proceeding of the Prætorian Guards made them the virtual arbiters of the destinies of the Empire more than half a century thereafter, during which period they made and unmade Emperors, the Senate being obliged to confirm their nomination.

The Prætorians found Claudius concealed in the palace, alarmed by his nephew's assassination, and literally compelled him to assume the imperial purple. He had been considered half-witted from his childhood, and had been kept out of public life. He was shy, weak and awkward, and in every way unfitted for the government of so vast an Empire, particularly at the time of its greatest corruption. However, as he was honest and well-meaning, he might have reigned with credit had he been permitted to rule alone; but, during his entire reign, this wretched idiot was a mere puppet in the hands of his wives and his worthless and unprincipled favorites, who profited by the Emperor's imbecility in carrying their infamous designs into execution. Messalina, the infamous wife of Claudius, was a monster of wickedness.

At the beginning of the reign of Claudius the conspirators against Caligula's life were punished with death, not because they had murdered the late Emperor, but because they were suspected of a design to restore the old Roman constitution.

The Romans now determined to obtain full possession of Britain, and Claudius sent his general, Aulus Plautius, to conquer the Britons. In A. D. 43 Plautius crossed the British Channel from Gaul and landed on the southern coast of Britain with four legions. After forcing a passage of the Thames, he was joined by the Emperor Claudius himself. The native tribe of the Trinobantes, inhabiting the territory of the modern Essex and Hertfordshire, were speedily subdued; and their capital, Camulodunum, became the seat of the Roman provincial government. This result was achieved in sixteen days.

After Claudius had returned to Rome, his able general, Vespasian, reduced the southwestern portion of the island as far as the Exe and the Severn. Ostorius Scápula extended the Roman dominion to the Wye and the Welsh mountains, where he met with a desperate resistance from the native chief, Carácatus, who reigned over a tribe in the region of the Severn. The army of Carácatus was routed by the Romans, and Carácatus himself was soon afterward captured and carried a prisoner to Rome. As this British chief was led through the streets of the great city of the Cæsars, loaded with chains, he exclaimed: "Alas! is it possible that a people possessed of such magnificence at home should envy my humble cottage in Britain!" The Emperor Claudius was greatly impressed by the bold demeanor of the captive chieftain, and gave him his freedom.

The Roman conquests in Britain were quickly organized into a compact Roman province; and Londinium (now London) soon became a town of great commercial importance. The conquerors brought that entire region under the influence of Roman civilization. The Romans not only extended their dominion over the Britons, but improved the conquered country as well. They constructed roads and bridges, and cleared forests. They established military stations which soon became centers of education and law. They deepened the Thames, and began those immense embankments of that river to which London really owes its existence, without being aware of the labor which they bestowed upon the work.

On the return of Claudius to Rome, the Senate granted him a magnificent triumph, in which his wife Messalina, whose scandalous conduct had now become notorious, accompanied her imperial husband in a stately chariot. The cruelty of this woman was equal to her infamy, and her name has become a synonym for female vice. She gratified her jealousy and hatred of the nobles at the cost of the lives of many of them. She audaciously went through the forms of a public marriage with one of her paramours, notwithstanding that her husband was still living. Her crimes finally became so intolerable that Claudius caused her to be put to death; and the Senate passed a law authorizing the Emperor to marry his niece Agrippína, the widow of Domitius Ahenobarbus, by whom she had one son, originally named after his father, but better known in history as Nero.

Agrippína caused the philosopher Seneca to be recalled from exile, and made him the tutor of her son Nero. She also raised the honest Burrhus to power as the Emperor's prime minister, and protected many of the accused nobles. She was, however, ambitious, avaricious and cruel. She ruled her imperial husband at her pleasure, appeared with him in the Senate, occupied the same throne during all public ceremonies, and gave audience to foreign princes and ambassadors.

Agrippína at length induced her husband to adopt her son Nero, and to bequeath to him the Empire, in preference to his own son Britannicus. When Claudius manifested a disposition to restore the succession to his own son, Agrippína caused the Emperor to be poisoned, with the aid of his own physician (A. D. 54). By previously gaining the commander of the Prætorian Guards over to her interest, she was enabled to conceal her husband's death until she had taken the necessary steps for her son's accession to the imperial dignity.

NERO.

The reign of NERO began full of promise, and for five years the Roman people found reason to congratulate themselves upon their change of Emperors. The oppressive taxes of the preceding reigns were remitted, and the poor and deserving were aided by land grants. The infamous class known as *delators*, who earned their living by accusing others of crime, were suppressed. Armenia was conquered by the Roman arms, and the country along the lower course of the Rhine was improved by the construction of dykes to protect that region against inundations. But these wise measures were wholly due to the eminent statesman, Burrhus, and the distinguished philosopher, Seneca, Nero's able and incorruptible ministers. The Emperor himself was from the very beginning a cruel tyrant and a profligate sensualist.

Nero had been nurtured in the midst of crimes, and had been educated more for the stage than for the imperial station. He was only seventeen years old at his accession, and regarded the Empire as merely a vast field for the indulgence of his passions. He soon wearied of his mother's imperious control over him; and Agrippína, seeing herself neglected, threatened to transfer the imperial office to her step-son Britannicus. Thereupon Nero determined upon the destruction of that young prince. Poison was accordingly administered to Britannicus by one of the Emperor's emissaries, and his body was exhibited to the public several hours after his death (A. D. 55). Nero displayed so little care in concealing his part in the murder of the young prince that preparations were made for the funeral before the poison was administered.

An infamous woman named Poppæa Sabína, the wife of Otho, became the Emperor's mistress and instigated him to the most atrocious crimes. Convinced that she would not be able to get rid of Octavia, Nero's wife, and thus herself become a partner in the Empire by marrying the Emperor, Poppæa urged Nero to murder his mother. Nero himself desired to be rid of one of whom he stood in such great fear; but he dreaded the resentment of the Roman people, who reverenced the last surviving representative of the family of Germanicus. After the failure of attempts to secretly take the life of Agrippína, Nero sent a body of armed men to her house, where they murdered her in her bed (A. D. 62).

Shortly afterward Burrhus, the Emperor's faithful minister, was murdered by poison at the Emperor's order. The death of this able statesman was a great public calamity, as his influence had restrained Nero from many extravagances in which he was disposed to indulge. The successor of the virtuous Burrhus as the Emperor's minister was Tigellínus, a man infamous for many crimes; and Nero gave free reign to his base propensities. The debauched Emperor banished Seneca from his court, divorced Octavia and afterwards caused her to be murdered, and finally married Poppæa.

In A. D. 61 Suetonius Paulínus, the Roman commander in Britain, determined to subdue the island of Mona (now Anglesey), the chief seat of the Druids, which afforded a refuge to the disaffected Britons. The strait separating the island from the mainland was crossed by the Roman infantry in shallow vessels, while the cavalry swam their horses across. The Britons sought to prevent the Romans from landing on the sacred island. The native warriors stoutly defended the shore, while the Druids and the women rushed about among their troops with flaming brands and disheveled hair, uttering the most terrible cries and imprecations. The superstitious Romans were for the time stricken with terror by these strange sounds, but Suetonius soon rallied his troops and led them to the attack. The Britons suffered an overwhelming defeat; the Druids were themselves burned in the fires which they had kindled for their.expected captives; and the sacred groves and altars of the natives were destroyed.

Suetonius was entirely mistaken in supposing that this bold blow at the Druidical religion would frighten the Britons into submission to the Roman power. While he was absent in Anglesey, the Britons on the mainland rose in revolt, being led by the valiant Boadicéa, Queen of the Iceni, whose daughter had been outraged by the Romans, while she herself had been scourged with rods by them. The revolted Britons suddenly and unexpectedly attacked the Roman colonies and garrisons in the island burned London and massacred seventy thousand Romans (A. D. 61). The next year Suetonius avenged the slaughter of his countrymen in a terrible battle, in which he defeated Boadicéa and slew eighty thousand Britons (A. D. 62). In despair at this defeat and to escape capture, Boadicéa committed suicide by taking poison. Suetonius Paulínus thus suppressed this formidable insurrection against the Roman power in Britain.

A tour through Italy afforded Nero an opportunity to appear as a singer on the stage at Naples, and he was exceedingly delighted by the applause with which the multitude greeted him. Soon after his return to Rome, in A. D. 64, a frightful conflagration lasting nine days destroyed ten of the fourteen *regions* of the city; and it was generally believed that the fire had been kindled by Nero's secret orders. It is said that, while the fire was raging, the Emperor was sitting upon a tower on the Esquiline Hill, enjoying the scene, and singing in a theatrical manner, to the music of his harp, *The Sack of Troy.*

In order to withdraw the blame of the cause of this calamity from himself, Nero charged it upon the Christians, of whom there were at that time quite a number in Rome; and the result was the first of the ten great persecutions of the Christians under the auspices of Roman Emperors. Thousands of these unfortunate people were cruelly tortured and put to death, among whom were the apostles Peter and Paul. Some were covered with the skins of wild beasts, and in that disguise they were devoured by dogs. Some were crucified, and others were burned alive. Nero himself, attired as a charioteer, witnessed their tortures from his gardens, where he entertained the people with their sufferings.

Concerning this fire and the relation of the Christians to it, the renowned Roman historian, Tacitus, who was born in Nero's reign, gives an interesting account. Alluding to the design of the Emperor to divert suspicion from himself, Tacitus says: "With this view, Nero inflicted the most exquisite tortures on those men who, under the vulgar appellation of Christians, were already branded with deserved infamy. They derived their name and origin from one CHRIST. who in the reign of Tiberius had suffered death by the sentence of the Procurator Pontius Pilate. For a while this dire superstition was checked, but it again burst forth; and not only spread itself over Judæa, the first seat of this mischievous sect, but was even introduced into Rome, the common asylum which receives and protects whatever is impure, whatever is atrocious. The confessions of those who were seized discovered a great multitude of their accomplices, and they were all convicted, not so much for the crime of setting fire to the city, as for their hatred of human kind. Some were nailed on crosses, others sewn up in the skins of wild beasts and exposed to the fury of dogs; others, again, smeared over with combustible materials, were used as torches to illuminate the darkness of the night. The gardens of Nero were destined for the melancholy spectacle, which was accompanied with a horse-race, and honored with the presence of the Emperor, who mingled with the populace in the dress and attitude of a charioteer. The guilt of the Christians deserved indeed the most exemplary punishment, but the public abhorrence was changed into commiseration, from the opinion that those unhappy wretches were sacrificed, not so much to the public welfare, as to the cruelty of a jealous tyrant."

Nero likewise persecuted the Jews. Only four of the fourteen regions, or wards, of Rome remained inhabitable after the great conflagration. Nero is believed to have ordered the burning of the city on account of disgust with its narrow and winding streets. At any rate, he availed himself of the opportunity to rebuild the city in more regular and spacious proportions. The houses were now constructed of stone and rendered fireproof; each being surrounded with balconies, and separated from other houses by lanes of considerable width; while an abundant supply of water was introduced into every dwelling.

Nero's palace having been destroyed by the fire, he erected a new palace, called his *Golden House*, on a scale of magnitude and splendor never before witnessed in Rome. The porticos surrounding this magnificent edifice were three miles in length, and rested on pillars. Within the enclosure formed by these porticos were artificial lakes, extensive woods, parks, gardens, orchards, vineyards, etc. An artificial lake filled the valley afterwards occupied by the Flavian Amphitheater, or Colosséum. The entrance of the Golden House was of sufficient height to admit a colossal statue of Nero himself, one hundred and twenty feet high. The roof of this splendid imperial mansion was covered with golden tiles. The walls were also gilded and elegantly adorned with precious stones and mother-of-pearl. The ceiling of one of the banqueting-rooms represented the firmament beset with stars, moving constantly, night and day, and showering perfumed water upon the guests.

The extravagant expenditures caused by this magnificent structure, by the rebuilding of the city, and by the Emperor's luxuries, exhausted the public treasury, and led to a system of plunder and extortion which almost brought about the dissolution of the Empire. Italy, the provinces, and the confederate nations were pillaged and laid waste. The temples of the gods and private dwellings were stripped of their treasures, but yet sufficient could not be obtained to support the Emperor's unbounded prodigality.

A conspiracy was formed against the tyrannical Emperor by Cneius Piso, and many of the Roman nobility became connected with it. The detection of this plot gave Nero an opportunity to glut his bloodthirsty disposition. Most of the prominent nobles were deprived of their lives, and among other victims were Lucan, the poet, and Seneca, the philosopher. About the same time Nero killed his second wife, Poppæa, by a kick. He openly encouraged the most shocking vices, and publicly participated in the performances of the circus and the theater, being ambitious of the reputation of a musician and a charioteer. In the very midst of his massacres, Nero appeared on the stage and won a prize for music.

Not satisfied with his Italian renown, he visited Greece to display his musical skill at the Olympic Games, and received great applauses. He won prizes at the Olympic Games in A. D. 67, the games having been postponed two years for his accommodation. He likewise personally engaged in the musical exercises of the Isthmian Games while on his visit to Greece, and on this occasion he caused a singer whose voice drowned his own to be put to death. On returning to Rome he entered the city through a breach in the walls, in accordance with the old Grecian custom; but the eighteen hundred garlands which the servile Greeks had showered upon him indicated the decay of the ancient Grecian heroic spirit more than the glory of the imperial victor.

The lower classes of the Roman people did not feel anything of the imperial despotism, and manifested no sympathy with the nobles in their calamities, still remembering the former oppressions which they had endured at the hands of the aristocracy. They were also won to the Emperor by a monthly distribution of corn, by occasional gifts of wine and meat, and by the splendid shows of the circus. In short, the times of imperial tyranny were the golden days of the Roman poor; and Nero's popularity with the mob vastly exceeded that of the most distinguished characters of the days of the Republic.

While Nero was visiting Greece, the Jewish rebellion began which finally ended in the destruction of Jerusalem and of the Jewish nation. Fear and suspicion hurried the Emperor on to acts of greater barbarity. By a rapid succession of executions and assassinations, he removed the wealthiest, the most powerful, and the most virtuous of the Romans, and all the descendants of Augustus. Finally he wreaked his vengeance on the Roman commanders in the remote provinces. The virtuous Córbulo, who won victories over the Parthians and conquered Armenia, was arrested and executed; while

Rufus and Scribonius, the commanders of the Roman army in Germany, avoided a similar fate by committing suicide. It now became apparent to the other Roman commanders that they could only save themselves by open rebellion. Accordingly formidable insurrections broke out simultaneously in the Western provinces of the Empire. Julius Vindex, the Roman Proconsul of Gaul, unfurled the standard of revolt in that province; while Servius Sulpicius Galba headed an outbreak in Spain. From that moment the detestable tyrant regarded his utter ruin as nearly certain.

Nero was informed of Galba's revolt while he was at supper, and was instantly stricken with such horror that he overturned the table with his foot, thus breaking two highly valuable crystal vases. He then fell into a swoon, and when he recovered consciousness he tore his clothes and struck his head, exclaiming that he was completely undone. He next asked for the aid of Locusta, a woman celebrated in the art of poisoning, to supply him with the means of death. As he was foiled in this design, and as the rebellion assumed alarming proportions, he ran from house to house, but all doors were closed against him.

Nero then desired that one of his favorite gladiators would kill him, but none complied with his wishes. Thereupon he exclaimed in utter despair: "Alas! have I neither friend nor enemy!" He then ran forth in utter desperation, seemingly determined to cast himself into the Tiber; but, as his courage failed him, he made a sudden stop, and asked for some sacred place where he would be able to summon his fortitude and encounter death with resolute spirit. In this dilemma, Phaon, one of Nero's own freedmen, offered the Emperor his country-house, about four miles distant, where he would be able to conceal himself for some time. Nero gladly accepted this offer, and mounted on horseback, with his head covered and his face hidden in his handkerchief, and attended by four of his domestics.

Though Nero's journey was short, it was full of adventures. An earthquake gave him the first alarm. The lightning next flashed in his face. He heard around him only confused noises from the camp and the cries of the people uttering innumerable imprecations upon his head. He was met on the way by a traveler, who said: "There go men in pursuit of Nero." Another inquired of him whether there were any news of Nero in the city. In the midst of these encounters, Nero's horse became frightened at a corpse lying near the road. The Emperor dropped his handkerchief, whereupon a soldier in passing by recognized him. The soldier addressed Nero by name; and the Emperor leaped from his horse, abandoned the highway, and entered a thicket leading toward the back portion of Phaon's house, making the best of his way among the reeds and brambles with which the place was overgrown.

The Senate, meanwhile, discovering that the Prætorian Guards had sided with Galba, proclaimed that commander Emperor, and condemned Nero to suffer death "according to the rigor of the ancient laws." When the tyrant was informed of this action of the Senate, he inquired for the meaning thereof, and was told that the criminal was to be stripped naked, to be set in a pillory, and to be beaten to death with rods. Nero was so terrified at this information that he seized two poniards which he had brought with him, and threatened to stab himself; but, as he again lost courage, he returned the weapons to their sheaths, pretending that the critical moment had not yet arrived.

The cowardly tyrant then desired Sporus, one of his attendants, to begin the lamentation which was in use at funerals. He next implored one of those around him to die, in order to give him courage by his example. He afterwards commenced reproaching himself for cowardice, exclaiming: "Does this become Nero? Is this trifling well-timed? No! let me be courageous!" In short, the fallen tyrant had no time to lose, as the soldiers who pursued him were just then approaching the house. When Nero heard the sound of their horses' feet, he set a dagger to his throat, with which he inflicted a fatal wound upon himself, with the aid of Epaphroditus, his secretary. Before the Emperor was quite dead, the officer sent by the Senate arrived and endeavored to stop the flow of blood. Nero looked at this officer sternly, and said: "It is too late. Is this your fidelity?" With his eyes fixed and frightfully staring, the Emperor then expired. His body received a private but honorable burial; and many of the lower classes, whose favor he had won by his extravagant liberalities, lamented his death, honored his memory, and brought flowers to decorate his tomb.

GALBA was proclaimed Emperor, upon the death of Nero, A. D. 68. He was descended from an illustrious family, and was in the seventy-third year of his age at the time of his accession. He proceeded slowly on his journey toward Rome; and Nymphidius, Nero's minister, took advantage of this circumstance to make an effort to obtain the imperial purple for himself, by bribing the Prætorian Guards. But the conduct of Nymphidius during Nero's reign had rendered him so deservedly unpopular that the very soldiers who had accepted his bribes assassinated him. This rash conspiracy caused Galba to sully the beginning of his reign by harsh proceedings, which offended his subjects, who had not anticipated such a policy.

Although the new Emperor was virtuous himself, it was soon observed that he was the mere instrument of unworthy favorites, who, under the sanction of the Emperor's name, plundered the people and deprived the soldiers of their usual donations. In consequence of a revolt of the Roman legions in Germany, Galba named Cneius Piso, who was highly esteemed, as his successor. But this appointment highly incensed Otho, Nero's favorite, and the first husband of Poppæa, Nero's infamous mistress and second wife. Otho had been the foremost to espouse Galba's cause. Profiting by the disaffection of the Prætorian Guards, he proceeded to their camp, and easily induced these turbulent soldiers to proclaim him Emperor; and Galba lost his life in the struggle to preserve his power (A. D. 69).

OTHO, the new Emperor, was simply a passive instrument in the hands of the licentious soldiery. His debaucheries had completely worn him out, and he was in no way fitted for the high station which he had usurped. He had been scarcely invested with the imperial dignity when he found a competitor in the person of Vitellius, the commander of the Roman legions in Lower Germany. Otho hastily left Rome to take the field against his rival. Both parties approached each other so precipitately that three considerable battles occurred within the space of three days.

Finally Otho's forces were disastrously defeated at Bedriacum, near Cremona; and when Otho was informed of this catastrophe, he assembled his remaining troops, thanked them for their loyalty, and announced his purpose of giving up the struggle, in order to avoid any further bloodshed. He committed suicide the same night, after a reign of only three months and five days (A. D. 69). His death was sincerely lamented by his soldiers, and his determination to die in order to save his subjects from the horrors of civil war had something truly heroic in it.

VITELLIUS was in the meantime proclaimed Emperor by the Senate (A. D. 69). He instantly pardoned all Otho's partisans, and then proceeded to Rome in all the splendor and magnificence which he was able to command. While he was sitting in painted galleys, bedecked with garlands and flowers, and feasting on delicacies, his licentious troops were engaged in plundering without restraint. The new Emperor entered Rome as if he were taking possession of a conquered city, and the Senate and the people marched before him as if he had taken them prisoners in battle. After he had harangued the citizens and received the homage which his liberal promises had drawn from the people, he quietly established himself in his palace, to enjoy the pleasures which his gluttony and his luxurious habits had caused him to regard as the main happiness of his life.

Vitellius entrusted the administration of

public affairs to the vilest of his worthless favorites, and the soldiers became effeminate and forgetful of the art of war amid their unrestrained debaucheries. The Emperor only thought of enjoying himself with costly viands, and had acquired the art of renewing the pleasure of his meals by disgorging the food which had already ministered to his appetite. His gluttony was simply indescribable. He invited himself to the various meals of the day with different individuals. The influence which his courtiers wielded over him depended upon the frequency of their entertainments and their skill in conducting them. His brother Lucius gave him a dinner consisting of two thousand dishes of fish and seven thousand dishes of fowl. A dish, called the "Shield of Minerva," was an olio composed of the sounds of the fish called *scarrus*, the brains of woodcocks and pheasants, the tongues of rare birds, and the spawn of lampreys from the Caspian Sea.

Not satisfied with the gratification of his appetite, Vitellius sought pleasure in deeds of cruelty. He even put to death without scruple those who dined or supped with him at the same table. While visiting one of his parasites who was lying ill with a burning fever, he put poison in a cup of water and administered it to the sufferer with his own hand. This imperial monster even asserted that he derived pleasure from the sufferings of his victims. On one occasion, when he had condemned a man to death, he caused the unfortunate man's sons to be executed for begging their father's life. When a Roman knight was led forth to be executed, and hoped to save his life by announcing that he had made the Emperor his heir, Vitellius examined the will, and, thus ascertaining that he was simply joint heir with another, he caused the death of both the knight and the associate heir for the purpose of obtaining the entire estate himself.

The intolerable tyrannies and cruelties of Vitellius soon exasperated even the most servile of the Romans. The legions in Judæa under Vespasian, then engaged in the siege of Jerusalem, rose in revolt and proclaimed their general Emperor; and the Roman armies in Mœsia, Pannonia and Egypt likewise revolted. The revolted troops at Alexandria proclaimed Vespasian Emperor without his consent, but his legions forced him to accept the imperial dignity. He assembled his officers to consult about what action should be taken in this emergency; and it was decided that Vespasian's son Titus should prosecute the war against the rebellious Jews, that Mucianus should lead the greater part of the legions to Italy, and that Vespasian should levy a new army in the East.

When Vitellius was informed of the revolt, he prepared for a struggle to uphold his power and dignity. His army, commanded by Valens and Cæcína, encountered the legions of Vespasian, commanded by Antonius Primus, near Cremona. On the eve of a battle, Cæcína deserted to Vespasian; but Antonius attacked the troops who remained loyal to Vitellius. The battle continued until night and was renewed the next morning, when the legions of Vitellius gave way and were routed with the loss of thirty thousand men. The victorious army of Antonius then marched toward Rome, but was opposed by a small body of troops who guarded the passes of the Apennines.

When Vitellius was informed that his fleet had pronounced against him, he offered to resign the imperial office to Vespasian. In the confusion which these proceedings occasioned at Rome, one Sabinus seized the Capitol, but was attacked by the troops of Vitellius; and the Capitol was set on fire during the struggle, and completely destroyed, with all its valuable furniture, ornaments, works of art, and ancient public records. The victorious An:nius disregarded all the messages and offers of Vitellius by marching to Rome without delay. He attacked the city on three sides, drove the defenders inside the walls, and slaughtered a vast number of them. The reckless and abandoned populace of the city appeared utterly insensible to the disgrace of the Empire. While scenes of bloodshed and horror appeared all around them, they celebrated the riotous feast of the Saturnalia, and thought of nothing but drunkenness and debauchery.

Amidst this chaos of slaughter, riot and vice, the miserable Vitellius wandered about deserted even by his own slaves. Finally the victorious army of Antonius obtained possession of the city, and the wretched Emperor was dragged from the obscure hiding-place in which he had sought to conceal himself. With the hope of prolonging his miserable existence, he humbly entreated to be kept in prison until the arrival of Vespasian, to whom he promised to communicate important secrets. But his petition was of no avail. The soldiers of Antonius bound his hands, put a halter around his neck, and dragged him half naked into the Forum, heaping upon him insults and curses. They tied his hair backwards, and held the point of a sword under his chin to prevent him from hiding his face. Some bespattered him with mud, some struck him with their fists, while others ridiculed his red face and his immense corpulence. At last they killed him with blows, dragged his body through the streets, and cast it into the Tiber.

Thus ended the reign of Vitellius, which had lasted but eight months and five days (A. D. 69). He was the most beastly of all the Roman Emperors. The soldiers took advantage of the opportunity for plunder by pursuing the fugitives into the houses and temples and committing every kind of rapine and cruelty. But these atrocities were stopped upon the arrival of Mucianus, Vespasian's general, and tranquillity was restored in Rome. The Senate and the army united in proclaiming VESPASIAN Emperor, and messengers were sent to him in Egypt, requesting him to return to Rome (A. D. 69).

Vespasian commanded the Roman armies in the East during the events which resulted in investing him with the imperial purple. His arrival in the city reëstablished tranquillity and spread universal joy throughout the Empire. He first applied himself to restoring the discipline of the army. He then revived the authority of the Senate, and supplied its diminished ranks with eminent men from the provinces and the colonies. He finally reformed the courts of law, which had longed ceased showing any regard for justice. Vespasian's virtues, supported by a firm temper, led to a vast improvement in the social condition of Rome. His excessive love of money was his only fault. He was the first good and able Emperor that Rome had after Augustus.

At the beginning of Vespasian's reign a dangerous revolt broke out in Roman Germany, under the leadership of Civilis, who endeavored to establish an independent state in that quarter. The revolt extended to the eastern portion of Gaul, and Civilis induced Sabinus and Classicus to proclaim a Gallic empire. The Gauls declined to take part in the revolt; and Cerialis, Vespasian's general, very easily restored tranquillity to that province, after which he passed into Roman Germany and drove Civilis across the Rhine (A. D. 69–70.)

The Jews, who had risen in rebellion against the Roman power during Nero's reign, were subdued during Vespasian's reign, when they were destroyed as a nation. Jerusalem was taken by the Roman legions under Titus, the son of Vespasian, after one of the most remarkable sieges on record, the Jews defending the Holy City with an army of six hundred thousand men. The city and the Temple were reduced to a heap of ruins by the conquering Romans; and many of the vanquished Jews fell by the swords of the Romans, or died by their own hands, while thousands were sold into slavery (A. D. 70). Among those taken prisoners by the Romans was the great Jewish historian Josephus, who wrote a complete history of the Jewish race in Greek. Ever since the destruction of Jerusalem by Titus, the Jews have been dispersed over every part of the earth.

Titus and his father were honored with a splendid triumph at Rome because of this great victory, and the rich ornaments of the Temple were displayed in the procession. A triumphal arch was likewise erected to

Titus, and on it were sculptured representations of his great deeds. This interesting structure is still in existence.

During the reign of Vespasian the Romans under Cerealis extended their dominions in Britain. In A. D. 78, Cneius Julius Agricola, a native of Gaul, was sent to Britain, and administered the Roman government in that country for seven years, during which he subdued the whole of what is now embraced in England. He was justly celebrated for his great abilities as a general and a statesman. He first recovered the island of Mona (now Anglesey) from the Ordovíces. His success was owing no less to his promptitude than to his valor. He made his appearance in the hostile country before the enemy were aware that he had passed the frontiers; and the Ordovíces, disconcerted by his sudden attack, consented to acknowledge the Roman sway. He attacked the Brigantes and other tribes between the Wash and the Tyne, and reduced the whole of Britain as far north as the river Tyne and Solway Frith, between which he erected a line of forts to protect the Roman dominions in the island against the incursions of the savage Picts and Scots from Caledonia (A. D. 79).

Having restored tranquillity to the Empire, Vespasian had the satisfaction of closing the Temple of Janus, which had stood open for six years. He next devoted himself to the task of securing the welfare of his subjects by moral as well as political reforms. He restored the old discipline of the Roman army. He likewise abridged and improved the course of proceedings in courts of justice, and it was said that no person suffered from injustice or from a severe decree during his entire reign.

Vespasian carefully fostered the arts and sciences, restored the public buildings, and improved the city. He patronized Josephus, the Jewish historian; Quintilian, the rhetorician; and Pliny, the naturalist. He invited the most celebrated masters and artificers from every part of the world to Rome. He restored the Capitol to its original splendor. He built the famous Flavian Amphi-

theater, whose ruins, now known as the Colosséum, bear testimony to the grandeur and magnificence of ancient Rome. He likewise founded new cities, and repaired the old ones which had suffered from the ravages of his predecessors.

Vespasian was as much celebrated for his clemency as for his wisdom. He settled a handsome dowry on the daughter of Vitellius, and refused to punish certain conspirators who had plotted against him. The only exception to his merciful and forgiving policy occurred in the case of Julius Sabínus, who had proclaimed himself Emperor on the death of Vitellius. After being defeated by Vespasian's army, this rash aspirant for the imperial dignity concealed himself for nine years in a cave, where he was attended by his faithful wife Empona, who provided him with the means of subsistence. Sabínus was finally discovered and conveyed a prisoner to Rome, where he was put to death.

Notwithstanding the wisdom with which Vesparian administered the government, he has been charged with avarice and rapacity. He revived taxes which had fallen into disuse, and was believed to have obtained large profits by speculations in trade; but may have had justification therefor in the impoverished condition of the public treasury at the time of his accession, and the necessities occasioned by the incursions of the barbarians, who ravaged the Eastern provinces of the Empire until they were finally defeated by Titus.

Vespasian died of an illness in Campania, in A. D. 79, after a reign of ten years, and was succeeded by his son TITUS, the conqueror of Jerusalem; though his other son, Domitian, made some opposition, alleging that his father's will had been altered. Titus had been fond of pleasure and dissipation in his youth; but, as soon as he obtained the imperial purple, he reformed his habits and became a model of regularity and moderation. He acquired the well-merited title of the "Delight of Mankind," in consequence of his generosity, his love of justice, his hatred of informers, his care to prevent dissensions, his obliging disposition, and his readiness to do good on all occasions. Having called to mind one evening that he had not performed any beneficent deed during the day, he exclaimed: "I have lost a day!"

In the first year of the reign of Titus (August 24, A. D. 79), occurred the most terrible eruption of the volcano of Vesuvius ever known, completely destroying the two cities of Herculaneum and Pompeii. The elder Pliny, the great naturalist, perished at the destruction of Pompeii. Though most of the inhabitants of the two cities may have had sufficient warning of the approaching calamity to enable them to flee, which most of them may have done, it is very evident that some of them delayed their flight until it was too late to save themselves, as is fully proven by the remains of human beings, found in situations showing how instantaneously they were overtaken by death.

The bodies of seventeen persons were thus discovered in the cellar of a house at Pompeii, inclosed in a hard substance, which probably burst into a liquid form into the vault and hardened as it cooled. When this cellar was excavated, the perfect mould of a woman with a child in her arms was found in the solid substance that had filled it; and two skeletons were inside this mould, the larger having a gold chain around its neck and rings on its fingers. In the barracks were found the remains of two soldiers chained to the stocks, who had doubtless been forgotten amid the terror, the darkness and confusion of that terrible day. Those who made their escape from the unfortunate cities would most naturally have taken all their most valuable effects with them; nor could they have imagined that what they left behind them would be of so much historical importance in subsequent times, when every other vestige of the domestic life of the Romans would have been obliterated long before.

STREET OF CORNELIUS RUFUS, POMPEII.

The houses of Herculaneum and Pompeii, and perhaps those of all other provincial towns of Italy in Roman times, were perhaps only one or two stories high, and consisted of a number of small rooms around a court, over the entrance of which the owner's name was written. The shops were open to the streets, with folding doors, like a coach-house, and which had signs painted over them, denoting the trade carried on inside the house. Many of these houses at Pompeii were taverns, where hot wine and

THE LAST DAYS OF POMPEII.

a liquor believed to have been mead were sold. Some of the wine was yet remaining in earthen vessels called *amphoræ*, and drinking cups were standing on the marble slabs, when the buried cities were unearthed. Olives were likewise found in a jar in a remarkable state of preservation. A box of pills stood on the counter of an apothecary. In a fruiterer's shop were chestnuts, walnuts and almonds, without any evidences of decay.

The articles for domestic and professional use closely resembled those which we use, thus showing that the Romans were absolutely familiar with the useful arts. Needles, scissors, compasses, fine surgical instruments, silver spoons, all kinds of kitchen implements, and tools for working at various trades, are among the relics so wonderfully preserved. The most wonderful specimens of Roman art are the metal stamps which the trades people used in marking their goods and in impressing letters on wax to teach children the art of reading.

During the reign of Titus, Julius Agricola continued his conquests in Britain; and, in his third and fourth campaigns, he reduced the Scotch Lowlands, extending the Roman dominion as far north as the Friths of Forth and Clyde.

The good Titus died of a fever in A. D. 81, after a short reign of only two years, and was succeeded by his brother DOMITIAN, who was suspected of having caused his death by poison. The new Emperor commenced his reign with the character of a liberal, just and humane sovereign. He refused the legacies which had been bequeathed to him, because the testators had children of their own. He sat for entire days engaged in the work of revising the sentences of the judges, and abhorred all kinds of cruelty to such a degree that he forbade the sacrifice of oxen. He furnished new books to the libraries which had suffered from fire, and sent persons to Alexandria to transcribe manuscripts for this purpose.

But these fair promises with which Domitian had opened his reign were soon blighted. His mind had become absorbed with the pursuits of archery and gaming; and his main ambition was to entertain the people with sports and exhibitions, and to preside in ostentatious pomp for the purpose of distributing rewards. He passed his hours of seclusion in killing flies. On one occasion, Vibius, one of his servants, was asked whether any one was with the Emperor, and replied: "No one, not even a fly."

Domitian also had a great passion for military glory, and this caused him to envy the reputation of his generals. One of these commanders was Julius Agricola, who still pursued his conquering career in Britain. In A. D. 83 Agricola invaded Caledonia as far as the low country north and north-east of the Frith of Forth, and defeated the Caledonians in several engagements, after which he explored the country. The next year (A. D. 84), Agricola again attacked the Caledonians, defeated their leader, Gálgacus, and threatened to conquer the whole country. His fleet explored the Caledonian coast as far as Cape Wrath and discovered the northern limits of Britain. By this naval expedition the Romans ascertained for the first time that Britain was an island, while they also discovered the Orcádes (now Orkney) islands.

Agricola resolved to confirm and secure the advantages which his military success had gained, by the adoption of an enlightened policy. He induced the Britons to lay aside their own barbarous habits and to adopt the Roman laws and customs, and instructed them in letters and science and in the arts of civilized life. Towns were built and roads constructed throughout the country. Having seen that they were unable to withstand the Romans, the Britons acquiesced in the Roman dominion, and were gradually incorporated into the mighty Empire of the Cæsars.

Domitian envied and hated Agricola on account of his brilliant achievements, and recalled him to Italy under the pretense of appointing him to the government of Syria (A. D. 84). But when the conquering general arrived at Rome, the Emperor received him with great coolness. Agrícola then retired to private life, and died of illness soon afterward, suspected of having been poisoned by the jealous Emperor.

For the purpose of making himself a great general, Domitian now organized an army, which he led into Gaul, under the pretense of undertaking a campaign against the Germans (A. D. 84). He led this expedition across the Rhine against the German tribe of the Chatti; and, although the Emperor did not encounter an enemy, this raid served to strike terror into the German tribes of that quarter. Domitian took the honors of a triumph for this expedition, returning to Rome in pompous array, taking a number of slaves with him and dressing them as Germans, thus pretending that they were prisoners taken in victorius battles. In A. D. 87 Domitian led an expedition against the German tribe of the Marcomanni, and their neighbors, the Quadi, and the Sarmatians; but his arms encountered reverses.

The most important of Domitian's wars was that which he waged with the Dacians, who occupied the country north of the Danube, east of the Theiss and south-west of the Dniester. The war with the Dacians began in the first year of Domitian's reign by an invasion of the province of Mœsia by the Dacians under their king, Decébalus, who defeated and cut off a Roman legion with its general, and ravaged the province to the foot of Mount Hæmus. Domitian made no effort to avenge this disaster for five years, until in A. D. 86, when his legions crossed the Danube and invaded Dacia, but were totally defeated. The next year (A. D. 87), the Romans won a victory; but three years later (A. D. 90), peace was concluded with these formidable barbarians on humiliating terms to the Romans, who consented to pay an annual tribute to the Dacians on condition that they would refrain from inroads into Mœsia. Thus for the first time did imperial Rome agree to purchase peace from an enemy.

Domitian now began to practice cruelty for amusement. During his reign occurred the second great persecution of the Christians. The Jews were also relentlessly persecuted by him. His avarice led him to seize the estates of all persons against whom he might be able to fabricate the most trivial charges. He was even more usurping and cruel than Nero, and revived the system of false accusations, forfeitures and death penalties which had caused the fall of that tyrant. But this monster of cruelty also died a violent death. His wife Domitia, whom he had designed putting to death, finally headed a conspiracy against him; and Domitian was assassinated, after considerable resistance, by Stephanus, the comptroller of the household, who was himself slain on the spot by some of the officers on guard (A. D. 96.) Domitian, who was thus murdered in the sixteenth year of his reign, was the last of the twelve Cæsars, including Julius Cæsar and Augustus and the ten Emperors who succeeded the latter.

Domitian's cruelties had so discredited the principle of hereditary succession that the Senate now asserted its right of naming a new Emperor—a right which that body had not exercised since the time of Augustus. It accordingly named the successsor of the murdered Emperor. The Prætorian Guards offered no objection to this action of the Senate, being satisfied with demanding the punishment of the assassins of Domitian. By thus taking advantage of the crisis, the Senate increased its power; and its prompt action gave it a position and a consideration of which it had been deprived for more than a century.

The Emperor chosen by the Senate to succeed Domitian was MARCUS COCCEIUS NERVA, who was then about sixty-five years old, and who was a native of Spain, in which country he had been born of an illustrious family. Nerva was the first of what are classed as the *Five Good Emperors*. He was of a mild disposition and of moderate abilities. As the Senate had chosen him solely from their experience of his talents and virtues, no doubt was entertained that he would do honor to the imperial dignity.

The horrors of his predecessor's reign induced Nerva to govern with the extreme of clemency and indulgence.

When he accepted the imperial dignity, he took an oath that no Roman Senator should be put to death during his reign. He was noted for his liberality in bestowing gifts upon his friends, and he sold all his gold and silver plate to enable him to continue his generosities. He abolished the oppressive taxes which his predecessors had imposed, and restored the property which Domitian had seized. In addition to originating good and wise laws, Nerva united a system of retrenchment with well-judged acts of liberality, more than any other Roman sovereign. He did not permit the erection of any statue to himself, sold all those raised to Domitian, and caused the gaudy robes and luxurious furniture of the palace to be converted into money.

Notwithstanding the benevolence and mildness which characterized his reign, Nerva soon began to experience the malignity which vice ever displays toward virtue. A conspiracy was formed to assassinate him, but was fortunately detected. The Senate desired to deal rigorously with the plotters, but Nerva was satisfied with driving them into exile. Nerva's clemency in this instance encouraged another plot against him, on the part of the Prætorian Guards, who pretended a desire to avenge the assassination of Domitian. Nerva employed all the gentle means at his command to suppress this mutiny. He presented himself to the mutineers, bared his breast, and desired them to take his life rather than bring new calamities upon their country. But his self-devotion did not avail to subdue the ferocity of the mutineers. They killed two of the Emperor's attendants in his very presence, and forced him to approve of their sedition. Happily, this was the limit of their insolence, and the ultimate consequence of this mutiny was most favorable for the Empire.

As Nerva was childless, he selected a successor, with the sanction of the Senate, in the person of Marcus Ulpius Trajanus, better known as Trajan, and adopted him with the usual ceremonies. This act established the future policy of the sovereign, and it became a recognized principle of the government that the Emperor should select as his adopted son and successor the one most fit for the place out of the whole population of the Empire. Before Trajan was able to arrive at Rome, Nerva died of a fever, said to have been caused by a violent passion in a dispute with a Senator (A. D. 98), after he had reigned but two years.

Nerva was succeeded in the imperial purple by TRAJAN, the greatest of all the Roman Emperors. Trajan was born at Hispalis (now Seville), in Spain, but of Italian parentage. His father had been elevated to the rank of patrician by Vespasian, and after various expeditions on the Euphrates and on the Rhine, in which he was accompanied by his son, he had been honored with the Consulate and with a triumph.

In this way Trajan acquired a considerable military reputation in early life. When he was intrusted with the command of the Roman army in Lower Germany, he lived in the most simple and unassuming manner. He performed long marches on foot with his soldiers, sharing with them all the dangers and fatigues of war. He knew all the old soldiers by their names, and conversed with them in the most familiar manner. Before retiring to rest, he personally inspected the camp, and satisfied himself of the vigilance of the sentinels and the security of the army.

Trajan's disposition was most amiable, mild and modest; and in his character he combined all those mental and moral qualities, along with all that experience and personal bravery in war, which appear rather to be possessed by a number of persons than to be united in but one individual. His personal character corresponded with his noble intellect; and when he entered Rome in the vigor of manhood, he inspired his subjects with the respect and admiration which they ever afterward attached to his name.

Trajan was distinguished for the most untiring industry. He administered public affairs almost alone, carrying on a voluminous correspondence with the various provincial governors and furnishing instructions to each for the government of his province. He sternly suppressed delation and scrupulously respected the rights of the Senate, allowing the members freedom of speech, and treating them as his equals in social intercourse. His financial administration was marked with success, and was so wisely and prudently conducted that it was never found necessary to resort to increased taxation or to confiscations of property. Yet the public treasury was kept so well filled that the Emperor always had funds sufficient for his great military expeditions, his great public works, and his measures to relieve the distresses of his subjects.

Trajan improved Nerva's poor law by extending and systematizing its provisions. He relieved the embarrassments of proprietors of encumbered estates by loaning them money at a low rate of interest. He caused the ravages occasioned by earthquakes and tempests to be repaired without delay. He founded colonies in remote portions of the Empire; erected bridges over the Rhine and the Danube; and adorned Rome and the provincial towns with many useful and ornamental works. The most important of these structures in Rome were the great Forum and the Ulpian Library.

While Trajan was so liberal in his treatment of his subjects, he spent very little upon himself; and found ample time in the midst of all his many engagements to give a

TRAJAN'S ARCH, BENEVENTO, ITALY.

patient hearing to all the numerous appeals made to him from the lower courts. Trajan's reign ranks next to that of Augustus in literature. Tacitus, the great Roman historian; the younger Pliny, the charming letter writer; Suetonius, the historian; and Plutarch, the eminent Greek biographer, flourished at this period.

The Romans always regarded Trajan as the ablest and the best of their Emperors, and he was considered the ablest man in

THE COLUMN OF TRAJAN, ROME.

Rome at the time of his accession. His faults were mainly his great fondness for wine and for sensual pleasures, but these were overbalanced by his numerous good and brilliant qualities.

Trajan's only error as Emperor was his desire to be ranked in subsequent ages as a great warrior and conqueror. As the time of Roman conquest had passed, he would have exhibited wisdom and policy in regarding the great rivers Rhine, Danube and Euphrates, as the boundaries of the Roman Empire, in accordance with the advice of Augustus.

No sooner had Trajan become Emperor than he was called upon to curb the insolence of the Dacians, who had ravaged the Empire during Domitian's reign, and who now demanded the tribute which that Emperor's cowardice had induced him to offer. Trajan chafed under this humiliating tribute, and in A. D. 101 he led a formidable army toward Dacia, and overawed the barbarians by suddenly appearing upon their frontier.

Trajan threw a bridge over the Danube, entered Dacia with his army, and occupied Zermizegethusa, the Dacian capital. The next year (A. D. 102) he defeated Decébalus in a great battle, thus obliging him to solicit peace, which was granted in A. D. 104 on severe terms to the Dacian king. The next year (A. D. 104) Decébalus broke the treaty and renewed the war. Thereupon Trajan again invaded Dacia, carrying all before him. Decébalus and his nobles committed suicide in despair. In the battle in which Trajan finally overthrew the Dacian king, the slaughter was so great that all the linen in the Roman camp was insufficient for dressing the wounds of the soldiers. Dacia became a Roman province; and Roman colonies were planted at Zermizegethusa, Apulum, Napoca and Cerna.

On his return to Rome, Trajan celebrated a splendid triumph; and the rejoicings continued one hundred and twenty-three days, during which the people were entertained with games, in which eleven thousand wild beasts and ten thousand gladiators, mainly Dacian prisoners, are said to have been slain. To commemorate his victories, Trajan employed the architect Apollodórus to erect a magnificent column in Rome, covered with sculptures, representing the events of his Dacian campaigns. This splendid structure still remains, and is one of the most remarkable objects of the city.

Trajan's next war was with the Parthian Empire. The pretext for the quarrel was the conflicting claims of the Romans and the Parthians to direct the affairs of Armenia. Trajan began the war by invading Armenia in A. D. 115, and conquering that country and reducing it to the condition of a Roman province; the Armenian king himself being taken prisoner. Trajan then invaded the territories of the Parthian Empire, overrunning and subduing Mesopotamia and Assyria, also reducing those Parthian dependencies to the condition of Roman provinces.

The next year (A. D. 116) Trajan marched southward and invaded the Parthian province of Babylonia, taking the cities of Seleucia, Ctesiphon and Babylon, and ravaging the country as far as Susa. When the Parthians had made a stand on the Euphrates, Trajan caused a large number of boats to be constructed among the mountains during a single night, brought them to the river suddenly, and transported his troops across the stream in the very presence of the enemy. In this campaign Trajan traversed countries which had never before been trod by the foot of a Roman soldier.

But revolts now broke out in Trajan's rear. Seleucia rebelled, but was retaken. The city of Hatra (now El Hadr) resisted Trajan with success. The inclemency of the weather and the inundations of the rivers almost destroyed Trajan's army; and the Emperor, suffering from the infirmities of age, and convinced of his untenable position, found himself obliged to retreat. He therefore relinquished the province of Babylonia to a Parthian prince named Parthamáspates, who consented to hold his dominions under the suzerainty of the Roman sovereign. Trajan then retired to Antioch, still retaining the provinces of Armenia,

Mesopotamia and Assyria as the fruits of the war.

Under Trajan, Arabia Petræa was also added to the Roman Empire by an expedition under the command of Cornelius Palma. Trajan established a king over Albania, a country bordering on the western shore of the Caspian Sea. He placed governors and lieutenants in the other Roman provinces. Trajan's reign was stained by the third great persecution of the Christians; and St. Ignatius, Bishop of Antioch, was torn to pieces in the amphitheater.

After arranging the affairs of the East, Trajan set out on his return to Rome, leaving his forces in Asia under the command of his adopted son, Adrian. The most magnificent preparations were made in the imperial city for the reception of the conquering Emperor; but Trajan was destined never again to behold that city. Exhausted with the fatigues of war, he was attacked with illness in Cilicia; and finding himself unable to proceed any farther, he was carried to the city of Selinus, where he died A. D. 117, at the age of sixty-five years, after a reign of nineteen years. His ashes were conveyed to Rome in a golden urn, and were buried under the column bearing his name.

Trajan was succeeded by his adopted son ADRIAN, who, like his illustrious predecessor, was a native of Híspalis (now Seville), in Spain, but of a Spanish family. Adrian was distantly related to Trajan, and had served under him with distinction. He was forty-two years of age at the time of his accession, and was childless. He resembled Trajan in many respects; being genial in disposition, affable in manner, and liberal in character. He expended the public funds lavishly in the service of the state and the improvement of the Empire, but managed the finances so skillfully that his treasury was never exhausted. Though he administered the government with firmness, he was moderate in everything, and scrupulously maintained the forms of a free government.

Adrian resembled Trajan in his capacity for and devotion to business, and never permitted his love of pleasure to interfere in his official duties. He liberally patronized the arts and wisely encouraged literature. Like most men of his time, he was lax in his morals, but he never permitted himself to become involved in any scandal. He was irritable and more jealous than Trajan, but these faults were overbalanced by his love of peace. He preferred the triumphs of peace to the victories of war, and wisely devoted himself to the improvement of his dominions without caring to extend them. He endeavored faithfully to promote the welfare and happiness of all his subjects.

Being quite satisfied with the old limits of the Empire, Adrian appeared in no way ambitious to make conquests, and abandoned all the acquisitions which Trajan had made, as he considered them more of a detriment than an advantage to the Empire, because it would require a greater cost of life and treasure to hold them than they were worth. Adrian was the first Roman Emperor who made a regular tour through the provinces of his Empire. He spent fifteen years in traveling over Gaul, Germany, Britain, Spain, Greece, and all the Roman provinces in Asia and Africa, in order to become acquainted with the needs of his subjects. He resided for protracted periods of time at the different provincial capitals—Eborácum (now York), in Britain, Athens, Antioch and Alexandria.

In Britain, Adrian vastly improved the city of Eborácum, and erected a wall of wood and earth from the river Eden, in Cumberland, to the river Tyne, in Northumberland, as a barrier against the predatory inroads of the savage Picts and Scots of Caledonia. He made no distinction in his treatment of the different races under his dominion, and left mementos of his presence in the great works which he constructed in every province which he visited. All portions of his Empire were thus benefited.

Adrian's reign was an almost unbroken period of peace and prosperity; the only wars which disturbed the tranquillity of the Empire being the struggle with the Roxolani in A. D. 118 and a revolt of the Jews under Barcochebas in A. D. 131. The strug-

FLOURISHING PERIOD OF THE EMPIRE.

gle with the Jews continued until A. D. 135, and terminated in the defeat of the Jews and their absolute expulsion from Palestine. A Roman colony was established at Jerusa-

On Adrian's return to Rome, the Senate decreed him a triumph, which he modestly declined. Adrian's virtues were not unalloyed. He tarnished his reign with the

MAUSOLEUM OF ADRIAN AT ROME.

lem under the name of Ælia Capitolina; and the Christians whom Titus had banished were freely admitted to this colony by Adrian.

fourth great persecution of the Christians, and also cruelly persecuted the Jews. He likewise permitted himself to be influenced by unworthy favorites, and listened to slanderers and informers. The excellence of his character was thus tarnished with darker shades. As his age advanced, his natural irritability of temper and jealousy were increased by his indulgence of these faults. He grew regardless of human life and put men to death for trivial offenses. He caused an architect to be executed for venturing to criticise some statues which the Emperor himself had designed.

As Adrian grew older, he became more reckless of the pain which he inflicted. He had a brother-in-law ninety years old, and this old man had a grandson eighteen years of age. Adrian caused both of them to be executed because he suspected them of a conspiracy. This double execution horrified the popular feeling. The old man protested his innocence, just before his death, and uttered a prayer of vengeance that Adrian might desire to die and find death impossible —an imprecation which was verified.

Tormented with disease, Adrian lingered long after he desired death, and entreated his slaves to kill him. He even stabbed himself with a dagger, but death still failed to relieve him of his suffering. He finally died after a prolonged illness, at Baiæ, near Naples, A. D. 138, after a prosperous reign of twenty-one years. With all his faults, he deservedly ranks as one of the greatest and best of the Roman Emperors. It was no little glory to have combined twenty years of almost unbroken peace with the maintenance of a contented and efficient army, liberal expenditure with a full exchequer not replenished by oppressive or unworthy means, and a free-speaking Senate with a firm and strong monarchy.

Adrian's successor was his adopted son, Titus Aurelius Antoninus, who is more generally known as ANTONINUS PIUS, the surname of *Pius* having been given to him because of his mild and merciful reign, which was the most tranquil and happy period which the Roman Empire ever enjoyed. He was fifty-one years old at his accession. His reign of twenty-three years was not prolific of events, as peace and prosperity prevailed throughout the whole Roman world.

A disturbance which ruffled the general serenity of the Empire was a revolt of the Brigantes in Britain (A. D. 140), chastised by Lollius Urbicus, who erected a barrier between the Friths of Forth and Clyde, known as the *Wall of Antonine*. Other troubles were a Jewish rebellion in Egypt, disturbances in Dacia, and the attacks of nomads from the African desert upon the Romans in Mauritania.

Antoninus Pius was blameless in both public and private life. He made no internal changes. He continued the liberal policy of his predecessors, Nerva, Trajan and Adrian, towards the Senate. He discouraged delation. He was generous in his gifts and largesses, but never exhausted the resources of the public treasury. He encouraged learning, erected many important edifices, watched over the whole Empire with a paternal solicitude, and made the happiness of his subjects his chief object.

The government of the provinces engaged the sovereign's earnest attention for the first time; and the Emperor's legates ceased oppressing the inhabitants of the provinces, as they saw that their conduct was very closely watched. The provincials were now gratified at seeing public schools established for the instruction of youth, harbors cleaned out and repaired, new marts of trade opened, etc.; instead of beholding their revenues squandered to maintain a profligate court or to pamper a degraded populace.

His liberality of conviction and his indulgence of temperament induced him to extend the leniency which was a principle of his government to the Christians, and he was the first Roman Emperor who actively protected that hitherto-persecuted sect. He suspended the persecutions against these people and ordered the punishment of their accusers as calumniators.

Antoninus Pius did not enjoy the happiness in his domestic life which his virtues deserved. His wife, Faustina, was notorious for her irregularities; his two sons died before he became Emperor; and his daughter, Annia Faustina, whom he married to the elder of his adopted sons, Marcus Aurelius

Antonínus, was not of blameless character. Nevertheless, Antonínus Pius enjoyed some compensation for his other domestic troubles in the affection, the respect and the growing promise of this excellent and amiable prince. He exercised a proper discernment in drawing a sharp line of distinction between the two adopted sons which Adrian assigned him. He showed the highest favor towards the elder, Marcus Aurelius, by marrying him to his daughter, associating him in the government, and formally appointing him his sole successor. He reposed no confidence whatever in Lucius Ælius Verus, advancing him to no public post, and giving him no prospect of the succession.

After a beneficent and tranquil reign of twenty-three years, whose prosperity is amply indicated by the fact that it afforded no materials for history, Antonínus Pius died of a fever at one of his villas, bequeathing to his family only his private fortune (A. D. 161). The Romans so highly venerated the memory of this excellent ruler that every Roman Emperor during the greater portion of the following century considered it essential to his popularity to assume the surname of Antonínus.

MARCUS AURELIUS, the adopted son and the successor of Antonínus Pius, was forty years of age at his accession, in A. D. 161. His attachment to his adoptive father and predecessor caused him to assume the surname of Antonínus. He was the last of the *Five Good Emperors*, beginning with Nerva. He was surnamed *the Philosopher*, because of his attachment to the doctrines of the Stoics. He shared the imperial power with Lucius Ælius Verus, to whom he gave his daughter in marriage.

Marcus Aurelius was personally one of the best of the Roman Emperors; having a love for religion, justice and peace, and sincerely endeavoring to promote the welfare of his subjects. He was a man of pure life and simple habits, and united all the virtues of the heroic age of Rome in his character. In disposition he was kind and affectionate, and was one of the first of the Cæsars in intellectual capacity.

Notwithstanding the worthiness of his character, the reign of Marcus Aurelius was clouded with misfortune. His wife, Faustína, the daughter of Antonínus Pius, was notorious for her dissoluteness; and his eldest son and daughter died during their childhood. The conduct of Lucius Ælius Verus, whom he had associated with him in the government of the Empire, caused him great grief and anxiety.

Though Marcus Aurelius desired peace, he was involved in war during his entire reign. The Parthians renewed the war for the possession of Armenia, in the year of his accession (A. D. 161). Severianus was sent against the Parthians, who had invaded Armenia, but was defeated and slain. The Emperor then took the opportunity of sending his unworthy son-in-law and colleague, Verus, with the command of an army against the Parthians (A. D. 162). Verus himself proceeded no farther than Antioch, where he established his residence and abandoned himself to every kind of debauchery, while his officers reduced some of the Parthian cities.

Avidius Cassius, Prefect of Syria, and Statius Priscus, assumed the offensive. Priscus drove the Parthians from Armenia; while Cassius invaded Mesopotamia, captured Seleucia, Ctesiphon and Babylon, burned the royal palace of the Parthian kings at Ctesiphon (A. D. 165), and forced the Parthians to solicit peace. Peace was concluded the following year (A. D. 166), by which Parthia ceded Mesopotamia to Rome, while Armenia was restored to its old condition of a semi-independent kingdom. Thus this war resulted in advancing the boundary of the Roman dominions on the east to the Tigris.

The tranquillity and happiness which Rome had enjoyed under the firm but merciful rule of Marcus Aurelius was interrupted by the return of Verus, who claimed a triumph for the victories which his officers had won. The Roman army which returned from the East brought the plague with it, communicating the infection to every province through which the legions passed. The violence of the pestilence lasted several years.

The year after the close of the war with Parthia (A. D. 167), the barbarians north of the Danube, pressed upon by the advancing wave of a formidable Scythian migration, were forced across that river into the Roman dominions. Both Marcus Aurelius and Verus took the field against the German tribes of the Quadi and the Marcomanni, who had ravaged Pannonia, crossed the Alps into Italy, and reached Aquileia (A. D. 167). On the approach of the Roman armies under the Emperor and his colleague, the Quadi and the Marcomanni retreated across the Alps. In A. D. 168 both Marcus Aurelius and Verus crossed the Alps, but returned to Italy, after having provided for the defense of the Alpine passes. Verus died the next year (A. D. 169) from the effects of his intemperate habits, thus relieving the Emperor of one of his troubles.

The weakness of the Roman efforts in these two years encouraged the tribes along the Danube to a general rising, and almost all of those tribes took the field against the Romans (A. D. 169). Marcus Aurelius then posted himself on the Danube, where he remained quartered for about three years (A. D. 169–172). In A. D. 174 he achieved a brilliant victory over the Quadi, who had enticed him into a barren defile, where his troops were in danger of perishing from hunger. In their distress the Roman soldiers were relieved by a thunder-storm. The rain relieved their wants, and the lightning struck the tents of the barbarians, who, believing this occurrence to be miraculous, at once submitted. This was the origin of the story of the "Thundering Legion"—one of the numerous monkish myths of the following age, in which it was pretended that the shower was sent in answer to the prayers of the Christian soldiers in the Roman army. When the Emperor received information that Cassius had revolted, he concluded peace with the Quadi (A. D. 175).

After the death of Verus, Cassius was induced to proclaim himself Emperor, and obtained possession of most of the Asiatic provices. Before Marcus Aurelius was able to arrive in the East, the rebel leader was slain by his own officers after a short reign of three months. Marcus Aurelius caused the papers of Cassius to be burned without reading them, and suffered no man to be punished for his participation in the revolt.

The Marcomanni soon broke the peace which they had made with Marcus Aurelius, and gained some successes. Marcus Aurelius and his son Cómmodus took the field against them in A. D. 178, and the barbarians were defeated the following year (A. D. 179).

Although one of the best of the Roman Emperors, Marcus Aurelius has been charged with being unfaithful to his marriage vows, and with neglecting the health and moral training of his offspring. His reign was stained with the fifth great persecution of the Christians. Justin Martyr was beheaded at Rome; while St. Polycarp—Bishop of Smyrna, and the friend and disciple of St. John—was burned at the stake. Multitudes of Christians likewise perished for their faith at Lugdunum (now Lyons), in Gaul, and at Vindobona (now Vienna), in Pannonia. As Marcus Aurelius had been a devoted follower of the Stoics, whose philosophical opinions he had imbibed in his youth, he may have been influenced in his treatment of the Christians by the advice of the harsh and arrogant members of that sect, who surrounded him. Nevertheless, as a distinguished divine truly says: "But the persecution of a sect so small and so obscure as the Christian was at that time is scarcely perceptible as a diminution of the sum of human happiness secured to the world by the gentleness and equity which regulated all his actions."

Marcus Aurelius, who was classed as a philosopher, was the author of a work on moral philosophy called *Meditations*, which has been transmitted to modern times, and contains a summary of the best rules for a virtuous life that have ever been devised by unaided reason or simple philosophy. He was one of the few sovereigns who attained a respectable rank as a writer, and was the last Roman Emperor who made the welfare and happiness of his subjects his main object.

THE CATACOMBS OF CALIXTUS AT ROME.

The mild and beneficent Marcus Aurelius died at Vindobona, in A. D. 180, after a reign of nineteen years. This ended the flourishing period of eighty-four years embraced in the reigns of the *Five Good Emperors*—Nerva, Trajan, Adrian, Antonínus Pius and Marcus Aurelius—from A. D. 96 to A. D. 180. With the death of Marcus Aurelius the glory of the Roman Empire virtually ended. The greater number of his successors were detestable and intolerable tyrants, who generally suffered violent deaths. From this time the Empire rapidly verged towards its fall. The barbarians from Northern Europe at length pressed heavily upon its northern frontiers, and finally put an end to its existence.

Unlike the first four of the Five Good Emperors, who were all childless, or at any rate without male offspring, Marcus Aurelius had a single dearly-loved son, in some respects promising. Allowing the tender partiality of the father to prevail over the cold prudence of the sovereign, and persuading himself that his son Cómmodus would prove a tolerable ruler, Marcus Aurelius had associated him in the government at the early age of fifteen (A. D. 177).

Accordingly, upon the death of his father, in A. D. 180, COMMODUS succeeded to the imperial purple, at the age of eighteen. He was but a weak youth, spoiled by self-indulgence, and easily influenced by favorites. Accordingly this wretched prince rapidly degenerated into a cruel, licentious and avaricious tyrant.

Cómmodus began his reign by purchasing a humilitating peace with the Marcomanni and the Quadi, abandoning all the castles and fortresses which the Romans held in their country, except those within five miles of the Danube. Equally disgraceful treaties were concluded with the other German tribes, and in some instances the Emperor bought peace with large sums of money. The wars of this reign were not important. Clodius Albínus and Pescennius Niger defended Dacia against the attacks of the Sarmatians and the Scythians; and in Britain, Marcellus Ulpius reëstablished the Roman dominion over the region between the Friths of Solway and Clyde, which had been again occupied by the barbarous tribes (A. D. 184).

The tyrannical career of Cómmodus began in A. D. 183, upon the discovery of a plot to assassinate him, organized by his sister Lucilla, who was aided by many of the most eminent Senators. The Emperor was attacked in a dark passage, on his way to the amphitheater; but the person who aimed the dagger at him, instead of striking him to the heart at once, raised the weapon, exclaiming: "The Senate sends you this." This delay enabled the Prætorian Guards to rescue their sovereign, and the conspirators were seized and put to death. Lucilla was exiled to the island of Capreæ, where she soon afterward met with a similar fate.

This plot aroused the natural ferocity of the Emperor's disposition. Fearing another conspiracy, Cómmodus plunged into the most excessive cruelties, and all who had the misfortune to incur his wrath suffered death. Delation was revived in its worst forms, and diminished the numbers of the Senate. The Emperor's ministers—Perennis, the Prætorian Prefect, and his successor, Cleander, a freedman—were permitted to enrich themselves by the most nefarious proceedings; and were sacrificed in succession to the Emperor's cruelty, as we shall presently see.

Soon afterward the Empire was disturbed by a strange revolt. Maternus, a common-soldier, with several others who had deserted from their legions, organized a band, which was gradually augmented by banditti from the various provinces. This band ravaged Spain and Gaul, and took several strong cities by storm. Pescennius Niger was sent with an army to crush the revolt; but Maternus, finding himself not sufficiently strong to cope with a disciplined army, divided his followers into small bands, sending them secretly to Rome by different routes. His design was to assassinate the Emperor at an annual festival and to seize the imperial purple. All the various bands arrived at Rome without being discovered, and some had already placed themselves among the guards at the palace. But the plot was disclosed by the treachery of one of the conspirators, whereupon Maternus was seized and executed.

A plague next broke out in Rome, and lasted two years, at times carrying off two thousand persons daily. The city was likewise set on fire by lightning, and a large portion of it was burned. This calamity was followed by a famine, which some believed to have been caused by Cleander, the Emperor's prime minister, who bought up the corn on speculation. The mob proceeded to the palace and demanded his head. Cleander ordered the Prætorian Guards to attack the multitude, many of whom were accordingly slain; but the City Cohorts espoused the popular side and routed the Prætorians. It was then that Cómmodus, on hearing of the tumult, ordered the head of Cleander to be thrown to the populace, thus quieting the insurrection. The Roman government at this period appears to have very much resembled the Turkish government in modern times.

As time went on, the conduct of Cómmodus became worse, and he indulged in the most disgusting cruelties and vices. Justice was bought and sold. Not caring for the administration of public affairs, he abandoned himself to the most debasing sensual pleasures. He is said, on one occasion, to have cut a man in two, while walking in the street, for the mere purpose of amusing himself by seeing his entrails fall on the ground. He displayed wonderful skill in archery, and performed many remarkable exploits with the bow.

Cómmodus also possessed enormous strength, and on this account he was called *the Roman Hercules*. For this reason he dressed himself in a lion's skin, and carried a knotted club in his hand. He ran his spear through an elephant; and is said to have killed a hundred lions, one after another, each by a single blow. He fought with the common gladiators in the amphitheater, where he conquered seven hundred and thirty times; for which reason he styled himself "Conqueror of a thousand gladiators." When the Senate granted Cómmodus divine honors at his request, he strewed such a quantity of gold dust on his head that it glittered in the sunbeams.

In the meantime population was declining, and production was diminishing in consequence, while luxury and extravagance continued among the higher ranks and exhausted the resources of the state. Worse than all, the general morality was constantly declining. Notwithstanding a few bright examples in high places, the tone of society became more corrupt everywhere. Except among the despised Christians, purity of life was scarcely known. Patriotism had disappeared, and loyalty had not supplied its place. Decline and decrepitude appeared in almost all parts of the body politic; and all classes were pervaded by a general despondency, in consequence of a consciousness of debility. But there was an extraordinary reserve of strength under all this apparent weakness. The Empire, which seemed to be tottering to its fall under Cómmodus, still stood, and for two centuries resisted the most terrible external attacks.

Under Cómmodus the decline of the Empire, which commenced after the death of Nero, and which had been checked by the Five Good Emperors, proceeded with wonderful rapidity. The discipline of the army had almost ceased to exist. The troops deserted their standards by hundreds. It was thus that Maternus was enabled to form a band that ravaged Spain and Gaul, and gave him hopes of being able to seize the imperial purple; while a deputation of fifteen hundred legionaries from Britain demanded and obtained the overthrow of Perennis. The different portions of the army were animated by no common spirit. The Prætorian Guards, the City Cohorts, and the legionaries had different interests; while the legionaries themselves had their own quarrels and jealousies. The soldiers were tired of military life, and, mingling with the provincials, engaged in agriculture or commerce, or else became banditti and plundered the inhabitants.

Finally some whom Cómmodus had proscribed and was about to put to death—Marcia, one of his concubines; Ecleċtus, his chamberlain; and Lætus, the Prætorian Prefeċt—ascertaining his design, anticipated their fate by assassinating him. Marcia administered poison to him; but as this did not prove effeċtual, a public wrestler of extraordinary strength was engaged to complete the work, and Cómmodus was strangled (A. D. 192). Upon receiving the intelligence of his assassination, the Senate declared him a public enemy, ordered his body to be cast into the Tiber, and his statues to be demolished. Thus perished Cómmodus, the last of the Antonines, after a reign of twelve years and nine months, during which the Empire began its decline.

SECTION XVII.—LATER LATIN LITERATURE.

MEANWHILE the Roman provinces of Africa, Spain, Gaul and Britain had become thoroughly *Latinized;* and the people of the whole Empire were called *Romans.* During this period Roman military virtue had entirely disappeared. The long period of peace had unfitted the people for war; and the Romans, enervated by luxury, ease and wealth, had become effeminate.

Roman literature began to decline after the Augustan Age. Many causes combined to make this decay more rapid than its previous progress and improvement had been. Among these causes were the establishment of despotism, the little encouragement which most of the successors of Augustus extended to literature, the great increase of luxury, and the consequent degeneracy of manners.

The changes in the moral and political condition of Rome paralyzed the nobler motives by which the citizens were aċtuated. Pure taste and delicate sensibility disappeared by degrees. Gaudy ornament was more admired than real beauty. Affeċtation took the place of nature, and the subtleties of sophistry that of true philosophy. Ultimately the barbarian invasions, the frequent internal troubles, the struggle of Christianity with paganism, the removal of the imperial capital from Rome to Constantinople, and the division of the Empire, all contributed to the extinċtion of Latin literature.

PHÆDRUS, an elegant Latin poet, was a native of Thrace and seems to have been a freedman of Augustus. Most of his fables are translated or imitated from those of Æsop. LUCAN, a famous Latin epic poet, was born at Córduba (now Cordova), in Spain, A. D. 38; and was educated at Rome and Athens. Nero created him Quæstor and augur; but Lucan, having imprudently competed with the Emperor in a poetical contest, aroused the jealousy of that remorseless tyrant, and was the probable reason why Lucan took part in a plot against him. Nero condemned him to death, with the privilege of choosing the manner of his death. Lucan was the author of an epic poem entitled *Pharsalia,* the subjeċt of which is the civil wars between Pompey and Cæsar. Its charaċter is historical and striċtly limited to faċts, but it contains excellent delineations of charaċter and finely wrought speeches.

PERSIUS and JUVENAL were celebrated Latin satirical poets. Persius was born A. D. 34, and died in his twenty-eighth year (A. D. 62). He wrote satires remarkable for their earnest and severe animadversions on the prevailing corruption of morals in his day. Juvenal was born A. D. 38, and reached a good old age, dying in a kind of exile, while he held a military command in Egypt. He wrote satires inveighing against the vices and follies of his times with a noble and animated spirit, but with rather too much freedom and indelicacy of language.

MARTIAL, a distinguished Latin poet, was born in Spain, A. D. 43. He went to Rome at the age of twenty-three, where his talents soon acquired celebrity for him. He enjoyed the favor of the Emperor Domitian, who heaped honors upon him; and these he repaid with the most extravagant flattery and servility. Pliny the Younger, Quintilian, Juvenal and other literary men were among the friends of Martial. After residing in Rome thirty-five years, Martial returned to Bilbilis at the close of A. D. 100, and lived on the estate of his wife Marcella. His works embrace fourteen books of short, metrical compositions, called *Epigrammata;* celebrated for their wit and exquisite diction, but likewise for their indelicacy. He died A. D. 104.

CLAUDIAN, the last of the ancient Roman poets, was born at Alexandria, in Egypt, about A. D. 365, and was there educated. He resided at Rome for some time, and at Mediolanum (now Milan), then the capital of the Western Roman Empire. He was patronized by Stilicho, the famous minister of the Emperor Honorius. Claudian was the author of panegyrical poems, epics, satires, epigrams, etc. His works exhibit great genius and poetic talents; but his thoughts, images and expressions are stamped with the impress of the artificial and unnatural taste prevalent in that age.

SENECA, the greatest Roman philosopher, was born at Córduba (now Cordova), in Spain, A. D. 3; and after many vicissitudes he became Nero's tutor at Rome, where he was sentenced to death by that tyrant, on a charge of being implicated in a conspiracy (A. D. 65). Seneca was permitted the privilege of choosing the manner of his death, and chose that of opening his veins; but as the blood did not flow readily, he swallowed poison. He was the author of tragedies, epistles and philosophical works. His style is severely criticised as being characterized by affectation, and abounding with sententious antithesis. Seneca says: "Will you call God the world? You may do so without mistake. For he is all that you see around you." "What is God? The mind of the universe. What is God? All that you see, and all that you do not see."

PLINY THE ELDER, the renowned naturalist, was born A. D. 23. He visited Africa in his twenty-second year, and spent some time in that Roman province. He afterwards served in the Roman army in Germany, practiced law at Rome, and held the office of Procurator in Spain. He commanded the Roman fleet at Misenum during the reign of Titus, and lost his life in the great eruption of Mount Vesuvius which overwhelmed the cities of Herculaneum and Pompeii (A. D. 79). Pliny the Elder was one of the most learned of the Romans; and was the author of a *Natural History,* which is a kind of encyclopædia, full of erudition, and one of the most remarkable of ancient literary productions. According to Pliny's own statement, it is a compilation drawn from almost twenty-five hundred authors, most of whom are now forgotten. He asserted that "all religion is the offspring of necessity, weakness and fear," and that "the best thing God has bestowed on man is the power to take his own life."

PLINY THE YOUNGER, nephew of the elder Pliny, was born A. D. 60. He studied eloquence under Quintilian, and achieved great distinction and influence at Rome as a judicial orator. During Trajan's reign he was appointed to govern Bithynia and Pontus, whence he wrote his interesting epistle to Trajan concerning the persecution of the Christians. Pliny the Younger was the author of rhetorical and epistolary productions; the former being lost, but the latter still remaining. Pliny's Letters possess considerable merit, both in matter and style, and may be regarded as models of epistolary writing.

QUINTILIAN, the illustrious rhetorician, was born in Spain about the same time as the younger Pliny. He was brought to Rome in his infancy, and was an eminent teacher of rhetoric in that city for many years. He was the author of a work entitled *Institutes of Oratory,* which was a work of education designed for the formation of a perfect speaker. It displays considerable talent and judgment on the part of its author, and is highly valuable on account of the information it gives us concerning the manner of education in the Roman schools of rhetoric.

TACITUS, the great Roman historian, was the most prominent prose writer of this latter period of Roman literature. He was born at Interamna, in Italy, about A. D. 50; but was educated at Massilia (now Marseilles), in Gaul. He began rising in office during Vespasian's reign, achieving some of the highest public honors. He was distinguished for his eloquence at the bar, when young. Tacitus recorded the events of the Roman Empire in his *History*, embracing the period from the death of Nero to the death of Domitian, and in his *Annals*, comprising the period from the death of Augustus to the death of Nero. He was also the author of the *Life of Agricola*, a *Treatise on the Manners of the Germans*, and a *Dialogue on Oratory*.

The name of Tacitus as a historian stands as high as any other, and his literary productions are a rich store-house of political and philosophical wisdom. He exhibits a profound knowledge of human nature, and of the most subtle influences affecting human character and conduct. His style displays remarkable conciseness, vigor, apparent abruptness and occasional obscurity; and his writings interest most those who study them best, as do all productions of great intellects. They have been translated into nearly all European languages. The precise date of his death is unknown.

QUINTUS CURTIUS, a Roman historian, of whom very little is known, and who probably lived about the middle of the first century of the Christian era, was the author of a *History of Alexander the Great*, a very interesting production, but much inferior in style to the works of Tacitus or Livy. LUCIUS ANNÆUS FLORUS, a native of Spain or Gaul, and who flourished about the beginning of the second century of the Christian era, was the author of an epitome of Roman History to the time of Augustus.

SUETONIUS, a Roman historian, who was also a famous grammarian, rhetorician and lawyer, flourished about the same time; and his most celebrated work is his *Vitae Duodecim Cæsarum*, or *Lives of the Twelve Cæsars*, which has the merit of candid impartiality and an easy and simple style, which has passed through many editions and been translated into nearly every European language. His other extant works are notices of grammarians, rhetoricians and poets. An English translation of Suetonius is included in Bohn's Classical Library.

SECTION XVIII.—COMMERCE UNDER THE ANTONINES.

DURING the reigns of the Antonines the Romans made great improvements in trade and commerce, particularly by the opening of new communications with India. Palmyra, in the Syrian desert—the Tadmor founded by Solomon twelve centuries before—distant but eighty-five miles from the Euphrates, and about one hundred and seventeen from the nearest coast of the Mediterranean, was the emporium of the traffic between Europe in the West and Persia and India in the East.

The great exports from the harbors of the Levant naturally caused by this trade induced many Syrian merchants to settle in Rome, where some of them attained the highest political honors. It is apparent that some merchants used a more northern route by the Caspian Sea and the Oxus river, as the Roman geographers seem to have had considerable knowledge of the countries now embraced in the Khanates of Khiva and Bokhara.

But the great caravan route across Asia began at Byzantium (now Constantinople),

2—69.-U. H.

which had been for centuries the emporium of a flourishing commerce before it became the capital and the metropolis of the Roman Empire. After passing the Bosphorus the merchant adventurers proceeded through Anatolia and crossed the Euphrates. Thence they proceeded to Ecbátana, the ancient Median capital, and Hecatómpylos, the capital and metropolis of Parthia proper; thence circuitously to Hyrcania and Aria; and finally reaching Baćtra, which had been the principal mart of Central Asia for centuries.

There were two caravan routes from Bactra—one to Northern India, over the western portion of the Himalaya mountain chain, called the Indian Caucasus; the other toward the frontiers of Serica, over the lofty mountain range of Imaus (now Kuen-lun), through a winding ravine which was marked by a celebrated station known as the *Stone Tower*, whose ruins are said to be yet in existence, under the name of *Chihel Sutun*, or the Forty Columns. The countries between the Imaus and Serica were almost unknown, being perhaps traversed by Baćtrian, and not by European merchants; but the road is said to have been remarkably tedious and difficult.

The progress of the caravans being liable to frequent interruption from the Parthians, and the transportation of manufaćtured silks through the deserts being very toilsome, the Emperor Antonínus Pius endeavored to open a communication with China by sea. No account of this strange transaćtion has thus far been discovered in the works of any Greek or Latin authors. But it is said that a French authority, M. de Guignes, has found, in a very old Chinese historical work, that an embassy had come by sea from Antun, the sovereign of the people of the Western Ocean, to Yanti, or Hanhuanti, who ruled over China in the one hundred and sixty-eighth year of the Christian era. The name and the date are sufficient to identify Antun with Antonínus, and the projećted intercourse was worthy the attention of that enlightened Roman Emperor; but the results of this embassy are unknown.

For a long time the navigation from the West to India was confined to circuitous voyages around the peninsula of Arabia and the shores of the Persian Gulf; but about a century after the establishment of the Roman dominion, Hárpalus, the commander of a vessel which had been engaged in the Indian trade for a long time, observing the regular changes of the periodical winds, undertook to sail from the straits of Bab-el Mandeb across the Erythræan (now Arabian) Sea, and the western monsoon wafted him to the Malabar coast. This great improvement was rightly considered highly important; and the western monsoon was called Hárpalus, in commemoration of the gallant navigator who had thus utilized it for commercial purposes.

Pliny has left us a tolerably accurate description of the route of the Egyptian trade under the Romans. Cargoes destined for India were conveyed in boats up the Nile to Coptos, whence they were transported by caravans to Myos Hormus, or Berenice. The latter was the usual route, though its distance was greater; on account of the excellent stati ns and watering-places which the Ptolemies had established at convenient distances along the road. The fleet sailed from Berenice, in June or July, for Ocelis, at the mouth of the Red Sea, and for Cane, a promontory and emporium on the south-eastern coast of Arabia Felix; whence it sailed across the Indian Ocean to the Malabar coast, generally making the passage in forty days. The return voyage commenced early in December; and the fleet usually encountered more difficulty on the way homeward, because of the unsteady winds. The principal imports from India were spices, precious stones, muslins and cotton goods. The chief exports were light woolens, chequered linens, glass, wine and bullion.

Cómmodus endeavored to open the old Carthaginian trade with Central Africa. He likewise devoted some attention to the corn trade, which was so essential to the prosperity of his central dominions when Italy had long ceased to produce sufficient grain for the support of its population; and he established a company to obtain corn from Northern Africa whenever the Egyptian crops failed, through the lack of a sufficiently-abundant overflow of the Nile.

The Euxine, or Black Sea trade, which had been so flourishing in the age of the Grecian republics, seems to have vastly declined after the Romans acquired dominion over the countries on both sides of the Ægean; and it appears probable that very little, if any, commerce passed through the Straits of Gibralter into the Atlantic Ocean. A result of this change was that the amber trade was transferred from the Baltic coasts to the banks of the Danube; and the barbarous tribes who brought amber from the Baltic shores are said to have been astonished at the prices which they obtained for what they considered a useless article.

Furs were purchased from the Scythian tribes; but this branch of trade seems never to have amounted to very much. The Romans appear to have neglected the British tin trade, which seems to have been monopolized by the Gauls, and therefore restricted to the British Channel.

SECTION XIX.—PERIOD OF MILITARY DESPOTISM.

HE assassins of Cómmodus hastened to the house of PUBLIUS HELVIUS PERTINAX, whom they elevated to the imperial dignity. The new Emperor had passed through so many adventures that he was called "Fortune's tennis-ball." He was descended from an obscure family, either a slave or the son of a slave; and followed the occupation of a charcoal-burner for some time. He afterwards became a petty shopkeeper in Rome; and then a schoolmaster in Etruria, where he taught Latin and Greek. He next became a lawyer; and subsequently a soldier, in which capacity he became distinguished for his courage, and was made commander of a cohort in the war with Parthia during the reign of Marcus Aurelius. After he had passed through the usual gradations of office in Britain and Mœsia, he was appointed to the command of a legion under Marcus Aurelius, who caused him to be made Consul for his eminent services. He was next assigned the government of the province of Mœsia, and at length was intrusted with the city government of Rome.

Under Cómmodus, Pertinax was sent into exile, but was soon recalled to reform the abuses of the army. During a mutiny which occurred among the legions, he was left for dead among a heap of slain; but he soon recovered, after which he punished the mutineers and restored discipline in the military ranks. He was next sent to Africa, where another insurrection almost cost him his life. He then returned to Rome, where he lived in quiet retirement for a short time, until Cómmodus made him Prefect of the city.

Pertinax held this latter office when Lætus, the commander of the Prætorian Guards and one of the assassins of Cómmodus, roused him from his sleep at night. Supposing that Cómmodus had issued an order for his execution, Pertinax prepared himself for death; but, instead of having to meet the executioner, he was greeted with the announcement that he was Emperor. He was at first unwilling to accept so exalted a trust, urging the pleas of old age and increasing infirmities; but his scruples were wholly disregarded by the Prætorian Prefect, whose followers, yielding to his entreaties, reluctantly accepted the new Emperor; while the Senate, highly delighted at the elevation of one of their own order, hailed him with unconcealed satisfaction.

The hopes which had been entertained respecting Pertinax were not disappointed. He was a man of unsullied character, and was one of the few remaining friends of

Marcus Aurelius. The public treasury was empty, and Pertinax endeavored to replenish it by introducing a wise system of economy into the administration of the government. By strict discipline and wise regulations, he restrained the licentiousness of the Prætorian Guards, and protected the citizens against the overbearing insolence to which they had been for so long a time subjected by this arrogant soldiery. He attended all the meetings of the Senate, and so scrupulously devoted himself to the public business that the humblest petitioner always obtained ready access to him. He melted down all the silver statues which had been erected to Cómmodus. By selling all his buffoons, jesters and horses, he obtained so large a sum of money that he was enabled to abolish many oppressive taxes which burdened the industry of the people.

The economy which Pertinax introduced into public affairs was obnoxious to the avaricious Prætorian Guards and to the citizens who clamored for public shows and games; and the strict military discipline which he adopted to reform the Prætorians incensed those insolent soldiers against him, and they accordingly determined to depose him. After assembling in the streets, they marched to the palace. The Emperor's attendants sought safety in flight; but Pertinax boldly faced the mutineers and advanced into their very midst, asking them if they had come to betray their sovereign and shed his blood. This act of personal heroism confounded the mutinous soldiers, who accordingly seemed disposed to retreat, when one of their number, a barbarian of Tongres, stabbed him in the breast with a lance, at the same time exclaiming: "The soldiers send you this!" Pertinax muffled his head in his purple toga and called upon Jupiter to avenge his death, after which he fell and expired under a number of wounds inflicted upon him by the murderous Prætorian mutineers, after a brief reign of less than three months (A. D. 193).

Rome was now in a most deplorable condition. Her unprincipled citizens had exhibited their readiness to submit to any usurper, however detestable and cruel, provided he gratified their desires for dissolute pleasures. Into such a depth of vice were they plunged that a good man appeared unfit as well as unable to govern them. But a degrading spectacle thus far without a parallel was now exhibited. The insolent Prætorian Guards put up the imperial dignity for sale to the highest bidder. Didius Julianus, a millionaire Senator, bid it off for a sum equal to more than fifteen million dollars of our money. The Prætorians who received and shared the money obtained by this infamous transaction proclaimed this wealthy Senator Emperor, and escorted him through the streets of Rome amid the hisses of the people; but the subservient Senate sanctioned their disgraceful proceeding by accepting DIDIUS JULIANUS as Emperor.

Having thus bought the imperial office, Didius Julianus determined to use it for his own personal gratification, and did not concern himself about public matters, but passed his entire time in feasting and entertainments. He became an object of general public contempt, and curses were lavished upon him whenever he went abroad. The people publicly reproached him in his very presence with being a thief and having stolen the Empire. The stupid Didius Julianus was so utterly insensible to shame that he patiently bore all these insults, bowing and smiling to those who lavishly bestowed their reproaches upon him, and meekly submitting to the whims and caprices of the city populace.

But amidst all this degradation of the national character, a part of the old Roman spirit still lingered in the provinces. Three generals—Septimius Sevérus in Pannonia, Clodius Albínus in Britain, and Pescennius Niger in Syria—determined to vindicate the honor of Rome. Pescennius Niger was instantly proclaimed Emperor by his troops, and the kings and princes of Asia sent ambassadors to acknowledge his title. Satisfied with this empty homage, he did not put forth any efforts to secure the imperial dignity, but abandoned himself to a life of luxury at Antioch.

THE REVOLT OF THE PRAETORIAN GUARD.

Septimius Sevérus acted with more caution and foresight, making himself master of all the strongholds in Germany, after which he marched for Italy at the head of a well equipped and disciplined army. Didius Julianus induced the Senate to declare Sevérus a traitor; but was unable to raise an army; and, embarrassed with divided counsels, he waited for the approach of his rival. When Sevérus advanced to Rome, Didius Julianus, with the consent of the Senate, sent ambassadors, offering to share the government with him. But Sevérus rejected this offer; and the Senate, seeing the hopelessness of the cause of Didius Julianus, deposed him from power and declared SEPTIMIUS SEVÉRUS Emperor. The wretched Didius Julianus was ignominiously hurled from his high station, after a short reign of three months, and was beheaded by the public executioner (A. D. 193.)

Before Septimius Sevérus had entered Rome, he ordered the Prætorian Guards, who had disgraced the Roman name by selling the sovereignty of the Empire, to be brought unarmed into his presence. He reproached them for their crimes, ordered them to be stripped of their military equipments, deprived of their military title and rank, and banished to the distance of a hundred miles from the city. The new Emperor then entered the city; the streets being strewn with flowers, and the Senate receiving him with the most distinguished honors.

After thus securing the imperial purple, Septimius Sevérus proceeded to get rid of his rivals. Pescennius Niger was reigning in the Eastern provinces under the title of Augustus, and Sevérus at once took the field against him. After many battles, Niger was finally defeated in the two decisive battles of Cyzicus and Issus, the latter place famous for the great victory gained by Alexander the Great over the Medo-Persians five centuries before; Niger himself being taken prisoner and put to death.

Septimius Sevérus next proceeded to rid himself of Clodius Albínus, whom he had made his partner in the Empire, and whom he had promised to declare his successor. Under the guise of messengers bearing despatches, Sevérus sent assassins into Britain to murder Albínus; but the lattle, receiving information of this design, proclaimed himself Emperor, and crossed over from Britain into Gaul. A civil war between the two rivals was carried on in Gaul for some time, and Sevérus was at one time in the most desperate straits. But he finally defeated Albínus in a terrible battle at Lugdunum (now Lyons), took him prisoner and put him to death.

The triumphant Septimius Sevérus soon showed his subjects that they had found in him a master. He was stern and cruel in character, and signalized his victory by putting forty-one Senators and a number of wealthy provincials to death, simply because they had supported his rivals. Under him the Roman Empire became a military despotism, and the Senate was deprived of its power and even openly insulted. He replaced the Prætorian Guards with a force of forty thousand select troops, which constituted the garrison of Rome and served in the capacity of the Emperor's body-guard. The commander of this force was the Prætorian Prefect, who ranked as the second person in the Empire; not only commanding the garrison in the city, but being also intrusted with the management of the finances, and with certain legislative and judicial functions; thus becoming a rival of the Emperor himself.

Septimius Sevérus was an able general, and endeavored to improve the discipline of the army, but failed in his efforts in this direction. In A. D. 197 he undertook an expedition against the Parthians, whom he defeated; capturing the cities of Seleucia, Ctesiphon and Babylon; conquering Adiabéné and annexing it to the Roman Empire; and thus ending the war the year after it had commenced (A. D. 198). After the triumphant close of his Parthian campaign, he visited Egypt, where he studied, with an inquiring eye, the different ruins and monuments which even in that day rendered the banks of the Nile interesting.

The Roman arms in Britain having experienced some checks, Septimius Sevérus determined to recover the territory which the savage Picts and Scots of Caledonia had conquered. After appointing his sons, Caracalla and Geta, his successors in the Empire, he landed in Britain, accompanied by his sons (A. D. 208). Leaving Geta in the South of the island, he took Caracalla with him in his march against the Caledonians in the North. As he pursued the inhabitants through their woods and marshes, he lost fifty thousand men in this toilsome expedition; but by so harassing the Caledonians, he forced them to sue for peace and to relinquish a large part of their territory.

For the purpose of securing his conquests in the North of Britain, Septimius Sevérus erected a wall from the mouth of the river Tyne to Solway Frith, a distance of sixty-eight miles. This wall was constructed of freestone; and was twelve feet high and eight feet thick, with a ditch on the north side, and a number of fortresses along its extent. This barrier prevented the Caledonians from making predatory inroads into the Roman territories south of it.

Septimius Sevérus retired to Eborácum (now York), where Caracalla attempted to assassinate his father. The aged Emperor was so shocked at his son's brutality that he summoned him into his presence and offered him a naked sword, saying: "If you are ambitious of reigning alone, imbrue your hands now in your father's blood, and let not the world witness your want of filial tenderness." Caracalla was little abashed by this reproof. He incited the troops to mutiny and to proclaim him Emperor. When Septimius Sevérus, who had now lost the use of his feet, was informed of this proceeding, he ordered his attendants to place him in a litter; and then summoned Caracalla, the Tribunes and the centurions, into his presence. They were so confounded with the Emperor's energy and boldness that they implored his pardon on their knees, whereupon the Emperor replied: "It is the head that governs, and not the feet." As his stern gaze fell upon Caracalla, the sword dropped from the hand of the would-be parricide. The spectators were utterly amazed when the Emperor forgave his son and put all whom he named as his accomplices to death with cruel sufferings.

The last years of the life of Septimius Sevérus were troubled by the animosity between his two sons, which their common dependence upon him did not restrain. It was that neither might be left at the other's mercy that he named both as his successors, giving them this parting advice: "Be generous to the soldiers and trample on all beside." Finding his disorder gaining upon him, Septimius Sevérus asked for poison, but it was refused him. He then swallowed an immense quantity of food to hasten his death, and this had the desired effect. He died at Eborácum at the age of sixty-five years, after a reign of eighteen years (A. D. 211).

He was succeeded by his sons, CARACALLA and GETA, who were proclaimed joint Emperors by the army. The two brothers soon manifested the most violent antipathy toward each other. They reigned together for a year, during which they returned to Rome. At the end of the first year of their joint reign, an effort was made to settle their quarrel by dividing the Empire between them; and when this failed, Caracalla murdered his brother in his mother's arms, thus becoming sole Emperor (A. D. 212). To prevent the consequences of this atrocious deed, the fratricide won the support of the soldiers by large gifts of money, and then induced the Senate to rank his murdered brother as one of the gods.

Caracalla was a cruel monster and tyrant. Remorse of conscience for the murder of his brother is believed to have deprived him of his reason. He endeavored to drown the reproaches of his conscience by putting to death all who might remind him of his murdered brother; and accordingly twenty thousand persons, whom he classed as "Geta's friends," among whom was a daughter of Marcus Aurelius, a son of Pertinax, a nephew of Cómmodus, and the eminent jurist Papinian, were thus removed.

Still the Emperor's conscience allowed him no rest; and he left Rome, beginning a series of aimless wanderings through the provinces of the Empire, thus passing the remainder of his life. He showed himself the common enemy of the human race, grievously oppressing the people wherever he went, and marking his progress by his cruelties. While angry at some trivial matter in Alexandria, he caused a general massacre of the citizens of that Egyptian metropolis, thus sacrificing the lives of thousands of people. Almost every Roman province thus suffered from his atrocities.

Knowing that he was hated by his subjects, he placed his sole dependence upon the army, and employed the most iniquitous means to obtain money to purchase the venal support of the troops, putting to death the wealthiest men in Rome on charges of treason, and confiscating their estates. In order to extend the incidence of the *succession-tax* (*vicesima hæreditatium*), Caracalla suddenly conferred the rights of Roman citizenship upon all the inhabitants of the Empire; at the same time increasing the tax from five to ten per cent.

Near the end of his reign, Caracalla undertook to conquer Parthia. He established his head-quarters at Edessa, in Mesopotamia, in A. D. 214, and crossing the Tigris, captured Arbéla; and by A. D. 216 he had driven the Parthians into their mountain fastnesses. He intended to continue the war the next year; but, before the campaign could be opened, the Emperor was assassinated near Edessa by Martial, a centurion, who had been engaged for the purpose by Macrínus, the Prætorian Prefect, who was obliged to resort to this act to save his own life, of which the detestable tyrant was about to deprive him (A. D. 217). Macrínus was not at first suspected of any complicity in the assassination of Caracalla, but the soldiers seized Martial and cut him to pieces.

After some hesitation, the army proclaimed MACRINUS Emperor, and the Senate confirmed him. He was a native of Mauritania, and was exceedingly popular with the Romans in the commencement of his reign; but this popularity was of brief duration, as we shall presently see. He began his reign by seeking to undo the evil acts of Caracalla. Being defeated by the Parthian king, he cowardly purchased a peace with a large sum of money. His constant affection for the virtuous Aurelius irritated the people and made him an object of popular contempt.

In his efforts to restrain the licentiousness of the troops, he found himself obliged to adopt some severe rules of discipline; and this produced a mutiny of the army. Julia Mœsa, the grandmother of Bassianus, who was an illegitimate son of Caracalla, took advantage of this rebellious spirit, and recommended Bassianus to the notice of the soldiers by distributing liberal presents among them.

While Macrínus was leading a life of luxury at Antioch, the troops at Rome proclaimed Bassianus Emperor. On hearing of this revolution in the imperial capital, Macrínus sent his legate Julian to Italy with some legions; but these troops killed their commander and declared for Bassianus. Macrínus then took the field in person; but, while a battle was in progress between his force and the troops who had declared against him, he cowardly abandoned the field to his enemies. He was pursued by the forces of his rival; and, while he was detained at Chalcedon by sickness, he was surprised and carried a prisoner to Antioch, where he was put to death by his enemies (A. D. 218). His son, Diadumenus, whom he had named as his successor, met a similar fate.

HELIOGÁBALUS, the name by which Bassianus was known as Emperor, was a Syrian youth of but fourteen years; and at the time of his accession was High-Priest of the Syrian sun-god Heliogábalus, in the great temple of Emesa (now Hems). He assumed the title of Marcus Aurelius Antonínus. His accession to the imperial dignity was ratified by the Roman Senate and people. He was surrounded by flatterers, who perceived that it was for their interest to gratify all his desires; and he soon abandoned himself to all the profligacy of the times. The Roman historians described him as a monster of sensuality and vice.

He appointed his mother and his grandmother his colleagues in the Empire. He created his grandmother a member of the Senate with rank next after the Consuls. He created a Senate of women to arrange the fashions of dress which were to prevail in the Empire, and to prescribe the precedence of ranks and the etiquette to be observed in visiting each other. He raised his horse to the office of Consul, and fed him with gilded oats. He compelled the Romans to worship the Syrian god whose name he bore; and the shrines of the Roman gods were plundered to embellish that of this new divinity, while the grave ceremonies of the Roman religion were replaced with the infamous orgies of Syria. He became enamored of one of the Vestal Virgins, forcibly took her from her sacred seclusion, and compelled her to become one of his wives.

Heliogábalus possessed no talent whatever, and was addicted to the lowest sensual vices, caring only for gluttony and debauchery. He painted his face, attired himself in female apparel, and publicly paraded his vices. He was so prodigal that he considered nothing worth eating that could be purchased for a moderate price, and is said to have squandered immense sums on the luxuries of the table. His dresses, jewels and golden ornaments were never worn twice, but after being once worn were given to his slaves and parasites. His apartments were furnished with the richest stuffs, covered with gold and jewels, and the floors were spread with gold dust. His mats consisted of the down of hares, or soft feathers from under the wings of partridges. His carpets were composed of gold and silver tissue; and his shoes were covered with precious stones, for the purpose of attracting the admiration of the populace.

The extravagances of Heliogábalus soon exhausted the resources of the Empire; and his grandmother was so annoyed by his disgraceful prodigality that she conceived the design of checking his extravagances by assigning him a colleague in the imperial dignity, persuading him to adopt his cousin Alexander Sevérus as his colleague and successor. Heliogábalus was soon annoyed at this restraint upon his vices, and desired to rid himself thereof. But the virtues of Alexander Sevérus, which were in marked contrast with the contemptible vices of Heliogábalus, soon gained many friends for the young prince, won for him the favor of the Prætorians, and drew upon him the Emperor's jealousy.

When Heliogábalus endeavored to remove Alexander Sevérus from office, a riot ensued; and the young prince would have been killed while walking in his garden had he not fled to save his life. But the seditious spirit thus aroused was not quelled so easily. The soldiers insisted upon guarding Alexander Sevérus and preventing any of the Emperor's favorites from corrupting him with their debasing associations.

Heliogábalus was now seriously alarmed; and perceiving the desperation of his cause, he made preparations for death suitable to his general habits. He therefore constructed a tower with steps of gold and mother-of-pearl; from which he might, in his last extremity, throw himself headlong. He kept cords of purple, silk and gold, about his person, with the design of strangling himself. He provided golden swords and daggers, and had boxes of emerald supplied with different kinds of poisons. In this condition of mind, he contemplated plans to take his rival's life by poison and by other means; but all these schemes proved abortive. Finally his soldiers mutinied against him, and followed him through the rooms of his palace. They dragged him from an obscure corner, killed him, and cast his body into the Tiber (A. D. 222). His mother and many others of his partners in crime met with a similar fate.

ALEXANDER SEVÉRUS was thereupon unanimously declared Emperor by the Senate. He was a very different kind of a man from his infamous cousin and predecessor, and was in every respect worthy of the high honor thus thrust upon him. He was the son of Mammæa, the younger daughter of Julia Mœsa, and had been educated with great care. He was a young man of pure and blameless morals, but he lacked sufficient energy and force of character to check the advancing tide of corruption that was threatening to engulf the Empire.

During his entire reign he shrank from the task of governing his dominions, submitting himself to his mother's direction. The tendency of his reign was for good. The young Emperor's good example had an excellent effect, and his mother's influence was elevating; but neither had sufficient strength of character to execute the reforms which they attempted. Nevertheless, his reign constitutes an agreeable contrast with the period immediately preceding it. Men distinguished for their wisdom and virtue were elevated to positions of honor and trust. The Senate was treated with a respect and a consideration beyond its merits, and an honest effort was made to administer the government upon principles of purity and economy.

Alexander Severus showed favor to the Christians and protected them from persecution, and admitted a bust of Christ among the images in his domestic place of worship. His accomplishments are highly extolled by historians. He patronized literature and devoted his leisure hours to the study of the Greek and Latin authors. He was likewise skilled in mathematics, music, painting and sculpture.

During the reign of Alexander Severus a great revolution took place in the East. In A. D. 226 the New Persians overthrew the Parthian Empire and established the *New Persian Empire of the Sassanidæ*. Artaxerxes, the founder of this new empire, aimed at recovering all the dominions over which Darius Hystaspes ruled seven centuries before, and demanded that Alexander Severus should instantly relinquish all the Roman provinces in Asia. The young Roman Emperor answered this demand by leading his army across the Euphrates in A. D. 231. In the short war which followed, Alexander Severus claimed entire success; but it would appear that he was barely able to hold his Eastern dominions. The Persian king was, however, so crippled by the struggle that he was unable to attempt to drive the Romans out of Asia; and peace was concluded in A. D. 232.

On the return of Alexander Severus to Antioch, after his campaign against the Persian king, his mother, Mammæa, sent for the famous Origen, one of the greatest of the Fathers of the Christian Church, to instruct the young Emperor in the Christian doctrines.

In the meantime the northern portion of the Empire was invaded by hordes of barbarians from Germany and Sarmatia, who crossed the Rhine and the Danube in such swarms that they spread alarm even to the very gates of Rome. The Emperor took the field in person against the German tribes who had invaded Gaul in A. D. 234. He took post at Mogontíacum (now Mayence); but the strict military discipline which he enforced in his army excited a mutiny among the German legions, which had been accustomed to every kind of indulgence during the preceding reigns. Maximin, one of the generals under the Emperor, fomented this seditious spirit; and finally the mutinous soldiers burst into the Emperor's tent and cut off his head. Thus the good Alexander Severus fell a victim to assassination, early in A. D. 235, before he was able to begin an active campaign against the barbarian invaders of Gaul.

MAXIMIN, the instigator of the murder of Alexander Severus, was instantly proclaimed Emperor by the mutinous troops. His father was a Thracian shepherd, and Maximin himself had exercised the same humble calling. By frequently leading his countrymen against the barbarians, he had acquired a knowledge of irregular warfare, and was actuated by a desire for military glory.

He accordingly joined the Roman army, where he soon became distinguished for his courage and discipline, as well as for his strength and gigantic stature. He was almost eight and a half feet high, and his physical frame was equally strong and symmetrical. He was said to have been able to draw a load which a yoke of oxen were not capable of moving. He was likewise credited with sufficient strength to break a horse's thigh-bone by a kick, and to strike out a horse's teeth by a blow of his fist. He is also represented as usually eating forty pounds of meat daily, and drinking six gallons of wine. Such are the wonderful stories related of Maximin's physical strength.

Maximin first exhibited his strength at the public games which Septimius Sevérus celebrated on his son Geta's birth-day. The gigantic Thracian had requested permission to contend for the prize of wrestling, but the Emperor permitted him to engage with slaves only. He surpassed sixteen persons in running, successively. He kept pace with the Emperor on horseback; and, after being thus fatigued, he overcame seven of the most active soldiers. These remarkable physical exploits induced Septimius Sevérus to take the powerful Thracian into his body-guard. He became centurion during Caracalla's reign; after which he experienced different vicissitudes of fortune, until Alexander Sevérus assigned him the command of a legion in Germany.

Maximin was an illiterate, coarse and brutal ruffian. The base ingratitude which he had displayed toward the virtuous Alexander Sevérus was followed by a system of tyranny and brutality which has scarcely a parallel in the reigns of the worst of his predecessors. The Senate having refused to ratify his elevation to the imperial dignity, he resolved to reign without the concurrence of that body. He put to death every individual whom he did not like, and determined to compel unwilling obedience from all ranks. He condemned rich men to execution, for the purpose of confiscating their estates. With the true spirit of a mean upstart, he put to death all who were acquainted with him in early life, and who remembered his low birth. He promptly sacrificed all whom he suspected of plotting against him, and four hundred persons fell victims to his suspicion. Maximin killed some of these by beating. He exposed others to wild beasts. He crucified others, and sewed up others in the carcasses of animals just slain. He also signalized his reign by the sixth great persecution of the Christians.

Maximin made war on the Germans, whose armies he defeated, and whose country he laid waste to an extent of four hundred and fifty miles. The soldiers were heartily devoted to him, because of the increased pay which he allowed them on his expeditions against the Germans, and because of the zeal with which he shared in all the duties of a common soldier, he being always found at the point of danger, fighting as a private, while commanding as a general.

But a rebellious spirit was excited in the Roman provinces in Africa, where Maximin's cruelties and extortions rendered his name odious. Gordian, the Proconsul of Africa, then in his eightieth year, and whose talents and virtues were well known in the Empire, was proclaimed Emperor, along with his son, by the people of Africa, who rose in rebellion in A. D. 238. As Gordian found it impossible to decline the office which the soldiers and people forced upon him, he informed the Senate of what had occurred in Africa, assuring them of his reluctance to accept the exalted station, and declaring that he would retain the imperial authority only long enough to deliver the Empire from its oppressor.

The Senate and people of Rome confirmed the elevation of the two GORDIANS to the imperial office, removed the governors, declared Maximin a public enemy, and ordered the provinces to acknowledge Gordian and his son as Emperors. When Maximin was informed of these proceedings, he burst into an ungovernable rage, raving like a madman and beating his head against the wall. But when he became somewhat cooler by reflection, he harangued his troops, promising to reward them with the estates of his enemies; after which he determined to march to Rome and gratify his revenge by an indiscriminate massacre. He therefore concluded peace with the barbarians and led his army toward Italy. On his march thither he was informed that Gordian and his son had been defeated and slain in Africa by Capelianus, one of Maximin's adherents in that province.

This intelligence raised the hopes of the tyrant and produced dreadful consternation at Rome; but the Senate, undismayed by the calamity, appointed PUPIENUS and BALBINUS joint Emperors. The populace were not satisfied with this choice. A great multitude assembled while the new sovereigns were offering the customary sacrifice, and loudly clamored for a prince of the Gordian race. After the Senate had in vain endeavored to quiet the mob, a youth of the Gordian family, only twelve years of age, was proclaimed Cæsar.

Meanwhile Maximin entered Italy with his army and besieged Aquileia; but that city was heroically defended by its inhabitants, who dreaded the cruelties of the tyrant. They threw scalding pitch and sulphur upon the soldiers who attempted to scale the walls. The old men and women fought upon the ramparts, and the women cut off their long hair to be twisted into bow-strings for the defenders. Enraged by this unexpected resistance, the tyrant vented his fury upon his own soldiers, putting several of them to death. This produced a mutiny in his army, and a large party of soldiers entered Maximin's tent at noonday and killed the tyrant, along with his son and his chief favorites (A. D. 238).

The assassination of Maximin restored internal tranquillity to the Empire, which was, however, soon involved in foreign wars. The barbarian Carpi and Goths crossed the Danube and ravaged the province of Mœsia; while the New Persians renewed hostilities on the eastern frontiers of the Roman dominions. Pupienus was making preparations to march against the New Persians, but was detained by serious events at home.

Jealousies had arisen between the two Emperors. Pupienus was universally regarded as superior to his colleague as a soldier and a statesman; but as he was a blacksmith's son, Balbínus considered him as his inferior. The petty quarrels resulting from this cause emboldened the Prætorian Guards, who were again as powerful and as insolent as they had been before they were humbled by Septimius Sevérus; and they now resolved upon an attempt at revolution in the government. They accordingly attacked the palace while the two Emperors were returning from the Capitoline Games, seized both of them and murdered them within six weeks of the murder of Maximin, and proclaimed the younger GORDIAN Emperor (A. D. 238).

The younger Gordian was the grandson and nephew of the prince of that name who had headed the revolt in Africa. As he was only twelve years of age, he was a mere tool in the hands of his ministers. At length he came under the influence of Timesitheus, the Prætorian Prefect, who acted as minister and guardian of the young Gordian. Timesitheus was well qualified for this duty, as he united the valor of a soldier with the wisdom of a statesman. As long as Timesitheus lived, the authority of the Empire was upheld with vigor.

The successes of the New Persians in the East attracted the attention of Timesitheus to that quarter. On his march against the Persians, he encountered an army of Gauls in Mœsia. The Gauls had attempted to settle in Thrace, but were driven back by Timesitheus after many battles. Timesitheus also defeated the New Persians in every battle and pursued them to the gates of Ctesiphon, their capital.

But these victories were overbalanced by the death of Timesitheus, who died suddenly, supposed to have been poisoned by Philip the Arabian, who succeeded him as Prætorian Prefect. The good fortune of Gordian appears to have deserted him with the death of his able minister. Philip the Arabian profited by the public discontents, managing to make himself the colleague of the Emperor, whom he then poisoned, thus making himself sole Emperor (A. D. 244).

PHILIP THE ARABIAN, the assassin and the successor of Gordian III., was a native of Bostra, in Arabia. His father had been captain of banditti in Arabia, and had in all probability educated his son to the same adventurous calling. During a visit to the scenes of his early life, Philip founded a city in Arabia, naming it Philippopolis.

Philip the Arabian began his reign by making peace with Persia, and defeated the Carpi on the Danube the next year (A. D. 245). The thousandth anniversary of the founding of the city of Rome occurred during this reign, and Philip celebrated the event by secular games with a magnificence corresponding to the occasion. He entertained the people of Rome with splendid shows, and two thousand gladiators fought in the amphitheater for their amusement (A. D. 248).

Dissatisfied with Philip's reign, the Syrians set up an Emperor in the person of Jotapianus; while the legions in Mœsia and Pannonia proclaimed Marinus Emperor. Both these leaders soon lost their lives; but the mutiny of the army still continued, and Philip sent a Senator named Decius to quell it. No sooner had Decius reached Illyricum than his soldiers forced him to assume the imperial title, threatening him with instant death in case of his refusal. He then led his legions into Italy against Philip, who took the field against the rebels; but Philip was defeated and slain near Verona, in A. D. 249, and DECIUS became Emperor.

Decius, thus made Emperor against his will, was acknowledged by the Senate and the people of Rome; and was surnamed Trajan, on account of the resemblance of his character to that of the virtuous Emperor of that name. During his brief reign of two years, he endeavored to restore the purity of religion and morals among the Romans. With this design he permitted the office of Censor to be revived; and Valerian, a man of the strictest morals, was intrusted with its duties. The Emperor guarded the dignity of the patrician class, as well as the interests of the lower ranks.

But Rome had now fallen into such a condition that no individual talent and no high example of virtue was sufficient to check the progress of corruption and prevent the national downfall. The constant and bitter controversies between the Christians and the Pagans throughout the Empire produced the most pernicious disputes in Rome itself; while the existence of the Empire was threatened by the increasing insolence of the barbarian hordes beyond the northern frontiers of the Roman dominion.

Decius tarnished his reign by the seventh great persecution of the Christians; thousands of whom in different parts of the Empire were driven from their homes and put to death in the most cruel manner, while many fled for refuge to the mountains and deserts. A general massacre of the Christians occurred at Alexandria, in Egypt; and the Bishops of Jerusalem, Antioch and Rome died the death of martyrs. This was the most dreadful persecution which the Christians had suffered since that of Nero.

The religious troubles which distracted the Empire were interrupted by a formidable invasion of the Roman dominions by the Goths, a fierce Scandinavian tribe, who in A. D. 250 ravaged Dacia and crossed the Danube and devastated Mœsia and Thrace. Decius marched against the barbarians; but was defeated in a great battle with them, the Goths, however, losing thirty thousand men (A. D. 250). The next year (A. D. 251) he made an effort to retrieve his ill-fortune; but was lured into an ambuscade by the treachery of his own general, Gallus; and the Roman army was surprised in a narrow defile near Forum Trebonii, in Mœsia, and was surrounded by the Goths. Seeing his own son shot by an arrow, and his troops routed, the Emperor in despair spurred his horse toward the enemy and plunged into a marsh, where he was instantly swallowed up and seen no more (A. D. 251).

The army now allowed the Senate to regulate the succession; and that body proclaimed GALLUS Emperor, with Hostilianus, the young son of Decius, and his own son,

Volusianus, as his colleagues. The first act of the new Emperor was to purchase a humiliating peace with the Goths by agreeing to pay to them an annual tribute on condition that they should abstain from invading the Roman dominions. This dishonorable peace cost Gallus his popularity at Rome, and the discontent which it occasioned was increased by the accumulating calamities with which the Empire was now visited in quick succession.

During the reign of Gallus occurred the eighth great persecution of the Christians. A destructive pestilence ravaged Rome and the whole Empire. The provinces south of the Danube were scourged by a fresh invasion of the Goths, who were repelled by Æmilianus, the governor of Pannonia and Mœsia. The victorious troops of Æmilianus at once proclaimed their general Emperor, and he instantly marched toward Rome. Gallus and his son took the field against Æmilianus, but were murdered by their own troops at Interamna, whereupon the Senate acknowledged ÆMILIANUS as Emperor (A. D. 253).

Æmilianus at once found a competitor for the imperial purple in the virtuous Valerian, who was recognized as the best and ablest man of his time. Gallus had sent him to bring the legions in Gaul and Germany to his aid. As he did not arrive in time to save Gallus, he turned his arms against Æmilianus, who was defeated and slain in battle after a reign of only three months (A. D. 253).

The Senate and the people promptly acknowledged VALERIAN as Emperor. He was then sixty-three years of age, and was therefore too old to grapple with the perils and difficulties which at that time endangered the Empire. Accordingly his reign was clouded with misfortune. He possessed an unsullied character, and powers which might have revived the sinking fortunes of the Empire; but the talents and virtues which had distinguished him in private life appeared to little advantage after his elevation to the sovereign power. He made some efforts to reform abuses; but tarnished his reign by the ninth great persecution of the Christians, when St. Cyprian, Archbishop of Carthage, suffered martyrdom.

The Northern barbarians no longer entertained any fear of the Roman name, and the rapidly declining Empire was now alarmingly conscious of their power. The Franks from the Lower Rhine and the Alemanni from Southern Germany ravaged Gaul, Spain and Italy; and even crossed the Pillars of Hercules (now Straits of Gibralter), extending their devastations to Africa. The fleets which the Goths constructed on the Euxine, or Black Sea, spread consternation and dismay along the coasts of Asia Minor and Greece; and Cyzicus, Chalcedon, Ephesus, Trebizond, Nicomedía, Nicæa and Prusa were captured and burned by the barbarians, who also took Corinth and Athens.

In the East the New Persians extended their territory toward the north-west at the expense of the Roman Empire; the valiant Sapor I., the second of the New Persian kings belonging to the dynasty of the Sassanidæ, having conquered Armenia and invaded Mesopotamia. Valerian took the field against the New Persian monarch, and attempted to drive him out of Mesopotamia. He imprudently crossed the Euphrates, and was surrounded by the New Persian army near Edessa, in a situation where neither courage nor military skill could be of any avail; and he was accordingly defeated and taken prisoner, and carried by Sapor in triumph to the Persian capital (A. D. 260).

Sapor refused all offers of ransom for his illustrious captive, and kept him loaded with chains, but clad in his purple toga, a constant prisoner at the Persian court for the remaining seven years of his life. The ancient accounts tell us that the captive Emperor was subjected to every brutal insult by his barbarous conqueror, who used his neck as a footstool whenever he mounted his horse; who put out his eyes and flayed him alive after he had languished in captivity for seven years; and who tanned his skin, painted it red, and nailed it up in a Persian temple as a national trophy. Such is the common account of the captivity of the unfortunate Valerian; but the particulars are not fully authenticated, and the story is undoubtedly largely an invention. Valerian had associated his son Gallienus with himself in the Empire as his colleague as early as A. D. 254; and upon his father's capture, in A. D. 260, GALLIENUS became sole Emperor. He received the tidings of his father's misfortune with secret satisfaction and with open indifference. He appeared to be familiar with almost all else except the art of government. Gibbons says that he "was a master of several curious but useless sciences; a ready orator, an elegant poet, a skillful gardener, an excellent cook, and a most contemptible prince." During his reign of eight years, the disasters to the Empire begun in the preceding reigns continued unabated.

At the time of the accession of Gallienus, the barbarians, encouraged by Valerian's captivity, invaded the Empire on every side. The Goths and the Scythians ravaged Pontus. The Franks and the Alemanni carried fire and sword into Rhætia, advancing as far southward into Italy as Ravenna. The Sarmatians and the Quadi entered Dacia and Pannonia. Other barbarous tribes made inroads into Spain, taking many strongholds in that province. Gallienus drove the barbarians out of Italy, and Regillianus defeated them in Dacia and Pannonia.

After these successes, Gallienus sunk into utter inactivity; and his indolence encouraged a number of pretenders to spring up in the various provinces of the Empire, who are usually styled *The Thirty Tyrants*. Most of them had short and inglorious reigns, and their kingdoms usually perished with them; the only two exceptions to this rule being the kingdom which Posthumus founded in Gaul and which lasted seventeen years under four successive princes, and the Kingdom of Palmyra founded in the East by Odenátus in A. D. 264.

Odenátus made himself master of Syria and the neighboring countries. He achieved several victories over the New Persians and besieged Sapor in Ctesiphon. Gallienus determined to convert Odenátus from a rival into a friend, and proclaimed him his partner in the Empire; but the Palmyrenian chieftain was assassinated by some of his own countrymen in A. D. 267, and was succeeded by his widow, Zenobia, who assumed the title of *Queen of the East*.

As none of the other rivals of Gallienus possessed sufficient strength to enable them to make a successful resistance against his arms, he maintained himself in the imperial dignity, while all his competitors suffered violent deaths. Gallienus himself was assassinated by his own troops, while besieging Mediolanum (now Milan), in A. D. 268.

The troops proclaimed MARCUS AURELIUS CLAUDIUS, one of their generals, Emperor. The new sovereign's wisdom and firmness for a time arrested the work of destruction which was threatening the dissolution of the Empire. He conquered the Alemanni and drove them out of Italy in A. D. 268, and vanquished the Goths in Mœsia in the following year. He then prepared to take the field against Zenobia, the Queen of the East, who had extended her dominion over Egypt and assumed imperial authority; but a pestilence broke out in the Emperor's army at Sirmium, in Pannonia, and Claudius himself was among its numerous victims, dying in A. D. 270, after a short but glorious reign of two years, during which he delivered the Empire from some of its greatest perils and gave it a new lease of life.

QUINTILLIUS, the brother of Claudius, was thereupon proclaimed Emperor by the army; but his efforts to revive the ancient military despotism gave so much dissatisfaction that he was killed by the soldiers after a reign of but seventeen days (A. D. 270). The virtuous AURELIAN, one of the leading generals of the army and a native of Sirmium, in Pannonia, whom Claudius on his death-bed had recommended as his successor, was then proclaimed Emperor by the soldiers, and was confirmed by the Senate, which body was well acquainted with his merits.

Aurelian was also a soldier of fortune, like Claudius. He was of humble origin, but was in every respect worthy of the

TEMPLE OF JUPITER, PALMYRA.

exalted position to which he had risen by the force of his own talents. His short reign of almost five years was one of the most brilliant in the annals of the Roman Empire. He routed the Goths in Pannonia in the first year of his reign (A. D. 270), thus obliging them to make peace. He then marched against the Germans, who had again invaded Italy. He was at first defeated; but he soon retrieved his fortune, cutting the whole barbarian army to pieces. He next vanquished the Vandals, who had just crossed the Danube. By reviving the rigid discipline of the army, he rendered it capable of winning its victories.

Determined to reunite the scattered fragments of the Empire, Aurelian, after securing the tranquillity of Europe, marched against Zenobia, the Queen of the East, in A. D. 272. This famous Queen of Palmyra was one of the most remarkable characters in history. She claimed descent from the Ptolemies of Egypt, and is said to have professed the Jewish religion. She was familiar with the principal languages of Asia and Europe, and was skilled in the leading sciences of the times. She had such a knowledge of affairs of state that the successes of her husband, Odenátus, were said to have been due to her counsels. Zenobia ruled Syria and Mesopotamia for almost six years, discharging all the duties of an excellent sovereign and an intrepid commander; but her ambition hastened her ruin. Not satisfied with the conquest of Egypt, she aspired to the dominion of Asia; and Aurelian resolved to extinguish this power which so audaciously encroached upon the dignity of Rome.

On his march against Zenobia, Aurelian defeated the Goths in a great battle in Thrace, and pursued them across the Danube and killed their king. He then crossed the Hellespont into Asia, and defeated Zenobia's army in an obstinate and sanguinary battle near Antioch (A. D. 272). After gaining a second victory, Aurelian was enabled to besiege Palmyra, Zenobia's capital, which the undaunted queen defended with remarkable spirit and resolution. Finally perceiving that there was no hope of succor, Zenobia attempted secretly to make her escape into Persia; but was betrayed by her servants and made prisoner (A. D. 273). Palmyra surrendered to Aurelian; but after he had taken possession of the city and garrisoned it, and begun his march for Rome, the Palmyrenians revolted and massacred the Roman garrison.

Aurelian promptly marched back to Palmyra, took the city by storm, and gave it up to pillage and massacre. The unfortunate inhabitants were mercilessly slaughtered, regardless of age or sex. Torrents of blood were shed. The wealth of the citizens became the prey of a rapacious and brutal soldiery. The temples were stripped of their magnificent ornaments. In short, the city was one scene of havoc, devastation and massacre. This great catastrophe proved the final ruin of Palmyra, and Zenobia's splendid capital fell from its ancient power and magnificence, to rise no more. The ruins of this famous city in the midst of the Syrian desert excite the admiration of the modern traveler by their beauty and grandeur.

As soon as the Palmyrenian revolt had been quelled, Aurelian was again obliged to exercise his arms against an insurrection. The troops in Egypt rebelled; but the celerity of Aurelian's march disconcerted this mutiny, which might otherwise have been formidable. The insurgents were speedily subdued; and after the Emperor had thus restored tranquillity in the East, he determined to recover Spain, Gaul and Britain, which Tetricus had united into one kingdom. Aurelian restored this Western kingdom to the Empire in a single campaign (A. D. 274), after which he returned to Rome and was honored with the most splendid triumph that the city ever witnessed.

Aurelian's generous treatment of his captives was most honorable to him. He assigned a suitable estate to Zenobia and her children, in the vicinity of Rome; and the captive queen, becoming reconciled to her lot, passed the remainder of her life in apparent contentment as a respectable Roman matron. Her daughters were married into distinguished families, and the race had not become extinct when the Empire fell, two centuries later.

In the meantime, for the purpose of securing his capital against a sudden barbarian attack, which the recent invasions of Italy had demonstrated could be easily made, Aurelian fortified Rome with a new wall which inclosed the suburbs that had sprung up just outside the wall erected by King Servius Tullius eight centuries before.

In the latter part of Aurelian's reign a violent outbreak disturbed Rome, caused by the debasing of the coinage. The imperial troops who attempted to drive the insurgents from the Cœlian Hill were routed, losing several thousand men; but the tumult was quelled by great exertions. The Emperor punished the instigators of this revolt with such severity that he became generally unpopular with the citizens. He accordingly retired from Rome, amusing himself with a campaign in Gaul, where some disturbances distracted his attention. He next marched into Vindelicia and restored that province to the Empire; but he relinquished Dacia to the Goths and Vandals, as that outlying province had proven more of a burden than a benefit to the Empire ever since its annexation by Trajan a century and a half before. He removed the Roman garrisons and inhabitants of the province to the south of the Danube.

The sternness of Aurelian's disposition, and the inflexible severity which he displayed in the exercise of his authority, finally caused his assassination. While he was preparing to march against the Persians, he discovered an act of peculation on the part of Mnestheus, one of his secretaries. As the Emperor had sentenced his own nephew to death, and the judgment was rigidly executed, the guilty official could not entertain any hope of escaping the vengeance of his sovereign. By means of a forged writing, Mnestheus caused a number of persons to believe that the Emperor had also marked them for destruction, thus inducing them to participate in a conspiracy to assassinate him. On the march to Byzantium, the conspirators attacked Aurelian and killed him by inflicting many wounds upon him (A. D. 275). But the fraud was soon discovered; and the soldiers, who were fondly attached to the murdered Emperor, tore the assassins to pieces. Aurelian had reigned only four years and nine months, but in that brief period he had reunited and reinvigorated the declining and dissolving Empire.

After this act of vengeance, Aurelian's soldiers manifested a remarkable amount of moderation and respect for the laws; quietly submitting the choice of Emperor to the Senate, instead of investing one of their own number with the imperial purple. The wretched fate of the Thirty Tyrants seems to have had the effect of checking that reckless ambition which characterized almost every Roman general, and on this occasion not one of them made any effort to claim the imperial dignity.

After a tranquil interregnum of more than half a year, the Senate elected MARCUS CLAUDIUS TACITUS, a descendant of the illustrious historian of that name, to the imperial office. Tacitus was in his seventy-fifth year; and at first declined the perilous honor thus bestowed upon him, retiring to his farm in Campania to avoid the importunities of the Romans; but the necessities of the State induced him to yield. Tacitus was a very wealthy Senator and a man of pure character. He was a model of temperance, moderation and impartiality. He devoted much attention to the morals of the people. He also patronized literature, and ordered ten copies of the great historical works of his renowned ancestor to be carefully and accurately transcribed every year to supply the public libraries. He likewise distinguished himself as a soldier, and drove back the barbarians who made an inroad into Asia Minor; but the fatigues of war proved too much for the Emperor's feeble age, and he died in Cappadocia after a reign of but seven months (A. D. 276).

FLORIAN, the brother of Tacitus, was

chosen Emperor by the Senate upon the reception of the intelligence of the death of Tacitus; but the army in the East proclaimed their general, MARCUS AURELIUS PROBUS, a Pannonian, Emperor. A civil war was averted by the course of Florian's soldiers, who refused to fight for their general, and who killed him in a mutiny after a reign of three months, thus leaving Probus as sole Emperor (A. D. 276).

Probus was an able general, and a prudent and vigorous monarch, sincerely devoted to the welfare of his subjects, which he believed he might be able to accomplish as well by the arts of peace as by conquest. After he had become undisputed sovereign of the whole Empire, he marched into Gaul, which had been invaded by the barbarous German tribes, whom he defeated in several great battles, in which four hundred thousand of them are said to have been left dead upon the field. He drove the Germans from the region of the Neckar and the Elbe, and subdued the Sarmatians; after which he passed into Thrace, where he vanquished the Goths, compelling them to sue for peace. In Asia Minor he conquered the revolted Isaurians, and divided their lands among his veteran soldiers. He made his power so feared in the East that rebellious Egypt likewise submitted; and Varanus, the New Persian monarch, alarmed at his victories, sent ambassadors to solicit peace, and submitted to the terms which he dictated to them.

Probus subdued three pretenders who started up in various parts of the Empire. The Goths and the Vandals, hoping to profit by these insurrections, again invaded the Empire; but Probus took the field against them, and drove them back to their native wilds; after which he devoted himself to the arts of peace. He endeavored to secure the frontiers of the Empire by settling them with colonies of barbarians, who, becoming civilized, served as a defense of the Roman dominion against their less civilized kinsmen. He likewise attempted to drain the marshy lands, and to improve the agricultural system of the Empire. He encouraged the inhabitants of Gaul and Illyricum to plant vines, and restored the seventy cities which had fallen into decay in various portions of the Empire.

Having passed through his native city, Sirmium, in Pannonia, Probus employed several thousand of his soldiers in draining a marsh in its vicinity by cutting canals to the sea. The troops so disliked this labor that they mutinied, and attacked the Emperor near an iron tower which he had constructed for the purpose of watching their operations. Probus made his escape into the tower; but, as he did not have any of his guards with him, he was overpowered and murdered by his soldiers (A. D. 282), after a reign of six years. His friends and enemies alike lamented his death, and aided in erecting an imposing monument to his memory.

CARUS, the Prætorian Prefect, was proclaimed Emperor by the army; and the Senate somewhat reluctantly confirmed this choice. The new Emperor bestowed the title of Cæsar on his two sons, Carinus and Numerian, associating the former with him as his colleague in the Empire. Carinus was one of the most depraved young men of the time, while Numerian was one of the most virtuous.

Leaving Carinus to govern the West, Carus started for the East, taking Numerian with him. He passed into Illyricum, where he defeated the Sarmatians; after which he took the field against the New Persians, marching into Mesopotamia, which he speedily conquered by defeating the New Persians, whom he pursued to the gates of Seleucia and Ctesiphon. The victorious Emperor crossed the Tigris, and seemed to be on the point of extinguishing the New Persian Empire, when he died (A. D. 283)—from disease, according to some writers; from a stroke of lightning according to others.

The superstitious fears of the Romans were excited by the Emperor's sudden death, and they obliged Numerian to retreat within the limits of the Roman dominions. Numerian's distress at his father's death was so great that he brought on a disease of his eyes by excessive weeping, and had to be carried in a close litter on the return of the Roman army from the Persian campaign. Arrius Aper, his father-in-law, the Prætorian Prefect, entertained the design of seizing the imperial purple, and hired an assassin to murder the young prince in his litter. For the purpose of concealing the deed, he announced that Numerian was unable to bear the light; and the deception was kept up until the odor of the corpse disclosed Aper's treacherous act, when an uproar was instantly excited in the army, and the soldiers at once proclaimed DIOCLETIAN, the commander of the body-guard, Emperor (A. D. 284). The new sovereign put the assassin to death with his own hands, and marched westward.

In the meantime Carínus was disgusting the West by his profligacy. When he was informed of Diocletian's advance, he marched against him at the head of a large army. Diocletian's army was defeated in a battle in Mœsia; but Carínus was slain in the moment of victory by a Tribune whom he had grievously wronged, and his troops immediately acknowledged Diocletian as Emperor (A. D. 285).

A new era began in the history of the Roman Empire with Diocletian's accession, putting an end to the license of the soldiery, who, from the time of the death of Cómmodus, claimed the right to set up and pull down Emperors at pleasure, while the imperial authority had likewise been hampered by the powers legally vested in the Senate. The tyranny of the legions which prevailed from the death of Cómmodus to the accession of Diocletian was unendurable, and would have long before destroyed the Empire had not the danger with which it was constantly menaced by the barbarians made the troops willing to submit to some kind of discipline.

With Diocletian's accession the period of military despotism ended; the imperial authority was strengthened; and the army was taught its proper position as the servant, and not the master, of the state. The reforms which Diocletian commenced were not completed until the reign of Constantine the Great. Though these reforms had the effect of vastly strengthening the imperial power, and giving a fresh vigor to the Empire by arresting its decline for the time, they tended very greatly to the division of the Roman world into two separate empires, which was already a question of time.

Diocletian was of low origin, his parents having been slaves. He received his name from Dioclea, a town in Dalmatia, where he was born. He had passed through the various gradations of office, having been promoted successively to the offices of Provincial Governor, Consul and Prætorian Prefect. He owed his elevation entirely to his abilities and merits, and was about forty years of age when he became Emperor. Diocletian possessed many virtues.

When Diocletian fully secured his authority, after the assassination of Carínus, in A. D. 285, he inaugurated the first of the measures by which he hoped to counteract the prevailing evils. As the cares of the vast Roman world were too great for one person, Diocletian divided the imperial authority, taking as his partner in the Empire one of his generals, Maximian, a brave and able soldier, but an ignorant and cruel barbarian. The two Emperors each assumed the title of Augustus.

Still the troubles of the Empire were so great that in A. D. 292 Diocletian and Maximian each took a subordinate colleague, or Cæsar, who were to occupy the position of sons and successors of the Augusti. Diocletian chose Galerius as his subordinate colleague, while Maximian selected Constantius Chlorus. These two Cæsars were younger than their patrons, and were able generals. Upon accepting the dignity conferred upon them, the two Cæsars repudiated their own wives; Galerius marrying Diocletian's daughter, while Constantius Chlorus married Maximian's stepdaughter.

Diocletian went a step farther, dividing the Empire between the four sovereigns; reserving the more settled provinces to himself and Maximian, and assigning to the Cæsars those requiring the presence of younger and more active men. Diocletian retained the government of Thrace, Macedon, Egypt and the Asiatic provinces. He assigned Italy and Africa to Maximian; the Danubian provinces, namely, Noricum, Pannonia and Mœsia, to Galerius; and the Western provinces, namely, Spain, Gaul and Britain, to Constantius Chlorus.

It was understood that the unity of the Empire was to be preserved, as the basis of this new arrangement. The two Cæsars were to regard the two Augusti as their superiors, and Maximian was to be guided by the influence of Diocletian, who was to be the chief of the four sovereigns between whom the government of the Roman world was thus divided. This very complex system worked smoothly during the lifetime of Diocletian, whose influence sufficed to preserve harmony in the government.

The results of the new imperial system were marked. Power was transferred from the legions to an imperial dynastic system. The principle of association, adopted on an extended scale, tended to give stability to the Empire. The ship of state was guided by firm hands; and various new arrangements were adopted, all tending toward strengthening absolutism, so that the old republican forms of the Empire were passing away, and the government of the vast Roman world was becoming a powerful imperial despotism, like the Oriental monarchies.

The restraint hitherto exercised by the Senate upon the despotic authority of the Emperors was completely removed by the transfer of the imperial capital from Rome; as Diocletian held his court at Nicomedia, in Asia Minor; while Maximian resided at Mediolanum (now Milan), in Northern Italy. Galerius had his residence at Sirmium, in Pannonia; and Constantius Chlorus held his court at Eborácum (now York), in Britain. When Rome ceased to be the capital of the Empire, the Roman Senate degenerated practically into a simple municipal body, directing the affairs of a single provincial town; and its lost privileges not being transferred to another assembly, "the Emperor remained the sole source of law, the sole fountain of honor, the one and only principle of authority."

For the purpose of guarding against the interference of the Prætorian Guards, who from their fortified camp at Rome had for so long a time been able to dictate terms to the Emperor, Diocletian reduced their numbers, with the view of ultimately suppressing them totally—a task which Constantine the Great finally accomplished. The multiplications of sovereigns, and the care taken to secure the throne against such a contingency as a vacancy, placed the imperial authority almost beyond the risk of danger and military violence.

In A. D. 286 a revolt broke out in Britain, where Cerausius, a naval chief, who had been intrusted with a large fleet for the defense of the coasts of Britain and Gaul, rose in rebellion against the Emperor, and having won the support of the legions in Britain, seized that island and established there an independent kingdom. He increased his navy by building new ships, and established his supremacy over the Western seas. Diocletian and Maximian made vigorous but fruitless efforts to reduce Cerausius to submission; but were finally obliged to accept him as their colleague in the Empire, with the title of Augustus (A. D. 287).

After Constantius Chlorus had been made Cæsar and assigned the Western provinces, he made war on Cerausius in A. D. 292. After a long siege, Constantius took Boulogne, in Gaul, on the shores of the British Channel, and prepared to invade Britain, where Cerausius was slain by his chief officer, Allectus (A. D. 293). In A. D. 296 Constantius landed in Britain, defeated Allectus, and reëstablished the Roman dominion over the island. He drove the Alemanni out of Gaul the next year, and settled his prisoners in colonies on the land which they had laid waste.

Maximian crushed a revolt which had broken out in Africa, vanquishing the revolted Moors in that quarter, and putting to death the pretender who had raised the standard of rebellion in that portion of the

Empire. Diocletian suppressed a rebellion in Egypt, taking Alexandria by storm, massacring several thousand of its inhabitants, and putting to death the pretender who had held the city against the Emperor.

Galerius was engaged for many years in defending the Danubian frontier against the barbarians, and maintained the renown of the Roman arms in that quarter; after which he took the field against the New Persians in the East. The Romans provoked the war with Persia in A. D. 286 by seizing Armenia and assigning it to their vassal, Tiridátes. The New Persians recovered Armenia in A. D. 296. Galerius invaded Mesopotamia in A. D. 297; and, after two indecisive battles, he was defeated by the New Persians near Carrhæ, the Haran of Abraham's time. After collecting a new army, Galerius advanced through Armenia upon Assyria, and defeated Narses, the New Persian monarch, in the mountains (A. D. 298). Peace was concluded the same year (A. D. 298), by which the New Persians ceded several small provinces beyond the Tigris to the Romans; while the dominions of Tiridátes, King of Armenia, the vassal of the Romans, were enlarged.

The evils of the imperial system established by Diocletian became apparent towards the end of his reign. The establishment of four imperial courts instead of one, and the increased number of officials in consequence, necessarily increased the rate of taxation, which was already exceedingly burdensome. The provinces were almost crushed under the burden of the imposts laid upon them; and the taxes were exacted from the people with the most extreme difficulty, it being usually necessary to employ violence, and sometimes even tortures, for this purpose. In consequence industry sank beneath this system which deprived it of all its earnings. Production steadily diminished, and a rise in the prices of all commodities followed. In A. D. 301 Diocletian attempted to remedy this evil by a decree fixing the maximum price for all the necessaries, and many of the luxuries, of life. But this violent interference with the natural laws of trade thwarted its very design, simply aggravating the evils it was intended to remedy.

Near the end of his reign Diocletian sullied his character by the tenth and last great persecution of the Christians. The rapid spread of the new religion, which at that time embraced about half of his subjects, alarmed him; and he resolved upon striking an effective blow for its destruction. In A. D. 303 he issued an edict which required uniformity of worship among all the inhabitants of the Roman world. The Christians were noted as the most orderly, the most industrious, and the most faithful of the Emperor's subjects; and their church in Rome numbered fifty thousand members.

The refusal of the Christians to comply with the Emperor's decree requiring them to repudiate their religion placed them outside the pale of the law. A war of extermination was waged against them in consequence, and thousands of them perished by rack and ax in every portion of the Empire; while their property was confiscated, their churches were burned, and the Scriptures were given to the flames. It was only in the extreme West, under the more enlightened rule of Constantinus Chlorus, that the Christians escaped the malice of their bigoted adversaries. But these violent persecutions, instead of stamping out the Christian faith, only increased the number of its adherents; as the Christian ranks were filled up with new converts as fast as they were thinned by the numerous martyrdoms. The epoch of this persecution was long observed in the Christian Church as the *Era of Martyrs*; and is still remembered by the Copts of Egypt, the Abyssinians and other African Christians.

In A. D. 305, after a glorious reign of twenty years, Diocletian, weary of the cares and trials of state, abdicated the imperial dignity in the presence of a vast multitude of people and retired to private life, compelling Maximian to resign his power on the same day. Diocletian never regretted this act, which he survived nine years. When requested by Maximian and others to resume the imperial purple, the ex-Emperor replied: "If you would see the cabbages I raise in my garden, you would not ask me to take a throne."

After the abdication of Diocletian and Maximian, in A. D. 305, GALERIUS and CONSTANTIUS CHLORUS were recognized as Emperors; and Galerius immediately appointed Maximin and Severus as Cæsars for himself and Constantius respectively. This appointment greatly offended the legions in Britain, who resented a proceeding which deprived their own leader, Constantius, of the choice of his successor.

Upon the death of Constantius Chlorus, the next year (A. D. 306), the dissatisfied legions in Britain proclaimed CONSTANTINE, the son of Constantius, as his successor. Galerius was obliged to condone this infringement of the new system, because he was unable to resist it. He therefore recognized Constantine as Cæsar, and promoted Severus to the rank of Augustus; so that there were now again two Augusti and two Cæsars, and the organization of the imperial college was maintained. Constantine retained his father's provinces in the West—Britain, Gaul and Spain. Severus ruled Italy and Africa. Maximin governed Syria and Egypt. Galerius retained for himself all the provinces between Italy and Gaul in the West and Syria in the East, comprising about three-fourths of the Empire.

The loss of the prestige and privileges of Rome in consequence of the division of the Empire and the establishment of new capitals had seriously offended the Italians, who actually rose in open rebellion in A. D. 307. The Roman Senate appointed MAXENTIUS, the son of Maximian, Emperor; whereupon Maximian joined his son and resumed the rank of Augustus, which he had resigned at the time of Diocletian's abdication. Severus marched to Rome for the purpose of suppressing the revolt, but was deserted by his troops, whereupon he committed suicide. By joining Constantine, Maxentius and Maximian were able to defeat the large armies which Galerius led to reduce Italy to submission, and Galerius was obliged to return to the East. A compromise was effected in A. D. 309, by which the Roman world was ruled by six sovereigns—Constantine, Maximian and Maxentius in the West; and Galerius, Maximin and Licinius in the East. Licinius had been appointed Cæsar by Galerius upon the death of Severus.

This arrangement lasted but a few years, and was first disturbed by a quarrel between father and son, Maximian and Maxentius. Maximian was forced to seek refuge at the court of Constantine, who had married his daughter. Maximian was well received by Constantine at first; but, being detected in a plot against his son-in-law, he was put to death in A. D. 310.

The next year (A. D. 311) Galerius, who was as cruel a persecutor of the Christians as Diocletian had been, died at his capital, Nicomedia, in Asia Minor; thus leaving the Roman world to four Emperors—Constantine in the West, Maxentius in Italy and Africa, Licinius in Illyricum and Thrace, and Maximin in Egypt and Asia.

Maxentius alienated his subjects by his cruelties and extortions, and they requested Constantine to depose him and to unite Italy and Africa to his own provinces. Constantine had displayed his military abilities by his successful resistance to the Franks and the Allemanni, whom he kept from invading Gaul; while his generous protection of his Christian subjects had rewarded him with the gratitude and affection of the Christians in every portion of the Empire.

Constantine sought to avoid the struggle with Maxentius; but, finding that his adversary was preparing to invade Gaul, he anticipated him by entering Italy with an army of forty thousand men, crossing the Alps by the passage of Mont Cenis without opposition, in A. D. 312. The struggle was decided by Constantine's vigor and rapid movements. Constantine won a victory at Turin, took Verona after an obstinate siege and battle, and finally encountered his rival before the gates of Rome. Constantine defeated Maxentius at the Milvian Bridge, and entered Rome in triumph; Maxentius being drowned in the Tiber (A. D. 312).

The victorious Constantine thus became master of Rome and Italy, and promptly devoted himself to the task of consolidating his dominions. His first act was the disbandment of the Prætorian Guards, which Maxentius had increased to eighty thousand men. By thus dispersing this formidable military force, Constantine deprived the Roman Senate of the last vestige of its dignity, and rendered Rome incapable of resisting his will (A. D. 312).

The next year (A. D. 313) a war broke out in the East between Licinius and Maximin. In the following year (A. D. 314) Maximin was defeated in a great battle near Heracléa, on the Propontis (now Sea of Marmora); and soon afterward committed suicide in despair at Tarsus, in Cilicia, thus leaving Licinius sole master of the Eastern Roman provinces.

Encouraged by his triumph over Maximin, Licinius aspired to the dominion of the whole Roman world by driving Constantine from power in the West; and, by his intrigues for this purpose, he provoked a war with his rival in A. D. 314. Licinius was defeated in a series of battles; and was thus obliged to cede Pannonia, Mœsia, Illyricum, Macedonia and Greece to Constantine in A. D. 315. Thus the river Strymon and the Ægean Sea became the boundaries between the Eastern and Western Roman Empires. Two sons of Constantine and one of Licinius obtained the title of Cæsar. Crispus, Constantine's son, defeated the Franks and the Alemanni on the Rhine; while, on the Danube, Constantine inflicted a terrible defeat upon the Goths, who had invaded the Roman dominions.

After a seven years' peace between the Eastern and Western Empires, hostilities were renewed in consequence of the ambition of Constantine, who had resolved to make himself master of the whole Roman dominions. Constantine defeated Licinius near Adrianople, besieged him in Byzantium, and finally overthrew him on the heights of Chalcedon (now Scutari), which commanded the latter city. Licinius was taken prisoner and put to death (A. D. 322).

By this triumph over the last of his rivals, CONSTANTINE THE GREAT, as he was now called, became sole sovereign of the vast Roman world; and under him Christianity became the state-religion of the Roman Empire, after he had personally embraced the religion of Christ and had thus become the *first Christian Emperor.* With this important event, the history of Pagan Rome ends, and the history of Christian Rome begins. In the following section we will trace the rise and progress of Christianity, and its ultimate triumph under Constantine the Great.

SECTION XX.—TRIUMPH OF CHRISTIANITY.

LREADY we have noted the birth of Jesus Christ—the founder of Christianity—during the reign of Augustus; his crucifixion during the reign of Tiberius; the propagation of his doctrines and teachings by his great Apostle, St. Paul; the rapid growth of Christianity throughout the whole Roman world during three centuries; and the Ten Great Persecutions of the Christians, beginning with that under Nero, and ending with that under Diocletian. With every persecution Christianity grew stronger and stronger, and "the blood of the martyrs became the seed of the Church."

The Romans were very tolerant of diverse faiths in the Empire, and the various pagan and polytheistic religions were unmolested by the Roman Emperors; but the Christians —whose virtues and purity kept them aloof from those around them in that corrupt age, and who held their meetings in secret—were looked upon with suspicion; and the perse-

THE ROMAN EMPIRE
AT THE DEATH OF AUGUSTUS
A. D. 13

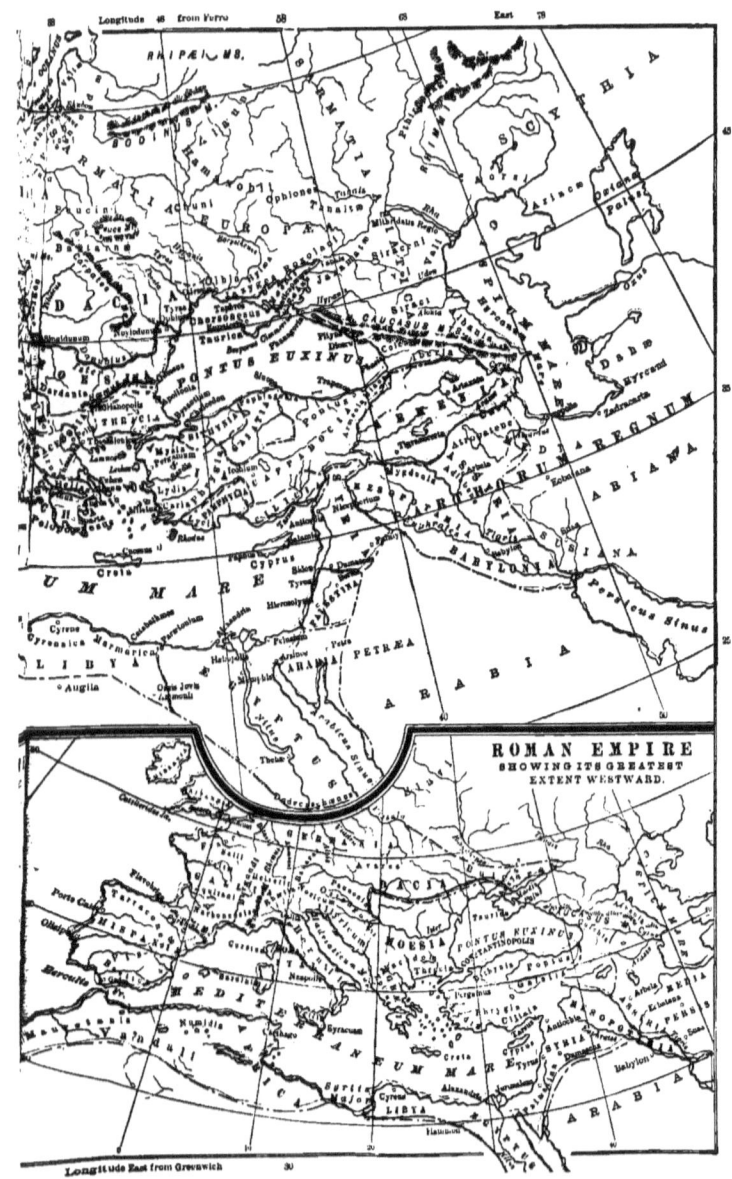

cutions were for political rather than for religious reasons. This accounts for the persecutions of the Christians by good Emperors like Trajan, Adrian, Marcus Aurelius, Decius, Valerian and Diocletian; while under the bad Emperors they were generally unmolested.

Below the hills surrounding Rome are excavated a labyrinth of galleries at three different levels cut out of the *tufa*, or volcanic rock. These galleries cross and recross each other, and would extend three or four hundred miles if stretched out in a single line. They are narrow passages, generally but three or four feet wide, with niches on each side for bodies. These Catacombs were the cemeteries of the early Christians at Rome. Seventy thousand of them have been counted, and Rossi has estimated them all to number more than three million. The Roman law carefully protected places of sepulture, both Christian and Pagan; and the Christians, gradually taking advantage of this respect for sepulchers, excavated chapels for prayer and rooms for love-feasts in the interior of the Catacombs. Afterwards, during the times of persecution, these interior rooms became the hiding-places of the Christians.

In A. D. 257 Valerian issued an edict forbidding Christian worship in the Catacombs, whereupon the Roman soldiers hunted the Christians through these underground recesses. Some of the unfortunates were blocked up and buried alive, while many were dragged out and tortured to death. An entire change then took place in the structure of the Catacombs, in order to adapt them to purposes of escape or concealment. The principal entrances were blocked up, and the stairways were destroyed. Lower galleries were excavated under the upper ones, and were narrower, darker, more complicated and labyrinthine. Many galleries were filled with earth or built up with masonry. Hiding-places were constructed in the deepest recesses, where bishops and other ecclesiastics were often concealed for years, and celebrated worship in the neighboring chapels. Wells were dug for the supply of water. Store-houses were cut out for corn and wine. Hundreds of lamps have been discovered for lighting up these gloomy recesses. The horrible tortures endured by those whose only crime was their religion have been fully related by Eusebius, who had witnessed them. The number who suffered such frightful deaths was sufficiently great to justify the ascription in the *Te Deum*—"The noble army of martyrs praise Thee!"

The courage of the Christians grew stronger in the midst of these perils and horrors. They were seized with an enthusiasm for martyrdom—a desire to gain an eternal heaven through a few hours of suffering. The universal Christian belief was that martyrdom was the surest way to heaven—better than all sacraments, all prayers, all good works. The Christians offered themselves to die—demanding tortures, seeking persecution, glorying in shame. The humblest Christian slave on his way to death saw a halo of immortal glory all around him. Said St. Basil: "These tortures, so far from being a terror, are rather a recreation!" Said Tertullian: "Kill us, rack us, grind us to powder; our numbers increase in proportion as you mow us down."

Galerius, just before his death, in A. D. 311, had issued an edict of toleration to Christians; and in A. D. 313 Constantine the Great also granted toleration by the *Edict of Milan*. Constantine's father had always shown favor to the Christians, valuing and honoring their virtues; and Constantine himself had grown up to regard their doctrines with favor, and for some time he wavered between Christianity and Paganism.

Eusebius, Bishop of Cæsaréa—the early historian of the Christian Church—asserted that Constantine declared that while marching against Maxentius he saw a luminous cross in the heavens, with the inscription in Greek: "By this conquer." This vision made a great impression upon Constantine and his army; and the Emperor, who had before been undecided in the choice of his religion, thereupon became a convert to Christianity, though he did not yet seek Christian baptism.

According to this legend Constantine's vision is said to have been followed by a remarkable dream the next night, in which Christ appeared before the Emperor and directed him to frame a standard under which his legions would march to certain victory. This was the origin of the famous *Lábarum*, afterwards borne by the Christian Emperors, and which scattered dismay among the opposing legions. The Lábarum had at the top a monogram of the mystic X., representing at once the cross and the initial of the Greek name for Christ. Constantine's victory over his Pagan rivals marked the complete triumph of Christianity over the Paganism of the Roman world.

In A. D. 324 Constantine the Great issued an edict exhorting all his subject to follow his example by becoming Christians. He did not, however, proscribe Paganism, as the office of Pontifex Maximus, which he held, required him to offer sacrifices to the heathen gods of Rome. Although he permitted his Pagan subjects to exercise their religion without molestation, the Emperor's example and the hope of gaining his favor induced thousands to renounce Paganism and to embrace the religion of the cross.

The lower classes being governed by imitation, the conversion of those possessing any eminence of birth, of power, or of riches, was soon followed by the dependent multitudes. Constantine's powerful influence extended beyond the limits of the Roman Empire. The education which he had given his sons and nephews secured to the Empire a race of princes whose faith was yet more earnest and sincere; they having imbibed the doctrine, if not the spirit, of Christianity in their earliest infancy.

War and commerce had been instrumental in spreading a knowledge of the gospel beyond the confines of the Roman provinces; and the barbarians who had looked with contempt upon an humble and persecuted sect soon learned to esteem a religion which had been so recently embraced by the greatest monarch and the most civilized nation of the world.

Constantine the Great did not receive Christian baptism until near the end of his life; but he summoned a Council of the Christian Church at Nicæa, or Nice, in Asia Minor, which convened in A. D. 325 and was attended by numerous bishops and deacons, and over which the Emperor himself presided. Christianity was now established on a firm basis as the state-religion of the Roman Empire (A. D. 325). The Council of Nice had been convened for the purpose of deciding certain disputed matters of faith; and it condemned the doctrines of Arius, of Alexandria, who denied Christ's divinity, and declared the doctrines of Athanasius, the other Alexandrian ecclesiastic, who maintained Christ's equality with God the Father and the doctrine of the Trinity in Unity, as the true, or orthodox, faith of the Catholic, or universal, Church. The Goths, the Vandals and the Lombards, who had become Arian Christians, were excommunicated as heretics.

Constantine the Great did not relinquish the right to direct the religious as well as the secular affairs of the state — a right which had always been claimed by the Roman Emperors. He treated the assembled dignitaries and ecclesiastics of the Church at Nice with every mark of reverence; but he refused to persecute Arius and his followers, the Alexandrian heretics, whom the Council had condemned. Nevertheless, he prohibited all the immoral rites of Paganism, and enacted rigorous laws against immoral practices, which Paganism had permitted, if not sanctioned.

Constantine the Great did not forbid Paganism until near the end of his life, seeking rather to bring that old worn-out religion into disrepute by ridicule. With public money Constantine the Great erected new Christian churches and repaired the old ones. He proclaimed Sunday (*dies solis*) a day of rest. He exempted the Christian priesthood from taxation and granted them other privileges, and allowed legacies to the Church. Constantine's ecclesiastical measures made the Christian Church a powerful organization, and it assumed a new form under the constitution which he gave it.

Before it had become the state-religion of the Empire, the Elders and Bishops were chosen from the entire Church community, and the principle of brotherly equality was held in honor. The Christian priesthood, or clergy, were thenceforth separated from the people, or laity; while degrees of rank were introduced, thus placing the bishops of the principal cities over the remaining bishops as metropolitans, and these again were superintended by the priests in their immediate vicinity. At the same time, the Church services, which previously consisted only in singing, prayer, and Bible reading, were succeeded by the so-called love-feasts, which were made more solemn by the aid of music and other arts.

Such was the foundation of that ecclesiastical organization which dominated Christendom for so many centuries, and which, under the Bishop of Rome, who eventually assumed the title of *Pope*, or Father of the Church, ruled the whole West of Europe during the Middle Ages, humbling even emperors and kings, and inspiring nations with awe by its power.

The establishment of Christianity as the state-religion of the Roman Empire was not only the greatest event in the history of the Empire, but also the greatest event in the history of the Church. From being a proscribed religion it became a legally-recognized and a legally-protected religion. Although Constantine did not fully carry out the teachings of this beneficent religion in his administration of public affairs and in his treatment of his family, the Christian world must ever owe him a debt of gratitude for the mighty impulse which the religion of the cross received by his action and policy. Although in becoming the state-religion of the Roman Empire, Christianity was obliged to accept and to incorporate into its organic system many heathen customs and practices and some heathen doctrines, as a concession to win converts and proselytes from Paganism, on the principle of give and take, this corruption of the new religion was far more than counterbalanced by the good results brought about by the substitution of the new monotheistic religion for the effete polytheisms of the ancient world.

From the time of Constantine's triumph over Maxentius, when the persecutions of the Christians ceased, the Catacombs were no longer places of refuge for that hitherto despised and oppressed sect. Thirteen years later the Roman Senate erected a triumphal arch near the vast amphitheater, where the Christians had been so recently massacred "to make a Roman holiday." This arch still stands in the Forum. The inscription on the arch declares that a trophy was erected to "the Emperor and Cæsar Flavius Constantènus Maximus Augustus, the Father of His Country; because through the instinct of Deity and the magnanimity of his mind, * * * he had overthrown the tyrant and avenged the Republic."

The first result of this event was that Christianity ceased to be an underground religion, and churches were opened above ground; while the Catacombs became sacred places to the Christians, and burials therein were now a matter of choice and not one of necessity, because of a desire to lay one's remains, or those of a friend, near the bones of the Christian martyrs. Wealthy Christians now enlarged the chapels and added new decorations. Pictures, sarcophagi and ornamentation were less simple and tasteful, but more magnificent, than previously. The tombs, pictures and inscriptions were afterwards restored by Damasus, Bishop of Rome from A. D. 366 to A. D. 384, who built piers of masonry to support the tottering galleries, cleared out the passages which had been filled up, and wrote poetical inscriptions on the martyrs' tombs. Basilicas were then erected above the Catacombs, to designate the martyr's grave below. The inscriptions of Damasus were executed by a fine engraver in an admirable manner. Charity, rather than theology, works rather than faith, character rather than creed, are recorded on these primeval records of primitive Christianity.

St. Jerome, A. D. 354, several years before Damasus began his restorations, thus describes a visit to the Catacombs: "When I was a boy, being educated at Rome, I used every Sunday, in company with other boys, to visit the tombs of the apostles and martyrs, and to go into the crypts excavated there within the bowels of the earth. The walls on either side as you enter are full of the bodies of the dead, and the whole place is so dark that one almost sees the fulfillment of those words of the prophet, 'Let them go down alive into Hades.' Here and there a little light, admitted from above, suffices to give a momentary relief from the horror of darkness; but as you go forward and find yourself again immersed in the utter blackness of night, the words of the poet come to your mind, 'Silence makes us afraid.'"

The Latin poet Prudentius, a little later, describes the Catacombs as they were after Bishop Damasus began his restorations. "Not far from the city walls among the well trimmed orchards, there lies a crypt buried in darksome pits. Into its secret recesses a steep path with winding stairs directs one, though the turnings shut out the light. The light of day, entering the doorway, illuminates the threshold; and when, as you advance further, the darkness as of night arrives, there occur, at intervals, apertures cut in the roof, which let in some rays of the sun. * * * Wondrous is the sanctity of the place. Here rests the body of Hippolytus. * * * Here have I, when sick in body and soul, often prostrated myself in prayer and found relief. * * * Wealthy hands have here put up bright tablets. Early in the morning pilgrims come to salute the saint; they come and go till the setting of the sun. Love of religion collects here natives and foreigners; they print kisses on the shining tablets of the tomb. * * * On the Feast of the Martyrs the imperial city pours forth her stream of Romans, plebeians and patricians alike, faith urging both to the shrine. Albano's gates also send forth their white-robed host. The noise on all the roads grows loud," etc.

Constantine's conversion to the religion of the meek and lowly Jesus did not prevent him from committing some great crimes—such as the murder of his wife, Fausta, and his eldest son, Crispus. At the age of seventeen, the virtuous Crispus had been made Cæsar, and was extremely idolized by the people. This popularity aroused the jealousy of his father, who suspected Crispus of treasonable designs. Constantine seized his son during the festivities at Rome in honor of the twentieth year of his reign, and caused him to be secretly tried and put to death (A. D. 326). At the same time Constantine caused his nephew Licinius, whom he also suspected, to be seized, tried and executed. Constantine had been instigated to these harsh deeds by his wife Fausta; and when too late he discovered his error, he caused Fausta and her accomplices to be put to death.

These horrible deeds of cruelty made Constantine the Great extremely unpopular with the people of Rome; but he no longer regarded their displeasure, as he had already determined to remove the capital of the vast Roman world to the Greek city of Byzantium, on the Thracian Bosphorus, in order to be nearer the center of his dominions. Accordingly, in A. D. 330, Constantine fixed his capital at Byzantium, on whose ruins he founded a new city, naming it *New Rome*, but which was thereafter named *Constantinople* (city of Constantine) in honor of the great Emperor. Constantine expended vast sums in fortifying his new capital with walls and towers, and in embellishing it most magnificently with splendid architectural works, adorning it with a Capitol, an amphitheater, a race-course, elegant palaces and churches, and works of art.

The removal of the capital of the Roman Empire to Constantinople was justified by considerations of the soundest public policy. The Eastern provinces of the Empire were exposed to the attacks of the powerful and vigorous New Persian Empire of the Sassanidæ, as that famous dynasty openly aimed to reëstablish the ancient empire of Cyrus the

Great over the whole of Western Asia. The Danubian frontier was not sufficiently protected against the ravages of the Goths and the Sarmatians. The Emperor would therefore have jeopardized the most faithful and wealthy portions of his dominions by continuing his residence in the West of Europe. A capital and metropolis on the confines of Europe and Asia was therefore recommended by the political advantages of its central location, and by the opportunities for the revival of the lucrative commerce of the Euxine and the Levant. A slight glance at the natural advantages of Byzantium will convince any one that it was worthy of being made the capital and metropolis of a great empire by the wise monarch whose name it has ever since borne.

The area of Constantinople is an irregular triangle, whose apex is an obtuse point advancing to the east and toward the Asiatic coast, meeting and repelling the waters of the Thracian Bosphorus. On the north side of the city is the winding harbor known in both ancient and modern times as the *Chryso Keras*, or the Golden Horn, which is about seven miles long, with good anchorage through most of its extent. The entrance is but five hundred yards wide, and can be easily defended against a hostile armament. The walls of the city on the south side are washed by the Sea of Marmora (the ancient Propontis), and the western walls form the base of the triangle which is connected with the continent. Thus favorably situated—with the Euxine sea to the northeast, and the Ægean sea to the south-west—Constantinople could be supplied with the richest productions of Europe and Asia; while its shape made it easily defensible against the assaults of the savage and plundering tribes of Thrace. The long prosperity of Constantinople, and the invincible resistance which it offered to barbarian aggressors for the thousand years during which it was the capital of the Eastern Roman Empire, demonstrate the sagacity of its founder in selecting it for his capital.'

The removal of the capital of the Roman world from Rome to Constantinople completed the change in the constitution of the Roman Empire which had been begun during the reign of Diocletian. Constantine reorganized the Empire, which was now again as compact and as powerful as in the time of Augustus; dividing it into four *prefectures*—1, Gaul, including Spain and Britain; 2, Italy, including Africa, Rhætia, Noricum, Pannonia and Dalmatia; 3, Illyricum, including Dacia and Macedonia; 4, The East, embracing Thrace, Egypt and all the Roman provinces in Asia. Each prefecture was divided into *dioceses*, and each diocese into *presidencies*, or proconsular governments.

The subdivision of the Empire gave rise to three ranks of officials, who constituted the nobility of the Empire and somewhat resembled the nobility of modern Europe. The old republican forms of government, which Augustus had so ostensibly cherished, had long since disappeared; and Constantine the Great made no effort to revive these forms, in the place of which was now established the elaborate ceremony of an Oriental court. Even the ten thousand spies, known as the *King's Eyes*, were maintained in the Roman Empire under Constantine the Great, as they had been of old in the Medo-Persian Empire under Darius Hystaspes and Xerxes the Great. On the frontiers of the Roman Empire was now maintained a standing army of six hundred and forty-five thousand men, composed of barbarian mercenaries; Roman citizens having now become averse to military service. The Franks, especially, occupied an important position in both the court and the camp of Constantine the Great.

Thus the Roman Empire became a simple despotism, with more of a political than a military character. After fixing his residence at Constantinople, Constantine the Great adopted Oriental manners. He affected the gorgeous attire of the Persian kings; decorated his head with false hair of various colors, and with a diadem of pearls and gems. He substituted robes of silk embroidered with flowers, in the place of the austere garb of Rome, or the unadorned purple toga of the first Roman Emperors. He crowded the palace with spies and parasites, and lavished the wealth of the Empire upon stately architecture.

Each of the four prefectures was governed by a Prætorian Prefect; but Constantine had taken good care that their power should not be rendered too dangerous by being united with military command. They were intrusted with the coinage, the highways, the ports, the granaries, the manufactures, and everything that could interest the public prosperity of their respective prefectures. They were empowered to explain, to enforce, and in some instances to modify, the imperial edicts. They were vested with authority to remove or punish the provincial governors. An appeal could be made to their tribunal from all inferior jurisdictions, and the sentence of a Prætorian Prefect was final.

Rome and Constantinople—the old and the new capital of the Empire—had each its own Prætorian Prefect. The superior dignity of their tribunals caused those of the Prætors to be deserted, and the most ancient title of Roman magistracy soon fell into disuse. The peace of each of these two great cities was preserved by a vigilant police. So many statues adorned each of them that a magistrate was specially appointed to preserve them from injury.

The first of the three classes of magistrates of the Empire were the *illustrissimi*, (illustrious)—the Consuls, the patricians, the Prætorian Prefects, the Metropolitan Prefects, the masters-general of the cavalry and the infantry, and the seven great officers of the imperial household. The titles of Consul and patrician were merely honorary, and were conferred by the Emperor at his pleasure; the distinctions being personal, not hereditary. The power of the Prætorian Prefects ranked next to that of the Emperor himself. The second rank of officials were the *spectábiles* (respectable), and the third rank were *clarissimi* (honorable).

There were seven great officers of the state and the court. The *Præpositus Sancti Cubiculi*, or Lord Chamberlain, was to attend the Emperor in his hours of state or amusement, and to perform about his person all those menial offices whose splendor can only be derived from the influence of royalty; and under him were all the *comites palatii* (lords of the palace), and the *cubicularii* (chamberlains), many of whom were eunuchs of great influence in later ages.

The *Magister Officiorum*, or Minister of the Home Department, was intrusted with the management of all correspondence between the Emperor and his subjects, such as memorials, petitions, letters and their answers. He was likewise inspector-general of the civil and military schools; and appeals could be made to his tribunal from every portion of the Empire in cases where the privileges of the imperial officers were concerned.

The *Comes Sacrarum Largitionum*, or Lord High Treasurer, was charged with the management of the finances of the Empire. His duties were not limited to the charge of the exchequer and the superintendence of the tax-gatherers; but he also had charge over manufactures and commerce, which Constantine, wiser than most of his predecessors, brought under the special care of the state.

The *Quæstor*, or Chief Secretary of State, was the representative of the Emperor's legislative power, and the original source of civil jurisprudence; some of his functions being apparently similar to those of the British Lord Chancellor. The *Comes Rei Principis*, or Keeper of the Privy Purse, had charge of the imperial private estates, which were scattered through the provinces from Mauritania to Britain. The *Comites Domesticorum*, or commanders of the household guards, presided over the *seven scholæ*, or troops or squadrons of cavalry and infantry that guarded the Emperor's person.

The *Magistri Equitum* were the commanders of the cavalry; the *Magistri Peditum* were the generals of the infantry; and the *Magistri Utriusque Militæ* was the commander-in-chief. Those commanding under them were called *duces*, or dukes, and *comites*, or counts; and were distinguished by wearing a golden belt. They received, besides their pay, a liberal allowance, sufficient to maintain one hundred and ninety servants and one hundred and fifty-eight horses. Constantine effected a total change in the constitution of the legions, diminishing their numbers to less than a fourth. For the purpose of securing a regular supply of young soldiers, he made it a condition, in assigning lands to the veterans, that their sons should be trained to the military profession. The necessity for such a stipulation is not the only evidence we possess concerning the decay of the Roman military spirit. The dislike entertained by the degenerate Romans for a soldier's life was such that many young men in Italy mutilated the fingers of their right hand to avoid being pressed into the military service. It was in consequence of this reluctance that the custom of employing barbarian mercenary soldiers became constantly more and more fatal; as they not only enlisted in the imperial army, but many of them were elevated to the highest offices of the state.

These changes in the constitution of the civil and military administration of the Empire rendered the government more costly, and required a wholly new system of taxation to maintain them. The first of the new taxes was the *indiction*, a yearly land-tax, levied in proportion to the fertility of the estates in possession of land-owners; and a general census, or survey of property, was made throughout the Empire every fifteen years, for the purpose of regulating this assessment. For this reason the name of *indiction* is assigned indifferently to the tax and to the cycle of registration. An impost called the *aurum lustrale* was levied on trade and commerce, and was collected every fourth year.

Says Gibbon: "The honorable merchant of Alexandria, who imported the gems and spices of India for the western world; the usurer who derived from the interest of money a silent and ignominious profit; the ingenious manufacturer, the diligent mechanic, and even the most obscure retailer of a sequestered village, were obliged to admit the officers of the revenue into the partnership of their gain; and the sovereign of the Roman Empire, who tolerated the profession, consented to share the infamous gain of prostitutes."

The *aurum coronarium* was originally a free gift, being a compensation for the crown of gold presented by the allies of the Romans to generals who had been instrumental in effecting their deliverance, or who had conferred some remarkable favor upon them. At length this spontaneous offering was exacted as a debt, whenever the Emperor announced any remarkable event which might give him a real or apparent claim to the benevolence of his subjects, such as his accession, the birth of a son, or a victory over barbarians. The municipal expenses fell almost entirely on the civic officers. There was no system of local taxation, but the wealthiest citizens were by turns obliged to provide for the administrative requirements of the towns in which they resided.

Although some evil resulted from these changes, Constantine's innovations were generally useful reforms. The despotism of the soldiery had been the great curse of the Romans for several centuries; but this military license was checked and restrained by "the pride, pomp and circumstance" which characterized the civil administration. The despotism of the army was superseded by the despotism of an imperial court, and the improvement in consequence of even this change is readily apparent to any one. Constantine saw very clearly the advantages resulting from a union of church and state; and for this reason he appropriated a large part of the revenue of cities to the endowment of churches and the support of the clergy, thus bringing religion to the aid of the police in checking turbulence. The Roman Empire might have enjoyed a long period of prosperity under Constantine's constitution had it not been for the crimes and follies of his successors.

Constantine's last years were harassed by fresh aggressions of the barbarians north of the Danube. The Goths attacked the Sarmatians, whereupon the latter implored the assistance of the Romans. Constantine thereupon marched against the Goths, but was defeated in one battle against them. In the next, however, he inflicted a disastrous defeat upon them; and one hundred thousand Goths who were driven into the mountains perished from cold and hunger.

The Sarmatians, dissatisfied with the division of the spoils, revenged themselves by making plundering raids into the Roman dominions. Constantine then allowed the Goths to defeat the Sarmatians, who were obliged to abandon their own territories in consequence of a servile insurrection, and to take refuge in the dominions of Constantine. The Emperor assigned lands in Italy, Macedonia, Thrace and Pannonia to about three hundred thousand Sarmatians, who were thus received as vassals of the Empire (A. D. 334).

With the hope of securing peace to his Empire after his death, Constantine now created his third son, Constans, and his nephew Dalmatius, Cæsars, and appointed another nephew, Hannibalianus, *Rex* (king); dividing the administration of the different portions of the Empire between his three sons and these two nephews. Constantine the Great died at Nicomedia, in Asia Minor, May 22, A. D. 337, after a glorious reign of thirty-one years, signalized by the greatest event in the history of the Roman Empire—the triumph of Christianity. Just before his death he received Christian baptism.

The character of Constantine the Great has been estimated differently, according to the light in which his patronage of Christianity has been viewed. The most impartial writers regard him as a man in whom vice and virtue, weakness and strength of mind, were strangely blended. His military talents and his power of organization are indisputable. His activity, courage, prudence and affection are unquestionable. But he was not as clement and humane as the first Christian Emperor was to have been expected to have shown himself. He was singularly superstitious; and what information we are able to gain concerning his religion, from his public acts and recorded speeches, his coins and medals, was a strange medley of Christianity and Paganism, unpleasant to contemplate.

Constantine's character deteriorated with the progress of time. His best period was that of his administration in Gaul from A. D. 306 to 312. As he advanced in years, he became more suspicious, more irritable, more harsh and severe in his punishments. The greatest stains upon his character are the executions of his wife Fausta, his worthy son Crispus, and his nephew Licinius; but it is hard to decide whether he punished an intended crime or whether he was actuated by a wicked and unworthy jealousy. The harmony prevailing between Constantine and his other sons, and the kindness which he exhibited toward his half-brothers and their offspring, would seem to indicate that in the great tragedies of his domestic life he may have been more unfortunate than guilty, and may have been swayed by the demands of state policy.

Although Constantine had bequeathed some portions of his dominions to his nephews Dalmatius and Hannibalianus, the Roman Senate and the imperial army ignored their claims, and unanimously proclaimed his three sons, to whom he had willed the greater part of his Empire, sole heirs of their father's dominions. CONSTANTINE II., the eldest son, received Gaul, Spain and Britain. CONSTANTIUS II., the second son, obtained Egypt and the Roman provinces in Asia; while CONSTANS, the youngest, was assigned Italy, Africa and Western Illyricum.

Constantine's three sons had been educated with the greatest care. The most pious of the Christian teachers, the most celebrated professors of Grecian philosophy and Roman jurisprudence, had been engaged to superintend their instruction; but the three princes resembled their mother Fausta more than their illustrious father, and were as similar in depravity of disposition as they were in name. Nevertheless some part of their faults are attributable to paternal weakness.

Before the three princes had reached manhood they were successively invested with the title of Cæsar and intrusted with a share in the government. This unwise indulgence necessarily surrounded them with a host of flatterers and exposed them to the corrupt adulations of the court. The three youths were summoned from their studies at too early an age, and were permitted to give up the pursuit of knowledge for the enjoyment of luxury and the expectation of a throne.

Constantius II. was the nearest to the imperial capital when his father died, and the soldiers, who were secretly prepared to second this incredible accusation, loudly demanded the punishment of the accused.

In accordance with these plans, all legal forms were violated, and a promiscuous massacre of the Flavian family followed. The great Constantine's two brothers, seven of his nephews, the patrician Optátus, who had married his sister, and the Prefect Ablavius, his leading favorite, were put to death without being allowed to say a word in their own defense. Gallus and Julian,

ARCH OF CONSTANTINE.

hastened to take possession of the palace; but his kinsmen, who were justly apprehensive of his jealous temper, forced him to take a solemn oath to protect them from all danger. A few days afterward a forged scroll was placed in his hands by Eusebius, Bishop of Nicomedía, the celebrated church historian. This document purported to be a genuine testament of Constantine the Great, in which the renowned Emperor was made to accuse his brothers of having poisoned him, and to exhort his sons to vengeance.

the youngest sons of Julius Constantius, were concealed with great difficulty until the rage of the assassins had subsided. A new division of the Empire then followed between the sons of Constantine the Great. Constantine II., the eldest, took the capital, along with Spain, Gaul and Britain; Constantius II. received Thrace, Egypt and the Asiatic provinces; and Constans obtained Italy, Africa and Western Illyricum.

Three years after this partition of the Empire, the ambition of Constantine II. kin-died the flames of a new civil war (A. D. 340). Discontented with his share, he wrested the African provinces from Constans, and invaded Italy by way of the Julian Alps, devastating the country around Aquileia. Constans marched against his brother, who advanced very imprudently and fell into an ambuscade near the little river Alsa, (now Ausa), where his army was cut to pieces, Constantine himself being among the slain. His body was cast into a river, but was afterwards found and taken to Constantinople, where it was interred. Constans took advantage of his victory by seizing Constantine's provinces, showing no disposition to allow his surviving brother, Constantius II., any share in them.

Constans reigned over two-thirds of his father's Empire for ten years, plundering his subjects by his rapacity, and disgracing himself by his vices. He generally resided in Gaul, in the forests of which province he found opportunities for hunting, the only manly sport in which he was in the habit of indulging. At the end of ten years (A. D. 350), while Constans was pursuing game in a neighboring forest, Magnentius, a German, who commanded the imperial forces at Augustodúnum (now Autun), caused himself to be proclaimed Emperor and closed the gates of the city. When Constans was informed of the revolt, he fled in the direction of Spain; but was overtaken at Ellíberis (now Elne), then called Helena, in memory of the mother of Constantine the Great, and was put to death.

The usurpation of Magnentius in Gaul was followed by that of Vetránio in Illyria; but the latter general assumed the imperial purple with great reluctance, being forced to do so by the clamors of his soldiers, and urged by the princess Constantína, who placed the crown on his head with her own hand. This ambitious woman was the sister of Constans and the widow of her cousin Hannibalianus, one of the murdered nephews of Constantine the Great. She was so eager for power, and so unscrupulous as to the means of gaining it, that she persuaded Vetránio to enter into an alliance with Magnentius, whose hands were still red with the blood of her murdered brother Constans.

In the meantime, while these civil wars and usurpations were distracting the Western Roman provinces, Constantius II. was engaged in a bloody war in Asia with the New Persians under their valiant king, Sapor II., who aspired to the dominion of all the territories which had formed a part of the empire founded by Cyrus the Great nine centuries before, and who was particularly desirous of recovering the five provinces that had been ceded to the Romans beyond the Tigris, and to assert the former supremacy of the Sassanidæ over Mesopotamia. Constantius II. hastened to the banks of the Euphrates upon receiving intelligence of the approach of this formidable invader, but the war for a long time was characterized by a series of petty skirmishes and predatory inroads.

After nine sanguinary but indecisive battles, the Romans were defeated in a decisive engagement on the Plains of Síngara (now Sinjar), near the ruins of Babylon (A. D. 348). Encouraged by this victory, Sapor II. besieged Nísibis; but after losing more than twenty thousand men before the walls of that city, he was obliged to raise the siege and to hasten to the defense of his eastern provinces, which were invaded by the fierce tribes from the country beyond the Oxus. This new war made it necessary for the New Persian monarch to propose a truce to Constantius II. which the latter readily accepted, because of the distracted condition of the Roman dominions.

After concluding the truce with Sapor II., Constantius II. intrusted the direction of affairs in the East to his lieutenants, but subsequently to his cousin Gallus, whom he elevated from a prison to a throne. He then hastened to Europe and entered Constantinople, deceiving Vetránio by offering to make him his colleague in the Empire. In a studied address to the assembled army and people, the artful Constantius II. asserted his claim to the Empire; and was greeted with outbursts of applause, followed by shouts for the deposition of the usurpers. Vetránio quietly submitted, taking the imperial diadem from his head, and tendering his homage to Constantius II. Constantius spared his rival's life and assigned him a considerable pension. Vetránio retired to Prusa (now Brusa), in Asia Minor, where he passed the remainder of his life in retirement, without ever expressing any desire to resume the imperial dignity.

Magnentius, seeing that he would be next attacked, led his army into Lower Pannonia, which became the seat of a fierce and bloody war. The armies finally encountered each other for a decisive engagement on the plains of Mursa (now Essek) in A. D. 351. The heavy-armed cavalry of Constantius II., sheathed in full panoply of plates of steel, decided the fate of the day, as the very weight of their onset broke the lines of the Western legions; while the light archers of Asia harassed the naked German auxiliaries, on which Magnentius placed his main reliance, and reduced them to such despair that battalions cast themselves into the rapid stream of the Drave. Still the battle was so obstinate that fifty-four thousand were slain, and the victors suffered more severely than the vanquished. The battle of Mursa seemed to have absorbed the vitality of the Empire, as the Roman rulers were never again able to collect such noble bands of veterans as fell on that sanguinary field.

After being defeated in a second battle at Mursa, Magnentius fled to Italy, and was pursued thither by Constantius II. the next spring (A. D. 352). The entire peninsula soon submitted to its legitimate sovereign, the usurper escaping into Gaul. After being defeated in a great battle at Mount Seleucus, among the Cottian Alps, Magnentius escaped the vengeance of his conqueror by commiting suicide; and his associates either followed his example or suffered the penalties of treason. Thus sixteen years after the death of Constantine the Great, Constantius II. became sole Emperor.

During the entire reign of Constantius II., the Christian Church was scandalized and distracted by bitter controversies produced by the Arian heresy. Constantius II. was the avowed partisan of the Arians, and encouraged them in their persecution of the orthodox party, particularly sanctioning their efforts for the destruction of the celebrated Athanasius, Bishop of Alexandria.

Constantius II. had given his sister Constantína in marriage to his cousin Gallus, conferred upon him the title of Cæsar, and assigned him the administration of the Asiatic provinces. Gallus was naturally of a sullen and morose disposition, and had been soured by the sufferings of his early youth, while his evil passions were stimulated by the ambitious intrigues of the princess to whom he was unfortunately united. His excesses ultimately obliged Constantius II. to send commissioners to investigate the condition of the Eastern provinces. These officers proceeded to Antioch, where they appear to have conducted themselves in a haughty and offensive manner; but their faults did not justify the crime of Gallus, who instigated the people of Antioch to put the commissioners to death with torture and insult, and then ordered their bodies to be cast into the Orontes.

Constantius II. did not openly resent this outrage, but invited Gallus to visit him. Gallus postponed his visit until further delay was impossible, when he proceeded on the way to Mediolanum (now Milan) safely through Asia Minor and Thrace; but when he passed the frontiers of Pannonia he was arrested, hurried to a distant castle in Istria, and secretly put to death (A. D. 354).

Julian, the brother of Gallus and the only surviving descendant of Constantius Chlorus, except the reigning Emperor, escaped a fate similar to that of Gallus by the generous interference of the Empress Eusebia. She caused the Emperor to grant Julian permission to pursue his studies at Athens, where he was so dazzled by the Grecian philosophy that he renounced Christianity and became a convert to Paganism, and for this reason he was surnamed *the Apostate*. After he had been in retirement for more than a year, he was summoned to court, married to Helena, the sister of the Emperor Constantius II., and was appointed to the government of Gaul and the provinces north of the Alps, with the title of Cæsar.

Constantius II. had achieved several victories over the Quadi in A. D. 357; but he remained in the West after Julian's departure for the purpose of supporting the Arian Christians against the orthodox prelates. Before he returned to the East he resolved to visit the old capital of the Empire; and, after an interval of thirty-two years, Rome was able to rejoice at the presence of its sovereign. Constantius II. was so delighted with the reception given him by the citizens of Rome that he presented to the city the splendid Theban obelisk with which his father had intended to adorn Constantinople. He was obliged to hasten his departure by the tidings that the Sarmatians had invaded Pannonia. Constantius II. instantly proceeded to the Danube, and gained several victories over the Sarmatians; but he had no sooner restored tranquillity on the northern frontiers of the Empire than he was menaced with the more dangerous hostility of the New Persians in the East.

After chastising the fierce Scythian tribes in the region of the Oxus, Sapor II., the New Persian king, resumed his attacks upon the Roman Empire; and, guided by a deserter from the Roman army, he led an army into Mesopotamia. Exasperated by the insolence of the inhabitants of Amida (now Diarbekr), Sapor II. besieged that city, which he finally captured, but thus lost the favorable season for invading Syria, and was obliged to content himself with reducing Síngara (now Sinjar) and Bezabdé (now Jezirah).

Constantius II. made an effort to recover Bezabdé, but was forced to relinquish the siege. Upon returning to Antioch he was mortified still further by tidings of Julian's brilliant achievements in Gaul. Julian showed himself in every way worthy of the important trust assigned him. He was a ruler of real ability and a man of the strictest morals. He defeated the Alemanni and the Franks in many battles within three years after assuming the administration of Gaul, recovered the territory which they had conquered in that province, and compelled them to retire to the east side of the Rhine; after which he invaded their country three times, thus pursuing his victorious career even beyond the Rhine. After ravaging Germany far and wide, and releasing twenty thousand captive Romans, Julian returned to Gaul, laden with booty.

Julian rebuilt the Gallic cities which had been destroyed by the barbarians, made Lutetia Parisiorum (now Paris) his winter-quarters, and adorned the city with a palace, a theater and baths; and encouraged agriculture, manufactures and commerce. Jealous of Julian's success, Constantius II. summoned his best legions from Gaul to defend the East, hoping thus to effect Julian's ruin by leaving him a military force insufficient to maintain his position. But Julian's legions refused to obey the Emperor's mandate and proclaimed their general Emperor (A. D. 360). The Roman world only escaped another civil war by the sudden death of Constantius II. in A. D. 361; whereupon JULIAN THE APOSTATE was joyfully acknowledged Emperor by the entire Roman world.

When Julian arrived at Heracléa (now Erekli), though he was yet sixty miles distant from Constantinople, the entire population of that imperial capital came to welcome him, and he made his triumphal entry into the city amid general acclamations. One of the first measures of the new Emperor was to constitute a court at Chalcedon (now Scutari) for the trial of those ministers who might be charged with peculation. Many of them deserved punishment for their oppression of the people, but the investigations were conducted with such indiscriminate rigor that many innocent persons suffered with the guilty. Julian also retrenched the luxury and extravagance of the court, banished the eunuchs and other ministers of luxury, and dismissed the ten thousand spies who had formed a part of the government since the reign of Constantine the Great.

Julian the Apostate was in his thirty-second year when the death of his cousin made him sovereign of the vast Roman Empire. Vanity was his characteristic weakness. He chose to be considered a philosopher rather than a sovereign, and in order to acquire that title he thought proper to disregard some of the common decencies of life. A treatise from his pen is still in existence, in which he dwells with remarkable complacency upon the filthy condition of his beard, the length of his nails, and the inky blackness of his hands, as though cleanliness were incompatible with the philosophic character.

In every other respect, Julian's conduct deserves the highest eulogy. He was just, merciful and tolerant. He had not sought the imperial purple, and his philosophic training had the effect of making him care little for the outward ceremonies of his exalted station. He styled himself "The Servant of the Republic," and his daily life was characterized by the most commendable simplicity and frugality.

His open renunciation of Christianity and conversion to Paganism, which acquired for him the surname of *the Apostate*, has been regarded as the great blemish upon his character; but, besides being a Pagan from conviction and through his love of Plato's philosophy, he was largely influenced in his conduct in this particular by his hatred of his Christian cousins, at whom he was exasperated for having murdered all of the family to which he belonged.

The great object of Julian's ambition was to revive fallen Paganism, and he zealously exerted himself to undo what had been done by the great Constantine. He revoked the edicts that had been issued against idolatry, under the plausible pretext of granting freedom of opinion to all his subjects. He put himself and his Empire under the protection of the "Immortal Gods," and substituted Paganism for Christianity as the state-religion of the Roman Empire.

Julian was, however, too good and too wise to engage in a violent persecution of his Christian subjects, as he allowed all the same right to opinion which he claimed for himself; but he attacked the religion of Christ in writing, and endeavored to bring it into disrepute by ridicule. He encouraged the philosophers to veil the most revolting mythological fictions under allegorical explanations. He manifested an intense dislike to the Christians who visited the imperial court.

Not content, however, with opposing the Christians with the weapons of argument and ridicule, Julian enacted several disqualifying laws, by which he deprived the Christians of wealth, knowledge and power. He also excluded Christians from all civil and military offices, filled their places with Pagans, and ordered the Christian schools to be closed. He excluded all Christians from schools of grammar and rhetoric, in order to weaken them in controversy and to degrade them in intellectual rank; but he disappointed the Pagan zealots by proclaiming universal tolerance.

For the purpose of disproving the prophecy of Christ, Julian the Apostate attempted to rebuild the Temple of Jerusalem on Mount Moriah and to restore the Jewish worship; but, according to both Christian and Pagan writers, this design of the Emperor was frustrated by balls of fire bursting out from the foundation, driving away the workmen and compelling them to abandon the work.

It was believed that this occurrence was some miraculous or supernatural agency, but a scientific explanation can be given. The numerous subterranean excavations, reservoirs, etc., beneath and around the ruins of the Temple, which had been neglected for three centuries, had become filled with inflammable air, which took fire from the workmen's torches, thus causing terrible explosions which drove away those who attempted to explore the ruins. Terrible accidents sometimes occur in deeply-excavated mines from a similar cause.

While Julian was vainly striving to check Christianity and revive fallen Paganism, he was called to the East to take the field against the New Persians, who had renewed their aggressions upon the Roman territories in that quarter. Julian invaded the Persian dominions and gained some successes, but was unable to bring the enemy to a decisive engagement. He advanced through the deserts of Hatra to the Tigris.

Deceived by treacherous guides, Julian at length burned his boats and advanced into a desert country, where his army was soon reduced to great distress from want of provisions. The enemy also laid waste the fertile country, burned the crops and destroyed the villages, in the line of march of the Romans. The physical powers of the Western veterans were weakened by a burning sun, and their sufferings became intolerable when famine was added to the severities of the climate.

Under these distressing circumstances, Julian at length gave orders for a retreat, and led his exhausted troops back over the desert plains which they had already passed with so much difficulty. But the retrograde march of the Romans was greatly impeded by the New Persian light cavalry, which harassed the flanks and rear of the retreating army, discharging showers of arrows and darts, but retreating, like their predecessors, the Parthians, whenever any effort was made to bring them to a regular engagement.

The Roman rear-guard was at last thrown into disorder by a charge of the enemy. Julian hastened to its rescue, with no other defensive arms than his buckler. The New Persians were routed, but the Emperor was struck by an arrow. As he was trying to draw it out, another pierced his fingers. He fell from his horse, fainting and bathed in blood, and was conveyed to his tent, where he died the same night (A. D. 363), after a reign of one year and eight months. It is said that as Julian drew the arrow from his wound, and as the blood spurted forth, he exclaimed: "There! Take thy fill, Galilean!"

On the death of Julian the Apostate, his army unanimously saluted the virtuous JOVIAN, a Pannonian and an able general, as Emperor. As Jovian had been educated a Christian, he at first declined the charge, on the ground that the people whom he was called to govern had relapsed into idolatry; but his scruples were overcome when the soldiers assured him that they preferred Christianity to Paganism.

The Roman army was now in great distress. So terrible was the famine in the camp that every Roman soldier and officer would have perished if the Persians had not offered peace. Though the terms were rather humiliating to the Romans, Jovian readily accepted them; thus surrendering to the New Persian king the five provinces beyond the Tigris, along with the whole of Mesopotamia, including the fortified cities of Nísibis and Síngara, which the Sassanidæ had so often assailed in vain.

Jovian at once reëstablished Christianity as the state-religion, and issued an edict repealing Julian's disqualifying laws concerning the Christians. But at the same time he established universal tolerance by an edict in which he allowed all rites, however idolatrous, except those of magic; thus securing the good will of his Pagan subjects. The zeal of the people for the Christian religion fully attested how ineffectual were the efforts of the apostate Julian for the restoration of fallen Paganism, as the heathen temples were immediately deserted and the heathen priests were left alone at their altars. Those individuals who had gratified Julian by assuming the dress and title of philosophers were assailed by such storms of ridicule that they relinquished the designation, shaved their beards, and were soon undistinguished among the people.

The good Jovian did not long survive this peaceful triumph of Christianity. While on his way to Constantinople, he slept in a damp room, which was heated with charcoal by his attendants. The Emperor was suffocated by the fumes of this burning charcoal, being found dead in bed, after a reign of eight months (A. D. 364).

TRIUMPH OF CHRISTIANITY.

The death of Jovian was followed by an interregnum of ten days, after which VALENTINIAN I. was proclaimed Emperor by the council of ministers at Nice, in Asia Minor, famous as the seat of the Church Council. Valentinian was a Christian and a brave and able general, who had distinguished himself in the campaigns against the New Persians and the barbarians. The army acquiesced in this choice, but required the new Emperor to associate a colleague in the government for the purpose of securing the succession in the event of his death. He appointed his younger brother VALENS his colleague, assigning him the Eastern provinces from the Lower Danube to the Persian frontier, and retaining the Western provinces for himself. Valentinian made Mediolanum (now Milan) his capital; but, as occasion demanded, sometimes residing at Augusta-Trevirorum (now Trèves), and sometimes at Durocortorum (now Rheims), in Belgic Gaul. From these centers Valentinian governed the West of Europe firmly and well. Valens held his court at Constantinople.

Valentinian I. gained great victories over the Alemanni on the Rhine and over the Quadi on the Danube, and secured the frontiers of that quarter by a new line of forts. The Picts and Scots of Caledonia having passed the Wall of Antonine and perpetrated great devastations in Southern Britain, an expedition was sent against them under Theodosius, the father of the future Emperor Theodosius the Great, and those wild hordes were driven back into Caledonia. Soon afterward Theodosius also achieved a great naval victory among the Orkneys over the piratical Saxons, who were ravaging the north-western coasts of Europe.

The rapid progress of the Picts and Scots in Roman Britain, and the discontent of the native Britons, would have lost that island province to the Empire had it not been for the heroic exertions of Theodosius, who, besides repelling the Picts and Scots, pacified the native Britons and partially restored the former prosperity of the province. The Emperor Valentinian rewarded him with the office of master-general of the cavalry, and he was appointed to protect the Upper Danubian frontier against the inroads of the Alemanni, until he was assigned a far more important post and was intrusted with the task of suppressing the formidable revolt in Africa.

The people of the province of Africa had been exasperated by the avarice and exactions of Count Románus, the military governor of that province. Complaints against him were made to Valentinian, and a commissioner was appointed to investigate his delinquency. By bribing the imperial ministers and commissioners, Románus purchased security from a venal court, and severely punished those who had been guilty of the treason of complaining to the Emperor. The Africans were so incensed at these accumulated wrongs that they revolted, and chose for their leader Firmus, the son of the wealthy Nabal, who had been summoned to appear before the governor's tribunal on a charge of murdering his brother.

The African rebels were already in possession of Mauritania and Numidia, when the arrival of Theodosius changed the whole face of the struggle. From the moment that he landed, the insurgents appeared to have lost all courage. Firmus abandoned his army after a feeble resistance, and sought refuge with the prince of a native tribe in the interior of the country; but was betrayed to the Romans, and only escaped a public execution by committing suicide.

Valentinian I. was harsh and cruel by nature, but was inclined to be inflexibly just; and the numerous undeserved executions that he sanctioned must be ascribed to the artifices of corrupt ministers. He was devotedly attached to the orthodox Christian faith, and readily afforded protection to the bishops and clergy who sought refuge in his court from the persecution of his brother Valens, who was a zealous Arian.

In the meantime Valentinian I. had been engaged in a war with the Quadi. He conquered those savage warriors, and they sent deputies to deprecate his resentment. While reproaching the barbarian ambassadors with national perfidy, he worked himself into such a passion that he burst a blood-vessel and fell upon the ground, dying instantly (A. D. 375); leaving the Empire to his son GRATIAN, whom he had made Cæsar as early as A. D. 367, and who, upon his accession in A. D. 375, had associated his five-year-old brother, Valentinian II., in the government of the West.

Soon after he had been assigned to the government of the Eastern provinces, Valens proceeded to Syria, which was menaced by an invasion from the New Persians; but before he was able to complete his preparations for war, he was alarmed by the revolt of Procopius, a kinsman of Julian the Apostate. The pretensions of this leader were acknowledged by a considerable portion of the army and the citizens of Constantinople. Valens failed in his first efforts to overthrow the usurper; but Procopius soon disgusted his partisans by his extreme haughtiness and tyranny, and was deserted by those who had been foremost in making him Emperor, and was taken prisoner with but little resistance and remorselessly executed in the camp of Valens. His chief followers shared the same fate, as Valens showed no mercy to vanquished rebels. Thus ended the revolt of Procopius, who ruled in Constantinople for a few months (A. D. 365).

Valens was next engaged in a war of two years with the Goths (A. D. 367-369); followed by a campaign against the New Persians, in A. D. 371, caused by an invasion of Armenia by King Sapor II., who was disastrously defeated. The Armenian prince Paras, on whose assistance the New Persian monarch relied, was treacherously murdered by the Romans; whereupon another truce followed. The next year (A. D. 372) the life of Valens was threatened by a conspiracy at Antioch.

A dangerous schism in the Church, in consequence of the heresy of Arius, was intensely aggravated by the intemperate zeal, and, in some cases, by the selfish ambition of the rival prelates. Valens openly encouraged the Arians and caused about eighty of the orthodox ecclesiastics to be murdered, because they maintained the election of a bishop of their own creed to the see of Constantinople.

The greatest event of the reign of Valens was the invasion of Europe by the Huns, who crossed the Tanais (now Don) and the Palus Mæotis (now Sea of Azov), driving before them the barbarian nations which occupied the country north of the Danube. These fugitive nations, being thus hurled upon one another, were driven across the frontier into the Roman dominions; thus beginning those great migrations of barbarian nations which occupied more than a century and brought about the dismemberment of the Roman Empire and the total subversion of the Western portion of it a century after they had commenced, and which changed the fate of Europe by laying the foundations of the modern nations.

The Huns were a fierce race of barbarians from Central Asia—more ferocious than any of the barbarian nations that the Romans had hitherto encountered. Gibbon considered the Huns to be the same people which the Chinese historians called *Hiung Nu* and whom they described as masters of the country between the river Irtish, the Altai mountains, the Great Wall of China, and Mantchoo Tartary. They were probably Mongols, Turks or Oigurs.

The personal appearance of the Huns was almost a caricature of humanity, and the Romans compared them to a block of wood which had been but partially trimmed. Their deformed shapes may have been caused to some extent by their singular custom of flattening the nose of their male infants as soon as they were born, so that the visor which they wore in battle might fit more closely to the face. Another cause of this deformity may have been the custom of plucking out the beard by the roots as soon as it commenced growing.

This fierce and relentless race of barbarians subsisted on raw flesh, or flesh sodden by being placed under their saddles and pressed against the backs of their steeds when they rode at full gallop. They passed their lives in war and hunting, leaving the

HUNNIC FESTIVAL AT THE COURT OF ATTILA.

cultivation of their fields to their women and slaves. They did not erect any cities or build any houses. They regarded any place surrounded by walls as a sepulcher, and never considered themselves safe under a roof.

About a century after Christ, the Southern Huns, aided by the Chinese and by the Mantchoos, expelled the Northern Huns from their ancient habitations, forcing them to seek refuge in the territories of the Bashkirs. In that country the Huns were brought in contact with the fiercer but less warlike Alans, whom they drove before them gradually, as they were themselves pressed forward by fresh hordes from the east.

About A. D. 370 the Huns, in their westward migration, entered Europe along the northern shores of the Euxine, or Black Sea, and occupied the vast steppes between the Rha (now Volga) and the Tanais (now Don) rivers. At that time the Gothic kingdom under its sovereign, Hermanric, reached from the Danube river and the Euxine sea on the south to the Baltic sea on the north; embracing the territory now comprised in South-western Russia, Poland and Eastern Prussia; and extending over various cognate tribes, of which the two most important were the Ostrogoths (Eastern Goths) and the Visigoths (Western Goths).

After being joined by the Alans and other barbarous tribes that they had conquered, the cavalry of the Huns crossed the Tanais (now Don), and swept like a devouring tempest over the rich fields of the Ostrogoths. The Ostrogothic armies were defeated; and at length the larger portion of the Gothic nation abandoned the country which they had so laboriously brought under a high state of cultivation, retiring beyond the Borysthenes (now Dnieper) river and the Danaster (now Dniester). The Huns slaughtered all who remained, including even the women and children; and all who did not save themselves by flight perished by the sword.

ARRIVAL OF THE HUNS ON THE DANUBE.

The triumphant invaders soon crossed the Danaster (now Dniester) and visited similar calamities upon the Visigoths. After suffering a disastrous defeat, Athánaric, the Gothic king, perceived that his only defense was to fortify himself between the Hierássus (now Pruth) and the Danube, by a wall extending from one river to the other; while the remainder of the country was exposed to the terrible ravages of this inundation of Central Asian barbarians.

The entire Gothic nation was reduced to despair. Their warriors, who had so many times fiercely withstood the Roman legions, now appeared as suppliants and fugitives on the banks of the Danube, imploring permission from the Eastern Emperor, Valens, to occupy the waste lands of Mœsia and Thrace as Roman subjects. Valens granted their request on condition that they resigned their arms. A million Visigoths alone are said to have crossed the Danube. The feeding of this vast multitude was of course a difficult task. The Roman commissioners who had been sent to enforce the stipulations concerning the disarming of the Goths were bribed to neglect their duty; and most of the Goths retained their arms, which they considered the means by which they might obtain more valuable lands than those which they had lost.

About this time the Goths had been thoroughly converted to Arian Christianity through the exertions of their celebrated bishop, Ulfilas, the inventor of the Gothic alphabet. This circumstance aggravated the antipathy of the Goths to the Romans, as the animosity of the Arian and orthodox sects toward each other at that time had become greater than the enmity between the Christians and the Pagans.

The officers who had been appointed by Valens to superintend the settlement of the Goths in Mœsia and Thrace were the most profligate extortioners of his corrupt court. Instead of supplying provisions to the new Roman subjects until their new lands would yield them a harvest, as they had promised, these officials closed the magazines, and enriched themselves by charging exorbitant prices for the worst and most revolting kinds of food. At length Lupicínus, one of the corrupt officials, attempted to murder Fritigern and other Gothic chiefs at Marcianopolis (now Pravadí), having invited them to a banquet there for that purpose. The plot was prematurely disclosed, thus enabling the Gothic leaders to escape, whereupon their followers massacred the larger portion of the Roman legions in revenge for the breach of hospitality on the part of the Roman officials.

In the meantime the advance of the Huns had obliged the Ostrogoths to cross the Danube, thus enabling them to join the Visigoths just as the war between them and the Romans was about to commence. Thus reinforced, the exasperated Fritigern desolated Thrace, Macedonia and Thessaly with fire and sword, and even approached the walls of Constantinople and destroyed its suburbs. The Eastern Emperor, Valens, wrote to Gratian, Valentinian's successor in the West, for assistance; and Gratian, although harassed by wars with the German tribes and with the Alans, marched to the aid of Valens, but was delayed at Sirmium by illness until Valens was no more. Baffled by Fritigern's artifices and enraged at his audacity, Valens marched against the Goths; but was defeated and slain in the decisive battle of Adrianople (A. D. 378)—the most disastrous reverse which the Romans had suffered since their terrible defeat by Hannibal at Cannæ—two-thirds of the legions, including thirty-five Tribunes and commanders of cohorts, perishing on the sanguinary field.

Gratian was unable to remedy this great disaster in the East without a colleague, as he could not advance against the Goths without leaving the Western provinces exposed to the ravages of the Germans. He therefore selected as his associate, and as the successor of Valens in the government of the Eastern provinces, Theodosius—afterwards so renowned as THEODOSIUS THE GREAT—the son of the illustrious general, Theodosius, whom he had unjustly put to death at the instigation of envious courtiers.

Gratian afterwards discovered by what gross misrepresentations he had been induced to sanction the execution of this gallant general, and he bitterly repented of his guilt in that great wrong, for which he sought reparation in the appointment of the victim's son to the government of the East. Gratian began his reign by punishing the ministers and Senators who had been guilty of extortion. He enacted several laws favorable to the interests of the Church, and ordained that all controversies concerning religion should be decided by the bishop and the synod of the provinces in which they occurred; that the clergy should be free from personal charges; and that all places where heterodox doctrines were taught should be confiscated.

Gratian was only seventeen years old at the time of his accession; and his first years, which were passed under the influence of the instructors of his youth, promised a beneficent reign; but when he arrived at manhood he gave way to his naturally weak and indolent disposition, devoting his time to hunting, and leaving the administration of public affairs to unworthy favorites, who cruelly abused the Emperor's confidence. The army despised a sovereign who neglected it, and their dissatisfaction soon manifested itself in open rebellion.

Maximus, the Roman governor of Britain, rose in revolt against Gratian; and the legions in Britain proclaimed him Emperor. Maximus crossed over into Gaul with the design of contesting the imperial dignity with Gratian; and the legions in Gaul joined him. Seeing himself thus deserted, Gratian fled from Lutetia Parisiorum (now Paris) to Lugdunum (now Lyons), where he was taken prisoner and put to death (A. D. 383). St. Ambrose, Bishop of Milan, one of the Christian Fathers, bravely went into Gaul and claimed the dead Emperor's body, which he obtained after some delay, and which he honorably interred in the sepulcher that he had constructed in the cathedral at Mediolanum (now Milan) for the Valentinian family.

In order to support his usurpation, Maximus had brought the flower of the British youth with him; and the province of Britain, thus deprived of its defenders, became a prey to the ravages of the Picts and Scots of Caledonia, who broke through the Roman wall and pushed their destructive inroads far into the South of the island.

Maximus now entered into a treaty with Theodosius, the Eastern Emperor, who consented to acknowledge the usurper's imperial dignity, while Maximus consented to recognize VALENTINIAN II. as Emperor and to leave him in peaceful possession of Italy. But in A. D. 387 Maximus broke this agreement by invading Italy and forcing Valentinian II. to take refuge with Theodosius, who was his uncle. After some hesitation, Theodosius espoused his nephew's cause, married his sister Galla, and defeated Maximus in two decisive battles in Pannonia. The usurper fled to Aquileia, in Italy, where he was arrested by his own soldiers, who carried him in chains to Theodosius, who caused him to be executed as a traitor (A. D. 388). It is said that the imperial ministers hastened his death, fearing that he might extort a pardon from their sovereign's compassion.

The generous Theodosius restored Valentinian II. to his dominions, and even resigned to him the provinces that had belonged to Gratian. After visiting Rome and sanctioning some severe measures in the city for extirpating Paganism, Theodosius returned to the East, where he made similar efforts to suppress Pagan superstitions and Christian heresies. The young Valentinian II. was eighteen years of age when restored to his throne, and was weak and indolent, like his brother Gratian. He permitted himself to fall under the influence of Arbogastes, a Frank, one of his officers, unwisely allowing him to assume a great share of sovereign power, himself becoming a mere instrument in that barbarian leader's hands. Valentinian II. soon became conscious of his real position, and made an effort to remove his powerful subject, but failed in the attempt. Arbogastes refused to submit to the Emperor's orders, and a few days later he murdered Valentinian II. (A. D. 392). Arbogastes did not dare to assume the imperial purple himself; but conferred the Empire on EUGENIUS, one of the imperial secretaries, trusting that he would be able to make him a mere instrument of his ambition.

Theodosius the Great refused to negotiate with Eugenius; but instantly prepared for war, levying a formidable army, which he led across the Alps to overthrow the usurper and to avenge the murder of his nephew. Theodosius routed the forces of Eugenius near Aquileía, whereupon the usurper was killed by his own troops (A. D. 394); and Arbogastes was obliged to flee for his life, and soon afterward committed suicide in despair. Theodosius the Great then became sole sovereign of the whole Roman Empire (A. D. 394).

During the reigns of Gratian, Maximus, Valentinian II. and Eugenius in the West, Theodosius the Great ruled in the East with a firm hand. He commenced his reign in A. D. 379, when, as we have seen, Gratian appointed him his colleague, assigning him the Eastern Roman provinces. Upon his accession, Theodosius immediately applied himself to the task of resisting the Visigoths, who had reduced his part of the Roman Empire to the verge of ruin.

During the first five years of his reign, Theodosius the Great fully displayed his remarkable military talents and his wonderful qualities as a sovereign, forcing the powerful Visigothic nation to submission, and even converting them into useful Roman subjects and employing their arms against his other enemies. He settled large colonies of Visigoths in Thrace, and Ostrogoths in Asia Minor; while he also enlisted forty thousand of the best Gothic warriors in the Roman army.

Many have thought that Theodosius the Great committed a blunder in colonizing these barbarians among his civilized subjects, as the Goths were not yet sufficiently civilized to amalgamate with the other inhabitants of the Empire; but the Emperor had only a choice of evils. Had he refused to allow the Goths these settlements they would have been driven to despair, and he would have had more to fear from their despair than from their fickleness and turbulence. As long as Theodosius lived, he showed himself fully able to manage the barbarians; and if his successors had possessed but a tithe of his genius, they might have made the Goths the main strength of the Empire, instead of permitting them to become its great peril.

The reign of Theodosius the Great was celebrated for the complete triumph of Christianity over Paganism. Although Christianity had now been the state-religion of the Roman Empire for about three quarters of a century, the practice of Pagan rites had been tolerated by Constantine the Great and his successors, until the reign of Theodosius the Great, who issued an edict positively forbidding any and all Pagan ceremonies on penalty of death, and closed all the heathen temples and confiscated their endowments.

The natives of Egypt believed that Serápis would signally avenge any desecration of his shrine; but when a Roman soldier entered the temple of that Egyptian god at Alexandria, and struck the idol a blow in the face with his battle-ax, the Egyptians opened their eyes and concluded that a god who was unable to defend himself was unworthy of worship.

Theodosius likewise enacted severe laws against the Arians and other heretical Christian sects, whom the Council of Nice, in A. D. 325, and the Council of Constantinople, in A. D. 381, had condemned. These heterodox Christians were forced to surrender their churches and to vacate their sees, and were forbidden to preach, to ordain ministers, or even to assemble for public worship; and all their property was confiscated and bestowed on the orthodox. The penalties attached to these rigorous laws were fines and exile. As it is a notorious fact that the acts of Theodosius the Great were far more merciful than his laws, his code is really no fair test of his administration of the imperial government.

The power of the Church during the

TRIUMPH OF CHRISTIANITY.

reign of Theodosius the Great is fully demonstrated by the celebrated encounter between the Emperor and St. Ambrose, Bishop of Milan, one of the Latin Fathers of the Christian Church. In a tumult in the Circus of Thessalonica, in Macedonia, a Gothic general in the Emperor's service and several other imperial officers were slain; and Theodosius avenged their death by an indiscriminate massacre of the Thessalonians—innocent and guilty alike—seven hundred persons being thus cruelly slaughtered.

The imperial court was at that time resident at Milan. When the Emperor, in an outburst of passion, had sent the order for the massacre, St. Ambrose remonstrated with Theodosius on his barbarity, and induced him to promise to revoke the cruel order. When, in spite of this promise, the massacre had actually taken place, and Theodosius repaired to the great cathedral of Milan, St. Ambrose met him at the door and sternly forbade him to enter the holy sanctuary until he made a public confession of his guilt. The Emperor pleaded David's example, whereupon the fearless bishop replied: "You have imitated David in his crime, imitate him in his repentance."

Theodosius was under an interdict for eight months, during which he was wholly excluded from church service; after which he acknowledged his crime in the presence of the entire congregation, and was obliged, not only to perform penance, but to sign an edict ordaining that an interval of thirty days should pass before the execution of any sentence of death or confiscation. After thus complying with all the demands of the relentless bishop, Theodosius was again received into the communion of the Church at Christmas, A. D. 390.

Theodosius the Great did not long survive his victory over the usurper Eugenius, which made him sole Emperor of the whole Roman world (A. D. 394); as he died at Milan four months afterward, January 17, A. D. 395; after appointing his elder son, Arcadius, Emperor of the East, and his younger son, Honorius, Emperor of the West. Theodosius the Great was the last Emperor who reigned over the whole Roman dominions; and after his death the Roman world remained divided into the Eastern Roman, or Greek, and the Western Roman, or Latin Empires. The Eastern Empire lasted over a thousand years, when it fell before the arms of the Ottoman Turks; while the Western Empire continued a little more than three quarters of a century, when it fell before the attacks of the Northern barbarians. We will devote the next section to the history of the Western Empire, and relate the annals of the Eastern Empire in its proper place in that portion of this work devoted to mediæval history.

Christianity had important intellectual results, as it furnished the mind of the age with new subjects for speculation; the imperial despotism having crushed out all political thought. The *Gospels* and the *New Testament* were written during the first century of the Christian era; and the Council of Nice decided which of the apostolic writings should be accepted and which should be rejected. The disciples of Jesus made many oral communications to their contemporaries, which are not found in the apostolic writings.

The Christian writers of the first five or six centuries are called *Fathers of the Christian Church*. Some wrote in Greek, others in Latin. On their works depend the traditional doctrines of the Catholic Church. The nearer they stand to the time of the Apostles, the greater is their authority. Four of these Christian Fathers flourished during the reign of Theodosius the Great— St. Chrysostom, St. Ambrose, St. Jerome and St. Augustine.

JUSTIN MARTYR was an early Greek Father in Palestine, and was born A. D. 103. He wrote several works in defense of Christianity, and suffered martyrdom at Rome in A. D. 165, during the reign of Marcus Aurelius.

ST. POLYCARP, one of the Apostolical Fathers of the Christian Church, was a Greek Father and a Christian martyr. He was the friend and disciple of St. John, who appointed him Bishop of Smyrna. He made many converts to the religion of the cross. He enjoyed the friendship of Ignatius, and opposed the heresies of Marcion and Valentinus. The only one of his writings remaining is his short *Epistle to the Philippians*. Like Justin Martyr, St. Polycarp suffered martyrdom at Rome during the reign of Marcus Aurelius, dying with the most heroic fortitude in A. D. 166.

CLEMENT OF ALEXANDRIA was a Greek Father, and was born A. D. 150. He flourished in the great metropolis of Egypt, and wrote several great works in favor of Christianity. He died A. D. 220.

TERTULLIAN was the first and one of the most renowned of the Latin Fathers. He was a native of Carthage, where he was born A. D. 160. He became a distinguished rhetorician, and was converted to Christianity. He reached the age of four score years, and wrote a great many works, some of which were lost very early. His *Apology for Christians*—the most important of his extant works—was addressed to the Roman magistrates in A. D. 198. Another of his remaining great works is his *Testimony of the Soul*, in which he endeavored to work out the idea of the preconformity of the human soul to the doctrine of Christ.

Tertullian's works are of four kinds—apological, practical, doctrinal and polemical. They are characterized by great learning, profound and comprehensive thought, fiery imagination and passionate partisanship, leading to sophistry and exaggeration. His style is often somewhat obscure. In one of Tertullian's lost works was taught the doctrine of Christ's millenial reign. Tertullian died A. D. 240.

ORIGEN was the most celebrated of the early Greek Fathers, and was one of the most learned men of his time. He flourishd at Alexandria, in Egypt, and was born A. D. 185. At the age of seventeen he lost his father, who was beheaded for professing Christianity. Origen then taught grammar in order to support the bereaved family; but he relinquished this occupation when he was appointed catechist, or head of the Christian school of Alexandria. From Alexandria he went to Rome, where he commenced his celebrated *Hexapla*, embracing five Greek versions of the Hebrew Bible.

Origen returned to Alexandria at the command of his bishop, Demetrius; and while on his way back through Palestine, in A. D. 228, he was ordained presbyter at Cæsaréa. He soon afterwards commenced his *Commentaries*, which are characterized too much by the fancy of allegory. In his other works he promulgated ideas more in consonance with the philosophy of Plato than with the Christian Scriptures. The pre-existence of souls and the finite duration of future punishment were to Origen's contemporaries the most obnoxious of his doctrines. Origen died A. D. 254.

ST. CYPRIAN, Archbishop of Carthage, was a Latin Father, and was born A. D. 200. He was the author of a work called *Unity of the Church*, and suffered martyrdom in A. D. 258, during Valerian's reign. The study of Tertullian had a marked influence on St. Cyprian, who was in the habit of asking his secretary for the works of the great Latin Father in the words "Da magistrum" (Hand me the teacher).

LACTANTIUS was an illustrious Latin Father, and was born in Africa, A. D. 260. His work entitled *Symposium* gave him such distinction that Diocletian appointed him teacher of rhetoric. He was the author of many works in vindication of Christianity; the most important being *Institutiones Divinæ* (Divine Institutions), in seven books. Because of the eloquence of his style, he was called the "Christian Cicero." The time of his death is uncertain, but it is believed to have occurred about A. D. 325.

ST. ATHANASIUS, Patriarch of Alexandria, was a Greek Father and one of the most renowned of the Christian doctors. He was a native of Alexandria, and was born A. D. 296. He spent some time in the desert with St. Anthony and took a leading part in the Council of Nice, where he was the great defender of the doctrines of the Trinity and Christ's divinity, which he

INHABITANTS OF GERMANY DURING THE 3D AND 4TH CENTURY.

ROMAN EMPEROR (ROMULUS AUGUSTULUS)— COURTIERS.

KING CHARLES THE BALD (10TH CENTURY).

FRANKISH KING AND QUEEN (10 CENTURY).

ROMAN EMPIRE, 4TH CENTURY. CARLOVINGIANS, 10TH CENTURY.

maintained with intense zeal and acuteness against the opposite doctrine of Arius, the other Alexandrian ecclesiastic; and his opinions on these points were declared by the Council of Nice to be the orthodox doctrines of the Church.

St. Athanasius was chosen patriarch of Alexandria in A. D. 326, the year after the meeting of the Council of Nice. For almost half a century he championed the orthodox doctrine with unshaken fidelity through all vicissitudes of fortune. Although he was condemned by councils, thrice exiled, alternately sustained and persecuted by the Emperors, a wanderer at Rome, at Milan, in Gaul, and in the desert of Egypt, he faithfully held fast to his convictions, and exercised an influence on the Christian world almost without a parallel. He passed the last ten years of his life at Alexandria, where he died A. D. 373. His works fill three folio volumes. The orthodox doctrines which he championed have been called *the Athanasian Creed.*

ST. CHRYSOSTOM, Patriarch of Constantinople, was a Greek Father and a native of Antioch, where he was born 347. He was called *Chrysostom,* which signifies *golden mouth,* on account of his eloquence. He was first intended for the bar; but being deeply impressed with religious feelings, he spent several years in solitary retirement, studying and meditating with the design of entering the service of the Church. After completing his voluntary probation, he returned to Antioch, where he was ordained, and where he acquired such renown for his eloquence in preaching that on the death of Nectarius, Patriarch of Constantinople, he was elevated to that exalted post.

St. Chrysostom exerted himself with such zeal in repressing Paganism, heresy and immorality, and in enforcing the obligations of monachism, that Theophilus, Bishop of Alexandria, instigated by the Empress Eudoxia, induced a synod convened at Chalcedon in A. D. 403 to depose him. The people, who had a deep affection for him, were so highly incensed at his deposition that the Empress was obliged to interfere to have him reinstated. But he soon aroused her anger by opposing the erection of her statue near the great church; and he was deposed by another synod in A. D. 404 and exiled to Armenia. He bore up under his troubles with wonderful fortitude; but being ordered to a yet greater distance from the imperial capital, where his influence was still dreaded by his enemies, he died during the journey, in A. D. 407. St. Chrysostom's voluminous works consist of sermons, commentaries, treatises, etc., abounding with information concerning the manners and characteristics of his times. His remains were removed to Constantinople thirty years after his death, with great pomp, and he was honored with the title of a saint.

ST. AMBROSE, Archbishop of Milan, was a Latin Father and a native of Gaul, being born A. D. 340. While still a youth he pleaded with such eloquence that Probus, Prefect of Italy, selected him as one of his council, and afterwards appointed him governor of Liguria, an office which he held five years. Upon the death of Auxentius, Bishop of Milan, in A. D. 374, the contest for the election of a successor to the vacant see was so fierce that the governor was called upon to suppress the tumult. He endeavored to do this by persuasion in the great church; and when he had finished his address, a voice in the multitude exclaimed: "Ambrose is bishop." This circumstance was regarded as a divine direction; and Ambrose was declared to be the object of divine selection, as well as of the popular choice.

St. Ambrose directed his first efforts, as Bishop of Milan, to the extermination of Arianism, which was then making considerable progress. He was likewise successful in resisting the Pagans, who were seeking the restoration of the ancient religion. When Maximus invaded Italy and actually entered Milan, St. Ambrose remained at his post to mitigate the calamities caused by the invading army. This fearless ecclesiastic vindicated the authority of the priesthood, even against monarchs, by condemning the Emperor Theodosius the Great to a long and weary penance for his massacre of the Thessalonians; as already noticed. St. Ambsose died A. D. 397.

ST. JEROME was a Latin Father and the guardian of monasticism. He was a native of Dalmatia, and was born A. D. 345. He visited Rome in A. D. 382 and was made secretary to Pope Damasus; but three years later he returned to the East, accompanied by several female devotees, who desired to lead an ascetic life in the Holy Land. St. Jerome was one of the most learned of the Christian Fathers and took a prominent part in the religious controversies of his time. Among the most important of his many writings are his *Commentaries* on different portions of the Scriptures. His chief work was a translation of the Bible into Latin, known as the *Vulgate version*. St. Jerome was particularly learned in the Hebrew. His style is wonderfully pure and classical. He died A. D. 420, while superintendent of a monastery at Bethlehem, in Palestine, the birth-place of David and Jesus.

ST. AUGUSTINE, Bishop of Hippo, in Africa, was the greatest of the Latin Fathers. He was a native of Numidia, and was born A. D. 354. He is known as the "Father of Latin Theology." St. Augustine had been very wicked in his youth. He took an active part in the Church controversies of his time. St. Augustine's doctrine of the predestined future fate of every human creature since Adam's fall, and man's consequent inability of himself to attain salvation, was accepted as the orthodox doctrine of the Church; while the opposite doctrine of Pelagius, a British monk resident in Africa, who maintained that man could of his own free will do good and partake of salvation, was condemned as heretical.

St. Augustine's influence over the Latin Church was powerful and permanent. He completed all that Athanasius had commenced; and, by his earnestness and logical clearness, he determined the form of the Catholic doctrines. Of his many works the most important are *On the Grace of Christ, Original Sin, City of God* and *Confessions;* the last being an autobiography. St. Augustine's writings constituted the special study of John Wickliffe and Martin Luther; and his doctrine of predestination or election, already alluded to, was adopted in modern times as the creed of John Calvin. St. Augustine died A. D. 430.

NESTORIUS, the renowned Patriarch of Constantinople, was a Greek Father and the founder of the sect of the *Nestorians*. He was a native of Syria, and flourished towards the middle of the fifth century of the Christian era. He was brought up in a convent, became a presbyter of the church at Antioch, and was celebrated for his austere life and for his fervid oratory. Theodosius the Great appointed him to the see of Constantinople in A. D. 428, and in that station he exhibited wonderful zeal against the Arians. At length he himself fell under censur; and the Council of Ephesus in A. D. 431 finally condemned him, deprived him of his see, and banished him. He died about the middle of of the fifth century; but his followers are yet a numerous sect in the East, and are organized with a Patriarch at their head.

LEO THE GREAT, a celebrated Pope, was a Roman, like most of his great predecessors and successors, and was born A. D. 390. He was devoted to the service of the Church at an early age. When Pope Sixtus III. died, Leo was absent from Rome on a civil mission, charged with the task of effecting a reconciliation between the two rival generals, Aëtius and Albinus, whose fatal dispute imperiled the Roman dominion in Gaul. There was no delay; and all Rome—clergy, Senate and people—by acclamation elevated Leo III. to the vacant see. With the self-reliance of a great intellect, he assumed the papal office in the pious confidence that the Almighty would give him power to fulfil the responsible duties thus imposed upon him.

Pope Leo III.—surnamed *the Great*—was no less a roman in sentiment than in birth. All that survived of ancient Rome—of her title to universal dominion, her inflexible perseverance, her haughtiness of language—might appear concentrated in this ecclesiastical potentate alone. His sermons singularly exhibit the union of the Roman and the Churchman. These sermons are remarkable for their brevity, simplicity and severity; being without passion or fancy.

Leo's sermons are peculiarly Christian, as dwelling almost wholly on Christ, his birth, his passion, his resurrection. Leo condemned the entire race of heretics, from Arius to Eutyches; but the Manicheans were the more immediate, the more dangerous, and the more obnoxious enemies of the Roman Church. That sect was continually rising in every portion of Christendom with a strangely obstinate vitality. Leo wrote to the Italian bishops, requesting them to search out these pestilent foes of Christian faith and virtue. By Leo's advice, the Emperor Valentinian III. issued an edict banishing the Manicheans from the entire world. They were rendered liable to all the penalties of sacrilege. The shameful and flagrant immorality of the Manicheans was the cause of the severity of the law. During the invasion of Italy by Attila's Huns, Leo was sent by the Emperor Valentinian III. to induce Attila to desist from his threatened march upon Rome, thus saving the famous city. Leo afterwards saved the city from being burned by the Vandals under Génseric. Leo the Great was the first Pope of whom we have any written records. He died A. D. 461.

EUSEBIUS, Bishop of Cæsarea, was a famous ecclesiastical historian, and was born in A. D. 264. During Diocletian's persecution, he aided the suffering Christians by his exhortations, especially his friend Pamphilus, whose name he assumed out of veneration. Eusebius was chosen Bishop of Cæsarea about A. D. 315. He was the friend of Arius, but still he took part in the Council of Nice. The Emperor Constantine the Great had a special esteem for him, and showed him many tokens of favor. He died A. D. 340. Eusebius was the author of an *Ecclesiastical History*, the *Life of Constantine*, etc. An English translation of his Ecclesiastical History constitutes a part of Bohn's Library.

PORPHYRY, the bitter and eloquent foe of Christianity, was a native of Tyre, born A. D. 233. In him the last feeble struggles of expiring Paganism against triumphant Christianity had their ablest champion, and he was the eloquent defender of a lost cause. Porphyry was a man of great talents and vast learning; as is fully apparent from what remain of his writings, and from the testimony of his Christian adversaries. His chief work was a book against the Christians. This work was publicly destroyed by the Emperor Theodosius the Great. The vigor of his attack on Chistianity aroused against him the severest maledictions and the fiercest vituperation. His name became synonymous with all that was silly, blasphemous, impudent and calumnious. Porphyry died A. D. 305.

SECTION XXI.—FALL OF THE WESTERN EMPIRE.

THE division of the Roman world into the Eastern and Western Empires upon the accession of ARCADIUS and HONORIUS marks the real and permanent separation of the Western, or Latin, provinces from the Eastern, or Greek, provinces. Hitherto the two portions of the vast Empire of the Cæsars were united together by an idea, at least, that they still constituted but one state; and there had been some appearance of an interest common to both. But from the death of Theodosius the Great and the accession of his two sons, this sentiment of unity gave way to a feeling of mutual jealousy and distrust; and the breach thus opened between the two sections of the Empire continually widened.

The real rulers of the two Empires thus

2—72.-U. H.

formed were Rufinus, the Prefect of the East, and Stilicho, the guardian of the youthful Emperor of the West. These two leaders entertained an inveterate enmity toward each other. Rufinus was a wicked wretch, but Stilicho was worthy to occupy the exalted station to which Theodosius had elevated him. Theodosius, on his death-bed, recommended the charge of both Empires to Stilicho; but Rufinus could only be deposed by a military force, for the assembling of which it was necessary to find some pretext that would not so alarm the vigilant statesman as to put him on his guard.

The war with the Goths afforded the desired excuse, and Stilicho led his forces around the Adriatic; but no sooner had he arrived at Thessalonica than he was ordered to return, being threatened with a declaration of war in case he approached nearer to Constantinople. Thereupon Stilicho left his army in charge of Gainas and returned to Italy; and Rufinus went out to review the Western army, believing all danger to be passed. But as he passed along the ranks, he was suddenly surrounded by a select band, pinned to the ground by a lance, on a signal given by Gainas, and mangled with innumerable wounds. If Stilicho had planned this assassination, he derived no advantage from it; as Gainas, the eunuch Eutropius, and the Empress Eudoxia, the newly-married wife of Arcadius, united to exclude the Western general from Constantinople; and their puppet Arcadius obtained a decree from his obsequious Senate, declaring Stilicho a public enemy, and confiscating all his property in the East.

Instead of risking a civil war, Stilicho exerted himself to crush the revolt excited in Africa by Gildo, the brother of Firmus. He assigned the forces which he raised for this purpose to Máscezel, Gildo's brother and mortal enemy. By accident, the imperial troops obtained an almost bloodless victory. Before giving the signal to engage, Máscezel rode to the front of the lines, making fair offers of peace and pardon ; and encountering an African standard-bearer, who refused to yield, he struck him on the arm with his sword. The force of the blow prostrated the standard-bearer with his standard. The whole rebel force considered this a signal of submission ; and all the revolted African legions hastened to return to their allegiance, flinging their ensigns to the ground, and unanimously submitting to their legitimate sovereign. Gildo, in his efforts at flight, was arrested by the citizens of Tábraca (now Tabarca) and cast into a dungeon, where he committed suicide to escape punishment for treason. Stilicho, dreading the hereditary enmity of the family of Nabal, afterwards assassinated Máscezel.

The Goths were now more formidable than they had ever been before. They were no longer led by several independent chiefs, but were united into a compact body under the famous Alaric. The withholding of the subsidy paid them by Theodosius the Great furnished them a plausible pretext for war (A. D. 396). Alaric disdained to ravage the exhausted lands of Thrace; but led his countrymen into Greece, making his way through the pass of Thermopylæ unopposed, and devastated Bœotia, Attica and the Peloponnesus, compelling Athens, Corinth, Argos and Sparta to submit to the barbarian invaders without any resistance.

Stilicho hastened to drive the Goths from Greece. His masterly movements forced Alaric into a small corner of Elis, whence his extrication seemed impossible; but when the Gothic king observed that the vigilance of his foes was relaxed, he gained the Gulf of Corinth by a rapid march, passed over the narrow strait between the headlands of Rhium and Antirrhium (the Dardanelles of Lepanto), and had made himself master of Epirus before Stilicho was able to renew his pursuit. The Romans were about to pass into Northern Greece, when they were informed that Alaric had made peace with the Eastern Emperor, and had even been appointed master-general of Illyricum by the feeble Arcadius.

Stilicho returned to Italy, and was soon obliged to defend that peninsula against

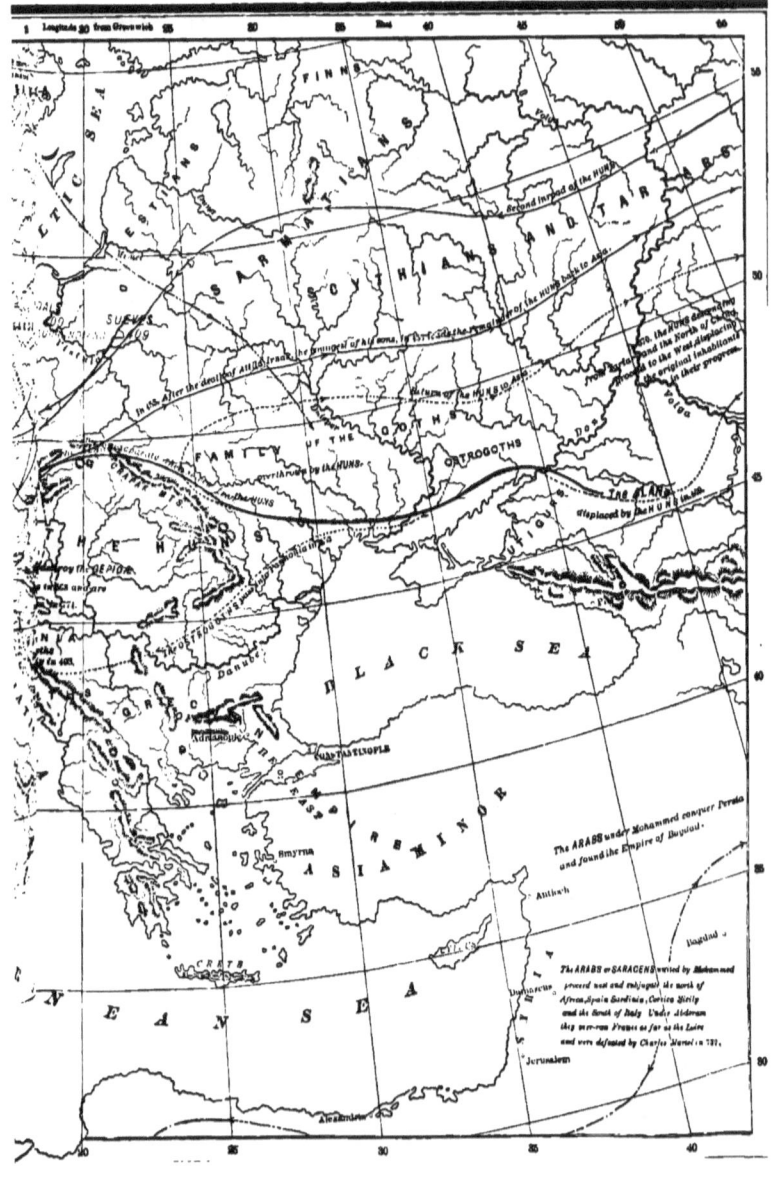

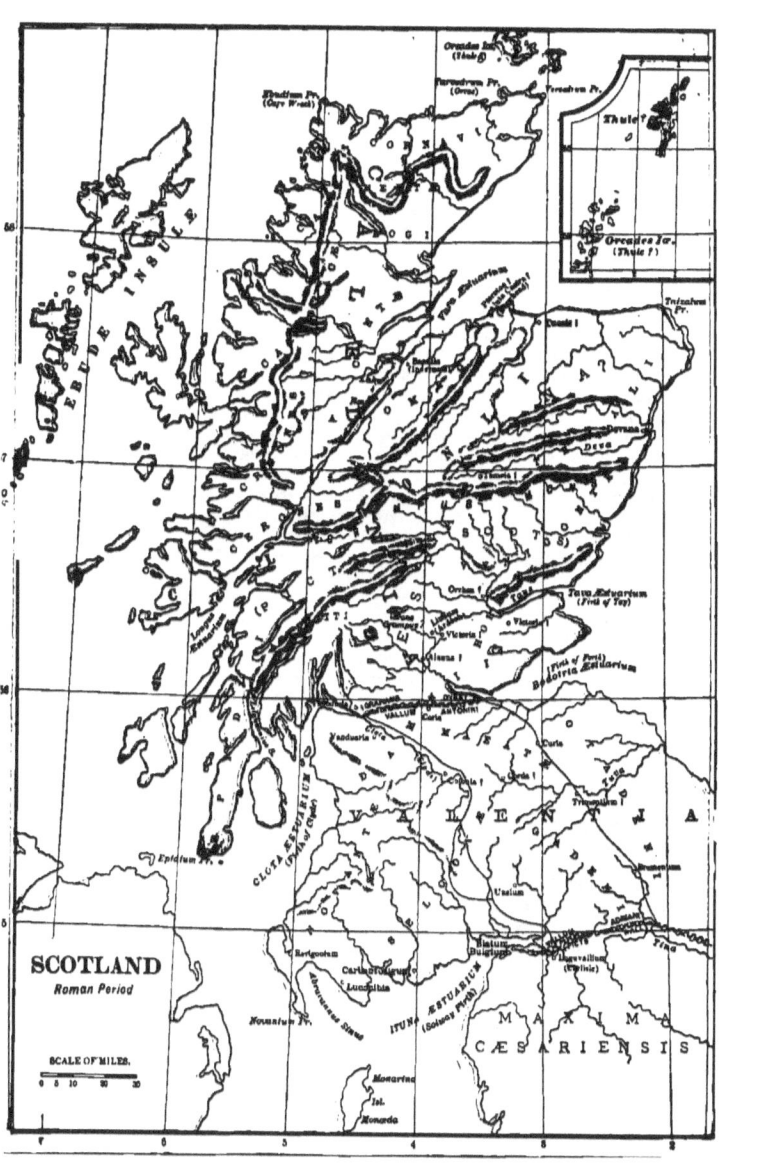

Alaric; who forced a passage over the Julian Alps and marched upon Milan (A. D. 403). Honorius fled from his capital, but was overtaken by the pursuing Goths and besieged by them in Asta. Stilicho hastened to the relief of the Emperor, and defeated the Goths with great slaughter at Pollentia, in Northern Italy. Instead of abandoning Italy after this defeat, Alaric rallied his shattered forces, crossed the Apennines, and marched directly toward Rome, which was saved by the diligence of Stilicho; but the withdrawal of the Goths from Italy was purchased by a heavy ransom.

Honorius then proceeded to Rome, where he received the empty honor of a triumph. The retreat of the barbarians caused great rejoicings. In the midst of the games, Telémachus, a Christian monk, sprang into the arena of the amphitheater; and, raising the cross over his head, ordered the gladiators in the name of the crucified Redeemer to cease their brutal sport. The enraged multitude stoned the monk to death; but a little later they were overwhelmed with remorse for their crime, and then acknowledged him a martyr. Honorius, profiting by the occasion, prohibited human combats in the amphitheater. The timid Emperor, greatly alarmed at the barbarian invasions, shortly afterward selected the strong fortress of Ravenna for his residence and seat of government.

No sooner was Italy freed from the ravages of Alaric and his Gothic followers, than another hostile inundation of barbarian warriors, consisting of Sueves, Vandals, Alans and Burgundians, led by the warlike Radagaisus, made its appearance and threatened Italy with slaughter and desolation. The barbarians crossed the Alps, the Po and the Apennines, and laid siege to Florence, which was well garrisoned and provisioned. But Italy was again delivered by the valiant Stilicho, who blockaded the besieging barbarians, and finally, after they had suffered greatly from famine, compelled them to surrender at discretion (A. D. 406). The barbarian leader, Radagaisus, was put to death, and his followers were sold as slaves; but about two-thirds of the barbarian hordes fell back upon Gaul, and laid waste that province from the Rhine to the Pyrenees.

As the people of Gaul received no aid from the Emperor Honorius, they proclaimed Constantine, the governor of Britain, Emperor. Constantine gained some successes over the Germans, and wrested Spain from Honorius. Stilicho concluded a treaty with Alaric against the usurper; but before this treaty could be productive of any results, the valiant general and able minister whose abilities had delayed the fall of the tottering Empire was treacherously assassinated by order of the jealous and ungrateful Honorius (A. D. 408).

Stilicho's successor as prime minister to Honorius was the unworthy Olympius, by whose advice the Emperor ordered the massacre of the families of the barbarians throughout Italy, instead of retaining them as hostages for the fidelity of the mercenary cohorts. This horrible order was cruelly executed, and the result proved that this measure was as impolitic as it was monstrous. Thirty thousand Gothic soldiers in the Roman pay at once revolted, and invited Alaric to come to Italy and avenge the slaughter of their wives and children.

At the call of his countrymen in the Roman service, Alaric again invaded Italy, and marched directly to Rome and laid siege to the city (A. D. 408). Within the walls, pestilence and famine raged with all their horrors. The Emperor Honorius, secure at Ravenna, made no effort to relieve his beleaguered subjects in the "Eternal City." Rome would have fallen into the hands of the barbarian chief, had not the Senate finally yielded to his demand and purchased the retirement of the besiegers by the payment of a heavy ransom. At first Alaric demanded all the gold and silver in the city, all the rich and precious movables, and all the slaves of barbarian origin. Thereupon the Roman ambassadors asked: "If such, O King, are your terms, what do you intend to leave us?" To this the stern chief replied: "Your lives." These severe terms were, however, somewhat modified, and Alaric agreed to raise the siege of Rome for a large ransom of gold, silver, and various articles of valuable merchandise.

Alaric then retired into Tuscany, where he was joined by forty thousand Goths and Germans, who had obtained their freedom in consequence of his victorious career. As the Emperor Honorius refused to ratify the treaty which had been concluded between the Gothic chief and the Romans, Alaric again led his army to Rome the next year (A. D. 409). After taking possession of Ostia, where the magazines were established for the corn that supplied Rome, and thus depriving the citizens of all means of sustenance, he demanded their surrender. Thus reduced to desperate straits the Romans were compelled to comply with his demand.

Alaric elevated Attalus to the imperial dignity, but soon deposed him and resumed his negotiations with Honorius at Ravenna. As the Emperor again refused to treat, Alaric marched against Rome a third time, and entered the city through one of the gates which the Gothic slaves in the city opened to him (A. D. 410). The captured city was given up to plunder; but the Goths, professing to be Christians, spared the churches.

After Rome had suffered six days from

BURIAL OF ALARIC THE GOTH.

the fury of the conquering Goths, the city was abandoned by them; and they marched into Southern Italy, where Alaric died. The body of the barbarian chief was buried in the bed of a small stream near Consentia (now Consenza); and the captives who prepared his grave were murdered, so that the Romans might never find the place of his sepulcher (A. D. 410).

Alaric was succeeded as King of the

ALARIC'S ENTRY INTO ROME.

THE LANDING OF THE VANDALS IN AFRICA.

Goths by his brother-in-law, Adolphus, who ravaged Southern Italy for two years; after which he made peace with the Emperor Honorius, married Placidia, the Emperor's sister, and led the Visigoths into Gaul (A. D. 412), whence he passed into Spain, which had been overrun by the Alans, Sueves and Vandals in A. D. 409. The Visigoths under Adolphus drove the Sueves into the north-western part of the Spanish peninsula, the Alans into the south-western part, and the Vandals into the southern part, since called *Andalusia*, the name being a corruption of *Vandalusia*. Adolphus thus founded the Kingdom of the Visigoths in Spain and Southern Gaul, which eventually embraced the whole of the Spanish peninsula and lasted three centuries.

About the same time the Franks established themselves in that portion of Gaul north of the Seine; while the Burgundians occupied that part of the same province east of the Rhone—in the region since called *Burgundy*. The Romans were now obliged to abandon Britain, which thus became entirely independent. Under the Roman dominion the Britons had become so peaceful and degenerate that they were utterly powerless to resist the savage Picts and Scots of Caledonia, and were therefore obliged to call in the aid of the warlike and savage Angles and Saxons from the North of Germany. These two German tribes quite willingly granted this request; but after they had repelled the Picts and Scots, they seized Southern Britain for themselves, expelling the Britons, and giving to that portion of the island the name of *Angle-land*, since contracted into *England*.

Thus all the Western provinces—Britain, Gaul and Spain—had been lost to the Western Roman Empire. The pretender Constantine, who had been proclaimed Emperor in Britain in A. D. 407, and who had made his son Constans his colleague, ruled Britain, Gaul and Spain in A. D. 408 and 409; but after the revolt of his general, Gerontius, in Spain, Constantine was defeated and put to death by Constantius, a general under the Emperor Honorius.

Constantius was rewarded for his great services by a marriage with Placidia, after the murder of her first husband, Adolphus, King of the Visigoths, and also by the imperial titles which he bore as her brother's colleague. Constantius only reigned a few months; and after his death his widow Placidia quarreled with her brother Honorius and took refuge at Constantinople with her nephew, Theodosius II., the successor of Arcadius as Emperor of the East, taking her two infant children, Valentinian and Honoria, with her.

Upon the death of Honorius, in A. D. 423, after a disgraceful reign of twenty-eight years, the throne of the Western Empire was usurped by John, his chief secretary; but Theodosius sent a fleet and army to uphold the claim of his cousin, Valentinian, the six-year-old son of Placidia. John was deposed, and was beheaded at Aquileia in A. D. 425; and VALENTINIAN III. was proclaimed Emperor of the West, under the regency of his mother Placidia, who governed the Western Empire for a quarter of a century, while her armies were commanded by two great generals, Aëtius and Boniface, who were enemies of each other. In return for the aid rendered by Theodosius II. in overthrowing the usurper John, the provinces of Dalmatia, Noricum and Pannonia were ceded to the Eastern Empire.

Aëtius induced Placidia to recall Boniface from the government of Africa. Boniface, who had been the most faithful friend of the imperial family, and who had been deceived by the crafty Aëtius, refused to relinquish the provincial government of Africa; and in revenge he invited Génseric, King of the Vandals, to his aid. The Vandal king very readily accepted this invitation, and immediately crossed over from Spain into Africa.

Count Boniface soon had reason to regret the effects of his hasty resentment. When it was too late, he endeavored to check the advance of the Vandals, and returned to his allegiance to the imperial government. He received the aid of auxiliaries from the Eastern Empire, but the combined forces of the two Roman Empires were irretrievably defeated. Boniface then retired from Africa, taking with him to Italy all the Roman inhabitants who were able to leave. Thus the Western Empire also lost Africa, in which country Génseric founded the Kingdom of the Vandals, in A. D. 429, which lasted one hundred and five years.

After returning to Italy, Boniface lost his life in a civil war with his rival, Aëtius. When Placidia discovered the double treachery of Aëtius, she proclaimed that general and minister a traitor; and Aëtius was obliged to seek refuge with the Huns in Pannonia.

The forced abandonment of Britain, Gaul, Spain and Africa to the barbarians, and the cession of Dalmatia, Noricum and Pannonia to the Eastern Empire, reduced the dominions of the Western Empire to insignificant proportions; as that Empire now comprised only Italy, Rhætia, Vindelicia and a small district in the South of Gaul. This small Roman territory in Gaul was gallantly defended against the Franks and the Visigoths by Aëtius, after he had been restored to Placidia's favor, until the Franks called in the aid of a new ally, who proved to be a more terrible barbarian invader than any that the Romans had hitherto encountered—Attila, King of the Huns.

Attila, justly called "the Scourge of God," had subdued all the Scythian and German tribes; thus extending his dominion from the Baltic on the north to the Euxine on the south, and from the Volga on the east to the Rhine on the west. His army of seven hundred thousand men was officered by a multitude of vassal kings. For nine years he had been ravaging the territory of the Eastern Empire to the very walls of Constantinople; and had only retired upon the promise of an enormous annual tribute, and the immediate payment of six thousand pounds of gold.

In A. D. 451 Attila invaded Gaul, in behalf of a Frankish king who had been driven to the east side of the Rhine, and who had solicited his assistance. Theódoric, King of the Visigoths—the son of Alaric—had entered into an alliance with the Romans. The united armies of the Romans and the Visigoths came up with Attila just as he had taken Genabum (now Orleans) by battering down the walls of the city. The King of the Huns thereupon retreated across the Seine to Châlons where his Scythian cavalry could operate to better advantage. Then followed the sanguinary battle of Châlons, one of the most memorable battles in the history of the world—in which Attila was defeated by the allied Romans and Visigoths under Aëtius; one hundred and sixty-two thousand of the barbarians being slain (A. D. 451). The Hunnic king at once retreated beyond the Rhine into Germany.

The battle of Châlons, gained by Aëtius, "the Last of the Romans," was the last victory won in the name of the Western Roman Empire. The rude civilization of the Goths, who had already become Christians, was well adapted to the laws and institutions of civilized society. The Huns were savage, heathen and destructive, being mighty in the work of devastation and desolation; but never, in the midst of their greatest power and wealth having made any effort to build and organize a state. The battle of Châlons was one of the great decisive battles in the world's annals. Had the Huns triumphed on that famous field, European civilization would have utterly perished, and all what is most admirable in European history would have been reversed. The next spring (A. D. 452) the Huns invaded Northern Italy and desolated the country, reducing Aquileia, Altinum. Concordia and Padua to ashes, and pillaging Pavia and Milan, the fugitives who fled in terror from their homes founded the city and republic of Venice on a number of small islands on the northern shores of the Adriatic sea. An embassy headed by Pope Leo the Great solemnly interceded with Attila for the safety of Rome; and the Pope's appeal aroused the superstitious fears of the barbarian chieftain, who thereupon made peace with the Emperor Valentinian III. and retired into Pannonia, where he shortly afterwards died from the bursting of a blood-

THE ARRIVAL OF THE HUNS.

SIEGE OF ROME BY THE VANDALS.

FALL OF THE WESTERN EMPIRE.

vessel. His empire at once fell to pieces; the Ostrogoths, the Gepidæ and the Longobards achieving their independence after a severe struggle; whilst the remnants of the nomadic Huns found their way back to the rich pastoral steppes of Central Asia.

The sudden death of Attila, and the civil wars among his followers, delayed the fall of the Western Roman Empire; but the assassination of the valiant Aëtius by the ungrateful Valentinian III. deprived the Empire of its last great general, and the ravages of the barbarians could no longer be checked.

The Emperor Valentinian III. was assassinated, in A. D. 455, by Petronius Maximus, whose wife he had corrupted. PETRONIUS MAXIMUS then became Emperor of the West; and on the death of his wife, which occurred soon afterward, he compelled Eudoxia, the Widow of Valentinian III., to marry him. In revenge, Eudoxia invited Génseric, the Vandal king of Northern Africa, to invade Italy. Génseric and his Vandal followers accordingly crossed the Mediterranean sea into Italy and besieged Rome (A. D. 455). The Emperor Petronius Maximus was killed in a tumult, which arose in the city. Rome soon fell into the hands of the besieging Vandals, who plundered the city of what the Goths had left, even despoiling the churches. After the victorious Vandals had pillaged the city of Romulus fourteen days and nights, their fleet waiting at Ostia returned to Africa, carrying with it the Empress Eudoxia and the plunder of Rome.

The Romans were so paralyzed by this terrible calamity that they were unable to proceed to the appointment of a new Emperor. Through the influence of Theódoric II., king of the Visigoths, the Empire received a new sovereign in the person of AVITUS, the commander of the legions in Gaul (A. D. 455). But after Avitus had reigned little more than a year, he was deposed by Count Ricimer, a Goth, who commanded the barbarian auxiliaries in Italy, and who had revolted and captured Avitus in a battle near Placentia (A. D. 456).

Avitus was made Bishop of Placentia, and

ALLEMANNI CROSSING THE RHINE.

died a few months later. Six months later (A. D. 457), Ricimer elevated MARJORIAN to the imperial throne. Marjorian's talents and virtues revived some appearance of justice and energy in the imperial government. A fleet was prepared to invade the Vandal kingdom in Africa to retaliate upon Génseric for his plunder of Rome, and to stop the ravages of the Vandal pirates upon the Italian coasts. This Roman fleet was betrayed to the emissaries of the Vandal king, in the port of Carthagena, in Spain.

Count Ricimer had already become jealous of Marjorian and forced him to abdicate the imperial throne, whereupon he elevated a new puppet to the imperial dignity in the person of LIBIUS SEVÉRUS, in whose name he hoped to exercise the real power himself (A. D. 461). But the nominal sway of the new Emperor did not extend beyond the frontiers of Italy; while two Roman generals—Marcellínus in Dalmatia and Ægidius in Gaul—exercised the real sovereign power, though without any imperial title. The Vandals constantly harassed the coasts of Italy, Spain and Greece; and two years after the death of Libius Sevérus, Ricimer solicited assistance from Leo I, the Eastern Emperor, against the common barbarian foe, promising to accept any sovereign in the West whom the Eastern Emperor would appoint.

Accordingly, Leo I. designated ANTHEMIUS, a Byzantine nobleman, as Emperor of the West (A. D. 467). The new Emperor was acknowledged by the Roman Senate and people, and by the barbarian auxiliaries. Ricimer's fidelity was believed to be secured by his marriage with the daughter of Anthemius. The combined forces of the two Roman Empires now made a formidable attack upon the Vandals; but this attack failed on account of the weakness or treachery of Basiliscus, the commander of the Eastern fleet, who lost his entire fleet through the secret contrivance of Génseric. The Vandals recovered Sardinia and obtained possession of Sicily, whence they were able to ravage Italy more constantly than hitherto.

In the meantime the Goths had become dissatisfied with the government of Anthemius. Ricimer retired to Milan, where he openly revolted, in concert with his countrymen, and led a Burgundian army to Rome, where he compelled the Senate to accept OLYBRIUS as Emperor (A. D. 472). Anthemius was killed in an attack upon the city. Ricimer died forty days after his victory, leaving his power to Gundobald, a Burgundian. Olybrius died less than two months afterwards, whereupon Gundobald elevated a soldier named GLYCERIUS to the vacant imperial throne (A. D. 473.) The Eastern Emperor, Leo I., again interfered, and appointed JULIUS NEPOS, a nephew of Marcellínus of Dalmatia, Emperor of the West (A. D. 474). The new Emperor was accepted by the Romans and the Gauls; while Glycerius was consoled for his loss of the imperial title by being appointed Bishop of Salóna.

Julius Nepos had no sooner been invested with the imperial insignia than he was driven from his throne and from Italy by a new revolt led by Orestes, a Pannonian, who commanded the barbarian auxiliaries. Orestes placed his own son, ROMULUS AUGUSTULUS, a mere youth upon the throne of the West (A. D. 475). This was the last of the sovereigns of the Western Roman Empire, and by a strange coincidence he bore the names of the founder of the city of Rome and the founder of the Roman Empire. He was called Augustulus—meaning Little Augustus—in burlesque of the imperial grandeur which mocked his youth and insignificance.

As the strength of the Romans diminished, the insolence of the barbarians increased; and finally, in A. D. 476—when the demand of the barbarians for a third part of the lands of Italy was rejected—they again rose in arms and killed Orestes, and Odoacer, chief of the Heruli, a German tribe, dethroned the youthful Emperor, Romulus Augustulus, and assumed the title of *King of Italy*, thus abolishing the title and office of Emperor of the West. In a letter to Zeno, the Eastern Emperor, the Roman Senate relinquished the claim of Italy to imperial rank, and acknowledged Constantinople as the capital of the Roman world, but requested that Odoacer should be invested with the diocese of Italy with the title of *Patrician*. Odoacer sent the deposed Romulus Augustulus into captivity at Naples, assigning him a pension for his support.

Thus ended the Western Roman Empire. The once-proud city of Romulus was occupied by barbarian warriors, and a barbarian chief was seated on the throne of the Cæsars. The Eastern Roman Empire—sometimes called the Greek Empire, or the Byzantine Empire—continued to flourish nearly

FALL OF THE WESTERN EMPIRE.

a thousand years longer; and was finally overthrown by the Ottoman Turks in A. D. 1453.

With the overthrow of the Western Roman Empire, ancient history ends; and the founding of new kingdoms by the northern barbarian nations marked the rise of a new era in the history of the world—an epoch, which, after a thousand years of feudal turbulence, opened into the varied and brilliant scenes of modern history.

The empire lasted five hundred and seven years from the accession of Augustus in B. C. 31 to the dethronement of Romulus Augustulus in A. D. 476. During this period seventy-seven Emperors swayed the destinies of the Roman world. The empire attained its greatest magnitude in the reign of Trajan, when it extended from the Pillars of Hercules (now Straight of Gibraltar) and the Friths of Forth and Clyde in the West to the Caspian Sea and the Persian Gulf in the East. During the fifth century of the Christian era it had gradually broken up and contracted its limits, until it had come to be almost confined to Italy.

The repeated invasions of immense hordes of barbarians—Goths, Vandals, Huns, Burgundians, Sueves, Alans, Alemanni, Franks and Heruli—had precipitated themselves in perpetual succession upon the regions which Roman civilization had converted into cultivated gardens, and poured in irresistible inundations over province after province. The West chiefly felt the force of the attack. After the first rush of the Goths across the Lower Danube, during the reign of Valens, the torrent of migration proceeded entirely in a westerly direction. The barbarian invaders occupied Pannonia, Gaul, Spain and Africa. Each more powerful spoiler was attracted to Italy, whose fertile plains were desolated by host after host of barbarian warriors. The city of Rome itself was taken repeatedly, and was twice sacked, first by Alaric the Goth and afterwards by Génseric the Vandal.

Rome perceived that she needed all her resources to defend herself, and was therefore under the necessity of relinquishing those outlying provinces which no enemy had yet captured. Thus Britain, most of Gaul, Vindelicia, and probably Rhætia, were abandoned. Pannonia, Noricum and Dalmatia were ceded to the Eastern Empire. Finally only Italy remained to the Western Emperors, and Italy was unable to defend herself.

The Western Emperors had for a long time ceased to put any confidence in Italian soldiers, and had obtained their recruits from the outlying provinces rather than from the heart of the Empire. Ultimately, the Emperors considered it excellent strategy to take the barbarians themselves into their pay, and to employ Goths to fight Huns, and to engage Burgundians or Vandals to fight Goths. But this policy had fatal consequences.

The barbarians, learning their power, resolved to exercise it, and to seize Italy for themselves. Tired of being servants, they determined to become masters. In fact the imperial power had been existing only upon sufferance for a long time. The structure lacked proper support, and only the touch of a finger was required to make it topple over. Ricimer could have done as easily what Odoacer did; but the facility of an enterprise is not always previously apparent.

The overthrow of the Western Empire was due to the operation of causes which had been slowly working for many centuries. The aggressive warfare of the early Romans, which had been continually extending the limits of the Roman dominion, was retaliated upon them in the fourth century of the Christian era by the barbarians against whom they commenced their attacks.

The Roman Emperors were no longer able to defend the provinces which they still pretended to govern; and they often observed, without regret, valiant foes become their guests and occupy the desert portions of the empire. The decay of the Empire was hastened by the advance of luxury and the decline of the military spirit. Its ruin was not caused by the barbarian nations which poured into it from the extremity of Scandinavia in the re-

ANCIENT HISTORY OF ROME.

mote North and from the steppes of Tartary and Mongolia in the far East. The Empire had for a long time been corroded by an internal ulcer. The decay of patriotism, the decline of military virtue, and the extinction of the national spirit had far more evil consequences to Rome than the arms of Alaric the Goth, Attila the Hun or Genseric the Vandal. Roman degeneracy made the gradual conquest and final subversion of the Western Empire an easy task.

ROMAN EMPERORS.

	FLOURISHING PERIOD OF THE EMPIRE.		PERIOD OF DECLINE AND MILITARY DESPOTISM.
B.C. 31	AUGUSTUS, } Julian Line of Cæsars.	A.D. 275	TACITUS.
A.D. 14	TIBERIUS,	276	FLORIAN.
37	CALIGULA,	276	PROBUS.
41	CLAUDIUS,	282	CARUS.
54	NERO,	283	CARINUS and NUMERIAN.
68	GALBA,	284	DIOCLETIAN and MAXIMIAN.
69	OTHO,	305	GALERIUS and CONSTANTIUS CHLORUS
69	VITELIUS,		
69	VESPASIAN, } The Three Flavii.		
79	TITUS,		PERIOD OF THE TRIUMPH OF CHRISTIANITY.
81	DOMITIAN,		
96	NERVA.		
98	TRAJAN.	306	CONSTANTINE THE GREAT.
117	ADRIAN.	337	CONSTANTIUS II., CONSTANTINE II., and CONSTANS.
138	ANTONINUS PIUS, } The Three Antonines.	361	JULIAN THE APOSTATE.
161	MARCUS AURELIUS,	363	JOVIAN.
180	COMMODUS,	364	VALENTINIAN I. and VALENS.
		375	GRATIAN in the West.
	PERIOD OF DECLINE AND MILITARY DESPOTISM.	378	THEODOSIUS THE GREAT in the East.
		383	VALENTINIAN II. in the West.
		383	MAXIMUS in the West.
		388	EUGENIUS in the West.
192	PERTINAX.	394	THEODOSIUS THE GREAT, sole Emperor.
193	DIDIUS JULINUS.		
193	SEPTIMIUS SEVERUS		
211	CARACALLA.		
217	MACRINUS.		
218	HELIOGABALUS.		LAST EMPERORS OF THE WEST.
222	ALEXANDER SEVERUS.		
235	MAXIMIN.		
238	GORDIAN I. and GORDIAN II.	395	HONORIUS.
238	PUPIENUS and BALBINUS.	423	VALENTINIAN III.
238	GORDIAN III.	455	PETRONIUS MAXIMUS.
244	PHILIP THE ARABIAN.	455	AVITUS.
249	DECIUS.	457	MARJORIAN.
251	GALLUS.	461	LIBIUS SEVERUS.
253	ÆMILIANUS.	467	ANTHEMIUS.
253	VALERIAN.	472	OLYBRIUS.
260	GALLIENUS.	473	GLYCERIUS.
268	CLAUDIUS II.	474	JULIUS NEPOS.
270	QUINTILLIUS.	475	ROMULUS AUGUSTULUS.
270	AURELIAN.	476	End of the Western Empire.

www.ingramcontent.com/pod-product-compliance
Lightning Source LLC
Chambersburg PA
CBHW032004300426
44117CB00008B/888